53/B

CURRICULUM IN THE
MODERN ELEMENTARY SCHOOL

Curriculum in the
Modern Elementary School

ROBERT H. BECK
Professor of the History and Philosophy of Education in the College of Education, University of Minnesota

WALTER W. COOK
Dean of the College of Education and Professor of Educational Psychology, University of Minnesota

NOLAN C. KEARNEY
Assistant Superintendent of Schools in charge of Curriculum and Curriculum Research, St. Paul Public School System

new york

Distributors:
BAILEY BROS. & SWINFEN LTD.
LONDON.

1953

PRENTICE-HALL EDUCATION SERIES

Harold Spears, Editor

First printing ....*May, 1953*
Second printing .....*September, 1953*

L.C. Cat. Card No.: 53-8394

$\mathcal{T}$HIS BOOK RELATES, in a manner significant to both parents and teachers, basic principles of psychology and the social sciences to the daily learning of children. The authors' technique has been to project the curriculum against a background of research on the nature of man and his interaction within the whole physical and social environment, and from this method to evolve principles that can be of great value when applied in the classroom. For the elementary-school teacher, or supervisor, the book serves the purpose of coordinating and organizing for classroom use the material from such courses as the teaching of reading, arithmetic, measurement and evaluation, educational psychology, and others.

Part One is devoted to the practical implications of work that has been done on ways to motivate children, to increase the effectiveness of group work and social learning, and, above all, to increase the quality, rate, and permanency of learning. Methods of dealing with individual differences and with the evaluation of student progress have been given special attention. These are the most vexing problems confronting the teachers and parents of children in elementary schools.

Those who deal directly with children sometimes have difficulty in spelling out their goals, in finding just the right ideas and materials to use with pupils in attaining these goals, and in using the printed outlines and other resources that are available. To meet this need, Part Two classifies and describes various types of curriculums—their content, strengths, and limitations.

Part Three is composed of three narratives illustrating how teachers in three different communities approach their classroom work and, working with parents in a community, develop instruction that applies the principles developed in Parts One and Two. These narratives also aid in understanding and utilizing these principles.

The authors wish to acknowledge the invaluable assistance given them by Mrs. Evelyn Thompson and her associates on the staff of the University of Minnesota Library, and the helpful advice of Professor Haym Kruglak of the Department of Physics, University of Minnesota. We wish also to express our obligation to Mr. Wilbur Mangas, Coordinating Editor of Prentice-Hall, Inc., who worked with us throughout the production of the book, and to Mrs. Halene Hatcher Visher for permission to quote from "Conservation Education or Tragedy," which appeared in the *Journal of Geography,* January 1949. For permission to quote, the authors also wish to thank Appleton-Century-Crofts, Inc., Ginn and Company, The Psychological Corporation, Henry Holt and Company, Inc., Harper and Brothers, The Ronald Press Company, The Macmillan Company, The University of Minnesota Press, William Sloane Associates, Inc., and Little, Brown and Company. In addition to these publishers, we are indebted to the American Council on Education for permission to use without direct quotation a portion of the thought elaborated by Walter W. Cook in Chapter I of *Educational Measurement.*

Finally, the authors wish to express their gratitude to the many excellent teachers whose work is reflected at various places in the book. However, all teachers' names and all illustrations of inept or poor practices are fictitious, and any similarity to real persons or events is purely coincidental.

ROBERT H. BECK
WALTER W. COOK
NOLAN C. KEARNEY

CONTENTS

PART ONE

INTRODUCTION

*N*EW RESEARCH findings in education and in psychology and other related sciences have made it necessary for curriculum-makers to re-examine many of the principles and practices of the past. In some cases the old practices have proved satisfactory. In other cases it has become obvious that the old methods were inefficient, cumbersome, and wasteful of time, effort, and money. In still other cases, and these have been far from infrequent, the effects of the old methods have been found to be positively bad. Some have interfered with learning more than they have aided it. Some have contributed to the growth of social attitudes and behavior that were the opposites of those desired.

Change, modification, and adaptation are necessary as further research in the field of education furnishes additional proof for or challenge to established beliefs. Part One of this book introduces a number of scientific discoveries that, if applied, will greatly enrich the elementary-school curriculum and the experiences of pupils and teachers alike. In addition, emphasis is placed upon the curriculum principles that are necessary for understanding and motivating students, for increasing the quality, rate, and permanency of learning, for increasing the effectiveness of group work and social learning, and for evaluating the growth and learning of children as individuals and as members of a group. Throughout, the ramifications of individual and trait differences of children are stressed.

AN HISTORICAL INTRODUCTION TO THE
ELEMENTARY-SCHOOL CURRICULUM

$\mathcal{T}$HE CURRICULUM is often defined as the educational experiences that children have in school. This is a broad definition and it includes far more than an outline of the learning of facts and skills, more than habits, attitudes, ideals, and appreciations. The personalities of the teachers, the janitor, and the principal are part of it. The school building has its influence. The impact of the community and of the whole culture on the child in school must be considered. The curriculum was not always so broadly conceived. Brief reference to some of its historical sources may serve to introduce our present broad conception of curriculum in general and of the curriculum of the elementary school in particular.

The elementary school over the years has taken many forms. The classic Greek and Roman variety emphasized physical training, wrestling, moral philosophy, and drama. The catechumenal and catechetical schools emphasized early Christian doctrine. After the Middle Ages, there developed the "hedge schools," the most informal elementary schools ever created. It was not until the middle of the nineteenth century, 1847 to be exact, that an elementary school with a graded program was established at Quincy, Massachusetts. These are but a few examples of the many organizational changes that schools and their curriculums have undergone.

In considering the long history of our present curriculum, primary attention should be given to the development of the ideas that have been important in shaping it, rather than to changes in subjects and courses of study. Many of the influential ideas of the last 50 years have resulted from the application of the methods and techniques of science to education. Though these are more useful to us than the earlier ideas that resulted largely from unscientific speculation, some of the earlier ideas had great influence in enriching and improving education. Much from the past, of course, is open to serious question. In some cases, it was not the ideas that were at fault; rather, the ideas were misunderstood and abused in practice. (Some of our inheritance is composed of contradictory and conflicting ideas that have slipped into practice and that exist today side by side, their disharmonies undetected except as they serve to perplex thoughtful teachers.) Nevertheless, what we may do to improve the elementary curriculum in the next decade will be influenced inevitably by what has been done in the past. Some of our rich legacy has not yet been accurately assessed for its value.

The philosophers who first influenced curriculum theory

Early Greek thinkers of prominence devoted much attention to ideas about "mind" and "knowledge." Foremost among them was Plato, whose writings on education and learning in his *Republic* proved to be the most important in educational philosophy for 1,500 years and more. Plato, however, was interested almost exclusively in the intellectual accomplishments of adults and had little feeling for the realities of child growth and development. He said, among other things, that reliable knowledge was not to be had through the analysis and generalization of experience; that emotions, the usual interests of children, and their exploratory activities had little to do with significant learning. His gifted student, Aristotle, was equally indifferent to the elementary level of schooling. He, too, dwelt on a type of thinking best exemplified by the geometrician. It was very abstract, altogether remote from everyday experience. The study honored by the Greek philosophers was a search for universal ideas; the here-and-now was less considered.

In the past, students of education rarely realized that neither Plato nor Aristotle had much to offer to curriculum theory. Had the study of the behavior of children been encouraged by Plato and Aristotle, the curriculum of the elementary school through the years of their influence might have reflected much greater insight into the needs of children. However, the prevailing practice of the elementary school was not to become enlightened by a realistic study of children until the child study movement hit its stride during the 1930's.

The references to Roman and Greek elementary schools are not intended to suggest that our elementary schools developed from them in a direct line. The more traceable ancestors of our schools were the haphazard schools of the sixteenth century called "hedge schools" by historians because often they were held behind a sheltering hedge. From that humble beginning have grown our graded elementary schools. The path traveled has many memorable landmarks but none more important than those brought about in the fifteenth and sixteenth centuries by the Protestant Reformation and the invention of the printing press. The Reformation stimulated the growth of elementary schools because Protestants were required to read the simple catechism and, if possible, the Bible. And the printing press greatly increased the availability of printed materials. As we know, what was read was religious and not primarily the secular study of geography, history, or the other subjects that were later to become conventional. New England Schools of the seventeenth century clearly showed this Protestant influence. [1] Perhaps the most memorable of the New England texts was the *New England Primer* of 1690. This book opened with the printed alphabet, whose letters were used in descriptive sentences ("In Adam's fall We sinned all"), succeeded by easy words of one, two, three, and four syllables. Then followed the Lord's Prayer, the Apostle's Creed, and, as a conclusion, the catechism.

From that day to this, reading has remained the most important of all elementary-schools subjects, but Puritan moral instruction lost ground when reading blossomed into grammar, declamation, literature, writing, spelling, and penmanship. Nor did reading remain the only subject of study, though as a skill it has retained its primary position.

Nineteen hundred years after Plato, John Amos Comenius (1592-

[1] Nila Banton Smith, *American Reading Instruction*. New York: Silver Burdett and Company, 1934, Chapters II and III.

1670) led a revolt against the Platonic tradition and its neglect of elementary education. There had been notable writers and reform-ers in the interim, but Comenius is worthy of special mention. He believed in the senses as the source of impressions from which knowledge could be constructed. Though not a scientist, Comenius learned enough about children to believe that their knowledge developed out of experiences within their environments. In this, he departed from the classic tradition that placed knowledge based on experience in an inferior position, well below the validity of speculative knowledge. Comenius' viewpoint explains why he was so committed to exercising the senses of children. Had he been more inclined toward Platonic values, he might have urged that children mature their power of reason through practice with verbal rules of grammar and drill in arithmetic or geometry. Comenius saw purpose in the rules of grammar and the processes of arithmetic and geometry, but he believed they were not sufficient preparation alone for youngsters feeling their way in the world. Children first needed time to put their sense experiences into some sort of order. They needed enough experience to become sensitive. Comenius ap-proached elementary schooling realistically in his monumental *Orbis pictus,* the first known picture-book text and one that aug-mented the "realistic" movement in education. After its publication other scholars were stimulated to study how children actually learn. The primacy of sense experience to which Comenius gave dramatic emphasis has remained prominent to the present day. It is a specu-lative idea from the past that scientific study later confirmed.

Another sense realist was John Locke (1632-1704). One of Locke's theories was that the mind is composed of separate faculties, an approach that today is called "faculty psychology." Faculty psy-chology went unchallenged scientifically until its philosophical con-clusions were challenged by the experiments of a hard-headed psychologist, Edward Lee Thorndike (1874-1950). Thorndike found no evidence substantiating the supposition that the mind was com-posed of separate powers or faculties such as reasoning, imagining, and willing, nor could he find support for the belief that special subjects (e.g., Latin or algebra) had special utility for disciplining the mind. [2] Thorndike's conclusion was that the disciplinary value

2 Edward Lee Thorndike, "Mental Discipline in High School Studies," *Journal of Educational Psychology,* Vol. 15, November-December 1924, 1-24, 83-98.

of a subject depended in part upon the attitudes or objectives of the student and in part upon the imaginativeness of the teacher in promoting critical thinking.

Locke must not be dismissed with the mere mention of his faculty psychology, though it was a dominant influence on curriculum for many decades and is still influential in the thinking of some people. Locke is also important because he helped greatly to break down Plato's theory of "innate ideas." He turned the attention of educators to the question of how children develop or acquire knowledge, and by showing that no evidence existed to prove that children are born with experience or knowledge he disposed of Plato's argument that children have innate ideas. Locke thoroughly agreed with Comenius that children learn from their contacts with the environment. To illustrate his idea, he pictured the mind at birth as a *tabula rasa* or translated literally, "shaved tablet." In classic times children employed a stylus to engrave their letters on a wax tablet. After their exercises had been corrected, the children or the master scraped the tablet clean. At birth, conjectured Locke, the mind is much like one of the schoolboy's tablets—neatly erased. Experience writes upon the mind by feeding into it experiences that the "faculties" of the mind make into ideas. This may seem to be a naive, literary description of learning, but it was as well as philosophy could do at this time without the aid of controlled scientific study.

Locke's view of the mind not only encouraged a very formal type of academic discipline but also had a humanizing influence on education. Formal cademic discipline was encouraged by the belief that the faculties needed exercise if they were to develop properly. In his *Some Thoughts Concerning Education,* Locke suggested that the exercise should be rigorous. "As the strength of the body lies chiefly in being able to endure hardships, so also does that of the mind." [3] One satirist said, "It does not matter what you learn as long as it is unpleasant." There is no denying that Locke set a hard row for youngsters, but his idea of the *tabula rasa* made some amends. If an educator took the conception of the *tabula rasa* seriously, he would believe that good teaching could overcome almost any handicaps. Locke's idea was advanced in the days before

---

[3] John Locke, *Some Thoughts Concerning Education.* London: Cambridge University Press, 1899, p. 21.

much was known about the relative importance of heredity and environment in determining learning ability. Educators felt that if the mind was a blank at birth they could do anything through effective teaching. Perhaps research into genetics has dampened some of this optimism, but we still agree there is no substitute for superior teaching.

Jean Jacques Rousseau (1712-1778) wrote in his book *Émile* that man comes "good" from the hand of God and becomes evil only through contact with the society around him. Few teachers of his day were completely in agreement with Rousseau's romantic optimism. Be that as it may, writers on the elementary-school curriculum were impressed with Rousseau and urged teachers to deal kindly with children. Rousseau's influence did more than promote the humane treatment of children. Along with Comenius and Locke, Rousseau's concern with the problem of educating the young drew attention to the need for more data on child growth and development. Much that he wrote proved highly controversial, but because of him education was advanced one step more toward the scientific study of child behavior.

The next significant step was taken by a Swiss, Johann Heinrich Pestalozzi (1746-1827). Pestalozzi rounded out the sense realist tradition. Less a theorist than Locke, Pestalozzi stood with Comenius in seeking ways of improving elementary-school instruction. The teacher was to take every opportunity to illustrate each idea with an object, an approach clearly in the sense realist tradition. He urged teachers to proceed from the concrete to the abstract, from the simple to the complex, and from the near to the far. Pestalozzi worked out his idea in detail, and left no stone unturned to make his theories practical. The schools Pestalozzi established were practical though very experimental. Doubtless this is what attracted normal school teachers to Pestalozzi. In this country, the first to exploit these methods was Edward A. Sheldon (1832-1897), who brought Pestalozzian "object teaching" to the normal school at Oswego, New York, where he taught teachers the use and value of field trips, shop work, and "inductive lessons."

Inductive lessons illustrate the Pestalozzian theory of learning. In an inductive lesson on coal, for example, the teacher might bring a lump of coal to class. The interests of the students in the subject of coal are presumed to be invited by the presence of the real substance. As the lesson develops, more illustrative materials are introduced. Ultimately the walls of the room might be lined with pictures of coal mines and steam engines, and exhibition cases in the rooms and halls might be filled with neatly labeled samples of various types of coal and peat, and with industrial exhibits outlining the uses of coal in chemical industries and steam production.

The theory behind all this is simple. The assumption is that learning is a process of generalizing upon a number of sensory experiences. To facilitate generalization and to insure that the desired generalizations are obtained, various sense impressions are afforded in a well-planned sequence. In the lesson on coal, the resultant generalizations may be an understanding of the chemical composition of coal, the extent of this natural resource, its uses, or its history.

Emphasis on the inductive lesson, however, should not lead the teacher to stress it to the exclusion of other methods. Following the inductive phase of a lesson or series of lessons, the students ought to be helped to make certain *deductions*. In the case of coal, such deductions might center about such topics as the conservation of coal, its place in the carbon family, and so forth. Teachers trained in Pestalozzian methods seldom heard about deductive instruction. Despite that lack, their teaching was no doubt more significant to children than was the instruction of teachers who started every discussion of a topic with abstract definitions.

Friedrich Froebel (1782-1852) continued Pestalozzi's emphasis upon the importance of the senses, and outdid Rousseau and Pestalozzi in urging teachers to be humane in their treatment of children. Froebel's attitude toward children was the quintessence of kindness. He gave us the kindergarten, which means "garden of children."

However romantic such men as Rousseau, Pestalozzi, and Froebel may have been in their attitudes toward children, we know that they also were shrewd observers of child behavior. In all their writings the reader is met with homely but perceptive references to the habits of children at the several stages of their development. With Johann Friedrich Herbart (1776-1841), the scientific study of human learning and maturation came to the fore, its scientific quality leavened by the humane sentiments of Rousseau and Pestalozzi. Perhaps they saved the modern elementary school from the chill of pure science.

Philosophy and psychology separate

Herbart marks the point in the history of educational theory where philosophy and psychology come to a parting of the ways. Although he was a professor of philosophy, Herbart will be remembered for his theories of psychology; certainly his influence on elementary-school curriculum theory has come through his theories on the operation of the human mind. Until Herbart's ideas became known to teachers, the relatively simple principles of John Locke were just about the only source constituting a widely accepted systematic "educational psychology." Before Herbart's writings were generally available, a teacher in the nineteenth century could find very little data on how children learned. It was impossible to find and follow well-defined or systematic teaching methods. The teacher who tried to base his teaching on a *tabula rasa* conception of mind was led to multiply the experiences of students with objects, field trips, and demonstrations. Books or pamphlets on teaching contained no conscientiously formulated suggestions on how the teacher might best organize the sense experiences of students or help children distill knowledge from their observation.

Herbart offered a very plausible picture of the human mind and of learning. He also offered advice to teachers on how to teach systematically. The theory Herbart described was not radically new, but it placed considerably less emphasis on having experiences for the sake of having experiences than had the earlier sense realists. Herbart certainly did not belittle experience, but he placed less trust in the ability of the unaided student to convert his experiences into wisdom.

Herbart wished the teacher to plan each step in the building of understanding in accordance with a functional theory of the human mind. He described the mind as an "apperceptive mass," intending to suggest a mind that devoured sense perceptions and shunted them into an orderly arrangement. The apperceptive mass included a continually replenished quantity of perceptions waiting to be sorted into generalizations. Not all these perceptions were equally lively, however. Those that had been experienced most recently and that had been clearly explained upon reception—by the teacher, for example—were lively enough to catch new perceptions. These were the experiences from which evolved ideas. On the other hand, ill-digested experiences were sent off to a discard pile, there to linger on and be subject to recall or join the host of dim memories. The less pains a teacher took to point out how today's lessons associated with yesterday's, the smaller was the student's apperceptive mass. Day by day, a competent teacher had to guide the student in associating his new perceptions with the old. As this was done, the student's store of knowledge grew.

The essence of Herbart's method was systematic preparation, presentation, generalization, and review. The same type of orderliness pervaded Herbart's thoughts about subject matter and its "correlation," a topic around which centered many of the educational controversies of his day. He thought subject matter should be correlated around some core, usually history and literature, although it might be geography. To help the teacher guide the pupil, Herbart suggested five steps.

Step. 1. *Preparation*. The teacher begins the lesson by recalling what he feels to be already familiar to the class. He misses no opportunity to make the students feel secure in their ability to extend their apperceptive mass. "Today's lesson is really very much like yesterday's. You remember that we were talking about water. Is water always like what comes out of the faucet? . . ."

Step 2. *Presentation*. Having established a common base, the teacher begins introducing the new ideas. "Let's see if we can jot down on the blackboard some of the ways water appears. . . ."

Step 3. *Association*. The teacher is most careful to show students that new materials cover points with which the students are already familiar, as well as information that is being covered for the first time. "Can anyone tell us whether snowflakes, hailstones, raindrops, and water vapor are alike in any other ways? . . ." Then the teacher works to see that these points of similarity are firmly established.

Step 4. *Systematization or generalization*. The teacher helps the students to generalize about new ideas. "Shall we see whether we can tell what might happen to water vapor on a warm summer day or on a cold winter day? . . . But it was always some form of water, was it not? Some day you will know more about water. You will know that any water you come across, whether it is ice or steam, has two things in it, hydrogen and oxygen, and that there is always twice as much hydrogen as there is oxygen. . . ."

Step. 5. *Application*. The teacher asks the students to make other illustrations of the new idea. In the good old days this often meant doing the problems at the end of the chapter.

The Herbartian method was a splendid aid to inexperienced teachers, educated in a day when little was known about scientific pedagogy and when instructional material was limited pretty largely to a single textbook. Herbart believed that the teacher should go to any length in developing associations (and hence meanings) between hitherto unrelated facts or impressions. In actual practice, however, his methods became identified with the rote memory of facts and principles and with the imposition of knowledge on children by subject-matter specialists. The drill masters neglected having the children work on insights. As might happen with any teaching method, even one firmly based in scientific research, the mass application of Herbart's methods failed in the hands of untutored, uninspired educators. More recently, thoughtless educators said that it was Herbart's theories that made American schoolrooms lifeless. They bemoaned an education that was a mere parade of teachers' knowledge before the children.

One of the reasons why Herbart's star set so quickly in this country may have been because of the violation of his judgments that we have previously cited. His ideas were soon rejected, however, on more intelligent ground—his theories had not been based on experimental evidence. For example, within a few years of its founding, the National Herbart Society, became the National Society for the Scientific Study of Education.[4] However, the scientific study of education was not a repudiation of Herbart or a reaction against him. Rather, it was a reaction against speculative philosophy. Herbart's right to a place in psychology is sustained by the fact that Edward Lee Thorndike, certainly one of our chief psychologists, carried on the Herbart tradition in the study of "associationist" psychology.[5]

Associationism

Since Herbart's time, the entire "associationist" position has come under fire by educators and psychologists who feel that the associationists are in error in their misinterpretation of *interest* and their

[4] Now the National Society for the Study of Education.

[5] Edward Lee Thorndike and Arthur I. Gates, *Elementary Principles of Learning*. New York: The Macmillan Company, 1930, pp. 247-250.

failure to recognize that purpose is the principal characteristic of human learning.[6] The discussion of this vital and important problem is a long way from being ended. No other is of greater importance for elementary-school curriculum theory. If the associationists are correct, the experiences of the child in school should be on the order of those recommended by Herbart. His steps, reviewed above, are models for what is meant by associationism. Their purpose is to associate new experiences with old experiences, new ideas with familiar ideas.

To appreciate why associationism has been viewed critically by both philosophers and psychologists, we must understand what associationism assumes about learning and the world in which learning takes place. Associationist learning theory takes on meaning when seen as a revolt against classicism and as the culmination of a tradition extending from Comenius through Locke to Pestalozzi and Herbart.[7] This is the tradition of sense realism. Each of its proponents has believed that the senses are the agencies through which men come to know reality, that reality is what the senses sense.[8] This is the heart of sense realism. Associationism enters the picture as the psychological explanation of how man associates his sense impressions into ideas, generalizations, or what we more familiarly call knowledge.

We have not described Herbart's associationist theory in any detail. It was the product of its day—a day that was lacking in experimental evidence. It is with Thorndike and Thorndike's associates that we must grapple if we would tilt at modern associationism.[9] Thorndike's sights were focused on human learning and the improvement of its efficiency. He wanted to find out how a teacher could help students eliminate wrong responses (mistakes) and assure correct ones.

As teachers, we think of these responses as answers to our questions or as solutions to the problems in the workbook or textbook.

[6] Ernest Hilgard, *Theories of Learning.* New York: Appleton-Century-Crofts, Inc., 1948, Chapters 2, 7, 11, 12.

[7] In the history of philosophy, this tradition is known as Empiricism. Francis Bacon is usually named as its first sponsor in Europe.

[8] In that branch of philosophy where problems of human knowledge are studied, sense realism is said to stumble over the fact that senses often give us false reports.

[9] Hilgard, *Theories of Learning.* Chapter 2.

As a psychologist, Thorndike employed a professional vocabulary, a form of shorthand, to describe his associationism. The letter *R* meant response and the letter *S* meant stimulus. Stimuli were anything coming from the outside world and affecting the individual through his senses. Responses were the reactions of the human being to these stimuli. How, asked Thorndike, shall we establish "bonds" or connections that would invariably join the correct response to any given stimulus? This was a question asked by a psychologist interested in helping teachers. Thorndike was also a "pure" or general psychologist eager to determine how learning took place and what "laws" governed the process.

Thorndike concluded that learning was a matter of trial-and-error, the trial of one response after another until the correct one was discovered. An efficient teacher could assist a student to fix upon the correct responses by rewarding him when a correct response was given and providing him with opportunities to drill on the correct response. In terms of psychology, Thorndike thus generalized what he thought to be two laws of learning, the laws of *exercise* and of *effect*.

Since Thorndike advanced his laws of learning (and they were based on considerable research when compared with what had been available to earlier associationists), they have been questioned by numerous psychologists and philosophers. Both as a philosopher and as a psychologist, John Dewey was one of the first to take exception to much of what is known as associationism. Dewey's views on psychology were formulated at the end of the nineteenth century when psychology was just beginning to separate itself from philosophy. Hence much of the data later used by psychologists in their attacks on associationism were not available to him. As a philosopher, Dewey more or less surmised (speculated) that human beings did not learn by a simple process of trial-and-error in which rewards were given to inhibit errors and punishments meted out to reinforce correct responses. Or, he believed, even if individuals did learn in this fashion, they certainly demonstrated a good bit of purposive behavior; they acted as though they could hope, plan, experiment, and generalize upon their experimentation. Dewey was interested in helping teachers encourage students to take the initiative in inquiry. He told curriculum-makers that the curriculum ought to *be* the child's experiences in the process of following out purposes to some conclusion. Dewey knew that the teacher faced a very difficult problem in motivating students to learn, but he believed that proper motivation lay not in using rewards or punishments but in the teacher's arousing in the student a genuine desire to learn. The way to do this, Dewey said, was to capitalize on the natural curiosity of children, their interests, and their ever-present activities. Today it is easy to see that Dewey had real need for some careful studies in two areas—the real interests of youngsters and the actual function of purposes and interests.

The problems that were faced by Dewey and Thorndike, and by those who came before them, were also faced by William James (1842-1910). James took to heart the tasks faced by teachers. His *Talks to Teachers*, was a down-to-earth discussion of the student's mind. James tried to get across to the teachers who read his books or came to his lectures that mental activity was *creative*. Though James was well aware that the "external world" placed obvious limitations on what the mind could invent, he was anxious to interest teachers in leading their students to do as much imaginative work as possible. James often has been characterized as a man caught up in curiosity. He felt that the world was made up of so many relationships that human beings should not be restricted in their development by a narrow range of experience. He urged people to "live dangerously," to be adventurous, and to teach others that the world was one of infinite possibility. Teachers found this doctrine exciting, but, although it captured their imagination, it did not supply them with basic scientific knowledge about children's behavior and interests. That type of information has been slow in coming. To gather it the psychologist has to be able to report accurately on the behavior of a great many children. He must depend upon careful accounts of every phase of child conduct made by many trained observers. He needs research bearing directly on children's interests and must be able to interpret what such research suggests for education.

The content of the elementary-school curriculum changed very slowly previous to 1900. The classical curriculum remained in use long after it was attacked by the sense realists. The impact of the associationists was not sudden, nor when its effect was felt did it fade quickly under the impact of the early development of psychology as a science. Curriculum change is slow even today; the actual curriculum as it may be seen in elementary classrooms today lags far behind theory. However, the curriculum is changing at a faster tempo than ever before in educational history.

Until about 1910, curriculum-making was pretty largely in the hands of private-school and college administrators. Associated with them were specialists in the various secondary-school subjects. In 1893 and 1895 respectively, the Committee of Ten and the Committee of Fifteen appointed by the National Education Association were dominated by the theories of faculty psychology. They recommended that time be economized in the elementary schools in order that a place might be found for secondary-school subjects and for introductions to secondary-school subjects. Their idea was to substitute algebra for most of the arithmetic in the seventh and eighth grades and to substitute Latin for English grammar in the eighth grade. These recommendations were made without any scientific data regarding the needs of children, the characteristics of children at different levels of development, or the psychology of learning. They were based on the assumption that certain subjects strengthen or sharpen the wits to such a degree that their study automatically transfers to all later living. Based on what was believed at the time, the recommendations were reasonable enough.

The scientific approach to objectives

In the early history of education, the objectives of the schools were considered in the same speculative way that was used to describe how learning took place and how teaching should be done. Greek learning had for its objective the training of superior young men to fight, philosophize, and be gentlemen. Roman education might have added that young men should know how to govern, and Roman Christian schools emphasized knowledge of Christianity. Under the influence of the Reformation, the schools stressed reading, particularly of the Bible and the catechism. A host of other subject and skill learnings were soon added. The sense realists had as one objective the development of man to his highest possible degree of intellectual ability, an idea carried to its ultimate in William James' thought that the world held inestimably more relationships than man was taking advantage of.

The first significant attempt to formulate objectives that might be scientifically verified was made by Herbert Spencer. His essay "What Knowledge Is of Most Worth?" had appeared in the July 1859 issue of the *Westminster Review*. It is a study in the process of social adaptation. Spencer believed that a scientific study of society would reveal certain types of information to be absolute essentials for human survival and for the progress of society. He divided adult living into such spheres as earning a living, rearing a family, or spending leisure time. Having made this analysis of living, his next step was to determine the information, knowledge, and skills that would make men efficient in each of these activities.

The measurement movement. The theories of the associationists and of faculty psychology might have persisted much longer had it not been for the rise of the measurement movement. Though Thorndike has been called an associationist himself, he saw clearly the need for scientific verification of many of the claims made about the disciplinary value or transfer value of the things that children were required to learn. Thorndike's work did throw grave doubt on the theory that certain subjects trained the mind or cultivated the intellect;[10] but his most significant contribution was in demonstrating measuring techniques, a development that marked a turning point in the professional study of education. By 1930, America led the world in educational research, and testing and measuring swept the boards in the name of science. First, handwriting was measured, in 1908; and from handwriting it was but a step to national "norms" for spelling and arithmetic. The march was on. City research bureaus were inaugurated and, in 1910, New York

10 Thorndike's examination of "faculty psychology," mental discipline, and automatic transfer of training extended from 1900 to 1930. Perhaps the first step was taken in experiments that were summarized in E. L. Thorndike and R. S. Woodworth, "The Influence of Improvement in One Mental Function Upon the Efficiency of Other Mental Functions," *Psychological Review*, Vol. 8, 1901, 247-251, 384-395, 556-564. In these articles Thorndike and Woodworth first suggest that there is little evidence for separate faculties of the mind. The educational corollary of this was that a course should not be taught to train the memory separately from training in critical thinking or imaginative response.
In the middle 1920's, Thorndike released a number of studies that upset the idea that Latin, or any other subject reputed to discipline the mind, was superior in mental training to any other subject. Perhaps the best known of Thorndike's writings on mental discipline is to be found in E. L. Thorndike, "Mental Discipline in High School Studies."

pioneered in a city-wide study of instruction and instructional results.

Needless to say, all this did not meet with universal approval. There were those who felt that too much attention was being paid to testing and measuring and too little to fitting objectives to the needs of children and society.[11] The educational scientists were challenged to produce the evidence upon which educational objectives could be firmly based. *The job of the schools was to teach these minimal essentials.*

Spencer had a tremendous vogue in the United States during the early years of the scientific movement in education. American educators found that he offered them utilitarian objectives suited to the technological civilization of this country. So well did Spencer fit the American scene that for years after the first American appearance of his thinking every important statement of educational objectives closely paralleled what he had done.[12]

It is not necessary to debate here whether Spencer was correct in his conception of the objectives of education. His criteria have been interpreted and applied without imagination in more than one case, just as were the ideas of Herbart, Thorndike, and others. In the final analysis, however, his objective, scientific attitude had a very commendable effect on curriculum-making. For example, the work of the 1893 and 1895 committees of the National Education Association gave little thought to what would be most realistic for the education of children. After 1915, however, various committees accepted Spencer's criterion of social utility: nothing was to be in-

[11] See the remarks of Harold Rugg writing in "The Foundations and Techniques of Curriculum Construction," Twenty-Sixth Yearbook of the National Society for the Study of Education. Bloomington, Illinois: Public School Publishing Company, 1926, p. 81.

[12] Compare Spencer's belief that education should function to advance self-preservation, the procurement of necessities of life, the rearing of children, social and political relations, and personal culture with the famous *Cardinal Principles of Secondary Education,* written by the Commission on the Reorganization of Secondary Education of the National Education Association. The Commission listed seven "cardinal" objectives of education: fundamental processes (the three R's, for example), health, home membership, vocational competence, citizenship, worthy use of leisure time, and ethical relationships. U. S. Bureau of Education, *Bulletin 35,* 1918.

Bobbitt, Counts, and a host of others, writing on educational objectives, went along with Spencer in almost every detail.

cluded in the *minimal* program of the elementary school that did
not have a direct bearing on preparation for successful adult life.

Under the philosophic spell of Herbert Spencer, American educators inaugurated the hunt for minimal essentials.[13] At first, these
essentials were selected without sufficient evidence. Furthermore,
some teachers and supervisors thought that the essentials were to
be drilled into students vigorously. This was a total misunderstanding of the Spencerian objectives *and* of the associationist learning theory with which the Spencerian objectives were coupled.
Both Spencer and Thorndike abhorred rote memorization and
dreary recitation as a steady educational diet. Perhaps one of the
most common errors in histories of education is the belief that a
scientific attitude toward education entails endless drill and unimaginative instruction. Actually, the science movement arose as a
revolt against faculty psychology. The patient work of E. L. Thorndike, G. M. Wilson, Ernest Horn, and many others, which resulted
in the devising of sensible spelling lists, realistic arithmetic problems, and interesting primers and readers *with controlled vocabularies*,[14] was done in part to avoid the errors intrinsic in dreary drill
methods.

New influences in the determination of objectives. Increasing
knowledge has made it possible to improve upon the utilitarianism
of Herbert Spencer. The new science of psychology has made the
greatest and most direct contributions to elementary education, but
many other sciences have aided also—for example, sociology, social
psychology, anthropology, public health, recreation, medicine, and
biology. Because of its significance in the study of the curriculum,
much material from these and other related areas is included in
later chapters. Advances in the physical sciences and in our tech-

13 For example, between 1925 and 1928 the Department of Superintendence
of the National Education Association published four yearbooks dealing with
minimal essentials.

14 Edward Lee Thorndike, *The Teacher's Word Book.* New York: Teachers
College, Columbia University, 1921; Edward Lee Thorndike and Irving Lorge,
The Teacher's Word Book of 30,000 words. New York: Bureau of Publications,
Teachers College, Columbia University, 1944; Ernest Horn, *A Basic Writing
Vocabulary: The Ten Thousand Words Most Commonly Used in Writing.*
University of Iowa Monographs in Education, First Series, No. 4, Iowa City:
University of Iowa, 1926; G. M. Wilson, *Survey of the Social and Business Uses
of Arithmetic.* Contributions to Education, No. 10, New York: Teachers College,
Columbia University, 1911.

nology generally have affected our ways of living and have changed the nature of the problems faced by man in his changing world. These also will be examined later in our study.

The teacher, aside from keeping abreast of new knowledge relating to education and the learning process, must also be widely informed in the areas of learning in which children will work. An elementary-school teacher must be able to join the physical and social sciences into units that build invaluable insights for students. Man in his environment, for example, is best understood when geography is complemented by many other sciences. It will be necessary that we increasingly break down the artificial boundaries of the conventional subjects. To do all this it is necessary that a teacher be well grounded in the knowledge bearing on the "lessons," that he know theory, method, *and subject matter.* As we are scientific in the knowledge that we gather, so must we be scientific in learning the art of teaching. This is the ultimate conclusion of the scientific movement in professional education.

"Essentialism" versus "progressivism." In 1926, the National Society for the Study of Education published one of its most interesting yearbooks, one dealing with the foundations and techniques of curriculum-making. The yearbook was written by the Society's Committee on Curriculum-Making, of which Harold Rugg was Director and William C. Bagley, George S. Counts, Ernest Horn, Charles H. Judd, and William Heard Kilpatrick were members.[15] Some of these men (Rugg, Counts, and Kilpatrick) saw the curriculum against the background of a social order that was changing rapidly from agrarianism to industrialization. These men emphasized that the curriculum should be thought of in terms of the perspective, understanding, and interests of children. Others among them (Bagley, Judd, and Horn) were more alert to the usefulness of tradition and felt that the curriculum ought to be aimed at helping children become adults by gaining possession of the accumulated wisdom of the centuries.

Both groups firmly declared themselves against parrot-like recita-

[15] The full membership roster of the Society's Committee on Curriculum-Making includes the names of William C. Bagley, Franklin Bobbitt, Frederick G. Bonser, Werrett W. Charters, George S. Counts, Stuart A. Courtis, Ernest Horn, Charles H. Judd, Frederick J. Kelly, William H. Kilpatrick, Harold Rugg, Chairman, and George A. Works.

tion, harsh discipline, and ignorance of scientific evidence on how children learn. The real difference between them was that the latter group was anxious to conserve the values created by civilization, while the former, though not rejecting that ambition, felt that civilization would be preserved best and improved most by aiding students to solve problems rather than to study the accumulated wisdom of the past. The group that emphasized the changing nature of society and man's role as a problem-solver felt that the curriculum had become a random miscellany of facts unrelated to the civic, artistic, and personal responsibilities of contemporary citizens. These men wished the schools to prepare students to work cooperatively with their fellows in solving the pressing problems of everyday living.

In the 1930's Rugg, Counts, and Kilpatrick wrote voluminously on the duty of the schools to develop responsible citizens, to create a new social order, and to build an awareness of the need for cooperative planning within an interdependent economy when social and economic change is accelerated. This emphasis was not evident in the later writing of the other group.

In the area of psychology, both groups were poles apart. With their avid interest in planning, problem-solving, and meeting the emerging issues of a changing world, Rugg, Counts, and Kilpatrick evidently disapproved of associationism, feeling that it was valuable only in rote learning and not helpful to students in promoting social progress. They wanted activities that invited insight and understanding.

As already mentioned, the essentialists, with some modifications, stood on the conviction that a realistic knowledge of man's cultural heritage was the most reliable guide for future action. In spite of this, no less than the progressives, the essentialists looked to the future and were equally reform-minded. In book after book, Judd flayed those who refused to allow free thinking and unfettered research. Time and again Bagley pleaded for less dogmatic, narrow, and provincial thinking and attacked isolationism and nationalism. Judd championed the cause of intellectual liberty; Bagley labored on behalf of cosmopolitanism and civilized, humane values.

The falling out between progressives and essentialists came during the 1920's, partly as the result of a failure to communicate. Men in each group failed to see that a difference in degree or em-

phasis was not a difference in kind or in basic viewpoint. Bagley, Judd, and Horn feared that if the interests and activities of children were given paramount attention teachers would not prepare units carefully. Horn, for one, had spent years evolving criteria for the selection of materials to be included in elementary-school books,[16] and did not wish to see his criteria lightly laid aside in favor of the transient interests of children. He could not accept the idea that the present concerns of a child should determine what the teacher teaches. As he put it, you do not teach a child as though he were going to die on his next birthday; i.e., what a child learns at any moment should be pointed to what he will need ten, twenty, or thirty years hence.

To allay Horn's doubts, the progressives should have been able to show that working with the present interests of children did not involve neglecting the knowledge, attitudes, and skills they would need as adults. It would have been necessary to prove that children *naturally* desire to read, to communicate, and to learn about living and the real world. At the time of the heated arguments between progressives and essentialists, educational psychologists did not have definitive data that might have resolved the conflict.

The authors of this book take the position that the teacher must be a student of the world and of human beings in order to guide students' insights into generalizations that can be demonstrated to be valid descriptions of reality. We do not believe that children, unaided by skilled teachers, will arrive at these insights. Only the most sophisticated teachers, after careful planning of their units of experience, can help a child to broaden his horizon.

We agree with the progressive argument against functionless subject matter. (Essentialists urged the same reconstruction of subject matter.) The progressives rejuvenated the tradition of those who tried to understand the ways in which children perceive themselves and their surroundings. We credit them with laboring ceaselessly to promote "integrative" social atmospheres in classrooms, to lessen

---

[16] His report was published in 1918. Under Horn's stimulation, discussions were going forward all over the country on utilization of the criteria of social utility: frequency of use with attention to the social status of the user, cruciality, and universality in time, geographic location, and vocation. As these terms suggest, Horn found a place in the curriculum for only those ideas, skills, and abilities which could be known to be of great social use because they were crucial, universal, and frequently encountered in life outside the school.

hostile teacher attitudes, and to use more of the principles of mental hygiene in teaching. Then, too, no other group in education has done more to champion a faith in democracy.

Unfortunately, the intensity with which the progressives wrote on behalf of children's interests and democracy offended many educators who were in essential agreement with them, but did not wish to wear their hearts on their sleeves and to wage crusades. Had there been less defensiveness in progressive ranks and less bitter criticism of progressivism by essentialists, both parties might have seen that they had common objectives and a common ancestry. Neither one would have had to claim to be the only group dedicated to advancing the science of education or, on the other hand, the "expressive" and creative activities of children.

Today there is no valid reason for continuing the essentialist-progressive quarrel. We believe that the issues of the Twenty-sixth Yearbook of the National Society for the Study of Education are dead and should be buried, without, however, scrapping the insights of the combatants. Judd has shown us that education is more than the interaction of subject matter with children. As he painstakingly demonstrated, education is a process of becoming acquainted with a culture and with a society. Of course, Judd worked at a time when sociology and cultural anthropology were in their infancy, but he saw their potentiality as did other educators. Sighting along the lines he defined, this book attempts to suggest what the social sciences have to offer an elementary teacher interested in the social foundations of the curriculum. Thus we ask what social and cultural influences play on students or on teachers? In another context, we are found to be Spencerian in inquiring into the social utility of the newer natural-science courses of study.

Agreeing with Rugg, Counts, and Kilpatrick that the survival of man calls for skill in human relations, we are vitally concerned to write about intergroup relations within the classroom, "integrative" teacher attitudes, and teaching for the advancement of original, creative, and critical thinking. Reminded that the understanding of facts means the ability to use them, we urge that units of study make ample provision for critical reflection on the relations of man to man and of man to his physical and social environment. Mindful of Rugg's pleas for people able to express themselves imaginatively, we urge greater attention to an arts program in the elementary school.

Horn, Judd, and Bagley—along with other realists—have taught us to honor organization in study. While we are quite unwilling to disregard the perspective, interests, and abilities of children, we do want teachers disciplined in their logic or thinking, generously conversant with the arts and with science, and schooled at working with materials in ways that are realistic for youngsters.

Both essentialists and progressives have advocated these goals for the elementary school, and the majority of sturdy, responsible, professional educators have endorsed them. We adopt them as the substance of our belief in education for human welfare.

This brief historical introduction and the short statement of the position of the authors in current curriculum discussions will serve only to introduce the interesting issues that lie ahead of us. The most intriguing and challenging aspects of the study of curriculum are the rapid changes in emphasis that are constantly taking place as research continues to open up new and exciting possibilities for those who deal with children in the schools. The conviction grows that elementary education will continue to develop and refine its curricular practices for many years to come. One of the most interesting places to start is with the consideration of individual differences—the subject of the next chapter.

Discussion Questions

1. Can you tell, after reading this first chapter, what two conflicting viewpoints the authors hope to reconcile?
2. Contrast essentialism and progressivism.
3. How much different were Spencer's objectives for education from the Cardinal Principles of Secondary Education?
4. The authors state their belief that education should serve human welfare—that is the basis of their philosophy. Is this objective too broad? What does it mean in terms of the details of the curriculum?
5. Does the philosophy of human welfare mean more for the curriculum when related to the idea of the interdependence of man and nature?
6. Does the idea of the interrelatedness of the various sciences and fields of human knowledge have implications for the curriculum?
7. The term "human relation" assumes relationships of various kinds between humans as individuals and groups. Does that assumption justify

the thought that teachers should know some of the basic ideas about culture and society and human personality?

8. Does the study of the artistic sensibilities and potentialities of man have implications for human welfare?

9. How can a philosophy of elementary education be developed from scientific sources?

10. What has been the effect of the thinking of Rousseau in education?

11. What is meant by "sense realism"?

12. What would you say were the limits of "testing" in education? Is everything in education subject to measurement? Can it be, ultimately?

13. What has the tests and measurements movement accomplished?

Selected References

Anderson, Harold H., and H. M. Brewer, Studies of Teachers' Classroom Personalities I: "Dominative and Socially Integrative Behavior of Kindergarten Teachers," *Applied Psychology Monographs*, No. 6, 1948.

Barker, Roger G., Herbert F. Wright, and Louise S. Barker, *et al., One Boy's Day*. New York: Harper and Brothers, 1951.

Dewey, John, *Democracy and Education*. New York: The Macmillan Company, 1916.

———, *How We Think*. Boston: D. C. Heath and Company, 1910.

———, *The Child and the Curriculum*. Chicago: The University of Chicago Press, 1903.

———, "Interest as Related to the Training of the Will," National Herbart Society Yearbook, 1895.

Judd, Charles H., *Education and Social Progress*. New York: Harcourt, Brace and Company, 1934.

Lippitt, Ronald, "An Experimental Study of the Effect of Democratic and Authoritarian Group Atmospheres," Studies in Topological and Vector Psychology, I. University of Iowa, *Studies in Child Welfare*, Vol. 16, 1940, 43-195.

Locke, John, *Some Thoughts Concerning Education*. London: Cambridge University Press, 1899.

Plato, *The Republic, Meno, and the Laws*. (Translated by B. Jowett). New York: Tudor Publishing Company, N.D.

Rousseau, J. J., *Émile; or, Education*. (Translated by Barbara Foxley). New York: E. P. Dutton and Company, 1911.

Spencer, Herbert, "What Knowledge is of Most Worth?" *Westminster Review*, July 1859.

Thorndike, Edward Lee, "Mental Discipline in High School Studies," *Journal of Educational Psychology*, Vol. 15, November-December, 1924, 1-24, 83-98.

INDIVIDUAL AND TRAIT DIFFERENCES

IN THE ELEMENTARY SCHOOLS

*W*HEN EXPERIENCED TEACHERS are asked to state the most difficult problems they face in the classroom, they emphasize those problems involved in adjusting the curriculum to the wide range of needs and abilities of individual pupils—how to motivate different pupils, how to find materials suited to the children's various levels of ability, how to differentiate assignments, how to make success possible for every pupil, how to diagnose and correct difficulties, how to present materials to different pupils, and how to test and evaluate achievement. As the teacher searches for the solutions to these problems, he continues to hope that some plan will be found to promote or to group children in classes in such a way that all members of each class are more or less alike in such things as abilities and interests. We shall see in this chapter why this is a vain hope.

There is much misunderstanding regarding the extent of individual and trait differences. The phrase individual differences refers to the dissimilarity among the various members of a class or age group in any characteristic such as intelligence, reading ability, spelling ability, and the like; while trait differences refers to the variability of a single person with reference to abilities and traits such as his own relative standing in reading, spelling, arithmetic, music, and art. There are some erroneous beliefs and attitudes regarding individual and trait differences. The following queries suggest what some of these erroneous beliefs and attitudes may be.

(1) Do you believe that grade levels signify rather definite levels of academic achievement?

(2) Do you believe that in a typical first grade made up of six-year-olds, there will be children with mental ages below four years and others with mental ages above eight years, or that in a typical sixth grade there are children with third-grade reading ability and others with tenth-grade reading ability?

(3) Do you believe that a measure of intelligence, either I.Q. or mental age, indicates learning capacity in the various school subjects with a high degree of exactness?

(4) Do you believe that the homogeneous grouping of pupils on the basis of general intelligence or general achievement materially reduces the range of specific abilities in the classroom?

(5) Do you believe that a teacher should be criticized for promoting a pupil who is not able to do the work for the next grade?

(6) Do you believe that the course of study for a given grade should be administered to all pupils?

(7) Do you believe that the promotion of all pupils, regardless of achievement, increases the variability of achievement in the upper grades?

(8) Do you believe that universal promotion tends to lower the average achievement levels of the various grades?

(9) Do you believe that the threat of failure causes pupils to work harder?

(10) Do you believe that a retarded pupil achieves more in the end than he would had he been regularly promoted?

(11) Do you believe that uniform textbooks and workbooks in the hands of all pupils constitute adequate instructional materials?

(12) Do you believe that the chief value of having the school furnish all instructional materials is that it enables the school to furnish each child with materials adapted to his abilities, interests, and levels of achievement?

(13) Do you believe that when teachers are under pressure to pass as many of their pupils as possible, they set examinations and learning goals that depend largely upon memory and neglect goals involving relational thinking, problem-solving, and creative endeavor?

(14) Do you believe that the same learning goals can be set for all pupils?

(15) Do you believe that the grade levels at which certain knowledges, skills, and abilities should be taught can be determined with a high degree of specificity?

(16) Do you believe that elementary teachers should consider themselves as highly specialized at a given grade level, for example, skilled as a first-grade teacher but not as a fifth-grade teacher?

(17) Do you believe that it is more important for the teacher to know the subject matter at a given grade level than to know the pupils?

(18) Do you believe that the number of pupils in a class should influence possible teaching procedures.

(19) Do you believe that individual differences should be accepted as

desirable in the scheme of things or as something undesirable, to be overcome?

(20) Do you accept the dictum, "Provide for individual differences and bring all students up to standard"?

The extent of individual differences
in the elementary school

Obviously our civilization requires the services of unskilled laborers, janitors, truck drivers, assembly-line workers, college professors, research specialists, industrial managers, lawyers, surgeons, and many others. There are approximately 30,000 different job classifications in the Department of Labor's *Dictionary of Occupations*. How fortunate it is that men are born with potentialities for the various abilities, interests, and temperaments necessary to fill these different jobs with more or less success, satisfaction, and happiness.

It is approximately true to say that public education in the United States is "committed" to at least 12 years of schooling for all the children of all the people. In the first grade, as well as in high school, the potential unskilled laborer sits beside the potential surgeon. This fact sets the problem with which the public schools are grappling. In some schools, both may be required to read the same material, solve the same problems, and be evaluated according to the same standards, the result being that the maximum intellectual possibilities of the prospective surgeon are not stimulated and the prospective unskilled laborer is required to do work far beyond his capacity and is faced with daily discouragement and humiliation when he fails. The problem has been apparent for a long time, but most of the remedies proposed have been based on an inadequate understanding of the nature and extent of individual and trait differences, and of the factors that influence them.

Although it is possible to overemphasize the importance of intelligence and achievement test scores in measuring individual and trait differences, it is more meaningful to describe some individual and trait differences on this basis. In a first-grade class made up of a random group of six-year-old children, 2 per cent of the pupils have mental ages of less than four years, and 2 per cent have mental ages of more than eight years. In other words, if we disregard the 2 per cent at both ends of the distribution and consider only the middle 96 per cent of the class, we have a four-year range in mental development.[1] If we administer tests designed to measure more specific traits, such as extent of vocabulary, acquaintance with the number system, reading readiness, and so forth, approximately the same range is found in these abilities as is found in intelligence. The various traits associated with educational achievement, measured at the six-year level, will show that there is a variability of four years between individuals at the 2nd and 98th percentile.

When we examine the variability in intelligence and achievement of children at the end of the sixth grade or at the beginning of the seventh grade (twelve-year-olds), we find it to be twice what it was in the first grade (measured in age units). At this level the range of intelligence and achievement (2nd to 98th percentile) is between seven and eight years. This has been found true in the achievement areas of reading comprehension, vocabulary, the mechanics of English composition, literary knowledge, science, geography, and history. In arithmetic reasoning and computation the range is slightly less, between six and seven years at the sixth-grade level.

Perhaps the most effective way of revealing the range of ability and achievement in the various subject areas of the elementary school is to present it graphically. Figure 1 shows the overlapping in grade achievement of two typical eight-grade elementary schools, one with a high rate of retardation, the other with a low rate of

[1] E. F. Lindquist, ed., *Educational Measurement*. Washington, D. C.: American Council on Education, 1951, pp. 9-14; Quinn McNemar, *The Revision of the Stanford-Binet Scale*. Boston: Houghton Mifflin Company, 1942, pp. 33-34.

Since the standard deviation of I.Q.'s for an unselected population is 16 I.Q. points (Lewis M. Terman and Maud A. Merrill, *Measuring Intelligence*. Boston: Houghton Mifflin Company, 1937, p. 40), we know that the individual at the second percentile will have an I.Q. of 68. If this I.Q. of 68 is divided by 100, it becomes .68, which means that the second percentile individual is developing .68 as rapidly as the normal individual. Hence, by multiplying .68 by any given chronological age, we find the mental age of the second percentile individual of that age. For example, six-year-olds, $6 \times .68 = 4.08$. This means that the second percentile six-year-old has a mental age of 4.08 years.

The 98th percentile individual has an I.Q. of 132. Following the same logic, we find that $6 \times 1.32 = 7.92$, which is the mental age of the 98th percentile six-year-old. By multiplying any chronological age by .68 and 1.32, we find the range in mental age between the 2nd and 98th percentile individual. For twelve-year-olds the range is from 8.16 to 15.84 years, or roughly from 8 to 16 years.

retardation. It will be noted that the grades are most homogeneous with respect to chronological age and mental age.[2] A study of Figure 1 reveals the following facts: (1) The chronological age distributions of the two schools is almost identical in the first two grades, but beginning with the third grade there is progressively more retardation in one of the schools. (2) The least variability in achievement is found in arithmetic, with a range of six years in the fourth grade, extending to eight years in the eighth grade. (3) In the mechanics of English, reading comprehension, science, geography, and history, almost the complete range of elementary-school achievement is found in each grade above the primary. (4) The mean achievement in the school with the low retardation rate is significantly higher than in the school that retains the low-ability pupils longer. (5) The range of achievement in the various grades with which the teacher must cope is not significantly different in the two schools. (6) The low achievers in any four or five successive grades have more in common with one another than they have with the average achiever in their own grade; likewise, the high achievers in four or five successive grades have more in common than they have with the average achiever in their own grade. (7) If the low achievers in the eighth grade were demoted to the fourth grade they would, in most instances, be below the average achiever of the fourth grade.

Conditions similar to these will be found in any school system when standardized intelligence and achievement tests are administered. They have far-reaching implications for curriculum organization and design. These implications will be outlined in detail in later chapters, but now, for the sake of contrast and hence for clarity as to desirable practice, we should consider briefly how the graded elementary school in the United States has, in the past, dealt with the problem of individual differences.

[2] Mental age was measured with the *Kuhlman-Anderson Intelligence Test.* This test yields a narrower range of mental ability at age and grade levels than the *Revised Stanford-Binet Tests of Intelligence,* probably because only ten tests of a possible 39 in the entire scale are given to any grade. The test manual cautions against this practice, but the cautions are rarely heeded. The use of the median mental age on the ten tests instead of the mean also tends to reduce the variability. Achievement was measured with the *Unit Scales of Attainment* battery.

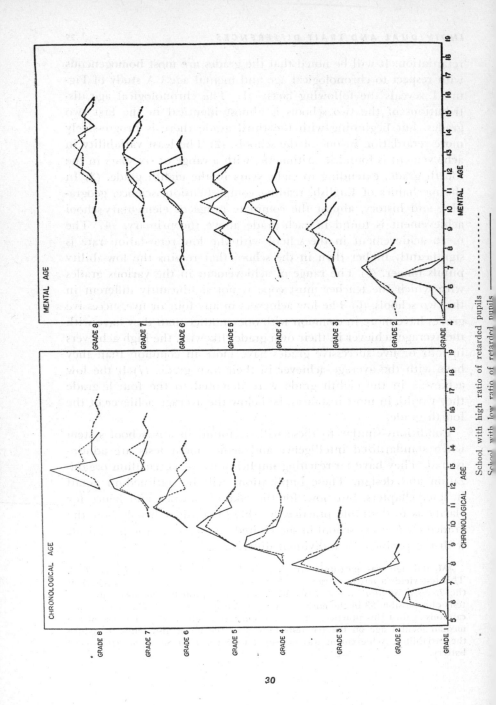

School with high ratio of retarded pupils ‥‥‥‥‥‥

School with low ratio of retarded pupils ————

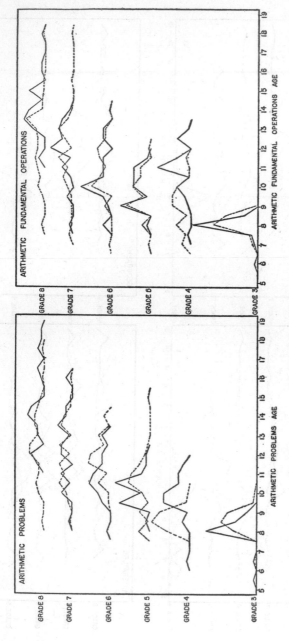

Figure 1. Variability in chronological age, mental age, and achievement ages of pupils in two eight-grade elementary schools, one with a high rate of retardation, the other with low rate of retardation. Frequencies computed as per cent of class at each age level.

31

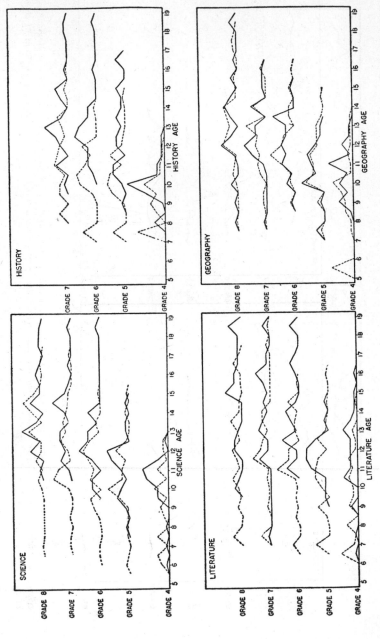

Figure 1 (continued). Variability in chronological age, mental age, and achievement ages of pupils in two eight-grade elementary schools, one with a high rate of retardation, the other with low rate of retardation. Frequencies computed as per cent of class at each age level.

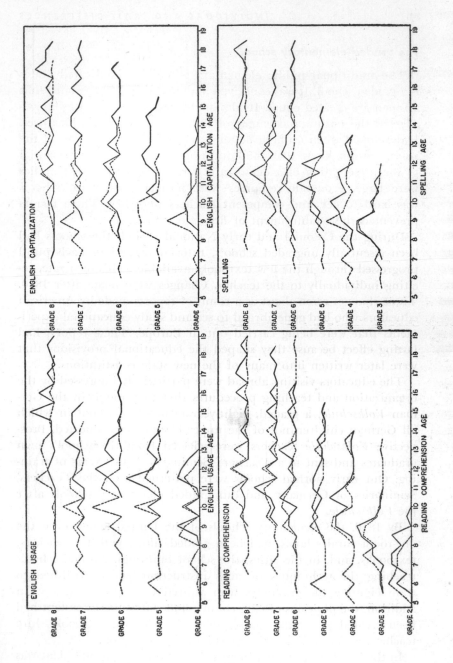

The graded elementary school

The traditional public elementary school in the United States is a graded school. It was conceived and established in the faith that all men are created equal. Its designers, however, had little knowledge of the nature and extent of individual and trait differences. It developed when nothing better was possible. The citizens of the young nation knew that the education of all youth was essential to the preservation of a democratic form of government. Families were large, economic resources were meager, money for schools was hard to get, and competent teachers were few. These factors prevented the establishment of first-rate schools.

During the Colonial and early National periods the schools had been essentially ungraded schools, tutorial in design. Each pupil progressed through the few textbooks available at his own rate, reciting individually to the teacher. Changes were made after 1840. These changes came about as a result of reports made by American educators who had gone abroad to see and study educational experiments that were being carried out in Europe. These reports had lasting effect because they shaped the educational provisions that were later written into many of the new state constitutions.

The educators visiting abroad were particularly impressed by the organization and teaching procedures that they found in the German *Volkschule*, a graded, eight-year elementary school in which all German children not of the upper classes were educated. Prospective *Volkschule* teachers were selected from the school's own graduates and sent to a Teachers' Seminary for two years of training. Our early normal schools were patterned after the Teachers' Seminaries of Germany and our graded elementary schools after the *Volkschule*.

By 1870, the elementary schools of the United States, even the one-room rural schools, had been graded, along with the teachers, textbooks, and, in the cities, the school buildings. Normal schools teaching the techniques of mass instruction were established to train eighth-grade graduates who aspired to become teachers. In addition, the positions of city, county, and state superintendent had been created to set up courses of study, approve textbooks, hire teachers, and coordinate the machinery of education.

In the latter part of the nineteenth century, a superintendent was prone to think he had a well-organized school system when he could take out his watch at ten o'clock on Monday morning, October 13, and say to his visitor, "The fourth-grade classes in every school in this city are at this minute beginning instruction in the division of whole numbers with single digit divisors, and the problem that is being presented is 24 divided by 2." The straight lines and lock-step procedure by which children entered and left the school building, the rigid attention, the harsh discipline, the pin-dropping atmosphere, the class lined up at attention, eyes right and heads snapping forward as each one recited in turn, were reflections of the *Volkschule* upon which our schools had been patterned.

Perhaps a clearer conception of what this type of schooling is like, its essentially mechanical nature, its disregard for individual differences, can be realized by comparing it with an assembly line in an automobile plant. Of course, the comparison is unfair. The most mechanical teaching in the world may be softened by a kindly manner. But there is some real similarity between the assembly line in a factory and unimaginative teaching. In a factory the chassis of a car is placed on a moving belt, approximately a half mile in length. On each side of the belt stand specialists, each responsible for attaching some part of the car. At the end of the line the car moves off under its own power, assembled by a group of workers, each with a minute task to perform, no one person on the assembly line having responsibilities requiring insight into the finished product or needing abilities approaching those of a mechanical engineer. Great credit is given the production engineers who first conceived the mass-production assembly line, though its psychological by-products are now being questioned by industrial management. The educators who first conceived the graded school anticipated the industrial production line by more than 50 years. In the assembly-line graded school, the six-year-old comes first into the province of the first-grade teacher, who is responsible for attaching certain specified knowledge, skills, attitudes, and abilities. He then moves on to the second-grade teacher, who again attaches certain knowledge, skills, attitudes, and abilities. By the time he reaches high school, the assembly-line workers are more specialized; one teacher is responsible for certain knowledge, skills, attitudes, and abilities in English, another in mathematics, another in social studies, and so on. Perhaps if children were as uniform in their aptitudes, interests, and abilities as steel is in its physical properties such a school could be defended on educational terms.

Early remedies for
uneven educational progress

Achievement standards required for promotion were determined subjectively by the authors of the graded textbooks and courses of study. Promotion policies were strict, and soon "laggards in our schools" became the major educational problem. In some schools the failure rate reached 50 per cent, and adolescent boys and girls were frequently retained in the primary grades.

Numerous panaceas for this situation were introduced and tried between 1875 and 1925. It was natural that changes in promotional policies should be suggested first. When it appeared that failing a pupil for a year was too severe, semiannual promotion, quarterly promotion, subject promotion, and special promotion were tried in different school systems. Then it was found that as the effects of non-promotion were made the less severe, the more often teachers resorted to its use. Semiannual promotion to a new room and a new teacher is still the policy in some schools. Its practice requires the teacher to learn the characteristics and needs of two classes each year instead of one, as under the annual promotion plan. Other remedies attempted to hold grade standards constant. In this approach, "assisting teachers" were appointed and vacation classes organized to increase the amount of instruction for slow-learning pupils. In some cities even today failing students are required to attend summer school. Another remedy was to hold the course of study and grade standards constant, and differentiate the time required to complete the elementary school—six years for the bright, seven for the average, and eight for the slow learners. Still another remedy limited the time spent in the elementary school to eight years, but differentiated the curriculum for slow, medium, and fast-learning pupils. Other plans divided the course of study in each skill area into units of specific activities and achievements, permitting each pupil to advance at his own rate in each skill, with group instruction being offered in the content areas of the curriculum. Several of these plans required that pupils be classified by their teachers into slow, medium, and fast-learning groups, the ability of teachers to make such an arrangement not being seriously questioned at the time.

A limitation on the effectiveness
of general-ability grouping: trait differences

Following World War I, the rapid development of group intelli-' gence and achievement tests suggested the practice of general-ability grouping to meet the individual needs of children. This plan was used on a large scale in the schools of Detroit in 1920. In that year 10,000 pupils entering the first grade were sectioned into three groups on the basis of scores they had made on a group intelligence test: the upper 20 per cent were designated as the X group, the middle 60 per cent as the Y group, and the lower 20 per cent as the Z group. The course of study was differentiated to provide the best possible experiences for each level of ability.

This practice of grouping pupils according to some measure of general ability (intelligence, general achievement, teacher opinion, or a combination of these) was extensively adopted in other cities. The extent to which courses of study were modified to meet the needs of the hypothetical slow, average, and bright pupil varied from school system to school system, as did the proportion of pupils placed in the different groups. Soon a lively debate was being carried on in the leading educational journals of the day as supporters and critics of the new system argued their respective points on educational, philosophical, sociological, and psychological grounds.[3] For a time everyone seemed to assume that the pupils really were grouped according to ability—that the groups were homogeneous. Little attention was given to the question of whether general-ability grouping reduced the variability of instructional groups in the specific subject areas of reading, arithmetic, spelling, music, art, and the like.

General-ability grouping is based on the hypothesis that trait dif-

[3] Thirty-fifth Yearbook of the National Society for the Study of Education, Part I, "The Grouping of Pupils," 1936; Twenty-fourth Yearbook of the National Society for the Study of Education, Part II, "Adapting the Schools to Individual Differences." 1925. Bloomington Illinois: Public School Publishing Company.

ferences may be ignored, that all traits with which the school is concerned are highly correlated, and that mental functions are organized around a predominating general factor that determines the general-competence level of the individual. In other words, the theory was that if a child was high, or low, or average in reading, he would be high, low, or average in arithmetic, in geography, in art, and in everything else—all because he was high, low, or average in general intelligence. Evidence from several overlapping fields of psychology tends to refute this hypothesis. This research is well summarized by Anastasi and Foley.[4] For our purposes, the conclusions based on Hull's [5] study of the variability in amount of different traits possessed by the individual are appropriate. His subjects were 107 ninth-grade boys to whom he administered 35 psychological and educational tests involving a wide variety of traits. Hull concluded that trait differences in the typical student in this group were 80 per cent as great as individual differences in the total group, that trait differences are normally distributed, that trait variability is twice as great in some individuals as in others, and that no relationship exists between the individual's general level of ability and the extent of his trait variability. If we assume that the traits measured by Hull are representative of the traits responsible for achievement in the various areas of the curriculum, general-ability grouping, if perfectly done, still would not reduce the variability of classes more than 20 per cent. That is, we should anticipate an overlapping of approximately 80 per cent between the X and Z groups in most subjects.

A more direct attack on the question of how the variability of elementary-school classes can be reduced through general-ability grouping has been made by Hollingshead [6] and Burr.[7] Hollingshead was concerned with determining the best measure of general ability for classification purposes. Educational achievement test bat-

4 A. Anastasi, and John P. Foley, Jr., *Differential Psychology*. New York: The Macmillan Company, 1949, Chapters 14 and 15.

5 Clark L. Hull, "Variability in Amount of Different Traits Possessed by the Individual," *Journal of Educational Psychology*, Vol. 18, 1927, 97-104.

6 A. D. Hollingshead, *An Evaluation of the Use of Certain Educational and Mental Measurements for the Purpose of Classification*. Contributions to Education, No. 302. New York: Teachers College, Columbia University, 1928.

7 Marvin A. Burr, *A Study of Homogeneous Grouping*. Contributions to Education, No. 457. New York: Teachers College, Columbia University, 1931.

teries were found to be the most effective basis for grouping. Burr attempted to determine the extent to which general-ability grouping reduces the range of ability of classes in reading and arithmetic. The variability of the typical X, Y, and Z section in reading and arithmetic was found to be approximately 80 per cent of the total grade range. That is, there was in general an overlapping of 80 per cent between the extreme X and Z sections. Individual pupils were found to be such complexes of more or less independent abilities that when sections were made non-overlapping in one phase of a subject such as arithmetic reasoning, they overlapped greatly in another phase such as arithmetic computation.

The important generalization to be drawn from studies of trait variability is that instructional groups formed by general-ability grouping are not sufficiently homogeneous, with reference to achievement or learning capacity in the various curricular areas, to warrant designing a curriculum for uniform mass-instruction procedures. For example, a typical sixth grade will show a range of almost eight years in reading ability. After X, Y, Z sectioning on the basis of educational age, each section will still show a range of from five to seven years. Thus, even when grouping is practiced, the teacher must adapt the curriculum to the individual child and must know his particular and immediate learning problems. The obligation of the school to furnish instructional materials with a range of difficulty commensurate with the range of ability in a class and to individualize instruction is just about as great when general-ability grouping is practiced as when it is not. General-ability grouping should *not* be confused with grouping for instruction in specific learning areas. If children are divided into small groups to work on various units and parts of units, the possibilities of caring for individual differences are enhanced. In Chapter 18, a desirable and necessary type of grouping will be described, and in the last three chapters of the book, illustrations of desirable types of grouping will be given.

Can promotion policies simplify the problem of meeting the needs of individual children?

Teachers and school officials frequently attribute the wide range of ability found in classes to lax promotion policies in the lower grades. Their arguments seem reasonable enough at first thought. They maintain that the practice of promoting almost all children regardless of achievement has been adopted by the elementary school as a means of hiding its failures and of keeping parents and children happy. What is needed, some critics insist, are meaningful grade standards that signify definite stages of educational development to which a pupil must attain before he is promoted. It is dishonest, they say, to promote pupils who have not earned a promotion. They assume that pressure and "discipline," if more rigorously applied would result in almost all pupils reaching a respectable standard; and that teachers, by bringing all pupils up to standard, would thus provide for individual differences. According to their argument, pupils of low achievement who are promoted are hurt more than they are helped because they suffer emotionally as they drop further and further behind the rest of their grade. They become discouraged, quit trying, and learn that they can "get by" without effort.

An investigation reported by Cook [8] tests several of these arguments on the basis of complete test records for 148 Minnesota school systems. These systems were first ranked on the basis of retardation. Then nine systems that approached the universal promotion end of the distribution were matched with nine systems that tried to maintain rigorous standards of promotion by failing many pupils. Matching was on the basis of type of community, size of school systems, socio-economic status of parents, and professional qualifications of teachers. It was found that schools that had relatively few failures and approached the universal promotion end of the continuum had significantly higher achievement and intelligence scores than those with many failures and much non-promotion. Those schools that had relatively high standards of promotion (retarded the slow and accelerated the fast learners) had a higher proportion of over-age, slow-learning pupils, one reason being that pupils remained in the elementary grades from one to several years longer.

The range of ability (2nd to 98th percentile) at the seventh-grade level of the two groups of schools also was compared. Eleven measures of achievement in addition to intelligence were available. No

[8] Walter W. Cook, "Some Effects of the Maintenance of High Standards of Promotion," *Elementary School Journal,* Vol. 41, February 1941, 430-437.

significant difference was found in the variability of the classes in the two groups. Thus, though we saw in the paragraph above that there was higher achievement in classes where there were fewer failures, we see here that the size of the range between the high and the low achievers is the same for both groups. The higher proportion of low-ability pupils in the schools with high rates of retardation tended to keep the variability of the classes large in spite of efforts to maintain standards. Pupils were rarely failed more than twice in the same grade and eventually reached the upper grades. The relatively high proportion of retarded pupils increased the range of ability found in classes in the schools with high failure rates.

When the achievement of pupils of the same chronological and mental ages in the two groups of schools was compared, there was no difference. This indicates that the schools were well matched and also that the constant threat of failure did *not* increase achievement in the schools with high rates of failure, and that non-promotion actually tends to reduce grade standards without alleviating the problem of the range of ability.

A considerable amount of substantiating evidence for these findings is available in books and journals in the educational field. If pupils were all promoted regularly, each grade would represent an age group: first-graders would all be six-year-olds, second-graders seven-year-olds, and so on. Hence it is possible to know what variability of classes would be produced by universal promotion. In the standardization of the *Stanford-Binet Tests of Intelligence,* both in 1916 and 1937, comparisons were made between the variability of age groups and grade groups (the median range of chronological age in the grade groups was six years). The conclusion was reached that age groups were no more variable than grade groups and that the problems of the teacher in meeting the needs of individual pupils would be no greater if universal promotion prevailed.[9]

Cornell has reported the variability of New York State school children in intelligence and achievement at three age levels—seven, ten, and fourteen. After comparing these age data with grade data from two previous studies by Coxe, Cornell concluded that, "both the range of the middle 50 per cent and the total range show no

[9] Quinn, *The Revision of the Stanford-Binet Scale,* pp. 23-25.

marked difference in favor of either age or grade groups. For practical purposes of classification, then, we could deal with an age group without any more difficulty due to diversity than we find in a grade." [10]

We are forced to conclude that it is impossible, in the public schools that all children attend, to reduce the variability of instructional groups significantly through promotion policies. If strict standards of promotion are followed, the efficiency of the school is reduced through the accumulation of low-ability pupils and the lessening of educational opportunities for the more able.

Can effective teaching make classes more homogeneous in achievement?

Many teachers believe that the wide range of achievement found in each grade is the result of poor teaching. "Too many teachers," they say, "are not willing to sacrifice the time and energy required to bring their classes up to a respectable minimum standard. Of course there are great differences in children, but if teachers will provide for these differences, be willing to give the slow learners extra help, have them work after school, give them more homework, and provide vacation classes, almost all pupils can reach a respectable standard."

The teachers who take this point of view are usually experienced, conscientious teachers, but frequently have very definite and very limited teaching goals. Such teachers know, or think that they know, quite exactly the experiences that fifth-grade pupils, for example, should have, the questions they should be able to answer, and the problems they should be able to solve. There is a list of words that must be spelled with at least 75 per cent accuracy; certain problems in addition, subtraction, multiplication, and division of fractions should be solved by a definite procedure. Pupils must know the 48 states and their capitals; the chief characteristics and products of the principal cities of the United States; the names and discoveries of early explorers; the causes, results, principal campaigns, and generals of each war in which the United States has participated; and

[10] Ethel L. Cornell, *The Variability of Children of Different Ages and Its Relation to School Classification and Grouping.* University of the State of New York Bulletin, No. 1101, Educational Research Studies, No. 1, 1937.

similar specific items of information. Success in achieving these goals depends largely upon memory. If a fact or a process or a relationship cannot be understood, at least it can be memorized.

In limited-goal schooling, information is substituted for education. Pupils get the idea that learning consists of memorizing the content of textbooks; they read to remember, not to understand. In such a scheme of education, little or no attempt is made to teach children to organize and integrate ideas, to see relationships, to draw inferences, or to make applications of what they have learned to new situations. The goals set by such teachers can be achieved by the majority of the class. The superior pupils can do it with ease, but they are bored and waste much of their time; the slower pupils do it with difficulty and work extra hours. But with respect to the limited goals, relative homogeneity may be attained in the group.

The problem with which we are dealing is concerned basically with the effect of a period of learning upon individual differences. Are pupils more alike or less alike with respect to a given ability after a period of instruction? Does good teaching decrease or increase the variability of the class? A considerable amount of research on this question has been published. It has been well summarized by Anastasi, Peterson and Barlow, and Reed.[11] Many technical problems are involved in the accurate interpretation of this research, but for our purposes the following generalization is warranted: If the responses to be learned are sufficiently simple, and if the goals that have been set are so limited that a high proportion of the group can master them during the period of learning, the variability in the learning of the group becomes less; if the task is complex and the goals unlimited, so that the abilities of the most apt members of the group are taxed during the period of learning, then the variability in the learning of the group increases.

[11] A. Anastasi, "Practice and Variability: A Study of Psychological Method," *Psychological Monographs*, Vol. 45, 1934, 1-55; J. Peterson and M. C. Barlow, "The Effects of Practice on Individual Differences," *Nature and Nurture: Their Influence upon Achievement*, Twenty-seventh Yearbook of the National Society for the Study of Education, Part II. Bloomington, Illinois: Public School Publishing Company, 1928, 211-230; H. B. Reed, "The Influence of Training on Changes in Variability in Achievement," *Psychological Monographs*, Vol. 41, 1931, 1-59.

That is the conclusion Mattson [12] reached in a study conducted to determine whether, for a given motor skill, degree of complexity of a task bore any relationship to the level of functioning attained through practice. He concluded, "The general trend of these data lends support to the theory that practice decreases differences in simple tasks and increases differences in complex tasks." [13] Hence, if the goals of a grade are sufficiently limited, the group can, through instruction, become homogeneous with respect to these goals, but if the goals are sufficiently difficult to tax the capacity of the superior individuals, the variability of the group will increase during the period of instruction. For example, a fourth-grade class may become homogeneous with respect to ability to recite a short poem, but in ability to comprehend or appreciate poetry the variability of the class will increase.

Unfortunately, when limited goals are emphasized in order to pass all pupils in a class, what is learned is frequently of little value and is retained for but a short time. Only rote memory, a low-order mental process, is required to pass the *name, describe, define, who, what, where,* and *when* type of examination by which achievement is measured. Investigations in various areas of the curriculum to determine how well a student can do on a final examination when it is repeated from three months to three years after a course is completed reveal that from 40 to 80 per cent of the information required by the final examination is lost. The forgetting curves for this material closely approximate those for nonsense materials, indicating that much of what is learned for examination purposes is no better organized, no more meaningful, no more useful to the pupil than are nonsense materials.

The relative permanency of different types of learning has been investigated by Tyler [14] and Wert.[15] In Tyler's study, a test in zoology measuring five objectives was administered to 82 students at the beginning of the course, and again 15 months later. Percentage

[12] Marion L. Mattson, "The Relation Between the Complexity of the Habit to Be Acquired and the Form of the Learning Curve in Young Children," *Genetic Psychology Monographs*, Vol. 13, April 1933, 299-398.

[13] *Ibid.*, p. 378.

[14] R. W. Tyler, "Permanency of Learning," *Journal of Higher Education*, Vol. 4, 1933, 203-204.

[15] J. E. Wert, "Twin Examination Assumptions," *Journal of Higher Education*, Vol. 8, 1937, 136-140.

'of loss or gain on each of the five parts of the test during the 15-month period was computed in relation to the amount gained during the course. On the part of the test requiring: (1) names of organs identified from pictures, the loss was 22 per cent; (2) recognition of technical terms, the loss was 72 per cent; (3) recall of facts, the loss was 80 per cent; (4) application of principles to new situations, there was no loss or gain; (5) interpretation of experimental data, new to the students, there was a gain of 126 per cent. Wert's experiment measured percentage of loss or gain over a period of three years in relation to the amount gained during the course. A gain of 60 per cent was found in application of principles to situations new to the student, a gain of 20 per cent in interpretation of new experiments. There was a loss of over 50 per cent in terminology, function of structures, and main ideas; and a loss of over 80 per cent in associating names with structures.

These experiments indicate that, in general, learning that involves problem-solving relationships and the operation of the higher mental processes is relatively permanent, whereas learning in which unrelated facts and mere unorganized information is involved is relatively temporary. Unless learning involves differentiation and integration of old and new behavioral responses into a meaningful and purposeful problem-solving type of mental process or into an organized behavioral pattern, it has little permanence or value. *How it was learned* determines the usefulness of learned behavior.

In thinking of the permanent results of his own educational efforts, the student may think in the following terms. If he has developed a usable vocabulary, it will remain with him. If he has developed the ability to read literary materials, or science materials, or social science materials, at a given level of difficulty, with a given degree of comprehension, he will not lose this ability. If he can solve complex reasoning problems in arithmetic or mathematics, this ability will not deteriorate. If he has developed the ability to write effective business letters or interesting personal letters, think on his feet and speak effectively to a group, to use the library and basic reference materials, to organize ideas for effective presentation, to conduct a meeting, to get along with people, and to maintain harmony in social groups, these abilities will be retained. The student will recognize that these statements are approximately true and that the learnings mentioned represent some of the most important results of education.

It is suggested then that the emphasis that some schools place on striving for homogeneity in classes, getting pupils over the passing mark, and trying to provide for individual differences by bringing all pupils up to a standard, encourages teachers to set limited goals for instruction and results in temporary factual learning involving mainly memory, a low-order mental process. When the ultimate goals of education, involving the higher mental processes and permanent learning, are striven for and each pupil is stimulated to capacity effort, the variability of instructional groups increases.

Meeting the needs of children
in heterogeneous groups

Materials presented up to this point in this chapter were selected to reveal the extent and nature of individual and trait differences and the general effect of educational experiences upon them. It was shown that in the first grade the typical range of ability in important educational traits is four years. In the sixth grade it approaches eight years. Administrative, supervisory, and curricular practices in the traditional graded elementary school have tended to ignore these facts. For the past century, educational experts have been trying to find some procedure for making instructional groups homogeneous, thus making possible the mass instruction of large classes and the use of uniform textbooks, uniform instructional procedures, and uniform standards of achievement. The object in most of this was to find a way to educate as many children as possible with a minimum expenditure of money. We have seen that most of the educational devices and procedures directed to this end have sprung from misconceptions regarding the facts and have oversimplified the problem. We have seen that the homogeneity of groups sufficient for uniform standards, materials, and procedures probably is unattainable. Certainly such groups cannot be achieved through general-ability grouping, judicious policies of promotion, or effective teaching. What then should be done? *Simply this: Accept the wide range of ability found in all classes as inevitable, accept it as something good, highly desirable, and necessary in the scheme of things. Then set about to find effective ways of meeting the individual needs of children in heterogeneous groups.* Modern educational thinking is quite largely devoted to this objective. It involves many modifications in administrative and curriculum policies, modifications that will be outlined in following chapters.

At various points throughout the remainder of this book, references will be made to the data presented here on individual differences. The significance of the existence of these wide differences in human characteristics will become increasingly clear, and will be illustrated by actual classroom examples in the final three chapters. The real implications for those who plan curriculums and for the teachers who use curriculums were not seen so long as major attention was devoted to overcoming individual differences. Now that we know we cannot wipe them out by any educational magic, we can proceed to take them into account.

Discussion Questions

1. The student should now answer the twenty questions asked at the beginning of Chapter 2.
2. Indicate the questions to which your answers have changed most as a result of reading Chapter 2.
3. Indicate the questions on which you would like to have additional information and class discussion.
4. With reference to the elementary school that you attended, what changes in organization, administrative procedures, instructional materials, and equipment would you recommend in order to meet more adequately the educational needs of children?
5. If we assume that in the first grade there is a range of four years and in the sixth grade a range of eight years in the various areas of educational development, what characteristics must the curriculum have to meet adequately the varying needs of the children? List as many suggestions as possible.
6. If children were admitted to the first grade in terms of mental development, what would be the typical range in chronological age of this grade? Who would learn most rapidly, the younger pupils or the older pupils? What would be the achievement status of the older and younger pupils at the end of the first grade?
7. If it is inadvisable to admit children to school regardless of age, whenever they reach a certain stage of mental development, is there any logic in promoting them from grade to grade on this basis?
8. In most grades the youngest pupil is the brightest and the oldest pupil is the dullest. What are the undesirable features of this situation? How

can it be avoided? Will your remedy tend to increase the range of ability in the various grades?

Selected References

Anastasi, A. and John P. Foley, Jr., *Differential Psychology*. New York: The Macmillan Company, 1949, Chapters 14 and 15.

Burr, Marvin Y., *A Study of Homogeneous Grouping*. Contributions to Education, No. 457. New York: Teachers College, Columbia University, 1931.

Cook, Walter W., *Grouping and Promotion in the Elementary School*. Series on Individualization of Instruction, No. 2. Minneapolis: University of Minnesota Press, 1941.

————, "Some Effects of the Maintenance of High Standards of Promotion," *Elementary School Journal*, Vol. 41, February 1941, 430-437.

Cornell, Ethel L., *The Variability of Children of Different Ages and Its Relation to School Classification and Grouping*. University of the State of New York Bulletin, No. 1101, Educational Research Studies, No. 1, 1937. 98 pp.

Hollingshead, A. D., *An Evaluation of the Use of Certain Educational and Mental Measurements for the Purpose of Classification*. Contributions to Education, No. 302. New York: Teachers College, Columbia University, 1928.

Hull, Clark L., "Variability in Amount of Different Traits Possessed by the Individual," *Journal of Educational Psychology*, Vol. 18, 1927, 97-104.

Lindquist, E. F., ed., *Educational Measurement*. Washington, D.C.: American Council on Education, 1951, Chapter I.

Mattson, Marion L., "The Relation Between the Complexity of the Habit to be Acquired and the Form of the Learning Curve in Young Children," *Genetic Psychology Monographs*, Vol. 13, April 1933, 299-398.

McNemar, Quinn, *The Revision of the Stanford-Binet Scale*. Boston: Houghton Mifflin Company, 1942.

Peterson, J. and M. C. Barlow, "The Effects of Practice on Individual Differences," *Nature and Nurture: Their Influence Upon Achievement*, Chapter XIV, Twenty-seventh Yearbook of the National Society for the Study of Education, Part II. Bloomington, Illinois: Public School Publishing Company, 1928, pp. 211-30.

Reed, H. B., "The Influence of Training on Changes in Variability in Achievement," *Psychological Monographs*, Vol. 41, 1931, 1-59.

Terman, Lewis M. and Maud A. Merrill, *Measuring Intelligence*. Boston: Houghton Mifflin Company, 1937.

3

MOTIVATING EDUCATIONAL BEHAVIOR

$\mathcal{M}$OTIVATING EDUCATIONAL BEHAVIOR means the process of making the activities and experiences in which the child engages under the direction of the school satisfying to the child. A motive stimulates and alerts the organism for action, initiates and directs activity into more or less definite channels, and sustains that activity to a more or less satisfying end. A motive is also a consciously sought goal of behavior. The well-motivated child is one who wants to do things, persistently tries to do things, and progressively improves his methods of doing them. The problem in curriculum development is to motivate the child along lines that are educational in nature. There will be as wide differences among the free motives of a group of children as there will be among any of their other intellectual or emotional traits.

The urge to get a satisfying grade in a final examination (the grade that will satisfy depends upon the student's level of aspiration) is sometimes given as an example of a motive. As students prepare for, take, and review their examination, this motive stimulates them; it initiates, directs, sustains, and also selects behavior. If the future conduct of the individuals is thus influenced in a socially desirable direction, then an educational experience is motivated.

But for those students who fail the examination or do more poorly than anticipated the anxiety state remains. It is important to understand that the examination is but one episode in a whole pattern of activities designed to satisfy the basic needs of the students. For example, why do young people want to pass the examinations that will enable them to become teachers? Is it because they feel it will give them social prestige and status? Is it because it will place them in a position to attract a more desirable mate? Is it because it will enable them to serve society in a significant way? Is it because it will give them economic security in the form of tasty food, attractive clothing, comfortable shelter, and flashy transportation? Is it because opportunities for travel, reading, study, and other forms of new experiences will be enhanced? Is it because they like people and love to work with children? Is it because learning is a fascinating enterprise for them? Perhaps all these are more or less involved in the examination incident.

Motive as part of an activity in process. The examination is but an episode in the process of going to college to prepare to teach more effectively, in order to hold a better position with greater success so that all the basic needs of the individual (ego enhancement, prestige, status, security, mating, new experiences, and so forth) may be more adequately satisfied.

If we are to understand the behavior of people, and especially that of our pupils, we must think not only in terms of motives but also in terms of such processes and purposes as going to school, going on vacation, associating with a specific group of friends, living in a specific family, working at a specific vocation, and living under a certain form of government.

Interest in terms of purposes, needs, and processes of living. If belonging to the college band, the library club, the Y.M.C.A., or any similar organizations, enhances our prestige or makes possible our acceptance by a congenial social group, we join. We are interested in those things that we *believe* meet our needs, although they may not always do so. Much has been written about the place of *interest* in education. We pay attention, work, concentrate, and give preferences in order to achieve the things in which we are interested. We are interested in those things that meet fundamental needs, that fit into or are related to our major purposes in life and enable us to achieve our goals. Interests, like motives, can only be understood in terms of the larger processes of living, the ways of our culture, and the over-all purposes and aims of the individual.

Learning to plan: long-and short-range goals

Long-range goals such as becoming a teacher, a doctor, or a grocer modify and determine motives and interests and are rather mature. Some students seriously choose such goals early in life, others later in life, while many may never seriously decide upon a vocation that requires long periods of planning and execution. Generally, the younger the child is the more incapable he is of conceiving such long-range goals. His motives and interests are more immediate and he is more impatient to achieve them. He is more subject to whims and fancies, is motivated and interested in the more immediate satisfaction of needs, is impatient, and has a short attention span.

One of the purposes of education is to emancipate the child from his dependence upon passing whims and impulsive desires and to tie in his purposes, motives, and interests with long-range goals. For example, the 14-year-old boy who bounces out of bed early on cold winter mornings to deliver his papers may have a definite long-range scheme in mind. He may be saving his money to buy a new bicycle so that he can extend his route, sell more papers, make more money, and eventually buy a trumpet and join the school band. Or he may be saving toward a college education. The people with whom he lives and comes in contact may plan their lives ahead in just such a way, and to act as they do probably bolsters his self-esteem.

In the intermediate grades it is possible to plan and organize activities in connection with learning units on a fairly long-range basis, thus avoiding the necessity for frequent planning periods. The activities and processes planned will furnish the motives and interests for the detailed and painstaking efforts required. Using the library and basic reference materials to find answers to certain questions that must be answered if the unit is to progress take on new meaning and purpose in terms of future goals. Pupils will see value in using an index, in writing letters, in alphabetizing, in map reading, or organizing material, in outlining, and so forth, if such skills aid them in writing a pamphlet on the early settlers of Minnesota, dramatizing some historical event, or making parchment for an illuminated manuscript. (See Chapters 19, 20, and 21.)

As far as primary-grade pupils are concerned, however, short-range and intermediate goals, and more frequent planning are necessary. Anyone who has taken children of primary age on an automobile trip recognizes the necessity of setting up intermediate goals for them along the way. The trip may involve eight hours of driving but after the first hour, six-year-old Bob's questions betray his impatience. "How soon do we get there? Will we be there pretty soon? How much longer? Will the next town be grandmother's?" We tell Bob that after passing through two more small towns, we will be in Cedar Rapids. After Cedar Rapids the next large city will be Davenport; then we will be at grandmother's. Later on, we will tell Bob that soon we will drive through four more towns and then stop for ice cream cones, or for lunch. If Bob is interested in horses, we count horses. Or it may be that tractors, silos, school buildings, trailer trucks, or Buicks will hold his interest as we ride along.

In the first grade, objectives should be such that the children can realize them almost immediately, frequently with no more effort on their part than answering simple questions. What does the sign in front of the circus tent say? What questions should we ask the grocery man when we visit his store? When our principal, Miss Smith, visits us this morning, she will want to know what we learned on our visit to the grocery store. What shall we tell her? How do animals prepare for winter? How do our fathers and mothers prepare for winter? What does the janitor do in the school? What does the principal do?

In building a play house, grocery store, or post office, elaborate and detailed planning is not necessary. A box placed on end, a few stamps, some envelopes, and a few pennies make a satisfactory post office. A few shelves with empty cereal cartons and price tags, become a grocery store. Pin a rope to the seat of a boy's trousers and he is transformed into a lion. A feather tied to the side of a boy's head makes him an Indian; and a toy gun in his belt makes him a cowboy. A board tied to a roller skate makes a wagon or an automobile. These activities are fast-moving and change rapidly. Continuity of activities is still largely in the planning of the teacher, not in the long-range sustained plans of the children. The world to the first-grader is full of interesting things to examine, to explore, and to play with, but the depth of his understanding and his background of experiences are not sufficient for him to devote too much time to any one thing.

Rich environment desirable
but not sufficient

It is the teacher's responsibility to set up goals for the children and maintain a continuity and sequence of activities so that the total process motivates and directs each part, gives it purpose and meaning, and leads to the satisfaction of basic needs. It is not enough that children find themselves in an environment that offers many possibilities for need-satisfying activities. They need help in the accomplishment of a satisfying achievement.

For example, the teacher may suggest a form of government for the classroom in which monthly elections are held and everyone gets a chance to hold some office. As each child is elected and serves, his self-respect and self-confidence will increase.

Or, let us take an individual case. John is not taking part in student activities; he feels neglected and left out of things. His teacher knows that John has some musical ability and feels that playing in the band would give the boy the assurance he needs; but his parents cannot afford to buy him an instrument. The teacher helps John plan. With her aid he finds work in a grocery store on Saturdays, saves money for an instrument, takes music lessons for six months, and gets to play in the band and wear a uniform.[1] His indifference has been successfully overcome. The teacher helps the child by suggesting a series of activities that lead from an unhappy situation to a satisfying one through educational experiences. The teacher is the most important figure in any educational situation.

Needs versus desires or wants

The word "needs" is frequently used to mean many things in books and journals dealing with education. It is important, here, that we clarify our meaning of it. A *need* is the lack of something that, if present, would further the welfare of the individual. The person may or may not be aware of the need and frequently is not. We consult many kinds of specialists concerning our needs: doctors

[1] Herbert F. Wright, "How the Psychology of Motivation is Related to Curriculum Development," *Journal of Educational Psychology*, Vol. 39, March 1948, 149-156.

about improving our health, architects with reference to what our houses should be like, and lawyers in regard to our civic security. All behavior is in response to some need. A boy's need for security and status in a group or for the love of his parents may be the real cause for his bullying behavior in class or on the playground.[2] Another boy's domineering attitude may represent an attempt to compensate for his small physical stature.

Writers on education also frequently assign many meanings to the term *felt need.* Correctly defined, it refers to a basic need that is conscious, but its meaning often is assumed erroneously to be synonymous with *desire* or *want.* Some schools that claim to meet the felt needs of children are actually concerned only with the child's superficial wants and desires. They fail to recognize that the basic needs of children refer to sound achievement, purposeful goals, and skills that give status and self-respect. A school that fails to recognize these basic needs and takes no steps to satisfy them may be adding to the maladjustment and unhappiness of its pupils. One of the great responsibilities of teachers is to motivate children so that they strive intelligently to satisfy their real needs in ethically and socially acceptable ways.

Organic needs [3]

Organic needs of children have their basis in the physiochemical nature and condition of the organism. The need for sleep, rest, food, water, fresh air, elimination, physical and mental activity, freedom from infection, and safety are examples. Most of these needs tend to change rapidly during maturation and to some extent throughout life. The teacher in the elementary school must be especially concerned with the changing nature and needs of children. It is important that the teacher, in considering the needs of a class, be aware of individual and trait differences as they apply to all areas of development. The pupils develop at different rates in the various traits. The same child shows varying rates of growth in his different abilities. The traits reach a mature level at different times and the level of development reached at maturity differs for

2 For a case in point, see Chapter 19.
3 The suggestions in Chapter 4 are intended to supplement and clarify the brief discussion of organic needs given here.

individuals and for the various traits of an individual. No two individuals develop in the same way or at the same speed, even though they tend to follow the same general pattern. Hence, as the needs of the typical child at different grade levels are described here, the teacher must remember that this is a device of convenience and economy. The teacher must be concerned most of the time with the needs of specific children.

The need for sleep and rest. The average six-year-old needs about twelve hours of sleep per day while the twelve-year-old needs about nine hours. This is a reduction of three hours in sleep need over a period of six years or about one-half hour reduction per year. Many children fail to get enough sleep. Parents who go out frequently and cannot afford "sitters" take the children with them to movies or card parties. The children fall asleep, are aroused to go home, and much of the sleep they get is only partly beneficial. Many small children roam the streets or go to movies at night without adult supervision. Children without enough sleep find it difficult to stay awake in school, are listless and inattentive. Indulgent or careless parents with radio and television sets are also frequent offenders. The teacher must use all the social ingenuity he possesses in broaching this subject to parents. When children are obviously sleepy during school hours, the proper procedure is to provide a place for them to sleep in the classroom. In any case, the child must get his rest—a primary need.

Elementary-school children do not adequately recognize the need for sleep and relaxation. Interesting things are usually happening at home and in the neighborhood during the evening hours, and children rarely want to go to bed. Sometimes they overexert themselves during the day and find it difficult to sleep at night. Finally, the teacher should recognize that a child's anxiety to "achieve up to standard" may also disturb his proper and normal sleeping habits.

The need for wholesome food, pure water, and properly conditioned air. The well-nourished, properly rested, elementary-school child is free from infection, has clear eyes, color in his cheeks, and tremendous energy and vitality. When this is not true, reasons for the condition should be sought. Although the school must rely on the cooperation of the parents in furnishing adequate and balanced nutrition for the child, there is much the school can do in improving the diets and eating habits of pupils and their parents. The study of foods and food groups should receive attention in the learning units at every grade level. This can be done regardless of the limitations of the school facilities. Ideally, the eating habits, likes, and dislikes of every child should be known to the teacher. Planning balanced meals is, of course, made more effective and easy if it can be done in relation to a school cafeteria. Some schools provide for school lunches in the regular school budget. Many manufacturers and processors of foods have available without cost educational material on nutrition that is scientifically reliable and free from obnoxious advertising. Not all free material is suitable or reliable and must, of course, be checked.

One of the most effective means of convincing children of the detrimental effects of unsatisfactory diets is to set up a controlled nutritional experiment in the classroom. One experiment requires at least two but preferably several cages suitable for white rats. These cages can be made or purchased. Two young rats are placed in each cage. The pupils plan the diets for each pair of rats, care for them, weigh them at regular intervals, and show the growth of each rat in tabular and graphic form. The weight, size, vitality, and glistening fur of the rats with the ideal diet will do much to convince children that drinking milk and eating a balanced diet are important. Such an experiment will attract the interest of the whole school but cannot generally be repeated with profit year after year, unless variations or extensions are introduced.

Nutritional problems sometimes arise because of parental anxiety over the child's eating habits. Growing children often assert their independence by refusing to eat certain foods. There are always a few homes in which the parents fail to get up early enough to get breakfast for their children before school time. In many homes meals are hurried because parents must prepare the children for school and report for work themselves.

The exact amount of water a child should drink each day cannot be determined with any great accuracy. The active child demands more water than the inactive one, and children drink more water on a warm day than they do on a cold day. Usually, the sensation of thirst can be relied upon to prevent any serious deficiency of water in the tissues, and drinking fountains should be provided in each classroom or on each floor to enable children to drink when they wish.

There is much controversy over what the optimum conditions are for school children insofar as heat and ventilation are concerned. Anyone who has visited many classroms in a day is struck by the difference in temperature, humidity, and odor of classrooms even in the same building. Variations of from 65 to 90 degrees Fahrenheit have been found in the same building. Some rooms are hot, stuffy, and malodorous. The bad effects from such conditions are not due to a reduction of oxygen or an increase in carbon dioxide in the air but probably to discomfort from improper temperatures, humidity, odors, and air circulation. In some rooms a group of children sit constantly in a blast of hot air, in others in a blast of cool air.

In the absence of evidence to the contrary, we may well assume that the motivation of effective school work is made easier when air conditions are pleasant and stimulating. It is generally recommended that the relative humidity of a classroom should be between 40 and 50 per cent and room temperature should be between 68 and 70 degrees Fahrenheit. The air movement should be mild but constant, allowing for sufficient change to prevent the accumulation of unpleasant odors. An excellent procedure for the teacher to follow would be to allow the pupils to make periodic checks of the heating and ventilating conditions of the room and integrate this activity with a unit in science. To see how this procedure is followed in connection with other classroom projects and associated learning units, see Chapters 20 and 21.

The good health that contributes to accelerated physical growth also contributes to accelerated mental growth. The extra physical vitality of healthy children leads them to apply themselves diligently to intellectual pursuits and they are likely to experience superior intellectual development.

The need for developmental activity—motor, intellectual, social, and emotional. The need for activity is obviously a biological need, the whole organism being structured for it. It is important, however, that the activity be suited to the level of the child's motor, intellectual, social, and emotional development, because if the curriculum is synchronized to the developmental needs of children, the problem of motivation is largely solved. The curriculum should be designed to broaden continuously the meaningful and related new experiences that are necessary to the maximum development of the child. The only basis for determining the developmental status and needs of a child is to observe his behavior either directly or indirectly.

Needs change from day to day. From early infancy the child is an explorer and his curiosity takes many turns. He wants to hear, see, taste, smell, handle, manipulate, and investigate everything that comes to his attention. Once he has learned to talk, he wants to know *what* things are for, *when* things are going to happen, *why* things are done the way they are, and *how* things work. He observes and listens to all that goes on about him, interpreting it in the light of his limited experience and information. He watches his father and mother at work; he observes the neighbors, the people who call at the home. If he lives on a farm, he is interested in the animals, the car, the truck, and the farm machinery. If he lives in the city, the policeman, the fireman, the milkman, the grocery man have a challenging fascination for him. He listens to the conversation of those about him, to stories, the radio; he probably has seen the movies and television. The things that don't make sense arouse his curiosity. Words with more than one meaning bother him when he hears them in a new context.

His toys are miniature reproductions of things about him—houses, dolls, trucks, animals, automobiles, airplanes. Much of his thinking is make-believe. He plays house with his sister and the neighbors' children. He plays delivery truck, mailman, railroad, aviator, cowboy. Dramatic play is a vital part of his life. When needed, he creates imaginary playmates with names and characteristics. With this imaginative capacity, the line between the real and the unreal is not always sharp. He may tell fanciful stories and invent incidents. Why not? They meet his needs as well as does the house he builds from boxes and blocks or the truck system he establishes to haul sand. They are part of his growing and learning. Despite all his eager observing, experimenting, building, playing, and listening, he has limitations from the adult point of view. Moreover, his observations, movements, thinking, and plans are very gross in the sense that he has not yet differentiated fine details. The control of the large muscles of arms, legs, and trunk has been differentiated. His purposes and goals have required it. But the differentiation required for control of muscles in detailed writing, drawing, and sewing, of course, are not far advanced. This will take time; he must differentiate details in terms of his purposes before they will have meaning to him and they must have meaning before he attempts to execute them. The extent to which the first-grader has differentiated the features of a man is evident when he draws a man: head, body, legs, arms, fingers, toes, ears, eyes, mouth, nose, hair, etc. Professor Goodenough [4] has shown that the extent of differentiation demonstrated by a child when he draws a man is a good indication of his over-all intellectual development. A child draws in an effort to make visible his ideas about the things that he has weighed carefully or that are familiar to him. For example, armholes are a very important part of a coat to a child who has had trouble putting his arms into them without help. It is not uncommon for children at this stage of development to draw carefully the armholes on an otherwise nude figure. Or, at a certain stage in the child's development, all coins become pennies or nickels, all animals dogs or cats. If the teacher is to plan meaningful activities for children and expect to see them successfully completed, he must know the extent to which children have differentiated details in any area of behavior.

The first-grader is not sensitive to sex, social status, or skin color to any extent, and selects his playmates without reference to these factors. But the boy with the ball, the girl with the big doll, the bad boy who hits him and smashes his house, and the nice little girl who helps him are differentiated in terms of his goals. He selects and rejects his friends in terms of their ability to further his objectives. Nor is he aware of time concepts as related to periods longer than a day, week, month or year, or of distances greater than those represented by the bounds of his neighborhood.

As one considers the spontaneous activities of children at various grade levels, it is important to keep in mind that individual differences increase from a typical range of four years in the first grade to a typical range of eight years in the seventh. The most advanced children in any grade are above the average child in the next higher two or three grades. The average second-grade child has advanced somewhat beyond his first-grade level, but in both years he is con-

---

[4] Florence L. Goodenough, *The Measurement of Intelligence by Drawings.* Yonkers, New York: World Book Company, 1926; and *Developmental Psychology.* New York: D. Appleton Century Company, 1934, pp. 332-336.

cerned with differentiating his environment in terms of his goals. Group plans grow more detailed and are effective for longer periods. As time passes, units of work can be made a little longer. Dramatic play becomes more mature in the sense of being more realistic, more detailed, and more sequential.

In the third grade, the average pupil has reached the point at which he can differentiate rapidly in reading and writing. A child has a large oral vocabulary when he starts to school. Somewhere between the third and the sixth grade, his reading vocabulary catches up to it. He is able to concentrate for longer periods, and is more attentive to detail in construction and art work. As his horizon gradually widens, his actions and desires become more socialized; as a result there is more identification of the individual with the group. Group planning and evaluation periods become more effective. Interests have extended his immediate neighborhood and community. He is interested in comparing his community with those in other regions of the world and other periods of time.

In the fourth, fifth, and sixth grades, the intellectual differentiation of the environment and of the responses to it continue to develop rapidly. At this stage of development, the child's curiosity is more detailed: he may have collections of stamps, of rocks, of insects, and so forth, in which small differences are important and fascinating to him. Time periods and distances begin to take on meaning, and work and play and the real and the fanciful are more clearly distinguished. Boys and girls tend to play and work in different groups, and much rivalry is displayed between the sexes. Generally, boys are attracted more by science, sports, and mechanical things; girls are more interested in home life, parties, trips, sewing, and clothes. Another indication of development during these grade years is that children have learned to differentiate between good and poor work. They are more critical of what they do, even to the point of refusing to show their work because it does not meet what they have set as their level of aspiration. In connection with this critical attitude, some children even adopt models of conduct and become self-conscious when their own behavior fails to measure up to the standards they have chosen.

Differentiation of the environment has reached the stage where differences may be explained in terms of causes. The building of boats, windmills, airplanes, and even electrical motors by the more

advanced boys with attention to the relation of design to performance is possible. These children not only differentiate cause and
effect, but also synthesize their experiences in the form of simple
generalizations such as: "The slope of the roof depends on the
amount of rainfall." "In dry climates flat roofs prevail." "The food,
clothing, and shelter of people are determined by the climate."

It should also be noted that children in the fourth, fifth, and
sixth grades are rather highly skilled in reading and writing, are
more attentive, and are developing the ability to center their conversations or group discussions around a single topic, paying more
attention to what other pupils are saying, and emphasizing less
their own first-hand experiences.

The shift in interests and social behavior that one finds in the
elementary school is revealed clearly in a study by Harold V. Baker,[5]
based on an analysis of "free" conversation materials in grades two,
four, and six. The findings reveal a shift in content emphasis from
the second to the sixth grade. Baker found that in the second grade,
69 per cent of the discussion involved the contributor's play, recreation, home, family, trips, and pets. In the fourth grade, there was
a decided broadening of interests with greatest emphasis, 45 per
cent, being given to trips, books, radio, and movies. In the sixth
grade, 52 per cent of the conversations emphasized the world, the
United States, and the cities and towns throughout the country.

As might be anticipated from the content, 83 per cent of the
second-grade contributions were acquired through actual experience. This figure dropped to 25 per cent in the sixth grade, where
the percentage of contributions arising through reflection and acquired by vicarious experience was highest. As children progress
through the elementary school, their contributions in general discussion shift from a consideration of that which is immediate in
time and space to that which is more remote, although the space
shift is more pronounced than the time shift. For example, the
study revealed that at the sixth-grade level, approximately 75 per
cent of the contributions were still focused in the present. Also, at
the second-grade level, there was little meeting of minds or discussion; less than 10 per cent of the contributions were continuations

5 Harold V. Baker, *Children's Contributions in Elementary School General
Discussion.* Child Development Monographs, No. 29. New York: Bureau of
Publications, Teachers College, Columbia University, 1942.

of topics already introduced. With fourth- and sixth-grade children, however, approximately 50 per cent of the contributions were of this type. Significant sex differences were few but their number increased in the upper grades. Boys favored such categories as "science" and "sports;" girls inclined more to "pleasure trips," "home affairs," "United States happenings," "pets" and "personal presence." Children in schools with a high socio-economic status gave evidence of having more information and better vocabularies. They displayed greater powers of concentration, were more inquisitive, and showed less evidence of intolerance, harshness, and interest in the gruesome than did children who were lower in the socio-economic scale.

Child development through the elementary school consists of a progressive emancipation of the child from dependence upon immediate interests in the present to reliance on direct experience. It moves toward a goal in which the here and now is considered in terms of the past, the future, and the distant future. As the powers develop, the child grows in his ability to profit by the experiences of humans in other times and places.

Social needs

Social needs are sometimes called *personality needs* or *psychological needs,* since they are rooted in man's intellect and emotions as well as in his culture. The specific form that these needs assume for a particular individual at a given time is dependent upon many factors such as age and developmental level, sex, socio-economic status, racial and nationality characteristics, and the home. Social needs display the same range of differences as do all human qualities and a study of them reveals much information that is helpful in understanding the motives and behavior of children. We have called them *social needs* because their existence and satisfaction assumes membership in social groups. It is not important what we call them. It is important how we deal with them.

An important characteristic of a good learning situation is a strong ego-involved purpose on the part of the learner to acquire the various socially approved behavior patterns with which the school is concerned. The behavior patterns fostered by the school, if valid, do increase the individual's *social acceptance, prestige,* and *status.* They increase his *security* in society, bringing *favorable attention* and *recognition* to him. They recognize and reward the individual's special aptitudes, abilities, and accomplishments. In this way they enhance the ego. They furnish a progressive broadening of significantly related and purposeful *new experiences.* In simple words, the school is designed to meet the social needs of the individual.

The curriculum and the school must be so organized and conducted that children's basic social needs are met and satisfied daily. Solving a page of long division problems merely for the sake of checking them with the answer key and getting a mark in the teacher's grade book will not satisfy a child's social needs. But an arithmetic exercise *can* be made a satisfying social experience, as can most sensible school assignments. (See Part Three.) Throughout this book, it is emphasized that man is essentially a social being.

The need to belong. It is probably correct to say that the child's social development starts at birth. At an early age he recognizes those who care for him, and before his first birthday understands many words addressed to him. Usually, by the time he is two years old, he is using language as an effective social tool. The passage of another year or two finds him eager to play with other children and willing, at times, to risk parental disapproval and punishment by "running away" to find companionship with those his own age.

Children, like adults, differ greatly in their sociability. Some children seem to get along well with adults and other children from a very early age. They are alert, responsive, considerate, and smiling. Others are timid and shy, or quarrelsome, rebellious, hostile, and unhappy and take part in group activities only reluctantly. Still others seem to be happy only when they are occupying the center of the stage and "showing off." The extent to which these differences are hereditary or environmental is a matter of controversy. Both influences are important and, with the exception of foster children, tend to operate in the same direction.

Of course, merely being with others of his own age does not satisfy the child's need to belong. There must be mutual acceptance, a feeling of mutual concern and affection, a commonness of purposes, goals, and activities. There must be a feeling of being a part of something bigger than self, of being wanted, respected, and liked.

It is a serious tragedy if a child is not accepted by the group in which he finds himself. For example, when children cross the street at the school patrol crossings by twos and no one walks with John, he feels it and thinks to himself, "They don't like me. Everyone wanted to walk with Bob. He is strong and has a new bicycle and is smart and the teacher likes him." If such occasions are frequent, the child broods and is troubled. He may develop feelings of hostility or inferiority or set out mistakenly to do things that he thinks will make him more popular.

A child who is loved and accepted at home but not at school may withdraw from other children and come to depend too strongly upon his parents for affection and the satisfaction of other needs. If he is not loved and accepted by his parents, he may seek compensation in the company of his mates and make a satisfactory adjustment to the situation, depending, of course, upon the type of children he associates with. But if he is rejected both at home and at school, serious maladjustment is indicated. In the early years, acceptance by parents and teacher is most important to the child; but beginning with the intermediate years, acceptance by the "gang" often becomes of more consequence. In some schools where teacher-pupil relations are strained, a child's rejection by a teacher may actually be a mark of distinction and a basis for status in the gang.

The school curriculum should insure that every child has a satisfactory role to play in achieving the purposes of the group. Solidarity is achieved when the class has common goals and common understandings, makes common efforts, and experiences common difficulties and common achievements.

The need for love and affection, the need for approval, acceptance, and status in the group, and the need for security are all closely related and this should be kept in mind even though these factors are treated independently.

The need for love. This, perhaps, is the most important need of the child and is related closely to many of his other social needs. When the need for love is satisfied, for example, the child inevitably feels more secure. Almost everyone, child or adult, is willing to admit that at times he grows more or less insecure and fearful over his own inadequacy, incapacity, and unworthiness. But when we feel we are loved by someone we respect and regard highly, our sense of security returns. The child feels secure in the love of his parents when he knows that even though he may be inadequate, fail, disobey, quarrel, and be punished, their love and acceptance of him will still remain. The security found in deep and abiding friendships, in the marriage relationship, and in religion is largely of this form.

It is especially important that children in the kindergarten and elementary school feel that the teacher is truly and deeply concerned with their welfare and happiness. If the teacher is kind, helpful, considerate, patient, just, understanding, and consistent, the pupils will feel secure in school. Such attitudes show in almost every move and action of the teacher, even in his tone of voice. Children are seldom fooled by the teacher who occasionally softens an otherwise harsh manner to disguise his dislike for his job.

Studies [6] have shown that most elementary teachers are highly concerned for the well-being of their pupils and are, in turn, accepted by them. Nevertheless, there are many teachers who are essentially hostile to children, who derive no satisfaction from their personal relations with their pupils, and seek security mainly by stressing conventional virtues, abusing their authority, or flaunting their superior knowledge.

The need for approval, acceptance, and status. It is necessary to satisfy these needs if we are to counteract our feelings of inferiority and unworthiness. We strive for achievement and for credit in order to convince ourselves as well as others that we are worthy, that we are somebody. The ten-year-old who gets up at an early hour to practice reading a story he has volunteered to read to the class, the student who works overtime on the really tough arithmetic problems, the pupil who spends extra hours on a special report, all realize that the successful completion of these tasks will increase their status with classmates, teacher, and parents. The problem for the teacher is to make certain that the learning process is integrated successfully with this prestige element.

The pre-primary and primary-school child looks to his parents and his teachers for acceptance, commendation, and recognition. If he succeeds in school, he will gain the approval of those he respects most. School is a new experience for him. He has no record of past achievement to encourage him if he should fail in his work, so it is important that he feel confident from the beginning. To insure

[6] Walter W. Cook, Carroll H. Leeds, and Robert Callis, *Manual, Minnesota Teacher Attitude Inventory.* New York: The Psychological Corporation, 1951.

this, the pupil should not be required to attempt tasks that are beyond his abilities, and should work with a group that is approximately equal to him in ability. If the child is not successful in his first attempts at reading, writing, or number work, he will soon come to think that he cannot learn these skills. When the child incorrectly concludes that he cannot do a certain thing, the teacher must then help the pupil "unlearn" this attitude and develop the ability to perform the task. A child's development may be delayed for years, sometimes for life, if he believes he lacks all ability to achieve in a given area. Many an adult can recall a deprecatory remark someone has made about his singing voice, artistic ability, or mathematical competence. If such a remark comes at a time when the individual also is questioning his ability, it may have disastrous results insofar as the person's self-confidence is concerned.

On page 64, it was stated that as pupils progress through the elementary school, they attribute less importance to recognition by parents and teachers and more to acceptance by others of their own age. Pupils in the intermediate grades seek acceptance by their groups with marked deliberation. Their choice of clothes, their mannerisms, enthusiasms, and choice of language show a gradual seeking of independence from adults and a deepening concern for the opinion of their peers.

Of course, the seeking of recognition from the immediate gang is not a lofty form of motivation. To seek status with a recognized group of authorities, or experts, or initiates, regardless of the opinion of the immediate audience is a higher ethical form. And to seek status with God, or in the ultimate decision of mankind, or with the masters of the ages, in spite of all current opinion, is higher still. Yet the teacher in the elementary school will do well to enlist group support for classroom endeavors that have educational value.

The need for security. Security is the same thing as the absence of fear. It is desirable within limits that individuals fear such things as loss of sustenance, love, prestige, or position. We should approach such fears rationally and feel secure in our belief that with some effort on our part we can overcome them successfully. The child's fear of failure at a task that is beyond his ability to surmount is undesirable, but some fear of failure at a task that is within his ability may be desirable. Irrational fears or phobias serve no useful purpose. But everyone needs to fear failure which may come through faulty or inadequate behavior. The fear of events or disasters that cannot be prevented is a useless, debilitating fear. It is useful to fear only those things that we can do something about. A youngster's feeling of helplessness in the face of a divorce that he believes will break up his home, or apprehension over his failure to please a teacher who is inconsistent in requirements and behavior are examples of fears to which children should not be subjected.

The need for new experience and adventure. The imaginative teacher with a broad knowledge of literature and science, some dramatic ability, and showmanship can make every school day an exciting adventure for the children. For example, Miss Watkins, a first-grade teacher, walks into the classroom with a shoebox under her arm. The lid is securely tied but there are air holes in the lid. She places the box on the desk and busies herself with activities in the room. The children's eyes are on the box. There is a scratching noise inside. Finally one child asks, "Miss Watkins, what is in that box? It sounds like an animal." Miss Watkins then tells them that there is an animal in the box and she would like to have them guess what it is. As the children ask questions, Miss Watkins prints them on the board with the answers, as follows:

Does it have fur?	Yes
What does it eat?	Insects
Does it have feathers?	No
Does it have two legs?	Yes
Does it have wings?	Yes
Can it fly well?	Yes
Does it have a tail?	Yes

The children read the questions and answers with rapt attention and expectation. Finally someone correctly guesses that the animal is a bat. The highly motivated reading lesson then is followed by a discussion of bats and their characteristics.

The teaching of literature, science, arithmetic, the social studies, art, and other subjects can be filled with the elements of exciting adventure and surprise. The teacher should be aware of these possibilities and seek to introduce them into every learning situation as far as possible.

Discussion Questions

1. From your own school experience give examples of motives and indicate how they initiate, direct, sustain, and select activity.
2. Give examples to show a motive that is effective because it is part of a goal-directed activity in process.
3. Give examples of goals that serve to motivate varied activity that would be difficult to motivate otherwise.
4. A child is kept after school because he did not complete an arithmetic assignment. After school he completed the work in a very short time. Discuss the possible motives involved. What feelings and attitudes are probably involved in this experience? To what extent is such an episode a reflection on the motivation of school work?
5. Give examples of educational goals that may be set through teacher-pupil planning in the first grade, in the sixth grade. In what ways do they differ?
6. Criticize the point of view of a teacher who believes that the fanciful tales of primary children should be treated the same as lying.
7. Give examples of how teacher-pupil planning may blaze a trail for pupil activity that leads to highly satisfying and rewarding achievement.
8. Why was teacher-pupil planning ignored in traditional elementary-school procedure?
9. What objections do you see to school procedure in which the teacher tells the pupils what to do, when to do it, how to do it, whether it is done correctly or not, and assigns rewards and penalties based on the performance?
10. Give examples of school room conditions, procedures, and practices that ignore the organic needs of children.
11. Give examples of school room procedures and practices that ignore the social needs of children.
12. What arguments can you present to show that love is the most effective shield against insecurity and anxiety?
13. Observe the speech, play, drawings, and other behavior of a first-grade child to determine what aspects of the environment he has differentiated. Speculate on why these elements were differentiated before others.
14. Give examples of how the social needs of children can be satisfied through educational experiences.
15. Distinguish carefully between needs and desires. Give some examples of each as they involve elementary-school children.

Selected References

Allport, G., *Personality*. New York: Henry Holt and Company, 1937, Chapter 7.

Bird, C., *Social Psychology*. New York: Appleton-Century-Crofts, Inc., 1940, Chapters 2, 3, and 4.

Blair, Arthur Witt and William H. Burton, *Growth and Development of the Preadolescent*. New York: Appleton-Century-Crofts, Inc., 1951.

Davis, W. Allison and Robert J. Havighurst, *Father of the Man: How Your Child Gets His Personality*. Boston: Houghton Mifflin Company, 1947.

Dollard, John, *et al.*, *Frustration and Aggression*. New Haven: Yale University Press, 1939.

Faculty of the University School, *How Children Develop*. Columbus: Ohio State University, 1949.

Kingsley, H. L., *The Nature and Conditions of Learning*. New York: Prentice-Hall, Inc., 1945, Chapter 6.

Prescott, Daniel A., *Emotion and the Educative Process*. Washington: American Council on Education, 1938.

Stroud, J. B., *Psychology in Education*. New York: Longmans, Green & Company, 1945, Chapter 16.

Thorndike, Edward L., *The Psychology of Wants, Interests and Attitudes*. New York: D. Appleton Century Co., 1935.

Young, P. T., "Motivation," *Encyclopedia of Educational Research*. New York: The Macmillan Company, 1941, pp. 735-742.

———, "Motivation," *Encyclopedia of Educational Research*. New York: The Macmillan Company, 1950, pp. 755-761.

4

A PSYCHOBIOLOGICAL APPROACH
TO THE CURRICULUM

$\mathcal{T}$HE BIOLOGICAL ASPECTS of learning and response are of basic significance for the elementary teacher. Biological experimentation is one source of that widely used phrase "teaching the whole child." It includes all the complex functions of an organism in its environment, every act that is guided by past experiences and designed to aid the organism in its adaptation to its environment. Learning by memorizing has no place in such an approach. He is a rare biologist (and a rare psychologist) who believes people learn by soaking up facts as a sponge absorbs water.[1]

This approach has many significant implications for elementary-school instruction, and a study of the principles involved will help the teacher to understand more fully the proposition that "the whole child should be the object of teaching." Properly understood, this statement has a great deal of hard, practical sense. Like so much phraseology in education, however, it is rarely explained in terms of the data from which it was derived.

The "holistic" concept

The concept of "holism" implies that human beings are wholes (organisms) that are *greater than the sum of their parts*. For example, just as we cannot tell time by examining the separate parts

[1] Gardner Murphy, *Personality: A Biosocial Approach to Origins and Structure.* New York: Harper and Brothers, 1947, pp. 40-41.

of a watch, so we cannot think of human beings, capable of activity and purposeful action, as nothing but a collection of arms, legs, and blood vessels. Men cannot be understood except as functioning wholes.

Back in the 1890's the biologist, Driesch, published the results of a number of studies of sea urchins in which he advanced the theory that the cells of these creatures were "equipotential"—that under certain conditions the cells could be made to grow into any portion of the organism.[2] The idea implicit in such a conclusion was that the cells of the sea urchin, and probably of other livings things, were intimately related. At this point, however, a question arose. If any bit of protoplasm, the building block of living tissue, could grow into any part of the sea urchin, why did it differentiate into distinguishable parts? A hypothesis was not hard to find; the "purpose" of this differentiation was to permit the organism to function in a variety of ways—digestive, motor, and so on.

A second idea that occurred to the scientists was that every part of an organism was necessary for the proper functioning of the whole. This point, however, must be stretched a bit in the case of living organisms because, as we know, many people live very happy and useful lives although physically handicapped in one way or another. This is possible because of the marvelous adaptability of human beings. This adaptability, in turn, points to the *purposiveness* of human living; our lives are organized and integrated around basic needs. Another way of stating the same thing is to acknowledge that the functioning of an integrated organism is something more than, and different from, the sum of its automatic responses to stimuli. It involves the drives, needs, and purposes of living beings. In this chapter we will outline the biological background of the purposive activity we call learning. Our approach is "holistic" in that we shall not refer to the human mind as though there were an organ, "mind," located somewhere in the body and separable from the feelings, emotion, or imagination of living organisms. In order to dodge the temptation to make any such distinction, the words "human organism" will be used often. They emphasize the idea of a functioning whole.

[2] Hilgard, *Theories of Learning*, p. 245.

Experimental embryology [3]

Experimental embryology is a wide field that has implications for psychology, educational psychology,[4] curriculum theory, and teaching. The experiments most suggestive of principles interesting to teachers are those in which tissues from a *newt* and *axolotl*, both small amphibious salamanders, were transplanted from one area of the body to another to determine if they would follow a predetermined growth pattern or develop subject only to the limitations of the area to which they were transplanted. It is interesting to see the development of field theory in all this. The experimenters, working on the newt and axolotl, came to think of an area of the body, the eye for example, as a field, an organism in just that sense of the word. The whole organism had sub-organisms, and these sub-organisms, in turn, had sub-sub-organisms, the lowest being the basic cell. A piece of tissue from one field, then, was being taken to live in another field, another area with its own characteristic pattern of life forces.

Hilgard quotes from Paul Weiss, as follows:

The head of the young larva of the *newt* carries ventrolaterally two rod-like excrescences, the so-called *balancers*. The larva of the axolotl, on the other hand, lacks them. The problem was to find out whether the balancer field of the newt, if confronted with undetermined axolotl ectoderm would

3 One of the most significant publications in this field is that of H. Spemann, *Embryonic Development and Induction*. New Haven: Yale University Press, 1938.
4 Among the psychologists who have embraced embryology is Raymond H. Wheeler. See his *The Laws of Human Nature*. New York: D. Appleton-Century, Inc., 1932. Students of educational psychology have long debated the merits of the argument advanced in Wheeler's and F. T. Perkin's book, *Principles of Mental Development*. New York: Thomas Y. Crowell Company, 1932. For a most enlightening discussion of Wheeler's position and the relation of embryological evidence to learning theory see Chapter 9 of Hilgard's *Theories of Learning*. Wheeler is by no means the only psychologist to exploit biology. One of the most lively and extensive discussions relating biology to learning theory may be found in Murphy, *Personality: A Biosocial Approach to Origins and Structure*. An excellent treatment of the subject may also be found in John E. Anderson, "Child Development and the Growth Process," *Intelligence: Its Nature and Nurture*, Thirty-ninth Yearbook of the National Society for the Study of Education, Part II. Bloomington, Illinois: Public School Publishing Company, 1940, pp. 15-49. Yet another excellent study, one which analyzes a great deal of experimental evidence, is Nathan W. Schock, "Physiological Factors in Behavior," in J. McV. Hunt, ed., *Personality and the Behavior Disorders*, Vol. I. New York: The Ronald Press Company, 1944, Chapter 19.

* be able to make these latter cells of a balancerless species form a balancer. Thus, belly ectoderm from a young axolotl germ was grafted over the lateral head region of a newt larva prior to the time when the balancer was due to appear. *No balancer developed in the strange skin graft.* The axolotl cells apparently did not know how to respond to the strange newt demand. In the reciprocal experiment, however, *belly ectoderm of a newt* (the balanced species) *when grafted over the head region of the axolotl* (the normally balancerless form) *did develop a balancer.*[5]

The explanation or conclusion is that the age of the transplanted cells is all-important. If the transplant is young enough—if it has not started developing past some crucial point—it will conform to the dictates of the host-field, which field is determined by the whole host-organism. Although the exact point at which transplanted cells no longer develop according to the established pattern of the host is not known, the best guess is that it is reached as soon as the cells of the area to be transplanted have begun to develop in terms of the needs of the parent organism.

This speculation bears upon the environment-heredity controversy and the importance of genetics for education.[6] In connection with it, teachers might reflect upon the universal tendency in living things to develop as organizations, as wholes, as patterns. Were we to be more detailed, which really is not necessary, we would speak, not of patterns, but of biochemical energy systems.[7] It may well be that the newt's head is an energy field of some sort. Then the experiment of transplanting one field into another could be broken down into terms of field physics. However interesting it might be to see whether living processes, cells, can be described in terms of mathematically symbolized equations of energy, the teacher can be satisfied with the insight into nature's persistent patterning of all living things. Since it is so common we will pause to summarize the theory, although it is a complex point of view.

Students in their first encounter with field theory may find it helpful to re-phrase certain terms into the language of a social scientist. Just pretend that instead of dissecting a newt or axolotl

5 Quoted by Hilgard, *Theories of Learning,* p. 245, from Paul Weiss, *Principles of Development.* New York: Henry Holt and Company, 1939, pp. 362-363.

6 See the works of Otis W. Caldwell and Laurence H. Snyder cited on pp. 78 and 81.

7 Murphy, *Personality: A Biosocial Approach to Origins and Structure,* pp. 29-34.

you were analyzing a community. Would not you find patterns there? Would not there be "fields"—social groups for example—organized with patterns of values, attitudes, beliefs, and manners? Instead of transplanting a group of cells from one field in a newt to a field in an axolotl, think of the adjustment required in moving from rural New England into New York City. Or, to try another example, would it not be easier to adopt a very young child rather than an older one? The infant would not have grown into the pattern of beliefs and values and mannerisms of another family or group other than your own. Of course, the parallels here are rather strained; human beings are much more complicated and adaptable than are newts; societies of human beings do not behave as do masses of cells. In both cases, however, insight into the broad patterns that are involved are most helpful.

This is offered here for any help it may give the reader in mastering the subtle idea of organism. In Chapters 6, 7, and 8 we will come back to the idea of organism and holism in more detail. First we are anxious to demonstrate that teachers are confronted with the consequences of *organization* as a persistent, universal fact of life. Forgetting the biological origins of the idea that life is lived through patterned fields, think of the influence of organization on everyday teaching. Each situation in which the teacher finds himself is a totality.

Consider a 14-year-old boy who is the lone eighth-grader in a one-room rural school in which there are five sixth-grade students, four fifth-graders, seven fourth-graders, and nine third-graders. This boy, because he is older and probably stronger than the other pupils, is respected by them, enjoys a certain amount of prestige, and usually is satisfied and cooperative. Contrast his situation, however, with that of another 14-year-old, in a graded schoolroom in town, who is two to five years older than anyone else in his room. This boy feels out of place, is uncomfortable and rebellious. One pattern is socially acceptable, the other is altogether undesirable. Each situation is patterned and the older boy fits into one but not into the other. In dealing with the problem of adjustment to a patterned situation, always keep in mind that every pattern, every situation that is organized, is resistant to change and to the introduction of anything strange.

A teacher or principal who has high hopes for a program of curriculum reorganization should be aware of this fact. A faculty member anxious to win his colleagues to a new marking system may fail unless he thinks of it realistically as changing the whole operational pattern of his school. A teacher new to a community is also up against a pattern. To communicate with the community—to have something in common with the community—the teacher will have to study that pattern.

The first experimental evidence of patterning within organisms dates from the classic experiments with the newt and axolotl that we have referred to previously. Serious speculation on organization and its characteristics, however, goes back to ancient times, to a Greek physician named Hippocrates (from whom today's physicians inherit the Hippocratic oath) who first proposed the idea of *homeostasis*. Homeostasis is the equilibrium of the human body. The concept of homeostasis is not self-evident; its conception was a stroke of inventive genius. The idea is much like a spinning top; Hippocrates put his finger on the gyroscopic quality of a human life.

A more recent and very interesting treatment of organization and its characteristics is to be found in Walter Cannon's book, *The Wisdom of the Body*.[8] Cannon interprets this wisdom in the light of various functions the body performs in satisfying its own needs. Thus, the sensation of thirst is communicated to us when the bodily tissues are in need of liquid. Or, if we need a great deal of energy in a hurry, we signal the body our need, and the adrenal glands respond by pouring adrenalin into the bloodstream to hasten the metabolism of energy-producing sugar.

Bodily equilibrium and interest. The wonderful organization of the body makes it responsive to its own needs. The needs children express, their interests—for needs and interests are closely related—are fundamental. It will not be soft-pedagogy, as some say, to tend to the satisfaction of these needs; meeting needs, interests, drives, and purposes is the most realistic course a teacher can pursue.

A child may be busy working away at some job, exerting effort or energy because he is interested. Interest and effort go hand in hand. It may be that he is interested in learning to play the drum—

[8] Walter B. Cannon, *The Wisdom of the Body*. New York: W. W. Norton and Company, Inc., 1939. See also by the same author, *Bodily Changes in Pain, Hunger, Fear and Rage*. New York: Appleton-Century Company, 1915; and "Organization for Physiological Homeostasis," *Physiological Review*, Vol. 9, 1930, 399-431.

that he has a goal and that he will have to expend energy and effort to reach it. Before he is successful he will *need* many hours of practice (notice the use of the word "need" in this connection; it does not suggest loafing or coddling). In psychological language, we have been describing the process of "drive reduction;" but whatever language is employed, tension is present. The child playing hard, "lost in his project," is interested. There is a sense of satisfaction, but the undertaking, also, is full of anguish and frustration.

If one takes the biological approach to learning, then interests, needs, and effort are inextricably linked. The idea that using student interest will make for a do-as-you-please school is quite wrong. Actually, much work and much self-discipline will be exerted by students whose motivation stems from interest.

Biological interrelatedness. It will repay us at this point to extend our investigation of the holistic theory. Its keystone is the fact of interrelatedness within organisms—one part influences another and in turn is influenced by it. An unfortunate example in children is the spinal curvature that often results from an attack of polio. Polio often weakens the muscles that are attached to one side of the spine. As the child grows, the stronger muscles, anchored to the other side, exert a constant, stronger pull and a spinal curvature results.

We have been illustrating the meaning of "functional" relationships that are characteristic of all life. The hand is shaped for grasping, for example; the nervous system is structured, as we shall see later, to permit the human being to learn, to remember, and to be imaginative. Many schools, however, disregard this fact of life. All materials presented to children or used by them should be enlivened by a functional setting. *They must be of use.* That is the order of nature, evidenced in the conditions governing adaptation and in the very body of man.

The organic system is flexible. But there is a companion notion to the holistic concept of the organism and its interrelatedness— that of flexibility. Organic systems, though characterized by a pattern and by infinite interrelations of parts and functions, are not rigidly organized. Man, for example, adjusts to drastic bodily abnormalities or deformities—the one-armed person learns to do the things his two-armed friend can do—and to environmental changes that are at times very radical. Of course there is a certain set of minimum conditions without which we cannot live (for example, the limits of temperature, oxygen concentration, and alkalinity-acidity circumscribe men); but otherwise we are flexible and adaptable. This should provide a hint for the teacher. *Survival in this changing world depends upon adaptability and education should focus on helping youngsters handle problems—some new only to him, others new only to his generation, and some new to all of us because we have just entered the Atomic Age.* The problem may be "childish," one that adults skilled in the growth and development of children will know to be common. However, this does not make the problem any less important for the child. The teacher should help the child approach and meet his problems confidently and satisfactorily, being careful, however, not to take away responsibilities that the child can carry and giving help only when needed.

The child should be allowed to explore freely in an effort to solve his own problems. The wonderful adaptability of the organism will insure that, in spite of rebuffs and disappointments, he will adapt to almost any circumstance. More space will be devoted to this matter in Chapters 5, 6, 7, and 8.

Development of man

Teachers who are not primarily concerned with biology and its related sciences will not feel compelled to master all the information about living organisms related to these fields. The purpose here is to generalize from a few of the ideas to be culled from the basic sciences—physical, biological, social, and psychological—as they apply to man. The biologists, anthropologists, and paleontologists contribute to our understanding of the amazing sensitivity and adaptability of man. Their comparisons of man with less developed animals further our understanding of man's educability.

Man, the superior animal. Man's progress has resulted from his being endowed with certain superior faculties and characteristics that have given him an advantage over other animals and have aided him in his struggle to survive within a treacherous environment. Walking erect, man is able to use his hands to grasp, mold, and shape objects, and his vision is free and unobstructed.

Hand and brain. The wonderful hands of man are coordinated, of course, with his brain.[9] It is most important that teachers grasp the idea that the hands and brain develop together and operate reciprocally.[10] We cannot train the hands without affecting the brain, and "brain work," so-called, will be improved by hand work. There is widespread agreement that human beings are an organic totality, much more than just a mind imprisoned within a body and the bonds of the emotions.

Skeletal structure. Another distinct advantage that man enjoys over many other animals is that he is equipped with an endoskeleton, that is, a skeleton inside his body. This living, internal skeleton is capable of growing with the body and does not need to be shed, as must an external skeleton, leaving vital organs unprotected during the molting season.[11]

Warm-blooded. Among the physical possessions of man that equip him to cope with the most varied types of physical environment, the circulatory system should not be omitted.[12] Man can maintain an even temperature of about 98.6 degrees Fahrenheit—if he is free from infection—whether the atmospheric temperature is higher or lower than his blood temperature.

The human nervous system. Standing upright and having a backbone enclosing the spinal column, man can balance his comparatively heavy head at the top of his nervous system. He can think while surveying his environs. When all is said that might be said about man's edge over all other species, it is the nervous system that is his treasure. With the aid of his nervous system man learned to use fire, to make tools and weapons, and to domesticate plants and animals, thereby freeing himself to some extent from the uncertainties of the hunt and of the season. He learned to communicate and to live an associated, social life. Gradually the mysteries of the physical world and the impediments of superstition and

[9] Ernest Albert Hooton, *Up From the Ape.* New York: The Macmillan Company, 1935, pp. 141-164. In these pages Professor Hooton not only discusses the development of man's brain but relates that development to the evolution of the brain case and the jaws.

[10] Otis W. Caldwell, *et. al., Biological Foundations of Education.* New York: Ginn and Company, 1935, p. 45.

[11] Hooton, *Up From the Ape,* pp. 115-131.

[12] George William Hunter, *et al., Biology: The Story of Living Things.* New York: American Book Company, 1937, pp. 310-311.

ignorance are giving way before man's inquiring mind. Nothing holds more hope for the future of man than the possibility that an increased knowledge of the nervous system itself will reveal the basic nature of learning and show how learning may be facilitated. This might short-cut many of the paths we must now travel in our search for psychological knowledge, and hasten the day when teachers can teach with something approaching maximum efficiency.

Irritability

Common elements in the nervous system. To understand the nervous system as far as one can, one must appreciate that its functions are based upon the general property of *irritability* common to all protoplasm. Even the simple, one-celled paramecium avoids obstacles. "Other reactions take place with reference to light, gravity, heat, dissolved chemicals, electricity, water currents, all of which, whether positive or negative, are coordinated by means of a so-called neuro-motor mechanism within the cell that enables it to adjust itself to its environment." [13] The paramecium's behavior is the first step, the least common denominator of nervous response. An organism, however simple, is reacting *as a whole* to the physical world cradling it.

Increased differentiation. Irritability and a nervous system sufficiently developed to carry messages from the sense organs to the muscles and brain and from the central nervous system to the muscles are the first prerequisites of human learning. To appreciate better the complicated physical structure and its flexibility and responsiveness, we suggest that the teacher reflect upon the degree to which the human nervous system is differentiated.

The hydra, a cut above the paramecium, shows greater differentiation of structure and function and is a very active organism. Its movements are coordinated in response to chemical stimuli, heat, light, and electricity, and in its outer or ectodermal layer there is a nerve circuit that receives stimuli from sensory cells and shunts these stimuli to muscle "fibrils." [14] In the hydra, there is some in-

[13] Hunter, *et al., Biology: The Story of Living Things,* p. 160.
[14] *Ibid.,* pp. 182-183.

dication of a spinal column, although it is a far cry from the verte-brate specimen.

The earthworm, the next step in development above the hydra, reacts positively to mechanical stimuli and has a simple type of *central nervous* system consisting of a ventral (stomach side) nerve cord with gangli (thickenings) in each segment, a dorsal (back) brain composed of two ganglia, and a "ring" of nervous tissue, ex-tending around his esophagus and connecting the brain with the ventral nerve cord. "Lateral nerves, which leave the brain and cord to end in muscles, skin, and other organs, form a *peripheral* nerv-ous system." [15] The skin of the earthworm is dotted with sensory cells that collect the sensations of light and, perhaps, odor, and transmit these stimuli to the central nervous system by means of nerves. The central nervous system has nerves connected with the muscle cells and stimulates them to contract, thus causing the worm's motion.[16]

Further differentiation. A comparison of man's nervous system with the simple nervous system of the earthworm, for example, shows how marvelously differentiated and specialized man's nervous equipment really is. The teacher who thinks that learning is simply a matter of storing knowledge in a "filing-case" brain is oversimpli-fying the process. One does not train humans; dogs are trained, although, in comparison with the paramecium, hydra, and earth-worm, even dogs are marvels of intricate nervous associations. Man, at least, even as a child, is worthy of something more im-aginative than the "conditioning" employed in training animals. Requiring students to drill on nonsense syllables, to memorize what they do not understand and do not enjoy, is to treat them as something less than human. To appreciate the complexity of his students, the teacher need think only of the tremendously com-plicated associative powers of the human nervous system, of the cerebro-spinal system alone.

The association neurons of these areas, which intervene in the neural paths between the sensory (receptor) areas and the motor (effector) areas, owing to the many ramifications of their fibers, make possible an almost infinite number of connections, or bonds, between any given sensory area and any given motor area. They make it possible also for the educator to

15 Hunter, *et al., Biology: The Story of Living Things*, p. 194.
16 *Ibid.*, pp. 194-195.

produce almost any given response by careful selection and association of stimuli.[17]

Heredity and environment [18]

Genetics. There has been endless discussion about the possibility of education in the face of hereditary limitations. The facts needed to settle the argument between believers in the force of heredity and those who pin their hopes on a good environment are not available. A few generalizations, however, may be advanced. The facts suggest that a man's characteristic traits are the result of inherited predispositions *and* interaction within an environment. All behavior is *within* an environment and is, therefore, conditioned by the environment. Human behavior, learning included, can be significantly altered by the individual's experience.

The egg at the very moment of fertilization is as dominated by heredity as it will ever be, but even at this stage environmental influences are operating.[19] In fact, the genes, small parts of a chromosome concerned with the transmission and development or determination of hereditary characteristics, do not act independently of the environment. On the contrary, ". . . the individual is produced by the interaction of genes and environmental conditions; so that the same set of genes may yield diverse characteristics under diverse environments." [20]

What a person will be depends upon how his environment, including his diet, influences his inheritance.[21] Special psychological traits may have genetic structure but this structure is probably no more than a biochemical disposition, which is realized in the process of growing up and living within an environment.[22]

Defining the environmental pressures as those observed by the physical sciences in terms of light, temperature, acidity . . . we shall reserve the

[17] Caldwell, *et al., Biological Foundations of Education,* p. 136. The emphasis on complexity made in this quotation may be accepted even if one rejects the "mechanistic" overtone in its concluding sentence.

[18] Laurence H. Snyder, *The Principles of Heredity.* Boston: D. C. Heath and Company, 1946.

[19] H. S. Jennings, *The Biological Basis of Human Nature.* New York: W. W. Norton and Company, 1930, pp. 201-202.

[20] *Ibid.,* pp. 228-229.

[21] Murphy, *Personality: A Biosocial Approach to Origins and Structure,* p. 45

[22] *Ibid.,* p. 50.

term heredity for the dispositions of the organism which allow these physical forces to produce greater or lesser changes in it or to manifest this or that type of qualitative variation in its response pattern. Heredity, then, will be the system of predispositions, throughout the life history of the individual organism, which, when different organisms are compared, is responsible for the varying effects of known environmental pressures.[23]

In sum, there is no assurance that a hereditary characteristic is not alterable. No teacher can say of a difficult student that he is hopeless because his older brother was a good-for-nothing and because his whole family is worthless. A child's behavior pattern can be radically altered if his "field" (environment) is favorable to the change.

Traits determined by genes? To say that dullness, slowness, laziness, indolence, or alertness and intelligence are genetically determined is to assume too much. It cannot even be said with certainty that metabolic traits are hereditary. There was a time when it was popular to speak of a successful person as one who was born to succeed, and to speak of the unsuccessful as doomed by their heredity. Careful study, however, does not reveal the children of indigent families to be unintelligent, shiftless, or unambitious. The poor family, or the state that is unable to raise enough money to finance adequate education, may foster children who are unable to perform well because they never had the opportunity to learn. Gene interaction is too complicated for one to point a finger at a successful or an unsuccessful child and account for his competence or incompetence in terms of his parents, in-laws, or grandparents. Of course, some abnormalities can be inherited,[24] but except in limited cases the genes work in man's favor. Strong genes tend to overbalance inadequate genes. When the data are analyzed, they provide ground for optimism. It will be man's unwillingness or inability to use the knowledge at hand and not the failure of his genes that will determine his prospects for a promising future.

[23] Murphy, *Personality: A Biosocial Approach to Origins and Structure*, pp. 52-53.

[24] Among the abnormalities that are inherited are haemophilia, microcephalic idiocy, cretinism, mongolian idiocy, epilepsy, Huntington's chorea, and perhaps, manic-depressive insanity. These, of course, are self-limiting—a mongoloid idiot, for example, is unlikely to reproduce. For further discussion see Chapter 28 of Snyder's, *The Principle of Heredity*, and Chapter VII of Jennings', *The Biological Basis of Human Nature*.

The psychological dimension

Consider a principal who is confronted by a second-grade boy who has been sent to the office with a note. The boy's forehead and upper face is vividly marked with varicolored crayon. Hesitantly he hands to the principal the note that reads, "When I asked Oscar why he did this he said that he wanted to be a monster and frighten the other children. Isn't that good! Miss J." This is not an unusual situation, but it is one that should be handled with great care. The worst that could be done would be to punish the child for having marked up his face, wasted crayon, and distracted the teacher and the class. Few principals or teachers would do that today. A somewhat more enlightened and common reaction would be to take the child to the washroom, help him wash his face, and talk to him kindly about ideal behavior in the classroom. He might then be sent back to his room with a kind and friendly admonitory remark.

But the *excellent* teacher with a background of reading in emotional and mental health probably would not have sent the child to the principal at all. If the teacher knew the child well, he would know, for example, that Oscar was relatively well adjusted and that what he had done was not likely to be a symptom of any *serious emotional trouble*. Instead of punishing the child, the teacher would be quick to see the advantages implicit in the situation for the class as a whole. Immediately he would show an interest in Oscar's behavior and seek to communicate his interest to the rest of the class by asking a number of questions designed to stimulate a group discussion of monsters with perhaps some reference to unobjectionable, fanciful children's stories. The discussion might, in turn, lead to the pupils' writing and performing a little dramatic play in which Oscar finally is revealed not as a monster at all but as a misunderstood elf who really was trying to do what was right. Oscar would have gained prestige from all this. He would have learned that his day-dreams and his fancies could be translated into activities, that others were honestly interested in what he thought and did, and that what he thought and did had something to do with the whole group of which he was a part. Any experienced teacher can carry this illustration much farther.

Let us assume, however, that the teacher has previously discovered in Oscar some symptoms of emotional difficulty. Perhaps he does not play easily with the other children and hesitates to recite in class. He always says "please" and "thank you" and always obeys the rules set by the teacher and the group, always tries to get his work in on time, tries to read the lesson assigned, and becomes worried and distraught when he cannot do so. Here is a child who may be compulsive. He is not well socialized and may be seriously disturbed. Such a child, "in the monster situation," would need careful attention. An inexperienced teacher might be inclined to pass over the incident because of Oscar's usual good "behavior," but the teacher with the proper background would be more careful. His paramount aim would be to try to discover anything possible about the basic need that led Oscar to act the way he did; and to this end he would seek to get the child to tell whether he dreamed about monsters, if he feared anything or felt insecure at home or in school, or why he wished to frighten people. There are cautions to be observed at this point, however. In his questioning, the teacher should avoid reading into the situation any of his own adult suspicions that are irrelevant, and should guard against the possibility that the child might invent reasons for his behavior that are not real. Such a teacher would need to know, too, that he could not go too far into this area without the trained assistance of a psychiatrist or a mental therapist. It might be wise to discuss with his principal or supervisor whether or not an expert should be called upon for assistance. Psychological research in personality development will be discussed further in Chapter 8.

Needs and the teacher. Needs influence the expenditure of energy, and teachers must use and direct them intelligently, not thwart or fight them. One of the most important lessons a teacher can learn from the study of motivation is that biological drives cannot be neglected. The teacher must not regard students apart from needs and drives as though they were a mere collection of disembodied minds.

Many classroom procedures seem to be planned around the idea that the child parks his life and ego at the dor when he comes into school and picks them up again when he leaves. Sometimes it seems that we consider the child to be in a state of suspended animation during his whole school career while we mold him and process him for life. But life is not passive in the classroom. The child has all his problems, needs, attitudes, interests, loves, fears, and dislikes with him all the time. He sees the teacher not solely as a person who is trying to teach him to read, spell, and compute, but more especially as an adult who has more knowledge, strength, status, and authority than he has and in whom he may find either security or insecurity, love or rejection, help or frustration, joy or unpleasantness, enthusiasm or discouragement, or inspiration or boredom.

A teacher who was not familiar with the complicated nature of human behavior was recently introduced into a school with a no-failure rule. This teacher said, "I am willing to mark in relation to ability, but I cannot see any justification for giving a passing mark to a child who has ability but who is too lazy to work." He did not know that laziness may be *organic* in nature as well as mental or emotional. Many a bright child (speaking of what the child might achieve in the way of a high intelligent quotient) may have glandular or other metabolic difficulties that are causing his laziness. Such a child cannot be other than lazy just as a furnace cannot give maximum heat with the draft closed. Under such circumstances, a child actually cannot burn up the energy stored in his body; until his basic difficulty has been overcome he *must* be lazy. No teacher can tell by inspection that a child has or has not a low metabolism rate. The normal rate of metabolism varies greatly from day to day. Even for those whose rate is below normal, these variations may be very great though the general level remains low. Such a condition may lead an inexperienced observer, unaware of a child's low rate, to deduce incorrectly that the child has abundant energy and should be led to use it at the right time. We can be sure that thousands of children are scolded, made to stay after school, receive low marks, are retarded, labeled as dullards, and deprived of status with their group and with their family, and, worse, have a sense of insecurity and guilt, because of circumstances over which they have no control. All this points to the conclusion that the teacher must approach each child with great humility.

Emotion and reason. In the tradition of Aristotle and Plato, it was proper to conceive of human beings as divided between the mental and physical, between passion and reason. Reason had as one of its functions the policing of the passions or emotions. It was assumed that the base part of man, the animal nature, was emotional; and that training consisted principally in disciplining the appetites, emotions, passions, and needs of the flesh. This ascetic attitude has led to any number of psychologically unsatisfactory ends, including the so-called "good discipline" of the authoritarian school, organized in the Prussian tradition. It is behind the resistance of certain people to family life education and teaching on human relations,[25] implicit in the approval of corporal punishment and most other controversial disciplinary practices, and lurks behind much of contemporary maladjustment evidenced outside the school in lax law enforcement, graft, and racketeering. In fact, maladjustment is so pervasive that it might be well to search the field a bit more thoroughly.

A few years ago a very excellent, though rather stern, teacher was criticized by parents for keeping children after school too much, slapping them too hard, and squeezing their upper arm muscles with the ends of her fingers when they were reluctant to obey. She told her principal (and it was true) that she taught her children many facts, that objective tests demonstrated her effectiveness, and that, in general, the children liked and respected her. The principal agreed, but said that these things were true not because children stayed after school or were slapped hard or had their arm squeezed, but rather because she loved to teach, was enthusiastic about teaching, believed in the subject matter with which she dealt, and had great pride in the group that was assigned to her. As an experiment, the teacher agreed for six months to abolish detention classes and to refrain from touching the children at all during any directive moments. The outcome of her experiment was a resolution never to revert to the use of punitive measures, corporal or otherwise. She discovered that her success and discipline resulted from something that was far more complimentary to her than that.

Emotion and learning.[26] Teachers often begin their careers by believing that the right environment can do almost anything for the child or young person. That is not a bad idea, but it can be merely a passing fancy if the teacher does not have some skill in dealing with human behavior. Many a parent has urged an authoritarian classroom because of a belief that children are little animals.

[25] In Chapter 5 and especially Chapter 8, the question of human relations in the classroom will be dealt with more thoroughly.

[26] Daniel A. Prescott, ed., *Emotion and the Educative Process.* Washington, D. C.: American Council on Education, 1938. Every teacher should be acquainted with this book as well as with some of the books and journals in the field of mental hygiene.

Of course children have seemingly unlimited energy, but there are ways to harness that energy without using a muzzle. In Chapter 8, in a discussion of teacher personality, it will be shown that the teachers who are convinced that children are little rascals, always up to mischief, are often the ones whom the principals, other teachers, students, and visiting experts tend to rate as poor teachers.

Discussion Questions

1. What does the phrase "the whole child" mean to you?
2. Is any learning "non-purposeful"? What about drill? Is it wrong to use drill, in the light of the extent to which children are motivated by their interests?
3. What is a biological explanation of "interest"?
4. If the teacher undertakes to make schoolwork interesting, is he in danger of making study too easy?
5. Is there any evidence on the "adaptability" of children? Do you know anything about the physical structure of the human being which would support your answer?
6. What is most likely to make children persevere in their schoolwork?
7. Can you capitalize on the needs of your students in motivating their learning? Which needs have you been able to detect? Which do you anticipate meeting in the future?
8. If a child knows that objectionable classroom behavior leads to unpleasant punishment, why does he persist in making a nuisance of himself?
9. A clinical psychologist at a famous hospital once remarked that "affection was the most important factor in a school." What did she mean? What would make you dislike a child? How would you show your dislike?
10. Since children actually are dependent upon adults, why should they not learn to do what they are told when they are told to do it?
11. If life is hard, and it is, is not a certain amount of failure in school absolutely necessary, at least enough to permit a student to know his limitations?
12. How can you tell which of your students were born "bright" and which were born "slow learners"? How dependable is that knowledge? What difference will it make in your attitudes toward the children?

Selected References

Anderson, John E., "Child Development and the Growth Process," *Intelligence: Its Nature and Nurture*. Thirty-ninth Yearbook, National Society for the Study of Education, Part II. Bloomington, Illinois: Public School Publishing Company, 1940.

Caldwell, Otis W., *et al., Biological Foundations of Education*. New York: Ginn and Company, 1935.

Cannon, Walter B., *The Wisdom of the Body*. New York: W. W. Norton and Company, Inc., 1939.

Dollard, John, *et al., Frustration and Aggression*. New Haven: Yale University Press, 1938.

Freeman, Frank S., *Individual Differences*. New York: Henry Holt and Company, 1934.

Hooton, Ernest Albert, *Up From the Ape*. New York: The Macmillan Company, 1935.

Hunt, J. McV., ed., *Personality and the Behavior Disorders*. New York: The Ronald Press Company, 1944.

Hunter, George William, *et al., Biology: The Story of Living Things*. New York: American Book Company, 1937.

Jennings, H. S., *The Biological Basis of Human Nature*. New York: W. W. Norton and Company, Inc., 1930.

Mowrer, O. H., "On the Dual Nature of Learning—A Re-interpretation of 'Conditioning' and 'Problem-Solving'," *The Harvard Educational Review*, Vol. 17, Spring 1947, 102-148.

Murphy, Gardner, *Personality: A Biosocial Approach to Origins and Structure*. New York: Harper and Brothers, 1947.

Murray, Henry A., *et al., Explorations in Personality*. New York: Oxford University Press, 1938.

Snyder, Laurence H., *The Principles of Heredity*. Boston: D. C. Heath and Company, 1946.

5

SOCIAL LEARNING AND THE

CURRICULUM

$\mathcal{T}$HE CLASSROOM contains a group of individuals whose feelings for each other make up an atmosphere. The teacher is the dominant personality in this group and his attitudes and behavior are the chief determinants of the atmosphere. If he is aware of how the members of the class feel about each other, he knows that some of them are greatly admired while others are actively disliked. He senses many of the frustrations and the hostilities. As these things become clear to him, his desire to make life more pleasant for the children drives him to investigate their homes, their out-of-school play groups, and their health. Within the classroom he distributes the actively disliked or ignored students throughout the class, pairing them with students who are able to help them bolster their egos and start them on the way to self-confidence. Through this concern for the welfare of the students, the teacher grows in sympathy and understanding. He develops into the type of teacher to whom students are attracted, to whom they are loyal, and for whom they will exert themselves.

But some teachers are not sympathetic, and will never become good teachers unless they change. In fact, unless they change, they may do positive harm. The prospective teacher can help himself to become a desirable type of instructor by taking the various aspects of social learning seriously into account. When he begins to experiment with social-learning situations, the enthusiastic response of the students soon will overcome his doubts.

The autocratic teacher

The autocratic teacher [1] attempts to dominate the classroom. He *may* succeed, but the result will be a classroom atmosphere marked by tenseness, fear, and submission. If he fails and, as a result, allows himself to grow nervous, fearful, and distraught, the student will be quick to recognize his confusion and will become restless, inattentive, and disrespectful. In either case, any wholesome attitude toward school work that may have been present soon vanishes, to be replaced by feelings of mutual distrust and hostility. Both teacher and pupils attempt to hide their inadequacies, their ignorance, and their mistakes from one another; ridicule, sarcasm, and sharp-tempered remarks are common. The teacher tends to think in terms of his status, the correctness of the position he takes on classroom matters, and the subject matter to be covered, rather than in terms of what the pupil feels, knows, and can do, and what is essential to his development.

The extremely autocratic teacher is insecure in his social relations.[2] He has never developed or cultivated attitudes and graces that insure success in the free exchange characterizing normal social intercourse. Such a teacher may be reasonably secure in dealing with recognized inferiors or superiors but until such a hierarchy is established he feels insecure. His sense of social inferiority may be the result of many factors such as autocratic home and school environments, poor physical appearance, failure to be accepted socially in high school and college, or some other disappointment; but whatever the cause, he has developed an aggression in the form of a general hostility toward people. He is convinced that it is unwise to trust anyone, that most people are sinful, that they are honest chiefly because they fear the consequences of a wrong act, and that most will use unfair means to gain profit. He believes that most children are disobedient (and they are, with him), do not appreciate what is done for them, cannot be trusted, and, in class, are continually conspiring against him. "I must be alert," he cautions himself, "and not let them get away with anything." It is impossible

---

[1] For a most informative study of the authoritarian personality, see T. W. Adorno, Else Frenkel-Brunswick, Daniel J. Levinson, and R. Sandford, *The Authoritarian Personality.* New York: Harper and Brothers, 1950.

[2] Cook, Leeds, and Callis, *Manual, Minnesota Teacher Attitude Inventory.*

for him to find security in his relations with other people, so he seeks refuge in asserting his power and authority.

Security through virtue. In seeking security through a pharisaic type of goodness and virtue, the authoritarian teacher holds rigidly to conventional standards and values. He does not see these virtues as means to human happiness or as moral-ethical values, but as behavioral ends in themselves. All misbehavior is serious to him and he feels strongly compelled to seek out, condemn, and punish severely anyone who violates a rule. There is little sense of humor in this teacher, but there is a strong sense of duty combined with a perverted sense of justice and a deep hostility toward people that condemns their wickedness and yet enjoys their suffering under punishment.

The authoritarian teacher is disposed to think in rigid, "all or none," "black or white" categories: "Children should be seen and not heard," "Children are too carefree." There is an exaggerated concern with sex: "It is better for a girl to be bashful than to be boy crazy." "Children have no business asking questions about sex." Another strong belief he harbors, one that is necessary to his security, is that he is always and unquestionably in the right, that "it takes a lot of argument to convince most people of the truth." Consequently, he condemns the methods and procedures of the more democratic teachers in the school, and is opposed to the new, the unusual, the different, the imaginative, and the creative. He believes that "Children nowadays are allowed too much freedom in school," or "the whims and impulsive desires of children are not worthy of attention."

Security through position and power. Power, position, authority, these are the principles the authoritarian teacher venerates. The winning of an advanced degree is vital in this respect, for he believes its acquisition will add greatly to his prestige and influence with other people. Regarding authority as he does, he emphasizes the dominance-submission dimension in his behavior—is submissive and uncritical toward authority from above and domineering and overbearing toward subordinates and pupils.

Security through knowledge of subject matter. The authoritarian teacher also seeks security through knowledge of subject matter. He is likely to assert that if one knows his subject, little else matters in teaching, and he believes firmly that a teacher should never acknowledge his ignorance of a topic in the presence of his pupils.

Often it is true that the authoritarian teacher will accept democracy and democratic procedures much in the same manner as he accepts conventional virtues. When this is the case, we find the anomalous situation of an autocratic classroom controlled through democratic procedures. Voting is maneuvered in such a way that the teacher's candidate or the teacher's policies always win. In pupil-teacher planning the discussion always continues until the pupils discover what the teacher has in mind all the time—the procedure degenerates into nothing but a guessing game.

Of course, this description of the authoritarian teacher represents the extreme. Seldom, if ever, would all the characteristics we have noted be found in one person. At the other end of the continuum is the extremely democratic teacher who has great confidence in people, loves children, and finds security and happiness in teaching and working with groups. Most teachers are somewhere between the two extremes. Unhappily, schools are perfect cloaks for authoritarians. The pupils are under parental and other compulsion to attend and to succeed, and will rebel only when the pressure becomes too great.

Usually, one tends to teach as he has been taught. The authoritarian mannerisms, then, are perpetuated despite the fact that a new teacher may be quite a different personality. Having been exposed to no other technique, he thinks that the authoritarian manner is the only method of instruction. Often enough, authoritarian or misled administrators themselves encourage that type of teaching. Woe to the teacher whose classroom is noisy! Yet it has to be somewhat noisy at times if the children are cooperating in groups, discussing their work, and helping one another.

Pupil behavior in autocratic and democratic atmospheres. The behavioral tendencies of pupils in autocratic and democratic social climates have been described by Lewin. His account was based on studies made by Lippitt and White at the Iowa Child Welfare Research Station involving clubs of ten- to eleven-year-old boys. (The purpose of the clubs was to make theatrical masks.) The autocratic group structure was not an extreme one. It was always friendly, and there was no attempt on the part of those in charge to suppress free expression. The leader merely told the children what to do, with whom to work, and how to proceed. The social atmosphere was that typically created by a friendly teacher who believes in order and strict discipline. In the democratic group situation, however, all problems of policy were discussed with the children. The leader acted as fully as possible as a regular member of the group, and decisions on what to do, when to do it, and how to do it, were made cooperatively. Lewin's report of the effect of the different social atmospheres upon the boys is as follows:[3]

(1) Probably the greatest quantitative difference (as between democratic and autocratic group structures or atmospheres) is the amount of *hostility* expressed among the members of the group. It is about thirty times as high in the autocratic group as in the democratic group.

(2) This is probably due partly to the greater *tension* which seems to prevail in the autocratic group. This tension shows itself in the fact that the *total volume of social interaction* is 55 per cent greater in the autocratic group, in spite of the fact that objectively there is less need of communication in regard to the ongoing activity because it is directed by the autocratic leader.

(3) The autocratic group shows a *less stable group structure.* Thirty-eight per cent of the time the members of the autocratic group work each by himself (group structure 1-1-1-1-1-1), or only one of the children works with another (2-1-1-1-1), whereas, in the democratic group such structure occurs only 18 per cent of the time. The more cooperative group structures in which all or at least four of the five children worked together (5, 4-1) occurred in the democratic group much more frequently; 56 per cent, against only 12 per cent in the autocratic group. In the autocratic group the more cooperative group structure had to be built up by the experimenter and had a tendency to break down rather quickly, whereas in the democratic group this cooperation developed spontaneously.

(4) The autocratic group shows more *dominating behavior and less objective behavior.* This difference was particularly great in relation to outgroups where the autocratic group showed 102 per cent more ascendant behavior than the democratic group.

(5) The democratic group showed 47 per cent more feeling of "we-ness" as expressed in language and in test situations; the autocratic group (expressed) 27 per cent more feeling of "I-ness."

(6) It is in line with this that the democratic group showed *more cooperative* endeavor. More often cooperation was offered and asked for, and there were many more instances of praise and expressions of friendliness.

(7) There was more expression of an objective, *matter-of-fact* attitude

[3] Kurt Lewin, "Experiments on Autocratic and Democratic Atmospheres," *The Social Frontier,* Vol. 4, July 1938, 316-319. See also Ronald Lippitt and R. K. White, "The Social Climate of Children's Groups," in R. Barker, J. Kounin, and H. Wright, eds., *Child Development and Behavior.* New York: McGraw-Hill Book Company, Inc., 1943, Chapter 28.

in the democratic group as against more personal feelings in the autocratic one. Many more constructive suggestions were offered in democracy and there was more give-and-take of objective criticism without personal involvement.

(8) The *constructiveness* was higher in the democratic group as shown in the superiority of the group products. Certain test periods where the experimenter left the room for a short while were introduced. In such periods, typically, the constructiveness of work in the autocratic group fell down very quickly, whereas in the democratic situation work went on with very little change.

(9) Feeling for *group property and group goals* was much better developed in the democratic group. The records show that the children at the close of the club had the tendency to destroy the masks or take them for themselves individually in the autocratic group, whereas in the democratic group they presented them to their leader and teacher.

(10) During the twelve meetings of the Club twice the situation of *scapegoat* arose (in the autocratic group), where the whole group ganged together against one of the members. At the fourth meeting most of the hostility was directed against one member. The next day he was still the center of hostility. As a matter of fact, he was treated so badly that he ceased to come to the Club. A few weeks later another member was made the scapegoat. He too quit, saying that he had bad eyes and that he could not come because his physician said his eyes needed the fresh air.

As a whole one might say that the autocratic situation was characterized by what one might call a state of higher basic tension, less objectivity, and more hostile aggressiveness. This aggressiveness was not directed openly against the autocrat (toward whom the children generally were rather submissive) but tended to find an outlet in the easy and less dangerous way of attacking a scapegoat.

Sometimes the behavior in the autocratic group is such that overtly everything seems to go along smoothly, and the children seem to like the situation. It was quite a revelation when the interviews with the children (which were conducted by a person not connected with the experiment) brought out a most intensive dislike of the autocrat. Not infrequently the dominant note in autocracy is not so much an atmosphere of hostility as one of (no) . . . initiative, and listlessness.

In summary, one may say that *autocratic classroom control tends to produce authoritarian personalities*—hostile, selfish, self-centered, sensitive, fearful, critical people who have little confidence in, or affection for, their fellows. They constantly need a leader to tell them what to do, and cannot act effectively unless constant guidance is assured them.

The autocratic teacher speaks. Here are some typical remarks an autocratic teacher might make:

(1) "I guess we must stop reading and, as usual, wait for Henry to catch up with the class." (Henry, who was having difficulty with his reading, was being punished for not keeping up with the pace the teacher has set as a standard. There was no provision for sub-grouping that might permit Henry to read with others whose reading level was closer to his own. In all probability Henry will be retarded further by this teacher's attitude.)

(2) "Oh, be quiet child! You chatter like a monkey." (The teacher, in this instance, was annoyed at being interrupted by a little girl.) Do you think that the teacher might have handled the situation without the scolding and comparison? Suppose that the teacher had said: "I shall try to make this story just as interesting as I can. Mary, will you help us remember what happens to Jo-Jo?"

(3) "Stand up when you recite! Where do you think you are?" (This teacher seemed to feel that it was necessary to have children stand at attention when reciting. His ego was flattered. There was no informality in the classroom; everyone was afraid of the teacher.)

(4) "Don't interrupt me! Hasn't anyone ever taught you any manners?" (Here was another insecure teacher, a little Napoleon.)

(5) "Stop contradicting me! Who do you think you are?" (This teacher felt that any questioning of his statements meant that the student was questioning his superior knowledge. By belittling the children the teacher may have hoped to magnify his own importance.)

(6) "Move over there, Michael, you're not made of glass." (The insecure teacher is often rude. He behaves as though the students were unimportant subordinates.)

(7) "I want to know who marked this map, but I don't suppose that I can get the truth out of you." (This teacher was abusive and insulting. Lacking respect and affection for his students, he made himself ridiculous by asking for a confession while making it perfectly clear that the guilty student would be punished. This certainly discouraged frankness and, if it accomplished anything, encouraged lying.)

(8) "Stop whispering! If you need help, raise your hand." (It would not occur to this teacher that students could possibly help one another and learn cooperation by doing so.)

The democratic classroom

Some of the essential characteristics of the democratic classroom have been referred to previously. In such a classroom the teacher and pupils are members of a cooperative group engaging in meaningful and purposeful activities directed toward the attainment of educational goals. Each member feels that his contributions to the group are worth while, are appreciated, and that he is accepted as a person of worth. The teacher and pupils work together in a social atmosphere of cooperative endeavor, of intense interest in the work of the day, and with a feeling of security growing from a permissive atmosphere of freedom to think, act, and speak one's mind with mutual respect for the feelings, rights, and abilities of others. Inadequacies and shortcomings in both teacher and pupils are admitted frankly and accepted as something to be overcome, not ridiculed. The varying abilities and strengths of the several group members are recognized and used to the utmost to further group goals. A sense of proportion involving humor, justice, honesty, and concern for the feelings of others is present. Group solidarity resulting from common goals, common understandings, common efforts, common difficulties, and common achievements characterize the class. The teacher in his every word respects the feelings of the students, shows faith in their good will and intentions, is confident of their ability and will to achieve, and recognizes the difficulties children encounter in attaining the goals set for themselves. The pupils constantly strive to prove themselves worthy of the high regard that the teacher and other members of the group have for them.

The democratic personality. The important single factor in creating a democratic social atmosphere in a classroom is the personality of the teacher. (This was true for the autocratic classroom, as well.) The democratic teacher has a deep affection for, and confidence in, people. He is sensitive to the feelings of others, and his greatest satisfaction comes from working to further their welfare. Being neither a reformer nor a perfectionist, he accepts himself and his limitations and is willing to accept others on the same basis. He is slow to condemn and quick to forgive and accepts criticism objectively without becoming emotionally upset. Because he feels secure in his social relations, he is not greatly concerned with his status as such.

The virtues he deems important are those that further harmonious and satisfying social relations. He recognizes that any form of behavior carried to excess may be harmful. Because he is secure, he seeks adventure and welcomes the imaginative, the creative, and the innovative. Unlike his opposite, the authoritarian, the democratic teacher is less inclined to be impressed by titles, degrees, or position. Also, he will seek ideas from the most humble, will try to establish what is true rather than who is right, and will not expect people to listen to him because of who he is but because of what he says. To him, subject matter is valuable only as it is related to the learning process and the development or maturation of the child.

Techniques of democratic control. The techniques of democratic discipline or classroom control have received much less attention in the past than have those of autocratic control. Autocratic procedures for making assignments, hearing recitations, questioning, testing, evaluating, and reporting have been the chief concern in methods classes for many years. The techniques of democratic procedure are only now receiving a hearing. We now turn to a consideration of the factors that increase the unity, solidarity, cohesiveness, and stability of a group.[4]

(1) *There should be no stigma attached to belonging to the group.* In a one-room rural school there is no stigma attached to a fourteen-year-old's being in the same room with a six-year-old. But in a graded school, where status is joined to grade label and developmental level is a criterion for grouping, it is difficult for a retarded pupil to accept younger and smaller children as his peers. Likewise, it is difficult for a group to accept a younger, smaller member who has been accelerated. Grade groups should be formed with reference to the most obvious criteria of status—chronological age and physical and social development.

(2) *Group achievements that are accepted and praised outside the group enhance its pride and cohesiveness.* The successful culmination of a unit of learning, publication of a room newspaper, a dramatic production, or any successful enterprise to which the entire group has contributed increases the group's stability.

4 See George V. Sheviakov and Fritz Redl, *Discipline for Today's Children and Youth.* Washington, D. C.: Department of Supervision and Curriculum Development, National Education Association, 1949.

(3) *Group suffering can be a cohesive force.* Children under a tyrannical teacher feel a bond of comradeship, mutual sympathy, and unity that makes their burden more bearable. Obviously, however, this is not a desirable way to increase group morale. Such a situation is productive of much hostility and the group, unable to release its resentment against the teacher, may turn its enmity against one of its own members.

(4) *The group undertaking must be broad enough to enable every member to make a contribution that the group and the individual recognize as important.* The role that the individual plays in the group enterprise should be suitable from the standpoint of his learning and personality needs, abilities, and values.

(5) *The members of the group should have common interests, needs, and values and yet be sufficiently different to complement each other in aptitude and abilities.* For example, a cohesive baseball team is made up of players approximately equal in ability, all interested in the sport and sharing similar ideas of sportsmanship and team play. But if too many of the players want to be pitchers, or catchers, or first basemen, there will be little cohesiveness within the group. In such circumstances, positions should be rotated. *Outside the school there is important work to be done by the individuals with I.Q.'s of 70, 80, and 90 as well as by individuals with I.Q.'s of 110, 120, and 130. In the democratic classroom the pupil with an I.Q. of 80 is as welcome as the pupil with an I.Q. of 120. Both should find valuable work they can do and both can be acceptable to the group.*

(6) *Secure groups do not need labels and trappings to give them prestige.* Usually, when a group is unified through common goals, common achievements, and common sufferings, there will be less emphasis on conformity insofar as clothes, badges, language, and standards are concerned. The imposition of a kind of mass orthodoxy in such matters generally indicates a feeling of insecurity in the group. They are essentially autocratic labels of prestige and may indicate autocratic group leadership. If a member feels secure in his membership, such constant assurances are not necessary. In a democratic group, each member feels that he is lending prestige to the group; he belongs because of his contribution, participation,

and skills. In an autocratic group, the member feels that he draws prestige from the group to which he belongs, hence the stress upon authoritative labels of prestige.

A warning. Successful group planning, execution, and evaluation requires social understandings and skills. A word of warning is in order here. The teacher should be alert not to allow secondary issues or problems to distract the group's attention from the main point of the learning unit. Invariably such issues will arise, but they should be recognized as being subordinate and dealt with in periods separate from those devoted to the chief topic. For example, it would be poor practice to interrupt a reading session devoted to meaning and interpretation to teach children the principles of phonetics. Instruction in phonetics could come later in some other period. To stop a serious discussion to point out a principle of group dynamics would be equally bad.[5]

An effective group—its nature and evaluation

Criteria of good workmanship. If the group is to make progress toward educational goals, by democratic procedures followed throughout the days, weeks, months, and years of working together, systematic planning is necessary and adequate records of progress and achievement should be kept. These records will provide a handy index of educational goals, and the procedures to be followed in achieving these goals. For example, they will serve as guides for future classroom conduct and will aid in the selection of learning units and the determination of correct standards for group discussion. Or they may be referred to if information is needed on preparing reports, on story-telling, oral reading, letter writing, study procedures, or other projects the class has developed. As an example, the following is a set of criteria drawn up by a sixth-grade class to guide them in their conversation periods.

[5] Free role-playing, non-directed play, and sociodrama are not being criticized in the above. They have definite purposes and are well planned, as well as expertly evaluated. Under censure is the so-called group work which spends the entire class time pretending to be getting prepared for a problem when there is no problem.

Standards for a Good Conversationalist [6]

1. The conversation should be kept going:
   (a) Keep on main points.
   (b) Change the subject smoothly.
2. The people should be polite:
   (a) Boys should stand when girls enter.
   (b) If a boy and a girl start to talk at the same time, the boy should let the girl go ahead.
   (c) If two boys or two girls start to talk at one time, the girl or boy who has talked more gives place to the one who has talked less.
   (d) Only one person should talk at a time.
   (e) Usually questions should be addressed to the group instead of to individuals.
   (f) The people in the audience should not attract the attention of the people in the conversation group.
3. The host or hostess should be polite to the guests:
   (a) The host or hostess should talk only when the conversation lags.
   (b) The host or hostess should talk only to encourage the guests to talk.
   (c) The host or hostess should greet the guests cordially.
4. Only people who have studied the *Weekly Reader* and read the local papers and listened to radio reports should accept an invitation:
   (a) People should think as they read.
   (b) People should be able to locate on the map places mentioned.
   (c) People should look up difficult words.
   (d) People should be able to give the source of their information.
5. People should talk about topics that are important now; that probably will be important for some time to come:
   (a) Talk about the causes of war and how war affects the people.
   (b) In connection with disasters talk about means of preventing them.
6. People should discuss sensible, interesting, and pleasant topics.
7. People should use good English:
   (a) People should make themselves heard.
   (b) People should pronounce words correctly.
   (c) People should use correct expressions, e.g., the *reporter* instead of *it,* an *interesting conversation* or a *pleasant conversation* or a *lively conversation* instead of *a nice time.*
   (d) People should omit unnecessary words.
   (e) People should try to add to their vocabularies all the time.

The group sets its goals and criteria. After the group has dis-

---

[6] Walter W. Cook, *Grouping and Promotion in the Elementary School,* Series on Individualization of Instruction, No. 2. Minneapolis: University of Minnesota Press, 1941, p. 14.

cussed educational goals and the essentials of proper procedure, the conclusions they reach may be placed on the blackboards or the bulletin board, or may be mimeographed or printed on large sheets of oaktag paper for ready reference during the planning, execution, and evaluation periods. The lists of criteria serve as a guide to behavior and as a basis for action, and are revised as the children mature and new insights into the activity are gained. Children can set goals suitable for their level of understanding and performance that are more meaningful in guiding learning and conduct than are those of curriculum committees or authors of textbooks. Children feel that unit activities that do not have definite learning goals are unimportant.

Pupil planning. Leadership in educational endeavor cannot be transferred to children until they are ready for it. What can be done at any grade level depends upon the previous experiences of the children. The social skills necessary for group cooperation— the assumption of responsibility, planning, carrying through, and evaluating work—must be learned. An atmosphere in which children feel free to express opinions, make suggestions, and criticize procedure is the first requirement. Even in the kindergarten and first grade, the children can help plan many activities such as the arrangement of a play house, a post office, a grocery store, and other similar enterprises. They can help plan a tea for their mothers, a trip to the bakery, an interview with the principal, and rules for the use of play equipment.

By the third-grade level, the children can plan and carry through a program designed to show their parents what they have learned. The whole complicated program involving a master of ceremonies, puppet show, the shifting of scenery, the telling of stories, gymnastics, and dancing can be executed by the students while the teacher sits in the audience with the parents.

Pupil planning and social learning. In almost everything he does and says, the democratic teacher impresses upon his pupils the importance of respecting the feelings of others. He is careful never to injure the pride of his pupils, for example; and they, sensing his solicitude, in turn display a similar attitude toward others. Or, as part of normal classroom procedure, the teacher may arrange to have every child play the part of a new pupil in a strange school. Thus, the children come to experience some of the hesitancy and uncertainty that normally accompanies such a situation and will be more tolerant of the newcomer. Also, ways may be discussed for welcoming the new pupil to the school. This may involv? helping him get his books, welcoming him into games, and seeing to it that someone walks home with him after school and to school with him in the morning. Subsequent planning may include a suggestion that the new pupil be given an opportunity to tell about his previous school experiences, where he lived, and something about his family. Children will plan and take responsibility for carrying out these friendly gestures with such enthusiasm that the coming of new pupils will be anticipated eagerly.

The pupils also can tell how they feel when they are not invited to play in a game or are not invited to a party, or when other children whisper secrets in their presence. Any and all forms of behavior that irritate and cause anxiety and insecurity can be brought into the open and discussed.[7]

Facilitating and blocking group progress.[8] In teacher-pupil planning, it is important that children ultimately become aware of the ways in which progress is made in group planning, and, also, of the ways in which progress is blocked. Such a recognition can be formulated through group discussion and, as progress is made, recorded for future reference. As already indicated, these records should be revised as additional information is gained; they should be used with this idea in mind. Of course, discussion guides should not be handed out and learned or memorized in a formal fashion.

When is progress being made? One of the best indications of progress is the development of a child to the point where he begins to show an awareness for the feelings of others in his group and tries by thought and action to understand the needs of every child in his class. Consequently, it should be regarded as encouraging when a pupil avoids misunderstandings in the class by restating and

[7] The example of planning the welcome of the new student fits the requirements of good sociodrama and activities that heighten perception (by teacher and students) of human needs for satisfactory human relations. Both will be discussed at some length in the rest of this chapter.

[8] There are many studies on membership roles in groups. See, for example Kenneth D. Benne and Paul Sheats, "Functional Roles of Group Members, I," *The Journal of Social Issues,* Spring 1948, Vol. 4, 41. For a very practical account see D. M. Hall, *The Dynamics of Group Discussion: A Handbook for Discussion Leaders.* Danville: The Interstate Printers and Publishers, 1950, pp. 12-16.

clarifying vague statements and stimulates other members to greater participation in discussions and class activities by encouraging them and helping them with their work. Progress also is being made when a pupil tries to relieve or compromise a tense situation with a humorous remark that clears the air, prepares and distributes materials that are helpful to the class in the achievement of its goals, and records accurately the action of the class for future reference and guidance.

When is progress being hindered? Many signs are indicative of progress being retarded. Progress is hindered when a child begins to attack the status of another, disapproves of suggestions and contributions others make, refuses to participate seriously in class activities, or seeks to attract attention to himself through boastful and cynical remarks and persistent questioning. Such behavior may in time result in his disagreeing with *every* proposal and adopting a completely negative attitude insofar as classroom activities are concerned. (At the same time, other pupils may be too docile, will blindly accept all suggestions without question—an equally bad situation.) Finally, progress is being hindered when a pupil tries to set one group in the class against another—girls against boys— or becomes so concerned with his own plans—often negative ones— that he fails to pay attention to what is going on around him.

A good teacher speaks. On pages 94 and 95, we noted typical remarks of an autocratic, hostile, and insecure teacher. A more effective instructor, one capable of enjoying work with youngsters, has learned how to help children who are not effective group members, who hinder the progress of the class in one or more of the ways suggested in the preceding paragraph. The teacher who tries to lead in supporting group spirit is quick to help a defensive or antagonistic child to regain status in the group. He never ridicules a child.

(1) "Some of us are having difficulty with this problem (subtraction). Subtraction is not easy. I wonder if there are some ways of making subtraction more sensible?" (The teacher is accepting subtraction as a real problem and is inviting all the class to suggest ways in which to approach it. No one experiencing difficulty is being singled out as a "dumb-bunny.")

(2) "You did a fine job of getting the room shipshape yesterday. Isn't it a pleasant place in which to live today? By the way, does

anyone know what 'shipshape' means? Why do you suppose that ship captains and the crews are so anxious to have things shipshape? Of course, when people have to live together in one room or in a small place, work and play are more fun if there isn't a great clutter." (The problem of replacing materials was no problem for this teacher. The group thought of the care submarine crews take to keep their confined quarters livable. Each child seemed to sense the need for keeping the room shipshape.)

(3) (Sam has just told the class that the thermometer outside the window shows the temperature to be about 35 degrees above zero. It is time for going out-of-doors.) "We will have fun in the nice crisp air but fingers will be pretty chilly if mittens are forgotten." (This teacher is not the type who insults a child for neglecting to dress warmly.)

The teacher whose experiments cause students to respond in ways that facilitate group progress will be a happy teacher, loved by his students and respected by his colleagues. Some helpful techniques have been mentioned in this chapter, and attention has been given to the qualities of personality a teacher must cultivate in order to succeed in his work. But this is not enough. Other devices and techniques that aid a teacher to understand the interrelations of personalities within his class and to overcome difficult behavior problems occasioned by students who have not become equal partners in the enterprises of the group, will be discussed in Chapters 6 and 7.

Discussion Questions

1. Is it fair to categorize teachers as "autocratic" and "democratic?" Are there better words we might use to describe them? What words would you suggest?

2. In the section dealing with security through virtue, did you feel that there was any intent on the part of the authors to discount the value of virtue as we commonly use the word? Why do you feel this way?

3. Is position or power bad or good in and of itself? Why?

4. Isn't mastery of subject matter important to a teacher? What is wrong in seeking security through knowledge of subject matter?

5. Why do pupils resent the exercise of autocratic powers by teachers? Do they *always* resent it? Did you?

6. Is the democratic personality as described here too "goody-goody?"

Have you known anyone who approached the ideal set forth here? Describe the person who came nearest to it.

7. Were you ever a member of a class or grade that developed democratic group control over itself? Describe how it was done.

8. How do you make children ready to assume leadership in a democratic group? How do you prepare them to select, follow, or replace their leaders?

9. Someone has said, "Children will never turn against a teacher if they feel he is on their side of the fence,—their team." What does this mean when viewed according to the context of this chapter? If this is true, could he be autocratic and at the same time loved, respected, and followed?

10. It has been said, "Happy teachers are good teachers." Could we also say, "Good teachers are happy teachers?" Does the happiness of the teacher in her class depend upon the class?

Selected References

Adorno, T. W., Else Frenkel-Brunswick, Daniel J. Levinson, and R. N. Sandford, *The Authoritarian Personality*. New York: Harper and Brothers, 1950.

Baxter, Bernice, *Teacher-Pupil Relationships*. New York: The Macmillan Company, 1941.

Cook, Walter W., Carroll H. Leeds, and Robert Callis, *Manual, Minnesota Teacher Attitude Inventory*. New York: The Psychological Corporation, 1951.

DeHuszar, George B., *Practical Applications of Democracy*. New York: Harper and Brothers, 1945.

Lewin, Kurt, "Dynamics of Group Action," *Educational Leadership*, Vol. 1, 1944, 195-200.

———, "Experiments on Autocratic and Democratic Atmospheres," *The Social Frontier*, Vol. 4, July 1938, 316-319.

Sheviakov, George V., and Fritz Redl, *Discipline for Today's Children and Youth*. Washington, D. C.: Department of Supervision and Curriculum Development, National Education Association, 1944.

———, "Engineering Research in Curriculum Building," *Journal of Educational Research*, Vol. 41, April 1948, 577-596.

Yauck, Wilbur A., *Improving Human Relations in School Administration*. New York: Harper and Brothers, 1949.

6

CULTURE, SOCIETY, AND
THE CHILD

CULTURE REFERS to the characteristic features—language, religious beliefs, dress, customs, attitudes, artifacts, and technology— of a place and a time. A neighborhood can have a culture, although it is more common to speak of it as having a sub-culture, leaving the term culture for the patterns of folkways [1] and mores [2] that are spread over longer time periods and greater space and that influence the lives of more people.

Society is not really separable from culture. All societies exist within cultures and all cultures exhibit themselves in societies. Society is the sum of the institutions through which we live and make our living. An institution, whether its purpose is educational, religious, recreational, or some other, is a sponsored and more or less organized way in which a group of activities are usually carried on. Churches, for example, are religious institutions. The family is an institution charged with such things as caring for children and old people and for the psychosocial and physical needs of husband and wife. Classes as they exist in society, on the other hand, are just as much parts of society as the family or churches, but they are *extra-legal*.

During World War II, the American Army and Navy needed

---

[1] A folkway is any way of thinking, feeling, or acting, common to a social group.
[2] Mores also involve customary behavior, but in addition, are imbued with ethical significance and have the force of law.

information from those who knew the ways of living characteristic of the people inhabiting the Pacific islands that were scheduled for invasion. They turned to the cultural anthropologists who had visited these islands before the war, and had studied terrain, climate, and the varied customs and habits of the inhabitants. The anthropologists' reports to the military were very useful in our dealings with the natives. This bears a moral for teachers.

Teaching and culture patterns

Consider the predicament of a young woman who taught a group of youngsters whose background was quite different from her own. This teacher undertook to "import" *her* values (ideas about what constitutes good manners, for example) into what amounted to an alien cultural pattern. Straight out of an up-state teachers' college, she was placed in charge of the sixth grade of an urban school located in a portion of town given over to Mexican and Puerto Rican families. Hers was a rural background and most of her friends and acquaintances were Scandinavians or Germans. She had never met a Mexican and knew nothing of Mexican folkways or mores. She was a Lutheran. Most of her pupils, however, were Catholic, lived amidst virtual slum conditions, came from large families, and did not behave as did the children she had known previously. She had never visited any of their homes, had no desire to do so, and, if she had, might not have been able to understand or make herself understood. Had she inquired, she would have discovered that the leader of the community was the parish priest who could have advised her on the means of communicating with or understanding the children and their parents. The principal of the school already had given her much information about the parents of the children and she had access to publications of a state commission established by the governor that would have given her some insight into the folkways and mores of the neighborhood had she chosen to use them.

Suspicion of the novel. But, confronted with children who did not look, behave, or respond in the ways with which she had become accustomed, her initial bewilderment changed to hostility. She felt (and said) that all these foreign children were dirty, told lies, lacked manners, were wanting in interest in the school's work, and, very likely, lacked intelligence.[3]

Happily, she resolved to persevere and to teach "those nasty children." On her own initiative she sought assistance, found it, and made significant progress. She was helped most when she realized that the behavior patterns of the Mexicans had been imported from a culture foreign to her experiences.[4] It had been very difficult for her to grant that these behavior patterns had any justification. Why did these people *have* to be so different (and objectionable)? Why could they not adjust to "our" ways?

These were legitimate questions. American customs and attitudes of the type with which she was familiar would have helped these Mexicans and Puerto Ricans to adjust. "When in Rome do as the Romans do" is good advice, *if* one can follow it. This teacher learned that a determined effort often is required to shift one's cultural perspective. There are several reasons for this and the teachers who know them will avoid some unnecessary disappointment and frustration.

Acceptance of the familiar. The psychologists tell us that children grow fond of what is familiar.[5] As the child matures, *his* family, neighborhood, friends, church, city, state, country ("right or wrong"), race, and standard of living appear to *him* to be the

[3] Many teachers, and administrators too, will be interested in the experiments undertaken in Springfield, Massachusetts. The "Springfield Plan" is described in Alexander Alland and James W. Wise, *The Springfield Plan.* New York: The Viking Press, 1945, and by Clarence I. Chatto and Alice L. Halligan in *The Story of the Springfield Plan.* New York: Hinds, Hayden, and Eldredge, Inc., 1945. One of the classics in intercultural research, a study that happens to focus on the American Negro, is Gunnar Myrdal, *An American Dilemma,* 2 Vols. New York: Harper and Brothers, 1944. Also of value are Hortense Powdermaker and Helen F. Storen, *Probing Our Prejudices.* New York: Harper and Brothers, 1944; Alice L. Sickels, *Around the World in St. Paul.* Minneapolis: The University of Minnesota Press, 1945; and William E. Vickery and Stewart G. Cole, *Intercultural Education in American Schools.* New York: Harper and Brothers, 1943.

[4] See Ruth Benedict, *Patterns of Culture.* Boston: Houghton Mifflin Company, 1934; Cora A. Du Bois, *The People of Alor.* Minneapolis: The University of Minnesota Press, 1949; Clyde Kluckhohn, *Mirror for Man.* New York: Whittlesey House, McGraw-Hill Book Company, Inc., 1949; and Ralph Linton, *The Cultural Background of Personality.* New York: D. Appleton-Century Company, 1945.

[5] Murphy, *Personality: A Biosocial Approach to Origins and Structure.* See especially Parts II and III.

most desirable. Sociologists call this tendency "ethnocentrism." It is cousin to prejudice, insularity, and narrow-mindedness. However, it is a natural inclination and actually helps to keep a culture united. Because people tend to accept the folkways and mores of their group, a pattern of culture emerges. When the pattern finally takes shape, it resists change. The psychologist would say that this is because people learn to think and act in accord with the folkways and mores of their cultures. Anthropologists affirm that the folkways and mores are built into the children by the adults or by the schools, for example. The maturing personality is conditioned to behave as the culture would have it behave. Only a long-time process of reconditioning, of un-learning, will ready an individual to live comfortably in another culture. The teacher cannot snap her fingers and expect that youngsters who are products of another cultural heritage will swing over to her perspective.

A corollary to the idea that people learn to like what is familiar to them is that they do not like what is strange or foreign. For example, "book larnin'" is suspect to a self-made man, and some people regard immigrants, displaced persons, or foreigners as inferior. This is perfectly understandable to the cultural anthropologist and the psychologist who study the ways in which people grow to learn and accept the familiar. There is a difference in the anthropologist's approach, however, in that he does not stress the tendency to learn and to like the commonplace, the old, and familiar. He emphasizes the *result* of this type of learning that produces a tightly woven cultural pattern resistant to change. Such a pattern, just because it is tightly woven, has little room for the strange, the new, or the experimental. Cultures, says the anthropologist, are conservative, and, as a result, people are also conservative. The person who is "different" runs the risk of being ostracized.[6]

The stranger. A student new to a country, city, neighborhood, or school usually is not familiar with the mores and folkways of his new cultural environment. The teacher, especially one whose class is composed of children from two different neighborhoods, is witness to this time and time again. It is the teacher's responsibility to see that the new student makes a satisfactory adjustment by helping

6 Margaret Mead, *Growing Up in Samoa*. New York: William Morrow & Company, 1928; and *Environment and Education*. Chicago: The University of Chicago Press, 1942.

him over the first difficult period of "practicing" the new "part." [7]

Provincialism. The short-sightedness and narrowness of peoples immersed in their own special cultural pattern is called "provincialism." The smothering effects of such an attitude rob us of rich experiences, of understanding, and of enjoyment.

Provincialism is a narrow, insular attitude of mind that springs from exclusive interest in, or overweening devotion to, the cultural pattern of one's own province, section, or, by extension, country. Inevitably, the provincial-minded person comes to regard with suspicion, distrust, or outright hostility everything that is foreign or alien to his beliefs or customs. The problem of provincialism arises to plague statesmen, religious leaders, politicians, and many others who have long sought ways to counteract its influence or eradicate it altogether. It is a problem with which the teacher must also come to grips.

The most promising start in overcoming provincialism is to make people secure within their own cultures. When an individual knows what is expected of him within his culture (in his school, for example) he is secure *if* he feels that he succeeds in his appointed role. The fellow who feels rejected, unwanted, looked down upon, unloved, despised, hated, laughed at, cut, or passed over, is insecure. An insecure boy takes out his feeling of inadequacy on himself and on his fellows. Likewise, a secure citizen does not need to depend upon a chauvinistic arrogance or provincial devotion. He does not need to feel superior to or "look down" on those from other cultures, classes, or communities. Secure men and women do not need to "compensate" whereas one who feels inadequate or insecure may become a bully.

This type of thinking has grave weaknesses. It is easy to say that frustration leads to aggression, but it is another thing to prove it. Because all the answers are not in, the idea of insecurity breeding hostility is advanced only as a hypothesis. Should one choose

[7] Too few studies by psychologists (on "individual differences") and by anthropologists (on the slowness of established cultural patterns to be modified by the new) show how the teacher can use the similarity in needs, wishes, fears, and reactions of children in making a newcomer feel at home. An adolescent in Germany, for example, is impelled by the same drives as the adolescent in this country; all children will respond to sympathy and warm-hearted interest. The ways of expressing needs will certainly differ, however, but the teacher should not be thrown off guard by these superficial differences. The stoic Indian child will cherish affection just as much as the more expressive Italian youngster.

to accept it for the moment, it suggests that students' fears and anxieties drive them to demean themselves and bully others. The causes of insecurity, if this hypothesis is correct, are to be reduced by every means at the teacher's disposal. This holds true even though many teachers feel that the very fears of their students may be used to motivate learning. To some extent they are correct. Unfortunately, such learning of subject matter is won at a tragic price in human relations.[8] There are other and more effective means to stimulate learning, many of which will be treated further in Chapter 9.

The cultural impact

Very often the need to be accepted by boys and girls of one's own age causes a child trouble at home. The storm might be weathered without too much sadness if the sympathy, affection, and love of one's parents were not so important. It is a perplexing situation for the child. No boy or girl will willingly offend his "gang," but on the other hand, he needs the acceptance and support of his parents. (At adolescence the youngster craves the friendship of his age-mates and imitates them with all his might. At home he sways between adulthood and childhood.) There are times when a girl expects her mother to braid her hair and others when she resents her mother questioning her about her friends and activities. The parents are bewildered. They watch their offspring run with the gang, act as a hoodlum, dress as a clown, and speak as a character from a comic strip. Is their son a man or a boy? The son, for his part, is sometimes a boy who desires unstinted praise and support from his parents and, almost at the same time, wants to be independent. This conflict situation usually blows over without undue unpleasantness but, if the incident is complicated by an exaggerated dislike of the parents for the folkways and mores their children are

---

[8] This injunction against frustration can be overdone by the sentimentalist. A little frustration is necessary for learning. If there is no frustration, no urge to solve a troublesome (frustrating) problem, there will be very little learning. However, the frustration is not to be so great that learning is undermined and students should not be driven to learn *in order to pass a test*. This is reasonable and supported by common sense and experiment. See S. Rosenzweig, "Outline of Frustration Theory," in J. McV. Hunt, ed., *Personality and the Behavior Disorders*, 2 Vols.

adopting, the insecurity of both parents and children is increased. Their relationship becomes so confused that trouble at home and in the school is unavoidable.

The child reflects his home. Teachers will run across many examples to illustrate these points. In one school the son of a bartender became a problem child. His teacher was an ardent champion of temperance. One day, when the class was engaged in discussing the effect of alcohol on the human body, one of the children mentioned that Billy's father was a bartender downtown. Billy soon grew unruly and disobedient. A clever principal inquiring into the matter was able to establish rapport with Billy and find out the reason for his behavior. Billy believed that he had lost caste with the other students because they agreed with the teacher in not respecting his father's occupation. He knew that the teacher regarded his father as a person who was engaged in an evil activity. The problem regarding Billy was not resolved easily. Fortunately his difficulties were diagnosed early, and he was placed with a different teacher and a different group. No one can tell what permanent marks such difficulties may leave. The teacher must be alert that they do not arise in the first place, for they may be productive of permanent harm. There are many other illustrations. The problem of the Jewish child at the time of the Christmas celebration may become a difficult one. In its solution the cooperation of Jewish people should be solicited. Many times gentile teachers with the best of intentions but with insufficient insight have aggravated rather than improved the tensions and psychological disturbances that often mark this situation.

Such incidents illustrate the importance a child attaches to acceptance by other children. It frequently happens, however, that neither the teacher nor the parents understand that the child's behavior is caused by his lack of status in his group. His unsocial behavior brings down upon his head not only the wrath of the teacher but the disapproval of his parents. There are, of course, many other ways in which the need for group approval creates tensions between the child and his parents. It may be that he is refused permission to attend moving pictures, cannot persuade his parents to buy a television set, must wear a style of clothing that is not popular, or be in bed earlier than the other children in the neighborhood. The difficulty can have its source in a purely domestic situation between parent and child and still have unfortunate repercussions in the school.

Often the teacher will find that a child's wish to be one of the gang may be utilized as a disciplinary aid. If the teacher knows something of the gang's *code,* he may be able to bring subtle and effective pressure to bear on the student who is disrupting the class. This is a rather well-known device. Less well understood are the troubles of the student whose parents do not appreciate his need to belong. It may be that his folks were born in another country—into a cultural pattern different from the one prevailing in school or in the neighborhood. In the old country, boys were expected to begin work at adolescence and girls worked at home. Now the boys and girls want to play afternoons, stay out late at night, and spend money. The children are urged by their teachers to stay in school, but the experience of the parents has been that in the old country, poor people rarely received more than a primary schooling, if that much.[9]

It is customary for the families of the foreign born to have difficulties similar to those just described. The elders are suspicious of the new cultural pattern and cherish the old, more familiar ways. Their children, on the other hand, are anxious to adjust to new surroundings and new friends, and add to this anxiety a typical "rejection of the parent." The teacher finds himself dealing with youngsters who are having trouble keeping the affection of their parents without losing the regard of their friends. These students are apt to be upset; their orderly inclusion in the classroom demands insight on the part of the teacher.

The prevalence of insecurity. Insecurity among students is widespread and although the causes of it are many, one that we feel needs stressing is the social *competition* in which many American

---

[9] The superintendent of a small five-teacher school in North Dakota was told when he noticed that a fifth-grade boy had been absent for a few days that the boy's father had decided to put the boy to work on the farm. He drove to the farm and found the boy at work in the field with his father. The father, a recent immigrant, said in broken English, "I work. He must work. That boy can read and he knows what he reads. He is too smart on books." It happened that there was a rich farmer nearby who, years before, had been an immigrant from the same country as this father. This farmer was known far and wide as a man who advised his neighbors on various points. The young superintendent talked with this man, who listened and said, "The boy will be back to school tomorrow." And he was.

parents indulge. Let us consider the Joneses, who are anxious to "measure up" to the Jacksons. Ann Jones, in the fourth grade, is the key figure in the contest. Her marks, her class-play parts, her manners, and her popularity help the Joneses compete with the Jacksons. The competition is really between the elder Jacksons and the elder Joneses, but Susy Jackson and Ann Jones do the competing for their mothers and fathers. At first glance this seems harmless enough. After all, competition is a good thing in business; why be suspicious of it in the home and school?[10] The answer is that countless instances are known where the Joneses and the Jacksons nagged their daughters. Ann and Susy grew to dread their report cards, unless they were good ones. To the extent that parental pressure assists teachers in their work, it *may* be condoned; but its dangers are not to be glossed over. Certainly, a class of neat, quiet, and hard working children is a splendid thing, but every teacher knows that a quiet, attentive, studious child may be extremely distressed and insecure. Studies in mental hygiene have stressed this point repeatedly. They tell how often the most cooperative, docile children are fear-ridden and, therefore, potential playground bullies, dropouts, wallflowers, and so on.[11]

However, the teacher who takes the injunctions of the mental hygienist seriously may encounter trouble from the parents. The parents are competing with one another. They like grades, gold stars, and awards for their children even though to motivate children in this way may be harmful. This difficulty may be more apparent than real. For example, the parents of the bright children may be competing with one another. They approve of grading and the bestowing of awards because they do not realize that such measures are undesirable and they derive pleasure from comparing the excellent marks their children get with the poorer marks received by the other children in the neighborhood. Such parents may protest bitterly when new reporting procedures or other methods are

10 John Dewey, *Individualism Old and New*. New York: Minton, Balch, and Company, 1930.

11 See for example Herbert A. Carroll, *Mental Hygiene,* 2nd ed. New York: Prentice-Hall, Inc., 1951; Lester D. Crow, *Mental Hygiene in School and Home Life*. New York: McGraw-Hill Book Company, Inc., 1942; Norman Fenton, *Mental Hygiene in School Practice*. Stanford, California: Stanford University Press, 1943; and Ernest W. Tiegs and Barney Katz, *Mental Hygiene in Education*. New York: The Ronald Press Company, 1941.

adopted to relieve pressures on their children. The majority of parents are secretly pleased and would come to the defense of the new methods if they were at all reassured that they were good. Unless they are reassured, they will remain passive while the parents of the bright children who received all the good marks will carry the fight to the teacher, the principal, the superintendent, and sometimes to the school board. Unfortunately, teachers themselves have frequently inherited this cultural bias. Very rightly they approve of scholarship and admire the good students, but sometimes this attitude carries over into an exaggerated respect for the opinions of the parents of the brighter students. However, most teachers today know the evils of competitive marking. Almost any teacher can relate how otherwise honest pupils cheated on tests because they feared the consequences of not doing better than they were able. The problem today is largely one of parental education. Parents will increasingly understand that pupils learn just as much or more about the things we want them to learn without being subjected to undue pressures.

Anthropologists and psychologists make a big point of fear and insecurity. They point out the middle class tendency to wean babies early, to make an early start on the toilet-training of infants or on teaching reading. They emphasize such things as thumb-sucking among middle class children. What difference do these instances of mildly neurotic behavior make? Can it be that the shame a child feels when he has wet his pants hurts his personality? One can choose to ignore these questions. Many do. It is not easy to measure the effect of scolding or shame. It is true that childhood experiences of fear are not the only factors in shaping adult personality. It is a fact, all the same, that children need affection, need the feeling that their parents do not think them fools. This is brought out in teaching reading. Teachers of reading advise that a child not be taught to read until he starts school. The reasoning behind such counsel is sound. Children usually have trouble learning to read, but the parent in our culture knows literacy and verbal facility to be a great asset in competition and may grow impatient with his or her offspring if the child is slow to read. The child responds in a perfectly natural way by fearing to make a mistake. No one knows how much stammering and stuttering may be attributed to a child's anxiety to please his parents. There may be more sentimentalism than science in this but the thought is worthy of consideration.[12]

Time is on the side of the teacher who is conscious of mental-hygiene. It would be safe to bet that in another decade every teacher-educating department or school will require prospective teachers to study the place of emotions in the educational process.[13]

There are some in this country who maintain that our democracy cannot long endure because Americans are not sufficiently mature or free of fear to enjoy freedom.[14] The mature person is not afraid or, to put it in another way, anyone who feels inadequate, afraid, persecuted, or disliked may, for example, become a bully or a hater of Jews. He will look around for someone he can "step on." Such behavior is not strange. Psychologists some time ago discovered that many animals have a "peck order." For example, some chickens, research showed, stood high on the peck order and could peck all chickens lower in the hierarchy. At the bottom was a "neurotic" chicken that was pecked by all the other chickens but could not retaliate. An interesting example of this "peck order" can be seen sometimes when a strange boy moves into a new school. This boy may have established a relatively high rating in the peck order in the school and community where he previously lived. In the new school community, however, his rank has yet to be determined and sometimes it is decided by his fists. The fights seldom occur on the school grounds because there is a rule against that, but they do occur. Perhaps a series of fights may be necessary before a boy's place finally is established. This may or may not be a serious matter, but it is well that teachers understand the process that is going on when it occurs. They may be able to assist the newcomer, as well as the members of the group into which the newcomer is entering, to understand the process that is going on and enable him to assume his place easier and with less of a clash taking place.

Some people jealously eye the leaders in the human peck order.

---

[12] Probably the most scholarly study of this issue is an unpublished Doctoral thesis by Helen H. Sorenson, "A Longitudinal Study of the Relationship between Various Child Behavior Ratings and Success in Primary Reading," University of Minnesota, 1950. See also Helen M. Robinson, *Why Pupils Fail in Reading*. Chicago: University of Chicago Press, 1946.

[13] That this is so may be judged by the growth of the guidance-counseling program, mental hygiene courses, and social psychology.

[14] The classic study on this subject is Erich Fromm, *Escape from Freedom*. New York: Ferrar and Rinehart, Inc., 1941.

The leaders, of course, are those who have won prestige because of their ability, their money, their beauty, or something else not possessed by, or not recognized in others. The only ego-satisfaction for the envious fellow comes from his sneering at someone else.

Mature people do not hate others because of differences that may exist in their race, color, or creed. Mature men and women shrink from compulsion and force. They favor a free press, free thought, free research, and free thinking generally. Only the immature do not. Those who are beset with fears are unable to accept responsibility for their own deeds and seek out scapegoats upon whom they can vent the fury of their frustration and suspicion. The immature find democracy to be strong stuff. They are overgrown children who demand coddling and who, in their fear, are forever looking for security.

While there is much in American culture today to suggest immaturity, insecurity, fear, and mob psychology,[15] America's cultural heritage has in it some of the most virile democratic thought ever expressed. Americans fearing for the future can draw strength from Ralph Waldo Emerson, Herman Melville, and Walt Whitman.[16] In the writings of these men—and there are others who can be mentioned—there are clear and convincing statements of man's ability to be mature. The teacher, who will first take the time to enjoy this inspiring literature, will find, upon turning to science, that the research in cultural anthropology, psychology, and sociology reaffirms the American democratic faith and pronounces it *the* intellectual, and emotional way of life for attaining and enjoying spiritual maturity.

The child in our society

This section deals with the structure of American society. The main source of the material in it will be sociological, but the reader should remain conscious of the inter-disciplinary aspect of all research into culture, community, society, and personality.

As a point of departure, let us assume that during the school year a recent graduate arrives at a teacher's college to address the

[15] Kluckhohn, *Mirror for Man*, Chapter 9.

[16] A most interesting study of this heritage is to be found in Ralph Henry Gabriel, *The Course of American Democratic Thought*. New York: The Ronald Press Company, 1940.

student body. The students, who are about to begin their teaching careers, are eager to learn all that they can from the speaker who has just completed his year's work as a teacher. Whether or not they are discouraged by what they hear will depend somewhat upon their knowledge of society and their preparation for meeting the real situations that face teachers in our society. In his prepared speech, the recent graduate might tell them about the many families in an average neighborhood that do not actively participate in the PTA or who do not vote at school board elections. Or, it is possible that he will choose as his topic crime and delinquency in the neighborhoods or problem children in class. Privately, however, the speaker might tell his audience much more. He might tell them about the squatters' settlement out at the edge of town and about the children who live there—how they talk and act and resent their teachers and lie whenever their status seems the least bit in question. To determine what light the study of sociology can throw upon such conditions, let us see how it influences the attainment of the American ideal of equality of educational opportunity.

Who drops out? Research shows that troublesome students—the drop-outs, truants, and so on—and indifferent or hostile parents have something in common. Both tend to come from that portion of society dubbed "the lower class," [17] and share the feeling that the school is either against them or useless to them. So strong is this belief that it constitutes the single most serious threat to the hope for universal education. Right now over 40 per cent of all fifth-graders drop out of school before they reach the twelfth grade.[18] The vast majority of these (as do the majority of truants and other problem children) come from low-income families. Future teachers should know that the average child from one of these families will

---

[17] A. B. Hollingshead, *Elmtown's Youth.* New York: John Wiley and Sons, Inc., 1949, Chapter 13 and especially pp. 175-176-185-192.

[18] One of the most helpful discussions of drop-outs is to be found in the report of the Work Conference on Life Adjustment, *Why Do Boys and Girls Drop Out of School, and What Can We Do About It?* Washington, D. C.: Federal Security Agency, Office of Education, Circular No. 269, 1950. There are at least three other monographs helpful in thinking through the drop-out problem: Charles M. Allen, *How to Conduct the Holding Powers Study.* Springfield, Illinois: Office of the State Department of Public Instruction; *Children Absent from School.* Citizens Committee on Children of New York City, Inc., 136 East 57th Street, New York City; and Harold J. Dillon, *Early School Leavers.* National Child Labor Committee, 419 Fourth Avenue, New York City.

tend to have a lower measurable I.Q. than the average child of a middle or upper class family.[19] There is a whole cluster of traits characteristic of children from the lower, the middle, and the upper classes. This section will aid the teacher to make valid interpretations of the data educators are given on the behavior of children from the several socio-economic classes. Since the bulk of the elementary-school population (and its problem children) comes from the lower and lower middle classes, the problems characteristic of such children are most significant to elementary-school teachers. Until recently, emphasis on these problems has not been greatly stressed in discussions of curriculum.

Class structure in the
social order

Social classes and their influence on education may at first be disturbing to an American brought up to believe in the idea that everyone is equal and that Horatio Alger was correct in thinking the log cabin to be good training for the White House. Pioneer traditions say with salty humor that any man is just as good as any other, if not better. Our history is replete with stories of men who rose from humble beginnings to positions of power and importance, and much is made of the idea that we have avoided the European concept of a hereditary aristocracy.

However, further study shows that our ideal of a classless society has not been entirely achieved. Europe's class structure may be primarily tied to blood and ours largely based upon wealth, but there are classes in America. Wealthy parents have an edge over the laborer in the matter of their children's schooling and medical care, jobs for their youngsters, travel for their families, and the good things that are associated with leisure time activities such as reading, music appreciation, and the like. However, we should not conclude that as a result of this situation evil is abroad in the land. The real challenge lies in providing a greater measure of opportunity for underprivileged children. As yet, neither economists or any other students of men and societies have agreed on a solution. It is a challenge for the future. The teacher's role consists in seeing

[19] Hollingshead, *Elmtown's Youth*, pp. 175-176.

that discrimination against children of any class or culture is avoided in the school.

The 60 per cent. Many teachers will say that no one discriminates against any child,[20] that talk about socio-economic classes is foolish.[21] Let us illustrate. The recent graduate talking to a group of future teachers may not have had a background in sociology. If not, he may not be conscious of many of the discriminations. For example, he may never have examined the illustrations in a typical primary reading book and seen that most of them show well-dressed, upper middle class children living in beautiful and expensive homes with well-kept yards and expensive playground equipment. It may have escaped his notice that the interiors of these homes are pictured as an architect's dream, with private rooms for each of the children, commodious clothes closets, and a bathroom that has a separate rack for each towel and each toothbrush. Sixty per cent of his pupils probably never have been in such a home and are familiar only with their own crowded quarters where they share the bathroom, if they have one, with other families, hang their clothes on hooks fastened to doors or to a wall in a corner behind a curtain, and brush their teeth and bathe in the kitchen. Children from such surroundings are hurt and bewildered when the reading book conception of home is completely different from their experience.

The five classes. Of course, one should not jump to conclusions about the composition of any class. The sociologists put the matter this way: There are socio-economic classes, all right, but one is never certain that Mr. A. is in Class I, II, III, IV, or V. A second warning involves statistics. When someone says that 95 per cent of

20 For example see Allison Davis, *Social-Class Influences Upon Learning.* Cambridge, Massachusetts: Harvard University Press, 1948. See also *Progressive Education,* Vol. 27, No. 4, February 1950.

21 There is a large and growing literature on the class system in America. The following are recommended: Allison Davis, Burleigh B. Gardner and Mary Gardner, *Deep South.* Chicago: University of Chicago Press, 1941; Hollingshead, *Elmtown's Youth;* W. Lloyd Warner, *et al., Democracy in Jonesville.* New York: Harper and Brothers, 1949; W. Lloyd Warner, Robert Havighurst, and Martin B. Loeb, *Who Shall Be Educated?* New York: Harper and Brothers, 1944; W. Lloyd Warner and Paul S. Lunt, *The Status System of a Modern Community,* Vol. II, "Yankee City Series." New Haven: Yale University Press, 1942; W. Lloyd Warner, Marcia Meeker and Kenneth Fells, *Social Class in America.* Chicago: Science Research Associates, 1949.

the teachers in New England, the deep South, and the Middle West
are middle class,[22] the student should begin to wonder if perhaps
the concept of middle class is not being stretched too far in including so many people.

But classes do exist. According to one classification, there is "the
400" or the old-family aristocracy, embracing perhaps 3 per cent of
a community. Just "beneath" it is the "upper middle class," constituting another 10 per cent. Teachers, it is noted, come in great
numbers from the "lower middle class," which makes up 28 per
cent of the population.[23] A step down from the lower middle class
is the "upper lower" class—the strata of the "common man, poor but
respectable." At the bottom of the scale is the "lower lower class"
composed of unskilled laborers, landless agricultural workers, social
isolates, and drifters.

Wealth, as already indicated, plays a part in such a classification,
but it is far from being the only factor. For example, the carpenter,
electrician, or plumber who may earn more than the teacher probably will not rank as high socially. Then, again, there are many
in the upper class who have less money than social climbers (nou-
veau riche) in the upper middle class. The members of the upper
class who are only moderately well-off usually have family backgrounds that maintain them in their class for some time, if they
remain relatively "respectable" otherwise.

Class structure and the school

A primary fact to remember and one that we have stressed in
Chapter 2, is that one cannot speak of "the" child. Children are
differentiated by the mores and folkways of their homes, neighborhoods, and churches, and by the class to which their parents belong.
At least two-thirds of the children who come to elementary school
come from very modest homes.[24] In some schools, one-third are
slum children, rural or urban. The normal accompaniments to the
lives of these children are insecurity, want, perhaps even privation.

[22] Davis, *Social-Class Influences Upon Learning.*

[23] These percentages will vary with the system of class stratification employed. They are referred to in W. Lloyd Warner, *et al.,* "*Yankee City Series,*"
Vols. I-IV.

[24] Davis, *Social-Class Influences Upon Learning,* pp. 22-23.

Often they must fend for themselves because both parents must work merely to maintain the household.[25]

The aspirations and fears of lower, middle, and upper class families are apt to be unknown to teachers from other classes, or at least not understood. Teachers may be inclined to favor children from homes and cultures similar to their own. Such children, for example the Mexican children of the previous chapter, may be "rejected" or they may "feel" rejected.

These are difficult problems. Consider the matter of stressing verbal ability. Being able to speak, read, and write are assets; but they are not the only accomplishments of civilized human beings and not the most important. Creative art work (fine, practical, and industrial arts included) and fine moral character are worthy of great attention. Yet when the child comes to school, be he from the home of a college professor or an illiterate, from the home of an industrial leader or a day laborer, from the home of a concert pianist or a handworker, a book is literally the first thing thrust into his hand, while any mechanical, non-verbal abilities and interests that he has may be pushed aside.[26]

Emphasis on reading. Why might this be true in an uncomfortable number of instances? When this question was put to a group of student teachers they suggested two reasons. The first was that reading (and, to lesser degree arithmetic) was a skill without which a student could not take advantage of the information carried by books, magazines, or newspapers. This reason is perfectly valid, is it not? Being able to read allows a person to have vicarious experiences. Short cuts are open to him who reads and is able to profit from descriptions of other people's experiences.

The second reason for the school's emphasis on reading was the pressure on the schools exerted by parents who are desirous of having their children compete successfully with others. These parents,

25 The lower one-third of incomes in this country averaged $471 for a family for the year 1935-1936. This lower one-third is below the national average of $780. In 1947 the lowest 20 per cent, in terms of annual family income, received only 4 per cent of the aggregate income of the country while the highest 20 per cent received 48 per cent of the aggregate income from the same year. See Mary Jean Bowman and George Leland Bach, *Economic Analysis and Public Policy*, 2nd ed. New York: Prentice-Hall, Inc., 1949, pp. 11-12.

26 Davis, *Social-Class Influences Upon Learning*, pp. 89-99.

at least the middle and upper class ones, correctly believe that verbal ability—ability to read, write, and speak—is essential.

History of the emphasis on reading. There is an historical reason, as well, for the emphasis. In a nutshell this is what happened. The Greeks of the centuries just preceding and following the birth of Christ were models of well-educated people. The Romans, who conquered them, instead of suppressing Greek culture, borrowed it. The core of Grecian education was training in language—in grammar, rhetoric, and oratory.

From Greece and Rome the belief in verbal training spread to Europe and to America. The Latin Grammar School of early New England was a perfect example of the Greek-Roman tradition. This tradition had been bolstered in Europe by two movements: the Renaissance of the fifteenth and sixteenth centuries and the Protestant Reformation. The Renaissance witnessed a re-birth of the Greek and Roman tradition that had been lost during the Middle Ages. The Protestant Reformation added *reading* to the classic emphasis on grammar, rhetoric, and oratory. The Protestants hoped each person would be able to read the Scripture, a desire made practical by the development of printing and the availability of paper.

As books became more numerous, the emphasis on "book larnin" in the schools increased. Our children learn about the world from books. There seems to be no other way. Our civilization is just too complex to depend upon any other method.[27]

Emphasis on verbal intelligence. Research is beginning to show that intelligence tests of the verbal type frequently use words and concepts that lower class children cannot be expected to understand.[28] Allison Davis cites the word "sonata" as an example. There is strong reason to believe that many of our present tests rate children as being less intelligent and less informed than they really are.

Evaluation. In Chapters 10 and 11 we will deal further with marking, testing, and measurement policies. Allison Davis' research led him to conclude that teachers report more failures among lower

---

[27] For the dangers inherent in our situation see John Dewey, *Democracy and Education*. New York: The Macmillan Company, 1916.

[28] See Davis, *Social-Class Influences Upon Learning*, and Hollingshead, *Elmtown's Youth*, pp. 172-180. See also Allison Davis and Robert J. Havighurst, "The Measurement of Mental Systems," *Scientific Monthly*, Vol. LXVI, No. 4, April 1948.

class children than among a proportionate number of middle or upper class youngsters.[29] From this, a pattern emerges. More of the lower class children (than middle or upper class) fail or drop out of school; and more lower class parents are indifferent to the school. Lower class children seem not to feel at home in our schools; they do not feel that the schools are designed for them. Many factors act to reinforce this attitude. For one thing, the child may have trouble with his class assignments and, as a result, may find himself set apart from the other pupils and stigmatized as a slow learner. Or, he is probably very conscious and sensitive of his shabby clothing and his parents' inability to give him money to pay for class dues and parties. Finally, he may grow spiteful toward the "better" children who receive most of the award and praise from the teacher while he receives little.[30]

Such a situation certainly makes for behavior or discipline problems. A child who feels that the teacher is against him, or that the whole school or society is against him, is a potential trouble-maker. Moreover, the child who feels that the teacher is hostile comes to feel that he himself is inadequate and becomes insecure.

Social distance. The teacher who tries to avoid bad discipline problems *must grow close to his pupils.* This does not mean that the teacher should fawn over his students. Psychologists have the right idea when they speak of "reducing the social distance." Perhaps the phraseology is a bit clumsy but the thought is proper enough. There is a social distance separating people. You may feel quite close to someone in your social class, for example, and quite distant from someone who is "above" or "below" you.

The teacher often is quite distant from his pupils. For one thing, he is an adult who sometimes sits on an elevated platform and is the cynosure of all eyes. In his position, he is to be obeyed and respected as an authority in all questions of conduct and knowledge. Unfortunately, the teacher by his actions often widens the gulf between himself and his pupils. If he forever lectures them about what is good and right and proper and if the things that he calls bad are not things that they have found out elsewhere in their

---

[29] A. B. Hollingshead also remarked that his study indicated that, although lower class children had the most scholastic failures, teachers spent less time in helping them than they did assisting middle and upper class children.
[30] Hollingshead, *Elmtown's Youth,* pp. 180-198.

experience to be bad, the barrier is raised higher. Children in such an atmosphere withdraw and sometimes grow resentful of the authority that they identify with the teacher. To them the teacher represents education and learning and they come to feel that education and learning is an unfriendly thing. They begin to have their little jokes about the teacher and the teacher's ignorance of things that are real to them. These jokes lead to trouble, to tensions, and to disciplinary problems.

There is no thought here that the teacher should discard his values or that children should not be improved by the educational process. The point, rather, is how this improvement is to take place. The teacher should not try to descend to the children's level or try to become one of them in thought and action. Such a posture would, at times, be ridiculous, and would be regarded as such by the children. To bridge the social distance, the teacher must be friendly. The friendly teacher will try to build a group feeling in the room or in the school and establish mutually acceptable group standards. He will not be shocked at innocent violations of these standards, but will seek to make them effective in the only way possible—by having the group willingly accept them.

Teamwork. In time, as social distances are lessened, the class becomes a team of which the teacher *can* be a most valuable member. Then it will not matter whether Mary is from an upper class home or Mike from a lower class home because the teacher's attitude toward individual students will be conditioned by the team of which the teacher is a part.

One might say that this is side-stepping democracy, because it would appear that the teacher was not seeing each child as an individual. Much has been written on democratizing the classroom—individualizing instruction. However, instruction cannot be individualized in the manner usually conceived, certainly not by "hearing recitations" individually. The only way instruction can be individualized (and the way it should be done regardless of class size) is to assign group work and to work with groups. By moving from one group to another—within the hour or within the term—the teacher sees how the various members are performing. The teacher and the group work as one, encouraging, criticizing, and helping.

Discussion Questions

1. How is the word "culture" usually used? How is the term employed in this chapter?

2. What set of values would you say is typical for the people of this country? Do variations in values appear?

3. What gives rise to the values of a people?

4. Is there more than one "culture pattern" present in the typical public elementary-school classroom? Does this have any bearing on the teaching?

5. How are you planning to learn about the cultural background of your students? What will you do with the information gathered?

6. Since no one is free from cultural "conditioning," what can you do to recognize your prejudices? What do you think might be done to keep those prejudices from appearing in class?

7. If some of your students evidence a prejudice against the race or religion of others of your students, will you punish them, lecture them on "equality" and "good sportsmanship," or try alternative means of getting them to work and play together? What is the reason for bringing prejudiced people into closer relation with those whom they dislike?

8. What do the terms "ethnocentrism," "insularity," and "provincialism" mean to you? Are there advantages as well as disadvantages implicit in provincialism? What are they? Ask yourself the same questions with regard to cosmopolitanism.

9. Does the study of geography, history, and the interdependence of man within the physical environment suggest anything useful in overcoming prejudice? Does their physical environment influence people to adopt certain value patterns and behavior?

10. In the community where you grew up, did you know any children whose parents may not have felt that they "belonged" in the community? What do you remember about these children?

11. Does the child of a foreign-born parent have any special problem?

12. When next you attend a PTA meeting, attempt to determine which parents almost never attend. On the basis of what you have learned about culture and cultural differences, can you explain the obvious reluctance of those who do not attend the meetings—assuming that the program is worth while.

13. If you were about to take a position in a new community, what would you wish to know about the community's cultural patterns?

14. What is meant by the phrase "social class?" Does the existence of social classes make "class warfare" inevitable? Can you suggest some things an elementary-school teacher can do to reduce "class conflict?"

15. In the United States everyone is urged to do his best. Illustrate what

an elementary-school teacher might do that would needlessly handicap a youngster in later life.

16. Many books and articles concerned with social class influences upon learning contain the suggestion that lower class children are discriminated against. Can you think of situations where children from upper middle and upper class homes might also be discriminated against? Is all prejudice directed against lower class children?

17. A teacher says, "Since two-thirds of all school children come from the homes of 'workers,' we should align ourselves with the interests of the lower class." Is this teacher guilty of advocating discrimination? Why or why not?

18. Do children of all classes need much the same sort of elementary-school education?

19. Is there a "spread" of I.Q.'s in all classes? What evidence can you find to support your answer? How do you interpret your findings?

20. What are some of the attitudes toward students that will assist the teacher to ignore social class distinctions?

21. Is it the business of the school to alter the class structure? What arguments have you used to support your conclusion? What do you know about the "role" the school has played in culture and in society?

22. Do you feel conscious of any "class-allegiance" in yourself? If you answer in the affirmative, do you feel that this allegiance will make a difference in your attitude toward students?

Selected References

Benedict, Ruth, *Patterns of Culture*. Boston: Houghton Mifflin Company, 1934.

Bowman, Mary Jane, and George Leland Bach, *Economic Analysis and Public Policy*, 2nd ed. New York: Prentice-Hall, Inc., 1949.

Davis, Allison, Burleigh B. Gardner, and Mary R. Gardner, *Deep South*. Chicago: University of Chicago Press, 1941.

Davis, Allison, and Robert J. Havighurst, "The Measurement of Mental Systems," *Scientific Monthly*, Vol. LXVI, No. 4, April 1948.

Davis, Allison, *Social-Class Influences Upon Learning*. Cambridge: Harvard University Press, 1948.

Dewey, John, *Individualism, Old and New*. New York: Minton, Balch, and Company, 1930.

Dillon, Harold J., *Early School Leavers*. New York: National Child Labor Committee, 419 Fourth Avenue, New York City.

Dollard, John, *Caste and Class in a Southern Town*. New Haven: Yale University Press, 1937.

DuBois, Cora A., *The People of Alor*. Minneapolis: The University of Minnesota Press, 1948.

Fenton, Norman, *Mental Hygiene in School Practice*. Stanford, California: Stanford University Press, 1943.

Hollingshead, A. B., *Elmtown's Youth*. New York: John Wiley and Sons, Inc., 1949.

Kardiner, Abram and Associates, *The Psychological Frontiers of Society*. New York: Columbia University Press, 1945.

Kluckhohn, Clyde, *Mirror for Man*. New York: Whittlesey House, McGraw-Hill Book Company, Inc., 1949.

Linton, Ralph, *The Cultural Background of Personality*. New York: D. Appleton-Century Company, 1945.

Mead, Margaret, *Growing Up in Samoa*. New York: William Morrow & Company, 1928.

Progressive Education, Vol. 27, No. 4, February, 1950.

Robinson, Helen M., *Why Pupils Fail in Reading*. Chicago: University of Chicago Press, 1946.

Stendler, Celia B., *Children of Brasstown*. Urbana, Illinois: Bureau of Research and Service, College of Education, University of Illinois, 1949.

Warner, William L., and Paul S. Lunt, *The Social Life of a Modern Community*, Vol. I, "Yankee City Series." New Haven: Yale University Press, 1941.

Warner, William L., Robert J. Havighurst, and Martin B. Loeb, *Who Shall Be Educated?* New York: Harper and Brothers, 1944.

Warner, William L., and Leo Srole, *The Social Systems of American Ethnic Groups*, Vol. III, "Yankee City Series." New Haven: Yale University Press, 1945.

Warner, William L., Marcia Meeker, and Kenneth Ells, *Social Class in America*. Chicago: Science Research Associates, 1949.

Warner, W. Lloyd, *et al.*, *Democracy in Jonesville*. New York: Harper and Brothers, 1949.

7

COMMUNITIES AND CHILDREN

*T*HIS CHAPTER serves as an introduction to the American community—city and town. The word community has two meanings, both of which are used in this chapter. The most familiar meaning equates community with a place where people live; the second suggests the "spirit" characteristic of a community. Because every school is greatly influenced by the community, our observations on community will be given in connection with their classroom implications. The conclusion of the chapter is that the same forces that build healthy or vigorous communities make for a healthy classroom atmosphere.

American communities are continually changing and in order for us to evaluate these changes, it will be necessary for us to distinguish between rural and urban communities.

The rural community [1]

The population of rural communities has declined greatly since the introduction of labor-saving farm machinery.[2] The tractor,

[1] One of the most scholarly studies in rural sociology is that of Lowry Nelson, *Rural Sociology.* New York: The American Book Company, 1948. Very helpful descriptions may be read in Robert L. Sutherland, and Julian L. Woodward, *Introductory Sociology.* Chicago: J. B. Lippincott Company, 1948, pp. 442-456. Teachers in rural areas will wish to read Kenneth MacLeish, and Kimball Young, *Rural Life Studies,* No. 3. Washington, D. C.: U. S. Department of Agriculture, April 1942.

[2] In 1920 there were about 246,000 tractors in use in the United States. In 1948 over 1,500,000 tractors were at work. Then again, in 1947, about 60 per

which has replaced the horse on many farms, has made possible the use of gang plows, multiple row cultivators, combine harvesters, two-row corn pickers, and many other machines that perform the work of many men. Knowing that they are not needed as workers, many young men and women born on farms have been moving to the cities. Hastening their exodus is the lack of entertainment characteristic of the more remote rural areas. Probably half the young people move to town or city before they are twenty-one.[3] The trend will not soon be reversed, even if a threat of atomic war makes cities seem less safe than farms. The fact is that few people could afford to buy and work farms of a size that would enable them to compete successfully with large-scale farming enterprises.

Tendency toward consolidation. As the rural population diminishes in size, farmers are altering their conventional political and economic policies. The economic change from rugged individualism is most apparent. For example, the price supports for farm products have resulted from the pressure of a "farm bloc." Traditionally farmers were not keen on organization; farmers today are organized. As farms grow fewer and larger, the practice of cooperative buying and marketing is also increasing.

A similar tendency toward larger units of administration seems to be developing in rural communities.[4] Students of rural life advocate replacing present township and village systems with new legal corporations coextensive with the "trade-area community." In other words, the city, town, or village would correspond to a natural social and trading area. The extent of this new community might well be determined by the attendance area of the local high school. *All this reflects the sociologist's hope that rural people will enlarge their areas of common interest.*

The schools must face up to the facts of rural life. About half the students in the rural school will at some time move to a town or city. This means that rural children must develop skills that

---

cent of America's farms were electrified. In 1920 only 13 per cent had been electrified. The trend is toward electrification, mechanization and, as a consequence, large-scale farming.

[3] Nelson, *Rural Sociology,* p. 404. By 1930 less than one-fourth of our people made their living on farms. See Newton Edwards, and Herman G. Richey, *The School in the American Social Order.* Boston: Houghton Mifflin Company, 1947.

[4] Nelson, *Rural Sociology,* Chapter 22.

will enable them to compete with city dwellers and to cooperate in urban affairs. In addition, the rural-school curriculum must provide for the needs of those children who will remain on the farm, and should include instruction in mechanical arts,[5] the principles and practices of producer-consumer cooperatives, and timber, mineral, game, water, and soil conservation.

Rural problems in the rural curriculum. None of these "realities" is remote from the elementary school.[6] In one school, a teacher undertook to introduce the principles of soil conservation to her pupils by having them observe and learn to cope with the gullies water had made in the road leading to the school. The children experimented with any number of ways of stemming the flow of water, and by so doing learned the value of check-dams, of grass cover, and of trees and shrubbery. In another school, one in a neighborhood of dairy cooperatives through which the farmers marketed their butter, milk, and cream, a group of students took the initiative in suggesting a study of cooperatives by organizing a cooperative in the school. The cooperative conformed to state laws and all students were members. The pupils elected a governing board and rotated the position of manager so that each child could supervise the purchase and retailing of school supplies. Reading, writing, and arithmetic—to say nothing of habits of cooperating— were taught through this method.

Bridging the gap. An imaginative and lively teacher can readily see the value of all such projects, not only as they encourage or motivate pupils to exercise their intelligence, but also as they inculcate in the pupils the principles of good living.

The ability to cooperate and to get along with others is highly important. Most people lose their jobs not because they are clumsy and incompetent or can't write, add, and spell, but because they are unable to live and work with others.[7] This inability is not inborn; its opposite can be learned, and practice will perfect it.

A warning. A word of warning is in order here. Some projects

---

[5] The rural boy will find mechanical arts useful (if not too specialized) should he go to a city to work in industry or should he join one of the armed services.

[6] See, for example, I. E. Schatzmann, *Country School at Home and Abroad.* Chicago: University of Chicago Press, 1942.

[7] Gertrude Forrester, *Methods of Vocational Guidance.* Boston: D. C. Heath and Company, 1944, pp. 284-299.

will involve teacher and students in controversial issues. This is fine *if* the community is not tremendously prejudiced against the discussion of the questions concerned. In many towns, the people have not become accustomed to having pupils work on "live" and controversial issues and may not understand the psychological principles involved in having children learn by studying "real" problems. Without meaning to be unfair, people often confuse open-minded, critical investigation with propaganda and indoctrination. The projects that will be most successful will be those that deal with problems of which the community is, or can easily become, aware. Then, people will understand what the schools are doing and will be eager to support new methods and to assist in their planning.

In one community in the heart of a dairy country, eighth-grade students became concerned over the decline of the dairy herds. The project that they launched led to an investigation of breeding and herd maintenance. The students consulted experts at the State's Agricultural College and learned enough to convince their parents that a few changes in dairying practice would pay. Their evidence was convincingly marshaled for they had learned about the collection and evaluation of data as well as its presentation to groups who had to be convinced. *They had learned lessons in science and also in communication. Those students wanted to get action on their findings and knew that the democratic way to get people to act was to help them see the facts in the case.* At least partly as a result of this project, the region's herds increased in value about a quarter of a million dollars in a relatively few years.

This project drew the entire community into the school's work. There is no better way of building a "community school," and of insuring support for the school and its curriculum. It is rich with opportunities to learn the types of knowledge *and* attitudes that people in rural communities need to know. Such an undertaking helps a child to understand his environment and to adjust to it satisfactorily. In the final analysis, that which is taught in the schools of a democracy must spring from that democracy—must be that which the people wish to have taught. The community school tends to bring out this type of curriculum.[8]

8 Some critics will say that children prefer fun—even antisocial pleasure—to the hard work involved in these cooperative projects. This is not so. One of our

The urban community

A good deal of what has been said of the rural community can be adapted to life in the city. A major difference lies in the relative lack of personal significance on the part of the urban individual. The larger the city the more impersonal and lonely it is and the more individuals need (and fail to find) the warmth, friendliness, and cohesiveness of the small town. The very anonymity of city existence explains the ease with which people move about and pick up the pattern of their lives amid different surroundings. More often than not, the city dweller has remained virtually unknown to his neighbors and his apartment has become nothing more than a place to eat and sleep, its attractiveness judged only by its proximity to one's job or transportation, and of course, by its reputation for respectability and, in some cases, "swank."

What is the city? Half of our elementary-school children are urban.[9] They have special problems, the scope and significance of which cannot be comprehended without some knowledge of what the city is.

Cities are both markets and reservoirs of manpower. They grow at the junction of trade routes, where it is possible to make steel with cheaply transported coal and iron ore. They grow as the frontier is closed to settlement and as rail and motor transportation becomes widely available. They grow with industry.[10] As cities grow, the demand for living and working space increases and the

---

great authorities on crime, delinquency, and other symptoms of social disorganization has this to say: "When opportunities are available to engage in complex projects, extending over periods of time, involving cooperation and yielding demonstrable results at the end, the preferences of most persons are for them, and physical pleasures take a minor place." Robert E. L. Faris, *Social Disorganization*. New York: The Ronald Press Company, 1948, p. 164. Although Faris was writing of older people, his observation holds true for youngsters, if the problem-topic is kept within their reach.

9 Sutherland, and Woodward, *Introductory Sociology*, pp. 930-932; Edwards and Richey, *The School in the American Social Order;* Austin F. MacDonald, *American City Government and Administration.* New York: Thomas Y. Crowell Company, 1945, Chapter 1; Ernest B. Schulz, *American City Government.* New York: Stackpole and Heck, Inc., 1949, Chapter 1; and Harold Zink, *Government of Cities in the United States.* New York: The Macmillan Company, 1948, Chapter 1.

10 Victor Jones, *Metropolitan Government.* Chicago: The University of Chicago Press, 1942, Chapters 1 and 2.

value of real estate soars. These values are somewhat enhanced by the attractions the city offers through its symphonies, museums, zoos, theaters, and art galleries. An apartment in the city is expensive and usually small. Many apartment houses will not rent to families with children or dogs, although a number will waive the restriction on dogs. It is not economically wise to have a very large family and many city dwellers are without children. Families with children often do not live near places for the children to play. Cities are not constructed for families but for consumers and producers.[11]

A city of specialists. Were a person to run an inventory of the skills possessed or needed by urban populations the number would be great. Most of the city's adults are specialists who work in a distant office, warehouse, or factory. Consequently children neither observe their parents at work nor share in maintaining the family. The rural child, although he may feel oppressed by the burden of his chores, knows that his contribution is necessary to his family's support and that he is not an economic liability. All this adds up to one fact: In cities children start life with a strike against them.

Social disorganization. Despite this gloomy picture of the urban child's lot, most children of the city mature into wholesome, attractive people. This is a tribute to human nature, especially since we have hardly begun to indicate all the marks of the city's hostility to children. There remains the whole atmosphere of overcrowding, lack of neighborhood spirit, crime, vice, corruption, wretched entertainment, and still other evidences of *social disorganization.*[12] It is not difficult to itemize a bill of particulars to support this indictment. *Anything that works against community spirit promotes social disorganization.* Community spirit is just a way of saying "communication." Unless the people of a city really understand and are interested in one another, there can be no community of interest. The factor of job specialization, previously referred to, is a bar to effective communication. In addition, we may mention the social distance between economic and social

---

11 Because this is true, it is important that cities maintain first-rate schools, adequate playgrounds, a variety of recreational centers such as parks, aquaria, zoos, museums, art centers, and theaters.

12 The literature on social disorganization (urban) is very large and ever-growing. One of the more comprehensive treatments is to be found in Faris, *Social Disorganization.*

classes as another contributing influence.[13] In this instance, social distance can be measured by the differential in rental scales existing between an exclusive neighborhood and a slum. The people who live in these neighborhoods almost never communicate and may not feel that they have anything in common.

To darken the picture a bit more, one might observe that what have been referred to as neighborhoods really are not neighborhoods. They are only places. The people in each have some things more or less in common—income, type of dress, entertainment, and other modes of living. But neighborliness is missing and neighborliness of the across-the-fence type is what makes a neighborhood into something that is more than a rental zone. In the cities of today, neighborhoods in a closely knit sense appear to be virtually nonexistent.[14]

Social disorganization and the family. Social disorganization shows up even more dramatically in terms of what is happening to our basic institutions—to the family for example. The family sees to it that children are nurtured and that the ill and weak are protected. Beyond this the family provides affection, intimacy, and love for its members. It is a center of loyalty, something around which all members "rally." Each year new evidence turns up to tell teachers how very important home life is for children. No one disputes this. The prime importance of the family is granted, an appreciation that heightens the tragedy indicated by statistics on divorce and delinquency. But this is getting ahead of the story.

What is the standard to be used in judging the efficiency of the family (or any other institution)? One eminent student of institutions has written [15] that an institution should be rigid enough to control and stabilize, but sufficiently flexible to change when conditions warrant new institutional forms and procedures. The family has done the latter—it has adapted to the needs of urban technology—but in so doing it has increasingly failed the individuals dependent upon it. That the family has adapted itself to the city is evident from the fact that it has grown smaller. As the economy

13 Sutherland and Woodward, *Introductory Sociology*, pp. 458-459, 463-466; Faris, *Social Disorganization*. Chapter 2.

14 Harry Elmer Barnes, *Social Institutions*. New York: Prentice-Hall, Inc., 1942, pp. 650-651, 655-657. See also Landis, *Social Control*, pp. 25-26.

15 J. O. Hertzler, *Social Institutions*. Lincoln, Nebraska: University of Nebraska Press, 1946, p. 270.

has called for more white-collar workers, women have gone to work. Then, too, the family has risen to meet the demands of production by increasing its consumption of goods—at the same time foregoing having children. The rural, patriarchal family, where father sat at the head of the table and headed the family, is now pretty uncommon. Moreover, there is an ever growing feminism. One certainly cannot say that this is a "bad" thing. Women do not think so, but working away from home, carrying on a career separate from homemaking, is incompatible with the old-fashioned home.

This line of argument need not be pressed. Whatever the causes, the American family is not doing what once it did and what it may be necessary for a family to do.[16] The family is giving up more and more of its educational functions. These are passed over to the school or to some other agency. Unhappily, even some religious functions slip away. Economically, the family is important only as a consumer unit. Recreation has left the home for the automobile, the movie, and other forms of paid amusements. It is doubtful whether television can be said to be a return of entertainment to the home. Even the protective functions of the home are few. Families dread having aged fathers and mothers with them. Birth and death are taken care of in hospitals. This is all evidence that the family changes. The change is rational; it is dictated by the type of civilization in which the family finds itself. Nonetheless the changes have not increased family stability. There is over three times as much divorce today as in 1890. The facts suggest that the city family is having a difficult time because of a new way of life inimical to family living.

As the community and family life grows disorganized there is an increase in neuroticism, crime, delinquency, insanity, and general maladjustment. Each of these makes the teacher's work more difficult.

Morale

There is every reason to believe that teachers are or can become effective morale builders. Perhaps it will be of help if we explain

16 Barnes, *Social Institutions*, Chapter 15; Hertzler, *Social Institutions*, pp. 103-111; Landis, *Social Control;* Faris, *Social Disorganization;* Sutherland and Woodward, *Introductory Sociology*, pp. 599-609.

more clearly what we mean by morale and how it can be detected. The easiest way to approach the problem of morale is to regard it as a "social condition." Of course, it is something that individuals feel but it still can be said to be social because *individuals are social beings*. When things are going well for us and we feel happy, our morale is high. We are not unduly afraid nor are we obsessed with feelings of guilt or inadequacy. To preserve this happy state the individual requires good physical health and assurance that his membership in the family, the neighborhood gang, or his school classes is secure.

Such a happy state is not likely to exist in a society torn by fear of war or famine. This point is made to emphasize that the condition of any and every individual depends upon the condition of his society. In Chapters 5 and 6, we mentioned a few of the forces that jar a person out of this security. Instead of repeating them, let us merely say that the more real neighborliness there is in a group, the better are the chances that any member of the group will feel secure.

The industrial model. Without spelling it out, we sense that a classroom where each student plays a lone game with the teacher— the one trying to outwit the other—is open to the charge of encouraging social disorganization with all its accompanying damage to group and individual morale. It follows naturally from this that every teacher should study ways and means of promoting morale in the class. Interestingly enough, some of the most practical hints on how to do this come from industry.[17] Studies point out the need for a high degree of *esprit de corps* or group morale among workers if there is to be a minimization of occupational fatigue, erratic output, recurrent absenteeism, and widespread frustration. The Western Electric Company discovered that teamwork was promoted by the workers' feeling that management was interested in them. All this can be taken to heart by teachers.

Group work and productivity. We have already had occasion to discuss the autocratic teacher. One of the ways to avoid autocracy

[17] Teachers can glean a great deal of useful information from Elton Mayo, *The Social Problems of an Industrial Civilization.* Boston: Division of Research, Graduate School of Business Administration, Harvard University, 1945. See also descriptions of the "Hawthorne Experiments" done in the Western Electric Company and discussed by F. J. Roethlisberger in *Management and Morale.* Cambridge: Harvard University Press, 1941.

(or the equally undesirable "do-as-you-please" or laissez faire approach) is to modify teaching methods in the direction of *more group work*. Group work can help develop student leadership, initiative, responsibility, and good work habits. Marjorie E. Shaw found that small groups were more efficient than were individuals in solving problems and that individuals *in the group* benefited from discussion they would have missed had they worked individually.[18] There is evidence also that group work, imaginatively handled, can be effective in classroom management and discipline as well as in problem solving.[19] Of course, this does not hold true of any type of group work. Group work—"committee reports" for example—are useless when they are employed by a teacher who is too lazy to prepare a lesson plan. Just as much preparation should go into planning for group activities as must attend a well-constructed lesson plan. It would hardly be common sense for a teacher to turn her students loose to pursue some fancy or whim. Where this has been done, the project broke down completely and the teacher was bewildered by the wild disorder that followed.

Such chaos was due to the students' lack of real interest. As a group they did not have an objective—except to have a little fun. This means that a first rule for the fruitful guidance of group learning activities is *to take enough time to define the problem*. This holds true for a graduate seminar quite as much as for an elementary-school class. Many a teacher back at college for graduate work has found himself in a class that is to be conducted through committees—each committee working on a special topic—where the topics were chosen so quickly that he never learned what the topic was all about, or why it was to be studied. The probable result of such careless instruction is that the students wish that the committee had never existed. They would prefer to hear the professor lecture. The moral is that although people may prefer to work cooperatively rather than competitively, the cooperative activities (group work) must be carefully engineered.

---

18 Marjorie E. Shaw, "A Comparison of Individual and Small Groups in the Rational Solution of Complex Problems," in T. Newcomb and E. Hartley, eds., *Readings in Social Psychology*. New York: Henry Holt and Company, 1947, pp. 304-315. See also Hubert M. Evans, "The Social Character of Problem Solving," *Progressive Education*, Vol. 26, April 1949, 161-165.

19 Milosh Muntyan, "Discipline: Child-Centered, Teacher-Centered, or Group-Centered?" *Progressive Education*, Vol. 26, April 1949, 168-173.

The group defines its problem. There are a few guides that may be followed to make group activity more useful than the old "assignment-study-recitation-test" technique.[20] One is to understand that in any group there will be differences in readiness and motivation. The teacher should practice to develop his sense of timing. All that this means is that he be patient enough to help his students define a problem and then see that each one works on that part of the problem he can handle most successfully. To do this the teacher must be familiar with his students' abilities, handicaps, strengths, and weaknesses, *both* social and academic.

By academic strengths and weaknesses we mean ability to read, write, speak, and handle arithmetical functions. Every elementary-school teacher is schooled in these communication skills. It is the *social skills,* however, that often are slighted in teacher education. To be the type of group member who will really contribute to the excellence of the group and, at the same time, learn from the enterprise, requires great self-discipline, social imagination, and constant practice. No one is born a "good group member." If it is difficult for well-mannered adults to get anything out of group work (or contribute anything to a group), how much more difficult for an elementary-school child. A child craves attention and is uninhibited enough to show his desire. He is restless and cannot be expected to display an adult's attention span or an adult's willingness to concentrate on what another person is saying.

Group membership. To be specific, we will attempt to treat briefly some of the types of behavior that will undermine the teacher's chance of success with group work. Domineering or showing-off is undesirable; it breeds resentment and jealousy. Abject submissiveness is quite as harmful. The presence of very submissive youngsters (who are doing themselves no good, of course) gives the more aggressive youngster an opportunity to dominate. Often the teacher can use group pressure to rein the unruly, and can use group spirit and cooperation to coax the submissive from his shell. The teacher then may have somewhat more time in which to try to diagnose what it is that is troubling the child. A first step is

[20] For more extended observation on learning activities see Chapter 9. A description of the assignment-study-recitation-test technique is to be found in William H. Burton, *The Guidance of Learning Activities.* New York: D. Appleton-Century Company, 1944.

to eliminate that which menaces the child's sense of security, status, or self-esteem. This threat may exist in his home or it may lie in the teacher's attitude, or in the way others in the group feel and act toward him. If it does repose in the group, the teacher will have to bring the problem adroitly into the open. Children are wonderfully able to open their hearts and to overcome their prejudices.[21]

Groups evaluate themselves. It always helps to allow plenty of time for the group to define a common goal (which should be re-defined and kept flexible as the work goes along) and to establish some simple rules for their discussions or desk work. In these rules the teacher will wish to keep the students clear in regard to their mutual obligations. Another dependable maxim is to allow time for self-criticism. Perhaps this last can be summed by the term "evaluation." For group work to be truly worth while, the group must periodically evaluate its progress. This evaluation might well be in terms of whether the group is keeping to its main objectives, working together as a team, and making sufficient speed. Privately the teacher will wish to know whether the three R's are being developed within the context of the group enterprise. In order to insure that these basic skills are learned and practiced, provision should be made for remedial instruction, appropriate drill, and constant practice. If this is integrated with the group work, the students will not fail to take advantage of the remedial and practice opportunities.

The elementary school is the place to nourish the skills needed for group living and cooperative enterprise. Our society, whether urban or rural, is suffering from the disintegration of common bonds and psychological "closeness" or friendliness (or neighborliness). Nothing will help to establish a type of living healthful for community growth and individual sanity better than the skills that characterize a "good" group member. Being a good group member, however, does not mean renouncing one's individuality or special skills. Specialization is here to stay and individuality will remain of prime importance. Within present-day communi-

---

[21] Truly psychotic students and those with severe neuroses cannot be treated by the teacher—any teacher. These cases need expert attention. If this is not understood, it is best for the teacher not to encourage the student to begin unburdening himself. This may seem cruel, but amateurish psychotherapy is much worse.

ties, however, the acquisition of social skills—competence in living with others—is absolutely essential.

Discussion Questions

1. Can you list some of the important changes that have come about in the community where you were born? (Changes in size, methods of earning a living, transportation, marketing, entertainment, and so forth.)
2. Do you plan to live in the community where you were born? Ask five of your friends whether they plan to return to the communities where they grew up. What do their answers indicate about "population shifts?"
3. How many people in your class come from rural areas? How many expect to return to rural communities? What does this suggest?
4. Try to find a classmate who was raised in a large city and one who passed his or her childhood and adolescence in a small town or on a farm. Compare and contrast their experiences. Ask each of them what they experienced of "neighborliness," of "community spirit." How do their responses to these questions differ?
5. Have you ever taught in a one-room rural school? What does the existence of such schools indicate about rural life? What does the "consolidated school" indicate?
6. What changes do you sense in rural life? What difference might these changes make in rural schools?
7. Does a rural community offer resource materials comparable to those of a city in which there is a park, museum, aquarium, art gallery, and zoo?
8. What does the phrase "community school" mean to you? Is the "community school" something reserved for rural locations?
9. Generally speaking, what are some ways in which a city influences children? Do these have significance for your teaching? Why or why not?
10. Can you think of any changes that have taken place in the family during the past century? Do these changes have meaning for the schools? Can you be specific in your answer?
11. Is there any truth in the statement that the school now is assigned many of the tasks that other social institutions once performed?

Selected References

Axtell, George E., Kenneth D. Benne, R. Bruce Raup, and B. Othanel Smith, *The Improvement of Practical Intelligence*. New York: Harper and Brothers, 1950.

Faris, Robert E. L., *Social Disorganization*. New York: The Ronald Press Company, 1948.

———, and H. Warren Dunham, *Mental Disorders in Urban Areas* (with an "Introduction" by Ernest W. Burgess). Chicago: University of Chicago Press, 1939.

Hertzler, J. O., *Social Institutions*. Lincoln, Nebraska: University of Nebraska Press, 1946.

Lewin, Kurt, *Resolving Social Conflicts*, edited by Gertrude W. Lewin. New York: Harper and Brothers, 1948.

Lippitt, Ronald, and Ralph K. White, "An Experimental Study of Leadership and Group Life," in T. Newcomb and E. Hartley, eds., *Readings in Social Psychology*. New York: Henry Holt and Company, 1947.

Roethlisberger, F. J., *Management and Morale*. Cambridge: Harvard University Press, 1941.

Zorbaugh, Harvey W., *The Gold Coast and the Slum*. Chicago: University of Chicago Press, 1929.

8

PERSONALITY

*S*TORY HAS IT that the late Robert Benchley, a great wit, met with difficulty in his last year of college. His school, given more to wisdom than wit, rejected the thesis Mr. Benchley submitted for graduation honors. Someone has said that it was titled: "The Newfoundland Fisheries from the Viewpoint of the Fish." The title explains Benchley's approach at once. He was doing his best to effect sympathy or empathy—to put himself in the other fellow's place—to see the problem from the fish's viewpoint. The story has a genuine relation to the object of this chapter. What follows is written from the angle of achieving empathy with another person's personality. This chapter will touch on some of the mechanisms that are at work as a personality develops.

The missing link. Some sociologists, economists, and cultural anthropologists tend to overlook the structure and the growth of individual personality and devote most of their attention to groups, societies, cultures, and, of course, patterns of living within each. Students have pointed out that some social scientists talk as though everyone behaved in ways that could be predicted were a person familiar with the cultures of people. In truth, man is something more than the sum of his folkways and mores. It would be an oversimplification to believe otherwise. Culture patterns influence all our thinking but they are not the whole story. Life does not reduce itself entirely to mores, folkways, institutions, and socio-economic classes.

The situation. The situation is a "figure-ground" arrangement. The individual is the figure, and the environment—social and physical—is the ground. The two are distinguishable but inseparable. You are a very real person yet you are aware of your physical environment. You are an individual, but you are well aware that you are also a part of many groups—of a social environment. It is not necessary to believe that personalities are *either* reducible to the forces at play in the situation *or* are altogether independent of them. It is not a black *or* white distinction. Personalities *develop* (they are not born mature) by the process of living.

A personality is not something lurking beneath one's outward appearance. The old concept of an "ego" haunting man is about as useful as the idea that there is a "real reality" behind appearances as we experience them. It is the appearances with which teachers must cope. The term "role" is perhaps better for our purposes than the word "appearance." If learning represents a change in behavior, the teacher's job is to effect changes in behavior, and for this purpose it may be well to consider that the organism is pretty largely what the organism does. Teachers are confronted with children who are learning roles. For example, from birth each child has been cast in a male or female role. Gender makes a substantial difference, for in any culture the sexes differ in their cultural roles.

Then, too, we may have brothers and sisters. We may be the first child, the second child, or the youngest. Many parents know what it means to say, "Oh! Dick is behaving as a typical first child who has been protected and bossed." In his case, Dick can tell you what it means to be hounded every time he has to cross a street, sneeze, or climb some stairs. Dick's recitation of his family situation is an illustration of what is sometimes called "positional psychology," the psychology that emphasizes the position and role that a person plays in his family.

For the elementary-school boy, age and sex are not the only items affecting his role. He also must cope with his friends. If he succeeds in establishing himself in their esteem, his father speaks of him as a "regular fellow" and rewards him suitably. Everyone knows what happens should a boy fail—undoubtedly he would be labeled a "sissy." Girls have their problems, too. All through life we strive to achieve status, to win approval and acceptance from those we respect.

Personality development

Developing personality. Apparently there are mechanisms by which personalities develop. No one knows all there is to know about these mechanisms or how personality evolves from them, but a great deal of useful information has been amassed.

The basic quality of all living is the satisfaction of needs (needs and satisfaction being used here in their widest sense). There are times when it is difficult to see just what compensation a person is looking for in his peculiar activities but he is trying, no matter how deviously, to satisfy some need or other.

The teacher in the elementary school can build constructive attitudes, values, and habits if he is able to associate them with satisfactions. This is not crude "conditioning;" more than sheer repetition is involved. Satisfaction is all-important, although some parents associate the word with laxity and are prone to reject it in favor of hard work and discipline. One can only suppose that this feeling that satisfaction cannot be found in hard work stems from the adult's dislike of work. But children refute this belief all the time. They enjoy hard work and its accompanying, necessary discipline. All that they ask is that they *feel* the purpose of the work, have some idea of the object for which the work is intended. After all, even adults do not enjoy working in the dark. Perhaps grownups are forced to undertake so much unsatisfying labor that they cannot believe youngsters capable of being interested in their school work.

The teacher or parent who says that children need to learn reading or arithmetic and neither can be interesting to the child—that person is on the wrong track. Children normally *want* to learn to read and count. The teacher's job is to make the processes familiar and at the same time stimulating. The methods that will help are available now, and better ones are being tested and introduced all the time.

The argument that encouraging satisfaction in learning is damaging to children is groundless. Nevertheless, there is a real danger and this menace is seldom noticed. Usually, it is the familiar that satisfies and if one tends to cling to the well known, the comfortable, the chance is that "egocentrism" and "ethnocentrism" [1] will develop. This is what we referred to previously under the heading of "provincialism" (Chapter 6). In that earlier discussion, it was pointed out that provincial-minded people are in danger of being cut off from understanding and sharing the values of other cultures.

Canalization, identification, and projection. The mechanisms of identification, projection, and canalization can be of real value to a teacher seeking to increase students' social skills. *Canalization,* for example, signifies that whatever satisfies a need today tends to do so even more adequately tomorrow.[2] If the children experience satisfaction with group work, with activities planned for increasing their habits of cooperation, their next contact with group work will profit from the good will created by the earlier activity. And, happily, this desire for cooperative enterprise will not disappear quickly.[3] It stands a good chance of being "carried over" into out-of-school life.

Although canalization does much to produce the *self,* it is important to make clear the fact that the self can be *social* rather than narrowly selfish. The process of *identification* helps to set in bold relief this principle of the social self. In identification [4] there is an assimilation of others to one's self. The child thinks that others belong to him—are really a part of himself—and that they feel as he feels. What are the implications of this? It is likely that sympathy has its origins in identification. As the child grows, more and more people are included in his sphere of sympathy. The time comes when the youngster understands that although others may be like himself in drives and motives, they may also be different from him in many ways. The differences are not likely to offend him if the process of identification has been fostered. This fund of feeling helps lessen the chances for the child's developing a sense of isolationism, of being "one against the world."

---

1 Egocentrism implies the feeling that "the world is my apple." Ethnocentrism suggests the idea that my race or my people are *the* cultured folk in this world.

2 Murphy, *Personality: A Biosocial Approach to Origins and Structure,* pp. 161-191.

3 *Ibid.,* p. 166.

4 *Ibid.,* pp. 491-495.

Projection[5] is essential to building the self or personality and is a term reflecting the fact that the child feels his experiences to be shared by others. It is presumed, then, that all other people are like ourselves. We "arrange" this world of other people and things in ways that make it acceptable to us. It is awfully nice to feel that the world is friendly to our needs, which it is when we believe that everyone has the same needs that we have. For the child there seems to be little thought that his needs are less satisfied when the needs of any other child or adult are admitted.[6]

Rationalization. Just as the radiator or pressure cooker has a valve that will open when the steam pressure becomes too great, so our personality is equipped with safety devices. One of these is the power to *rationalize,* the ability to find convincing reasons for having done what is not approved. Dick, for example, will find such an excuse for having failed to live up to his father's expectations. There are times, however, when teachers feel that students overwork this safety valve. Then we say that the pupil is rationalizing too much. The danger is that the student may get into the habit of avoiding difficulties and thus become overly timid and irresponsible. There would be real cause for worry if a child rationalized so much that he seemed to find it necessary to escape from every little problem.

Rationalizing is closely related to the habit of day-dreaming and wishful thinking. In our day-dreams we see ourselves as heroes or as martyrs, the objects of much adulation if the former, and of heartfelt lamentation if the latter. Day-dreams are nothing about which to be concerned unless, as with rationalization, they indicate that a student too frequently feels himself altogether incompetent and driven to embrace this convenient escape. If the day-dream merely represents a brief flight of fancy from a boring lesson, grant the child his moment of release.

Regression. The student who resorts freely to escape mechanisms is in need of help. It is very likely that he is unable to do his class work—perhaps he cannot read—or is being shunned by his classmates. Something can and should be done in both situations. If the teacher hesitates to embark on a remedial reading program or

[5] Murphy, *Personality: A Biosocial Approach to Origins and Structure,* pp. 495-503.
[6] *Ibid.,* pp. 241-243.

psychotherapy, and both are tasks for highly trained people, he should consult his supervisor, or department head, or principal for advice and assistance.

Not all cases are difficult. Almost everyone has seen a class start forming itself into small groups. Often, there is a child who walks up to each group—rather shyly—and turns away because no one welcomes him. Is he an "isolate," a "rejected" child? In such a circumstance, the teacher can be of great help either by introducing the child into the group or by trying to learn the reason for his rejection and helping him overcome it.

If neglected, an "isolate" or rejected child may get worse. Temporary flights of fancy, day-dreaming, or rationalization no longer compensate him. The child may actually regress, become as a babe in arms again. He resumes the infantile state in order to win back the loving care and carefree times that were his during his days of complete dependence. This child needs psychiatric help and needs it quickly.

In all this discussion, the idea that repeats as the major theme is that each of us needs security. No one can be very happy unless he is assured of acceptance and approval. Children, too, need support and assurance. They need it more than an adult because they have achieved so little. They are dependent, at the mercy of arbitrary and often neurotic adults. Do not add to their burdens.

Compensation. This much is certain: Every adult will try to picture himself in the most flattering terms possible to insure his being accepted.[7] Every child, too, wants approval, feels a strong compulsion to be good. Often, when we walk through the looking glass in an attempt to analyze ourselves, we find our habits such that others will not like them. It is not our intention to develop unattractive habits. Our wish is to be liked, to succeed; but often we try so hard that we give offense. Here is the clue to many a child's behavior. It is what the psychologists call *compensation*.[8] Compensatory behavior may be mistaken for intentional aggression—something distasteful to all teachers. Not *all* objectionable action should be excused as compensation but some of it must be. To begin, we incorporate what others think of us (as manifested

7 Murphy, *Personality: A Biosocial Approach to Origins and Structure*, p. 535.
8 *Ibid.*, Chapter 24.

by what they do to us and say about us) in our own self-portrait. This has placed quite a burden on us from birth. In infancy, we experienced the frustrations occasioned by being unable to walk and talk. Then, when walking and talking were accomplished, we were "treated as children"—fenced in, warned constantly, and scolded. We threatened both the leisure and the furniture of our parents, and they were quick to let us know about it. If we did not adopt a pretty domineering attitude (which teachers certainly do not like) we hardly received any attention. If this did not work, we could always fall back upon the whine-and-fret technique.

One of the shortcomings of any particular compensation is that it does not cure the situation that brought it on. Compensating for one's lack in some respect will not rectify the inferiority. That still remains to be overcome. Another fault of compensation is its proneness to fit only one developmental level.[9] Gardner Murphy cites the case of the short, ten-year-old boy, who succeeded in compensating for his small size by dint of athletic prowess. (In a society where size and strength is supposed to characterize the male, short stature is something for which one may compensate. This is an example of the influence culture has on personality.) Four years later, when the tastes of his group change, this athletic prowess may not serve to win him prestige. Then, the compensation likely to be most effective would be "smooth" manners, glibness, and dancing ability.

There are significant lessons for the teacher in all this. (1) Try to determine what aspirations and what needs students feel. (2) Do not set up barriers to success that will crucify any particular child. Unduly high "levels of aspiration," as the psychologists put it, invite compensatory behavior. (This compensatory behavior may be directed toward getting attention and approval from the class and not from the teacher, which is bound to involve misconduct.) (3) Be on the alert for compensatory behavior (it is not easy to detect) and help the student to overcome the fear that prompts the compensation. If the teacher does feel capable of this, and he should hesitate before essaying the role of psychoanalyst or therapist, he should do what he can to make the child's compensatory activity acceptable. (4) Never be blunt or cocksure in pointing

[9] Murphy, *Personality: A Biosocial Approach to Origins and Structure,* p. 572.

out compensations. Do not attempt to deal with them at all if totally unaware of their cause. Overlook them and proceed to do what can be done to build up the student's self-confidence in the everyday work of the class.

Beyond good and evil. Thus far, the attitude of this chapter has been typical of almost every book on education and of almost every work in the psychological and social sciences. In each of them an author urges his readers to be aware of the social dimension of the classroom. The hope is that students become well adjusted, social, human beings; a "group altruism" is most heartily endorsed. This is the accepted and approved manner. Our culture sanctions it for this is a civilization in which getting on and getting along are valued. The idle dreamer is rejected. Men are to be extroverted, hard workers, and known by their accomplishments. This has become part of our national philosophy. Sharing in it, as one inevitably does, the educator preaches the doctrine of "adjustment."

However, one hears a still, small voice saying that man does not live by action alone, that there is a private world of fantasy, dream, and idle curiosity. These are parts of personality, too, though they belong to introversion. Sometimes dream and fantasy are but escapes and, in our culture, escape is often frowned upon.[10] But escape is useful in maintaining balance. It is to be feared only if it develops to the point where it permanently veils reality.

Even this is too utilitarian. Dreams can be fun; day-dreams can be rich; fantasy does not need excuse.[11] Children's imaginations are vivid and legitimate and ought not to be dismissed as something less valuable than their intellects. Usually children can be easily persuaded to return to reality, to "be themselves."

If this is heresy, we hasten to remark that fantasy and imagination are not enemies of reason or intellect. All are involved in anything creative. After all, what is creativity? To some extent, certainly, it is being original. What type of person is original? It is

[10] It may be that John Dewey's philosophy of education is accepted so widely because it stresses problem-solving as the end of all schooling.

[11] "Fantasy ideas are as much a function of a healthy, active mental life as motor achievements and skills are of healthy muscles." Murphy, *Personality,* pp. 453-454. We would not deny that genuine differences between thinking and dreaming do exist. While imagination is common to both, dreams are less restrained by reality. The dreamer indulges in "wishful thinking."

the fellow with curiosity, the person who challenges the accepted or the stereotyped. The teacher who realizes that this is a changing world will help his students develop confidence in their curiosities and imaginations. These are not "faculties" that only artists need. Not only the fine arts teacher but *every* teacher should be alert to stimulate the imagination. Speaking practically, this means that our classes should have great *spontaneity*.[12] Students should be allowed to have an idea, to react in their own manner. Artist-teachers are famous for permitting their students to give free rein to their imaginations. They sense the value of student originality. In their rooms, one finds "originals" in arithmetic or geometry, the children's art work has a flair, the poems collected often tell a personal story with an intimate rhythm that suggests folk music, folk dancing, and folk literature. These master teachers appreciate the primitive or spontaneous expression of comedy, tragedy, or straight narrative so many children find natural. On this native foundation of needs crying for expression, our best teachers build skills and techniques through drill, practice, and exercise. They labor to keep alive the driving interest, and to equip that interest with the tools that will allow it to mature. One can see that this is not a hand's-off policy. The good teacher is more than an amused observer. He encourages the student to learn what he will need to know if his interest in expression is to remain vivid. All too often teachers sit back and wait for the student to "grow." They are amazed to find that John, such a creative youngster, outgrows his creativity. Of course he will *if* his skills, perceptions, and techniques are not improved. The smearing of colors that pleased him when he was six will not satisfy him when he is ten. The trick, if a trick it is, is not to force his skills. Patience is the virtue that will be rewarded. Patience and persistence the teacher must have and to these two it would be well if imagination were added.

Teacher personality

The teacher's personality is a part of the curriculum because it is a part of the learning situation. In fact, it has been said that the teacher is the curriculum. The teacher is as much the posses-

[12] J. L. Moreno, *Psychodrama*. New York: Beacon House, 1946.

sor of a personality as is the child, and his personality is as much in need of analysis and understanding as is that of the child.

In Chapter 5 reference was made to investigations carried on by Walter W. Cook and others over a ten year period. Those studies indicated that the attitudes of teachers toward children and school work can be measured with high reliability.[13] Cook learned that these attitudes correlate highly with types of teacher-pupil relations found in classrooms. Teachers whose attitudes were friendly and permissive or encouraging of student trust had close rapport with their students. The investigations also revealed that principals rated the friendly, congenial teachers far above those who lacked rapport with their class.

What is our aim when we encourage teachers-in-training to develop desirable personality traits? The question is answerable. Cook assured that a teacher whose "scores" on his teacher attitude inventory were high (who had the attitudes that successful teachers were known to have) should be able to maintain relations with his pupils that were characterized by mutual affection and sympathetic understanding. It is to be expected that, in the classroom of the teacher with these attitudes,

. . . the pupils should like the teacher and enjoy school work. The teacher should like the children and enjoy teaching. Situations requiring disciplinary action should not occur. The teacher and pupils should work together in a social atmosphere of cooperative endeavor, of intense interest in the work of the day and with a feeling of security growing from a permissive atmosphere of freedom to think, act, and speak one's mind with mutual respect for the feelings, rights, and abilities of others. Inadequacies and shortcomings in both teacher and pupils should be admitted frankly as something to be overcome, not ridiculed. Abilities and strengths should be recognized and used to the utmost for the benefit of the group. A sense of proportion involving humor, justice, and honesty is essential. Group solidarity resulting from common goals, common understandings, common efforts, common difficulties, and common achievements should characterize the class.[14]

Cook and his associates warn us, however, that the mere inculcation of attitudes that characterize superior teachers will not necessarily result in the maintenance of superior teacher-pupil re-

---

[13] Cook, Leeds and Callis, *Manual, Minnesota Teacher Attitude Inventory.*
[14] *Ibid.,* pp. 3-4.

lations by the new teacher. The neophyte may not have the ability to maintain a classroom atmosphere in which he can win the affection of students. In order to be helpful to the beginning teacher, the discussion that follows will undertake to suggest desirable personality factors for the new teacher.[15]

High among the unfortunate traits that warp a teacher's personality is "social insecurity." As was remarked, this may be caused by many factors such as general appearance, failure in heterosexual adjustment, low social status of family, or failure to be accepted socially in high school.[16] Experience has demonstrated that one of the most effective means of overcoming a sense of social insecurity (in an adult) is to participate in adult social activities. Through them, the insecure teacher may soon discover that others are quite willing to take him for what he is. Participation in good professional groups is equally important. Many universities sponsor summer workshops. They are almost always informal and in them teachers reluctant to make suggestions in front of other adults discover that their contributions are encouraged by their fellows. The camaraderie of the workshop further draws teachers from their shells.

Similar personal reinforcement can be gained from working in church groups, study groups, and recreation and hobby groups. The purposes of such groups are legion. They may be to identify birds, to hike, to collect tropical fish, or to raise funds for a worthy purpose. The point in such participation is to provide opportunity to learn that people are not hyper-critical, unfriendly, or cruel. Anyone interested in associating with others will be accepted in most groups on his own terms and for what he is. There is no need to "play upstage," to "put on airs," to pretend to be what one is not, or to pretend to origins that are not real.

In any situation where teachers feel socially insecure, they feel insecure in relation to one or more other persons. Feeling thus, they tend to become unresponsive, cold, distant, and distrustful of the motives prompting others in the group. Anyone having such feelings may help to overcome them by putting himself in the place of the other fellow. He should try to decide *why* the other

---

15 See Chapter 5.
16 Cook, Leeds, and Callis, *Manual, Minnesota Teacher Attitude Inventory,* pp. 3-4.

person does what he does rather than spend time thinking about whether what others do is good or bad.

In the classroom situation where a teacher is prone to be overly critical of children's behavior in general, an interesting device frequently successful is to have the teacher select, somewhat at random, a single child for intensive study. The object of the study is to understand the causative factors in that child's behavior. As the teacher comes to understand many of the factors involved in the behavior of a single child, he tends to develop better attitudes toward the behavior of all other children. In time the teacher comes to understand the wisdom of the old saying that to understand everything about a person is to forgive all that the person does.

Teachers who have difficulty in achieving a sense of security often tend to avoid talking about their problems. While no one wishes to be burdened constantly with tales of woe from those around him, the teacher who is willing to be a sympathetic listener will discover that he can be of great help to his colleagues.

To be at home (secure) in the school situation, the teacher must be well prepared in his subject and have confidence in his methods. Knowledge of his subject is important in sustaining the interest of pupils, and a reasonable degree of confidence in one's methods will contribute to the pupils' confidence in all that goes on in class. Both will give the teacher confidence, too, in experimenting with new methods.

Teachers will be more secure if they understand and are able to take into account the duties and responsibilities of administrators. The realization that principals and supervisors also sometimes feel insecure may contribute to the teacher's security in dealing with them. Greater rapport between people on different levels of authority or influence in a school system also will be achieved as better communication between various groups is developed.

In these remarks on teacher personality, it is the hope of the authors that young men and women expecting to teach will reflect upon their own attitudes. They will ask themselves whether or not they have confidence in their students-to-be. They will permit students to adventure in ideas and to create with freedom. Many of these points will be developed more thoroughly in later chapters, particularly in Chapter 18 that deals with administration and curriculum change, and in Chapters 19, 20, and 21 that contain numerous illustrations of teachers, supervisors, and principals meeting both the routine and unusual situations that arise from day to day in the school and community.

Some years ago a professor of psychology reported that one of his graduate students insisted on taking a toy canary into her Ph.D. examination. The bird brought her luck, she said, although she knew that her own behavior was "compulsive." Socrates, it will be remembered, once declared that knowledge is virtue. He felt that no one would do what was wrong if he knew what it was proper to do. Socrates was in error. The student of psychology knew a great deal about compulsions, but this did not free her from her own constraint. So teachers, too, may be able to rattle off important mental hygiene principles but continue to treat students after a fashion quite unhygienic. Practice what you preach—if you can.

Discussion Questions

1. The term "personality" has as many different meanings as has "culture." Can you think of some? Have they anything in common?
2. Can you distinguish among the types of personality evidenced in your class? How do you account for these differences? What evidence have you for your judgment?
3. Do you feel that a child's "position" in the family influences his personality?
4. As a teacher, do you think that the personalities of your students will or should have any effect upon your teaching?
5. Recall the chapter on motivation. Does the discussion of needs and satisfactions in this chapter relate to motivation of learning? Recall the chapter on the psychobiological foundations of the curriculum. Does it throw light on an important relation between satisfactions and needs and their relation to the motivation of learning?
6. Can you sketch some plans for aiding the development of personality among your students? What types of behavior do you feel should be discouraged or encouraged? Why?
7. Have you ever "identified" yourself with someone whom you wished to be or resemble? Do you think that this is common practice? Is it something that you would wish to eradicate? Why or why not?
8. Can you illustrate the processes of "projection" and "canalization?" In what ways do the two differ? Have you ever noted their existence in the behavior of children or adults?
9. What is your conception of the term "inferiority complex?" Do you think that everyone who behaves as a bully or who continually "blows

his own horn" is suffering from a feeling of inferiority, is "compensating?" Can these useful descriptions of behavior be carried too far?

Selected References

Anderson, John E., "Child Development and the Growth Process," *Yearbook, National Society for the Study of Education,* Vol. 38, Part I, 1939, 15-49.

Cattell, R. B., *Personality.* New York: McGraw-Hill Book Company, Inc., 1950.

Chein, I., "The Awareness of Self and the Structure of the Ego," *Psychological Review,* Vol. 51, 1944, 304-314.

Dennis, W., "Does Culture Appreciably Affect Patterns of Infant Behavior?" *Journal of Social Psychology,* Vol. 12, 1940, 305-317.

Dollard, J., N. E. Miller, L. W. Doob, O. H. Mowrer, and R. R. Sears, *Frustration and Aggression.* New Haven: Yale University Press, 1939.

Erikson, E. H., "Problems of Infancy and Early Childhood," *Encyclopedia of Medicine, Surgery, and Specialties,* 1940.

———, "Studies in the Interpretation of Play: I. Clinical Observation of Play Description in Young Children," *Journal of Genetic Psychology,* Vol. 22, 1940, 557-671.

Greenberg, P. J., "Competition in Children: An Experimental Study," *American Journal of Psychology,* Vol. 44, 1932, 221-248.

Gordon, K., "Samples of Students' Originality," *Journal of Genetic Psychology,* Vol. 49, 1936, 480-494.

Horowitz, E. L., "Spatial Localization of the Self," *Journal of Social Psychology,* Vol. 6, 1935, 379-387.

Moreno, J. L., *Who Shall Survive?* Washington, D. C.: Nervous and Mental Disease Publishing Co., 1934.

———, *Psychodrama.* New York: Beacon House, 1946.

Murphy, Gardner, *Personality: A Biosocial Approach to Origins and Structure.* New York: Harper and Brothers, 1947.

9

PRINCIPLES OF LEARNING BASIC

TO CURRICULUM DEVELOPMENT

$\mathcal{T}$RADITIONALLY, textbooks have been assigned to teachers who, in turn, have been expected to supervise the "learning" of the texts by the pupils. There are a number of assumptions implicit in this traditional process of schooling. One of them is that everything that students need to learn can be found in the books assigned. This overlooks what students learn in the way of *attitudes* toward teachers, school, other pupils, books, and reading. Similarly ignored are what students learn about themselves—about their abilities, interests, and social responses. This exclusion of what we might call "incidental learning," or the emotional and feeling accompaniment of the schooling processes, indicates the inadequate conception of learning that formed the basis of the traditional curriculum.

Of course, a person cannot learn a book in any meaningful sense. A person learns only what the reading of the book causes him to do. If he memorizes it in a rote sense for factual recitation and examination purposes, little if any valuable learning takes place. Books deal with man's relationship to the physical universe and man's relationship with man and are designed to influence feelings, attitudes, beliefs, understandings, insights, and meanings. They are intended to modify man's behavior, to enable him to have more wholesome purposes, and to achieve these purposes with greater ease and skill. For example, this book you are reading now is designed to impart insights, meanings, and understandings to students about modern man and his social institutions—especially his schools —and his place in the universe. Also, it has been planned to give the student some idea of how the individual is adapted and adapts to his environment. If it does not give the prospective teacher more insight into his own behavior and the behavior of children and cause him to modify his teaching procedures in certain respects, the reading of it will be a waste of time. As already indicated, the purpose with which one reads is all important. One may read to understand, to gain insight, and to see relationships; or one may read to memorize. But rote memorizing inhibits understanding and the ability to relate and apply facts and information. The student may test this for himself. Read three or four paragraphs of this book with the idea of remembering them verbatim. Then, read three or four paragraphs for the purpose of understanding them and relating them to past experiences, methods of study, and beliefs about learning. Reading to remember may be temporarily useful insofar as it enables a child to meet the demands of a particular recitation or examination; but devoid of practical applications and meaningful relationships, any information thus obtained is soon forgotten. Reading to understand, however, enhances perspective and insight and may thus influence behavior in a salutary direction.

School books that merely present a series of unrelated facts for the student to swallow and digest wholesale contribute to the development of faulty reading habits and create the wrong impression of what reading is and what constitutes an education. One might as well try to read a dictionary or an encyclopedia in alphabetical sequence. Human organisms are equipped with sensory apparatus enabling them to *appraise* their environment and to direct their own *purposeful* action. The key words in this last sentence are *appraise* and *purposeful.* Mental activities must be aimed at helping a child make successful, efficient adaptations to his environment. Perhaps the term adaptation is not the best to employ in this connection. Adaptation is not a passive process. For one thing, the environment is too changing to make a once-and-for-all-time adaptation. This does not mean, however, that there are not essential skills to develop. However much the environment changes, reading, writing, and arithmetic are truly basic tool skills. But, granting this, the teacher must not lose sight of the fact that students learn most efficiently if they are driven by purpose and insight rather than by fear of failure or ridicule. It is insight that the teacher strives to stimulate.

What do we mean by insight? A student may be said to have insight if he is able to perceive meanings. What are meanings? Meanings are diverse. The meaning of a thing, an act, or an event may be linked to its usage. For example, a table has an "operational" meaning that is spelled in terms of the uses to which tables generally are put. Young children are more in need of operational meanings than of abstract meanings and definitions (such as, a table is an article of furniture consisting of a flat top resting on legs or on a pillar). Youngsters have not *learned* the inter-connections with their environment; e.g., their dependence upon the school helpers (janitor, for example) upon the milkmen, grocers, mailmen, firemen, and policemen. They do not *understand* the function (operation) of their own body or of the simple physical and chemical changes that go on around them all the time. Nor do they recognize their interdependence with one another; e.g., the reasons for sharing toys, standing in line, telling the truth (if there is no fear of punishment), hanging up clothing, being honest, and learning to read, to count, to spell, and to write.

Because of their immaturity, young learners might well be treated as explorers who are just finding out the use of maps, compasses, and other similar instruments. Through purposeful use and practice, skills, attitudes, and essential information are mastered.

Importance of the goal in learning

The goal (purpose) of the learner is the most important single factor in the learning situation. Not only does it determine what is learned, when it is learned, how it is learned, and within the limits of capacity, how well it is learned, but also, to a considerable degree, the permanency of the learning and the emotional (feeling) accompaniment of the learning process.

In the traditional curriculum, school work to the pupil was merely a series of assigned tasks requiring the reading of certain materials, the memorization of certain rules and processes, and the manipulation of symbols according to prescribed procedures. The real purposes of the process were frequently not clear even to the teacher. His function was to follow the course of study or the textbook and to keep pupils busy with the ritual of the schooling process. The pupils were mainly concerned in getting good marks and behaving reasonably well so that their teacher was satisfied and their parents pleased. Arithmetic was the most popular subject with most teachers and pupils because it made sense, one could prove his answers, and it obviously had value outside of school; but even the good student couldn't conceive of a use for diagraming sentences unless perhaps some day he might become a teacher. Then one would have to know it.

In Chapters 3, 4, 5, and 8, it was emphasized that the interests, purposes, and goals of the learner grow out of the purposes, activities, and values characteristic of the environment. Interests in reading, in writing, in good English, in the arts, and in science, for example, develop in environments in which these things are esteemed. The school is one of the most important aspects of that environment, and one of its most important functions is the development of wholesome goals and purposes. The necessity and value of teacher-pupil planning in setting meaningful goals also were stressed in these chapters, as was the importance of the on-going, planned activity that serves as a motivating force for the detailed drill and learning exercises necessary for the attainment of goals; e.g., drill in the mechanics of writing good English takes on meaning if one has a purpose in learning to write well. Here we are more concerned with showing the influence of pupil goals on the learning process.

Differentiation takes place in terms of the learner's goals. The child differentiates the armholes in his coat when he has trouble finding them in the process of dressing himself; he differentiates the eyelets in his shoes, the shoe strings, and the movements necessary for handling them when he wants to put on his shoes. Or, he differentiates the "boy who has the football" when he wants to play football, and makes a distinction between "stop" and "go" in the process of crossing busy intersections, and between "fl" and "d" when he uses the words floor and door.

The situations to which we respond are always complex. Until one has learned to attach meanings to certain cues in the complex of details any situation or experience is meaningless. Only the gross characteristics are noted. To the child who cannot read, the printed page is merely a mass of unintelligible black marks on white paper.

An American adult trying to comprehend a page of Chinese writing can sense the feelings of the child and realize with some accuracy the problems the child faces in learning to read. Learning to read will require that a child direct his attention to certain details in the mass of symbols, and that he will associate meanings with these details. The clues (symbols) will be differentiated in terms of the youngster's purposes. Even before he can spell or recite the alphabet, a child can distinguish words that have come to be important to him, much in the same manner as one differentiates the face of a friend, by its general configuration. In the modern school, the child reads for meaning (a functional goal) from the moment he begins to read. He may at first recognize short sentences or even paragraphs from their general outline or their location on a page after he knows what they say. He then differentiates words that are repeated in different sentences. He learns to read fluently for meaning with a "sight" vocabulary of from 100 to 150 well-chosen words before he runs into difficulty with different words that look much alike. It is then that a distinction in terms of letters and spelling is made. The sounds of letters and combinations of letters are then distinguished in terms of the "sight" words he already knows. Differentiation has taken place from the beginning in terms of the child's goals—the acquisition of meaning from the printed page. In the old-fashioned approach, the child's attention was focused from the beginning on the letters of the alphabet, the sounds of these letters, and articulation and voice inflection. This greatly impeded the reading process, made it unnecessarily complex and stilted, and led to the development of faulty reading habits. The good reader reads by glimpsing rapidly the general configuration of words, and fixes his attention on the flow of meaning. When the symbols are differentiated in terms of acquiring meaning from the printed page, meaning is always associated directly with the symbols, and learning is promoted. For those who are learning to read, a page that contains more than two or three words that require analysis may prove too difficult for developing good reading habits.

When teaching children to write and when stressing such things as exact form of the letters, uniform spacing, correct position to take when writing, and other formal requirements, situations should be created so that it is obvious to the child that mastery of these elements is necessary if he is to communicate his ideas to others rap-

idly, accurately, and concisely. In other words, the child should
have a purpose for writing and communicating ideas. Learning to
write involves giving the learner a clear conception of what good
writing is and how to go about learning it. The beginner then makes
a series of approximations to his goal, sensing cues (differentiating
elements) that lead to it or having them pointed out by the teacher.
There is greater retention and greater economy of effort in learning
to write or in any other learning when it is undertaken with purpose in a meaningful situation.

Integration takes place in terms of the goals of the learner.
Learning involves not only the process of differentiating meaningful elements and cues from a total situation, but also the act of
combining elements that have been differentiated in previous learning into new combinations to achieve new goals. For example, a
student may wish to write the script for the dramatization of an
historical event. What he already knows (has differentiated) about
the historical period—contemporary characters, important events,
political issues, social problems, manner of dress, popular and classical music, tools and weapons in use, and the furnishing of houses—
will all be integrated in terms of his new purpose, as will his knowledge of sources of information—the use of the library card files, the
ability to use an index, to skim for information, to organize materials, to sense dramatic situations, to characterize, to write dialogue,
and to punctuate. The situation calls for the integration and reorganization of what is known, the use of communication skills, and
it also gives purpose to the differentiation and learning of many
other things that are not known.

Problem situations such as this require the integration of previous
learnings in the achievement of new purposes. They are the most
effective educational experiences, being creative in character, involving the operation of the higher mental processes, giving a feeling of mastery and accomplishment to the learner, and endowing
the development of all the fundamental intellectual skills with
purpose.

*Retention and elimination of trial responses in the process of
learning takes place in terms of the goals of the learner.* Most learning involves a period of trial and error. Some psychologists prefer
to say trials are made and success occurs, or to call it simply a period
of provisional trials. In any activity, many mistakes are made by

the learner. The responses that he makes in the beginning are awkward and incorrect; he cannot make his fingers, his body, or his feet behave as smoothly as does the skilled performer. In learning to write, the beginner's whole body seems to be involved and some time may elapse before he is able to coordinate it properly. When beginning to read, if meanings are not clear, he makes a guess according to the cues he perceives from the context. Or, if this does not make sense, he makes another guess based upon additional cues until he perceives the correct meaning. In solving an arithmetic problem, many attempts and different approaches often are required because the quantitative relationships are so complex that it is difficult to integrate all the relationships and still be certain that they are correct. Learning involves practice, which is essentially a series of provisional trials.

The teacher's aim is to reduce as much as possible this period of provisional trials by helping the learner associate his beginning activity with the ultimate goal. In dancing or writing, the teacher does it by showing the movements slowly and explaining the correct form; in reading, by giving the correct meaning or cues to the correct meaning; and in arithmetic, by demonstrating with concrete objects the relationships involved.

Among the provisional trials that the learner makes, some are better than others, are almost correct, and from these the beginner gets the feeling of partial success. If his goal is clearly perceived, the responses that are all but accurate tend to be retained and repeated; incorrect responses are not. This indicates the importance of clearly understood goals. Responses are retained and learned or are rejected and not learned in terms of the learner's goals.

Teaching, a process of helping pupils set goals. Teaching, then, is largely a process of helping the pupils perceive their goals accurately. In some instances it is necessary for the teacher to explain and demonstrate the goals of learning. For example, this is true of voice training, pronunciation, reading a poem, dancing, holding a pencil, and tying a knot. But in all learning it is well to give the pupils an opportunity to set and state their own goals, to say themselves what they are trying to do. Children can set highly acceptable goals for classroom behavior and for conduct in the halls, and in the lunch room. They can also set goals for study, oral reading, conversation, letter writing, behavior on field trips, story telling, and report writing.

Much of the embarrassment and confusion in learning, after children have set goals for themselves, results from a child's having to practice (make his provisional trials) before the group. He knows that he has not yet achieved his goal, that his performance is not correct, and it is embarrassing to have to make mistakes before the group. In oral reading, for example, we are concerned with a very complex learning process. In some schools, children are called upon frequently to read materials at sight and then are criticized and ridiculed for their mistakes. Most teachers would be embarrassed if called upon to read to a group of adults material that they had had no opportunity to practice. Oral reading is a complicated speech art; children should be given an opportunity, after the goals of oral reading are clear to them, to practice the selections they are to read in private or before a small friendly group before being required to read it to the class. Of course, materials read orally should be new to the group in order that a real audience situation prevails. Under no conditions does embarrassing ridicule have a place in the learning situation. It inhibits and confuses the learner.

The learner must believe he can achieve his goals. The learner must be constantly encouraged and led to believe that improvement is possible, that the goals may be achieved. This is especially true in the elementary school. Numerous experiments have shown that praise and encouragement are more effective than criticism in securing improvement. However, being ignored is probably even less effective than being criticized. The learner should feel that others are interested in his accomplishments. Children in elementary school who try to learn and who fail, frequently have had few outstanding learning successes in the past that they can rely upon for comfort. These children need sympathetic encouragement. On the other hand, individuals who find learning easy and are quite confident of themselves, may be stimulated by failure. The coach of a college football team may find it necessary to be severe and sarcastic in criticizing mistakes made by players who consider themselves stars. Likewise, a professor can establish high standards and expect them to be met if the members of his class are highly intelligent. This is possible only because of the self-confidence of the students. In the elementary school, pupils frequently lack the confidence necessary to profit from criticism. The teacher must do everything possible to build self-assurance and the feeling that progress is possible and is being made.

Adequate goals include intention to learn. Learning is a complex process and although application of the principles of learning enables one to learn with greater efficiency, it still requires effort and determination. There is no easy road to learning. Practice without clearly perceived goals and the intent to learn will not result in progress. Many an individual's penmanship has been poor for years simply because he has not made a conscious effort to improve it. He has not become sufficiently annoyed with his scribbling. For the same reason, people can speak, walk, dance, play bridge, and typewrite for years without improving their techniques and abilities. Practice alone does not bring improvement. It is necessary also to understand one's mistakes, know what type of behavior (goals) will insure progress, and have a definite desire to improve.

The modern school emphasizes instrumental learning. When something is learned in order that the knowledge obtained may function to some purpose, and when the learning takes place at a time when the purpose is of importance to the learner, the learning may be called *instrumental* learning. Such learning must not be considered haphazard or accidental. It is often called incidental learning, but it must be kept in mind that it is incidental learning *with a purpose.* Most people cannot tell you whose likeness appears on one, five, and ten dollar bills, although they have handled them many times, nor can they tell you the nature of the numerals on their watches in spite of the fact that they look at them many times each day. This is because such information is not useful to them. Instrumental learning is emphasized because it enables the learner to see the purpose of the learning and to set goals that are realistic in terms of the uses to which the learning is put. The indispensable tools of writing, spelling, punctuation, capitalization, proper word usage, and sentence structure cannot be left to chance. Proper goals, acceptable usage, good form, and good models must be kept before the beginner and presented in their proper functional settings. When the learner is doing much writing—letters to friends, relatives, absent schoolmates, and "pen-pals," or articles for the school paper—these mechanical aspects of composition take on new meaning and purpose and drill in them becomes effective. A basketball player may shoot baskets effectively in a game but that does not mean his skill was acquired entirely in the game. He probably has drilled for hours shooting baskets from various positions on the floor. The game and the drill are both necessary; either one without the other is inadequate.

Achievement in arithmetic involves the development of a hierarchy of interrelated skills and understandings involving comprehension of an internally related and consistent system of quantitative logic. It cannot be learned adequately if it is used only in a functional way in connection with unit activities. Attention must be devoted to it daily and systematically. The daily functional use of arithmetic does give more clear-cut and purposeful goals for the work of the arithmetic period, but drill in problem-solving and an understanding of the system are essential also.

In a modern school, approximately one-half the time may be devoted to a functional, purposeful use of the skills, abilities, and understandings that are being and have been developed. The other half of the day may be devoted to the improvement of the specific skills required in developing the learning units. The two halves are closely related and both are essential. They insure that attention is being given to subject matter and to the intellectual skills through which subject matter is made significant (meaningful).

Most learning results from goal-directed activity. The teacher's purpose is to give the learning child a clear and detailed conception of the goal toward which he is striving and convince the youngster that it is possible of attainment. If the child is not convinced that eventually he can succeed, he will remain confused and frustrated. During the provisional trials, the learner should be praised for his progress and made aware of his successes. The sooner he recognizes that a response was successful, the better. Also the reasons for his failures should be pointed out in detail, *if he does not know them,* in order that he may avoid them in the future or profit from them. However, the teacher should not call attention to more errors than can be corrected at once; the number will vary with the maturity of the child. It is also helpful to the beginner's morale if he realizes that others are experiencing the same difficulties that he is. The slow pupil will grow more and more discouraged if he is placed in company with children whose rate of progress is much more rapid than his own. Often pupils may be arranged or seated in such a way that common difficulties characterize the group. As provisional trials are made, with some success occurring and errors being pointed out in a sympathetic way, the child gains a clearer and clearer conception of the goal, a development necessary if further learning is to take place. Success in attaining goals strengthens the desire to learn.

Emotional learning may not be goal-directed. Many school children come to dislike reading, arithmetic, music, art, poetry, and other subjects because of the frustrations, disappointments, and embarrassments associated with the teachers and the study of these subjects. The teachers certainly did not intend that the students learn these negative attitudes, but many times the methods used could not have achieved the result more directly if this intent had been present. Requiring an individual to read orally day after day in the face of failure, criticism, and embarrassing remarks is too much for even an adult to tolerate. If a child is asked to solve meaningless (to him) problems in arithmetic, he will soon develop a strong aversion to the subject. The required reading of literature that is beyond the student's comprehension defeats the first purpose of literature—to bring enjoyment to the reader.

The learning of ideals, values, and attitudes is largely incidental to the purposes of the learner. Seldom does a learner say to himself, "I want to develop a new attitude, ideal, or value . . . along this or that line." They can be developed, but to do so the total situation should be such that the learnings are incidental even though the arrangement is purposive. For example, the church uses prestige, architecture, music, literature, liturgy, color, lights, vestments, processions, symbols, and cadences to instill a sense of reverence. Similarly, the army uses music, uniforms, decorations, parades, formations, literature, flags, symbols, and cadences, to foster discipline. A home, a business office, a school room creates an emotional effect. Environments create democratic and autocratic attitudes. The social atmosphere of the classroom determines emotional learnings. This feature has been dealt with already in Chapters 5 and 8. Emotional learning takes place as a result of the emotional responses to the total situation.

Organization is essential for effective learning

Organization is a central concept in learning; it is an essential of the learning process. The student may test this statement for himself by writing a list of ten nonsense syllables and trying to memorize them. Although it is known that the syllables are unorganized and devoid of meaning, the first step in memorizing them, in fact almost the whole process, consists in trying to organize them, to find some meanings or relationships that will enable them to be remembered. Some syllables may rhyme, some may sound like parts of words that are related in some way, or some may sound like the nicknames of friends. The syllables are learned largely as a result of attempts to find relationships and order. In remembering the number of days in the various months of the year, perhaps everyone relies on the rhyme, "Thirty days hath September, April, June and November . . ." Poetry that has a distinct meter and rhyme (one form of organization) is easier to memorize than prose because the meter and rhyme offer cues for remembering the specific words. A sequence of related ideas is also involved—this affords other cues. Poetry properly read and understood can be memorized almost without effort.

The emphasis that the paragraphs immediately preceding place on nonsense material and rote memory is not intended to emphasize the importance of such learning in the school, but merely to show that *even with* such materials, organization and meaning are at the heart of the learning process. Chapter 4 emphasized the fact that in a wide variety of sciences the idea of organization and relatedness is essential.

Importance of sequence. Since the school curriculum for a specific child may be defined as all the experiences that the child has while in school, it is very important to know *how* these experiences should be organized. What principles for organizing experiences will facilitate learning?

(1) All learning is dependent upon previous learning and serves as a basis for future learning. This generalization may be stated in many ways and all of them, perhaps, add something to its meaning. *All learning is a reorganization of previous learnings.* A word is defined in terms of other words. If the meanings of these other words are not known, the definition does not help in understanding the new word. Professor Thorndike used this principle in organizing his

dictionaries. Each word was defined in terms of words that had a higher frequency; i.e., were used more often and hence were more likely to be known than the word being defined.

(2) A new experience is always interpreted in terms of previous experience. A child whose only experience with the word "poker" has been in connection with a stove poker is likely to assume when he first hears of a game called "poker" that it is played with stove pokers. If it is referred to as a game that is played in secret by people of questionable reputations, his suspicion that it is played with stove pokers is confirmed. If a child knows the word *crane* only as it refers to a kind of bird, and he reads about a crane that was a feature of colonial fireplaces, he interprets it to mean that a bird was in some way connected with the fireplace. Or, when the only ministers the child has ever heard about are local clergymen, it is no wonder that he thinks Benjamin Franklin was a French clergyman when the child's history books refer to Franklin as the "minister to France."

(3) An educational experience is one that stimulates, enriches, and makes future experiences meaningful. Here the emphasis is on the value of the experience. Learning to read, for example, makes possible the constant enrichment and broadening of experience, with the ultimate possibility of communicating with the great minds of the past and present. A person's reading is always interpreted in terms of his own past experiences, either real or vicarious. Only in so far as an individual's experience is similar to that of Shakespeare does he get the meaning that Shakespeare intended. *A non-educational experience is one that limits or inhibits future experiences.* Again the emphasis is on the value of the experience. A child in learning to read may be hurried through books that are too difficult for him. As a result, he fails to get meaning from his reading, is embarrassed frequently in class by mistakes, is told by his teachers that he never will learn to read, becomes convinced that he will not, and learns to dislike reading to the extent that all through life he avoids it whenever possible. The future experiences of this child are limited and inhibited by this non-educational experience. Children who lack resourcefulness, independence, and a zest for new experiences have experienced a host of similar non-educational experiences. The so-called "spoiled child" has learned his behavior and it prevents and limits his future experiences.

(4) One sees in a situation only what one knows. Students in teacher-education courses frequently observe superior teachers teach. It looks simple, easy, and natural. Anyone would do it that way. The better the teaching, the easier it looks. The students recognize only those features in the performance that they know something about. Most of the artistry of the teachers is missed completely. The same is true in watching a dramatic artist on the stage. Again it is easy, simple, natural. Anyone would do it that way. One sees only the dramatic techniques and skills that one knows something about. In the elementary schools, a thing can have meaning only in terms of what the child already understands. For example, if a very young child has grown familiar with the name of a certain car or truck, he is apt to use this name in referring to all cars and trucks. Likewise, *what one gains from the reading of a selection depends entirely upon what one brings to the reading in the nature of past experiences.* Readiness to learn is an important consideration in all learning at all levels. Much attention and research have been devoted to the problem of when to begin reading. Reading readiness tests and preparedness programs are used in the primary grades of most modern schools. There is no magic in these materials; readiness is not really indicated by a test score. Unless the teacher understands the ideas back of a reading readiness program, it can be misused and become formal, stilted, and meaningless. The child can only learn to read in terms of previous learnings. He must have a speaking and "understanding" vocabulary that will enable him to comprehend what he reads, and he must be able to speak in thought units and to express ideas. Also he must be able to recognize words as such; i.e., in a sentence that he speaks, he should know that it is made up of words. This is called *auditory discrimination* of words. As this ability is developed, the child can recognize such words as his name, *stop, go,* and perhaps the labels that have been placed on articles in the classroom, such as *desk, chair, table, wall, ceiling, window, door, closet, blackboard, and bulletin board.* He has learned that words differ from one another in appearance and he has learned to make visual discrimination between words and letters. The ideas and words that appear in the reading matter must be discussed or experienced until they are meaningful for the child. He must, of course, be able to listen with understanding, and be able to follow simple directions. Finally, he must have heard stories

told and read to him, and have learned to follow the sequence of events and be able to tell about something he has experienced.

Readiness to read is developed through experience. One never waits for readiness to occur but seeks to provide for children the experiences that develop readiness. In a sense, readiness to read is a consideration through all education and life. There are articles in mathematical journals that the professor of mathematics is not prepared to read; i.e., his previous experiences in mathematics have not fitted him to read a certain technical article with understanding. This is true in every field at the most advanced levels. Developing readiness to read and the ability to solve problems, to understand, and to perform, is what education is all about.

Importance of individual differences in learning capacity. The pacing of the learning sequence for an individual should depend upon his learning capacity. Some children after reading two or three pre-primers are ready to read primers, whereas others will have to read five or six or perhaps more pre-primers before they can move comfortably to the next level of reading difficulty. Slow learners require more experiences at each level of a learning sequence. In the traditional school, a prescribed number of books were to be read by each child. As a result, the fast learners were kept at each stage of a learning sequence longer than necessary, and the slow learners were not provided with enough experience at each level. The teacher frequently "pulled" the slow learners through materials too difficult for them, leaving them confused and uncertain of their abilities. When a young child is required to read a page containing more than two or three unfamiliar words, the material very probably is too difficult for him. Reading skills grow more rapidly if one reads material that he can comprehend easily and pleasurably. What has been said about the development sequence in reading applies equally to arithmetic, writing, and all other complicated skill areas. Each step must be based on previous steps and the steps for each child must be taken slowly enough so that he moves from one to the next with confidence. They are not really steps at all, but rather represent gradual adaptations to new concepts. Only the teacher can judge the stage of a child's development and adjust the materials comfortably to the child's learning ability. The curriculum must be sufficiently flexible to enable the teacher to provide the experiences that the child needs rather than force him through misadapted materials.

Organization is essential to meaning. By placing specific items in a broad pattern of relationships they are invested with meaning. Education consists in learning *the meaning and doing of things.* This requires that learning experiences be properly organized and that relatedness, generalization, and understanding be emphasized rather than itemization, specificity, and verbalization.

Experiences and learning may be organized in any number of ways. There are as many forms of organization as there are types of relationships. The question is, what organization produces the most valuable learning? Let us consider first a rather poor or academic type of organization from the standpoint of learning, yet one that is frequently used in school. The student may recognize that some of his courses have been organized in this way.

Suppose we are organizing a course in "golf" at the high-school level in a typically academic fashion. It might look something like this:

Golf

I. The Derivation of the Word *Golf*
   1. The order of forms.
   2. Various theories regarding its derivation.
II. The History of Golf
   1. Golf in the Middle Ages.
   2. Development of the game in Holland.
   3. Development of the game in Scotland.
   4. Golf in England.
   5. Golf in France.
   6. Golf in the United States.
   7. Golf in the Modern World.
III. The Game of Golf
   1. The nature of the game before 1700.
   2. The nature of the game in the eighteenth century.
   3. The nature of the game in the nineteenth century.
   4. Twentieth-century golf.
   5. Factors influencing changes in the game of golf.
IV. The Language and Technical Terms of Golf
   1. The 150 most commonly used terms in golf and their meaning.
   2. Names of various golf grips.
   3. Names of various golf strokes.
   4. Names of various golf stances.
   5. Names of various golf clubs.

V. Practice on the Fundamentals of Golf
  1. The grip, (2) the stance, (3) medium pitch, (4) full pitch, (5) the chip shot.
  2. Fundamental positions for use of the (1) brassie, (2) driver, (3) driving iron, (4) mashie, (5) mashie iron, (6) mashie-niblick, (7) mid-iron, (8) mid-mashie, (9) niblick, (10) putter.

After a semester of studying about golf and another of formal drill in the gymnasium on the fundamental grips, stances, drives, approaches, and putts the student could probably play the game of golf with the same confidence that he speaks or reads French after a typical two-year, high-school course in the subject. Such an organization might be satisfactory for an article on golf in the encyclopedia but it is not for teaching because the goals are wrong. Such a procedure demands the memorizing of a great deal of material in a one-two-three fashion, out of its functional (operational or instrumental) setting. The emphasis is on teaching rather than learning, and the skills are not practiced in relationship to the game. Learning to play golf by this method would be a boring process to all but the academically minded, those who have good memories or who may be satisfied with "a mere bookish sufficiency." It can be understood why gold stars, grades, and honor rolls would be necessary to motivate such learning. This organization is an ideal refuge for the teacher of golf who is very inexpert at the game. It can be taught out of a book, and one can avoid showing his ineptitude on the links. Of course, all this is not to deny that a few students who followed such a course might ultimately become experts at the game and claim that it was their thorough grounding in the fundamentals that made their expertness possible.

A second unsatisfactory way to teach golf might be called the "ultra-progressive method." Here the teacher misapplies some *not-too-well-understood* principles of personality development and learning. "Understanding" the necessity of learning ideas and skills in their instrumental relationship to the goal, the students are required to play the game of golf from the beginning. Everything must be learned in the game, any special and concentrated drill on driving or putting, regardless of the obvious need for it, is considered a violation of the principle. Isolated drill is considered always formal, meaningless, and a waste of time. Believing that the school should avoid teaching competitive behavior, the teacher dispenses with keeping score. Keeping score leads to competition. It also leads to disappointment, frustration, aggression, cheating, and other personality aberrations. After all, it is the social nature of the game that is important. Why clutter it up with competition and frustrating experiences? Not having a good understanding of what is meant by freedom and a permissive atmosphere, the teacher and the pupils are not bound by the order in which the holes are meant to be played. Each pupil feels free to drive through the next foursome if they are too slow. The social learnings of the *whole child* in the *total situation* are of utmost importance, and the child must be allowed to structure the game for himself!

One would be surprised if anyone learned to play golf at all under this form of organization. Certainly no one would learn to play well. Perhaps this description is overdrawn, but there are those who recommend that *all* learning *must* be in connection with the unit activities, that examinations (and other means of keeping score) should be abolished, and that children should not be frustrated or placed in situations where anxiety exists because of fear of failure. (There are at least three types of fear and anxiety: (1) irrational fears or phobias, (2) fear of failure when the level of expectation is beyond the capacity of the individual, and (3) fear of failure when the level of expectation is within the capacity of the individual. The first two should be avoided but the last type is essential to effort, achievement, and development.)

The teaching of golf, like all other teaching, should be organized to avoid the errors in both of these extreme illustrations. It should be organized in terms of the goal of the game; i.e., keeping the number of strokes at a minimum. The novice should play the game with an expert (the teacher) who takes him over the whole course, pointing out the nature of the game, the proper stances, the proper clubs for each shot, giving reasons and explanations, pointing out the reasons for poor shots and explaining the proper cues for the good shots, using the technical vocabulary of the game in the process of playing it, discussing the reasons for and the goals of special drill in driving, putting, and various types of approach shots. The learner should keep a careful record of his scores to measure progress. Competition with self and others adds zest to the game. Awareness of correct form and incorrect form should come as soon after the performance as possible. Perhaps in the beginning, one-half of the time should be devoted to playing the game and the other half to special drill in developing form and eliminating the most glaring errors. This insures that all the practice is related operationally to the over-all goal of the game; i.e., keeping the score down. Learning about the history and development of the game should be postponed until a person has become competent at the game and such facts are interesting to him.

Organizing instruction in the elementary school. In the elementary school, the experiences of the child with reference to generalization, details, time, space, and so forth, are very limited. Consequently, his attention span is short—he knows and sees little in any situation and moves quickly to the next interest. He wants to handle things, to try them out, to explore, and to play with them in make-believe fashion up to his limit of understanding. As he grows and develops, his ability to generalize, to think abstractly, and to be concerned with details and relationships increases. Buswell [1] has described this maturing of interest and activities as follows:

Any person can identify this developing process in any interest which has developed to a mature stage. Any boy's interest in model airplanes illustrates it equally well. At first he simply wants a plane that will fly. Then he wants it to fly faster and longer. Then, through comparing (relating) the flight of his plane to that of those of his friends, he wants to know how to improve the flight of his own. His interest now veers to the scientific; he wants some general knowledge, some principles that will direct him. Gradually, he comes to be interested in technical aspects of aerodynamics and spends hours in reading 'abstract' material that provides a systematic and organized framework for his problem. His interest now is habitual and the time he devotes to 'concrete' flying of a plane is far less than the time he willingly gives to furthering his abstract understanding of aviation.

One of the important advantages of teacher-pupil planning is that the maturity of pupils' interests is reflected in their analysis and organization of topics. They tend to set goals and suggest activities that are appropriate for their level of development.

Many of the interests and learning activities of pupils in the ele-

[1] A. L. Buswell, "Curriculum Organization and Sequence," *Psychology of Learning*, Chapter XIII, Forty-first Yearbook of the National Society for the Study of Education, Part II. Bloomington, Illinois: Public School Publishing Company, 1942, p. 455.

mentary school involve an investigation of the workings of such establishments as a bakery, dairy, fire department, police department, grocery, airport, oil station, or shoe repair shop. In such units of work the nature of the service or business itself gives the clue as to how the study should be organized and conducted. If, for example, the unit involves the study of baking processes and a trip to the bakery is planned, the procedure should involve the following steps: The children should first have an opportunity to tell and discuss all they know about bakeries. Here is the "known" out of which the "unknown" will develop. The process of learning will involve a reorganization of these past experiences in a constantly expanding and developing body of knowledge, meanings, and understandings. The new experiences must make sense; they must be organized in relationship to what is known and what is not known. After telling what they know and raising questions and expressing a need for more information, these questions are organized in terms of the baking process. The children understand this and will come out with something like this: (1) What kind of bakery goods do people buy? (2) What are the things necessary to make bread, pies, rolls, buns, and cookies? (3) Where does the bakery get these things? (4) How does the baker know what things to put in bread, in pie, and so forth? (5) How are they mixed? (6) How does he make all the loaves uniform in size? (7) Does the baker do anything else with the mixture before it is baked? (8) How does the baker keep the oven hot? (9) How long does it take to bake bread? (10) What happens after the bread comes out of the oven? (11) How is it wrapped? (12) How does the baker know what to charge for a loaf of bread? (13) How does the baker know how much to bake? (14) What happens if the baker bakes too much? It can be seen that the questions can be organized roughly in terms of the sequence of events in the process of baking bread or other products. When the children visit the bakery, they have definite things to look for and definite questions to ask the baker. The observations should start at the beginning, the bringing of the ingredients into the bakery, and end with the finished product leaving the bakery. The experiences are organized in terms of the processes of the bakery. If an unorganized discussion of baking takes place and is followed by an unorganized sequence of observations, much of what is said and observed fails to take on meaning because the relationships that would have given them meaning are absent. The bright child will strive to give his experiences meaning by reorganizing them in terms of the baking process, but for most children this is leaving too much to chance.

Learning is a creative process. Meaningful, functional learning is a creative process because it involves discovery, insight, and problem solving. Of course, rote memorization is not creative except in the discovery of relationships that enable the memorized material to be remembered; but such learning is only temporary and of limited usefulness. Learning in the modern school is concerned with the techniques of investigation and the search for relationships and meanings. Children are taught how to carry on a personal or business correspondence and to compose original plays, poems, and dramas. Reading is consciously directed toward certain definite objectives designed to enable a student to follow directions, increase his ability to interpret and summarize information, aid him in locating references bearing on particular problems, and generally to broaden his interests. Other activities accented are field trips, experiments into the nature and structure of working objects, preparing indexes, and helping prepare issues of the school newspaper. This is the type of learning that is creative, self-stimulating, and easily adjusted to the maturity level of the child.

Learning is a developmental process. If we were to ask the median pupil of each grade from the first through the nineteenth to state what the words, *justice, democracy, duty, water, and river* mean to him, we would get a series of statements showing a constant development of the meaning of these concepts through the various educational levels. However, the fact that primary children might be asked or required to memorize the most advanced and adequate definitions would not indicate necessarily that the children understood them. Education cannot be short-circuited in this manner. Verbalization is *not* education. It is perhaps one of the greatest enemies of true education because it gives an impression of great learning where little exists. Traditional education with its emphasis on reading and reciting consisted largely of this kind of verbalization.

A word means something a little different in every new context in which it is used. Some words have a surprisingly large number of connotations; *The American College Dictionary,* for example, gives 104 meanings for the word "run." The hundreds of relationships in arithmetic take on additional meaning in every new situation in which they are encountered, and each generalization in the natural and social sciences takes on added significance in every situation to which it gives meaning and understanding. Since learning is always a reorganization of previous learning and must serve as the basic material for new learning, it is essentially developmental in character. There is no short cut to each new degree of learning; each step must be taken in the order in which it has purpose and meaning. Improvement in a skill or an increase in understanding must come through attention to new details, new clues, new insights, and a new organization of behavior. Progress requires effort and the intent to improve.

Discussion Questions

1. Make a list of the intellectual skills that you practice when you study. What are some of the important intellectual skills you neglect? Why do you neglect them?
2. Defend the statement, "One learns from a book only those things that the reading of the book causes him to do."
3. Find out what proportion of your class has developed the habit of reading textbooks merely to remember rather than to understand.
4. Examine textbooks in history and geography from the standpoint of the degree to which they can be read to understand relationships and gain insights. To what extent do they give factual material that can only be memorized?
5. Why are "operational" meanings more important than abstract meanings in the elementary schools? Give examples of operational and abstract definitions for several things of interest to children in the elementary schools.
6. Give examples of long-range and short-range learning goals characteristic of children in the elementary school. What are the important factors in setting goals? (See Chapter 3.) Why are goals important in learning?
7. What are the difficulties and problems involved in teacher-pupil planning?
8. Assume that, in order to find out more about your students, you assign them the task of writing autobiographies. Set up for the class a sequence of experiences leading to this goal Defend your approach from the standpoint of learning.

9. List a few of the most effective learning experiences you have had. Give the reasons why they were effective.
10. Show how the goals of the learner change in the process of learning to dance, skate, or play a musical instrument.
11. Give examples of school experiences that had no purpose or meaning for you.
12. Explain the reasons for your negative attitude toward certain school subjects.
13. Point out the relationships between the processes of differentiation, synthesis, and organization.
14. What do you consider to be the most important principles for guiding the organization of learning experiences in the elementary school?

Selected References

Anderson, G. Lester, Chairman, in Nelson B. Henry, ed., *Learning and Instruction*, Forty-ninth Yearbook of the National Society for the Study of Education, Part I. Chicago: University of Chicago Press, 1950.

Brownell, W. A., *The Development of Children's Number Ideas in the Primary Grades*. Chicago: University of Chicago Press, 1928.

Dewey, John, *Experience and Education*. New York: The Macmillan Company, 1938.

Gates, Arthur I., Arthur T. Jersild, T. R. McConnell, and Robert C. Challman, *Reading Readiness*. New York: Teachers College, Bureau of Publications, Columbia University, 1939.

———, *Educational Psychology*, 3rd ed. New York: The Macmillan Company, 1948, Chapters 9, 10, 11, 12, 13, 14, and 15.

Hilgard, E. R., *Theories of Learning*. New York: Appleton-Century-Crofts, Inc., 1948.

Kingsley, H. L., *The Nature and Conditions of Learning*. New York: Prentice Hall, Inc., 1946.

McConnell, T. R., "Reconciliation of Learning Theories," in Nelson B. Henry, ed., *The Psychology of Learning*, Forty-first Yearbook of the National Society for the Study of Education, Part II. Bloomington, Illinois: Public School Publishing Company, 1942, Chapter 7.

McGeoch, J. A., *The Psychology of Human Learning*. New York: Longmans, Green and Company, 1942.

Stroud, J. B., *Psychology in Education*. New York: Longmans, Green and Company, 1946.

10

EVALUATION, OBSERVATION, TESTING, AND MEASUREMENT

*E*VALUATION is an inherent part of the learning process. The learner seeks through practice and provisional trials to improve his behavior in solving problems, in writing, in swimming, in reading, in spelling, in composing letters, in organizing a report, and in explaining to himself the relationships involved in a situation. During and after each provisional trial, the learner evaluates it. Certain aspects of the trial behavior are judged correct and these are retained; others are determined to be undesirable and the learner attempts to avoid them in the future.

Evaluation also is essential to improvement. The beginner must have a clear conception of his goal, because it is in terms of this goal that he constantly *evaluates* responses. The superior teacher seeks through every means possible to give the learner a clear conception of the goal. This is done by showing and explaining the desirable features of behavior. In motor behavior such as handwriting, the teacher helps the learner set his goals by showing him good specimens of handwriting, by going through the process and demonstrating it slowly, and by pointing out the features of good penmanship. Of course, all the characteristics of good writing are not presented to the pupil at one time. They are described to the child as he shows a need for them in the process of evaluating his writing. By descriptions, demonstrations, pictures, models, and teacher-pupil discussions, the goals of learning grow in meaning and become the basis for the learner's constant evaluation of his behavior.

It is important for the teacher to realize that in all this learning it is essential that the child know in detail what is right in his behavior and what is wrong, why a detail is right and why a detail is wrong. The teacher must observe carefully the pupil's performance in order to help the pupil evaluate it. Unless the child understands the goals toward which he is aiming and strives to reach them by constant evaluation of his progress, improvement cannot take place. In school, children frequently try to solve a problem without knowing what the problem is; they try to organize and outline materials without knowing what the essential relationships are. In arithmetic, for example, children are too often taught to follow routine procedures in solving problems without understanding the relation between each step of the process and the goal. The process rather than the solution of the problem becomes the goal. When this is true, the pupil is unable to evaluate his work effectively.

Effective preparation for teaching involves learning to observe children at work and play and knowing the significance of what is observed for the planning and organization of future experiences for the children. It is only through observing the behavior of a child that the teacher knows the extent of the youngster's readiness for various educational experiences; e.g., his readiness for the various stages of learning to read. In determining a child's position in the sequence of learnings necessary for reading, the teacher observes the extent of the child's vocabulary, his ability to speak in complete sentences, his ability to follow verbal directions, his ability to listen, his ability to relate an experience in sequence, his ability to distinguish between sounds that he hears and symbols that he sees, and his ability to work cooperatively with other children.

In learning to observe children, knowing *what* to observe is of primary importance, although perhaps in the past more attention has been given to the technique of *how* to observe. During and after observing, the teacher evaluates; i.e., makes judgments concerning what the future educational experiences of the child should be or what was the value of past experiences. It is important for the teacher to understand that tests and measurements are simply more exact methods of observing behavior and that evaluation is the process of making value judgments on the basis of what is observed. A person may *evaluate* a curriculum; i. e., judge the value of the educational experiences to the children; but a person *measures* the growth in reading comprehension or in reasoning ability in arithmetic upon which the judgments are based. Measurement does not involve a value judgment. It is simply a process of determining the amount or the relative amount of something.

Levels of evaluation

There are several levels at which the educational process involves evaluation: (1) the learner's level, (2) the teacher's level, (3) the school officials' level, (4) the parents' level, and (5) the community level. The nature of evaluation at these five levels should receive attention, though it is difficult to discuss evaluation at one level without discussing other levels at the same time.

The primary importance of the learner's evaluation of his own behavior. The beginner must understand clearly what his goals are, must evaluate each response (provisional trial) in terms of his goals, and know that he has it within his capacity to attain them. If his objectives are clearly formulated, if he has had a large share in setting his goals and they are meaningful and reasonable to him, he will be eager to improve until he achieves them.

When tests and measuring instruments are used in evaluating pupil progress, it is essential that these instruments serve to clarify significant educational goals for the child. For example, the various types of information that may be obtained from a map or from a dictionary are clarified by questions that require him to go to the maps or dictionary in ferreting out answers. Reading tests should clarify such goals in reading instruction as learning to follow directions, to predict what will happen, to summarize, to organize, to make inferences, to note details, to get the meaning of a word from context, to skim, and to change pace according to the difficulty of the materials and the purposes of the reading.

The attention and emphasis commonly given to reporting educational progress to parents (conferences and report cards), to school officials, and to the community frequently neglects the fact that the student is the most interested of all in knowing his progess. Children should be encouraged and taught how to keep a record of their progress. Many textbooks in the basic skill areas make systematic provision for "self-testing drills" and provide the materials for keeping a graphic record of progress. Properly guided, such records have great interest for children, and furnish a strong desire to improve on past records. Some teachers feel that the keeping of such records is embarrassing to some pupils and hence do not make use of them. This is like an individual's trying to improve his golf game without keeping score, because keeping score is embarrassing at times. Not knowing when improvement occurs takes all the zest out of learning as well as out of a game.

Care must be taken to maintain pupil morale during all evaluation procedures. Many batteries of tests are designed to measure achievement over a range of grade levels; i.e., a test is designed to be used in grades three, four, five, and six. When this is the case, the low achievers in all grades, and especially in the lower grades, will be discouraged by the many questions that they are unable to answer. To prepare children for this ordeal, the teacher should tell them that the test is designed for more advanced pupils and that they should expect to find many questions that are too difficult for them to answer. Pupils should be protected from educational experiences that are unnecessarily frustrating.

Teacher evaluation of pupil behavior. The teacher's evaluation of pupil behavior has two over-all purposes: (1) to determine the learning experiences most appropriate for the learner or his *readiness* for certain experiences, and (2) to ascertain the amount of *growth* resulting from learning experiences. The readiness purpose is concerned with observing and evaluating those aspects of pupil behavior that reveal what the child is ready to learn and what experiences will have educational value to him. This may involve intelligence testing, readiness testing, diagnostic testing, and aptitude testing. The evaluation of achievement involves a judgment about whether the educational experiences of the child have been valuable in attaining educational goals.

Using readiness tests. In evaluating a child's behavior from the standpoint of determining his readiness for certain educational experiences, the teacher's point of view is extremely important. When readiness, diagnostic, and aptitude tests are used, the teacher may think that the scores on these tests are important. This is true

only in a limited sense. One must know a great deal more about
a pupil than his test score if educational experiences are to be
planned intelligently. One cannot convert a test score into planned
educational experiences. Specific information about the child's vocabulary, ability to express himself, interests, ability to think
quantitatively, physical development, motor skills, social skills,
emotional peculiarities, and many other characteristics is essential
in planning learning experiences.

For example, when reading readiness tests are used, the teacher
should study the tests to determine what aspects of child development are essential in learning to read. The better reading readiness tests are based on extensive research designed to determine
what aspects of child development are most closely related to reading achievement in the primary grades. Such tests measure the extent of the child's speaking vocabulary and his ability to follow
directions, to distinguish between printed words, to distinguish between sounds of words, to identify numbers and letters by name,
to speak in complete sentences, to remember a story, and to see
certain types of relationships. The readiness test reveals to the
teacher certain aspects of child behavior that are important and
that should be observed in the daily class work. The idea that tests
must be used to observe these factors is unfortunate. The tests
afford an over-all checkup and save the teacher much time, but the
teacher should be constantly on the alert in observing these afore-
mentioned factors. The use of the test should develop the teacher's
powers of observation in that they direct attention to important
aspects of behavior, suggest situations in which the various aspects
of behavior can be observed, and point out the importance of
that behavior in planning educational experiences for the children. As far as the scores of the pupils are concerned, two pupils
making exactly the same total score may need different experiences
in order to further their reading development.

Using diagnostic tests. Diagnostic tests should be studied in the
same way. Good diagnostic tests are based on research designed to
reveal the specific difficulties that children experience in learning.
By studying the tests, the teacher becomes aware of these difficulties and is prepared to observe and avoid these difficulties in the
daily work with the class.

Measurement has an important function in the diagnosis and

treatment of learning difficulties. Effective learning experiences result in complex behavior patterns that for observational purposes may be differentiated into habits, skills, understandings, feelings, and desires. The learned behavior, however, is infinitely complex with the habits, skills, understandings, feelings, and desires all interrelated in a more or less smoothly flowing behavior pattern. Oral reading is a good example of what we mean here. It involves the rapid recognition of verbal symbols, the reorganization of past experiences with these symbols into a consistently flowing sequence of meanings, the conversion of the written symbols into spoken symbols, the manipulation of the complex speech mechanism, the expression of the emotional content in the inflection of the voice, and an over-all emotional reaction toward the whole process.

Although oral reading is very complex, the process of learning it appears to be to some extent linear and to a high degree sequential. The ability to articulate each of the verbal symbols and to sense their various meanings must receive individual attention at some time. However, the rapid recognition of thought units, the interpretation of punctuation marks, and the integration of the visual, oral, and emotional aspects of the situation into a smoothly flowing performance of oral reading is a complex and difficult feat. In many schools, children are subjected to this task without adequate preparation, and embarrassment and a dislike for reading result.

The role of the school is to determine, within the limits of the pupil's capacity, the level of educated behavior to be achieved and then to determine the most effective sequence of experiences to bring it about. If sequence in experiences was not important, there would be little need for schools. The mere fact of our living in a complex culture would be sufficient to develop the necessary involved learnings. Sequence and the various criteria for determining it are important points in educational thinking today.

Determining optimum sequence of experiences. In general, the criteria for determining optimum sequence of experiences are of two kinds: (1) those related to the physical, intellectual, social, and emotional maturity of the child, and (2) those related to the nature and complexity of the behavior to be learned. These are really different aspects of the same developmental process. Properly conceived, they both result in sequences that are challenging, purposeful, and meaningful to the learner. The "child development" approach emphasizes the maturation process and tends to ignore definite goals, while the "culture centered" approach emphasizes the selecting, refining, and grading of experiences in the direction of definite behavioral goals.

That the development of motor, social, and intellectual abilities is sequential in nature is attested by the highly reliable age scales that have been constructed. The facts presented in Chapter 2 dealing with the nature and extent of individual and trait differences are based on the application of such scales. In general, we know that individuals differ greatly in the rate at which a given trait develops and in the level of development attained at maturity. We also know that the various traits of an individual develop at different rates and reach different levels at maturity.

Because of the waste and discouragement involved in attempting to teach again what the learner already knows or attempting to teach him at a level far beyond his present attainment, it is important that procedures be instituted for economically revealing to both the teacher and the learner his position in a given sequence and what the nature of the next educational experiences should be if optimum development is to be achieved. Whether the process of determining the learner's status in a given developmental sequence should ever be called "remedial teaching" is questionable. It would seem to be simply good teaching procedure. It has been called remedial teaching because of faulty conceptions of the nature and extent of individual and trait differences and erroneous ideas of how the schooling process should be adjusted to them. The common criteria of need for remedial instruction have been: (1) discrepancy between measured intelligence and achievement in a given area, and (2) achievement status below grade status in a given area. The first criterion assumes that individuals have equal aptitude in all areas of learning and that this aptitude is measured by an intelligence test; the second assumes that all children should achieve up to the norms established for their age or grade group. In Chapter 2, it was pointed out that studies of trait differences refute the first assumption and the second is unsound because half the pupils at a given age or grade level are always at or below the (norm) median. The best measure of what an individual should achieve in a given area is past achievement in that area. The need for remedial attention is indicated when progress in an area is stopped or markedly slowed down over a period of time.

Determining pupil learning status. The determination of pupil status in a given area of learning and the adjustment of instruction to status should be an inherent part of the teaching process. The proper use of tests in this process results in an economy of effort. Achievement tests have some value in the process, but diagnostic tests are by far the most important. A diagnostic test is one in which scores have little or no significance. It is designed to reveal the specific difficulty the individual learner is having with his work. A test, for example, that divides the whole field of English correctness into such parts as word usage, sentence meaning, grammar, punctuation, capitalization, and spelling is of use only in revealing those areas in which more specific testing is needed. Even a diagnostic test devoted entirely to punctuation in which the divisions are devoted to the use of the comma, period, colon, semicolon, and so forth, is of value largely in indicating whether or not it is desirable to test further on all the situations in which the comma, for example, may be used.

The teacher should be warned that often when diagnostic testing is first instituted, a discouraging situation is revealed. It seems that most children need some special attention on all aspects of the learning that is tested. However, confidence in the correctness of the approach and persistence in applying it over a period of time will reveal its effectiveness. Desire to improve and knowledge of how to improve in any area of learning result in optimum achievement.

The considerable amount of time devoted to this type of diagnostic testing and remedial teaching in the modern elementary school is not generally recognized in books and journals dealing with educational topics. The fact is that almost all the time devoted directly to the teaching of spelling and handwriting is consumed in the search for, and the correction of, specific errors of specific children. In arithmetic, reading, and the mechanics of English, many modern schools systematically devote no less than one-fifth (one period per week) of the time allotted to the development of skills to finding the specific habitual errors of individual pupils and to correcting them. The sooner such errors are detected the easier they are to eliminate. Many of the diagnostic devices are pupil-corrected; in this way self-diagnostic procedures are stimulated.

In the "readiness testing" approach to determining pupil status in a learning sequence, certain cautions are in order. Such tests frequently are based on an analysis of the learnings essential to satisfactory progress in a predetermined instructional sequence. Too frequently the emphasis is placed on discovering pupils who cannot profit from a given course of instruction rather than on determining the optimum course for each pupil. That is, readiness is considered as something to wait for, rather than something that should be developed. Instead of adjusting the curriculum to the individual child, children are sorted in terms of an inflexible curriculum.

The "diagnostic testing" approach to determining pupil status in a learning sequence involves the administration of a test after a period of instruction. The test is designed to determine points of faulty or inadequate learning in a detailed and analytical manner with a view to correction. Competent teachers constantly carry on the process of checking learning through direct observation of behavior and informal testing. Expertly devised "readiness" and "diagnostic" tests have certain advantages: (1) They save the teacher much time and work, and allow more hours for individual remedial work and instruction. (2) They are based on research and expert analysis, making it possible for the teacher and pupils to become more aware of the important elements, necessary order, and difficulties of the learning sequence. (3) They help the pupil recognize his learning needs by systematically revealing his errors. (4) Remedial procedures are usually suggested or provided that not only save the teacher's time but also help to systematize the teaching process, thus bringing about better learning.

Criteria of a test designed to determine pupil status. In order that a test designed to indicate a pupil's status in a learning sequence be most effective, it should meet the following criteria: (1) The test should be based on experimental evidence designed to reveal the sources of learning difficulties, misunderstandings, and faulty thinking. (2) The test must be an integral part of the curriculum, emphasizing and clarifying the important objectives. (3) The test items should require responses to situations that approximate the functional as closely as possible. (4) The responses should be such as to reveal the mental processes of the learner. (5) Instructional procedures should be provided to correct the various errors or provide needed learning experiences. (6) The tests should be segmented, organized, and spaced to cover systematically a substantial sequence of learning. In fact, the testing should continue at regular intervals through the elementary-school period. (7) The tests, by affording the opportunity for a constant, systematic review of difficult elements, should reduce forgetting as well as detect faulty or inadequate learning. (8) Provision should be made for the pupil to keep a record of learning problems and to measure and record his progress systematically. Tests of this type are likely to deal with the more mechanical features of a learning sequence, neglecting the higher elements that require imagination, the capacity to solve problems, and creative ability. This can be defended only if the efficient handling of the mechanical aspects of the sequence result in more time being available for the application of the learning in situations that involve the more complex and creative mental processes.

The measurement of growth and status using the more general type of achievement test battery has considerable instructional value if used properly. This is discussed at greater length in Chapter 18. There is danger involved in using these general achievement tests, however, particularly if supervisory and administrative officers emphasize the test results in such a way that the teacher feels he is being rated in terms of the progress of his pupils as measured by these tests. If such is the case, the teacher will tend to emphasize only those skills that the tests measure, and since these are always limited in number, the curriculum tends to become unbalanced. For example, certain skills in reading and English may be overemphasized but achievement in art, music, speech, and the social sciences may be neglected.

In general, a sound achievement testing program meets the following criteria. The tests should be given systematically; i.e., the same skills should be measured year after year at about the same time of year, affording an opportunity to measure growth and status in the most important functional skills and enabling a graphic portrayal of the results to be placed on the permanent record of each child. This graphic record of growth and status over a period of years becomes indispensable in the educational and vocational guidance of the pupil.

Fall testing desirable. The tests should be administered three or four weeks after the beginning of the fall semester. There are several reasons for this: (1) It prevents the results from being used as a basis for promotion. (2) It avoids the tendency of teachers to feel that, primarily, they are preparing pupils to pass examinations at the end of the year. Thus it reduces the tendency to drill pupils only in the learnings to be tested. (3) It discourages supervisory and administrative officers from putting too much emphasis on the limited results of the tests and rating teachers in terms of these results. (4) The tests will tend to measure the more permanent learnings, because, coming after the vacation period, the temporary learnings will be reduced to a minimum. (5) Most important of all, the results of the tests give the teacher a sound basis for grouping within the class and planning the instructional program for the year. The use of test results in planning educational experiences for children thus becomes more important than the practice of using them for post mortems after a period of instruction is ended. The tests should focus attention on as many of the important and ultimate objectives of education as possible.

Objectives that achievement tests should measure. Achievement tests should measure the skills and the abilities that are necessary to perform tasks essential to what we call "good" daily living, such as: (1) the ability to comprehend and appreciate literature, both prose and poetry that have not previously been studied in school; (2) the ability to read, comprehend, and interpret new natural science materials and to solve simple problems in this area (knowledge of facts should be necessary but not sufficient by themselves to solve the problem); (3) the ability to read, comprehend, and interpret new social materials and to work out easy problems in this field (this would involve such skills as the evaluation of evidence, the sensing of relevancy, generalizing, judging relative significance, and interpretation of tables, graphs, diagrams, and figures); (4) the ability to use the library and all sources of information such as encylopedias, dictionaries, atlases, and almanacs; (5) the ability to apply the principles of arithmetic and mathematics in the solution of quantitative problems; (6) the extent of the understanding vocabulary (If an over-all measure of intelligence is needed this is an excellent measure to use. The teacher and all concerned know what it is—vocabulary.); (7) the ability to organize materials and use the mechanics of English effectively in speaking and writing; (8) the ability to write legibly with satisfactory aesthetic qualities this does not mean standardized handwriting, but it does mean that the basic features of legibility should be combined with individual characteristics to give an aesthetically pleasing and at the same time legible hand); (9) the ability to think through a problem and plan an approach to its solution before beginning actual work (this includes the planning of social activities or programs, construction activities, field trips, interviews, and conversation, as well as reports of events, imaginative stories, and artistic creations); (10) the attitudes necessary for effective cooperative work with others (this embraces feelings of general confidence in and willingness to help others, a sense of humor, feelings of "we-ness" rather than "I-ness," a sense of responsibility, confidence in self, and an optimistic attitude toward life and its problems); and (11) the attitudes and understandings necessary for satisfactory personal and social hygiene. The ideal battery of tests described here is not yet available but certainly will be before many years. The tests that are available should be judged in terms of the extent to which they cover these various areas. Some of the batteries of tests in the basic skills areas are reasonably adequate for this type of testing. Tests of mere factual memory should be avoided. The tests used to measure over-all status and growth from year to year should serve constantly to focus the attention of pupils, teachers, school officials, parents, and the community on the defensible objectives of education.

It is possible to measure achievement in such a way as to distort the objectives of education. For example, a test in literature that requires detailed information on plot, events, characters, dates, and other factual information of a selection covered in class focuses attention and effort on the least important characteristics of a literary selection, making such study a pedantic task rather than an aesthetic experience. If tests do not clarify educational objectives they should not be used.

An adequate achievement testing program provides a basis for predicting individual pupil achievement in the various learning areas. When attention is given to individual rates of development in the various learning areas, a pupil's potential achievement is most accurately judged by what he has previously accomplished. Properly measured, rate of development is continuous in a given area; usually the instruments used show more rapid development in the early stages with a slowing down as the higher levels are attained. In general, achievement tests give a much more accurate indication of what to expect from a pupil than do intelligence tests. They also indicate areas of special aptitude.

The achievement testing program carried on in the early weeks of the first semester affords a basis for the preliminary grouping of children in each learning area. It also gives the teacher an accurate idea of the books a child can read with profit and the degree of complexity of the problems that he can solve in various areas. Problem scales are available in the better textbooks in arithmetic, but books, in the natural and social sciences do not yet provide adequate problems for developing problem-solving abilities. Many formulas are available for determining the reading difficulty of books.[1] The teacher should learn how to apply at least one of these formulas and in the process of using it, develop his ability to judge rapidly the level of difficulty of a book.

Tests as a motivating condition

A defensible achievement testing program stimulates the learning activities of pupils. A test is a relatively powerful motivating condition and can be said to have three functions in furthering the learning process: (1) an *energizing* function, to increase the general level of activity and effort; (2) a *directive* function, to direct the variable and persistent activities of the learner into desirable channels; and (3) a *selective* function, to help determine which responses will be fixated and retained and which will be eliminated. Testing procedures properly conceived and executed places the control of the learning process within the teacher's power as no other teaching device does. The three functions of a motivating condition are inherent in the test situation and should serve as important criteria in the evaluation of measurement procedure.

The energizing function. The energizing function refers to the

[1] Rudolf Flesch, *The Art of Plain Talk*. New York: Harper and Brothers, 1946, Chapter VII.

extent to which tests increase the level of learning activity and effort. This influence is attested by the cramming sessions that precede examination periods in high school and college. It is hardly necessary at this place to point out the many undesirable features of "cramming." The types of tests recommended here require consistent, long-sustained, and effective learning experiences. However, in many schools the examination is the "payoff." Examinations determine to a great extent when students study, what they study, and how they study. Students will scrutinize instructors throughout a course in an effort to determine what he will emphasize and what type of questions he will ask in the final examination. Unless the examinations truly measure the real objectives of the course, the value of such motivation is highly questionable. This procedure is an example of the use of tests for the purpose of marking. In the elementary school, tests are used to determine what learning has been achieved and what future learning experiences will be most beneficial for each child. They are used for educational guidance, not for rating. Nevertheless, the tests are stimulating to the pupils because each child is usually eager to make a good showing and to demonstrate what he has learned and can do.

The directive function. The directive function refers to the extent to which tests determine what teachers teach and how they teach, and what pupils learn and how they learn. The fact that the results of tests have some power to do this is well established. In regional, statewide, and local school testing programs in which schools, teachers, and pupils are rated and judged to some extent by the test results, the nature of the tests largely determines the quality of the educational process. When tests are imposed upon the teacher and pupil, with important quality judgments involved, they become powerful instruments for determining educational goals and methods. The effects may be good or bad, depending upon the nature of the tests.

If the tests are based on traditional curriculum materials of the factual type, designed to determine the amount of textbook material that has been memorized, they have the effect of "freezing" the curriculum and making both teachers and pupils satisfied with the *status quo.* Such tests encourage memorizing or cramming rather than the understanding approach to study. They emphasize the traditional standardized curriculum and prevent teachers from making adaptations in terms of the peculiarities of the local community, of their pupils, and of their own interests.

If, on the other hand, the tests measure the basic study skills, problem-solving and creative abilities, emphasize the application of generalizations in new situations, clarify important but frequently neglected objectives, and focus attention on the ultimate objectives of education—the permanent learnings—(the nature of these has been outlined previously in Chapter 2) then they have the important function of "thawing out" the traditional curriculum of the schools, and of stimulating more acceptable, meaningful, purposeful, and effective learning experiences. This kind of test encourages the teacher to use more vital and stimulating materials and to improve the learning experiences of his pupils. Certainly the most important criteria of the value of an achievement test is the degree to which it directs teaching and learning procedures into desirable channels resulting in the achievement of important educational objectives.

The selective function. The selective function concerns the degree to which the tests help fixate and retain desirable behavior and eliminate errors. This function depends not only upon the nature of the test but also upon how it is scored, and upon the emphasis placed on individual errors, remedial work, and follow-up procedures. Achievement test batteries tend to be too general for diagnostic purposes. The sampling of items is too limited and the organization too lacking in specificity for such tests to be considered as adequate guides for planning and directing educational experiences for individual children. A detailed analysis of the errors made on such a test has value but its possibilities are limited by the too-broad sampling of materials and skills.

The selective function of measurement is related to the diagnostic function previously described. In diagnostic testing, emphasis is placed on informing the teacher and pupil of the nature and causes of the errors that characterize the learning behavior of the pupil. Maximum learning of a selective nature occurs when students are permitted to score their own papers and then discuss immediately their errors and begin their remedial work. Logic and experimental evidence indicate that in the test situation the more immediate and direct the student's knowledge of when and why he is correct and when and why he is in error, the greater the likelihood that he will fixate and retain the correct response.

Pupils should think of their achievement in objective terms. A comprehensive achievement testing program enables pupils to think of their achievement in objective terms rather than in terms of the subjective appraisal of teachers. For example, it is stimulating to a child to know that during the past year he has gained nine, twelve, or sixteen months in reading comprehension. It is difficult to imagine a boy who is practicing the high jump being satisfied with the appraisal that he has "done very well, probably better than he has done before." It is more stimulating to know that he cleared the bar at four feet, nine inches and that this is three inches higher than his previous record. Objective measures make it possible for the pupil to compete constantly with his past records and performances and to think in terms of individual progress, rather than be rated solely on his relative standing in the group. Of course, objective knowledge of progress is only stimulating when progress is being made, but since almost all pupils show rapid progress in the elementary school most pupils will be stimulated.

A comprehensive testing program of the type recommended here enables the teacher to know the effectiveness of learning experiences in the various areas of the curriculum. It indicates those areas in which modifications in the curriculum are desirable and where, perhaps, supervisory aid is needed.

The test period is a learning period. The importance of systematic testing procedures in the development and maintenance of skills and abilities should be recognized. When the tests are functional; i.e., the items are such that they approximate the situations in life in which the learning will function, they may be considered not only good test items but also excellent teaching questions as well. Such a test becomes an effective learning device because it requires relational thinking and problem-solving effort, and not mere recall or recognition of previous learning. It is probable that the additional motivation resulting from the test situation together with the problem nature of the items result in one of the most effective learning experiences that the school affords.

The potentiality of tests for stimulating learning, especially in the skill and problem-solving areas (notably reading, arithmetic, science, and English correctness) has resulted in the publication of sets of bound tests in which the development and maintenance of skills and problem-solving abilities are more important than the measurement function. Of course, standardized scores are furnished to measure week-to-week progress but the real purposes of the tests are to develop and maintain problem-solving skills.

The characteristics of such drill-tests are: (1) The maintenance program is integrated with the developmental program. (2) The administration of the drills is spaced to afford maximum maintenance and review with a minimum expenditure of time. (3) Each drill is graduated in difficulty to enable each pupil to solve problems up to the limits of his ability. (4) Difficult aspects of problem-solving occur with planned regularity to afford a systematic basis for the diagnosis of specific difficulties. (5) Remedial work is provided for each type of deficiency revealed by the tests. (6) Practice on all aspects of the skill developed prior to the testing is provided for.

Materials of this type have been available in the better-designed workbooks and in the form of self-testing drills for many years. If teachers are to use them effectively, it is necessary that they understand in detail how these workbooks and drills are constructed and what is their proper place in the sequence of learning experiences. It is necessary to provide such materials at several levels of difficulty if provision is to be made for the range of ability in a grade. Such materials have frequently been overused and reduced in effectiveness to the level of meaningless drill materials. However, when the teacher and pupils understand the purposes for which the materials are designed and they are used correctly for the maintenance of skills, diagnosis of difficulties, and measurement of progress, they are very effective.

The evaluation of the schools by school officials, parents, and the community at large should be a continuing process. However, it should not be necessary to administer special tests for this specific purpose. If the battery of tests described previously for the purposes of measuring growth and achievement is administered regularly each September or October, it will afford a wealth of information regarding the effectiveness of the schools. The tests were selected primarily for their influence in clarifying and stimulating the achievement of the more defensible types of educational goals.

The influence of tests on the instructional program should always be the central consideration in a testing program regardless of the immediate purposes for which the tests are given.

Studying child behavior

Teaching involves the constant study of child behavior in order that learning activities may be appropriate to the needs, interests, and abilities of the child. We learn about the behavioral peculiarities of a child in three ways: (1) observing directly the child's behavior or a product of that behavior (free observation, directed observation, and test scales of various types); (2) asking others who have observed the child to submit objective reports on behavior or relative ratings of behavioral traits (questionnaires, anecdotal records, and rating scales); and (3) directly questioning the child about his behavior, his attitudes, his beliefs, his interests, and what he does under described circumstances (questionnaire). Refinements in these three methods of studying behavior have come about through more exact descriptions of traits, more rigorous control of the conditions under which traits are observed, and the quantitative treatment of observations. These make possible the placement of an individual with reference to such things as the distribution of various traits in a specified population, the determination of the relationship among traits, and the relationship between trait development and the various aspects of educational procedure.

Directed observation. Refinements in the procedures for observing behavior have resulted in two types of instruments, those of *directed observation* and *tests.* When the situation in which the behavior occurs is not controlled but the aspects of behavior to be observed are specified, and the observations are recorded, analyzed, weighted, and expressed quantitatively, the technique is called *directed observation.* Behavior traits that are likely to be seriously influenced by the requirements of a test situation or that are to be observed in children too young to be controlled for the requirements of a test are assessed by this procedure. Examples are: (1) "nervous" habits, such as sucking the thumb, biting the nails, twisting the hair, tics, posture, and so forth; (2) behavior involving the virtues of honesty, kindness, courtesy, respect for authority, and the like; (3) interests in objects, people, and activities; and (4) characteristics of motor behavior requiring coordination and skill.

Tests. When the situation to which the child responds is precisely controlled and the responses recorded, weighted, and treated quantitatively, the technique is called testing. In testing we are concerned with what the child can do under prescribed and standardized conditions. Although tests have been devised for measuring physical, motor, emotional, and social traits, their chief use up to now has been in measuring intellectual development. Because testing is an integral part of educational programs, emphasis on certain of its other phases is desirable.

Whenever the results of tests are used in a systematic manner to gauge the efficiency of instruction in terms of the progress and present status of pupils, the items of knowledge, the specific skills, the attitudes, and abilities measured by the tests have a strong tendency to become the objectives of both teachers and pupils. This is true whether the tests used in the evaluation of an educational program are constructed by an agency outside the school system (state department, county superintendent, research bureau, or test publisher) or by the teachers and supervisory staff of the school. If the tests measure only the ability to recall or recognize isolated bits of information chosen at random from textbooks and other curriculum materials, educational procedure tends to stagnate into a mechanical process of memorizing the answers to the test questions. If, on the other hand, the tests are devised by individuals who have insight into the true objectives of education and possess ingenuity sufficient to devise ways of measuring such development, the influence of the tests may be highly beneficial.

The *criteria that tests must meet* if their effects are to be in harmony with the objectives of a modern curriculum are as follows:

(1) All the important objectives must receive attention, otherwise those neglected in the evaluation program will be neglected in the instructional program.

(2) The mental processes required by the tests must be those required in intelligent behavior in life outside the school. For example, what are the mental processes required in such situations as planning, building, and decorating a home, planning nutritious meals, buying insurance of various kinds, making an investment,

evaluating the effectiveness of a social agency, reading newspapers and journals, selecting and succeeding in a vocation, voting intelligently, and cooperating in community projects? Certainly the following are among the most essential: (a) the ability to read literary and factual materials rapidly, and with comprehension; (b) reading for different purposes such as to follow directions, to skim for information, to summarize, to organize, to outline, to criticize, to evaluate, to remember, to enjoy, and so forth; (c) the capacity to use basic reference materials effectively: dictionaries, encyclopedias, atlases, handbooks, almanacs, library card files, and reference books of a more specialized nature; (d) the ability to interpret a wide variety of maps, graphs, tables, charts, diagrams and figures; and (e) in the various content areas, the proficiency to reorganize and to analyze data, to generalize, to apply principles in new situations, to propose and test hypotheses, to draw inferences, and so forth.

(3) The tests should measure the results of good teaching practices with such precision that they will help to clarify the true educational objectives for teachers and pupils.

(4) The tests should reveal not only the results of a mental process but also the steps in the process in order that specific deficiencies may be diagnosed.

(5) The tests should be of such a nature that effective preparation for them results in good teaching procedures and effective study habits.

Rating scales. Refinements in the procedure of asking others their opinion of an individual's behavior have resulted in the rating scale. Ratings may be made by the teacher, the parents, or the pupils themselves. Perhaps the best known scale for rating school behavior is the Haggerty-Olson-Wickman *Behavior Rating Schedule.*[2] Most report cards of the past have contained such items as deportment, punctuality, courtesy, citizenship, respect for the rights of others, and industry that were rated by the teacher. Many modern report cards provide for ratings by parents as well as by teachers. Ratings by pupils under favorable circumstances should be defended because it directs the pupils' attention to the criteria of good behavior.

[2] M. E. Haggerty, W. O. Olson, and E. K. Wickman, *Behavior Rating Schedule.* Yonkers, New York: World Book Company, 1930.

Although ratings of behavior characteristics have been found to be highly unreliable from the standpoint of accuracy and consistency of measurement, their use in the school can still be justified from the standpoint of their influence upon those being rated and upon the rater. Rating technique requires that the rater be analytical in his judgment, breaking down behavior into many elements and devoting his attention to each. If used properly, it stimulates the person being rated, focusing his attention on those aspects of behavior that require attention and keeping alive within him the desire to improve. Self-rating is most defensible from this point of view.

Questionnaires. Perhaps the most natural method of learning about an individual's behavioral characteristics and the factors that influence them is to question him. Of course, his answers may be influenced by the degree of his willingness to tell the truth, his interpretation of the questions, and the accuracy and extent of his knowledge of the facts. Considerable research has been undertaken to determine the degree to which these factors influence responses to various types of questions at different levels of development. Questionnaires have been developed for measuring the educational background of pupils, the socio-economic status of the home, the nature of pupil adjustment to various aspects of his environment, and pupil attitudes and interests.

Discussion Questions

1. Explain why both observation and evaluation are inherent parts of the learning process.
2. Explain and give examples of how observation differs from evaluation.
3. Explain and give examples of how evaluation and measurement differ.
4. Explain and give examples of how your courses in education have made you a better observer of child behavior.
5. Give instances in which you have carefully observed your own behavior with a view to evaluation and improvement.
6. Give instances in which the taking of a test has helped clarify educational goals for you.
7. When objective tests were first developed, they were used in the traditional framework of school organization and teaching (as examinations had always been used), to determine grades, promotion, and the classification of students. Show how the uses of tests emphasized in this

chapter differ from the traditional uses. Defend and criticize these new uses.

8. Obtain a copy of a reading readiness test. Make an analysis of the abilities necessary for beginning the teaching of reading and discuss how these abilities can be developed in the kindergarten and primary grades. In what situations may these abilities be observed apart from the test?

9. Obtain a copy of a diagnostic test in arithmetic or in a language field. Analyze the test from the standpoint of common errors and difficulties. What can a teacher, possessing such knowledge, do to increase the effectiveness of instruction?

10. Make a list of important educational objectives that cannot now be measured by tests. How can pupil development toward these objectives be observed?

11. What are the dangers inherent in a testing program designed to measure the effectiveness of teaching?

12. Make a list of cues or criteria that a teacher can use to determine a proper sequence of learning experiences.

13. To what extent is the development of motor, social, and intellectual abilities sequential in nature?

14. What are the disadvantages of sporadic attempts at remedial teaching?

15. What are some of the characteristics that tests must possess if they are to be used to measure status and growth systematically?

16. Point out the faults of the testing program of any school with which you are acquainted. Point out the desirable features of the program.

Selected References

Broom, M. E., *Educational Measurement in the Elementary School.* New York: McGraw-Hill Book Company, Inc., 1939.

Brownell, William A., "Some Neglected Criteria for Evaluating Classroom Tests," *Appraising the Elementary School Program.* Sixteenth Yearbook of the Department of Elementary School Principals, 1937. Washington, D.C.: National Education Association, pp. 485-492.

Brueckner, Leo J. (Chairman), *Educational Diagnosis,* in Henry B. Nelson, ed., Thirty-fourth Yearbook of the National Society for the Study of Education. Bloomington, Illinois: Public School Publishing Company, 1935.

Buros, Oscar K., *The 1938 Mental Measurements Yearbook.* New Brunswick, New Jersey: Rutgers University Press, 1938.

———, *The 1940 Mental Measurements Yearbook.* Highland Park, New Jersey: The Mental Measurements Yearbook, 1941.

———, *The Third Mental Measurements Yearbook.* New Brunswick, New Jersey: Rutgers University Press, 1949.

Cook, Walter W., "Tests, Achievement," *Encyclopedia of Educational Research*, Rev. ed. New York: The Macmillan Company, 1950, pp. 407-414.

Green, Harry A., Albert N. Jorgensen, and J. Raymond Gerberich, *Measurement and Evaluation in the Elementary School*. New York: Longmans, Green and Company, 1942.

Hawkes, Herbert E., E. F. Lindquist, and C. R. Mann, *The Construction and Use of Achievement Examinations*. Boston: Houghton Mifflin Company, 1936, Chapters I, II, III, V.

Nelson, M. J., *Tests and Measurements in Elementary Education*. New York: The Cordon Company, 1939.

Ross, C. C. *Measurement in Today's Schools*, 2nd ed. New York: Prentice Hall, Inc., 1947.

Achievement Test Batteries

Hildreth, Gertrude E., *Metropolitan Achievement Tests*. Yonkers, New York: World Book Company, 1947.

Kelley, Truman L., Giles M. Ruch, and Lewis M. Terman, *Stanford Achievement Tests*. Yonkers, New York: World Book Company, 1923-1940.

Lindquist, E. F., ed., *Iowa Every Pupil Tests of Basic Skills*, New ed. Boston: Houghton Mifflin Company, 1940-1945.

Lindquist, E. F., *Iowa Tests of Educational Development*. Chicago: Science Research Associates, 1942.

Tiegs, Ernest W. and Willis W. Clark, *Progressive Achievement Tests*. Los Angeles: California Test Bureau, 1943.

Young, Robert V. and Willis E. Pratt, *American School Achievement Tests*. Bloomington, Illinois: Public School Publishing Company, 1941-1943.

Reading Tests

Dvorak, August and M. J. Van Wagenen, *Diagnostic Examination of Silent Reading Abilities*. Minneapolis: Educational Test Bureau, 1939-1940.

Gates, Arthur I., *Gates Primary Reading Tests*. New York: Bureau of Publications, Teachers College, Columbia University, 1926-1943.

———, *Gates Advanced Primary Reading Tests*. New York: Bureau of Publications, Teachers College, Columbia University, 1926-1943.

———, *Gates Basic Reading Tests*. New York: Bureau of Publications, Teachers College, Columbia University, 1926-1943.

———, *Gates Reading Diagnostic Tests*, Rev, ed. New York: Bureau of Publications, Teachers College, Columbia University, 1926-1945.

Green, H. A., A. N. Jorgenson, and V. H. Kelley, *Iowa Silent Reading*

Tests, Rev. new ed. Yonkers, New York: World Book Company, 1927-1943.

Pond, Frederick L., *Inventory of Reading Experiences*. Stanford, California: Stanford University Press, 1940.

Stone, C. R., *Record for Reading Diagnosis*. St. Louis: Webster Publishing Company, 1936.

Reading Readiness Tests

Binion, Harriet Seay and Roland L. Beck, *Binion-Beck Reading Readiness Test for Kindergarten and First Grade*. Rockville Centre, New York: Acorn Publishing Company, 1945.

Gates, Arthur I., *Gates Reading Readiness Tests*. New York: Bureau of Publications, Teachers College, Columbia University, 1939.

Hildreth, Gertrude H., and Nellie L. Griffiths, *Metropolitan Readiness Tests*. Yonkers, New York: World Book Company, 1933-1939.

Lee, J. Murray and Willis W. Clark, *Lee-Clark Reading Readiness Test*. Los Angeles: California Test Bureau, 1943.

Monroe, Marion, *Reading Aptitude Tests*. Boston: Houghton Mifflin Company, 1935.

Stevens, Avis Coultas, *Stevens Reading Readiness Test*. Yonkers, New York: World Book Company, 1938-1944.

Stone, Clarence R. and Clifford C. Grover, *Classification Test for Beginners in Reading*. St. Louis: Webster Publishing Company, 1933.

Van Wagenen, M. J., *Reading Readiness Test*. Minneapolis: Educational Test Bureau, 1932-1938.

Young, Robert, Willis E. Pratt, and Carroll A. Whitmer, *American School Reading Readiness Test*. Bloomington, Illinois: Public School Publishing Company, 1941.

Arithmetic Tests

Lindquist, E. F., ed., Basic Arithmetic Skills: *Iowa Every Pupil Tests of Basic Skills*. Boston: Houghton Mifflin Company, 1940-1945.

Moore, B. V., *Arithmetic Reasoning*. New York: The Psychological Corporation, 1941.

Ruch, G. M., F. B. Knight, H. A. Green, and J. W. Studebaker, *Compass Diagnostic Tests in Arithmetic*. Chicago: Scott, Foresman and Company, 1925.

Schorling, Raleigh, John R. Clark, and Mary A. Potter, *Hundred-Problem Arithmetic Test*. Yonkers, New York: World Book Company, 1926-1944.

Wrinkle, William L., Juanita Sanders, and Elizabeth H. Kendel, *Basic Skills in Arithmetic Test*. Chicago: Science Research Associates, 1945.

11

THE EVALUATION
OF SOCIAL LEARNING

THIS CHAPTER is a continuation of the last. In it we shall describe some ways in which a teacher can evaluate the social atmosphere of the classroom and we will suggest others. After studying how the teacher becomes acquainted with the feelings of the students—the pattern of likes and dislikes—we will move into a discussion of techniques for improving the learning atmosphere.

There are teachers who never think and never worry about the relations that exist between the children in the class. What one student feels about another is no concern of theirs, unless the feelings result in "misconduct." Any disturbance is handled quickly; chronic offenders are transferred to another teacher's class. If they disturb all teachers, they may be sent to another school or expelled from school altogether. Everyone is sorry for these children, but after all, what can be done for them? The entire class cannot be sacrificed because of one malcontent. The teacher with 30, 40, or more children has not the time to play mother or father to every unhappy child.

A heavy burden is placed on the teacher, but through diagnosis and prevention, with which this chapter deals, many of the problem personalities in the classroom can be restored to good citizenship.

No one should expect a teacher to be a paragon of all the virtues. Certainly that will not be presumed in our discussion. The teacher can have worries, can be tired or disappointed, and still have a happy, productive class with which he enjoys living and working. Do we not have to take these teacher problems into account? Perhaps one of the faults of so many of the books and articles written on discipline, mental hygiene, classroom atmospheres, and teacher personality is that they are unrealistic. Few teachers have unbounded energy, easily satisfied ambitions, thick skins, and all the other attributes that would guarantee them wholly happy, carefree lives. Often they must work in spite of the fact that they may be burdened with a variety of woes. As a consequence, they are often *entitled* to exhibit any amount of hostility, suspicion, and anxiety that they wish.

This is, of course, far too dismal a picture. The point to consider is that good classroom relations among students and between students and teacher are possible even if the teacher is not a Mr. Chips. *What is to be suggested can be tried with good chance for success by any teacher.* All that is required is curiosity. The delightful part of this duty is that the inquisitiveness is not improper prying into the affairs of other people. Rather, it is a most approved sensitivity to student needs.

Chapters 3 and 4 examined students' needs from many sides. The need for a feeling of self-respect is the crucial need upon which this chapter concentrates. In all likelihood, the chapter would be unnecessary if the self-respect of children could be insured without help and attention from teachers. Unhappily, juvenile self-esteem is constantly under fire, not necessarily from the teacher, but from other children and from parents, too. Think how often parents compare their children. "Susan, just see how nicely Timothy eats his spareribs!" or "Jane, why do you tell lies when your sister doesn't?" Was it necessary to make a fuss about the spareribs? And what about Jane and her fibbing? Jane was not born a storyteller. Perhaps she is afraid to tell the truth—afraid of the consequences—or she is adding to her self-esteem by giving free rein to her imagination. Both Jane and Susan could be subjected to the same sort of trials in school. Someone passes a note in a class. The machinery grinds to a halt while the teacher pulls on his dignity and glowers about for the malingerer. Even if his bark is worse than his bite, it is usually bad enough to prevent anyone from volunteering that he or she was the culprit. Perhaps he is obnoxious enough to insist that the note-passer be tattled on, "else the whole class stays after school and writes, 'I will not pass notes' a thousand times." The subject is just too dreary to dwell upon longer. Let us hope that things like this will soon cease to transpire in our classes everywhere.

Punishment of children by other children also poses a problem. So much has been said about what ogres parents and teachers are— to say nothing of principals—that we sometimes forget how cruel children themselves can be. They can make life miserable for their little brother, the boy from across the tracks, or the little girl who wears glasses.

The hostility that children sometimes feel towards other children must not be exaggerated. It is only one dimension of their feeling. More often children are kind and considerate and seek affection. Actually there is no end to the variations in the feelings and responses children possess and make to other children. The question is, how can the teacher get these feelings (about the self and about classmates) out in the open where she can examine them and do something about them?

Sociometry

Sociometry is the study of patterns of acceptance and rejection within groups. Simply stated, sociometry undertakes to define and measure [1] the likes and dislikes of group members—likes and dislikes for others in the group. It is a first step in revealing the interaction within the classroom to the teacher. But sociometry helps the teacher even more. As we shall see, it is not something that the teacher does without the cooperation of the children. They do the basic work; the teacher does his most important work in interpreting and applying the test results. For example, the teacher may ask the children to state with whom they would like to sit and then see that their first reciprocated choices are honored. This helps to increase the children's interest in one another, to widen mutual ap-

---

[1] Helen Hall Jennings, "Sociometric Grouping in Relation to Child Development," *Fostering Mental Health in Our Schools,* 1950 Yearbook, Association for Supervision and Curriculum Development, 1950. Washington, D. C.: Association for Supervision and Curriculum Development, National Education Association, Chapter 13.

preciation of one another's abilities, and to maximize opportunity for the satisfaction of the individual need for self-respect.[2] We hope, through sociometry, to find a program for helping individual students develop self-respect or personal security by giving them a chance to play a useful and satisfying role in the group. If the child can locate his niche, he then may be motivated to do his work and to cooperate with the other children and with the teacher. It is becoming increasingly evident that the child who has located himself, who is accepted by the group with which he is seated, is not going to be a disciplinary case. Think of the effort that is saved for other activities when teachers do not have to supervise *every* child *all* the time.

The sociogram. The sociogram is a type of seating chart. It sketches the pattern of rejection and attraction in the class by indicating which friend each child would prefer to have in the next seat as a companion in class, on the school bus, or as a partner on the next classroom committee that is organized. The sociogram indicates to the teacher what the pattern of interaction is *at the time;* it does *not* enlighten the teacher concerning the *reasons* for the likes or the dislikes manifested. Personal interviews, thematic apperception tests, Rorschach tests, projective techniques, group play, anecdotal records, or other instruments must be employed if the teacher is to learn what cues the responses. John may not wish to sit with Henry, but the reason for this aversion lies hidden. Henry may be from the "other side of the tracks" or he may be of a racial group that John has been taught by his parents to despise. The sociogram is only a beginning. It provides the raw material with which one must be familiar before undertaking the more subtle diagnosis of motives.

Grouping by attraction. Some benefits from the use of sociometry are relatively direct and easy to achieve. For example, even before the teacher starts to study the social motivation of the children, he will find that he has obtained a natural grouping [3] in his classroom.

---

[2] Helen Hall Jennings, edited in association with the Staff of Intergroup Education in Cooperating Schools, Hilda Taba, Director, *Sociometry in Group Relations: A Work Guide for Teachers.* Washington, D.C.: American Council on Education, 1949, p. 47.

[3] Helen Hall Jennings, "Sociometric Grouping in Relation to Child Development," *Fostering Mental Health in Our Schools,* p. 203.

This natural grouping (seating children with others whom they like) increases "academic production." [4]

Procedure. Although making sociograms and deducing simple inferences from them is not at all difficult,[5] there are a few "rules" that it is well to follow. In the first place, the sociogram should never be made (in a school) merely to do research, to gain material for a colloquium paper or Master's thesis.[6] *The sociogram is an aid to teaching.* This is a first guiding principle of sociometry applied to teaching. To live up to it, the teacher should select a real situation, such as a seating arrangement, where the ultimate distribution of children may serve to improve working conditions *in the near future.* A second important principle for the teacher to observe is to *guard* the secrecy of the children's answers. Most sociograms are built from the written responses of children, indicating to their teacher their first three choices of companions (and, at the bottom of their slips, the three *least* desired). These slips should be worked into a sociogram at the very earliest opportunity and then destroyed. They should not be made a part of the classroom file of anecdotal records, test results, or other information.

The third essential, guiding the use of sociograms, is that the teacher *carry through.* This is part and parcel of making the sociogram improve working conditions in the class. After the children are asked their choice of companions, the teacher should be certain that the seating arrangement that is worked out reflects the choice given by the children. If Jim indicates that the fellow with whom he would prefer to sit is Henry, and Henry tags Jim as his selection, Jim and Henry should be seated together. And what of the "isolate," the little boy or girl whom no one chooses? He or she should be seated with his first choice. The chances are that the rejected young-

4 Ruth Cornelius, "Reading with Six-Year-Olds," *Childhood Education*, Vol. 26, December 1949, 62-163.

5 For an account of how to begin sociometric procedure, the teacher might be interested in the filmstrip, *Know Your Children,* produced by the Metropolitan School Study Council, Teachers College, Columbia University, New York City. It is recommended by Helen Hall Jennings, an outstanding student of sociometry.

6 " . . . the sociometric test should primarily meet the felt needs of the members and not a research need of someone studying their interactions." Helen Hall Jennings, edited in association with the Staff of Intergroup Education in Cooperating Schools, Hilda Taba, Director, *Sociometry in Group Relations: A Work Guide for Teachers*, p. 42.

ster will be so pleased with getting his first choice that he will do his level best to please his "buddy"—the child whom *he* chose. This does not penalize the student chosen by the isolate. The isolate, Joe in this case, is not the only pupil seated near Henry. Henry has children of his own choice with him. Henry should not have been seated with Joe if Henry had indicated that he definitely disliked this arrangement. When it is suggested that an isolate be given his first choice, the condition governing this choice is that the object of his first choice, Henry in this instance, shall not have rejected him previously. It is wise procedure to be certain that each child is placed with at least one of his choices.

With these guideposts in mind, we may now turn our attention to the procedure that is followed in introducing the class to the sociometric "test" and how the sociogram is constructed.[7] An excellent occasion for sociometric testing of the pattern of acceptance-rejection is at the beginning of the school year when the first seating chart is to be made. Changes in the pattern of acceptance-rejection between pupils can be followed throughout the year by sociograms drawn at eight-week intervals (minimum), perhaps just before committees are regrouped for a new unit of work or a new activity—if the eight weeks have elapsed.

The teacher must be certain that the class does not feel that a *test* is being administered; they should not be self-conscious in their choosing. The sociogram will be meaningless if the choices and rejections are made merely to please the teacher. The students should be told that a seating chart must be made and that each of them will have a chance to sit near a child whom they like. Perhaps the teacher will have given the pupils cards on which to write the full names of three students, ranked in order of preference. In addition, it may be suggested to the pupils that at the bottom of the card they jot down the names of the youngsers with whom they do not wish to be seated. The reasons for suggesting that there might be children with whom it would be less fun to be seated can be completely natural and off-hand. The children with whom they do not wish to sit—with whom they think that they might not have as much fun—are to be ranked. "Perhaps you would like to write down the

[7] Horace Mann-Lincoln Institute of School Experimentation, *How to Construct a Sociogram*. New York: Bureau of Publications, Teachers College, Columbia University, 1947.

names of three children with whom you would rather not be seated. I want to do my very best to seat you with the children with whom you wish to work. We all know that there are some children who are awfully nice but whom we do not like quite as much as certain others. We often change our minds about these things as time goes by but right now let us see if we can make a very pleasant arrangement for the beginning of the new year."

After the slips of paper or cards are returned to the teacher, he can prepare his sociogram. The first step is to tabulate the choices. One way of doing this is to write the names of each child, including absentees, on the left-hand side of a large sheet of paper that has been ruled off into squares. Graph paper is excellent for this purpose. The left-hand column lists the names of the children in their role as choosers. Across the top of the sheet list these names, but this time in their role as choices. Finding Grace's name in the left-hand column, trace across to a square under Patrica's name and place there a 1. Then by inserting a 2 and 3, indicate the second and third choices. Follow this procedure for every child in the class.

When this tabulation is complete, it will be a simple matter for the teacher to summarize who was chosen once, twice, five times, or not at all. There is an illustrative sociogram on page 465, and extracts from sociograms appear in Figures 2, 3, 4, and 5. These reveal what an isolate looks like in a sociogram; the "lines of choice" never lead *to* him. The diagrams also furnish us some information about the "clique." The clique is a group that chooses among its own members with no "outsiders" being selected. Figure 2 pictures a clique. The normal situation is a "chain pattern." The choices of the youngsters run from one person to another with two or three "stars" [8] (recipients of many choices), and one or more "isolates." In a moment we will suggest one way of "breaking" a clique. First, however, let us note the simple directions for drawing a sociogram. The teacher looks through the cards and writes down the names of the children chosen most often. The "stars" (Figure

[8] Sometimes the "star" deceives the teacher. He may actually be an "isolate." Suppose that an upper class child (in the socio-economic sense) were chosen by many of the children. He would be a "star," but *if* he did not choose the other children, you would realize that he preferred being alone. Wishing to be alone makes an "isolate" just as readily as does being rejected. It may hurt the "isolate" less, but he is not a bit less isolated.

5) will come from this list. They are to be drawn toward the center of the sheet of paper. Conventionally, a boy is indicated by a triangle, with his name clearly printed within, and a girl is indicated by a circle, with her name plainly printed within the circle. The same figure is used in representing an absent child, but in this case the lines are dotted or broken.

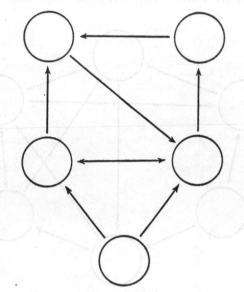

Figure 2. A clique-and-isolate pattern.

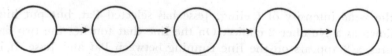

Figure 3. The "chain" linkage, a very common occurrence in the classroom.

In expressing acceptance, the teacher uses a straight line tipped with an arrow in a line-of-choice. If the acceptance is reciprocal, the line should have an arrow at both ends. Of course, the lines are not always straight. They do not cut through Hank's triangle to get at Angelo, but use an "off-set" or angle bend to by-pass Hank.

The absent children will not have any lines-of-choice stemming from their figures. However, they may be chosen and the teacher

should tell the class to feel perfectly free to name their absent classmates.

The teacher will wish to indicate whether a line-of-choice indicates a first, second, or third choice. This can be done by putting
a small Arabic 1, 2, or 3 on the line-of-choice. Let us take as an
example a reciprocal line-of-choice between Pat and Jesse. Pat has
named Jesse as his Number 1 choice. Jesse reciprocates, but not with

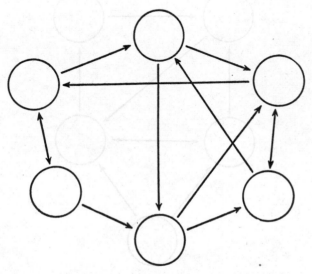

Figure 4. A stable arrangement often encountered.

the same intensity of feeling. Jesse has selected Pat, but put him
down as a Number 2 choice. On the line that touches the two figures, a 2 appears on the line running between Pat and Jesse. It is
near Jesse. A1 appears on the same line but close to Pat.

One of the things against which the teacher must guard is *prece-
dent*. The teacher must make it perfectly clear that *any* choice is
permissible. It may be customary in some schools for boys to sit
with boys and girls to sit with girls. If the teacher does not make
possible a free choice, the boys will tend to choose only boys and
the girls will confine their choices to girls.

Reading the sociogram. When a teacher reviews his sociogram,
he must keep in mind that he wishes to know the "motive and the

cue for passion." Why did Thomas, Joe, and Mary choose one another and no one else? They are a clique. Why are they a clique?
This is the point at which you begin to write down your questions
and to collect data for answering them. Do Thomas, Joe, and Mary
go to the same church, live in the same part of town, attend the
same dancing class?

The problem of cliques becomes acute when more than one ap-

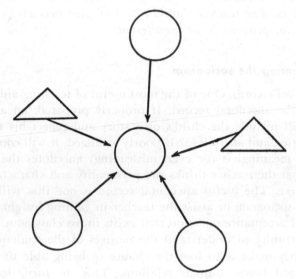

Figure 5. This distribution highlights the "star."

pears in the classroom. If they become very exclusive, rivalry and
antagonisms are often engendered. Moreover, where there are
cliques, there will be isolates. Actually the clique pattern is not
usual but it is the one that is most difficult to handle. Their appearance may suggest that there are patterns of value within the
community to which the teacher has not been sensitive. The clique
problem cannot be handled successfully unless the teacher is aware
of the nature of the value patterns that characterize his community.[9]
In handling the problem, the teacher must look for occasions when

[9] In Chapters 5, 6, 7, and 8, every effort was made to analyze a variety of cultural value patterns and to indicate the causes of cleavage that occasion the
cliques in our schools.

a project promises to be of such size that the several groups will have to pool their resources in order to carry it through. When the children are all at work, the cliques can be re-grouped. This must be done with great reserve and vigilant attention to the reaction of the cliques. If the children sense that the teacher is trying to manipulate them for some purpose inimical to their organization, the benefit of sociometric testing will be lost.

An improvement in classroom atmosphere is not to be expected immediately. *The teacher should allow at least two weeks after regrouping for progress to be manifested.*

Supplementing the sociogram

Anecdotal records. One of the most useful of teaching aids, if well done, is the anecdotal record. If properly prepared, an anecdotal record will include the child's own story and reflect his real feelings, worries, and attitudes.[10] If poorly arranged, it will consist only of a few meaningless (or even misleading) anecdotes that merely reflect what the teacher thinks the personality and character of the child is like. The useful anecdotal record is one that will supplement the sociogram or assist the teacher in gaining insight into the pattern of acceptance-rejection that exists in his classroom. To miss the opportunity to understand the motives of the students in the choices they make is to lose the chance of being able to lead the class toward better human relations. This, in turn, leaves the teacher with nothing to do but hand out information, listen to recitations, give tests, and issue grades. The assignment-study-recitation-test technique does not require that records be kept, except those relating to attendance and grade. Such information alone will not make the teacher an educational engineer,[11] able to design learning situations and improve the atmosphere of the classroom.

Criteria for judging the anecdotal record. As already mentioned,

[10] Helen Bieker, "Using Anecdotal Records to Know the Child," *Fostering Mental Health in Our Schools,* 1950 Yearbook, Association for Supervision and Curriculum Development. Washington, D.C.: Association for Supervision and Curriculum Development, National Education Association, pp. 184-202. See also Arthur E. Hamalainen, "An Appraisal of Anecdotal Records," *Teachers College Record,* Vol. 45, October 1944, 351-352.

[11] H. A. Thelen, "Engineering Research in Curriculum Building," *Journal of Educational Research,* Vol. 451, April 1948, 577-596.

a good anecdotal record is one that reveals the feelings of the child and that includes a brief digest of many of his conversations, samples of his drawings or stories, examples of typical and atypical behavior with other students, and glimpses into his home and neighborhood life. The ideal is that whatever appears in the record be clear-cut, specific, factual, and *absolutely* uncolored by the teacher's opinions. It does not matter what the teacher feels about Rachel's attitude toward her mother. If that attitude appears to have some significance for understanding Rachel's behavior in the class and the attitude of Rachel's classmates toward her, that is enough. The teacher's reactions to Rachel are altogether gratuitous and *never* appear in the anecdotal record. Rather than the teacher's sentiments, the anecdotal record carries precise references to the time of day the incident occurred, the persons who were involved, and the phases through which the incident developed—if it transpired over a rather long time.

The student of child growth and development will recognize that these criteria are almost the same as those that apply to any observation of behavior. The anecdotal record, as a matter of fact, is subject to the very limitations that psychologists have discovered in connection with the biographical sketches of an infant's behavior compiled by parents or other untrained observers. These people obviously were well-intentioned, but they did not write all that they saw or all that they might have seen. Then, too, the reports did not cover a sufficient variety of behavior (feeding habits, sleeping habits) to permit reconstructing the total behavior pattern. If an anecdotal record is to serve the teacher or anyone else, it must be objective and characteristic of the child's over-all behavior.

Procedure. Entering upon anecdotal recording is not as easy to plan in advance as making sociograms. When the teacher compiles a sociogram, he has the entire class for a subject. This is not the case with anecdotal records. Each child is a subject by himself, although, to be sure, the record traces his interaction within the class. When each child has been recorded, the teacher is in the position of a novelist who has the story of a number of unrelated people and can proceed to interweave these into a composite drama.

Generally, the teacher starts with a child who interests him. It may be the little boy who stars in the sociogram. What is so attractive about him? Is it that he has a large allowance and buys candy for the others or is he the object of pity, an obvious "underdog" whom the other children take satisfaction in sheltering? Is he pleasant and easy to get along with? He certainly reads well. Maybe he could be a help in encouraging Mary, who has not been reading as quickly or as comprehensively as Mabel, Skinny Thompson, and "Andy's bunch," the "eager-beavers" from Sculpin Avenue.

Supplemental observations. The anecdotal records should contain more than the report of a variety of situations in which the child played a role. Any clues to personality, to emotional drives, to unfulfilled hopes, or pressing worries belong in the record. Intimations of all these can often be discerned in the drawings and paintings of children that often are "projections" of secret fears, "dragons of the mind," or aspirations and intense pleasures.[12] We will return again to this topic in Chapter 17.

Many, many times the teacher can learn something of the child's attitude toward home life by listening to his conversation with a doll or with a friend whom the child imagines to be his parents, or his older brother or sister.

An Inadequate Anecdotal Record

(Kindergarten)

Ray is a shy boy. I can't get him to like me, it seems. He does what the others do, but he does not react to me at all. His tests show him to be a little above average in ability, but he seems to depend on other children for most of his ideas.

His mother is nice, but a typical proud Mamma. Talks about Ray by the hour, but doesn't say much.

(First Grade)

I wouldn't call Ray shy. He's quiet. He doesn't listen to instructions. He is careless in doing as he is told but he isn't mean or bad.

(Second Grade)

Hasn't learned to read. Likes to play with toys and construction materials. Doesn't make very much. Won't try to learn to read. Isn't interested in drawing or projects other children do.

---

12 William E. Henry, "The Child Tells About Himself Through His Creative Products," *Fostering Mental Health in our Schools.* 1950 Yearbook, Association for Supervision and Curriculum Development. Washington, D.C.: Association for Supervision and Curriculum Development, National Education Association, Chapter 15.

(Third Grade)

Reads like a beginner. Won't try to read. Probably isn't well. Two times lately, Ray went home from recess without asking, on days his mother wasn't home. Won't tell why he did it.

(Fourth Grade)

Ray may be quiet, but he is irritating. He does little things to distract the other children. He pulled the wire out of the plug so the lights wouldn't go on at the proper time in our dramatization. He dug up the beans the children planted so they could watch them sprout. He planted them at home and said they had sprouted there and he would bring the old things if anybody wanted them. He is very difficult and talks very little.

(Fifth Grade)

You have to watch Ray, but he is no worse than some of the others. I let him know I'm the boss. His achievement is low for his ability. He won't try to learn. His sight and hearing are sound.

I talked to his mother. You can't tell her he isn't perfect. She says we don't understand Ray. She's right! I don't think she is a good influence on Ray.

(Sixth Grade)

Ray skipped school two days the first week. Didn't go home. Won't say where he was. Won't listen when you try to talk to him.

Last week he tripped Robert on the stairs. Robert's arm was broken. Robert never fights or causes trouble so it must have been Ray's fault. The Principal took Ray into the Superintendent's office and perhaps they can do something with him.

Ray has been a terror lately. He doesn't do any of his work. Just scribbles. He doesn't sass me. Just pays no attention. He doesn't fight. It's just the underhanded things he does.

He skips school more frequently this spring. Seems to want to be alone. . . .

This record certainly gives an unfavorable story of a young boy. Let's see what we would get out of it if we were to have charge of Ray in the seventh grade. We would see that Ray started out as a shy child, who didn't make friends with his teachers, and was content to take his cues from the other pupils. He didn't follow instructions to learn to read as early or as well as most children. According to the teacher's standards, his work was desultory. He began to skip school in the third grade, and in the fourth, revealed a clear negativism toward the projects of the other children. These tendencies increased. He was not openly disruptive, but quietly rebellious.

The record does not tell us much that will serve as a basis for helping Ray. It contains very little about his intelligence or ability, and almost nothing upon which to base a guess concerning his real interests. We are not told how he behaved on the playground or in other specific instances. There is something about his mother, but nothing about father, home, or socio-economic status. No clue exists to his behavior except the third-grade teacher's note, "Probably isn't well." There are but few specific illustrations of his conduct and there are concerned only with violations (skipping school, tripping Robert, the incidents with the wire and the beans). The rest of the remarks are general and not very revealing.

He has gradually become a "bad" boy in the judgment of a succession of teachers, but we do not have any idea why this is so. We do not know what, if anything, was done to interest Ray, to help him find his place in class, to gain his trust, affection, cooperation, and approval. We know nothing about how his group reacted to him. We do not know if he has any friends or enemies. Apparently the only effort made to find out the reason for Ray's skipping school was to ask him about it. Had he given reasons, they might not have been the real ones, but would probably have been useful in providing leads even if they were not sufficient as answers in themselves.

We are not told anything about his achievement outside of reading. Such matters as Ray's health, his early childhood, and his basic social and organic needs, fears, emotions, and motives were completely neglected.

The tripping incident is highly significant, and we are told little about it. Why did he trip Robert? Could it have been someone else just as well? Was this typical or unusual aggressiveness? Ray probably did not think of a broken arm or other serious consequences, but after the arm was broken, it may have been more serious to him than to Robert. Did Ray feel guilty because of it? Was he rejected by his group more than ever? Did it inflate his ego? There are thousands of possibilities, the least probable one being that Ray learned a good lesson from it. Does the record seem to indicate that Ray's behavior got worse after the tripping episode took place?

It should be emphasized that this record, though rather poorly put together, is still better than nothing *if it is not misinterpreted* by the teachers into whose hands it falls.

An anecdotal record, to be of value, should be made up of little revealing stories. It should tell something that might be used in helping the child. Illustrations of how a teacher may start, and build up, anecdotal records while the class carries on its activities are given in Chapter 19. Anecdotal records, in their most valuable form, will reflect a knowledge of much that has been provided as background thus far in this book. Such records do not necessarily have to be exciting or dramatic. Many of them are orderly, helpful records about the abilities, interests, and activities of normal children.

The sociogram, the anecdotal record, and various supplemental techniques have been named. There still remains the *good, old, reliable, informal visit with parents.* We ask an awful lot of our teachers, but a visit with the parents of each and every child—at least once a year—would be of great help to the teacher in understanding the child, to say nothing of the excellent public relations to be had from home visitation and the visit of the parents to the school. Messages sent home with children are not adequate substitutes for a face-to-face discussion with parents.

When talking with a parent, there are several things that the teacher will wish to remember. For one thing, the parent naturally is emotionally involved with his child. The mother or father have great hopes for their offspring and, of course, just as great fears for them. Nothing should be said that will lead the parent to place increasing pressure on the youngsters, particularly if it seems that there may be too much pressure already. "Pedagese" should be avoided. The professional jargon infuriates some parents, intimidates others, and in no case increases the chance of gaining the parents' confidence. Charles Dickens first sounded the warning we are passing on to the teacher. Mr. Squeers, a teacher of sorts, is speaking.

If there's a screw loose in a heavenly body, that's philosophy, and if there's a screw loose in an earthly body, that's philosophy too; or it may be that there's sometimes a little metaphysics in it, but that's not often. Philosophy's the chap for me. If a parent asks a question in the classical, commercial, or mathematical line, says I gravely, "Why, sir, in the first place, are you a philosopher?" "No, Mr. Squeers," he says, "I ain't." "Then, sir," says I, "I am sorry for you, for I shan't be able to explain it." Naturally the parent goes away and wishes he was a philosopher, and equally naturally, thinks I'm one.

Discussion Questions

1. Observe a teacher working with a class and make a record of the teacher's statements. Classify these statements into three categories (1) those indicating autocratic attitudes toward children, (2) those indicating democratic attitudes toward children, and (3) those that cannot be classified.

2. Make a list of statements made by teachers that impart confidence to children, lift their spirits, and increase their eagerness to achieve.

3. Make a list of statements made by teachers that depress and discourage children.

4. Observe children at free play (dramatic play). They may be playing house, grocery store, cops and robbers, Indians and cowboys, and so forth. Make an objective record of what one or more children do that you believe gives insight into feelings, beliefs, attitudes, fears, hates, or anxieties. Discuss these in class.

5. Recall teachers you have had who experienced considerable trouble with "discipline" and others who had no such problems. Analyze as best you can the behavior of the teachers that caused the difference in pupil responses to them.

6. Give reasons why respectable individuals who tend to be hostile to people generally hold closely to the conventional virtues.

7. Discuss the proposition that children who come from authoritarian homes need authoritarian teachers and children who come from democratic homes need democratic teachers.

8. Why do you think the chapters on social learnings were not entitled *School Discipline?*

9. Defend the proposition that the behavior of a child can be explained in terms of the personalities of his parents and teachers.

10. Observe a committee meeting or a teacher-pupil planning session and make a record of the contributions that furthered the work of the group and of those that hindered group progress.

11. Give reasons why it might be undesirable for a teacher to become too concerned with group dynamics, sociograms, anectodal records, projective techniques, sociodrama, psychodrama, and the like. What are the dangers of a little knowledge in this area? Should this vocabulary be used in discussion with parents or pupils? Write the meanings of one or two of these terms in simple language that any teacher or parent would understand.

12. Discuss the proposition that the teacher's insights into human behavior (gained from reading these chapters or from references cited or techniques of observation suggested) should be used so casually that they are not obvious to pupils or to casual visitors to the classroom.

13. To what extent are sociograms and anecdolal records merely observa-

tional techniques? How will the teacher know what to do with the information gained through such observation? Will the authoritarian teacher use it in a different way from the democratic teacher?

14. Defend the proposition that the most important single factor in determining social learning in the classroom is the personality of the teacher.

Selected References

Axline, Virginia Mae, *Play Therapy*. Boston: Houghton Mifflin Company, 1947.

Bales, Robert F., *Interaction Process Analysis*. Cambridge: Addison-Wesley Press, Inc., 1950.

Bieker, Helen, "Using Anecdotal Records to Know the Child," *Fostering Mental Health in Our Schools*, 1950 Yearbook, Association For Supervision and Curriculum Development. Washington, D.C.: Association for Supervision and Curriculum Development, National Education Association, Chapter 12.

Haas, Robert B., ed., *Psychodrama and Sociodrama in American Education*. New York: Beacon House, 1949.

Hamalainen, Arthur E., "An Appraisal of Anecdotal Records," *Teachers College Record*, Vol. 45, October 1944, 351-352.

Henry, William E., "The Child Tells About Himself through His Creative Products," *Fostering Mental Health in Our Schools*, 1950 Yearbook, Association for Supervision and Curriculum Development. Washington, D.C.: Association for Supervision and Curriculum Development, National Education Association, Chapter 15.

Horace-Mann-Lincoln Institute of School Experimentation, *How to Construct a Sociogram*. New York: Bureau of Publications, Teachers College, Columbia University, 1947.

Jennings, Helen Hall, "Sociometric Grouping in Relation to Child Development," *Fostering Mental Health in Our Schools*, 1950 Yearbook, Association for Supervision and Curriculum Development. Washington, D.C.: Association for Supervision and Curriculum Development, National Education Association, Chapter 13.

———, "Sociodrama as Educative Process," *Fostering Mental Health in Our Schools*, 1950 Yearbook, Association for Supervision and Curriculum Development. Washington, D.C.: Association for Supervision and Curriculum Development, National Education Association, Chapter 16.

———, R. Lippitt, and R. K. White, "Patterns of Aggressive Behavior in Experimentally Created Social Climates," *Journal of Social Psychology*, Vol. 10, 1939, 271-299.

Moreno, J. L., *Psychodrama*. New York: Beacon House, 1946.

Roethlesberger, Fritz J., *Management and Morale*, Cambridge: Harvard University Press, 1943.

PART TWO

CURRICULUM

*B*UILDING UPON a background similar to that presented thus far in this book, the curriculums in our country take shape and are put into practice. Curriculums in this sense may be regarded as important educational tools. There are many types of curriculums and many conflicting theories regarding their organization and use.

The authors believe that there are common elements of agreement running through most of the differences of opinion. Most curriculums represent a compromise between what is done in the actual situation and what the best theory would indicate should be done. Some of these compromises are due to a lack of adequate experimental knowledge about how to practice what is clear in the laboratory situation. Some of them are due to shortcomings in teacher education and preparation.

This part of the book shows some of the most common ways in which curriculums are organized and some of the kinds of units and activities that are used. It demonstrates some of the relationships of content and subject matter to curriculum organization and to the learnings that are outlined as objectives. In addition, it attempts to identify the important elemental characteristics of curriculums as instructional tools so that descriptions of classroom procedure given in Part Three may have meaning in terms of the curriculum tools with which teachers are provided.

Because the authors feel that the subject is crucial to future human welfare, two full chapters are devoted to the importance of certain insights regarding man's physical world and of the sciences through which he comes to know it. Mathematics is emphasized in these same chapters. The authors also feel, that there has been inadequate development of art experience in the elementary schools. For this reason, one chapter is devoted to a discussion of esthetics in the schools.

12

CURRICULUM STRUCTURE

*I*T IS POSSIBLE to study curriculum organization at five levels. These are:

(1) The written official state, county, or city curriculums.
(2) The resource units or resource materials and experiences that are drawn upon.
(3) The experiences planned by the pupils and the teachers.
(4) The experiences as they work out in the classroom.
(5) The curriculum, as it influences each individual child.

Let us define briefly these five curriculum levels, why they were planned, and what they purport to do. Only a few suggestive illustrations will be used to identify the five levels since the concepts are not difficult to grasp. *The official state, county, or city curriculums* seek to insure that objectives important to society are achieved through the schools, particularly objectives having to do with the American traditions and the preservation of our democratic way of life: the signalizing of patriotic holidays and events, the display of the flag, the pledge of allegiance, and knowledge of the Constitution and of American history. They tend to prescribe subject matter that is of state and local concern, and that might not appear in books prepared for sale all over the country. For example, state and local heroes, history, and social and civic problems are stressed.

The resource units tend to set the bounds or expand the limits within which the teacher may feel free to select curriculum materials, activities and experiences, objectives, and subject matter.

They are meant to insure a broad, creative experience for teachers and children.

The curriculum as it is planned by teachers and pupils seeks to take into account the interests, motives and individual differences of all the children. It seeks to promote good mental health, emphasize democratic procedures, develop individual and group abilities, meet the real needs and interests of children, and broaden the contacts of children with the world around them.

The curriculum as it works out from day to day adds to the other levels all the resources that the school can draw upon—library, laboratory, shop, gymnasium, playground, home, church, camp, and community (this last is immensely broad and rich in its resources). Through the use of these resources it tries to provide the children with effective learning experiences. The day-to-day curriculum is helped or hampered by the customs and mores that characterize the particular culture in which it operates, by the personalities of the teachers, supervisors, and other school personnel, and by the children themselves who are in various stages of social adjustment.

The fifth level, *the curriculum as it influences each individual child,* is the one that is of most importance for us, and the one that we must keep in mind as we plan, write about, or study any of the others. This is true because it is on this level and through this curriculum that all other levels of curriculum effort become effective. What are the characteristics of this curriculum that are bound up with each individual child? It is to answer that question that this whole book has been written.

We have defined the curriculum as the sum of the educational experiences that children have in school. This is a broad definition. The experiences that the child has in school may "educate" him in undesirable as well as in desirable directions. For example, a child may learn in school to dislike arithmetic or literature, or he may learn to enjoy and appreciate both of them. It is necessary to remember that education in a broad sense may be either good or bad. If bad, it may be consciously bad—planned to be bad. Witness the indoctrination in schools in Fascist and Communist countries. On the other hand, unfortunate results may derive from a curriculum that is meant to be the best in the world; thus the first problem in achieving a desirable curriculum is to determine satisfactory objectives, and the second problem is to be alert constantly to see that the means selected are used so as to contribute to the objectives we are seeking.

The need and basis for clear objectives

It follows, then, that we must plan if the objectives of the schools are to be achieved. These plans have been variously called events, experiences, content, activities, contracts, projects, assignments, or subject matter. Each of these words has at various times held special connotations for those who worked with curriculums. They are joined together here to indicate the universally admitted idea that it is the function of the school to provide some sort of learning situations in the school program. These learning situations are expected to have a good effect on children and ultimately on all society. What follows is an effort on our part to determine what is or is not "good" education.

The nature and quality of the real curriculum of a school system is determined very largely by the ideals and values held by the teachers and other staff members, by the pupils and their parents, and by the community. The educational goals of the teachers, the pupils, the parents, and the community are all interrelated; they influence each other and determine the quality of the educational system. A school cannot be much better or much poorer than the aspirations of those concerned with it.

Much attention has been given to the formulation of educational objectives that should guide the schools. For example, most curriculum guides developed for use by state and city school systems begin with rather comprehensive lists of educational objectives. The value of such lists is frequently questioned. Unless they become more than pious hopes and perfunctory gestures, their fomulation and publication are a waste of time. However, the time given to the setting up of objectives is well spent if it leads to deep insights into the nature of education and a clear conception of the place of education in the promotion of human welfare and happiness. To be worth while, a statement of objectives should make itself evident in changes in teaching procedures, in supervisory and administrative policies, and ultimately in the ideals, values, skills, and behavior of the people of the community.

Outlines of the characteristics of man and of the universe in which he lives may serve as a frame of reference for a discussion of educational goals. They suggest some of the factors that must be considered in setting up adequate objectives for the schools, and provide a frame of reference for a discussion of educational goals that contribute to the realization of the fundamental needs of human life.

The Characteristics of Man

(Characteristics)	(Implications for Elementary Education)
1. High intelligence a. High capacity to learn, to profit from experience, to do abstract thinking, to adapt to new situations. Plasticity and modifiability b. A social being whose goals are: 　1. Social approval and status 　2. Intimate response 　3. Security 　4. New experiences	1. Man's highest aspirations depend upon the exercise of his intelligence in the solution of problems in the realms of family life, health, economic production, government, education, philosophy, art, science, and recreation. That man is intelligent and that intelligence must be free is the fundamental assumption of democracy. Freedom of thought, conscience, speech, the press, assembly, etc., follow from the free exercise of intelligence.
2. Organic needs A limited range of food, drink, air and temperature requirements. Rest and action Sex Tender body, highly sensitive to pain	2. The bases of the human needs for food, drink, clothing, shelter, fuel, heat, light, power, etc., are organic.
3. Articulate speech	3. Articulate speech is the basis for communication, for the accumulation, transmission, and symbolic manipulation of the social heritage.
4. Human hand—opposable thumb	4. Man is a tool-using and instrument-manipulating animal. Manual skills are as characteristically human as intellectual skills. Man is a working animal.
5. Upright posture	5. Man is a forward- and upward-looking animal with forearms free

The Characteristics of Man (Continued)

(Characteristics)	(Implications for Elementary Education)
	to handle tools, to manipulate objects, and to gesture.
6. Long period of maturation, infancy, and dependency	6. The long period of childhood is one of the main biological bases of the family, a basic social institution from which all others have evolved.
7. Wide range of individual and trait differences	7. The irreducible variation within grades or classrooms makes a broad flexible curriculum essential. The elimination of single or limited standards and the substitution of a multiplicity of personal and vocational goals is necessary.
8. Racial groups, based on biological differences in color, hair texture, etc.	8. Intercultural relations and problems must be understood.
9. Emotions and mechanisms of adjustment to self, society, and the culture	9. The dynamics of human behavior as a means of attaining a sound emotional and social adjustment must be understood.

The Characteristics of the Universe

(Characteristics)	(Implications for Elementary Education)
1. The solar system, the planets, the stars, and galaxies	1. Children may be introduced to the interfunctional relationship of the universe and solar system, to the sun's role in the solar system, to the science of astronomy, to some of the fundamental physical laws, to the earth's role in the solar system.
2. Geological processes	2. Children will see the active forces in geological processes and the changes that have taken place as a result of these processes.
3. Matter and energy	3. Some elementary-school children will understand some of the simple

The Characteristics of the Universe (Continued)

(Characteristics)	(Implications for Elementary Education)
	physiochemical relationships. The concept of the indestructibility of energy will be of interest to some, as will be the idea of elements as "the building blocks" of physical reality, and the concept of atomic structure. Simple items include the energy of coal, steam, etc.
4. Fundamental chemical processes	4. The interaction of the elements and the role of interaction in geological and biological change can be introduced to those who are interested.
5. The nature of life	5. The fundamental cellular structure, protoplasm, can be identified and the differences between the organic and the inorganic can be pointed out.
6. Bacteria	6. Some of the functions of single-celled organisms—in other forms and levels of "life" and growth and in deterioration processes—can be learned.
7. The plant kingdom	7. Plant matter is essential to all organic life.
8. Plants and their environment	8. Again, the inter-dependent relationships of the organic and inorganic can be illustrated.
9. The animal kingdom	9. Children can be introduced to the zoological sciences.
10. Man	10. The concept of the progress of civilization and the implications of man's capacity for thought or reasoning can be pointed out. Children will understand that man has an individual and a social nature.
11. The dynamics of living proc-	11. Children are interested in the

The Characteristics of the Universe (Continued)

(Characteristics)	(Implications for Elementary Education)
esses including human physiology and hygiene	normal, efficient maintenance of man's mental and physical endowments, in health vs. disease, in the normal vs. the abnormal, and in adaptation to change.

If man were to live in his physical environment without various forms of social organization, it is doubtful that he could survive even in primitive fashion. If his social organizations remained fairly informal, his society would probably be classified as some form of anarchy. The fact is that man has shown a great deal of ingenuity in creating and using social institutions for his purposes. Certain basic social institutions exist in some form in every culture to satisfy man's needs. The particular form these institutions take in a given culture and the specific needs that they fulfill are modified by man's cultural history, cultural contacts, natural resources, inventions, discoveries, and biological characteristics. The vital goals of education may be organized around these institutions. In the more or less detailed study of these institutions, all the things that children (or adults for that matter) need to learn may be learned. To round out the two preceding outlines that showed the characteristics of man and the characteristics of his environment, a third outline on man's social heritage is given below.

The Social Heritage of Man

(Basic Social Institutions and Their Functions)	(Some Suggested Educational Goals)
1. *The Family* with its kindred customs such as marriage and those of the home serves to propagate the race, furnish protection and care of young and aged, provide for intimate social and sex relations, and for early childhood education.	1. Knowledge, skills, attitudes, and abilities essential to happy family life, hereditary strength, courtesy, cooperation.
2. *The Economic System* with its vocations, professions, trades, indus-	2. Efficiency in production and consumption of goods and services,

The Social Heritage of Man (Continued)

(Basic Social Institutions and Their
Functions)

try, commerce, and insurance serves
to sustain life and insure comfort
by furnishing food, clothing, shelter, transportation, communication,
tools, utensils, weapons, and luxuries.

(Some Suggested Educational Goals)
finding a suitable occupation, economic security.

3. *The Democratic State* in its various governmental, political, and ju-
dicial forms provides for property
control, welfare, health and police
protection, etc., and serves to protect life and property against the
enemies and exploiters of the
group, both external and internal,
and to insure life, liberty, and the
pursuit of happiness.

3. Fulfilling the duties of a citizen
of a democracy in peace and in war.
Understanding social justice and
tolerance.

4. *The Schools* and related institutions such as libraries, institutes,
etc., transmit and further develop
the cultural heritage by organizing,
refining, selecting, graduating, and
enhancing the culture for transmission to each succeeding generation.
Through mathematics and science
the schools furnish a language of
precision for quantitative thinking.
They refine, check, and order the
products of intelligence.

4. Understanding and appreciating
the social and scientific role of the
school. Acquiring the ability to live
purposefully and dynamically in a
democratic world. Learning to
think quantitatively and scientifically. Learning to do accurate quantitative thinking. Understanding
the physical and social environment
and the scientific method as a technique for problem solving.

5. *Philosophy and Religion* with
their spiritual values, standards,
and mores give motive, purpose,
and understanding to life and system to the universe.

5. Acquiring a sustaining philosophy of life and criteria of values.

6. *Language* through reading, writing, vocabulary, spelling, and all of
its other manifestations, serves to
transmit, communicate, and preserve the culture. It is a fundamental cultural tool.

6. Communicating effectively.

7. *Public Opinion and Information*

7. Distinguishing between fact and

The Social Heritage of Man (Continued)

(Basic Social Institutions and Their Functions)	(Some Suggested Educational Goals)
through newspapers, journals, radio, and public forums promote and direct civic and cultural progress.	opinion and separating issues and news from propaganda.
8. *The Arts* through painting, literature, drawing, sculpture, music, architecture, drama, and humor, serve to control and direct the emotional, to communicate, and to inspire.	8. Learning to appreciate the place of art in everyday living. Learning to be creative.
9. *Medicine* with its hospitals, its clinics, and its preventive measures promotes both physical and mental health.	9. Keeping physically fit, insuring community health and safety.
10. *Recreation* serves to give diversification to life.	10. Living a more complete life through recreation.
11. *Philanthropy* as seen in the Community Chest, the Red Cross, etc., promotes human welfare in distress areas not served by other institutions.	11. Practicing the ethics of sacrificing for the welfare of others.

Objectives are based on philosophy and science

A consideration of the above characteristics provides a good basis for a discussion of the objectives of the schools through which man seeks to perpetuate and improve his culture and insure the welfare of future generations.

The educational philosophy of the authors is summarized in the statement that education should serve welfare. This is, of course, the kind of a statement that, taken alone can mean everything or nothing. It must be interpreted in terms of the background provided throughout this book. Human welfare has been taken to consist of the welfare of individuals. The nature of individual differences has been stressed. Human welfare depends upon the successful and efficient learning of many things. We have emphasized the research bearing on the nature of intellectual and social learning, and, with reference to basic sciences, the psychobiological nature of man. Motives, as they spring from organic and social needs, have broad implications for human welfare, as have the techniques by which we measure the extent and effectiveness of learning. We have shown that man lives in groups in his society, in urban and rural communities, and that his society has definite structural characteristics. Man lives in a culture marked by certain customs and mores, and as an individual in a society he develops a personality. Though it has been mentioned at many points, we will emphasize again in succeeding chapters the peculiar problems that man faces in reacting to and controlling his environment in order to insure his welfare. We reject altogether the idea that there is any collection of facts in social science, natural science, art, or even in the basic skills or tool subjects that can be itemized and prepared for injection into all students on a graded, standardized basis. We reject, too, the idea that existing research in all the fields available to educators is complete and that we are now able to chart the course for each individual child and for all society with the sure hand of either a confirmed essentialist or reconstructionist. The ideas regarding curriculum content that we have given are not bits of subject matter intended to be pre-digested by teachers and later spoon-fed to students. Rather, we have made an effort to collect in one place some significant illustrations of the most influential ideas uncovered by artists, social scientists, and natural scientists, and to suggest some of the educational theories the teacher may apply using many of the subtle and abstract arguments from these fields. Our purpose is to stimulate ideas and generalizations that will help teachers to enrich their teaching. These ideas and generalizations are foundation stones for a curriculum; they are the basis upon which to build the child's elementary-school experiences.

Throughout, we have stressed the twin ideas of interrelatedness and interdependence. The interdependence of man upon man, and of man upon his environment is in constant evidence. Interrelatedness is also becoming more clearly understood. For example, we have seen that you cannot regard a child from the psychological standpoint without also considering the biological, the social, the anthropological, and others. All the natural sciences are interrelated, too, as witness some of their joint names: physical chemistry, biostatics, biochemistry, and astrophysics.

The child will not necessarily sense this interdependence and interrelatedness; it is the teacher's responsibility to make him aware of them.

In their more theoretical books, progressive educators warn us against "atomistic" thinking that separates children into such components as mind, emotion, and physique, and oppose mechanical teaching, which takes subject matter out of its functional setting. This line of thinking, with its reference to "wholes"—including social wholes or class groups—is part of a broad cultural movement that was started first in physics and was furthered in biology and in sociology, and last, in psychology. This movement led to the formulation of the phrase "common learnings" on the elementary level, "core curriculum" on the secondary level, "general education" on the college level, and "the unity of science movement" or "interdisciplinary research" (work carried on jointly by anthropologists, sociologists, psychologists, and economists) at the graduate-school level. There is much current research that will contribute further to our knowledge of children and their environment if we can come to understand this move away from the "atomism" of the nineteenth century.

A suggested statement of objectives

Implicit in the two ideas of interdependence and interrelatedness is the assumption that the promotion of human welfare is the concern and responsibility of everyone. With this premise in mind, we may be able to agree on more detailed but still very general objectives of education.

Objectives of General Education [1]

1. To understand other persons' ideas correctly by reading and listening, and, in turn, to express ideas effectively to others.

2. To understand the dynamics of human behavior as a means of attaining a sound emotional and social adjustment.

3. To improve and maintain personal and community health.

4. To enjoy a wide range of social relationships and to work cooperatively with others in common enterprises.

[1] The first six objectives and 8, 10, 11, 12, and 13 are taken with slight adaptation from T. R. McConnell, "Liberal Education After the War," *The Annals of the American Academy of Political and Social Science,* Vol. 231, January 1944, 86.

5. To acquire the knowledge, attitudes, action patterns, and values that are necessary for a satisfying family, social, civic, and vocational life.

6. To take an active, intelligent, and responsible part in the affairs of the community, state, nation and world.

7. To become acquainted with the principles of the natural environment, and of physical and biological phenomena.

8. To understand the application of scientific facts and principles to human affairs; to understand and appreciate scientific method and attitude, and to use them in the solution of a wide range of personal, social, and scientific problems.

9. To understand and enjoy the natural environment.

10. To understand and to enjoy literature, art, and music as an expression of human experience in the past and in the student's own time; also, if possible, to participate in some form of creative literary, artistic, or musical activity.

11. To recognize the values implicit in conduct and in concrete social issues, to examine these values critically, and to develop a coherent set of principles for the evaluation and direction of personal and social behavior.

12. To think critically and constructively in dealing with a wide range of intellectual and practical problems.

13. To choose a vocation that will enable one to utilize his particular interests and abilities to the fullest and to make his work socially useful.

14. To enjoy and participate in games, sports, and other recreational activities suitable to one's level of development and aptitudes.

15. To develop motor control essential to graceful coordination of bodily movements and to adequate skill in handling and using the common tools and implements.

If we have a fairly definite idea of what our educational objectives are, we can discriminate in, and increase our knowledge of, the selection of procedures that may be used in their attainment.

Necessary as they are, there are many dangers involved in using sets of stated objectives. One is that we use them merely to rationalize or justify what we are already doing, regardless of its fundamental appropriateness. A second is that we assume that the child, without assistance from us, can see the worth of the objectives we have selected. A third is that we think all children can progress equally toward our objectives. A fourth is that we assume all adults or all school systems must agree on the objectives we find valid. A fifth is that we do not relate our objectives to our methods and procedures. A sixth is that we cease to examine and refine the meanings and insights that are involved in our objectives and that, as a consequence, our objectives serve to crystallize our aims and ideals far short of their potentialities.

One further danger in using lists of objectives lies in the temptation to multiply them indefinitely until they are broken down into hundreds of atomized items. The teacher who attempts to see the objectives of the school in such a list is hard put to bring sufficient interrelatedness into them to make them interesting or meaningful. It cannot be emphasized too often that the "organization" of learning is of paramount importance.

Statements of objectives must be used in a scholarly way if they are to serve their purposes.

Four types of curriculum

Chapter 1 dealt briefly with the historical background of the elementary schools, particularly in reference to the development of the curriculum. We saw that at the turn of the century, and for some time thereafter, the typical elementary-school curriculum was composed of subjects all of which were taught separately. Even today this type of curriculum organization is found in many elementary schools, though in recent years the trend has been away from it. As curriculum theory has advanced, different types of curriculum organization have made their appearance. Though they are classified and described variously by different writers, it may be convenient to classify them according to four categories.

Separate-subjects curriculum. In a separate-subjects curriculum, arithmetic, geography, history, spelling, writing, and all other subjects are taken up in separate periods of the school day. The children study arithmetic, for example, in a group. As the weeks pass, they progress from the simple to the more complex processes, learning to solve problems that grow progressively more difficult. Many of the brighter children are not adequately challenged by the work and many of the slower children become hopelessly confused as they fall behind, for the work in such a curriculum is generally geared to those whose abilities, in this case arithmetical, are about average. The problems that the children work with are artificial and have little functional relationship to the other subjects. Spelling words are selected by someone who thinks that he has organized them in terms of their increasing difficulty or of the child's need for them. Geography is taught separately from history; frequently the historical illustrations necessary to understand geography, and the geographical background necessary to understand history, are so much out of relationship to one another that the intrinsic "oneness" of the two subjects is never understood by the children. Where such curricu'.ıms are in use, one frequently hears the complaint by teachers that other teachers are to be criticized for failing to insist on good grammar during the geography or the history period or to require good composition in papers on history or in science. In such a curriculum, children may run across geographical discussions of relative humidity or percentage figures relating to population or agricultural production before they have been introduced to such concepts in their science and mathematics. They may be studying about children of Holland or Japan in their geography while their history is dealing with colonial life. Educators have tried desperately, but have not been able, *in the separate-subjects curriculum,* to overcome the barriers in the way of caring for individual and trait differences while integrating learning so that all that is learned may be brought to bear in a meaningful way in thinking and in problem-solving.

Correlated curriculum. In an effort to overcome the confusion, inefficiency, and unwieldiness of the separate-subjects curriculum, some educators, early in the nineteen hundreds, developed the idea of a correlated curriculum. Immediately a lively debate arose in educational circles over the merits of the new system. Essentially, the thought behind the new theory was that the various subjects in the curriculum should be related and organized so that one reinforced and complemented the other. Advocates of correlation attempted to defer the use of arithmetical concepts in other subjects until such time as those concepts had been adequately covered in the arithmetic courses, and to teach the geography of a region at the same time that the history of that region was studied.

One of the most fruitful attempts at a "correlated curriculum" arose from choosing one of the main subjects as a *core* subject. This core subject was generally broadened somewhat and the subject-matter organization of the other subjects was made to fit as much as possible into its scope and sequence. This was not insurmountably difficult in *some* of the social science subjects, but it presented special difficulties in the natural sciences, in mathematics, and in special subjects such as art, music, literature, and the like. This was particularly true because the content of many of these subjects had become "frozen" into special forms. For example, certain poems and passages "had" to be read and learned; no others could be substituted for them. Some subjects had certain prerequisites that were traditional in nature, but neither logical nor scientific in their basis.

Broad-fields curriculum. The tendency in the correlated curriculum to depend upon a core subject finally led to a third form of curriculum organization generally known as the broad-fields curriculum. In this form of curriculum organization, several cores of "broad fields" are chosen. Within each one, because of the similarity of the subject matter, a great deal of correlation is possible. One of the broad fields sometimes selected is language arts, or communication. It includes reading, writing, spelling, grammar, punctuation, oral speech, and listening. Social studies is another, and includes history, geography, civics, the American way of life, the Constitution, and so forth. Other broad fields are health and physical education, the arts, and arithmetic-science. Under the broad-fields curriculum, the number of periods during the school day was greatly reduced and the opportunities for sustained activity, motivation, and more meaningful learning were greatly increased.

Developmental-activity curriculum. The fourth type of curriculum organization may well be called the "developmental-activity" curriculum. This plan seeks to provide learning experiences for children in terms of the youngsters' biological, intellectual, and social growth. The separate-subject curriculum, the correlated curriculum, and the broad-fields curriculum are dependent for their organization, essentially, upon a consideration of subject matter, of content-set-out-to-be-learned. The developmental-activity curriculum on the other hand depends for its organization upon the various stages of development through which the young learner passes, upon the range of individual and trait differences that must be taken into account for effective learning, upon the needs of children as we understand them today, and upon the problems facing the learners in their culture and their community—their area of experience.

Curriculum types overlap in practice

In actual practice, however, these four types of curriculums cannot be rigidly separated. They merge into and overlap each other. Teachers, for example, were able to relate the various subjects in the separate-subject curriculum to one another in various ways and the more capable teachers did so. Strong teachers frequently dared to violate the rigid prescriptions of the curriculum outline and the time schedule in bringing about more effective learning situations. In the actual classrooms, it is frequently difficult to classify a curriculum as a broad-fields curriculum rather than as a developmental-activity curriculum because so many of the characteristic elements of both may be present and overlapping. Finally, it seems necessary to admit that the developmental-activity curriculum must itself compromise at many points with one of the various other types of curriculum organization that places primary emphasis upon subject matter.

In general, it may be said that the developmental-activity curriculum is better than any of the others. It seems to the authors to incorporate more completely than the other three types the best curriculum information now available. It should not be inferred from this, however, that recourse to this type of curriculum will solve all the teacher's problems.

The authors recommend that the school day be divided roughly and flexibly into two approximately equal parts. Half of the day may be devoted to developmental activities and half to specific practice on essential learnings. As much as possible, this practice, drill, and study should grow out of, and be motivated by, the developmental activities of the children. There will be occasions, however, when it will be necessary that certain things be learned regardless of whether or not their need has become obvious in the experiences of the units as they develop. It will be necessary that these be taught according to the principles of learning as we know them. They must be related to what children already know. They must be introduced in terms of the individual differences of children. There may come a time when teachers will develop sufficient skill so that all these learnings will emerge from the developmental-activity curriculum. The breadth of the learning involved in the elementary curriculum and the extensive nature of the criteria by which curriculum content may be determined are indicated in the next section.

Many writers who have dealt with curriculum problems have emphasized the complexity and the highly professional nature of teaching. Children's problems are always complex; they occur in different situations and in new combinations. They are never surely solved but reappear in different forms and phases.

Criteria of content

In discussing the content of the curriculum, many writers spend page after page setting up rules, standards, and principles for the selection either of subject matter or of activities and experiences. No matter how they are phrased, most of them may be summarized under headings that are an outgrowth of the scientific effort to determine textbook and curriculum content. There are seven chief criteria:

Frequency of use. This criterion should be stated thus: Those knowledges, skills, attitudes, and abilities most useful in life are to be given primary emphasis. The over-all selection, the determination of what should be taught, can be based largely on *adult* use. The *time* (developmental level) at which they should be taught can be determined on the basis of the ability of children to learn the knowledge, skills, abilities, and so forth, required in various stages of their development. Since 1920 much research has been done on determining such things as which words are most frequently used, or most often misspelled. The pioneers in the field of determining basic reading vocabulary were E. L. Thorndike, Irving Lorge, and Ernest Horn. G. M. Wilson undertook a similar study in the field of arithmetic. The point of all this to us is that textbooks are based on much sound research.

Quality. Quality assumes that the knowledge, skills, attitudes, and abilities that are useful to people "of status and quality" in our culture should be given more emphasis than those common to people lower in the socio-economic scale. This may sound very undemocratic, but a little thought shows that it is absolutely necessary if the criterion of frequency is not to lead us to absurdity. For example, suppose that a school were in the process of deciding upon a marking system. Employing the criterion of frequency, the Principal might send out a questionnaire to comparable schools and ask the faculties of those schools to indicate the type of marking system used there. If one type of marking system proved more popular than any other, if it received a majority of votes, that one would be accepted. But such a decision would be foolish and illogical. Before any conclusions are arrived at, one should know the basis for the choices made in the other systems. The verdict of a school or faculty that had done research into the part a marking system plays in the total instructional program would be of greater value than a choice not buttressed by such data. Finally, greater weight should be given to what has been done in schools with a good reputation.

This means that all selection should be guided by research rather than by popularity. Of course, many problems immediately become apparent. It is difficult to reconcile the criterion of quality with a child's readiness to learn. For example, in reading it is essential that children begin at the level, and with the vocabulary, they can understand. Even within the range of the most limited vocabulary, however, there is some "quality" literature; and each year there is an increase in the production of good, simply-written children's literature.

Cruciality. This criterion propounds the belief that the knowledge, skills, attitudes, and abilities that are useful in crucial situations should be emphasized *even though their frequency of use is low.* Artificial respiration is one that comes to mind immediately. It is taught because it is crucial when needed, not because it is frequently used. You do not purchase life insurance very often, but it is most important that you buy the right policy for your needs.

Universality in time, place, and use. Application of this difficult criterion calls for unusual intelligence. It assumes that the knowledge, skills, attitudes, and abilities that have been useful to a social group over a long period of time have greater value than those that have only recently become useful. Knowledge, skills, attitudes, and abilities useful over a wide geographic area (in addition to being useful over a long period of time) are of greater value than those that have a limited geographic application. For example, vocabulary lists made up of children's spoken language at the four-or five-year level are frequently drawn from limited geographic areas. (There is considerable difference between the vocabularies of rural and urban children.) These are not suitable for inclusion in a reader that is intended to be widely used in all parts of the country. In the same way, knowledge, skills, attitudes, and abilities are important if used in a wide variety of occupations or in a great many situations. The use of tools is an example. The hammer, perhaps, has more uses than a level or a square. Another illustration could be chosen from the study of elementary-school science. The principle that the higher the temperature of the air, the greater the amount of moisture it will absorb has a host of applications involving man's welfare, and many of them will be pointed out later, in Chapter 15.

Decreasing returns. This rule assumes that in any area of learning there are principles, facts, usages, and understandings that are of the greatest value and that there are others of less value. We are concerned with educational efficiency. We ask about ways to save time in teaching arithmetic in the fourth grade, for example. Too often a decision is made without using the criterion of decreasing returns.

Imagine a superintendent of schools in Midtown who wishes to advise the Midtown teachers on the length of the arithmetic period in the fourth grade. J. M. Rice studied such problems at the turn of the century. Mr. Rice, editor of *Forum* at that time, had come to the conclusion that American schools were spending entirely too much time in teaching the three R's, and that there was too little attention given to the subject matter of social science, geography, history, and hygiene. Spelling skill was the first object of his curiosity. Rice wished to know how much time was being devoted to spelling [2] and, more important, to determine the amount of time that might most profitably be allotted to spelling. Rice discovered that some cities in the United States at that time did not devote any time to spelling, while others allotted more than an hour a day to it. He prepared a spelling test and tested thousands of pupils in schools that devoted an hour, 45 minutes, half an hour, 15 minutes, and no time at all, daily, to the formal teaching of spelling. When he compared the test results of the several cities, there was not as much difference in the scores as one might think. It was quite disconcerting to see how ineffective the instruction in spelling really

2 Joseph M. Rice, *The Public-School System of the United States.* New York: The Century Company, 1893, pp. 42, 70-73, 84-87, 115-116.

was. Rice's findings and those of other investigators are the basis even today for the general principle that the teaching of spelling for a period of 15 minutes daily, if done efficiently, is sufficient.

It is only fair to point out that the modern teaching of spelling is much different from the formal instruction of Rice's day. Rice's study is mentioned here only as a neat illustration of the criterion of diminishing returns.

Difficulty. This criterion assumes that valuable knowledge, skills, attitudes, and abilities that are so difficult that they would not be learned outside of school should be given emphasis in school.

Educational shortages. This criterion assumes that needed knowledge, skills, attitudes, and abilities that are found lacking in the general population should be emphasized in the school. The other criteria would help you to decide which of these learnings, abilities, attitudes, and skills you valued.

This concern with criteria may strike many as being old-fashioned. It is. However, no logician would wish you to jump to the conclusion that the old-fashioned is necessarily useless. Old-fashioned or not, research into the usability of materials is important. It is true that many of the early inquiries were overly "mechanistic," and it is dangerous to classify a list of "minimum essentials" with the idea of cramming them down the throats of students. Unhappily, that is the manner in which these sound criteria have been abused. This mistake has done as much as anything else to give rise to the criticisms of elementary schools. When we speak of the abuse of the criteria for selecting material, one of the abuses we have in mind is the belief that students should have no part in this selection. They should, of course.

These criteria have grown out of the attempt by Herbert Spencer in 1859 to determine what knowledge was of most worth. He asked his question because he was disturbed by what impressed him as the careless, thoughtless manner in which subject matter and courses drifted into and out of use. He looked for criteria for determining the essentials. His desire is related to our criteria; his criteria were not. They sprang from a consideration of adult activities and were not based on research. The seven criteria given here are based on research and are capable of being tempered (and must always be tempered) by a consideration of the child's stage of development.

. In the next chapter we will consider the curriculum from the standpoint of the units that make it up.

Discussion Questions

1. Is there any value in distinguishing among the five levels of curriculum organization? What is this value, if any?
2. Should the curriculum be defined in a more limited and specific way than the authors do it? Try your hand at such a definition or defend the one used here.
3. Can you think of any human characteristics that are missed or slighted in the outline? Would you wish to write the authors about any oversights?
4. What, if any, basic social institutions are ignored or slighted in the outline of the social heritage of man? What is included that might be dropped?
5. Does human welfare mean something to you that it does not apparently mean to the authors?
6. Do the objectives follow logically from the philosophy outlined by the authors, including the three outlines?
7. Would you add other objectives? Would you drop any?
8. Would you favor one of the first three types of curriculum rather than the developmental-activity curriculum favored by the authors?
9. Do you believe that the compromise the authors make in recommending one-half day for activities and units and one-half day for specific practice in essential learning is a point of weakness? How would you resolve it?
10. What do you think of the outline of the broad basis of the modern curriculum? Is it too broad in presentation? Is it not broad enough?
11. Are the criteria for content old-fashioned? Are they useful in selecting what should be included in a modern curriculum?
12. Which of these criteria seem most useful?

Selected References

Adams, Fay, *Educating America's Children.* New York: The Ronald Press Company, 1946.

Benjamin, Harold, *Saber-Tooth Curriculum,* including other lectures in the history of paleolithic education. New York: McGraw-Hill Book Company, Inc., 1939.

Caswell, Hollis Leland, *Education in the Elementary School,* 2nd ed. New York: American Book Company, 1950.

————, *et al., Curriculum Improvement in Public School System.* New York: Teachers College, Columbia University, 1950.

Havighurst, Robert James, *Developmental Tasks and Education.* Chicago: University of Chicago Press, 1948.

Lee, Johnathan Murray and Dorris May Lee, *The Child and His Curriculum,* 2nd ed. New York: Appleton-Century-Crofts, 1950.

Macomber, Freeman Glenn, *Guiding Child Development in the Elementary School.* New York: American Book Company, 1948.

Meyer, Adolph Erich, *The Development of Education in the Twentieth Century,* 2nd ed. New York: Prentice-Hall, Inc., 1949.

Stratemeyer, Florence Barbara, *et al., Developing a Curriculum for Modern Living.* New York: Teachers College, Columbia University, 1947.

13

THE USE OF UNITS

$\mathcal{I}$N THE PRECEDING CHAPTER, we outlined and described four types of curriculum. For our purposes in discussing the nature and use of units in the classroom, these four can be considered under two headings: (1) subject-matter curriculums, including separate-subject, correlated, and broad-field curriculums, and (2) developmental-activity curriculums.

When units are used with the subject-matter curriculums, they are generally called subject-matter units, and within limits are easy to identify. Developmental-activity curriculums are generally implemented by what we call "experience units" when we observe them in the classrooms, and "resource units" when they are prepared in written form for teachers' use.

Subject-matter units. Subject-matter curriculums are no longer widely defended among school people. There are but few strictly subject-matter curriculums being written today, but many are prepared in the subject-matter tradition. They are organized in sub-ject-matter "units" instead of logically organized outlines. The idea of organizing subject matter into units came about primarily as the result of early experimentation into the nature of human learning. When educators discovered that isolated facts were hard to remember and that isolated skills were hard to retain, they began to emphasize "relatedness." To some extent, they substituted a *psychological* for a *logical* organization of the things to be learned, but they retained the stress on facts and skills. In some cases, textbooks and curriculums were quite thoroughly revised in an attempt to organize subject-matter outlines into unit outlines. In many cases, however, the same outlines were used as had been used previously, with the subdivisions in the old outlines and with the chapter headings in the old textbooks now being labeled as "units." As this change came about it was rather common, for example, to see textbooks in elementary history organized around subject-matter units in such areas as "Discovery and Exploration," "Colonization," "The Period of the Revolution," "Westward Expansion," "The Old South," and so forth. An examination of such a textbook might reveal that the content within the various units had been changed but little if any from a previous edition in which the author had outlined the history in what was largely its logical or chronological sequence.

Subject-matter units are of various kinds. During the days when they were more popular and when they represented a really constructive departure from what had gone before, they were sometimes characterized as falling into four types: (1) topical units, (2) generalization units, (3) survey units, and (4) problem units. In a topical unit the subject matter concerned itself with a theme such as the French and Indian Wars or the fishing industry in New England. A generalization unit pointed up various conclusions such as, "Where the forests are destroyed, floods sweep the lower drainage basins," or, more narrow in scope, "To pluralize words ending in 'y', change the 'y' to 'i' and add 'es'." A survey unit covered a subject such as the cultural resources or the recreational resources of a community. Problem units dealt with such subjects as, "Why did Slavery Flourish in the South more than in the North?" or "How did the Rivers of North America help the Explorers and the Settlers?"

Experience units. An experience unit is a cluster of educative experiences, organized through pupil-teacher planning, placed within the functioning framework of the developing child in his social and physical environment in terms of the needs and purposes of the child and his society, and utilizing, to as great a degree as possible, the useful resources of the material and cultural environment, to the end that the democratically determined purposes of the schools may be achieved.

The phrase "cluster of educative experiences" stresses that the unit hangs together because of the psychological relationships that exist in the various learning activities involved in it. This follows from the factors in meaningful human learning that were emphasized in Chapter 9, and from the material on the psychobiological nature of man in Chapter 4. The phrase "organized by pupil-teacher planning" places emphasis on the great range in individual and trait differences. When pupils participate in the planning, then it is possible to assess the educational tasks in terms of the children's abilities, needs, interests, and motives. The development of a child's ability to participate in group enterprises, both as leader and as follower, is also emphasized. These factors were emphasized in Chapters 2, 5, and 9.

The term "pupil-teacher planning" does not belittle at all the paramount influence of the teacher in planning. The fact is, and this is shown clearly in Chapters 19 and 20, that children rely upon the teacher's judgment when a real teacher-pupil rapport is established on a democratic, cooperative basis.

When we define an experience unit as being placed in "the functioning framework of the developing child in his social and physical environment," we mean it to embrace the whole field of developmental psychology as the child grows and matures from infancy. The definition also includes the society of which the child is a part and the various socio-economic classes to which the child may belong and to which he may owe his loyalties and his patterns of action, and his physical surroundings—the climate, soil, water, air, and other factors—that have such great impact on living.

To insure that this is to be done "in terms of the needs and purposes of the child and of his society," we return again to the nature of the learner, to his basic needs, as outlined in Chapter 3, and to the society that needs mentally and physically healthy and effective individuals to insure its growth and development.

We conclude our definition with a phrase that returns us to the democracy in which our schools have their being, and from which our schools draw their meaning and purpose. We organize experience units (and curriculums and schools in general) "to the end that the democratically determined purposes of the schools may be achieved." In America, we believe that the public schools belong to the people. It is the citizens of our country, in the final analysis, who determine the purposes for which public education exists and the means that shall be used to achieve those purposes.

Subject-matter versus experience units. There is no desire on the part of the authors to "load" unfairly the definitions of subject-matter units and experience units. One springs from the conceptions underlying the subject-matter curriculums and one from the conceptions underlying the "developmental-activity" curriculums. In actual practice, good teachers of subject-matter units have always included many of the characteristics of experience units.

There is no doubt that many teachers follow well-developed courses of study organized into logically compact subject-matter areas. Such courses are often well implemented with supplies and equipment, including provision for activities and experiences and for wide reference on various ability levels. Though this falls short of the ideal, it is better than trying to develop "experience units" *without* understanding how it should be done and *without* some of the basic materials and supplies at hand. The authors are convinced that the crucial element in deciding which choice a teacher makes is the preparation, the ability, and the conviction of the teachers involved. The authors are also convinced that as teachers gain insight into the nature of young humans in their environment, and as they gain power in the use of techniques of instruction, broad experience units will be used whenever it is possible to do so. There is nothing to be gained by claiming to be a teacher of "experience units" unless this really means something in terms of the way the teacher understands children and the way he teaches.

The use of experience units is increasing. Those who gain their impressions of modern education from textbooks on curriculum and method, and from demonstration schools in some of the better teachers colleges, may have an idea that units are in almost universal use today. This feeling is partly the result of the attempts by some of the writers of textbooks for the elementary and secondary schools to revise their books into units rather than into chapters and parts. The term experience unit, as used in this book, has a meaning far different from that. The experience unit is what the children actually experience in the classroom.

Resource units. A resource unit is generally well developed and extensive in scope. It can be centered around many interesting ideas and generalizations. The main qualifications of a topic for a resource unit are (1) that it be in line with the real interests of the children for whom it is designed, (2) that it be concerned with ideas and generalizations that are of importance, and (3) that this importance be determined in terms of the broad aspects of human welfare. The typical resource unit states its purpose and objectives and suggests ways in which its use may be initiated, developed, and evaluated.

A resource unit should reveal to the teacher various ways in which he can take advantage of the principles of motivation and learning. The purposes and objectives of all units should be governed by the over-all objective of promoting human welfare. The teacher should encourage integration of subjects at least to the extent that the substance of education is not falsified by being pictured as a mere collection of geographical, historical, and physical facts.

The experience unit, to return to it for a moment, is the actual classroom procedure planned by the teacher and pupils who draw upon the background presented in the resource unit. There should be no compulsion in the classroom to attempt to duplicate or exhaust the material in the resource unit. In fact, many resource units are so voluminous as to make this impossible. The experience unit, as it develops, draws upon the suggested materials and procedures in the resource unit in terms of the interests and abilities that the children display.

Written resource units appear in a variety of forms. Most of them have a title that gives or suggests the general area or theme to be developed in the unit and most of them contain lists of general or specific aims and objectives or expected results. Many of them describe ways to start the unit, carry it on, and terminate it by a "culminating" program or by written or oral reports. Some few suggest evaluation techniques, by which to assess the success of the unit. Increasingly, written resource units are coming to contain long lists of materials, films, plays, places to visit, things to build, books to read, pamphlets to secure, letters to write, and other activities to conduct.

Resource units frequently are written for teachers by curriculum supervisors and consultants, but increasingly they are being prepared by committees of teachers who are freed from their regular responsibilities to prepare them. Often they are prepared in curriculum workshops. In any case, they almost always include much more material than can be covered by any one class or one teacher.

Frequently some of the suggestions do not fit certain communities. A resource unit is designed to suggest a wide range of activities, materials, teaching techniques, themes, motivational and interest-arousing situations, significant facts, and valuable skills from which teachers may gain assistance in selecting units and activities and giving them direction.

Choosing activities for units

The seven criteria governing curriculum content have already been referred to in Chapter 12. We will now consider some of the factors involved in selecting the activities that go to make up experience units.

In the selection of activities, pupils should always be allowed a large degree of free choice. This is not said with any intent to resolve the argument over whether or not the child would select the ideal curriculum activities by himself if he were presented with wide enough opportunities (under ideal emotional, social, and physical conditions, of course). We do not know whether he would or not. We do know that teachers can learn to see which choices children make and to use those choices whenever they are sound. We know that when the children and the teacher gain confidence and skill, the teacher's job seldom requires that he suggest or initiate activities. Rather, his responsibility is to select from among the activities that constantly pop up those that seem to promise the greatest educational return in terms of the objectives (long-term or immediate) that are held valid.

Let us see what occurred as a capable teacher went through the process of selecting an activity. In a free discussion period, two of the children had confessed that they did not like their "language" lesson, especially oral language. "Nobody don't talk that way, anyway," the little boy had said, and the little girl had added, "Teachers, they do."

At this point, many teachers would have stopped the discussion, fearful, perhaps, that further references to themselves either as people or as a profession might injure their status before the class. The teacher in question showed interest in the discussion and thus encouraged it to continue.

"Nobody wants to talk like a teacher."

"Mrs. Baker does. She ain't a teacher."

"Yeah, she yells all-a-time 'bout her old flowers."

Then a third voice joined in, "Teachers *have* to talk that way."

"What do some of the rest of you think?" the teacher asked.

The conversation was a fortuitous circumstance. They happen frequently. Teachers can hear only a few of them, but if sufficiently alert, they can hear enough to "season the potpourri" of each day's learning. As the children contributed various reactions of their own to their study of language, the teacher listened carefully to see how to use the discussion to answer the question that had been raised. The question, though it had not been so stated, was whether or not the study of correct usage was worth while. She thought she might direct the thinking of the children if she identified some of their generalizations more clearly for them. She wrote a few on the blackboard, pronouncing the words carefully as she wrote them.

(1) Nobody uses school language, anyway.
(2) Teachers have to talk that way.
(3) Boys don't talk the way girls do. (Suggested by, "It's all right for girls.")
(4) Negroes don't talk the way white people do.
(5) School language is used in books.

After this had gone on for some time, the teacher had a decision to make. Did the interest of the children and the importance of the subject (they are bound together and cannot be separated in the real situation) merit broad emphasis on the question or not? Were they as interested in this question as they were in others? If the teacher had decided to try to make major use of the new idea, she might have suggested that the children remember the statements on the board and ask their parents that evening what they thought about them.

We have already mentioned in another place the necessity for closer cooperation between parents and school. One obvious way to accomplish this is to enlist the aid of parents in projects such as this and treat their contributions with dignity and tact. Thus closer home-school rapport may be established and eventually a real relationship by which teacher and parents can work at solving the child's problems together, not at cross purposes.

The next day, after the parental suggestions had been studied, the teacher might have had the pupils interview the principal, the nurse, the local playground supervisor, the Sunday school teacher, their physician, the corner grocer, and others. Undoubtedly the children would have had many ideas themselves. They might have suggested studying how their various comic-strip characters talk. Or, if the teacher knew who their heroes were and what their budding interests and hobbies were, she could have led a discussion of the language used by the children's "heroes" or the style of the books dealing with the pupils' interests and hobbies. This teacher did know because she listened a great deal to the conversations of the children. She was able to slant her teaching in the direction of their interests, thus avoiding the necessity for nerve-wracking driving, endless talking, and scolding. She let the children waste too much time chattering, the old-fashioned third-grade teacher across the hall said.

In this case, the teacher decided not to make an expanded topic of the incident. The children were already busy on numerous units and activities. Instead, she asked, "How many know what baby talk is?" After this subject was discussed, the pupils discussed other kinds of talk. Again using the blackboard, they finally came up with the following list.

(1) Baby talk.   (4) School talk.
(2) Home talk.   (5) Work talk.
(3) Play talk.   (6) Office talk.

After some discussion, they decided that many kinds of talk have their place and that school talk is very important. The conclusions were not hard to work out. Most experienced teachers could do that. The skill comes in sensing that an incident or a remark springs from real need and real interest and that it should be heeded intelligently.

This short incident illustrates many of the vital elements of good procedure. Let us see what the important ones are.

(1) The children felt free enough to discuss "teachers" in the presence of the teacher. She *never* went back to the original statements of the little boy and girl who started the discussion nor did she force them to "admit" that "people do talk that way, not only teachers." To have done so, even at the very end, would have been

tragic in that the children in their embarrassment would have seen to it that she overheard no more of their real thoughts.

(2) The teacher noticed the reference to Mrs. Baker and her "old" flowers. Here was a real interest. Mrs. Baker lived in a corner lot across from the school and perhaps in their play the children had trampled Mrs. Baker's garden and had been reprimanded by the lady. Did the children feel a little guilt or only childish resentment? Was this an area where some early steps could be taken to build some of the ethical concepts related to property, trespass, beauty, and so forth. The teacher made a note of Mrs. Baker and ,her flowers to use later, if possible, not as something to preach about, but as a subject for the children to study and think about. A week later at a garden party where flowers were sold to help provide a camp for crippled children, the teacher found herself saying to Mrs. Baker, "From something I overheard, I guessed that perhaps some of our children have been into your flowers. The children are anxious to understand about flowers and to be good citizens, I wondered if sometime we couldn't plan some little. . . ." The teacher's textbooks had stressed the necessity for stimulating the community's interest in the schools. She was following the advice.

(3) The teacher taught reading as she wrote on the board, using simple words wherever she could. The children paid attention and read back what was written as they carried on the discussion.

(4) The teacher showed her pupils how to "generalize" and to test generalizations, an early lesson in scientific thinking, but she did not identify it for them just then.

(5) Without preaching, scolding, or embarrassing anyone, the teacher showed her pupils that there is a place for many kinds of language usage, and that the standard for usage in the school has merit.

(6) The teacher made no great fuss about being progressive or modern in all this. The situation arose; she saw its possibilities. She did not (as some critics say the modern teacher does) ask the children, "Now, children, do you want to study language any more or do you just want to talk any old way?" That is foolish and no sensible person would try such a thing except perhaps as an experiment. Instead, she directed the children's interest and attention to some of the significant features that were inherent in their problem.

(7) The teacher did not approach the children with a "package"

to sell. She did not decide in advance to interest them in this or that. The interest was there; she discovered it and capitalized upon it briefly.

It is interesting to speculate about what would have happened had the teacher tried to let interest in "school language" develop into a long unit. The story so far is a real incident. The teacher in question told her visitor later that if a similar situation arose again, she would be tempted to let the children go much further. "Think of how much they could learn by bringing examples of their own baby vocabularies to school—baby words that persisted in family use through childhood or longer. Think of the insights into word meanings that they would gain. Then they could identify family words and words that reveal national or regional origin, and thus learn a lot about intercultural life. Think of the books to read, the letters to write, the people to interview, the parental and community participation to call upon, the writing and spelling and language skills to learn, the outlining to do. Think of the range of difficulty of the items that would come up. There would be something for children of every level of ability to do successfully and profitably. Think of the opportunities for dramatizing, for culminating activities that parents might attend. I'm almost sorry I didn't carry it on. But there are always so many more things popping up than we can possibly do." She sighed, "It's like the extra helping at a tasty meal. You have to refuse ultimately."

In textbooks today, there are hundreds of illustrations of curriculums in progress. The sad fact, however, is that few of them reveal the dynamics of what makes things function in the good classroom. For example, how does an activity get started? How is it kept going? Typical of the printed illustrations are opening statements such as the following:

"The class was to have a store. Plans for operating it got under way at once," or "The group decided that they would appoint a committee to interview the Mayor." These may be adequate for the teacher who is experienced in knowing just how stores come into the picture in the first place and how the plans for such things get under way. For most teachers, however, this opening begs the whole question. The reasons for these inept openings are hard to assess until you see the difficulties of their authors in discussing such things as pupil-teacher planning, determining the day's schedule of activities, day-by-day and long-term planning, caring for individual differences, deciding on which unit to choose, directing the interests of children into constructive channels, and evaluating what a good unit is. It becomes clear then that many of the authors could not go into a classroom and start the units they are discussing, or units similar to them, without resorting to authoritarian imposition of plans and ideas.

Some actual day-to-day examples of how teachers start work on an experience unit, motivate and initiate variegated units, and carry them through are given in Chapters 19, 20, and 21.

Choosing topics for units

Let us examine a list of topics that are suggestive of things in which children are interested and that, when studied, contribute to the commonly accepted objectives of education.

Instruction in the elementary schools is, in general, organized around social studies and natural science content. It is recognized that if reading, thinking, speaking, writing, computing, and other skills are to be developed effectively, the content through which they evolve must have meaning and purpose to the children. Likewise it is recognized that social skills and attitudes, appreciations, ideals, values, loyalties, and the like, cannot be developed in any real sense except in relation to meaningful and purposeful content. The content through which intellectual and social skills and spiritual values are achieved gains meaning and purpose for children as it is related to their immediate environment and interests. It should deal with their relations to other people and with their relations to natural (physical and biological) surroundings. This is the ideal toward which the supervisory, administrative, and teaching staff of the school is working. To expect it to be completely achieved is akin to expecting the millennium.

In this type of curriculum organization, a frame of reference is set up with many centers of interest around which units of subject matter may be organized. In Chapter 3, we pointed out that the units of the kindergarten and first grade are centered in the family, the home, the school, and the immediate neighborhood. In the second grade, children move out farther into the local community.

In the third and fourth grade, other types of communities of men are studied emphasizing life in different climates and geographic regions and peoples of different racial and cultural types, always contrasting them with the home community. In the fifth grade, the study of the development of modern man is emphasized—his industries, business, and arts and crafts, with special reference to the United States. In the sixth grade, the development of modern European countries is emphasized.

An outline of such a frame of reference follows. It is a modification of one originally made by Nonilee Saunders of Eastern Illinois State College.

Possibilities From Which Units May Be Chosen for the Elementary School

1. Family
   a. Members
   b. Responsibility of members
      (1) Father earns money for food, shelter, clothing, and pleasure
      (2) Mother cares for the family
      (3) Children have home duties and care for pets
      (4) Interdependence for pleasure
      (5) Family helpers
          (a) Laundry man
          (b) Grocery man
          (c) Garbage man
          (d) Postman
          (e) Vegetable man
          (f) Milkman
          (g) Baker

2. Home
   a. Surroundings
      (1) Trees—orchards
      (2) Lawns
      (3) Gardens
          (a) Flower
          (b) Vegetable
   b. Types of houses
      (1) Duplex
      (2) Apartment
      (3) Bungalow
      (4) Two-story house
   c. Builders
      (1) Architects

      (2) Carpenters
      (3) Plumbers
      (4) Electricians
      (5) Painters
      (6) Plasterers
  d. Materials
      (1) Lumber
      (2) Brick
      (3) Stucco
      (4) Shingles
      (5) Stones
  e. Rooms—uses and furnishings
  f. Houses provide shelter for man and for animals

3. Communication
  a. Telephone
  b. Newspaper
  c. Radio
  d. Television
  e. Moving picture
  f. Telegraph
  g. Postal service
  h. Cable

4. Transportation as it applies to the home
  a. Automobile
  b. Horse
  c. Airplane
  d. Ships
  e. Truck
  f. Street cars
  g. Trains
  h. Bicycles
  i. Busses

5. School
  a. City schools and rural schools
      (1) Transportation
      (2) Environment
      (3) Buildings
      (4) Uses
      (5) Organization
      (6) Personnel

6. Neighborhood
  a. Types of buildings
  b. Transportation facilities
  c. Workers and their work

7. Farm
   a. Use of buildings for animals
   b. Source of food supply
   c. Care of animals
   d. Use of machinery
   e. Farm workers and their tasks
   f. Communication
   g. Transportation

8. Production
   a. Food production
      (1) Grocer
      (2) Baker
      (3) Farmer
      (4) Dairyman
   b. Clothes production
      (1) Tailor
      (2) Factory worker
      (3) Cobbler
   c. Building, iron, steel, wood
   d. Power
   e. Toolmaking
   f. Buying and selling, money and credit

9. Protection
   a. Fireman
   b. Policeman
   c. State Highway Patrol
   d. Health organization
   e. Doctor
   f. Nurse
   g. Dentist
   h. Armed Forces

10. Transportation as it applies to the community
    a. Boats (ocean, streams, canals, sailing, steam)
    b. Wagons, buggies, stage coach
    c. Trains
    d. Street cars
    e. Busses
    f. Automobiles
    g. Trucks
    h. Airplanes

11. Building
    a. Architect
    b. Carpenter
    c. Bricklayer

    d. Painter
    e. Plumber
    f. Electrician
    g. Engineer

12. Other workers
    a. Minister
    b. Teacher
    c. Lawyer
    d. Social worker
    e. Librarian
    f. Surveyor

13. Primitive people (food gatherers)
    a. Cave man
    b. Tree dwellers
    c. Eskimos (cold climate)
    d. Jungle dwellers (hot climate)
    e. Nomads (desert type)
    f. Indians

14. Modern people
    a. Scandinavians and Swiss (cold climate, mountainous)
    b. Japanese (isolated, island group)
    c. Dutch (damp lowland)
    d. German village
    e. English village

15. Examples of racial types
    a. Equatorial Africans as examples of Negroid
    b. Japanese or Chinese as examples of Mongoloid
    c. American Indian as an example of Mongoloid
    d. Pacific Islanders as marginal types—Micronesians, Melanesians, Polynesians
    e. Dutch as an example of Caucasians

16. National Cultural patterns
    a. American
    b. Dutch
    c. Japanese

17. Lowland types
    a. Holland
    b. Jungle

18. Mountain types
    a. Switzerland
    b. Norway

19. Christmas in other lands

20. Contrasts between what the explorers found and what the modern tourist sees in any one of the following:
  a. Mexico
    (1) How the early explorers conquered Mexico
    (2) The advanced civilization they found
    (3) How they changed the civilization
        (a) A nation largely of a handicraft culture
        (b) Called the "Land of Eternal Spring"
        (c) A region of wide range of climate and products
        (d) A region of wide cultural contrasts
  b. Florida
  c. California
  d. Brazil
  e. Argentina

21. Contrasts of colonial and modern life along the Atlantic seaboard
  a. Colonial life
    (1) Why the colonists came
    (2) What they brought
    (3) What they learned from the Indians
    (4) How their environment affected their:
        (a) Food
        (b) Clothing
        (c) Shelter
        (d) Amusements
        (e) Agriculture
        (f) Industries
  b. Modern life
    (1) How people along the Atlantic seaboard today adapt themselves to their environment
    (2) The rise of industrial marketing, processing, and transportation centers (New York, Boston, Philadelphia)
        Buildings, iron, steel, toolmaking, buying and selling, money and credit, Industrial Revolution, interdependence

22. Contrasts of pioneer and modern life in
  a. The great Central Plains (Pittsburgh, Detroit, Chicago, St. Louis)
    (1) Why the pioneers moved westward
    (2) How they traveled
    (3) How the type of region determined their way of living
    (4) How people of the same region have learned better use of the land and resources today
  b. The South (New Orleans, Birmingham, Houston)
  c. The West (Santa Fe, San Francisco, Seattle)

23. Life in Medieval Europe
  a. In the town
  b. Among the craftsmen

c. On the farm
d. In the monastery

24. Life in areas of modern Europe whose social significance and international activities warrant consideration as centers about which pupils may build up geographic concepts
    a. The British Isles
    b. Progressive Scandinavia
    c. The Mediterranean Lands
    d. The industrial areas of western Europe with emphasis based upon the significance of the location of the natural resources of the continent.

25. The coming of modern medicine and sanitation
    a. Conditions in the Middle Ages and those in modern Europe contrasted according to:
       (1) Size of town
       (2) Water supply
       (3) Sewage disposal
       (4) Medical care
    b. Factors contributing to the changes
       (1) Scientific discoveries
       (2) Changes in governmental organization

It is recognized that more topics are suggested here than can be developed adequately during the period of elementary-school instruction, but this allows for wide freedom of choice by pupils and teachers at each grade level. An important factor in choosing an area of the outline for unit development at any grade level is the adequacy of reading materials that are available. Equally important are the laboratories, shops, other school equipment, and the resources of the community. Most of the textbook materials (readers, arithmetic, language, science, geography, history, social studies, health) that have been developed in recent years are written on the assumption that the subject-matter content of the elementary-school curriculum will center in the areas covered by this outline.

Criteria for evaluating a unit

The child becomes educated through individual and group activities. In the modern school with its experience units, pupils are doing, making, and learning things. Thoroughness and proficiency in all this, whether in academic pursuits or in the arts and crafts, is one of the leading objectives of the modern school. But what a person can *do* is more important than what a person *knows*. The value of developmental activities has been demonstrated. Our concern is not that some bit of knowledge be learned but rather that it be used well. One of the common weaknesses of this idea has been, and still is, that teachers have failed to make a critical, unbiased evaluation of the results of developmental units. *The activity unit should be directed toward definite goals in child growth and development and carry with it a high standard of educational achievement.* Such units should be constantly evaluated so that they may be further improved.

Because there must be this careful weighing of values, there must be some criteria by which the teacher and the pupils may judge a unit while they are planning it and as they proceed with it. Such careful weighing of their plan is most important, but of almost equal importance is the check of actual gain in knowledge, skills, attitudes, and habits that must be made constantly as the unit progresses, as it passes into some other interest, or as it closes. For all this, the same standards may be used. These criteria listed below stand for *some of* the definite objectives or goals of a unit. They overlap one another to some extent, but they will serve their purpose despite their lack of mutual exclusiveness.

Criteria for Evaluating a Unit

1. A good unit should be broad enough to provide various types of learning to meet all the needs, interests, and abilities of children.
   a. Knowledge
      (1) Of interest and value to the pupil at the period of his life in which he engages in the study
      (2) On topics of fundamental social significance that serve as bases for drawing generalizations basic to successful living
   b. Skills
      (1) In using various sources of information: books, pictures, maps, excursions, experiences, people, current literature, and so forth
      (2) In expressing information gained in a variety of ways:
         (a) Dramatization
         (b) Oral and written reports
         (c) Pageants
         (d) Costuming individuals or puppets
         (e) Selecting and using tools and media of expression
         (f) Drawing
         (g) Construction

     (h) Music
     (i) Interviews
     (j) Parliamentary procedure
   (3) In planning and evaluating work
  c. Habits
    Many of the desirable learning outcomes should become so well established ultimately as to be largely automatic in use. Each unit should make its contribution to this habituation of response.
  d. Attitudes
   (1) Of cooperation
   (2) Of appreciation
   (3) Of high standards of workmanship
   (4) Of persistent application
   (5) Of thoroughness
   (6) Of leading or following as the case warrants
   (7) Of inquiry
   (8) Of tolerance
   (9) Of resourcefulness
  (10) Of open-mindedness

2. A good unit should provide real purposes for the development of the skill subjects.
   A good unit should facilitate learning of the skill subjects by associating mastery of these subjects—reading, speech, writing, art, manual arts, arithmetic—with the student's aims and purposes. When children feel the need for learning certain facts or acquiring certain abilities learning becomes much more effective and rapid. (Important skills not developed adequately within units should be taught and maintained without reference to the units.)

3. A good unit should lead into many subject-matter fields. This means, essentially, that the materials for studying the unit should not be limited by subject-matter lines and that the pupils should follow into whatever fields the search for information naturally leads them. The more fields that are entered the better, provided the research and study is carried out in response to a felt need and with a definite aim in mind. There is always the danger that too much subject matter may be "dragged" in and too many fields entered without sufficient justification. Such needless accumulation of data may lead to misunderstanding or a clouded appreciation of the unit rather than to comprehension and clearness. *The criterion, then, for selecting any item of subject matter should not be its subject field, but rather a felt need for that item as a contributing factor to the understanding of the unit.*

4. A good unit should be compatible with the child's understanding, vocabulary, interests, and abilities in order to insure its successful accomplishment. It should deal with the child's environment, and the materials used and experiences elicited should provide sufficient range to care for

individual needs. The range of types of material should include the fictional, the informational, the graphic, and the visual.

5. A good unit should provide a wide balance and variety of activities—dramatic, constructive, creative, research, experimental, and exploratory.

6. A good unit should familiarize the group with the processes of selecting, planning, carrying out, and evaluating an experiment. A unit should provide opportunities for selecting the work that is of interest to the children and on their level of understanding so that they may be able to think independently and have a widening conception of their place in the group and society at large. In planning and carrying out the work there should be continuous growth and satisfaction from many activities in the various fields in which the unit is developed. Opportunity must be provided for children to evaluate the work they have done.

7. A good unit of work should stimulate the children to acquire further information concerning the topic at hand and other related topics. The interests of the children should carry the activity from one phase to another. There should be small units within the large unit that the children can pursue and investigate. Natural relationships should be established between topics that will stimulate definite interests in other later study or major unit of work. There should be much evidence of growth on the part of those participating, both teacher and pupil.

8. There should be an abundance of reading material dealing with the subject matter of the unit. This should have a range of difficulty comensurate with the reading abilities of the pupils participating in the unit. The material should be in book or pamphlet form and have an adequate table of contents and index. The units above the second grade should involve the use of basic reference tools such as encyclopedias, library card files, and the like.

9. An important objective in every unit should be to develop the essential meanings underlying the facts. The subject matter must not remain as isolated facts. Instead, these facts serve as cases from which the pupils are able to draw their conclusions. These conclusions are, of course, temporary. More facts (greater knowledge) may direct thinking to other conclusions, also tentative. These tentative conclusions are merely intermediate goals. In every case, however, the facts are being assimilated so that the essential meaning involved is being developed. Information from many situations serves to substantiate conclusions or basic ideas already partly formed.

10. Throughout the unit, emphasis should be placed on problem-solving. Emphasis should be placed not only on the applicability of a special method made up of a series of steps used to solve the special problems of a particular unit, but on the general procedures followed in an approach to the solution of any new problem.

11. Any unit should take into account the conditions affecting the various

children involved in the unit. In addition to a child's understanding, interests, and attitudes, this includes various factors contributory to them, and to the whole personality of the child—his culture, socio-economic background, nationality, color and religion, mental and physical health, place of residence, acceptance by his group, and past fortunate and unfortunate experiences.

Discussion Questions

1. Try to relate subject-matter units to the subject-matter curriculums, and experience units to developmental-activity curriculums.
2. Examine the definition of an experience unit. Try to write an equally explicit definition of a subject-matter unit. Why do you think the authors were not as explicit in defining a subject-matter unit as in defining an experience unit?
3. Is there danger in the freedom recommended by the authors for teachers in the use of resource units? How would you avoid such dangers?
4. Who should prepare resource units? Why?
5. Discuss the knowledge and skills needed by teachers in selecting activities to pursue in experience units.
6. What do you think of the outline of topics for use in units? Is it too mechanical? Is it a crutch? Will its use serve to give teachers self-confidence?
7. Are there other good criteria for evaluating a unit besides those mentioned in this chapter? Do these criteria neglect the basic skills? How? Do they neglect attitudes and problem-solving ability? Would you suggest any changes in emphasis?
8. What is your reaction to the story of the teacher who had the lesson on the different kinds of language? Did she see the problem clearly? Would this problem be different in communities with different socio-economic levels?

Selected References

Bayles, E. E., *The Theory and Practice of Teaching*. New York: Harper and Brothers, 1950.

Bode, B. H., *Modern Educational Theories*. New York: The Macmillan Company, 1927.

Caswell, H. L., *Education in the Elementary School*. New York: American Book Company, 1942.

Hildreth, G., *Child Growth Through Education*. New York: The Ronald Press Company, 1948.

Jacobs, L. B., J. B. Burr, and L. W. Harding, *Student Teaching in the Elementary School*. New York: Appleton-Century-Crofts, Inc., 1950.

Lee, J. M. and D. M. Lee, *The Child and His Curriculum,* 2nd ed. New York: Appleton-Century-Crofts, Inc., 1950.

Macomber, F. G., *Guiding Child Development in the Elementary School.* New York: American Book Company, 1941.

Millard, C. V. and A. J. Huggett, *Growth and Learning in the Elementary School.* Boston: D. C. Heath & Company, 1946.

Otto, H. J., *Principles of Elementary Education,* 2nd ed. New York: Rinehart and Company, Inc., 1949.

Phillips, C. A., F. H. Gorman, and J. H. Dougherty, *Elementary School Organization and Management,* Rev. ed. New York: The Macmillan Company, 1950.

Stratemeyer, F. B. and others, *Developing a Curriculum for Modern Living.* New York: Teachers College, Columbia University, 1947.

14

SUBJECTS AND BASIC SKILLS

REGARDLESS OF CURRICULUM THEORY, teachers must continue to teach in actual situations. The schools, like other institutions and professions, are in a state of change and will so continue. Through research in the various sciences that affect educational procedures we will learn more and more, and provision must be made for the use of this new knowledge in the schools. The schools are now engaged in this process. While some schools lag more than others, all schools change with the growth of the science of education. The changes in our technology and our society also bring about changes in the schools. This last does not mean that there is nothing stable in the objectives of the elementary school. Basic skills always will be taught but new knowledge and conditions will demand changes by the schools.

It is possible to designate certain school systems that, although far from perfect, are good, and are in the process of becoming better. They are the type of school systems in which teachers may feel fortunate to teach. In such schools, the curriculum is frequently organized around social studies and natural science content. The curriculum bulletins generally state that if the basic skills are to be developed effectively, the content through which they are to be developed must have meaning and purpose for the children. Social skills, attitudes, appreciations, ideals, values, loyalties, and the like, cannot be developed except in relation to meaningful and purposeful content.

A good curriculum in action

In visiting a school system, there are many things that a visitor may look for in order to *begin* the process of curriculum evaluation. Such criteria must be used with care, of course, because classrooms are full of young human beings with almost infinite possibilities for variation in individual and group behavior.

Teacher-pupil planning. In a modern school, one that is attempting to break with the traditional assignment-study-recite regimen, the observer looks for evidence that the children and the teacher recognize that improvements can be made in almost every aspect of their environment and in every activity in which they engage. These improvements can be planned in great variety. They involve such things as the removal of safety hazards, proper nutrition, conduct in the lunchroom and halls, speech habits, promptness, neatness, skill in multiplication, a better school paper, more courteous behavior, or better handwriting. The children work closely with the teacher in planning activities, practice exercises, field trips, and other undertakings designed to bring about the desired improvements in their behavior.

Organizing and outlining. Evidence should be available in the classroom that children are developing the ability to organize ideas. When pupils read different reference books, interview authorities, and report their findings it is important that all this material be organized, that the important relationships be emphasized. Organized knowledge becomes meaningful and is retained; unorganized facts lack meaning and are soon forgotten. For example, a field trip should be jointly planned and organized before it is taken. The learnings that result from a field trip must be organized after it is taken. The organization must be for some specified purpose and in terms of significant relationships.

Dramatic play. Dramatic play is perhaps the most natural activity of children. Playing house, baking mud pies, playing cops and robbers, playing Indians and cowboys, building bridges, building houses, playing railroad, playing truck driver, publishing a newspaper, writing a book, and playing mechanic are activities in which the child engages. Dramatic play gives the child's activity purpose and meaning to him. Children strive to make their dramatic play authentic and realistic, and in so doing they become effective observers. They read, study, ask questions, and in fact, do research at their level of understanding in order to make their play as satisfying and as real as possible. In school, the free dramatizing of stories, historical events, dramatic episodes in science, tribal ceremonies, occupations, current affairs, and so forth, gives purpose and drive to the children's reading, writing, speaking, singing, dancing, painting, and research activities. Dramatic play can furnish the motivation for every type of educational experience if the possibilities are sensed by the teacher.

Construction activities. The use of tools, weaving and sewing, working with wood, paper, metal, and leather, building models of all kinds—boats, cars, houses, airplanes—and the pursuit of other hobbies should be emphasized. These are important educational experiences. Many classrooms are unfortunately too small to make effective use of workbenches and tools. Such activities should not be allowed to absorb too much school time, but they should be stimulated, given recognition and encouragement. When interest is aroused, children often carry on such activities outside the school. Each room library should contain many books on hobbies, or how to make things, on the building of models, and on popular science and popular mechanics for both boys and girls. Hobby displays are an evidence of good curriculum procedure.

Field trips. The schools that use field trips to enrich the curriculum are making use of an ideal tool for the study of the history, the culture, and the economic life of the community.

The use of audio-visual teaching materials. Audio-visual teaching materials include models, dramatic presentations, demonstrations, field trips, exhibits, museums, motion pictures, still pictures, photographs, slides, film strips, television, radio, recordings, charts, maps, graphs, globes, and other devices. The possibilities of using such materials in achieving educational goals have only recently been recognized.[1]

The use of the library. In judging the nature of the instructional program that prevails in an elementary classroom, no factor is more important than the nature of the classroom library and reference materials. One expects to find in each classroom no less than 100 books of a literary nature. These should be carefully selected with

[1] Edgar Dale, *Audio Visual Methods in Teaching.* New York: The Dryden Press, Inc., 1946.

reference to their interest appeal and range of reading difficulty. In each classroom there should be from 30 to 100 factual reference books bearing on the units that the children are developing. These should have a wide range of difficulty and interest appeal.

In each classroom, from the third grade through the sixth, there should be at least two children's encyclopedias. The two most highly recommended are *Compton's Pictured Encyclopedia* and the *World Book Encyclopedia*. Perhaps in the third grade, but certainly from the fourth grade on, each child should have a dictionary. Some authorities think these should be uniform for purposes of instruction; others think they should vary so that brighter children could have dictionaries suitable to their degrees of understanding and comprehension.

In addition, newspapers and journals published for children should be circulated through the classroom libraries. Some schools ask the children to subscribe to one or more of them. Many elementary schools use the daily newspapers or the weekly community newspapers to good advantage in teaching children the parts of a newspaper and how to locate information quickly.

Teaching the basic skills

The modern elementary-school curriculum is integrated by organizing it around meaningful (to the child) social studies and natural science content. It is recognized that if the skills of reading, thinking, speaking, listening, writing, computing, and so forth, are to be most effectively developed, the content through which they are developed must have significance and purpose to the children. Likewise it is recognized that the social skills (skills necessary in working with people) and attitudes, appreciations, ideals, values, loyalties, and so forth, cannot be developed in any real sense except in relation to meaningful and purposeful content. The content through which the intellectual skills, the social skills, and the spiritual values are developed has meaning and purpose to children when it is related to their immediate environment, interests, and needs. It deals with their relations to other people and with their relations to the natural (physical and biological) surroundings. (The ideas expressed in this paragraph are more adequately developed in Chapter 18, under the section heading *Skills, Subject Matter, and Attitudes.*)

It would be impossible to treat here all that a teacher needs to know about the development of the basic intellectual skills of reading, thinking, speaking, writing, computing, and so forth. The material that follows in this section is designed to give a few illustrations of how the principles and practices described throughout this book carry over into these specific areas of instruction.

Reading. Reading has long been and will long remain the most important basic skill to be learned in the elementary school!. It is a highly specialized subject and the well-prepared teacher will have taken one or more courses devoted exclusively to it. A pupil's failure in other subjects is often traceable to his inability to read up to the level these subjects require. In schools where pupils are required to repeat grades, the great majority who are not promoted fail because of poor reading. Poor achievement in reading has many causes such as faulty teaching procedures, low level of intelligence, poor health, poor vision or hearing, lack of a desire to read, fear of the inability to read, or a lack in the basic experiences necessary for reading.

In teaching reading, the teacher must approach each child as a separate problem. The pupil's readiness for a stage of reading instruction and all its contributory factors must be explored. In many cases, children are required to begin reading from books too early. Some may begin before they enter school, the majority in the first grade, some in the second, and some should not begin until the third grade. There is much evidence available now to support the idea that the ultimate level of reading and of general school success is improved if reading instruction is postponed until the learnings necessary for success have been achieved. The fear that the child will feel inferior to his classmates if many can read and he cannot has not proven out. The failures he encounters as he tries to perform tasks that he cannot do are far more damaging.

Reading in accordance with grade-level standards has been abandoned as more and more has become known about individual and trait differences. When children do begin to read, they learn and improve *by reading*. Most of this reading should be silent. The great amount of time consumed as groups of children listen while one child reads aloud is difficult to justify. It is boring and discouraging both to the very bright and to the very dull in the group. To give practice in reading before groups, children should have frequent opportunities to read a selection that is new to the other pupils, but the passage should be well within the reading ability of the one who reads, and he should have adequate opportunity to practice beforehand.

Many of the bad habits that teachers worry about, such as lip movement and verbalization, are caused by the teacher's demanding too much in the way of a high level of accomplishment or too much in the way of rapid progress from the child. Frequently these habits represent actual *props* that are of value to particular children. Study of such habits in individual cases may help to reveal what the child's real difficulties are.

Reading that involves the searching of reference materials in various subject areas will grow naturally out of unit activities. In this reading, pupils will seek the answers to specific questions that come up. They will develop the ability to grasp the general significance of a paragraph and to predict the results of given events. These abilities require imagination and originality. Here the pupil must relate, infer, imagine, and predict. Matter-of-fact reading as a means of getting facts from the printed page is usually overemphasized. Thoughtful, imaginative reading in which the reader's interpretation is of more importance than the material *per se* is usually underemphasized.

During the reading lesson, the teacher should ask questions that require the children to make inferences, to be critical, to test the logic of what is said, to think in terms of a sequence of ideas or events, to make summary statements of what a paragraph is about, to give the author's purpose or the author's point of view, and to suggest additional material that the author may not have included. The goal should be to have the pupil learn to think more effectively about what he reads. The pupil in this situation will, of course, be reading materials for which he is "ready." Through such reading he should learn to follow precise written directions, to note details, and to use all the other skills required for the comprehension of written materials.

In order to insure a proper sequence in the development of skills in reading, the teachers should in general pay close attention to the manuals that accompany the readers. The use of teachers' manuals cannot be overemphasized. In many schools, instruction in reading suffers because teachers fail to see the purpose of the various types of materials in the readers. For example, an article designed to develop the ability to organize materials might be used inappropriately as oral reading material. Of course, there may be instances in which the author of a set of readers lacks certain understandings and neglects certain aims, and consequently his recommendations may be unreliable. For example, the author of one well-known set of readers compliments a teacher who found it necessary to have three reading groups at the beginning of the year, but at the end of the year had all the pupils in one group reading the same materials. This certainly is not the ideal toward which a teacher should work. When this happens the fast learners are being held back.

Language. Language expresses ideas or thoughts. This is done through what appears to be the use of words. Actually, however, ideas generally are expressed through the use of "combinations of words." As this has become more clear, there has been less and less emphasis on grammar that stresses word study—nouns, action words, pronouns, and so forth. The same thing applies to the teaching of sentence structure, paragraphing, and punctuation through the use of rules and drill. There is nothing to indicate that these approaches are efficient. In general, authoritative opinion favors the teaching of grammar through instrumental rather than through formal procedures. This means that grammar should be taught as it is needed by pupils in writing themes, letters, reports, and the like.

In all language teaching, the importance of meanings and concepts must be kept in mind. Children will not want to learn language rules that they do not understand. Language is the tool for expressing thought. To teach language without reference to thought is like carrying to the garden imaginary water in empty pails. No child should be required to write or speak the thoughts of others that he has mechanically mastered without understanding their meaning.

Careful attention must be given to such aspects of language as speech development. Oral language makes social intercourse possible. Through its use, the majority of the ordinary, everyday affairs of life are directed. Oral language is of primary importance in entertainment and an essential instrument in the stimulation of individual and group thought and action. The general motives of language expression are socially and biologically deep-rooted in man. They involve the fundamental drives of self-expression and social communication. The specific motives for oral expression may be identified as follows: to entertain, to improve one's social relations, to instruct, to plan, to make decisions, to persuade, to influence, to report on activities or findings, to spread views, to conduct meetings, to unify or disrupt group thinking, and to carry on business.[2]

There are many opportunities to use speech in meaningful situations in a good elementary-school program—teacher-pupil planning, conversation, discussion, story telling, explaining, arguing, speechmaking, and oral reporting. Pupils are often quite well aware of what effective speech is; they are able to identify what makes a report stimulating and interesting. Much should be done through teacher-pupil planning to help pupils set the goals toward which they strive. Goals imposed by the teacher may be rejected by the pupils.

Handwriting. For years handwriting was taught and rated mechanically. Today, the consideration of its proper teaching in the elementary school largely depends upon what we know about the growth and maturation of the child. Motor skills grow slowly and depend upon many physical and neural factors. Children, when they begin to learn a particular skill, are necessarily awkward. They should be allowed and encouraged to use large letters without attaining great beauty or regularity in form. The evidence in favor of using manuscript writing has been widely accepted and some authorities believe it will soon be universally adopted. Others believe its usage will be limited to the lower grades, after which the change will be made to cursive writing. The advocated change depends upon evidence in regard to speed that is not as yet conclusive. Some authorities believe the evidence shows greater speed in the upper grade and secondary school with one method, some

2 Ernest Horn, "Language and Meaning," *Forty-first Yearbook of the National Society for the Study of Education*, Part II. Bloomington, Illinois, Public School Publishing Company, 1942, pp. 377-415; R. I. Johnson, *English Expression: A Study in Curriculum Building.* Bloomington, Illinois: Public School Publishing Company, 1926; C. S. Pendelton, *The Social Objectives of School English.* Nashville: Published by the author, 1924; T. C. Pollock and others, *The English Language in American Education.* New York: The Modern Language Association of America, 1945.

with the other. One point of agreement seems to be that no very great difficulties are involved in changing from manuscript to cursive writing at about the fourth-grade level. Teachers and educators should remain alert to additional research in these areas and be ready to adjust procedures in terms of the evidence. A main consideration in the adoption of manuscript writing in the lower grades is its legibility, ease of learning, and its assistance in teaching children to read printed material.

Some schools attempt to teach handwriting instrumentally. As in all other skill subjects, this is psychologically sound as long as it is understood properly. There still *must be* practice or drill on the skills involved whether this occurs at regularly scheduled periods or whether it occurs as the needs arise. Certainly the concepts and meanings involved are best learned in relation to the meaningful activities that are being furthered by the use of the particular skill. The instrumental method can be used to teach handwriting in the lower grades upon countless occasions when children must make signs, name objects, make labels, copy outlines and rules, write notes, make programs, and so forth.

Certainly there should be no formal drill in ovals, strokes, letter repetition, arm movement, and the like. Whenever children write, they may be helped in learning to hold the pencil and pen, in placing the paper, and in assuming the correct posture. This work should be largely individual and should be done gently and with great care, since the effect on the personality and on various speech and brain dominance factors seems related to some of the writing difficulties or to have common bases. There is much that we do not know about such things, but we are sure that undue pressure and impatient and unsympathetic teacher and parent attitudes can do nothing but harm.

Much foolishness has been written and practiced about the use of old-fashioned pens, fountain pens, ball point pens, and so forth. For example, some have insisted that the first use of pen and ink be with old-fashioned pens that must be dipped in the ink well. There seems to be no corresponding advocacy that people first learn to drive Model T Fords with planetary transmissions before they learn to drive modern cars with automatic transmissions. In the absence of real evidence to the contrary, why not let children use effective tools they enjoy using as soon as they are able to use them at all efficiently? Perhaps a fountain pen with a rugged point would be very good for a child in the second or third grade. Perhaps, too, there are times in a child's development at which he might be expected to use finger, wrist, or arm movement, or a combination of all three. The fact is that most children, if left alone, start with finger movement, which is natural, since the small muscles are best adapted to precise movements. It seems sensible to use small muscles for precise and delicate movements. Outside the traditional teaching of handwriting, we recognize this quite clearly. Can you imagine a watch repair school where the students practice arm movement?

In general today, a standard of about 60 on the Ayres scale is considered sufficient for the purposes of the ordinary citizen. Others say that an average literate adult should write 80 letters per minute legibly. A great deal of research is needed in this area.

All writing should be for a definite purpose and be integrated with the unit activities and the social life of the children. Writing that is merely an exercise or an assignment, with no other purpose than to be handed in to the teacher and marked, should be avoided. For example, letters may be written to a sick schoolmate, to a baker thanking him for permitting the class to visit his bakery, to the pupils of the sixth grade thanking them for the use of reference books, to last year's teacher, to a pupil who formerly was in school, to the Home of the Aged offering to present a Christmas program, to the people from whom Christmas gifts were received, to a class in a school in a neighboring city, to the children of a school in England, and so forth.[3]

Of course, it is through discussion and teacher-pupil planning that the criteria of good writing are made clear to the pupils. What makes a personal letter interesting? What are the things about our school that an English pupil would like to know? What are the essential facts to be included in a letter to General Mills requesting materials on nutrition? Through group thinking and planning in answering such questions, each child gains insight into the problems and subtleties of effective communication.

[3] Maude McBroom, *The Course of Study in Written Composition for the Elementary School*, University of Iowa Monographs in Education, No. 10. Iowa City: College of Education, University of Iowa, 1928.

Spelling. There is still much controversy between those who would teach spelling instrumentally and those who would teach it formally. Instrumental spelling, taught in connection with classroom activities, does not involve a definite word list and a specific number of minutes for its mastery each day or week. The words taught are the new and important ones that arise as the work of the class progresses and as the children's inability to spell them becomes obvious. Since learning to spell, like all learning, is not an atomistic skill, the mastery of the spelling of a large list of words carries with it the power to spell many other words. Those who advocate the instrumental method stress the wide range in individual differences and the inability of spelling experts (or content experts in any other field) to arrange spelling words accurately in grade-placement categories. When a child reaches school age, his average vocabulary consists in the neighborhood of 2,500 words and the size of this list increases rapidly. The words that children know and use will furnish a good starting place for beginning spelling. Instrumental teaching of spelling, if well done, takes individual differences into account and provides motivation springing from real purposes. There is no reason to discard drill in this method; it may or may not take place in regularly scheduled periods. As words arise, they are put into lists and learned. Some good examples of this procedure in actual teaching are illustrated in Chapters 19, 20, and 21.

Some authorities who would subscribe to the instrumental method in theory cannot agree that it will accomplish the desired spelling competence in actual practice. Primarily they are afraid, not of good instrumental teaching, but of neglect. They advocate a modified formal approach that has much to recommend it for teachers who are just gaining experience in the new techniques.

These authorities advocate starting with the words most frequently used in adult and children's writing.[4] These are sufficient to enable the curriculum-maker to select 4,000 or 5,000 words and be reasonably confident of their wide usage. The 4,000 words most frequently used account for approximately 99 per cent of the "run-

---

[4] The two best summaries of research in spelling are Thomas George Foran, *The Psychology and Teaching of Spelling.* Washington, D. C.: The Catholic Education Press, 1934; and Ernest Horn, "Spelling," in Walter S. Monroe, ed., *The Encyclopedia of Educational Research.* New York: The Macmillan Company, 1950, pp. 1247-1264.

ning words" that the average adult uses.[5] In this method the systematic teaching of spelling is continuous through the elementary school. The words taught at each grade level are those words that the children are using at their correct level of thinking and reading, and that they are misspelling. Comprehensive studies of children's usage have been made by McKee,[6] Fitzgerald,[7] and Rinsland.[8] These studies should be consulted by those who determine at which grade level words should be studied and reviewed.

The time devoted to drill in spelling should not be considered a time for increasing the "meaning" vocabulary of children. This is done more pleasantly and effectively through reading, discussion, and the daily experiences of the children with language. The words that the child studies in spelling are those that he uses and needs to spell, but does not yet know how to spell correctly. The principal purpose of a spelling period is to allow the child to learn to spell correctly the words he has learned to read.

Learning to spell a word means learning to write the word correctly in legible form. Insofar as oral spelling is used, its purpose is to establish associations between written symbols and sounds. In beginning spelling in the primary grades, the child should never be asked to learn to write a word he cannot already read. What he writes should always have purpose and meaning to him. The child should know the letters in the words he writes, or learn them in the process of learning to write it. For example, in learning to spell *funny* the elements of the following procedure should be present:

(1) The child pronounces the word either aloud or silently. He must know how to pronounce the word correctly.

(2) The child writes *fun* saying to himself the letters *f, u, n* as he writes them; he then pronounces *fun* to himself. Then he writes

5 Horn, *A Basic Writing Vocabulary: The Ten Thousand Words Most Commonly Used in Writing.*

6 Paul McKee, *Language in the Elementary School.* Boston: Houghton Mifflin Company, 1939, pp. 329-430.

7 J. A. Fitzgerald, *Letters Written Outside the School by Children in the Fourth, Fifth and Sixth Grades,* University of Iowa, 1935; "The Vocabulary and Spelling Errors of Third Grade Children's Life Letters," *Elementary School Journal,* Vol. 38, 1938, 518-527; "Words Misspelled Most Frequently by Children in the Fourth, Fifth, and Sixth Grade Levels in Life Outside the School," *Journal of Educational Research,* Vol. 26, 1932, 213-218.

8 H. D. Rinsland, *A Basic Vocabulary of Elementary School Children.* New York: The Macmillan Company, 1945.

the letters *n*, and *y*, saying *n* and *y* to himself as he writes them and pronouncing *ny* as he finishes.

(3) He then pronounces the word *funny* again as he looks at his writing of the word.

In the beginning, the teacher may have to repeat this process with some children time after time with each word until the habit ,of spelling in terms of syllables and letters is established. The first words learned will, in general, be one-syllable words. After a child has learned to write the word with a model before him, he then practices without the model. As soon as a child has learned to spell enough words to make sentences and to express thoughts, further practice should take the form of contextual and meaningful writing.

The system of having a child write his spelling words in context is good, especially in the first three grades, providing the child is taught how to learn to write the new words, know the letters, and relate the sounds to the letters.

A child can and frequently does learn to write words correctly without knowing the letters; he simply has a visual image of the word. The visual image of a word is important in learning to spell correctly. It is derived when the child learns to read the word. The pupil knows what the word looks like in print, manuscript, or script form when he has learned to read it in these various forms. A pupil should see the word in the form in which he is expected to write it. Good readers are, in general, good spellers and poor readers are poor spellers. Nevertheless, it is unreal to expect that all children will develop the habit of spelling by visual imagery alone. The child who needs it should be helped to know the letters he is writing, and to have a feeling for the relationship between the letters and their sounds.

Beginning with the fourth grade in this modified spelling method, the *test study* method of teaching spelling is often followed. This procedure provides for individual differences and enables the pupil to devote his spelling period to the study of words that he misspells. A general outline of this method is as follows:

(1) The words for the week are pronounced by the teacher and written by the pupils on Monday.

(2) On Tuesday each child studies the words he missed on Mon-

day's pre-test. Children who spelled all the words correctly on Monday work at other school tasks.

(3) On Wednesday all pupils are tested again. Sometimes review words, systematically selected, are repeated along with the 20 words for the week.

(4) On Thursday the pupils study the words missed on Wednesday.

(5) On Friday the words pronounced by the teacher and written by the pupils on Wednesday are tested again.

(6) This procedure requires five different testings of each word in the spelling list and each pupil is required to study only those words he has misspelled. Teachers should excuse "good spellers" from the re-tests and allow them to do more rewarding work.

(7) Each pupil keeps in his spelling notebook a list of the words he misses on Friday and also words he has missed in his written work. At regular intervals during the "free study" periods (these are periods during which each child works on his most pressing learning problems) the children are paired off to pronounce to each other the words in this "spelling demon" list.

In order to check on the efficiency with which spelling is taught, and to provide for individual differences, the following procedure is sometimes used. At the beginning of each semester the teacher selects at random 50 words from the spelling list to be taught that semester and administers them to the pupils in the form of a written spelling test, pronouncing each word clearly before the child writes it down. The score of each pupil is recorded as a percentage (multiply the number of words spelled correctly by two). The average score of the class also is recorded. Those pupils who spell more than 90 per cent of the words correctly on this pre-test may be excused from spelling during the semester. The pupils who spell less than 30 per cent of the words correctly continue to study words from the first 1,000 most commonly used words before going to the study of the second thousand, and spend additional time on the second thousand before going to the third thousand. Since the first 1,000 most commonly used words make up 90 per cent of "running words," [9] these should be mastered by the poor spellers first, regard-

---

[9] The number of separate words of all kinds, no matter how often repeated, on a page or in a book or newspaper is called the number of running words on that page, or in that book or newspaper.

less of the grade in which the pupil is found. The average speller can master the list of 4,000 or 5,000, and the superior speller does very well with the 10,000. At the end of each semester, the 50-word test is repeated again and the gain in percentage of correct spellings is recorded for each pupil and for the class as a whole.

No matter how spelling is taught, a pre- and post-test on the words studied each semester gives a useful check on the efficiency of learning. This is especially important when teachers are experimenting with various methods of teaching spelling. Standardized tests are not effective in measuring achievement over the period of a semester because they test too many words that may not have been taught in class.

Arithmetic. The volume or extent of the literature and research regarding the teaching of arithmetic is second only to that regarding reading. In recent years, formal, atomistic methods of teaching arithmetic have given way to an approach that stresses meaningful use through integration and experience. Readiness for learning arithmetic is as important as reading readiness. Readiness comes after wide experiences in dealing with recognizable quantities (amounts, shapes, sizes, and the like). As the importance of the factor of experience has been recognized, automatic habits and mechanical skills such as the memorizing of tables and combinations before they are understood have come to be emphasized less and less. Based on research, the formal teaching of various aspects of arithmetic has been deferred until later in the elementary school. Evidence shows that this serves to increase rather than decrease what is known at the end of the elementary period (yet it lightens rather than increases the load placed on both lower- and upper-grade teachers). In other words, it is better all around not to try to teach counter to the way humans learn. In the first three grades, as much time can be devoted to teaching arithmetic in a meaningful, integrative way as was formerly used for memory work and formal drill. With the new method, however, the subject is taught informally as it is used and no effort is made to go beyond the child's understanding.

Some curious things are indicated by some of the research. Children do not necessarily learn arithmetic in logical order from the simple to the complex. Primary children who needed and wanted to use fractions, learned them far earlier than most teachers would have thought possible, and continued to remember and use them because they understood them. There is much similar evidence to prove that many aspects of arithmetic are hard for children because they are taught poorly and according to how adults think the aspects of the subject are best learned. This is an error in scientific thinking on the part of educators.

Drill and practice in arithmetic will serve a purpose if they follow rather than attempt to precede the development of enough intelligence and ability to manipulate quantities with insight. Elementary teachers should take special courses in arithmetic instruction. In Chapter 16 there is a more extended section on certain aspects of mathematics, particularly on how teachers may help children to understand the basic nature of quantity as expressed in numbers.

Science

The authors of this book believe that the teaching of science is underemphasized in the elementary schools. Children should gain an appreciation of the progress made in the field of science and the effect of such progress upon our modern life, understand the relations of science, as it has developed historically, to society, and gain some respect and understanding for the methods, processes, and objectives of science. They may also learn to feel akin to the "naturalist" who studies birds, animals, flowers, and the natural environment in general, from the standpoint of personal enjoyment and appreciation. This is somewhat different from appreciating the "scientist" who is interested in systematic knowledge and the means of extending it.

In science education in the elementary schools, the important objectives are: (1) the development of a scientific attitude, of problem-solving skills and the methods of science, (2) an understanding of the principles and laws of science and their application in everyday life, and (3) an understanding of the pervasive application of the principles of interrelatedness and interdependence.

In many instances, the absence of aquariums, herbariums, low-power microscopes, magnifying glasses, magnets, batteries, test tubes, and other elementary scientific equipment in the classroom is in itself indicative of the fact that the teaching of science is neglected.

Usually, the elementary teacher needs much more help in the teaching of science than he needs in teaching music, art, and physical education. In the elementary school, the teaching of science is not likely to improve greatly until school administrators and the public begin to recognize its value and importance.

There is no objection to integrating the teaching of science with units in social studies or with other units providing it is properly done. This requires partial sets of all the best elementary-school textbooks in science, much supplementary reference material, and laboratory equipment suitable for each developmental level. It requires that the teacher know how to teach elementary science from the problem-solving point of view and to have an interest in doing so. It requires, in addition, that science be regarded as important. In being integrated, it *must not* be watered down or lost, but instead emphasized in its various implications.

Science in the elementary school is relatively new. So important do the authors regard the subject that we have devoted the next two chapters to it and to its implications for social studies, health, mathematics, and the whole curriculum.

Fine arts

Fine arts education is planned to meet different abilities and interests of children. Through it, opportunities are provided for freedom of expression. The merit of a fine arts program is that it recognizes the personal and expressive creations of the child as deserving of honest acceptance and acclaim. The modern school focuses attention upon individual personalities, their strengths and their needs. In this way, development is secured—development that would not be possible if the individual child were subordinated to materials, processes, and techniques, and his art products evaluated by adult standards. In the modern school, children's art is not evaluated according to adult standards. No criticisms are made that would tend to discourage the less talented. There are no competitive exhibits, no drive to discover and train young artists. The aim is to have every child enjoy his art experiences, and the range of art materials is considered in terms of providing adequately for individual pupils' abilities and interests. For example, the children constantly strive to create an attractive schoolroom environment.

Outside exhibits and visual aids are used in order that children may know and enjoy their aesthetic heritage. A high level of democratic cooperation is fostered by having the children in groups work on murals, puppets, displays, and theatricals. Children are given the opportunity to work with wood, plastic, metals, and the like, thus combining the fine arts and industrial arts programs. All curriculum experiences are vitalized and given a high level of reality through the integrated art experience.

In music, as in art, it is essential that the program be adapted to the child and not the child to the program. Attention should be focused upon the musical needs and capacities of the individual pupil and not upon musical skills, technical terms, and superior performance. It is somewhat difficult to avoid judging the musical accomplishments of children according to adult standards, but it is necessary insofar as possible. The less talented child needs to be protected from criticisms that cause him to be fearful and unwilling to participate. The aim should be to have each child enjoy to the utmost his musical experiences. It should not be to discover and train young artists. The program should be judged in terms of how much the children enjoy it and not in terms of public performances judged by adults.

A most important criterion of the effectiveness of the music program in a school is the joy the children get from the various musical activities and the anticipation with which they approach the music period. Group singing, dramatization of songs, folk dancing, square dancing, rhythm responses, and so forth, can improve the social relations throughout the school, impart cohesiveness to school groups, and lift school morale.

Music education should be integrated with the rest of the curriculum. Every social studies unit involving the study of a cultural pattern or a social institution lends itself to appropriate musical accompaniment. For example, through music the children may develop a feeling of comradeship with children of other countries, races, and cultures. Music is a universal language.

Opportunities for music participation should be varied. In addition to classroom periods devoted to group singing, various types of musical programs should be developed and presented by the children throughout the school year. There should be assembly singing accompanied by the school orchestra, choral groups of various types, instrumental and piano classes, rhythm bands in the lower grades, and periods set aside for listening to recordings.

The importance of aesthetics has appeared so essential to the authors that Chapter 17 has been devoted to art experiences. The fine arts have implications for many of the key objectives of the curriculum of the elementary schools.

Health and physical education

Every phase of a child's development is dependent upon the state of his health. Susceptibility to disease, physical defects, or habits that endanger health and safety are handicaps to successful living. For normal physical development a child requires an adequate, properly balanced diet; freedom from remediable defects, illness, and injurious environmental influences; and a personality that is based upon and springs from mental, emotional, and moral health. Provision should be made in school for the gradual acquisition of habits, attitudes, and knowledge that will guarantee a high level of personal hygiene and that will in time raise the health level of the whole community.

A complete health program should include: (1) the daily observation of the physical condition of children by properly educated teachers, (2) the immunization program against smallpox, diphtheria, and tetanus, and tuberculin skin testing and chest X-rays to detect tuberculosis, (3) the detection and control of communicable diseases, (4) periodic medical and dental examinations, (5) correction of physical defects, (6) periodic testing of hearing and vision, (7) safety inspections as regards hazards of fire and traffic in buildings, playgrounds, and playrooms, (8) the physical education program, (9) first aid equipment and training, (10) the school lunch and nutritional education program, (11) health instruction at all levels, (12) regard for health in making up the school schedule, (13) school sanitation, (14) health and safety habit training, (15) mental hygiene program, (16) school nursing, medical, dental, and psychiatric services, (17) the physical examination of athletes, (18) summer roundup program for getting children to the doctor and the dentist before they enter school, (19) special classes for exceptional children such as those who are hard of hearing, defective in vision, physically handicapped, or mentally retarded, (20) school health records and reports, and (21) the coordination of the school health program with other health and welfare services of the community.

A physical education program in the elementary school should provide an opportunity for every child, unless physically handicapped, to participate in a well-balanced program of physical activities that have educational value. The school must provide for the innate physical activity interests of children in the form of happy play situations and experiences. The physical education program offers a fine opportunity for the development of social and moral standards such as good sportsmanship, faithfulness to duty, teamwork, leadership, the ability to adjust and contribute to a play group, to develop playing skills, and to obtain a repertoire of activities and games for use outside the school. A good physical education program should provide activities that will continue to be used creatively and fruitfully in the future life of the child. The competitive aspect of sports and games should not be overemphasized; the child who is motivated to perform beyond his physical capacity may injure himself permanently. The paramount aim should be that the child derive pleasure from his activities.

Health lessons should parallel and be a part of the physical education program. They should contribute to an understanding of the steps taken in the health program and to the need for such steps. A functional, vital health curriculum should supplement, facilitate, and devote time and effort to execute the health program of the school. This is, in its best sense, functional education in a developmental-activity curriculum.

The social studies

Considered as subjects, social studies in the elementary schools include geography, history, civics, economics, sociology, and so forth. Considered more broadly, social studies include all man's group skills and attitudes, all the knowledge of man's interdependence with other men and with nature, all his social customs and mores, and all his moral and spiritual values as they affect his living with his fellows. The growing and expanding nature of the child's social world as the basis of his curriculum was outlined in Chapter 3. The nature of man, his universe, and his institutions were summarized in the outlines in Chapter 12 and the objectives of education stemming from them were suggested in some detail. Culture, societies, and communities were covered in Chapters 6 and 7.

Some further relationships of man to his physical world and to his social environment will be outlined in chapters to follow. The whole organization of the modern curriculum as it has been outlined in this text has been structured to provide adequate emphasis to the social studies.

Kindergartens

The objectives of the kindergarten are the development of language ability, physical growth, motor development, intellectual, social, and emotional development, and an over-all adjustment to the school situation.

The kindergarten today is an integral part of the elementary-school organization. It is administered and supervised by the same staff that administers and supervises the elementary school. At one time there was pressure from first-grade teachers and supervisors to emphasize kindergarten as preparation for first-grade work, especially for the first-grade reading program. Such a conception of the purposes of kindergarten work is very narrow and restricted. This "reading" emphasis is no longer present in the kindergartens. However, the "pre-reading" experiences furnished by the kindergarten are tremendously important. Kindergarten activities centering around speaking, listening, story telling, small-group work, field trips, and adjustment to the school situation in general are all important in preparing children for the first grade; but a reading readiness program in the narrow academic sense of formal exercises is no longer followed.

Promotion to the first grade from the kindergarten should be automatic. In the past, when reading readiness was accepted as a valid kindergarten objective, many kindergarten teachers hesitated to promote children who could not read at the first-grade level, fearful that the child's lack of reading ability would reflect upon their own competence as teachers. Consequently, many children were retained in kindergarten an extra year. However, in the last few years with the broadened conception of child development and a recognition that no matter what the promotional policy, not all first graders are ready to begin the reading program, this condition has changed. Only in the most rare and exceptional cases should a child be required to spend two years in kindergarten. Today, more and more first-grade teachers realize that a wide range of ability should be expected and cannot be avoided in the first-grade, and that it is a mistake to retain pupils for more than one year in the kindergarten.

In stating the objectives of the various types of kindergarten work and in making suggestions of various types of activities designed to achieve these objectives, there must be a very adequate balance between large-group, small-group, and individual activities.

Many books and periodicals dealing with the kindergarten emphasize specific aspects of child development without offering guides that would help the teacher to foster this development. Curriculum guides should supply supplemental material that will enable the teachers to develop excellent programs that contribute to the objectives of the kindergarten.

It is necessary that the kindergarten teacher learn in a short time a great deal about each child. In order to organize his kindergarten program effectively, the teacher should be familiar with the child's home environment, his physical condition, particularly in relation to vision and hearing, and a multitude of other facts. This information begins to accumulate when the teacher first confers with the mother during the spring "roundup." Systematic check lists and questionnaires are filled in. In these conferences it is best to have the parent do most of the talking. It is through listening and asking questions that the teacher learns about the pupil and his problems. Instruction of the parents is kept at a minimum in these conferences. In the typical "good" school system, audiometer and visual tests are given to the pupils by the nurse or the examining physician. Frequently, a school psychologist is available to give psychological tests where the need for such tests seems to be indicated.

It would be desirable to have all kindergarten teachers learn to administer an individual intelligence test such as the Stanford-Binet under the supervision of the school psychologist. These teachers should then spend the two weeks (with pay) before school starts testing their youngsters. These tests would not only furnish an intelligence quotient for each pupil but also provide the teacher

with insight into the over-all developmental status of each child—
the extent of his vocabulary, his ability to follow directions, his
breadth of experience, his ability to follow stories, to see patterns
and relationships, to speak in complete sentences, and a host of
other characteristics that would be valuable to the teacher in planning the work for the year.

Discussion Questions

1. The authors constantly compare and contrast *two* different types of
   classes—one that they think is good and one that they think is bad.
   Is this helpful? Defensible? Confusing? Unfair to some types of
   teaching?
2. What other factors, besides those mentioned by the authors, are indicative of a good curriculum in use?
3. What do you think of the authors' statement about reading? Do you
   believe in promoting non-readers to the third grade when they are old
   enough? Should poor readers be given more drill? Can this last question be answered "yes" or "no?"
4. What do you think about language being taught "instrumentally?"
   Do you believe the study of grammar helped you to write or speak
   correctly? Explain.
5. Are businessmen correct when they sometimes say that the schools
   neglect spelling? What are the reasons for your answer? Should you
   have research evidence to support your view? The authors suggest
   two viewpoints about teaching spelling. Which do you favor?
6. Try to describe how you would endeavor to get children to adopt
   for themselves high standards of handwriting excellence.
7. Do you think that a knowledge of science is crucial in the modern
   world? Try to make a short list of major learnings in science that
   elementary-school children should master.
8. What about deferring arithmetic until children are ready? Can arithmetic be taught by skipping around without regard for the logical
   nature of the subject? When should the logic of arithmetic become
   clear to children?
9. Are discussions of the fine arts and music filled with too many general
   and somewhat meaningless words such as "creativity," "self-expression," and the like? Pick out such words and try to define them to
   your satisfaction. Why do such terms abound in the area of aesthetics?
10. Evaluate the school health program outlined in this chapter.
11. What implications do the main points in the discussion of kinder-
    gartens have for all the primary grades? For the whole elementary
    school?

12. In view of the organization of this book so far, should more or less have been said about social studies? Does the whole book so far place too much emphasis on social studies?

Selected References

Blough, G. O., *Materials and Apparatus for Teaching Elementary Science,* Education Brief No. 1. Washington, D. C.: U. S. Office of Education, 1947.

Bond, G. L. and E. B. Wagner, *Teaching the Child to Read,* Rev. ed. New York: The Macmillan Company, 1950.

Brownell, Clifford Lee, *Principles of Health Education Applied.* New York: McGraw-Hill Book Company, Inc., 1949.

Brueckner, L. J. and F. E. Grossnickle, *How to Make Arithmetic Meaningful.* Philadelphia: John C. Winston Company, 1947.

Craig, G. S., *Science for the Elementary School Teacher.* Boston: Ginn and Company, 1947.

Dawson, Mildred Agnes, *Language Teaching in Grades One and Two.* Yonkers, New York: World Book Company, 1949.

Gates, A. I., *The Improvement of Reading.* New York: The Macmillan Company, 1947.

Gray, W. S., *On Their Own in Reading.* Chicago: Scott, Foresman and Company, 1948.

Hildreth, Gertrude, *Child Growth Through Education.* New York: The Ronald Press Company, 1948.

Michaelis, J. U., *Social Studies for Children in a Democracy.* New York: Prentice-Hall, Inc., 1950.

Myers, Louise Kilfer, *Teaching Children Music in the Elementary School.* New York: Prentice-Hall, Inc., 1950.

Preston, Ralph Clausius, *Teaching Social Studies in the School.* New York: Rinehart & Company, Inc., 1950.

Quillen, Isaac James and Lavonne A. Hanna, *Education for Social Competence: Curriculum and Instruction in Secondary-School Social Studies.* Chicago: Scott, Foresman and Company, 1948.

Saucier, W. A., *Theory and Practice in the Elementary School.* New York: The Macmillan Company, 1951.

Stack, Herbert James, *Education for Safe Living,* 2nd ed. New York: Prentice-Hall, Inc., 1949.

Witty, Paul Andrew, *Reading in Modern Education.* Boston: D. C. Heath & Company, 1949.

Wesley, Edgar Bruce, *Teaching the Social Studies in High Schools,* 3rd ed. Boston: D. C. Heath & Company, 1950.

15

TEACHING ABOUT THE PHYSICAL WORLD

*A*s NEVER BEFORE, man is coming to understand the impact of the physical world in which he lives. Everything that has been discussed in the preceding chapters about man as an individual or as a member of a group is tied in with the question of how the physical world affects man. The technological developments of the past century and particularly of the last few years have greatly increased man's control of his physical environment, and at the same time have multiplied in number and complexity the problems he faces. In the elementary-school curriculum during the next decade, there will be many changes designed to bring about a more adequate emphasis on science.

For the teacher, all this must be regarded in two ways. First, the teacher must always consider the child in relation to the physical world in which he lives. In considering him as an individual or as a member of a class living in a community, his problems must be seen in relation to the world around him. Second, the teacher must be constantly alert to acquaint the child with the world, and with the sciences that reveal his world to him. The knowledge basic to these two thoughts cannot be divided into two categories. The teacher must be adept in using the same knowledge for both purposes. The teacher uses his knowledge of society both to interpret for himself the nature of a child in society and to make the child's study of society more interesting and meaningful. The same thing is true of the teacher's knowledge of biology and the physical sciences.

The teaching of science in the elementary school may be defined as the process of bringing children into a functional relationship with their physical environment. By functional we mean "can and will be used." The material that can and will be used develops skills and attitudes and imparts information concerning the vital problems of scientific progress, human welfare, and survival.[1] The best introductory science teaching utilizes the natural curiosity of pupils about their physical world. That is part of what is meant by the oft-repeated phrase, "starting where the student is."

The student is a "common sense realist." Children accept as real the impressions they gain from their sensory experiences. Thus to them the world is flat because it seems to be flat. This we must keep in mind. In addition, children do not know that adults can be effective in making the environment serve human welfare. Another way of saying this is that students are unaware, as children, of adult responsibility for using the physical environment for man's benefit.

Consider first the idea that children believe that what they see, exists as they see it. It is natural and normal to be a common sense realist. We saw in Chapter 1 that this belief has a long and distinguished tradition behind it. Aristotle, for example, thought that heavy objects *must* fall faster than light objects. For centuries intelligent men were certain, too, that the earth was flat. These were but two of many beliefs founded on common sense realism. The lesson in this for the elementary-school science teacher is that he must help the students to know that in addition to the senses (and common sense knowledge) there is the power to test, to refine observations, to be critical, and to generalize from tested data. This is the scientific way.

This returns us to the second idea, which was that children do not know that adults can be effective in making the environment serve human welfare. Children usually are aware of the physical world only as it impresses itself upon their senses. Because they are common sense realists, they realize that they did not have a hand in fashioning it and consequently feel powerless to control it for their own needs. This attitude could lead children to be indifferent

[1] See the criterion for selection of knowledge, skills, and attitudes as listed in Chapter 12.

toward their responsibilities as adults. The conservation of natural resources, for example, might seem unimportant to them.

Such widespread indifference would be fatal to mankind. That is why elementary teachers increasingly take every opportunity to help children understand their physical environment. When children do understand it, they come to see that man can control the physical environment for his own benefit. This is a step in the direction of assuming responsibility for human welfare. In order that students may have confidence in their own intelligence, they must see and experience the benefits that go with intelligent control of the physical world. No opportunity is to be missed for impressing upon students the hazards of indifference.

The child in the primary unit who studies water, soil, forests, and edible plants in relation to man's needs is beginning to learn about man and his world—the interdependence within all nature. Units built around field trips will help acquaint pupils with their environment. If it is granted that man is dependent upon his environment even though he is constantly modifying it, then it is possible that, fortified and disciplined with information that is valid about the world and its potentialities, man could create for himself and his fellows a very decent future. But progress is not inevitable. "Utopia" will cost hard work, study, experiment, restraint, and above all, a willingness to cooperate. This goal of human welfare is pretty abstract to an unaided child. It is the teacher's responsibility to help him progress from common sense realism to a more sophisticated perception of the world around him.

Physical environment shapes the way of life

Cultural anthropologists, studying primitive people in an effort to understand the nature of "culture," always dramatize the degree to which geography affects living.[2] Two of the more famous examples are the studies that have been made of the Sioux and the Yurok Indians.

The Yurok Indians.[3] The Yurok Indians lived in the narrow,

[2] Ralph E. Turner, *American Civilization.* New York: Alfred A. Knopf, Inc., 1925, p. 57.
[3] Erik Hamburger Erikson, "Childhood and Tradition in Two American Indian Tribes," in Clyde Kluckhohn and Henry A. Murray, eds., *Personality in Nature, Society and Culture.* New York: Alfred A. Knopf, Inc., 1948.

densely wooded river valley of the Klamath River that empties into the Pacific Ocean just below the Yurok village. Hemmed in by the cliffs of the river, these Indians looked upon their valley as a world in itself. Travel was unnecessary, for each year the salmon run brought to the Yurok an abundance of food. Erikson describes the tribe in these words: "They were peaceful and sedentary, gathering acorns, fishing, and preparing themselves spiritually for the annual miracle of the salmon run, when an abundance of fish enters and ascends their river, coming from the ocean like a gift from nowhere." [4] Yurok culture revolved about the salmon. The hopes and fears of adults and children were shaped by the salmon. Religion, mysteries, rites, and rituals were touched with the image of the salmon.

The Sioux. Similar studies have been made of many other Indian tribes: The Saulteaux, Hopi, Ojibwa, and Pepago. Erikson found all of them stamped by the environment in which they lived. "The original image of the Sioux is that of the warrior and the hunter, endowed with manliness and mobility, cunning and cruelty." [5] As a tribe, the Sioux were loosely organized, belligerent, usually generous, and certainly brave. Apparently their environment accounted for these personality traits. Loose tribal organization was a product of the life of the plains. The buffalo and antelope wandered and so did the hunters. Much of the day was spent on horseback. Family possessions had to be few, light, and easily moved. Belligerence might have been a result of the dangerous occupation followed by the men and the warfare engendered when Sioux encountered alien peoples, often agrarian and settled. Generosity stemmed from the possibility of having too much meat one day and none the next. The successful hunter shared his game with others in order that on a less successful day they would share with him.

The stories of the Sioux and the Yurok show the way that man's living habits are influenced by his physical setting. This remains but an interesting bit of information if the teacher does not understand that in these simple cultures, the people were at the mercy

<hr>

4 Erikson, "Childhood and Tradition in Two American Indian Tribes," p. 177.

5 *Ibid.* For further data see Erik Hamburger Erickson, "Observations on Sioux Education," *Journal of Psychology,* Vol. 7, 1939, 101-156.

of their environment—their lives were restricted and determined by forces that *they did not attempt to control.*

The analysis of man's dependence upon the physical environment and his intelligent adaptation to his surroundings assists the study of history, geography, and social science in general. For example, what a country is, depends to a very great extent upon its areal and regional shape and size, topography, location, and natural resources. It depends upon the shoreline, natural harbors, navigable rivers, arable land, grazing land, deposits of coal, oil, iron, and non-ferrous minerals. The United Kingdom is well situated in regard to world shipping routes and can obtain and market raw materials, which Australia, for example, cannot because of her isolated location.[6] Chile is 2,500 miles long but only about a hundred miles wide. She is less favorably situated than would be the case of a more compact but otherwise comparable area.[7]

The physical environment also is a determining factor within countries. Steep slopes, to employ a topographic illustration, allow topsoil to be washed away, leaving shallow and poor residue and curtailing the amount of available arable land. Pittsburgh, Pennsylvania, and Gary, Indiana, became great steel producing centers because of their accessibility to the iron ore deposits of northern Minnesota and the coal beds of Pennsylvania, Kentucky, and Ohio. Nature also chose the site for Kansas City, Missouri. Located at the travel and commercial crossroads of the nation and the logical center of a large and rich agricultural and cattle producing area, Kansas City expanded as the West was developed.

Two important ideas and their relation to curriculum organization. The first of the ideas illustrated in this chapter was that the physical environment determines the way people live. Twin to this concept, its hopeful counterpart, is an assumption that man is intelligent and able to curb his appetites, discipline himself, and plan in order to advance human welfare. Regardless of how the curriculum may be organized, these two basic ideas can be used by the elementary-school teacher. If the curriculum is organized into subject-matter areas, it can be done as indicated on pages 298 to

[6] Darrell Haug Davis, *The Earth and Man.* New York: The Macmillan Company, 1942, p. 143.
[7] *Ibid.*

305. If organized as units, either subject-matter units or experience units, the approach indicated on pages 306 to 314 can be used.

Emphasizing the environment
in the subject-organized curriculum

Teachers whose prescribed course of study or whose personal-professional conviction requires that various subjects be taught as separate subjects in separate periods under their traditional names will still wish to stress (1) that the physical environment determines the way people live, and (2) that man is able to influence and control this environment to his own advantage or disadvantage. In Chapter 12, we outlined four types of curriculums, and in Chapter 12 we divided these into two groups: (1) subject-matter curriculums, and (2) developmental-activity curriculums. Subject-matter units are generally used with the former, experience units with the latter. The illustrations that follow show how various basic ideas or generalizations about man and his environment can be taken up in the history, geography, and health-hygiene courses typical of the subject-organized program of study in many elementary schools. Examples show how these ideas and generalizations can be used in *correlating subject matter* and making the content of the curriculum more meaningful to the pupil. If teachers are to correlate two, three, or more subjects, it must be done through ideas and generalizations that are common, and preferably basic, to all the subjects.

Teaching geography with an emphasis on interdependence within nature. Geography can be one of the most instructive and interesting subjects in the elementary school because it deals with the environment as it affects man's welfare. In order to make this point clear to the youngster, the elementary-school teacher will do well to exercise care in selecting topics that can be interrelated. Four topics have been selected here—one on relative humidity, one on frost, one on oceans, and one on geographical regions.[8] These were arbitrarily chosen. In an actual classroom, the teacher who follows a rigid curriculum might find them in the written course of study.

[8] For children's books that emphasize similar materials see Bertha Morris Parker, and Ralph Buchsbaum, *Balance in Nature.* Evanston, Illinois: Row, Peterson and Company, 1941. See also, Glenn O. Blough and Bertha Morris Parker, *An Aquarium.* Evanston, Illinois: Row, Peterson and Company, 1950.

The teacher who plans the work himself might suggest or prescribe them to the pupils. The teacher who plans with his pupils might find that they did or did not select these topics. However, any teacher alert to the discussions that go on in the geography class when the children are allowed to talk freely about their lessons will find topics such as these constantly coming up. The topics selected have no magic in them. Many others could be selected just as well. Their purpose here is to illustrate a method by which interest is aroused, work and study stimulated, and a realistic understanding of the interdependence that is characteristic of our world attained. This interdependence is one of the highly important facts with which men must learn to live intelligently.

Relative humidity as a topic. The study of relative humidity is one of a variety of topics that can serve to acquaint students with their physical environment and its influence on human life.[9] The relative humidity of any geographical region affects the water supply and hence the kind of crops that may be grown. This relates the topic to the ways in which men make a living.

Plants adapt themselves to the humidity characteristics of the regions in which they grow. In arid regions, plants are small-leaved to prevent excessive evaporation of moisture that would cause the plant to wither and die. In humid areas the reverse is true—plants are broad-leaved to encourage evaporation.[10] A crop planted in a hot, dry area of Texas would require more moisture than the same crop planted in a cooler, more humid area of Montana. A wise farmer, thinking of planting a broad-leaved plant requiring much rainfall and an atmosphere that has a relative high humidity (in order that the plant's moisture not be drained off) would take steps to insure an adequate supply of water. Were the water unavailable he would be courting disaster to plant the crop. Geography is a study that *can* profit man.

9 Relative humidity or the water content of air may be expressed as a percentage relationship between the amount of water by weight in a definite volume of air and the amount an equal volume of air can contain under the same conditions of temperature and pressure. For example, if a cubic foot of air at 70 degrees F. contains four grains of water, it contains one-half or 50 per cent of what it is able to hold at that temperature. Its relative humidity is 50.

10 An example of the many books available on the geographic aspects of the subject is J. R. Whitaker, *Geography in School and College*. Nashville, Tennessee: George Peabody College for Teachers, 1948.

We all need food whether we live in cities or in rural areas. Relative humidity is a topic that is of universal importance because of its relationship to agriculture. It also meets the other criteria for selecting knowledge and attitudes discussed in Chapter 12. And let us not forget these criteria. If we do, we may teach geography with but superficial reference to how the physical characteristics of a region affect such things as the types of crops, the typical work habits, and way of life of the people inhabiting the region.

Beyond geography. Relative humidity is not a topic that relates only to geography. Nor is it a concept that originated with geographers or one that geographers can explain as adequately as can physicists. No science stands alone. Just as interdependence characterizes the real world, the connection and interdependence of the sciences typify the study of the physical world. The elementary teacher who fails to understand this point may be tempted to give students an isolated definition of relative humidity and fail to reveal its interrelatedness to a discussion of crops and the conservation of water supplies. That will not do for children. Most of them will not be satisfied with, or understand, an abstract definition of relative humidity. The geography lesson will have to include some classroom demonstrations that show some of the properties of hot and cold air, and should be made to include the effects on health of various climatic conditions. In geography, children need to have the physical principles brought down to their level of comprehension and this can best be done by simple demonstrations of physical principles.[11]

Frost as a topic. Outside of certain "favored" spots in our country, almost every gardener knows the significance of the phrase "killing frost." [12] It typifies one of the facts of nature that, although beyond man's ability to prevent, still can be dealt with intelligently. Man is not helpless in confronting it and in this fact lies a point that the child should learn. The small gardener can cover his

---

[11] See, for example, Bertha Morris Parker, *Clouds, Rain, and Snow,* 1950; and *The Air About Us,* 1950. Both books are published by Row, Peterson, and Company, Evanston, Illinois.

[12] Plants die when there is a killing frost because their watery sap freezes and, in freezing, expands, rupturing the cell walls. In many regions, the teacher who wishes a class to understand that water expands when freezing and desires to have that understanding useful will find the world about him replete with illustrative materials.

plants, this is common knowledge; but it may not be financially possible for a farmer to protect his large crop in this way. However, if he is free to relocate near a large body of water, his knowledge of the physical world will stand him in good stead for there is a relation between the temperature of the air and the presence of large bodies of water. The air near a lake or ocean is warmer in fall and winter than air over land in the same latitude. Water "gives off" heat while cooling. Crops in the neighborhood of large bodies of water, then, have a measure of frost protection. The farmer can still protect his crop, even if there are no stretches of water to ameliorate the killing frost, by using blankets of smoke in his orchards. At least he should know that since warm air rises and that cold air sinks, crops planted at the bases of slopes will be frost-killed sooner than those growing higher on the slopes.

This much would be pure geography, but the principles of "convection currents"—of the relative density of cold and warm air— these also are a part of physics. The alert geography teacher will introduce his student to these principles with the help of simple experiments. Thus, the children will begin their acquaintance with the "laws of nature." The acquaintance, moreover, will be a lively one for having been met in human geography, in the study of things vital to living.

Oceans as a topic. Oceans cover 72 per cent of the earth's surface. They are the source of most rainfall and can easily work into any discussion of weather, atmosphere, or climate. A more obvious way of acquainting students with oceans would be in connection with a unit on transportation. Today and in the past, oceans are and have been important avenues of commerce and travel. In addition, they are important sources of food and have a profound effect on the temperature and moisture of the land adjacent to them. The Pacific Ocean and the leeward and windward slopes of the Sierras exemplify the relation of an ocean, prevailing winds, and a land mass. The slopes of the Sierras facing the Pacific precipitate the moisture borne by the prevailing winds sweeping in from the sea. The leeward slopes are dry. Many pupils will be interested in learning the practical economic geography that is related to a discussion of living conditions on either side of the mountains.

These examples show how the ocean can be studied in ways that are significant for human geography, economic geography, physical geography, physics, and other subjects. Fortified with a broad background, later study of the sciences will not lead to the common, though utterly false, conclusion that the sciences are not interrelated or that scientific knowledge is an end in itself.[13]

The upland region as a topic. One of the most interesting lessons that may be learned from geography is that the topography and location of a geographical region has a good deal to do with a person's life in all its aspects. The mountainous areas of our country are relatively uninhabited. Here the water, through the centuries, has robbed the steep slopes of topsoil, streams are too swift for navigation, surface irregularity is great and cultivation is decidedly difficult, temperatures are low, and communications are poor. People live by choice where there are optimum conditions for agriculture, manufacturing, or commerce and trade. Thus mountains are sparsely populated.

In studying the lives of hill folk and the lack of development in the "hills," students have but to apply the facts about climate and soil. They could go a step further in their generalization and ask themselves what difference it makes to the nation as a whole that the birthrate is high in these regions and that the excess population tends to migrate to the cities because the bare mountain land cannot support large numbers of people.

In these four topics different portions of the country have been considered. Some teachers live near the oceans, some in the hill

[13] The facts about nature, the principles and so-called laws students learn, must be carefully scrutinized. For example, the persistent discussion of our need for water may lead the student to think that rain is a blessing of which one cannot have too much. That certainly is not true. Unless the earth is able to absorb and hold the rain, erosion results from rapid run-off. "The exact amount which will be the optimum varies with the form, distribution, intensity, rate of evaporation and other factors such as natural drainage and soil types." "In general rainfalls of from 20 to 60 inches are advantageous. Below 20 inches, agriculture normally becomes hazardous; above 60 inches, the excess precipitation is not beneficial. Inspection of a population map of the world will show that at least 90 per cent of the world's inhabitants live in those areas favored by precipitation conditions." Davis, *The Earth and Man*, p. 135.

There is a lesson in conservation in this, too. Often water runs off too rapidly in the area, because the land has been carelessly logged-off. When trees grow their roots hold the water in the soil and slow the run-off. The fact that unsettled areas where the precipitation averages more than 60 inches a year is poor farming country, because the water washes valuable minerals from the soil, means that we cannot allow erosion to ruin our present farming country in the vain prospect of opening such unsettled areas to agriculture.

country, others near agricultural areas—all where the conditions of relative humidity, topography, climate, and other physical factors make a crucial difference to living. We might have suggested topics for the teacher who works near Pennsylvania's coal mines, Indiana's steel plants, or Minnesota's iron range. These topics, too, would have fitted the teaching of economic geography. We might have pointed out that the industrial might of the United States is linked to our possession of about two-thirds of the world's coal supply. In northern Minnesota, vast deposits of iron ore lie close to the surface of the earth, so close that they can be extracted with giant power-driven shovels and loaded onto railroad cars that travel *downhill* to a fine natural harbor in Duluth, where ore boats haul their cargo to the smelters and mills of the lake shore steel centers of Gary, Indiana and Buffalo, New York. There is a natural interdependence between the coal of Pennsylvania, West Virginia, and Ohio, the iron of Minnesota, and the limestone of Indiana—to say nothing of the lake route for transporting iron ore.

There are many other topics in geography illustrative of the connections that exist within nature and which man, armed with knowledge, can exploit. Let us go on to consider the relation of nature's interdependence with an important elementary-school subject, health and hygiene.

Teaching the interdependence of health and hygiene with nature. All science instruction in the elementary school, or in the secondary school for that matter, can and should teach about man's dependence upon the environment (of which he is a part, of course) and the control he can exercise over it, if he knows its interconnections or the principles of these relations. The subject of soil and soil conservation [14] is illustrative of the many promising avenues that can be used in making an approach to a study of health and hygiene. Let us examine a brief illustration of man's dependence upon the soil, as far as health is concerned.

Many farms produce large yields but the minerals necessary to human health and to healthy farm stock have been "mined" from much of the soil. Consequently, the crops lack the vitamins and

[14] Bertha Morris Parker, *Soil.* Evanston, Illinois: Row, Peterson and Company, 1943. This is yet another book suitable for children that illustrates the important facts about soil that children can comprehend and that they need in order to understand the physical environment and their duties as citizens.

minerals necessary for health. This is one reason why crop rotation is urged by the county agricultural agent. A class looking into the question of diet and good health will need to understand that growing the same crop in the same patch of ground season after season removes the same minerals until these vital elements are exhausted. Not all crops, however, require the same minerals for growth. Hence, the rotating of crops and the use of chemical fertilizer replenishes the soil of some of its minerals. There is at present no way of knowing how many illnesses result from dietary deficiencies resulting from the lack of minerals in the soil. But there is reason to suspect that the number is large.

In all this, the teacher will see that two ideas, health and conservation, both indispensable for human welfare, emerge from the same scientific study of the interrelated environment. Both emerged naturally and easily since man has his roots in nature, every part of which is related to every other part. The things we eat, animal or vegetable, take their nourishment from the air, soil, and water. Whether one starts the scientific study of nature from an analysis of air, soil, and water or whether one begins by studying agriculture and animal husbandry, man and man's welfare is dependent upon natural resources.

Teaching history with an emphasis on its interdependence with other subjects. When we talked of relative humidity and of frost we noticed that science instruction cannot comfortably be squeezed into the limits of any one subject. Similarly, history cannot be limited to the mere chronological recitation of events. There is a place for that at the college or graduate-school level, but it has no place in the elementary school. History is the story of man. This story involves a study of nature, too, for as we have continually stressed, man lives within an environment. In what follows, we are talking about history *plus* geography, history *plus* economics, and history *plus* nature study.

A good example to use in illustrating the way in which history, geography, economics, and nature study are interrelated is the story of how the American West was won. The episode of the westward expansion, the pioneer, the unlimited land, and the prodigal waste of resources that attended the conquest should become familiar in some form or another to most children. The opportunities here for the teacher are almost limitless.[15] The presentation could include a discussion of the bare, rocky soil of New England that led many "Yankees" to undertake the long trek; a study of the inland waterways—the Ohio River and its tributaries and the Great Lakes—over which many of the pioneers traveled; the magnetic attraction of "free land" in the West and the story of how this land often was ruthlessly exploited and the implications today of such exploitation in the field of conservation; and finally, the West as a kind of social laboratory and incubator of democracy, drawing people together from different regions and lands, blending checkered cultures, and providing a testing ground for new social and religious theories—the Owenite community at New Harmony and the Mormon experiment in Utah. These are but a few of the many illustrations that could be used to emphasize the idea of the interrelatedness of the historical, geographical, and social. The elementary-school teacher is not being asked to teach about unnatural connections. The relationships exist and the teacher should be able to help the student explore them.

In the past, history was taught in an isolated, chronological way as dealing only with wars, warrior kings, treaties, and the like. Students who are forced to memorize long lists of virtually meaningless dates come to regard history as a bore and a drudge. But there are ways in which the teacher may resolve this dilemma. Interesting parallels may be drawn that reveal the interrelatedness of the historical, the economic, and the geographical. Opportunities abound for instructing students in the concept of the balance of nature during the course of the history lesson. One striking example is afforded in our own West where farmers and ranchers must spend large amounts of money and time to control the gopher because earlier they had all but wiped out the coyote, the natural enemy of the gopher, and thus upset nature's delicate balance.[16] A similar example concerns the case of the Australian rabbit. Introduced into that subcontinent to supply sport for resident Englishmen, the rabbit, having no natural enemies, soon so increased in numbers that its control has come to be a perplexing and expensive task for the Australian government.

---

[15] Davis, *The Earth and Man,* p. 171.
[16] *Ibid.,* p. 343.

The environment in the unit-organized curriculum

We have been talking in terms of separate subjects that are correlated. Now we will change our approach and think in terms of experience units rather than subjects. Because the separate subjects do overlap in any realistic teaching approach, there is a trend toward teaching in terms of units planned in such a way that they consciously and thoughtfully draw on such subjects as geography, history, and the sciences. This is a realistic trend. As we have said again and again, nature is one and the subjects are separate only for convenience. No one could be master of them all. In the elementary school, however, children need to sense the unity of nature. There is time enough for specialization. Children are so ignorant of the forest that it is almost foolish to have them memorize the names of all the trees.

These remarks follow from the discussion in Chapter 13 of insights useful in planning units containing material from more than one subject. They follow from the discussion of the developmental-experience unit and of the extensive resource unit that includes a wealth of material from which selections are made in terms of the objectives of elementary education and the interests, needs, and abilities of the children. An experience unit takes place in the classroom; the written unit from which it springs, at least in part, should be thought of as a resource unit.

As was said before, the authors of this book advocate unit instruction. However, there is much excellent teaching done in subject-organized courses. The environment, the physical world, is the same whether it is approached from the standpoint of units or subjects. The class that keeps its eye on the essential unity, the interdependence within nature, gets at facts and principles crucial for all students. Then the choice of units or subjects reduces itself to one of efficiency and adequacy, as well as of convenience, training, preference, and experience. The major *potential* weakness of subject-centered instruction, aside from restrictions caused by fragmented time schedules, interruptions in developing and holding interest, and other mechanical limitations, is that it may lean too heavily on *a* textbook and on one, single, non-functional organization of ideas. It may neglect the nature of the child as a learner and as a member of his society. It should be admitted that teachers who claim to teach through "experience units" can fall into the same trap. There is much more to good teaching or good curriculum organization than the mere decision to organize material into either integrated subject courses or into experience units.

In the material that follows, background will be suggested that might be included as a *part* of various resource units. The four background areas are on (1) conservation, (2) China, (3) population, and (4) soil. It must be held clearly in mind that these four discussions do not constitute units, unit outlines, or outlines of subject matter that children will necessarily learn. They represent the type of materials that go to make up good resource units, but a single complete resource unit sometimes is as lengthy as a small book. The four brief discussions that follow point out some materials and insights that children should learn and understand, but they also include material that will be of value only for the teacher. These are not discussed in this chapter in such detail that the teacher or prospective teacher who is untrained in physical science will necessarily follow all the discussion or understand precisely the meaning of all the terms. The purpose of the four discussions, in part, is to point out the importance of scientific insights for the pupil *and* the teacher and to illustrate the nature of some of the insights useful to both.

Some background for a resource unit on soil conservation. Children in the elementary schools of many of our western states can find in the study of the Dust Bowl, much information that will clarify and simplify their thinking and the thinking of their communities relative to such matters as the dependence of animals and men upon the soil, the causes of soil depletion, and how soil erosion may be checked.

In the nineteen-thirties topsoil from the Dust Bowl dimmed the sun as far east as Washington where legislators were faced with the problem of conservation. Anyone who had seriously thought about the problem realized its implications, but the majority of citizens were apathetic and few knew what might be done to check and to prevent a similar disaster from ever occurring again.[17]

[17] Halene Hatcher writes, ". . . widespread apathy toward conservation is reflected in the fact that of our total national income for 1945 approximately one-half of 1 per cent was spent on conservation research, education and operations. Further evidence of prevailing complacency is apparent when we consider that of over 1,000 foundations in the United States, only two are devoted to

What happened in the Dust Bowl had happened before. Conservationists estimate that during our national history, wind and water have, between them, blown or washed away three inches of topsoil. There were nine inches originally. A third of America's heritage in soil is gone. Six inches stand between today's standard of living and starvation.

The Dust Bowl resulted from winds dispersing the dry, pulverized topsoil. In analyzing the sequence of events, with an eye to cure and prevention, the student and the citizen must know something about the nature and movement of winds. Winds that are dry evaporate large quantities of moisture. Blowing in force they will dry out and then sweep away as much topsoil in half a day as is carried off by water erosion in months or years. The winds that denuded the Dust Bowl of topsoil would have blown strong and dry across the plains, but they probably would have moved little earth had there been windbreaks of trees or had the area been left untilled with its original covering of Buffalo grass. The Dust Bowl area is often dry and subject to drought because of its geographical location. That fact cannot be changed. But the farmers flew in the face of the facts, plowed under the grass, and then were taken unaware when the winds blew away the exposed, pulverized, dried topsoil.

Not all Americans think seriously about the soil. After all, 55 per cent of Americans live in cities. Some of the indifference may be because there is so much soil that it appears to be inexhaustible. Actually, neglect of the soil costs Americans 4 billion dollars every year. About 3 billion tons of soil materials are lost annually.

Man will always live within a physical world and knowledge of that world, its limitations and possibilities, will be essential at any time. The judicious use of natural resources is not a passing need. No one can foresee the day when men will be free to overlook natural resources.

China, background for a resource unit illustrating the results of unsuccessful adaptation. China represents a case history in the consequences of not living intelligently with the facts of nature.[18] After

---

renewable natural resources." "Conservation Education or Tragedy," *The Journal of Geography,* Vol. 48, January 1949, 20-26.

18 Gerald F. Winfield, *China: The Land and the People.* New York: William Sloane Associates, 1948.

the fashion of peasant rebellions the world over, the Chinese recently fought for a redistribution of their crowded land, although any further subdivisions of Chinese acreage can only be detrimental. The Communists took advantage of the conditions they found in China to get the people to redistribute into smaller parcels the inadequate farm land now available. The real trouble in China is the failure of the people to adjust to their interdependence with their physical environment. What China needs is greater agricultural production (now high per tillable acre but low per man) and more tillable land. A 13-acre farm uses its labor supply almost twice as efficiently as the more usual small Chinese farm of two to five acres. Thus, contrary to Chinese Communist promises, some 180 million of the present farming population will have to be moved into city industries if the farms are to be made more productive. All this is a lesson in world history that finds a counterpart in many countries such as India, Hungary, Poland, and throughout the Balkans. A broad general education will enable the teacher to draw valuable lessons similar to those mentioned here from almost all activities that develop in the classroom.

There is a second aspect to the Chinese story. It is concerned with health, a subject that can always be related to the land. In this story, the central figure is the pig and his sty. In China, the pig plays the same role as the snail in an aquarium. The snail transforms fish waste into organic materials used by the plants, the plants, in turn, supplying oxygen used by the fish. The pig sty usually is located adjacent to the Chinese peasant's latrine. In China the life expectancy is 30 years as compared with more than 60 years in this country. About 25 per cent of all deaths in China are caused by fecal-borne diseases: hookworm, liver flukes, and intestinal flukes (that kill their victim by preventing the assimilation of food). These diseases could be checked by sterilizing human waste, a process no more elaborate than composting it. Unfortunately, this would require mixing vegetable waste with the human waste and the poor Chinese farmer must use whatever vegetable matter can be spared for fuel. The snail in the classroom aquarium will provide a link with far off China in such a discussion.

The interdependence of elements within an economy enter the picture at almost every point and is shown in other aspects of the study of China. China has extensive coal deposits and vast poten-

tial but undeveloped hydroelcctric resources. However, her transportation system is not sufficiently developed to allow the coal to
be transported to different points in the country where it can be
used for industry. Her lack of dams, generators, power lines, and
factories leaves her water power untapped. These are some of the
points about the geography of China that elementary children can
understand. They meet the test of cruciality and the other criteria
used to test material for the elementary school.

Population, background for a resource unit on current events.
People have tended to settle where living is easy, there to work and
raise families. Usually the growth in population was not accompanied by any concern for the resources needed to support the
growing numbers of people. Perhaps the people never learned
enough about their physical environment to know that its resources
were expendable. Gradually the standard of living declined. Health
was impaired because as the soil was depleted it did not impart
sufficient minerals and vitamins to the plants that were consumed
by animals and men. Perhaps farms were sub-divided with the passing generations and became too small for efficient cultivation. At
last a day came when it seemed that the nation must acquire new
lands and new resources if life was to be sustained. Since there was
no free land to exploit, a neighbor's country was coveted. War
broke out; men died that others might live a while longer. Before
the war, all available land within the country had been converted
to farming, although most of it should never have been plowed.
There were portions of the nation where strong, dry winds blew
and little rain fell. To plow those sections invited dust storms. The
tale is an unhappy one. Had the people understood man's interaction with his environment, they might have avoided some of
their errors.

Population experts have a fondness for figures and upon occasion
their statistics can "make iron tears run down Pluto's cheeks." Before recounting any of them it would be well to acknowledge a few
cautions. It is probable that if the world could not support over
two billion people, they would not be here. It is also likely that
self-discipline, intelligent administration, and wise consumption
could lighten the problems of people in economically "backward"
areas.

The statistics are impressive, nevertheless. Mr. Vogt puts it this way: the population of Germany was about 25 million in 1800 and (will be) about 71 million in 1950. Italy will have come from 18 million in 1800 to 47 million in 1950. Japan's increase will be over 300 per cent, from 25 million in 1800 to about 80 million in 1950. England and Wales will have grown in population from about 8 million in 1800 to about 41 million in 1950.[19]

Russia furnishes another illustration. The U.S.S.R., a vast country, faces the severe problem of increasing the potential of her land. The Atlantic Ocean is the source of most of the rain that falls in Russia, and most of the rainbearing winds drop their moisture before reaching her fields. Thus she receives a relatively small amount of rainfall in proportion to her area. This climatic factor becomes a most interesting instance of how world affairs are touched by a country's geographical situation. Most of Russia's fertile soil lies on the steppes East of the Caspian Sea. The rainfall on these steppes is between 12 and 16 inches annually and unless the government is able to find underground water supplies—low in alkalinity (in order not to sow the soil with salt) and inexhaustible—this region will not be able to feed the growing population of the country. This is true despite the fortunate circumstance for Russia that much of the rainfall occurs during the growing season. This appears to be the region on which the Soviet government is depending to feed its rapidly growing population. If the gamble on the agricultural productivity of these soils should turn against Russia, she might become more aggressive than ever before.

The children who are studying the geography of Europe should learn something about these relationships bewteen men and the resources around them. It is more important to know how rainfall and geographic positions affect Russian policy than it is to know the names of the great cities and rivers, even though they are important too. It is necessary, in studying the British Isles, to understand that her increase in population since 1800 kept pace until recently with increasing productivity and profit from the whole Empire. British prosperity was further dependent upon a vast world trade and an efficient merchant marine. Now that the Empire no longer contributes as it formerly did, and British profit from

[19] William Vogt, *The Road to Survival*. New York: William Sloane Associates, 1948, Chapters 8 and 9.

world trade is greatly reduced, the problem of maintaining her large population becomes very difficult.

The point in all this is that children need to learn these things, if not about Russia and Britain, then about some other countries, in order to understand that all peoples are dependent upon the geography of the world and of their particular place in it. One important way to get children to understand these things clearly is to relate them to their own region, state, or locality in their own country.

Soil, background for a unit on human geography. Since the world's people are so dependent upon the land, geography is a "human" subject. Within human geography, which is a study more broad than geopolitics or economic geography, soil is the main subject. Soil presents innumerable problems. Fairfield Osborn summarizes them succinctly: "The problem is," he says, "how to conserve the remaining good natural soils that exist on the earth, together with the complementary resources of forests, water resources, and the myriads of beneficial forms of animal life." [20] The teacher, having stated the problem clearly, can proceed to a study of how to encourage students who may think them insoluble. Children lose interest in problems that they feel to be impossibly difficult. Unless the teacher feels that control of the situation is within man's capability he should not undertake the unit. Most problems of men, problems involving adaptation to material things, are theoretically capable of solution. This is not something that is to be handed students on a platter in order to reassure them. It is much more advisable for the teacher to undertake, on his own and with the students, such research as will give him a clear picture of the problem's dimensions and the types of material that the resource unit must contain if the students are to make progress in their experience units. Let us see what the teacher might do with the problem of soil.

A very little research reveals that only inertia keeps people from saving topsoil that, today, is being lost in this country at the rate of 240 acres daily. This waste is not necessary and students who are concerned with the future must be helped to see what can be done to prevent it. One manner of accomplishing this is pretty much

20 Fairfield Osborn, *Our Plundered Planet.* Boston: Little, Brown and Company, 1948, p. 75.

arithmetical. It will aid students to see that there may be arithmetical relationships between numbers of people, amount of arable land, and a standard of living.[21]

The first step for the student is to see the actual dimensions of the problem. In 1948 the world population stood at roughly $2\frac{1}{4}$ billion persons or 43 persons per square mile compared with a United States population of 145 million and 48 persons per square mile. Thinking of the future, the student should realize that the recent rate of population growth in the United States, to single out this country, has been about 1.5 to 2 million people a year. There are about three people now where there was only one 200 years ago. The world over, there has been an increase of about 45 per cent in the last 50 years, with the increase mostly in the Asiatic countries. Population experts estimate there may be an additional 900 million mouths to feed in the next 50 years, or a total world population of 3.3 billion people.

The student then makes an assumption, based upon the findings of specialists in dietetics. Assuming a world population of $2\frac{1}{4}$ billion persons and estimating very generously, 4 billion arable acres, and 2 and one-half acres required to support each person, it follows that 66 per cent of the world's population is poorly fed. It has been said that 250 million people could be supported in the United States, but only at the Chinese level, as the remaining potentially arable land is largely marginal in productivity and our increase in science and technique is insufficient to keep pace with population growth.[22] Human society is inviting trouble unless it learns to conserve its natural resources.

Children become interested in various aspects of erosion relatively early in their experience. Many of us have seen children playing in

[21] Without any doubt our land resources can be made to support the world population for some time to come by applying known methods of technique and science as we have a world food potential of some additional 1.3 billion acres. Needed are increased production, increased conservation, a higher standard of living for rural people, full use of farm family labor, and sufficient insight into the problem to encourage the self-discipline that is needed.

[22] Professor Hatcher suggests that 4 billion acres of arable land might be an overestimate. She writes: "Pearson and Harper, after considering the portions of the earth that have a favorable combination of temperature, moisture, soils, sunlight, and other factors, give a more conservative figure of 2,600,000,000 acres as the total amount of land suitable for food production. This means little more than one acre for each person." "Conservation Education or Tragedy," 20-26.

the running water when winter's snows are melting. Older children have seen gullies in the rural areas. If they can be made curious about such things, they can be led to study erosion. There is much material available concerning erosion. Much of it can be obtained from state and federal conservation agencies. Also, there are many books on the subject suitable for teachers and for brighter children.

Reference to Osborne, Hatcher, Davis, and Vogt will provide much background and many ideas for projects and activities in a classroom. For example, reference to Hatcher will reveal that two and one-half acres of land of average productivity are barely adequate to provide the minimum essentials necessary to sustain one person in good health for one year. From the same source the student can learn that Europe has a ratio of only .88 acres per person. There are countless other examples of ratio in regard to productive land and population. Young people who become interested in this subject will have ample opportunity to exercise their skill in arithmetic in the solution of real problems involving the earth and the welfare of the people who live on it. Similar projects involving arithmetic may be developed regarding the 2,600,000,000 acres of arable land in the world that is best adapted for cultivation, the percentage of this land in various countries, and the rate at which it is being depleted or destroyed.

In all this study, the background is the earth that has been washed or blown away through erosion. Students will learn about the land that is left, the inferior clay, and the flat land after the valuable topsoil is lost. Students who relate this study to the South will discover that our southern states are the worst victims of erosion in our country. This erosion has resulted from too much destruction of forest cover, from too intensive cultivation, and from heavy rainfall over ground that does not freeze in the winter and hence is subject to rapid erosion the year round. When students begin to wonder if there is anything that can be done about this destruction, they may be introduced to the classification developed by the United States Soil Conservation Service, which divides land into eight groups or classes. The top three classes are (1) very good land, (2) good land, and (3) moderately good land, all of which can be cultivated, though greater care and additional precautions are necessary in class 3 than in class 1. Class 4 is fairly good land,

but is best suited to pasture, while class 5 is not suitable for cultivation at all, but may be used for grazing or forestry. Class 6 is used
for grazing, but must be protected against over-grazing. Class 7
must be carefully protected if used at all, and class 8 is suitable
only for wild-life or recreation.

As students discuss what can be done to conserve our land by
protecting it from erosion and waste, many opportunities will arise
for creative planning and problem solving. Reforestation can be
considered. Children are always interested in game and fish, hence
wild-life conservation can become an interesting project. The conservation of water, the elimination of waste in water usage, will
involve the study of improper storage of water, the tremendous
cost of floods, the value of irrigation, and the necessity for large
amounts of pure water as cities grow and develop.

The community school
and the community's environment

The idea of the community school that is developing so widely
in our country today has been given great publicity in educational
books and magazines. Those familiar with this concept should remember at this point, however, that the idea has vitality and meaning primarily when it is tied to an intelligent utilization of man's
physical and social environment.

Russell H. Conwell delivered his famous sermon, "Acres of Diamonds: or How Men and Women May Become Rich," some 6,000
times. The moral of his sermon was simple: There are riches in
one's backyard; it is not necessary to travel to the end of the rain-
bow to find wealth. Conwell urged his audiences to make the most
of the resources at hand. This was good sense. There are acres of
educational diamonds in the vicinity of every school. An illustration might be introduced at this point to show how the physical
environment can be used in giving dynamic substance to the community school idea.

There comes to mind a certain school, combined elementary
and secondary, located in the southern portion of one of our
larger western states. The school is in the heart of the state's
sheep country and the locale of some very bitter feuds between

sheep and cattle interests.[23] Forty miles away are mountains where there is water that could be brought to the desert for irrigation. This desert, by the way, now 6,200 feet above sea level, was once ocean bottom and the sands are strewn with fossilized sea life. Geologic history of the most interesting type is at hand. Strange as it may seem, however, the area has never been used to enrich the curriculum for the students. The teachers in this school continue to stress textbook mathematics, textbook literature, and foreign language, and to neglect the rich environment around them. Their course content was almost identical with similar schools in the cities of Illinois or the towns of Maine. To a degree, this may be both necessary and desirable. The criterion of universality should be used. However, the curriculum should take into account the everyday interests of the students. These interests will reflect the students' own environment. Pushing these interests aside misses the acre of diamonds. It will not avail that the teacher thinks in terms of human welfare. The phrase will degenerate into another uninspiring, inactive, broad, social objective. On the other hand, anchoring the school's work to student experience and interests can lead to knowledge and insight of the greatest worth. The students of that western school should have grown to understand the needs of their area and the relation of that area's prosperity to the welfare of the entire country.[24] Starting with the student's environment, "universal" principles could have been reached.

The physical environment is best understood when met head-on through resources across the street, across the city, or out in the country. Some schools are located near farming land, some close to mines, others near lumbering operations, still others in cities, and not a few are situated on rivers and on the shore of an ocean. The natural environment of these schools differ. Necessity demands that the program "step-off" from the unique location of the school, the

23 Cattlemen fought the incursion of sheep because of the latter's eating habits. Sheep eat to the roots of plants, killing them. Their small, hard hoofs trample dirt hard, further harming plant growth. Because of the thoroughness with which sheep graze it is very easy for them to overgraze a range.

24 At the moment not 50 miles away from this school, oil companies have begun the commercial extraction of oil from the "shale"—oil-bearing rock—of the mountains. One wonders if the school will use this occasion to bring students into contact with the physical environment (the facts about oil)—the possibilities are limitless. Students can learn what developments led up to the exploitation of the shale, glean something of the earth's history from the facts that shale is made from mud—indicative of the fact that the area was once covered with water.

environment peculiar to its students. The young people in the western school must of necessity appreciate the role played by the physical world in a way quite different from that of the student whose school is located near the Mesabi Range of northern Minnesota, the coal mines of Pennsylvania, the oil fields of Oklahoma and Texas, or the copper mines of Montana. But all students have much in common—the resources of their area.[25] The resources of an agricultural area are consumed or processed in cities, which in turn, supply agricultural centers and mining areas with manufactured goods. An economy embraces all regions (and all the nation's schools) and connects them to the larger world beyond. These are the ties that interrelate the social sciences with the earth sciences or natural sciences, revealing how the environment influences our economic and political problems.

Discussion Questions

1. Does it make sense to say that "men help to make their own physical environment?" Can you give three examples of changes in the environment men have helped to produce?

2. On the basis of your answer to Question 1, would you say that your teaching in civics or citizenship should contain any units dealing with man's understanding of his place in the physical environment?

3. Do you think that there are any habits you could encourage youngsters to develop that would make them more intelligent when, as adults, they are confronted with the problems of conservation of natural resources?

4. In what aspects of his environment is a first-grader interested? What changes in interest accompany his development through the elementary grades?

5. In the chapter you have just read what limitations of "common sense" were suggested? Did pointing out the limitations of common sense realism mean that students should not be encouraged to display common sense?

6. Learn what you can about the history of the city or town where you were born and about the background of the place where you now reside. Did geography play a part in determining where the community was located, how fast it grew, who came to live in it, and how the inhabitants earned their living?

7. Would you wish to introduce geography into a history lesson? Why? Why not?

[25] Bertha Morris Parker, *The Earth a Great Storehouse*. Evanston, Illinois: Row, Peterson and Company, 1950.

8. Of what use is the concept of "relative humidity" to you? to a farmer? to a lumberman? to the school nurse? to the school architect?

9. Recall the story of the Dust Bowl. In what ways did that story illustrate the interdependence of men and physical environment?

10. Does the principle of "crop rotation" concern boys or girls who will live all their lives in the city?

11. Can you give two illustrations of how a knowledge of geographical factors would improve a current events discussion?

12. How might "culture" be affected by prevailing winds, amount of precipitation, range of temperature, and type of soil?

13. Can you describe a simple experiment that elementary-school children of any grade might perform to illustrate the dependence of plants upon light and moisture? the dependence of animals upon plants? the dependence of men upon plants and animals? the interdependence of plants, animals, and man?

Selected References

Bennett, H. H., Soil Conservation. New York: McGraw-Hill Book Company, Inc., 1939.

Croxton, W. C., Science in the Elementary School. New York: McGraw-Hill Book Company, Inc., 1937.

Davis, Darrell Haug, The Earth and Man. New York: The Macmillan Company, 1942.

Erikson, Erik Hamburger, "Childhood and Tradition in Two American Indian Tribes," in Clyde Kluckhohn and Henry A. Murray, eds., Personality in Nature, Society and Culture. New York: Alfred A. Knopf, Inc., 1948, Chapter 14.

Hatcher, Halene, "Conservation Education or Tragedy," The Journal of Geography, Vol. 48, January 1949, 20-27.

Osborn, Fairfield, Our Plundered Planet. Boston: Little, Brown and Company, 1948.

Science Education in American Schools, Forty-sixth Yearbook of the National Society for the Study of Education. Chicago: University of Chicago Press, 1947.

Vogt, William, The Road to Survival. New York: William Sloane Associates, 1948.

Whitaker, J. R., Geography in School and College. Nashville, Tennessee: George Peabody College for Teachers, 1948.

Whitaker, J. R., and A. E. Parkins, eds., Our National Resources and Their Conservation. New York: John Wiley and Sons, Inc., 1936.

Winfield, Gerald F., China: The Land and the People. New York: William Sloane Associates, 1948.

16

BEYOND THE EARTH SCIENCES

$\mathcal{T}$ODAY'S ELEMENTARY TEACHER faces a serious problem in communicating with his pupils. His students have their minds on sonic barriers to be crossed by jet- or rocket-propelled aircraft. From the first grade on, many of the boys take pride in knowing about internal combustion engines and elementary electronics. Even if his sister is not encouraged to bone up on compression ratios, little brother will soon know a great deal about the comparative advantages of high and low compression engines. In all probability his big brother will have told him about the infra-red "scopes" on the sniper's rifles used in the army. Although girls are presently conditioned to show a lack of interest in things scientific, this will not last. Right now, the average middle class housewife each day operates more machinery, more intricate machinery, than does her husband. Moreover, she knows a good deal more about machines than she "lets on." It must be admitted that today a goodly section of an elementary-school class is fairly well acquainted with science. All this poses a problem of communication between teacher and pupils. For example, there are those who say the good elementary teacher must project herself or himself into the phantasy life of a child. To accomplish this projection today requires a respectable grasp of atomic physics and chemistry. Children navigate in imagination from planet to planet at supersonic speed.

Students, as we noted in Chapter 15, are common sense realists, but the sciences have now explored far beyond the ken of the simple realist who tried to know only the things that he saw about him without the assistance of instruments or teachers. The youngster should be helped to gain an appreciation of the new worlds that are being revealed to him. He will not be able to understand most of the technical or abstract detail, but some basic and general principles are within his grasp; there are many ideas that will fit his maturity. This chapter will illustrate a few of these ideas. From the fields of physics, chemistry, and mathematics a small selection of fundamental concepts will be made.

Let us examine our objectives. The illustrations we use are not examples of ends in themselves—of facts to be learned. It is most important in reading this chapter to understand that we are not setting up subject matter for courses in elementary-school science. That has been well done many times. Our purpose is more fundamental than that, and in view of the neglect of science in elementary education, far more important. Our first aim is to train children in the scientific method from the very beginning. *Scientific habits of thinking and scientific attitudes,* developed by students during their science study, *are a great deal more significant than is the subject-matter* content of the science that they learn, though that is important, too. After all, the habits and attitudes will remain with the pupils for a much longer time than will many of the memorized facts. Some of these habits and attitudes we all know. They are characteristic, in greater or lesser degree, of practicing scientists. Without spelling out their precise meaning, they include (1) sensitivity to relevant evidence, (2) the willingness to suspend judgment until a conclusion has been warranted by experiment and observation, (3) the *ability to make warranted deductions* from evidence, and (4) the ability to make disciplined observations. In addition to these, there is the over-all characteristic of precision and patience. These abilities or attitudes are qualities to be strived for. They are desirable, *if* a person values the behavior to which they lead. *Scientific study in the elementary school can help, but only to the extent that the teacher teaches scientifically,* and helps pupils to *think* scientifically.

This brings us to the second major objective of the chapter, which is to show that science must be taught properly. Not all science teaching brings out the need for the scientific method. We shall try to make this clear by citing some of the "fallacies" scientists themselves commit when they stray away from scientific attitudes and habits. Hardly a week goes by without some scientist, perfectly competent in his field, making a statement about something of which he is totally ignorant. Presumably this can be accounted for by the fact that scientists are but human. That is the very thing our second objective should demonstrate. Not any type of special scientific training will make people genuinely scientific in all their dealings. There is a type of training or general education that will do it more surely. This form of education in science emphasizes the need for patience, for disciplined observation, imaginative experimentation, and an inquiring mind. It puts faith in the use of intelligence. It does not defer scientific education until the age of specialization in college, but starts in the lower grades and conditions a child to think scientifically in all areas that are susceptible to scientific analysis.

A third major aim of this chapter might be described as providing background for the teacher concerning the unity of science. Chapter 15 stressed this same point. Now we will approach it from a more abstract perspective. The unity of science has significance for human welfare. The ties that bind physics to chemistry and both to mathematics illustrate this unity. Students in the elementary schools soon must take over in a world where the "unity of science" must be accepted and developed if man is to avoid catastrophe. Even though most children do not aspire to become scientists, their support as adults will be needed for scientific research and for the control of science in the interests of human welfare. There are many potential scientists and engineers in our elementary schools, however, who never sense the romance and excitement of scientific work. In view of the demands of our modern world, this must be rectified.

The concluding section of this chapter suggests an enlargement of the place of arithmetic and mathematics in the elementary school. There is no more important source of ideas for the young than the field of mathematics. Despite its importance, arithmetic is not always taught in such a way as to develop and hold student interest. All too many boys and girls leave school hating it, which is both regrettable and unnecessary. There is no mystery about why this happens. It is because arithmetic concepts are taught as the manipulation of abstractions having little or no meaning. The problems often are too difficult and sometimes absurd. Arithmetic is further abused by treating it as though it had no function but to "discipline the mind." There are better ways to teach mathematics and some of these will be indicated.

Today, far too many people, people with years of formal schooling, stand in complete awe of science and scientists. They do not understand these modern mystery men or the results of their labor. But scientific progress continues and the problems and implications of this progress will have to be handled intelligently by future generations. Children must be made familiar with the ways of science. Theirs will be a scientific world whose growing complexity demands that they be introduced to it without loss of time.

Fundamental scientific ideas. Although they are extremely technical subjects, this chapter will touch on atomic structure, light, radiation, electricity and magnetism, relativity, and "field theory." Someone will say: "Surely these are far beyond the reach of the elementary-school child and perhaps even of his teacher." They certainly are, if you think of them in terms of a program in an institute of technology. We will not treat them as college courses. Our objectives can be better attained if we pick from these topics some ideas that most of us have thought about, but never troubled to set down in any order. Take as an example the most difficult of all the topics, *field theory.* Field theory is a concept for graduate students in such sciences as physics, mathematics, chemistry, biology, psychology, sociology, and electrical engineering. We first came across the word "fields" in Chapter 4 of this book. Field theory was discussed in Chapter 15 under the heading of "interdependence within the environment." Man is "related" to soil, to water, to wind, and so forth. What men do with the soil, with trees, or with water makes a difference to the environment and, of course, to man's welfare. This interrelatedness is the most simple meaning of "field." In other words, when a scientist talks about a field he is emphasizing the relations (forces) between things rather than the individual, distinct, separate thing.

Common sense realism, which is our everyday form of thinking, envisions electricity as something "running" through wires. It explains magnetism as a force but never explains what "force" means. Common sense realism pictures light as made up of bits of luminous stuff. It has no good explanation for gravitation. Without some knowledge of field theory, the elementary-school teacher cannot hope to explain such concepts as electricity, magnetism, and gravitation satisfactorily to his class. Although it is beyond hope to try to explain these phenomena in great detail to the students, children can be enlightened about a few of the crucial principles. This will remove much of the mystery from these principles and encourage the students to go on with their thinking and study.

The objective we have in mind in speaking of field theory and the other subjects of this chapter is now before us. It is to help the teacher understand some of the basic principles that scientists use to sketch the nature of the physical world.

While we cannot hope to become specialists in these fields, we can acquaint ourselves with some of their fundamentals. With this broad understanding, we may be able to see relationships, possibilities for putting meaning into the bare framework of skills and facts, and thus give pupils the power to use what they learn in constructive thinking and doing. We hope that elementary-school teachers will stimulate in their students the ambition to work for *knowledge* rather than "hearsay." Much can be done to counteract the idea that all one has to do to discover the truth is to memorize a few pat answers. A few years ago, Albert Einstein, talking with a newspaper man about education, remarked that it had taken him a year or two to get over his own scientific schooling. It took him a while to dare ask some fundamental questions. We all know what he meant. It may be that at this very moment some college, high-school, or elementary-school student is grinding out a "cook book" experiment in chemistry. All he needs to do is go through the motions outlined in his laboratory manual. He will take a few measurements, write down the findings, and wind up another experiment. By looking ahead a few pages, he knows just how the "experiment" should come out. This is not the best way to develop the scientific method of attacking problems. Little, if anything, has been accomplished. At best the student learned that he had to be careful, but he could have been taught that precaution without taking precious time and using expensive laboratory equipment.

Science includes so much that the question arises where the elementary teacher should start. We know that children are wondering about the make-up of their world. In adult language the question they put to themselves is, what is the nature of reality?

The analysis of matter

Starting at home. Every student has a chemistry laboratory in his home.[1] His mother's kitchen and bathroom shelves are stocked with chemicals: salt, vinegar, caustic soda, baking soda, baking powder, household ammonia, cream of tartar, lye, boric acid, iodine, and alcohol to name a few. At home he learns any number of scientific facts; e. g., water is an excellent solvent but lemon juice is a more effective bleach when stains are of a particular type. He will learn much more from the great laboratory of the world about him if the school pulls its resources into the classroom.

A basic fact of life a child can observe is the difference between physical and chemical change.[2] We say that this distinction is basic because thinking about it will serve to furnish background for fundamental scientific insights into the molecular and atomic structure of any substance whether it appear as liquid, solid, or gas. This probing into the physical structure of things was first done successfully in chemistry. It may be, then, that for many children, *elementary* chemical analysis is a most natural first step in science education. Even in the early steps of elementary science, the paramount idea is to experiment. Sometimes this means refraining from giving explanations read from a text and instead encouraging the children to explore ways of finding answers. There would be no science, and none of its benefit, had men been willing to stop with some other person's answers. Units must be developed in which students go home and watch mother, help mother, and try to understand the reasons behind what mother does. Thus, a day in the kitchen will be a chance to experiment with yeast and baking powder. Mother may not be able to explain what the baking powder is and why it has the effect it does, but she may become interested and become a learner along with her children. In any case, the teacher should be interested and helpful.

1 See, for example, Carleton Lynde, *Science Experiences With Home Equipment,* 1937, and *Science Experiences with Ten-cent Store Equipment,* 1941, both published by the International Textbook Company, Scranton, Pennsylvania.

2 Physical changes—boiling, melting, solidifying, condensing, dissolving, and dividing—do not affect the chemical properties of things. Products of chemical change are different from the parent elements. Common salt is a product of chemical change. It is composed of both sodium (Na) and chlorine (Cl) but NaCl, salt, has properties not possessed by either sodium or chlorine.

States of matter. Whether the teacher discusses cooking and baking or chooses to experiment with evaporation, condensation, and freezing, the student's initial explorations into "quantitative analysis" will bring him to the realization that the same "substance" can turn up in any one of three forms—gaseous, solid, or liquid. This is a great discovery and may prove to be a source of real insight into the nature of the physical sciences. Once appreciated, the groundwork has been laid for much learning in elementary science. The initial awareness that matter has the three physical states exemplified by water vapor, water, and ice can be followed by experiments with the typical properties of matter in each of its three forms. The youngsters will gain much information from such a procedure.

Gases. Children know that hot air rises; they have seen "heat waves" rising from the hot pavement in summertime. The pressure of steam on the kettle's lid has offered them visual proof that gas expands when heated. From these beginnings, further experiments or illustrations may be used to acquaint children with other properties of gas, particularly in their practical application. (For example, what happens to Dad's tires if they are over-inflated and he drives fast over a heated road surface?)

Our eye is still on that rather distant objective—learning to think scientifically through dealing with the currently crucial questions basic to atomic structure. Children can advance to this objective one step at a time.[3] The nature of gas is an excellent approach to the idea of molecules, which, in their turn, leads into the realm of the atomic and sub-atomic. Gas can be conceived of as "material," as matter. Let the students think about an odorless, colorless gas. They can detect its presence in many ways. Here young children may make a start with rubber balloons. How far they go will depend upon their maturity. As the class discusses the question of whether the air inside the balloon exists, the suggestion is almost certain to be made that it may exist—be something—but it is awfully thin. Not only is it thin, but it is spread out. The teacher must bear in mind that the quality of being spread out suggests that the very minute gas particles are not as closely spaced and have more freedom to move about than do the particles in liquids or solids.

[3] Phillipp Frank, "Foundations of Physics," in *International Encyclopedia of Unified Science,* Vol. I, No. 7. Chicago: The University of Chicago Press, 1946.

Should the children go on to discuss the fact that gases may be compressed and expanded, the concept of molecular motion may become more meaningful.[4] The chances of such a discussion are greatly increased by having a store of science books and pamphlets in the room library. It may be desirable to direct the attention of those with scientific interests to such reading.

A danger. This illustration of easing into an understanding of molecular and atomic structure through analyzing matter in each of its three states presents the possibility of error. The danger, again, really comes from common sense realism. When the student imagines that gas is made up of small bits of matter, he may think that gas, or anything else, can be divided and divided again indefinitely. He may begin to see the least divisible parts of matter as composed of the same material as the large piece. That would be an error. The atoms in a piece of wood do not have the temperature, color, or density of wood. If the student really conceives that the wood or steel in his desk contains things—very very tiny things—called molecules and atoms, both of which are quite unlike the wood or steel in the desk, he will have avoided one of the pitfalls of common sense realism.

More about gases. Some students may appreciate that the expansion or contraction of gas is related to the speed of the particles that make up the gas. The relation between molecular motion, heat, and work (energy that is used to do a job) will be much easier for youngsters in the upper elementary grades to understand. They can grasp the principle of the steam engine, which, after all, was the classic illustration of thermodynamics in the early years of the Industrial Revolution. The steam engine demonstrated the usefulness of knowledge about the gas known as steam. Steam is one kind of gas in a highly expanded state. The gas molecules are far apart and in exceedingly rapid motion. Harnessing that motion allowed men to use "the mechanical equivalent" of heat. The discovery was significant for human welfare for it freed men from bondage— human power was not as cheap as coal.[5]

---

[4] In 1811 Avogadro announced his principle of gas volume. Experiment revealed that equal volumes of gases, measured at the same temperature and under equal pressure, possessed an equal number of molecules.

[5] An interesting unit could be called "setting men free with science." The unit might follow the study of energy. It could be developed as a sequential story: energy from the conversion of water into steam in coal burning engines, the

Liquids. Elementary students can and do learn about the liquid forms that matter sometimes takes. It is sometimes more difficult to devise simple experiences that lead children to understand as much about liquids as they do about gases. It is more difficult to suggest the atomic or molecular structure of liquid. For one thing, the effect of pressure on gas—something which makes it possible to guess that gas is made up of particles spread thinly over a lot of space—is much easier to demonstrate than the effect of pressure on liquids.

Solids. Once the molecular composition of gases and liquids has been glimpsed, the nature of solids can be studied. This involves no simple concept. It was not until late in the nineteenth century that scientists made any significant headway in describing, first, the molecular structure of matter and, then, its atomic composition. Until that time all manner of theories had been advanced; a crude form of atomism had been most popular but it was as crude as the imaginings of any bright child in the advanced elementary grades. We need not expect that pupils in the elementary school will be able to follow the fine analysis of matter with which scientists in this century are familiar. If they have traced the topic from the structure of gases, through liquids, to solids, they will have some background for further thinking later. They will have avoided some blind spots and misconceptions that might later handicap their thinking.

The synthesis of matter

Thus far, we have insisted that children must learn to think and act scientifically, that this requires proper teaching and some background in science on the part of teachers. We have given some illustrations of how the study of the states of matter (analysis) can spring naturally from experiences children have in the home and community. This leads to an introduction to synthesis.

The chemical industry. Any drugstore will have "flowers of sulfur." Sulfur is a very common element. It is a perfect vehicle, being most inexpensive and harmless, for the child to use in the study synthesis that follows so easily upon his introduction to analysis.

conversion of water power into electricity, and finally nuclear energy. Thus man is freed more and more from drudgery.

Sulfur is indispensable to industry. It is the key element in sulfuric acid, without which there would be no metal industry. Were sulfuric acid suddenly to become unavailable tomorrow, no more steel and no other metals or products of the metallurgist could be produced because the acid is used in the manufacture of dynamite that miners use in extracting ore from the earth. In addition, sulfuric acid is used in refining processes and is important to the textile industry.

Long ago alchemists found that sulfur, when burned over water, caused the water to turn acid and that if the burning took place in the presence of saltpeter, the acid became very strong. This was not the product of analytic, scientific research, however. It was an *accidental* discovery, *incidental* to the alchemist's search for the "philosopher's stone" with which to change such "base" or common metals as lead into gold. The modern methods by which sulfuric acid of great strength is synthesized cheaply depends upon *careful analysis of the properties of sulfur and upon experimentation conducted in the light of this knowledge.*

Many simple experiments can be worked in the classroom with the sulfur that comes from the corner drug store. The more intelligent children, if they are interested in science, can thus be provided with activities that will absorb their interest while other children work at other things. They learn a valuable lesson from working with a yellow powder that they know to be basic to so much of America's industrial development. This will be particularly true if the teacher can relate this simple chemistry to the industries of his community.

More synthetics. Sulfuric acid synthesized in laboratories is but one of the discoveries that have resulted from *research* [6] into the composition of gases, liquids, and solids. From coal tar chemists have synthesized the famous aniline dyes, saccharine, and literally hundreds of other products vital to human welfare and comfort. Rayon and artificial rubber are chemists' discoveries. The list is interminable, but the aniline dyes tell the story of all the rest. It is a tale that goes back to the ancient Phoenician traders who gained

[6] There is a most important idea to be gained from a study of the history of science. It is that luck, accident, or inspiration have been publicized although the real advance of science is accomplished *only* by the painstaking, plodding labor of scientists, schooled in their work and disciplined in their search.

much wealth selling Romans and other Mediterranean people a wonderful purple dye. This dye was collected from the Mediterranean sea slug. It was costly and so little was available that only the aristocracy used it in edging their togas, whence comes the expression "the royal purple" or "born to the purple." Today much more lasting and more beautiful purple is made synthetically and sold in every dime store. The teacher who knows the history of these scientific developments, and is able to refer to their sources will have a valuable resource in interesting children in science, in history, and in the other social sciences.

In many units that deal with health and with diet, either directly or indirectly, various vitamins and drugs are almost certain to be included. In order to make the study of health more attractive, a scientific approach is recommended. Then the study is pertinent not only to health, about which so many children are lectured at every meal, but also to many other aspects of the physical environment in which problem-solving and scientific method are involved. A good example of the application of scientific method to health and diet occurred in 1912, when it was shown that rats fed on chemically pure foods ceased to grow, but that growth began when minute quantities of fresh milk were added to their diet. The vitalizing agent of the fresh milk was called an "accessory food factor." This was the beginning of research into vitamins that led, in 1929, to synthesis of Vitamin A, a substance like the yellow carotene of plant pigment (carrots, for example) and necessary to the health of the nervous system, retina of the eyes, and the skin. Then a chemist synthesized Vitamin B and it is now known that there is a Vitamin B complex that includes a number of substances such as riboflavin and nicotinic acid. About six Vitamin B compounds are under study. Today, Vitamins C, D, E, and K have already been synthesized.

Implications for social studies. We have suggested ways that children may learn that science, judiciously applied, advances human welfare. Through such study, they can see that in its practical application science has lessened drudgery, harnessed energy, and contributed to progress in medicine and industry. But the lesson must not stop there for some students may be led to believe that progress through science is inevitable, that science is the key to utopia. Science is more than a laboratory affair. It is of great concern to the social scientist. It is not automatically helpful. For example, it is readily perverted to the use of a tyrant or, as in Russia, is easily thwarted to conform to the dictates of a party line. The elementary-school teacher of science should take every opportunity to make clear to students that, in a sense, science is a method of thought and hence must be free if it is to make progress and to serve human welfare.

A teacher of sixth-grade geography interested his class in the nitrate fields of Chile. Later he made a point of the struggle against Germany in World War I, and the strength that she gained as the result of her skillful scientists. Then, later, the topic of human relations and of racial and religious prejudices arose. He then brought all three topics together in the story of the great German chemist Haber, who synthesized ammonium nitrate. This synthesizing was most important, for nitrates are indispensable both in agriculture and in war. During World War I, Germany was cut off from the nitrate fields of Chile's highlands. It seemed that she would lack both the nitric acid needed for explosives and the nitrates her farmers needed for fertilizer.[7] Had the time been 1714, or even 1814, rather than 1914, it is unlikely that Germany could have eased the situation. But in 1914, she had many experts in chemistry to call upon. Haber, working to solve his nation's critical problem, came to realize that nitrogen and hydrogen, both readily available in the atmosphere, heated together at high pressure and in the presence of a "catalyst," [8] formed ammonia. It was but a step to the manufacture of the ammonium nitrates that made Germany independent of Chile's saltpeter. She was able to fight World War I without lacking nitrate fertilizers and the nitric acid necessary for the production of gun cotton, dynamite, TNT, and other explosives.

Haber was a distinguished scientist and a national hero. Years later, when Hitler came to power, Haber was working in Berlin's famous Kaiser Wilhelm Institute. He was a Jew. Because of this, Hitler ordered him removed from his position. Prejudice has no

---

[7] The decay of organic matter in the earth, and its change by soil bacteria, produces nitrates, but these are quickly used up unless both crop rotation and nitrate fertilization are employed to replenish them.

[8] A catalyst speeds chemical reactions but does not become a part of the reaction's product. Just how the catalyst functions is not precisely known.

respect for intelligence, but science lives only as long as intelligence is unfettered. Haber and his genius were lost to Germany. Nor was his loss the only one that Germany suffered from the same cause. Einstein left Germany, as did Meitner and Hahn. These three, together with Fermi who left Italy, were key personnel in America in the experiments that resulted in the atom bomb.

The atom

Role of the physicist. The physicist may soon bring about a revolution in civilization by supplying mankind with almost limitless amounts of atomic energy. Many people, pondering the marvels of scientific discovery, look upon the physicist as a man who is one step ahead of the Wizard of Oz. He is glorified as having the power of Zeus, holding in his hand atomic energy capable of drastically modifying modern civilization. Geiger counters and atomic piles have made him the supreme gadgeteer. He is the leading candidate to become the future school-boy's hero—a marvelous mechanic *and* a whiz at mathematics.

Although physicists are mortal, they have done remarkable things with the analysis of matter. The broad outlines of this experimentation will enrich the storehouse from which the teacher draws ideas for resource units and experience units. It should be noted that nothing has been said about translating this material for the student. Much of it is too difficult, although some success has attended efforts to discuss atomic structure in the upper elementary grades.[9]

A new age. The explosion of the atomic bombs toward the end of World War II dramatized the fact that mankind had entered the atomic age. The children in our elementary schools must live in such an age. The concepts involved in its understanding are difficult. It is essential, however, that children be introduced in some way to the background and problems of the atomic age, just as they have been introduced to reading, geography, history, hygiene, and other subjects. Knowledge about the atomic age is crucial knowledge, yet textbooks in curriculum have largely ignored it. Some teachers who have a background in science have experimented in many ways with attempts to give a background in science.

[9] For example, see Bertha Morris Parker, *Matter and Molecules*. Evanston, Illinois: Row, Peterson and Company, 1947.

Models of the atom. In introducing youngsters to the atom, one sixth-grade teacher made use of models of the hydrogen atom and of the helium atom. Though these could be built in class, since there is no need to be absolutely precise, the teacher in question obtained ready-made models. Because there are over 90 distinct types of atoms, he used a large chart of the periodic table so that the children could see the elements arranged according to their weight. The light elements or atoms, hydrogen being the lightest, are at one end of the chart. The heavy elements, uranium, for example, are at the other end. A model could be built or obtained for each of the atoms but that would serve no real purpose. At the center of each model was the nucleus made up of the protons and neutrons. The proton is the heaviest part of the hydrogen atom and, in the model, was colored black. This was meant to indicate that it had most of the weight or mass of the atom, though it is not mass in the usual sense of "stuff." It really is a charge of positive electricity. The nucleus of the helium atom is made up of two protons and two neutrons. Circling the nucleus with its protons and neutrons are the electrons. There are just as many electrons, which are charges of negative electricity, as there are protons in the nucleus. In the model of the hydrogen atom there is one proton (no neutron) and one electron. In the model of the helium atom there are two protons in the nucleus, two neutrons, and two electrons. The electrons circle the nucleus in orbits in the manner of the planets circling the sun. In fact, the electrons are often called planetary electrons. In the models, the electrons are very small. The nucleus is the size of an orange, and the electrons, the size of grapes, and are placed at quite a distance from the orange.

In this teacher's class, many of the children had heard about uranium 238. With his model of a simple atom as background, and with his periodic table, the teacher was able to show how complicated the uranium atom is. He showed that it had 92 protons, 92 electrons, and 146 neutrons. The number 238 is the sum of the number of neutrons and protons. The children were very interested in the models of the hydrogen and helium atoms. They handled them, and some of them studied the periodic table to discover other names they knew. A few asked pointed questions that showed good understanding of what the teacher was trying to teach.

The whole discussion problem about atoms had arisen during

study of the combat in Korea. There was an expression by some of the children that atomic bombs should be dropped there by the United Nations. The authors do not recommend that teachers equip their classrooms with models of atoms and periodic tables, nor that the pupils learn such things as the definitions of protons, neutrons, and electrons. The brief description of one teacher's efforts is meant to show the facility in discussions in science that can result from a background of general education in science. It is meant to show the use of some of the advanced concepts in science to challenge those students whose abilities are high. It is meant to show how a teacher used models to help make concepts clearer, since children learn by manipulating things. It is meant to show that many students have a rather extensive science vocabulary and much interest in science.

Arithmetic and mathematics

Arithmetic and science. We have placed the discussion of mathematics after the sections on experimental science in order to emphasize the unique role of mathematics in modern scientific research. Neither arithmetic nor mathematics—both of which we shall refer to as arithmetic—is experimental, but both are indispensable for science. Arithmetic is non-experimental because it can be studied independently of any observation of real life situations. Arithmetic is *deductive.* Experimental science is *inductive.* Experiments are conducted so that the scientist can *induce* from the results generalizations about the way the physical environment functions. The mathematician, on the other hand, is concerned with accurate deduction. He shows what can be said on the basis of a few assumptions. The word "said" in this connection refers to numbers or geometric figures. Arithmetic is the language of numbers or, more precisely, it is the grammar (the manipulative rules) regulating the quantitative measurement of dimensions and numbers.

In the work-a-day world induction and deduction go hand in hand. The experimental scientist uses arithmetic and geometric language in describing his findings. Here, the elementary-school teacher enters the scene. He must prepare students to think in terms of this quantitative language. The introduction must be skillful or the student may form a "block" against it for the remainder of his life. Everything that can be said about teaching any other language applies to arithmetic. For example, it must be taught "conversationally" before its grammar is practiced. Students must become acquainted with arithmetic communication. When youngsters work at a task where counting or measuring of any type is possible, the teacher should allow them "to talk their quantities." After they have familiarized themselves with number language, the rules of multiplication, division, subtraction, and addition can be taken up. It is the same with learning any other language. The student progresses much more rapidly if the grammar is postponed until he has begun to feel at home in the language. When this stage has been reached, the rules of grammar become meaningful because they govern usage or, better, tell the student the *conventions* of usage. Conventions develop as the race acquires experience. Grammar in arithmetic is a set of rules that experience has shown to be useful in making language of quantitative measurement more efficient. This viewpoint has emerged and won increasing recognition within the past two or three decades. Elementary science must work hand-in-hand with arithmetic.

Present errors. Many unwise educational practices stem from the divorce of arithmetic from science. Much arithmetic could be taught as an aid to students in exploring, describing, and controlling their environment. Arithmetic, essential for accurate and general description, is a necessary accompaniment to a course in science.

Using the history of arithmetic. The story-telling and story-reading periods of the day can be used by the science-arithmetic teachers to develop in their students a realistic appreciation of arithmetic communication. How did this grammar of size develop? There was a time, we know, when people could not even count. When the teacher "calls the roll" he is repeating a very primitive type of census-taking, for primitive folk gave a special name to each person in a group and called these names at various times when the tribe was assembled to discover if any change had taken place in the size of the group. The teacher can use this illustration to clarify for the child this aspect of arithmetic. Even the seating chart is handy for the same purpose. It is a primitive counting device.

The elementary-school child may have counted on his fingers or he may have observed his teacher doing it. The counting of fingers will help him to understand the decimal system. Finger counting is a process that no doubt helped to make arithmetic possible. Our Arabic system of numbers is a ten's system; we count by tens and tens of tens. A very convenient system it is, too.

As part of the intercultural school program, a study can be made of the manner in which people count in other parts of the world. Tracing counting around the globe is a way of demonstrating the simplicity of our counting system. This applies equally to the writing of numbers. When certain American Indians wished to write that eight men had camped in the vicinity, they put all eight men in a picture. Of course, in keeping the score we still "tally" by drawing short vertical lines close together. To avoid confusion that might result from too many lines being drawn close together, it is common practice to group the lines by fives by drawing a slanting line across each four vertical lines. This procedure is quite primitive.

Zero, the place holder. All the figures that the master mathematician uses are combinations or representations of the numbers one through ten. The teacher may find it profitable to move slowly into these abstractions and a long pause at "zero" has much to recommend it. Too many people are unfamiliar with the Arabic numbering process and consequently are never able to grasp the meaning of such things as zero and the minus quantities in algebra. The concept of zero is indispensable for using algebra, algebraic graphs, trigonometry, and the higher mathematics. The concept of zero is not a simple idea to grasp, either. It expresses no quantity. The teacher should explain that zero is used only to keep the quantitative numbers in their places. For example, 3 written with a zero means 30, but 3 written or used with two zeros at its right means 300. The zeros are being used to keep the three's in one of the ten's columns. The function of "carrying," of moving from the ten's column to another, is simple when the theory of zero has been clearly understood. It may take a little time to develop it with the students but, then, it took a long time for the Hindus to work it out originally and for the Arabs, who borrowed it from the Hindus, to convince Europeans of the value of its use.

Utility in mathematics. People will accept a new idea when they become convinced of its utility. Europeans were skeptical of the Arab-Hindu number system, but its remarkable usefulness con-

vinced them of its value. The concept of the zero is but one example
of the utility of mathematical abstractions and of the wisdom of
broaching any mathematical abstraction from the viewpoint of its
usefulness.

As students begin to learn to use the Arabic number system, they
see how useful it is to be able to add, multiply, subtract, and divide.
Students have need to "sort" and to count all the time. An interesting way in which children can be made aware of the utility of
mathematics is given in Chapter 21 in connection with the operation of a classroom store.

To the right of zero. The Arabs knew nothing of decimals. They
worked to the left of the zero but never to the right. That is, they
did not use their algebra to find laws of combinations for tenths
and hundredths. These rules, first worked out by the Flemish mathematician, Simon Steven, in the 1590's, are really the same as the
rules for combining tens and hundreds. It took centuries to make
this advance and students must not be expected to swallow it at a
gulp. It is a fact that very intelligent people 250 years ago stood
in awe of ideas and calculations that an eleven-year-old today is
expected to grasp with ease. To contemporaries of Pythagoras, the
Greek arithmetician, numbers and geometric constructions were so
new and wonderful that they held them magical. Plato thought
mathematics so special that he held it as one of the chief studies
and pleasures of the rulers. Philolaus, a follower of Pythagoras,
established a club to preserve the secrets of arithmeticians.

The utility of arithmetical signs. Among the more utilitarian
devices are the arithmetical signs that mean *equal, plus, minus,
multiplied by,* and *divided by.* Students rarely know that even these
simple devices were long in originating. William Oughtred used the
multiplication sign, perhaps for the first time, in seventeenth-cen-
tury England. Johann Rahn, in the same century, introduced the
Swiss to the sign for division. The German, Johann Widman, two
centuries earlier, wrote a book that used both the plus and minus
signs. All these signs came into common use when arithmetic demonstrated its value for the new sciences—navigation and merchant
accounting. They were invaluable then and have persisted because
no substitute for them has been invented. Teachers will understand
better the difficulty of mathematics for children if they understand
how long it took to develop some of the devices and procedures that

now seem so obvious. Many children will be enthused when they find they are learning things that wise adults struggled for centuries to learn.

Mathematics and civilization. Mathematics has developed with civilization. In countries and times where counting was limited to numbering sheep in flocks and in helping keep count of the seasons of the year, arithmetic was not as developed as that now taught in the lower grades of the elementary school. In Egypt, mathematics developed as there was use for it. Measurements of the rise and fall of the River Nile were made. Construction of the pyramids and the surveying of the land required a working knowledge of geometry and trigonometry, both unknown to more primitive societies.

At a later date, the sailors of western Europe needed mathematics to navigate the seas. Hundreds of years later, mathematics developed along with engineering, as in the development of the steam engine, the internal combustion engine, and the use of electricity. When mathematics is studied with reference to its development and its broad use today, it becomes easier to understand and to adapt it to everyday uses as well. These brief historical references indicate the interesting history of science and mathematics, and suggest how it can be used to motivate and give meaning to mathematics.

Discussion Questions

1. List and discuss the reasons for affirming or rejecting the statement: "Science has no place in the elementary-school curriculum."
2. What are the differences in classroom approach as between the "nature study" and "systematized science teaching" approach? Did the increase in knowledge in the special sciences bear any relation to the introduction of the "systematized science teaching" idea? Can nature study and systematized science teaching be brought into harmonious relationship within the elementary grades?
3. What does the phrase "scientific method" mean to you? Has it any place in the elementary school?
4. Ask several elementary-school children for their definitions of the word "matter." How much, according to their definitions, do the children know about "matter?" Could you make "matter" meaningful to the children of your class? How would you go about it?
5. Does it help in understanding the physical and chemical composition of matter to distinguish between its liquid, gaseous, and solid states?
6. Do you think that the children in your class could become interested

in the chemical industry, in the making of synthetics? What synthetic products does your classroom contain? Is there any chemical industry in your community? Is there a pharmacist? Could your children have the opportunity to observe "chemistry at work" in the community?

7. Do you think that most children in the upper elementary-school grades have heard about the atomic bomb? Do you think that they could be interested in the story of the atom? How would you tell it or discuss it with them? Can you think of any visual aids that would assist you?

8. If you were planning to emphasize the "One World" concept in your year's teaching, would the story of the discoveries that have been made about the atom's structure be of any use?

9. Has arithmetic done its share in lightening our burdens? How many of your students are interested in arithmetic? Do they know some of the story behind addition, subtraction, multiplication, and division? Have you ever attempted to multiply Roman numerals?

10. You will have heard the expression "reading readiness." Do you think that there might be such a thing as "science readiness?" Can you illustrate this concept?

11. Can you give two examples of the way the questions of a youngster in the second, fourth, and sixth grades can lead into scientific study?

Selected References

Bridgeman, P. W., *The Logic of Modern Physics*. New York: The Macmillan Company, 1927.

Chubb, L. W., *The World Within the Atom*. Pittsburgh: Westinghouse Electric Corporation, 306 Fourth Avenue, P. O. Box 1017, 1946.

Craig, Gerald S., *Science for the Elementary School Teacher*. Boston: Ginn and Company, 1940.

Croxton, W. C., *Science in the Elementary School*. New York: McGraw-Hill Book Company, Inc., 1937.

Frank, Phillipp, "Foundations of Physics," in *International Encyclopedia of Unified Science*, Vol. I, No. 7. Chicago: University of Chicago Press, 1946.

———, "Modern Physics and Common Sense," *Scripta Mathematica*, Vol. VI, No. 1, March 1939, 5-16.

Gamow, George, *One, Two, Three . . . Infinity*. New York: The Viking Press, 1947.

Lynde, Carleton J., *Science Experiences with Home Equipment*. Scranton, Pennsylvania: International Textbook Company, 1937.

———, *Science Experiences with Inexpensive Equipment*. Scranton, Pennsylvania: International Textbook Company, 1939.

————, *Science Experiences with Ten-cent Store Equipment.* Scranton, Pennsylvania: International Textbook Company, 1941.

Noll, Victor H., *The Teaching of Science in Elementary and Secondary Schools.* New York: Longmans, Green & Company, 1939.

Science Education in American Schools, in Nelson B. Henry, ed., Forty-sixth Yearbook of the National Society for the Study of Education, Part I. Chicago: University of Chicago Press, 1947.

Superintendent of Documents, *Atomic Energy Education.* Washington, D. C.: U. S. Document 9480, 1949.

Whitehead, Alfred North, *Science in the Modern World.* New York: The Macmillan Company, 1928.

17

ART AND THE

ELEMENTARY-SCHOOL CURRICULUM

*L*IFE, to be prized, must have quality;[1] survival is not enough.[2] If this is true, then art, the cultivation and enjoyment of *human sensibility,* holds a commanding place in education. It is neither fad nor frill.

A work of art is original in design or in the interpretation of the worker's experience and feeling. In this chapter, art is thought of as subtle and personal, not a subject for an "art class" alone, but a branch of learning intended to reach and stimulate the *sensibilities* of all students.

In order to clarify our meaning of sensibility let us look at an example. Keats writes: ". . . Can burst joy's grape against a palate fine. . . ." [3] This line is an example of response or sensibility. Sensibility means the ability to perceive or to receive sensation, though more than ordinary perception is implied. Sensibility refers to a peculiar susceptibility to impression, or acuteness of feeling. Only a person who has learned to *discriminate,*[3] to contrast things and qualities, to savor events, can "extract" great pleasure from living.

[1] Ray, Faulkner, "Art and Its Relation to Society," in Nelson B. Henry, ed., *Art in American Life and Education,* Fortieth Yearbook of the National Society for the Study of Education. Bloomington, Illinois: Public School Publishing Company, 1941, pp. 427-441; and Lawrence K Frank, *Society as Patient,* New Jersey: Rutgers University Press, 1949.

[2] Whitney Griswold, "Survival Is Not Enough," *The Atlantic Monthly,* Vol. 187, April 1951, 25-30.

[3] John Keats, "Ode on Melancholy," in H. Buston Forman, ed., *The Poetical Works of John Keats.* London: Oxford University Press, 1934.

Often the artist's sensitivity is expressed through symbols to which he gives an order or design or shape. Because these symbols often represent a unique, personal, or intimate expression, and because the artist uses them in ways that are not familiar to many of us, we often protest the difficulty of art. However, unique, personal, deeply-felt responses usually are not obvious. Some art is relatively inaccessible. So is some science.

The artist gets at the essence of an experience and seeks to "internalize" it. He expresses his understanding *and* his emotional response or feeling. The two (understanding and emotion) are dovetailed. A "response" evolves from experiences that have been lived with, reflected upon, internalized. When the artist feels that he wishes to "state" his reaction to an experience, he paints, shapes, composes, writes, dances, weaves, or sings his interpretation of it.

Much of the trouble we encounter in establishing rapport with the artist stems from our lack of experience with the process of response. There is too much passive enjoyment and too little personal creativity in our society today. Let us take sports as an example. Men and women in physical education have been fighting spectator passivity for years. They do not want athletics limited to stars. Everyone, or almost everyone, can get pleasure and benefit from some form of exercise and game. Art is also open for mass participation. Of course, "great" art is not common. Neither is great blocking, tackling, passing, high-jumping, running, or putting. To produce a distinguished work of art requires years of work and practice. The master here as in other fields will have to limit some of his other pleasures. "Artists must be sacrificed to their art. Like bees, they must put their lives into the sting they give."

However, we are not concerned here with the exceptionally gifted and persevering artist. We are thinking of children. What does art mean where children are involved? Clue number one was given us by Keats. As he told us, art is a matter of feeling, of susceptibility to impression. Children develop response as they are given opportunity to enjoy, to savor, to perceive. Perhaps this can be clarified by listing what should be avoided in children's art instruction. Heading the list of "don'ts" is a warning against insisting that responses be meaningful. That does not mean that they ought to be, or need be *nonsense*. It only means that they need not look like something, or tell a simple story, or express an obvious idea.

For many years, art programs in the schools were aimed at having children produce a poem, or a picture, or a bit of music that was a miniature of an adult effort. The study of child growth and development shows us that children are not to be expected to behave like miniature adults. They are at another stage of development altogether. Children do not perceive as adults; their feelings are less seasoned with experience. This very lack of experience helps make a child's responses much less conventional. Of course, the child is naive, but the curriculum must be designed to exploit that freshness, that mine of untrammeled imagination. It must give children the opportunity to respond freely and not demand imitation or parrotry.[4]

In childhood, preparation should be made for the originality and *intensity* of feeling that characterizes the most vigorous of adult art. Youth's spontaneity and sensitivity are the basis for that originality and intensity. Neither is likely to develop from a restricted, conventional art experience or from a narrow-minded interpretation of art. Rather, youngsters are to be encouraged to feel, to react, to admit their responses. It is through these that the teacher comes to understand how the child conceives his art work. One child, when asked about his drawing explained, "When I make a picture, I make a think and draw a line around it." There is a purpose in encouraging this free responsiveness so that the child may reveal his true feelings, wishes, likes, and dislikes. It is to provide sources of pleasure in his surroundings by way of imagination, to give him a personal claim to his mode of life, and by so doing to sharpen his perception of all things. It supplies the child with

4 M. Edmund Speare illustrates the difference between literal-mindedness (the manner in which most adults think) and imaginative conception (natural to children) by telling a story about William Blake. "Somebody asked him: 'When the sun rises, do you not see a round disk of fire something like a guinea (an English gold-piece)?' 'Oh! No, no!' Blake replied. 'I see an immeasurable company of the heavenly host, crying 'Holy, Holy, Holy is the Lord God Almighty!'" M. Edmund Speare, "Introduction," *The Pocket Book of Verse*. New York: Pocket Books, Inc., 1940.

"The Poet's eye, in a fine frenzy rolling
Doth glance from heaven to earth, from earth to heaven;
And as imagination bodies forth
The forms of things, unknown, the poet's pen
Turns them to shapes and gives to airy nothing
A local habitation and a name."

William Shakespeare, *A Midsummer-Night's Dream*. Act II, Sc. 2.

the desire and the opportunity to observe his feelings and tastes. In his art production, for example, a child can express a dread, a hope, or a fantasy that influences his behavior but that he may keep hidden from ordinary observation. Art contributes in this way in helping a person live realistically with his uncertainties, his ambitions, and his dreams.

In our curriculum, we must provide for the freedom and intensity of response. It is well to recognize the *universality of response* because it is available to everyone. It does not depend upon expensive material and special equipment. In everything that we do, at every moment, there is a chance for sensibility. We can learn to detect individuality, to respond to the feelings of others; we can learn to react to sounds, colors, shapes, and ideas. There is no merit in going through life with a "poker face," "dead pan." The studied reserve of a cold and aloof person hardly is satisfying. Better too much emotion than no feeling at all. Human beings are born to comedy and tragedy, to emotion, and to personal declarations or responses. These things must not be stifled in our classrooms. When we say that children should be seen and not heard; when we laugh at their observations, impressing the children with our indifference or superiority—we are teaching them to hide their feelings, to keep secret their reactions.

This plea for emotional freedom in *response* does not imply that response need be a "fine frenzy," developing into a stunning bit of art. Sensibility can be a quality of all living. We ought to be able to take pleasure from simple things: the sound of the wind in the trees, the flowers that can be grown in a window box, the rain. Specially trained art teachers have much to offer, but they cannot do the job alone. Each of us must share their vision and intent.

Appreciation

Everywhere in our work-a-day world is monotony, drudgery, and confinement. Wars and rumors of wars shock us daily. We seek consolation and escape. Sometimes the only escape is the inner consolation granted by the use of our personal resources.

Perhaps the quickest antidote to anger, depression, shock, the deteriorating effect of monotony or close quarters is a sense of appreciation.[5] Children seek change and stimulation in each other. Later in life they find companionship with other adults on the basis of common interests. In the inevitable effort to keep himself and his family as comfortable as possible, for example, few men have the money or the time to find perfect friends or the perfect occupation that will provide the comfort and mental activity that give purpose and color to their immediate surroundings. As a result, people will absorb the nearest most convenient device for the diversification it offers from the numbing effect of routine. In what way, then, can the schools supply a remedy for the methodical, the wearisomely uniform?

We have stressed the individuality of response and its value. All about us are the products of mass production—identical houses, identical clothes, even identical entertainment. In all this the individual is missing. The individuality of the owner rarely is seen in the planning or decorating of a house. His own imagination is missing. In what way can he ever find pleasure or further purpose to his life if he cannot take dullness out of his job, add his personal convictions to the walls of his home, or project into his children enough of the specialties and untrodden ideas of life so that they can be of interest to him in return? How can education give him enough exultation within himself to enliven his daily task?

A program of arts and crafts may be a partial solution. Not too elaborate at the start, it could afford participation by children in both appreciative and creative activity. For example, most elemen-

---

5 There are many excellent studies on the place of appreciation in the classroom. Each makes the point that teachers should not speak or think of appreciation as something passive. Appreciation is active. It embraces understanding, analysis, interpretation, and emotional sensitivity. See for example, Cleanth Brooks and Robert Penn Warren, *Understanding Fiction*. New York: F. S. Crofts & Co., 1943; Gertrude E. Johnson, *Studies in the Art of Interpretation*. Appleton-Century-Crofts, Inc., 1940; Ludwig Lewison, *A Modern Book of Criticism*. New York: The Modern Library, 1919; Thomas Munro, "Powers of Art Appreciation. and Evaluation," in Nelson B. Henry, ed., *Art in American Life and Education,* Fortieth Yearbook of the National Society for the Study of Education. Bloomington, Illinois: Public School Publishing Company, 1941, pp. 323-348; William Van O'Connor, *Sense and Sensibility in Modern Poetry*. Chicago: The University of Chicago Press, 1948; Stephen C. Pepper, *Principles of Art Appreciation*. New York: Harcourt, Brace & Company, Inc., 1949; Henri Peyre, *Writers and Their Critics*. Ithaca, New York: Cornell University Press, 1944; and M. D. Voss, "A Study of the Conditioning of the Art Appreciation Process at the Child Level," *Psychological Monographs,* Vol. 48, 1-39.

tary schools have at least the elements of a music program. Each year more recorded music becomes available for children. Very early it becomes possible to make adjustments to the wide differences in music interest and ability among children. There is opportunity to teach some children to read music in the second grade, when their reading of words is well in hand. During the second or third grade the reading of music can be supplemented by attendance at children's concerts, if they are available, or by listening to orchestras through recordings. Many children will learn to recognize the instruments.

The recreation crafts offer another example. With workbenches designed for children, a few good tools, and suitable supplies, the curriculum can be expanded to include work with clay, wood, leather, and metals. Many schools that provide for expression in art and music have not yet ventured into the crafts. The trend is for more teacher education in art. When this trend hits its stride, the incidence of handicrafts will increase. Again, this will allow for the wide differences in abilities that are found in children. Boys and girls to whom singing, instrumental music, dancing, poetry, drawing, or painting holds little fascination may show great interest in the various crafts.

Enjoyment of the simple. The good teacher can make it unnecessary for children to depend wholly upon toys for pleasure. The child can be taught to react to the natural objects around him—the light, darkness, figures, sounds—and can be taught to perceive variety in the commonplace. A child told to look at an apple and copy it may also be shown that there is more to an apple than its taste, color, or nutritional value. In addition to these, there is the relation of an apple to its surroundings seen in contrasts or in parallels with the shape and position of other objects. As a result of being introduced to all this, the child may develop a sense of proportion or a perception of contrast. As he matures, his perceptions may sharpen and his responses include more and more. If so, he is becoming an individual with imagination, with feeling, with taste. He will have identity as a person.

It may be said again that achievement in creative accomplishment does not require constant immersion in "works of art." The poet does not necessarily seek inspiration in a palace. What surrounds a person indoors and out is the raw material for the perceptions that are woven into reactions. As Wordsworth made clear in the *Preface* to the second edition of the *Lyrical Ballads:* "Low and rustic life was generally chosen, [for the setting of the ballads] because in that situation the essential passions of the heart find a better soil in which they can attain their maturity, are less under restraint, and speak a plainer and more emphatic language; because in that situation our elementary feelings exist in a state of greater simplicity and consequently may be more accurately contemplated and more forcibly communicated. . . . the great national events which are daily taking place, and the increasing accumulation of men in cities, where the uniformity of their occupations produces a craving for extraordinary incident which the rapid communication of intelligence hourly gratifies. . . ."

Over 150 years ago this poet felt the pressure of fabricated, material stimulation that thwarted the individual's ability to select and personally enhance his own environment. In the century and a half since, it has become much harder to put the signature of personal quality into life. If this is true, we need ever more opportunities for expression; ever more satisfying gratification in the sound of rainfall, the path of the electric light across the bare corner of a room, or simply the bright color of an apple.[6]

Teacher education institutions must help teachers to instill in children the power of choice, expression, perception, and skill in terms of their abilities. We do not want our children to become so much alike in their taste as to lose individuality and, as men and women, be continually on the hunt to find satisfactions that their imaginations have not learned to point out for them.

The encouragement of individuality and originality should be begun in the child's earliest years. A child of kindergarten age

---

[6] Much has been written on the subject of creative expression. See for example, Gertrude Hartman and Ann Shumaker, eds., *Creative Expression*. New York: The John Day Company, 1932; Viktor Lowenfeld, *Creative and Mental Growth*. New York: The Macmillan Company, 1947; Hughes Mearns, *Creative Youth*. New York: Doubleday, Page and Company, 1925, and *Creative Power*. New York: Doubleday, Doran and Company, Inc., 1929; and Thomas Munro, "Creative Ability in Art and Its Educational Fosterings," in Nelson B. Henry, ed., *Art in American Life and Education*, Fortieth Yearbook of the National Society for the Study of Education. Bloomington, Illinois: Public School Publishing Company, 1941, pp. 289-322. This is the most helpful analysis available. In addition, see Henry Schaeffer-Simmern, *The Unfolding of Artistic Activity*. Berkeley, California: The University of California Press, 1948.

probably can see, feel, and hear much more freely than a child in the fifth grade. The frost on a window may be anything for the younger child—a skyscraper, a balloon, or a stalk of celery. The older child will name a much more "likely" object. His imagination has been circumscribed by experience and by the accumulation of the meanings all his fellows have in common.

Response. By slowly bringing the ever-present, but unspoken commentary of children to the surface, a teacher can eventually ask youngsters to draw what they are thinking about. A child might draw a giant. The continuous recurrence of such themes might lead the teacher to surmise that the child was ridding himself of some troublesome giant that was lurking in his mind. Making mud pies has helped generations of children to satisfy cravings and has shown many the road to further articulation. Sometimes it is through the simplest methods that the large unconscious scenery of the mind can be evoked. A child will paint or notice what is lovable or hateful to him. It is here that the teacher's guidance is needed to encourage him to draw not what looks like a dog or a tree, but what suggests a tree-like feeling or a dog-like quality.

Specially trained art teachers will have less difficulty with such things than will teachers to whom the field of art is all very new.[7] A traditional teacher of plane geometry may experience difficulty in trying to redirect her teaching so that students have an opportunity to see "analysis of space" as the artist sees it. But geometry is of help in achieving "balance" or design in painting, sculpting, or building. The Greeks discovered how to use the study of ratios and proportions for designing temple pillars. There is no reason to deny children the opportunity to combine appreciation of spatial

[7] *A Guide for Instruction in Art: Elementary School, Grades 1-8,* Curriculum Bulletin No. 5. St. Paul: State of Minnesota Department of Education, 1948; Polly Ames, "Children and the Teaching of Painting," *Progressive Education,* Vol. 41, December 1939, 535-542; Alice Dalgliesch, *First Experiences with Literature.* New York: Charles Scribner's Sons, 1932; George E. Hubbard, *Music Teaching in the Elementary Grades.* New York: American Book Company, 1934; Minnie McLeish, *Beginnings: Teaching Art to Children.* New York: The Studio Publications, 1941; James L. Mursell, "How Children Learn Aesthetic Responses," *Learning and Instruction,* Forty-ninth Yearbook of the National Society for the Study of Education, Part I. Chicago: University of Chicago Press, 1950, pp. 183-191; Owatonna Art Education Project, *Art Units for Grades 1 to 3* (by the Project Staff) and *Art Units for Grades 4 to 6* (by the Project Staff). Minneapolis: The University of Minnesota Press, 1944.

and quantitative relations with arithmetic or geometry, or any other subject or skill.[8]

Even in such subjects as arithmetic and geometry, art may be introduced without reducing the scientific content. This is a point worth making. Think for a moment about "form" in art.[9] Then reflect upon the "content" of artistic creation. Form is design—rhyme, rhythm, balance, harmony, and all the other terms expressing such things as the spatial arrangement of colors and shapes in a picture or statue, or cadence in a poem or prose passage. This form is learned in order to facilitate expression. Grammar, as a case in point, helps to make prose effective. The rules of rhetoric, spelling, punctuation, arithmetic, or geometry have been devised mainly to facilitate expression and description.

Art and feelings. Because art is more than form; because it is substance as well, an artist must be more than just scientific. Artistic designs and forms must be evocative, must provoke an emotional reaction and afford emotional satisfactions. Science is not meant to provide this emotive or emotional content. For the elementary teacher the most rewarding source of inspiration will be his students' imaginations. Imagination is an exhaustible source of imagery, fantasy, insight, and perspective. It *may* be, although it is not always, exploited. When a student works in a colorless schoolroom atmosphere, his imagination is curtailed, dulled, perhaps even deadened. Even today many of our schoolrooms are drab; little more than a random miscellany of seats and closets. Often the pictures that adorn the walls are not meant to please children or to tell a story but to illustrate a virtue. Often, there is little in them to stimulate and challenge students' imagination. For example, Washington is shown standing in the prow of a rowboat crossing the Delaware in winter. Presumably, the picture is supposed to impress the children with the bravery, the staunch devotion to duty of our first President. It is good to remember Washington's character, but that is beside the point. The fact is that the picture that is charged with this responsibility is so colorless, so artificial, so

8 A mathematician's interest in mathematical analysis of art is revealed in George D. Birkhoff, *Aesthetic Measure.* Cambridge: Harvard University Press, 1933.

9 Kenneth Burke, *The Philosophy of Literary Form.* Baton Rouge: Louisiana State University Press, 1941.

removed from children's living that it may serve only to catch dust. In this instance, art is betrayed or at least made subordinate to some abstract purpose, some adult thought of instilling virtue and honesty in children.

A pathetic example of a missed opportunity in the teaching of literature is illustrated by the experience of a young married teacher in a small town. He was a teacher in an eighth grade. One of his pupils, a mature girl, thought that she had fallen in love. This girl had always had a wonderful record, but after falling in love, her grades suffered. The teacher summoned the girl and told her that her test scores had fallen off and that she was averaging 78—whatever that would mean as a mark of literary ability. The girl was accustomed to meeting the demands of the school. She snapped out of her romantic mood and got down to business, writing a "perfect examination."

This teacher really thought he had accomplished something important and perhaps he had. But he had missed a great chance. That girl was in the mood to have wallowed in the poetry of almost any romantic lyricist. But the teacher did not make the most of the opportunity, perhaps because he himself had not derived satisfaction from literature. Perhaps, for him, literature was meant to be suffered for its noble sentiments. If a teacher cannot understand the feelings of an artist and the feelings of people, he will be incapable of moving his students in the direction of appreciating creative art.

Imagination and understanding. What is the lesson in all this for the elementary teacher or curriculum-planner? What, for example, might the children be reading? Elementary-school reading might well begin the formation of literary interests both critical and creative. The quality of the reading material available to children has improved immeasurably in the last few years. Illustrations of the use of such literature are given in Chapters 19, 20, and 21.[10]

Fantasies, if fed to children as a steady diet, invite indolence. There is no excuse for that to happen since children possess, in almost all instances, noteworthy imaginations. After all, children are wide-eyed; their wishes are many. They have much to dream about,

---

[10] Louise M. Rosenblatt, *Literature as Exploitation.* New York: D. Appleton Century Company, 1938.

to express, and to project. For them life is adventurous and mysterious, not disillusioning. The night is still magic; a trip into the country or into the city holds unbounded joy. There is little need to overwork the fairies, ogres, giants; and no need to introduce brutal stories of any type. Fanciful stories are a part of our heritage and, if otherwise harmless, should not be denied a place in teaching. But taken alone they do not foster and will often destroy that imagination that leads to creativity. Imagination is really perception and understanding. There are innumerable things to be perceived and to be understood in the every-day world. Stories, properly chosen, will enhance this perception and understanding.

Increasing skill. While we are on the subject of uncovering artistic response, we might note that for the younger students, there must not be too much stress on form, on design, on plot-of-the-story. The *architecture* of art is quite difficult to learn and it tends to inhibit the beginner. Later, as the student makes progress in controlling his art medium, the need for form and mastery of technique will appear. That is the time to practice the skills. At the outset, the teacher should not set art tasks for the pupil, such as copying a bowl of fruit. Teacher direction is useful to the student not in defining jobs to be done or things to be expressed (something, of course, which cannot be commanded), but in discovering talents and desires for expression. The techniques and insights that will enable the student to work more efficiently in his particular art medium can be developed later.[11] The teacher, of course, will have to be able to offer help of this kind when the time comes.

Art is disciplinary. Many adults demand that music be rhyth-

---

[11] On this very point a further word of warning is in order. Do not require a finished piece of work whenever students begin to create. The student may not wish to complete his undertaking or his sense of completion may be different from the adult's. There are two temptations an effective teacher will learn to avoid. One is the urge to make a student come through with a complete bit of work, something that looks like something, something that can be hung on the wall or sent home. Hidden in this desire is that old Puritanical dislike of play, of "fooling around." In many situations, "stick-to-itiveness" is good, but this is not one of them. If insisted upon, art becomes dour, disciplinary, subservient to some ulterior moral purpose. The second temptation to be avoided at all costs is to hurry. A competent teacher may think that she knows what the child should produce by way of a finished product. Watching the neophyte struggle, she feels the urge to step in and help. All the while the child is feeling his way toward a better understanding of himself and his environment. He must be allowed time to do both without interference from adults.

mical, that a picture resemble a model, or that poetry have a definite rhyme and message. (This tendency is apparent in the usual criticism of abstract painting, atonal music, or rare poetic construction.) It may be that such people look upon art as entertainment and as skill in reproduction. It is both, certainly, but much more. Art is individual perception and individual expression.[12] Parenthetically, the art that many of us find so difficult to understand would be much more comprehensible to us and much more enjoyable if art had been a part of our education from our early years. The intricate forms would not seem so odd. Nor would we demand that the artist do something so obvious that it made no demands upon the imagination, perception, or understanding. We would have come to understand and respect the discipline that real art calls for, whether it be in its appreciation or in its creation.

The thought of art as discipline is not inconsistent with creativity and sensitive response. For years art teachers were trained to conform to strict standards of design. For example, a painting was to reproduce a scene much as a camera would. It was inevitable that artists would rebel against such restriction. Man has imagination and feelings to express. This talk of discipline is not to advocate interference with what children and young people feel and wish to express.

When we speak of the discipline of art, our motive is to assure those who think that art is idle pastime. Creative art calls for intelligence in its planning.[13] Nothing could be sillier than to think that an artist when expressing himself is relaxed. Far too much has been made of inspiration in art. Perspiration outweighs the moments of "divine inspiration." Just watch children seriously engaged in handicraft or painting or music. They are tense and strained. Art is taxing.

The effort expended by the artist, whatever his level of ability, is due partly to the amount of energy it takes to organize one's ideas, feelings, media, and technique. This concept of organizing is at the

[12] Norman C. Maier, "Recent Research in the Psychology of Art," in Nelson B. Henry, ed., *Art in American Life and Education,* Fortieth Yearbook of the National Society for the Study of Education. Bloomington, Illinois: Public School Publishing Company, 1941, pp. 379-400; and Thomas Munro, "The Nature of Art and Related Types of Experience," *ibid.,* pp. 249-288.
[13] John Dewey, *Art as Experience.* New York: Minton, Balch, 1934.

heart of art. Perhaps that is one reason why art is often good therapy for bewildered, unhappy youngsters or adults. Confusion usually results from disorganization.[14] The child whose intelligence is insufficient to permit him to compete successfully with other children is often unhappy, frustrated, confused, and *disorganized*. The teacher cannot give him more intelligence—although much can be done by way of permitting him to function at what is par for him. This is where a teacher sensitive to art has an opportunity. He can offer the child a chance to "work out" his feelings. Art is two-edged. Not only is it "catharsis," but in a certain sense it also results in a "work of art." Of course, only rarely does a finished work of art appear. Children are very generous, however. They will give approval to forms of expression that less sensitive adults would snub. This little approval means worlds to a youngster who may be struggling, for example, to overcome a sense of incompetence or physical ugliness. Art returns dividends out of all proportion to the self-discipline, training, and effort expended in creating it. We must remember, of course, that this "mental hygiene" value of art is extra, pure velvet. It comes along with the pleasure that art affords, the spiritual gratification that it gives.

It is not too much to expect that the fine arts will supplement one another and all the other proper activities of the curriculum, as well as make their individual contributions. Art, for example, has an affinity for science, and can blend with it and supplement it in many subtle though desirable ways. In Chapter 15 we employed a scientific background to demonstrate the need for conservation of our natural resources. Perhaps a more effective means for reaching the same end—the harboring of our resources—could be achieved by imbuing in children a love of nature. The child who has seen and felt the beauty of wild geese as they flock in South Dakota will, as an adult, hesitate to consent to schemes that would destroy their breeding grounds. The child who has come to love the wild forest for its peace, flowers, animals, and lakes or streams will not wish them destroyed by careless timbering, fires, or thoughtless camping. The love of color, tone, and form can be a mighty fortress of the human spirit. Without that spirit, welfare is nothing more than survival.

14 Schaeffer-Simmern, *The Unfolding of Artistic Activity.*

Discussion Questions

1. What does the phrase "human sensibility" mean to you? Do you feel embarrassed in expressing your feelings about something that moves you? Do children? Have you noticed at what point children become self-conscious about the expression of feelings?

2. Is there any point in encouraging children to be expressive? Will it "spoil them?"

3. What types of expression can you name and which of them are appropriate for the elementary grades? Can experiences of the type you have been discussing be "graded," i.e., be treated differently at different stages of development or maturation?

4. What distinction, if any, do you make between "creation" and "appreciation?" Is the one to be preferred over the other? Is one necessary for the other?

5. Is it the purpose of art in the elementary school to help the children make more complicated designs, rhythms, rhymes, patterns. . . ?

6. How would you compare and contrast the terms "insight" and "sensibility?"

7. Does the expression of feeling interfere with the development of intelligence?

8. How do you relate processes of "imagination" and "understanding?"

9. Is the art program of the elementary school a program of play or one of work—or both?

10. How would you describe the place of art in our culture? Does the place of art in our culture influence the place afforded art in the elementary-school curriculum?

11. Discuss aesthetics from the standpoint of the moral and spiritual nature of man.

Selected References

A Guide for Instruction in Music: Elementary School, Grades 1-8. Curriculum Bulletin No. 5. St. Paul: State of Minnesota, Department of Education, 1948.

A Guide for Instruction in Art: Elementary School, Grades 1-8. Curriculum Bulletin No. 5. St. Paul: State of Minnesota, Department of Education, 1948.

Art in American Life and Education, Fortieth Yearbook of the National Society for the Study of Education. Bloomington, Illinois: Public School Publishing Company, 1941.

Munro, Thomas, *The Arts and Their Interrelations*. New York: The Liberal Arts Press, 1949.

———, "The Nature of Art and Related Types of Experience," in Nelson B. Henry, ed., *Art in American Life and Education*, Fortieth Yearbook of the National Society for the Study of Education. Bloomington, Illinois: Public School Publishing Company, 1941, pp. 249-288.

Owatonna Art Education Project, *Art Units for Grades 1 to 3* (by the Project Staff). Minneapolis: University of Minnesota Press, 1944.

Art Units for Grades 4 to 6 (by the Project Staff). Minneapolis: University of Minnesota Press, 1944.

Teague, Walter Dorwin, *Design This Day*. New York: Harcourt, Brace & Company, Inc., 1940.

18

SCHOOL ADMINISTRATION
AND THE CURRICULUM

A PERSON cannot consider the curriculum of a school apart from the administrative policies of the school. All aspects of a school system are related. An individual cannot adopt modern curriculum policies without adopting modern administrative policies. The truth of this statement will be demonstrated by the remainder of this chapter.

To direct the educational experiences of each individual child in such a way as to bring about his optimum development and adjustment to his culture presents one of the most complex problems imaginable. The approach should always be experimental and tentative to a high degree, since interpretations and implications, even when based on carefully observed facts, are subject to error. Administrative decisions must always be made in terms of what happens to individual children in classrooms.

Administrative policy and individual pupil needs

The administrative policies necessary to enable teachers to meet the various needs of all the pupils in heterogeneous groups should be directed toward two main goals: First, to make it possible for the teacher to know the pupil better—to know his abilities, his interests, and his deficiencies well enough to direct his learning experiences; and second, to provide instructional methods and materials with a range of difficulty and content commensurate with the range of abilities and interests of the instructional group.

The measurement program of the school should be systematic and comprehensive. The measurement program should furnish the teacher with up-to-date information regarding the record of growth and status of each of his pupils in at least the fields of English, reading comprehension, arithmetic, and study skills. The tests should measure at regular intervals the permanent learnings that have been achieved toward the major and ultimate objectives of education. Knowledge of the pupil and his record of achievement should be considered basic data for guiding the educational process.

Measurement should begin with a relatively undifferentiated test of the individual Binet type at the pre-primary level and reach a considerable degree of differentiation in terms of improvable skills, abilities, and attitudes by the intermediate-school level. During the primary-school years, the differentiation should be in terms of (1) specific abilities related to developing number concepts, (2) reading readiness, some aspects of beginning reading achievement, and (3) specific behavior related to health and socialization. Group tests that require reading ability generally are unsatisfactory below the fourth grade. During the intermediate-school years, however, the approach to complete differentiation of learned behavior in terms of ultimate educational objectives can be made.

The results of the testing should be recorded in some well-known, easily interpreted unit of measurement showing the growth in each differentiated ability from year to year. It is also helpful to have these scores portrayed in graphic profile form. This test record should be kept by the teacher in a permanent record folder, which also should contain other important information about the child—his health record and information on social and emotional development and pertinent information about the child's family, his interests and activities outside of school, and samples of his best handwriting, art, poetry, and composition produced each year. Additional pertinent information may be secured by having each child write an autobiography.

Systematic testing should be carried out at the beginning of the school year; end-of-course testing should be avoided. Testing early in the school year has several distinct advantages. In the first place, it provides the teacher with up-to-date information regarding the educational status of each child at the beginning of the period of instruction when attention should be focused on planning in terms of individual needs. When tests are given at the close of the school year, the efforts of the teacher are more likely to be centered on preparing children for the tests and hence may result in undesirable cramming procedures. Also, tests that are administered at the end of a vacation period will reveal the more permanent learnings. Finally, by testing at the beginning of the year, the temptation to use the tests to determine promotion or failure is minimized. When a child knows his status in improvable skills at the beginning of a year and considers his progress during the preceding year, there is usually an urge on his part to better his previous record.

Other tests of a more diagnostic nature in reading, arithmetic, and the language areas should be available to teachers at all times in order to determine individual needs and to measure progress in the skills being emphasized in instruction. Informal tests developed by the teacher often are effective for diagnostic purposes. These tests should always be selected and used strictly from the standpoint of their instructional value. Detailed attention to measurement procedures was given in Chapter 10.

Grouping within the class on the basis of status and needs. Grouping in specific learning areas is one of the most essential procedures in meeting individual needs. The within-class grouping in reading, for example, may involve grouping on the basis of four specific types of reading activity.

In the basic reading program in which the child is taught how to read and in which the development of the various reading skills is undertaken, the grouping should be in terms of the development in these skills. In most classes, with the range of ability that is common, it will be necessary to have at least three groups, each using reading tests suitable for their level of development. In many schools where but one basic reader is available, an attempt is made to adapt questions and exercises to ability. This is very unsatisfactory. If three or four fifth-graders have second-grade reading ability, they should use a book suitable to their level and not a fifth-grade book. If four or five have seventh-grade reading ability or higher, they should use a seventh-grade reader or one equal to their competency. Of course, these groups are informal; if a name is attached to the group it should probably be the name of the book they are using.

(Modern reading texts have names and the grade difficulty is not emphasized on the cover. A key number or symbol reveals to the teacher the level of difficulty of the book.) There may be five children in one reading group, fifteen in another, and ten in another. The size of each group will depend upon the distribution of reading ability in the class. A child may be shifted from one group to another at any time that the re-assessment of his ability warrants. Each child is given a book that he can read and exercises that he can complete successfully.

In the experience unit phase of the reading program, children usually are grouped in committees each with a different problem to solve, report to prepare, questions to answer, and so forth. These committees are formed and their chairmen chosen on the basis of several factors: the reference books available, the difficulty of these books and the interest appeal of each book; the interests, reading ability, and other abilities required by the committee's work; and the needs of certain children to assume responsibility, to be successful, to develop self-confidence, and so forth. The groups here are called committees but they are formed in such a way as to give each child tasks that he can do, books that he can read, responsibilities that he can shoulder. The learning activities associated with the unit development are so varied that every child can make a contribution that is satisfying to him regardless of his level of ability.

The free reading program is an individual matter. The teacher helps each child select books from the library that are suitable to the child's interests and level of ability. If this phase of the reading program is handled properly, the average elementary child will read perhaps 20 books during the year simply for the pleasure of reading. The important thing is to help the child select a book that he is certain to like. If the teacher tries to make the child read a particular kind of book or requires him to make book reports, the program will be irreparably damaged.

The remedial reading program may involve only a few pupils in the room who are reading below their potential level. Generally, by the fourth grade, the median or average child should be able to read any material that he is able to understand when it is read aloud to him. The reading level cannot be higher than the thinking level, but it will normally approach or equal the thinking level. This means that there will be some children in a fourth grade, for example, with second-grade reading ability who do not need remedial attention. They are reading as well as their intellectual development permits. The grouping for remedial reading instruction is based on specific needs of individual children.

Pupils also will have to be grouped in terms of their arithmetic ability. However, in this field the use of diagnostic tests and the realization by the teachers that most processes in arithmetic can be applied to either simple problems or very complex problems will enable the teacher to make adjustments to individual pupils with less specific grouping than in the reading area. In the mechanics of writing it is possible for the whole class to write on the same topic, for example, "thank you" letters for Christmas presents. But the letters will reveal that grouping is desirable for meeting the needs of certain children.

The important consideration in informal grouping within the class is to form groups in terms of specific needs in the various areas of the curriculum.

Much of the work of the class, however, will still involve the entire group. This should be kept in mind in planning, coordinating, and unifying the over-all activities and goals of the class. A pupil needs to feel most strongly his membership in and acceptance by the total group. The use of smaller groups, however, should be on a matter-of-fact basis for meeting special needs and purposes that are subsidiary to the over-all purposes and undertakings of the total group. The use of groups is demonstrated in Chapters 19, 20, and 21.

In naming or designating a group, care should be taken to see to it that no hint or connotation of brightness or dullness is allowed to impress itself upon the minds of the children. Groups usually are designated in terms of the purpose of the group, the title of the book being used, or the name of the pupil who is chairman.

Since different texts, reference books, materials, and procedures are used with each sub-group, the necessity of buying complete sets of readers and texts is avoided. A much greater range of materials may be purchased at no greater expense.

The teaching load should be limited. Teachers skilled in the art of adapting group procedures to the needs of individual pupils insist that no primary teacher should be responsible for more than 25 pupils and that 30 pupils should be the maximum load for intermediate-grade teachers. Of course, there are individual differences among teachers as well as among pupils. Some teachers can direct 40 pupils with greater effectiveness than others achieve with half that number. Some teachers follow the same "ritual" in teaching a class of 20 that they use with a class of 40. However, the size of classes should be limited to the number that a competent teacher who is sensitive to individual pupil needs can manage successfully.

Teachers should remain with the same pupils longer. Many elementary schools permit the teacher to remain with the same pupils for more than one year. In some schools the pupils have the same teacher from kindergarten through the sixth year; in others, one teacher through the primary years and another through the intermediate years. Of course, in one- and two-room rural schools this has always been accepted practice. The continuing teacher plan eliminates the concept of a grade teacher and gives a teacher the opportunity to know more completely the abilities and peculiarities of his pupils, to become better acquainted with his pupils' parents, and to think in terms of child development rather than merely of the subject matter to be covered. The teacher is enabled to start each year with a thorough knowledge of his pupils and can plan the work of the year in terms of specific needs. The process of promotion is eliminated; there are no failures in the sense of repeating the same materials and exercises. Each child works with materials suitable to his level of development and starts each September where he left off in June.

This plan need not be adopted for all teachers in a school. For example, if a first- and second-grade teacher are willing to try the plan and if it is acceptable to parents and principal, each teacher can keep the same class for two years. If a third-grade teacher is willing to enter into the plan, each teacher may work with the same pupils for three years. Some parents may object to having their children with the same teacher for more than one year. If the school is large enough, such children may be transferred to another teacher. Also, when personality conflicts occur between pupils and teachers, it should be possible to transfer the child to another teacher. Under this plan, pupils and teacher who work well together remain together.

The traditional method of reporting to parents should be modified. The plan of reporting to parents in terms of percentage marks, or letter grades, based on relative standing in the class, is not consistent with the policy of meeting the needs of individual pupils. Likewise, the practice of simply marking a pupil satisfactory or unsatisfactory in terms of his general learning capacity is inadequate. The weakness of these marking and reporting methods is not that they convey too much information about the pupil, but rather that they tell too little and their meaning is ambiguous. What is needed is a reporting system that involves a mutual exchange of information between teacher and parents and that will result in a better understanding of school and home conditions and aid the child's development. The child also should be informed about how well he is progressing. In many instances the child is more concerned with the report than are his parents. It is important that he be able to evaluate his development realistically. Certainly in the intermediate grades and above, he likes to think of it in objective terms.

It takes some time in a traditional school to prepare teachers, parents, and pupils to understand, accept, and profit from an improved reporting system. Such changes must be made slowly and with every effort to show those concerned how the proposed system is better and how they will profit from it. It is easier to start the system with a specific primary class and advance the practice through the school with this class.

If proper preparation is made, it is beneficial and revealing to all concerned if the teacher once or twice a year, or more often when desirable, sits down with the parents of each child and discusses the youngster's achievements and needs, going through the pupil's record folder and pointing out signs of his growth and status, his achievements in the basic study skills and progress toward other major educational objectives, samples of his work, his behavior charactcristics, and his personality strengths and weaknesses. The teacher will of necessity study each pupil in preparation for this conference and plan to learn much of value from the parents regarding the out-of-school life of the pupil. Teachers using this system of reporting keep records, study growth and development, make case studies—become better acquainted with their pupils, and in addition, get to know their pupils' parents. Because of the time such interviews take, most schools may find it necessary to work out a combination of parent-teacher conferences that are supplemented by an improved periodic report form.

The primary bases for grouping children into classes should be general social and physical development. During the years of maturation, the traits most important to the child in determining membership and status in a congenial group are chronological age and general physical development. Together with general social development these are also the most obvious. In a graded school it is very important to a child that he be grouped with his peers. To deny him this privilege is to violate one of the most important requirements of a favorable learning situation. A child will always put forth effort to gain the approval and acceptance of his peers; but if he is grouped with children he considers chronologically and physically his inferiors, he cares less about their approval. In addition, democratic control in such a group is much less effective. Therefore, throughout the period of maturation, these traits should constitute the fundamental basis for educational grouping; that is, when a child is five he enters kindergarten, when six he enters the first grade of the elementary school, when twelve he enters the junior high school, and when fifteen the senior high school. Since chronological age is not perfectly related to physical and social development, some adjustments may have to be made, especially at the primary level, with the physical and social developmental level taking precedence over chronological age. A child should live and work in the group he most obviously belongs with, which accepts him and is accepted by him. It will be recalled that both intelligence and achievement test data show that age groups are no more variable than grade groups. Hence this basis for grouping will not increase materially the range of ability with which the teacher must cope.

Some school officials have considered the possibility of admitting children to the first grade in terms of mental age rather than chronological age. If this were done, there would be children in the first grade ranging from a chronological age of four to eight years. The eight-year-olds would learn to read with great difficulty but the four-year-olds would learn easily and rapidly. Few experienced first-grade teachers would recommend this policy. But the illogicalness of admitting children to the school on the basis of chronological age and then shifting to achievement as a basis for progress through that school should be seen with equal clarity.

When a 13-year-old boy moves into a new school district, he is sent to the junior high school on the basis of no more evidence than that he is 13. But suppose he cannot read. There are already pupils in any junior high school who cannot read; he will be grouped with them for instruction.

Suggestions have been made that children should be grouped on the basis of the average of their chronological and mental ages. This means that a fifteen-year-old boy with a mental age of ten will be grouped with a ten-year-old boy who has a mental age of fifteen. One does not need to be a psychologist to see the absurdity of such a grouping; it places the very slowest with the very best.

If chronological age and physical and social development are accepted as the primary bases for grouping in the school, all assumptions that a grade level indicates anything specific regarding intellectual competence or educational achievement must be given up. Evidence has been presented in Chapter 2 indicating that grade level, *per se*, never truly signifies intellectual competence or educational achievement. The assumption that it does has led to indefensible practices, subterfuge, and confusion in meeting individual needs. Diplomas will be given on the basis of years attended, age attained, and courses taken, but they will be assumed to convey little or no other meaning. They never did have any other meaning. The school period, at least through the high school, should probably be the same length for all pupils. No attempt should be made to bring the slow pupil up to standard by keeping him in school a few extra years. No attempt should be made to accelerate the bright pupil through school at any early age. As instruction is adapted to individual needs and capacities, information on the level of achievement attained in the various areas of learning will be determined through measurement procedures and reported to anyone who has the right to such information.

The traditional inflexible daily program of the elementary school should be modified. A daily and weekly program is necessary: (a) to give the teacher and pupils a sense of security; (b) to insure that the various areas of the curriculum are given attention; and (c) to conform to life and activities outside the school, that necessarily run on a very rigid schedule. However, if the teacher is to be free to meet the individual needs of children, the program specifying the amount of time to be devoted to each learning area must be made more flexible. The week rather than the day should be the unit of program-making. Certain periods, such as the current affairs or the library period, may be held once each week. Other periods, such as art and construction work, may require long periods twice or three times each week. Free periods near the close of the day when each pupil works on his most pressing problems or does what he wishes should be provided almost every day. The program should always be considered as a guide rather than a requirement. Sufficient flexibility to meet the requirements of planning and executing the unit activities should always be possible.

A wealth of instructional material must be provided. Instructional materials should have a range of difficulty, interest appeal, and content commensurate with the range of abilities and interests of the class. Classroom libraries in the elementary school should be given special attention. They should contain all the basic reference materials suitable for the abilities represented in the room: dictionaries, atlases, children's encyclopedias, yearly almanacs of information, *Who's Who in America,* and so forth. It is not sufficient that these books be in the school library; they should be in each room library. The room library also should contain books at appropriate levels of difficulty on the units to be developed by the class, children's literature in abundance, and books on popular mechanics, hobbies, science, and how to make things. The school library should constantly feed into and supplement the room libraries, but it should never supplant them in any way.

In addition to a wealth of books, there should be in the elementary classroom children's magazines and newspapers, art materials, woodworking tools, a workbench, simple science laboratory equipment, a science cabinet and sink with running water, bulletin boards equal in space to the blackboards, colorful, well-chosen pictures, visual aids of all types, movable desks, tables and chairs, heavy and light screens for dividing the room, and a combination radio-phonograph-television for watching and listening to educational programs. The room should be large enough to provide at least 25 square feet of floor space (30 square feet is desirable) for each pupil. The classroom should be a self-contained unit with equipment and facilities for scientific experiments, construction activities (the building of scenery for use in dramatics, for example), painting, modeling, and other art forms, and the publishing of a room newspaper. In addition, a place or places in the room should be set aside where the children can engage in concentrated reading and study, hold committee meetings, and entertain guests, as the occasion warrants.

School room environments of the past were highly restricted and needlessly standardized. Learning activities were limited (by the fixed, screwed-down seats, blackboard sidewalls, and cramped quarters) to reciting, reading, writing, and listening. Unnecessary restrictions on communication and movement limited social experiences and social learning. A more unstimulating environment for a group of children is difficult to conceive. In no place outside of school has man duplicated such surroundings for his adult activities.

Curriculum policies and practices
adjustable to individual pupil needs

It is obvious, that if all pupils in the elementary school are required to follow the same course of study, read the same books, do the same exercises, solve the same problems, and pass the same examinations, there can be but slight recognition of individual interests and abilities. Whenever a school purports to accept all the children of all the people and to meet their individual needs, the curriculum must be developed according to policies that recognize individual and trait differences. The policies outlined have two purposes:

(1) To strive for a curriculum sufficiently broad and flexible to recognize and reward the great variety of combinations of aptitudes and interests of its pupils, enabling them to learn what their peculiar strengths and weaknesses are and preparing them to fit into our complex society with its multiplicity of demands for workers with varying aptitudes.

(2) To free the teacher from rigid procedures and prescribed subject matter to be covered in order that he may adapt procedures and subject matter to the abilities, interests, and aptitudes of pupils. Since the teacher knows the pupil better than does the supervisors and administrators, he is, when unhampered in regard to procedure, the person best qualified in the school system to plan for the optimum development of the pupil.

Skills, subject matter, and attitudes

It is helpful in thinking about the curriculum, its objectives, content, and organization, to differentiate three major aspects of learning. The three aspects are all important and essential in any learning activity. It is difficult to say that one is more important than another; they are highly interrelated and go on at the same time. Perhaps one of the most significant faults of the traditional curriculum has been that the various aspects of learning were thought of as independent and treated as such. The three aspects are: (1) the skill aspect, (2) the content aspect, and (3) the attitudinal or feeling aspect.

The *skill aspect* of learning is concerned with the techniques and procedures of performance. Excellent performance requires the integration of properly adjusted and related behavior. Skill in thinking, for example, requires ability to organize material, to see relationships, to make inferences, to hypothesize readily, to systematically test possible solutions, to recognize clues, to see things in new relationships, to be critical of superficial relationships, and so forth. But thinking always involves subject matter or content; we must think about something. Thinking always takes place in a context that gives it significance. It also always involves attitudes and feelings toward the process and the context. The communication skills (listening, speaking, reading, writing, gesturing, and the like) always involve content and attitudes. We have attitudes and opinions about the things we listen to and speak, read, and write about. Skill in quantitative thinking (arithmetical processes, computation, the logic of mathematics) always involves content or at least a context that gives it significance and meaning, and it always involves attitudes. Even the skills of walking, running, and playing games of all kinds involve situations that give them meaning and value.

The *subject-matter aspect* of learning is concerned either with man's relationships to man (the social sciences and the humanities) and/or man's relationship to the universe (the natural sciences). To deal with these relationships requires, always, some of the skills mentioned above and involves attitudes and feelings toward the subject matter and skills involved.

The *attitudinal aspects* of learning always involve a context and content and a way of behaving. A person's attitudes toward man-kind or the universe may range from the extremely hostile to the extremely friendly. All attitudes and feelings are related to these two continuums in some way, directly or indirectly.

In the traditional curriculum, *skills, subject matter,* and *attitudes* were thought of as being independent of each other, as things to be developed in special classes in different periods of the day. There were subjects such as reading, writing, arithmetic, spelling, and the like, in which the development of abstract skills was the primary objective. The meaningful and purposeful content of the subjects was ignored.

In other subjects such as history, geography, science, hygiene, government, and so forth, the mastery of subject matter was the primary objective, mastery usually taking the form of rote memori-zation of isolated facts and dates. Here the skills (reading, thinking, inferring, reasoning, relating, organizing, proving, understanding, writing, computing, and so forth) for dealing with subject matter were largely ignored. In fact, even when all the important intellec-tual skills are neglected, the ability to memorize still remains and almost everyone can do it. Attitudes toward subject matter and the skills of dealing with it again remain neglected.

There were still other subjects in which appreciations and atti-tudes were supreme: art, music, literature, ideals, morals, and na-ture. These were subjects to "Oh" and "Ah" and "preach" about. Here both content and skills were neglected.

With special subjects used to develop skills, certain subjects in which content was regarded as all important, and other subjects in which appreciation was stressed, it is no wonder the curriculum lacked integration, organization, and direction.

Integrating the curriculum

If the curriculum is to be integrated, it should be organized around content (subject matter) that has significance, meaning, and purpose to the learner. In saying this we in no sense mean to place skills and attitudes in minor roles. In fact they are "co-equal," for learning cannot be effectively achieved in a vacuum free of skills, content, attitudes, and everything else. It is the subject matter (something about something), that is manipulated as children learn.

Since all subject matter is related to man's relationships to man and to the physical universe, the content at each maturation and developmental level will deal with significant aspects of the social and natural environment of the child. It will begin at the kindergarten and first-grade level with the home, the family, the school, and the neighborhood and move out gradually at succeeding levels to include the community, the state, the nation, the world, and the universe. It must not be forgotten that the understanding of the immediate cultural and physical environment requires ultimately an understanding of other cultures in other environments both past and present as they are determined and influenced by historical, geographic, physical, and biological factors.

Providing for individual differences

Because there is such a wide range of abilities, skills, and attitudes in every class, it is important to recognize that any aspect of the social or natural environment can be experienced, thought about, read about, and partly understood at all levels of development from the kindergarten through the university graduate school. The first-grader can study the family, the school, the airport, the grocery store, the dairy, the bakery, and so forth, and so can and does the graduate student. Both may find in such topics enough to challenge the highest abilities. They think, read, and study at different levels depending upon different skills, understandings, and backgrounds. Increasingly, there are books dealing with any aspect of the environment (automobiles, airplanes, cows, boats, and the like) at every reading level from pre-primer to the highly technical level. In a fifth-grade class with a range of reading ability of seven years, every student can experience, read, discuss, and solve problems at his level of understanding about any aspect of the social and physical environment. The subject matter related to a given unit of work may differ for children at various stages of development as will the skills utilized in dealing with it and the understandings and attitudes that result from it, but all the work of the class can be integrated in terms of the varied aspects and problems of the unit. The organized type of subject matter usually found in textbooks is the end product of such study, not the starting point. Given adequate reference materials and guidance, classes in the upper elementary school can write more meaningful and instructive texts than many that were required reading a few years ago.

The curriculum units in the social and natural sciences should be selected to organize subject matter around purposeful and meaningful problems, with a view to:

(1) Making possible the use of a *wide variety* of stimulating educational material from *factual* source books, literature, and visual and auditory aids, with the *local social and physical environment* as a laboratory.

(2) Making possible an appeal to many and *varied interests.*

(3) Making possible the utilization of reading material with a *wide range of difficulty,* content, and interest appeal.

(4) Stimulating and giving purpose and meaning to a *wide range of educational activities* in reading, research, problem-solving, discussion, use of reference materials, writing and giving reports, letter-writing, organizing materials, planning, observing relationships, drawing conclusions, formulating generalizations, dramatizing, understanding and using all art forms, construction activities, using arithmetic in a functional way, taking responsibility and co-operating in *group projects,* conducting meetings, giving talks before groups, panel discussions, and interviewing to *develop skills, understandings, ideals, values, beliefs,* and *attitudes.*

(5) Giving purpose to, and affording the functional use of the *basic skills* in the language arts, reading, and mathematics. Skill in these areas must be given constant, definite, and systematic attention. The *developmental sequence* of each must be followed in the *development of each child.* Much practice in their use should come in the social and natural science units.

The grade levels at which certain knowledge, skills, and abilities should be learned cannot be determined with any degree of specificity. Despite this, it has been common practice until recently in courses of study to specify what should be taught in a given skill area in a given grade. For example, it has been common in the mechanics of capitalization to specify that children should learn in the third grade to capitalize "Mr.," "Mrs.," and "Miss;" in the fourth grade, the names of cities, states, streets, and organizations; in the fifth grade, the names of persons and firms and the first word in a line of poetry; in the sixth grade, the names of the Deity, the Bible, and abbreviations of titles and proper names. Experienced teachers know that some pupils will learn all these by the close of the fourth grade; others will not have learned them by the time they graduate from high school or college. The teacher must be sensitive to the developmental level of each child, determined not by a score on a test but by observation of what the child can and cannot do. The teacher should be prepared to lead the child patiently through the next steps in his development, regardless of the level he has achieved.

Similar graded lists of things to be learned are provided in instructional materials in all subjects: lists of words in spelling, lists of processes and problems in arithmetic, lists of exercises in handwriting, lists of capitalization, punctuation, and usage rules in language, lists of skills to be developed in reading, and many others. When based on experimental evidence with reference to the social value of the skill and its place in the sequence of development, and if properly used, these lists of essential learnings have some value in that they identify subject matter that those who prepared the lists thought to be important. We shall mention two of the values. First, they serve as guides for the teacher. Exercises for teaching these skills may be introduced and emphasized when their purpose is clear or when there is a need for them. The purpose of the most essential skills is clear even for the first-grade child. He knows why he came to school (to learn to read) and if he doesn't make progress in that direction, he is disappointed and provoked. Graded lists should never be considered as things to be learned by all children once and for all,[1] in a one, two, three, four sequence, out of their functional setting and natural context. Neither should they be considered as centers around which all instruction should be organized. The practice of organizing the curriculum almost entirely around these piecemeal, itemized goals has been the greatest limitation of the traditional school.

The second use to be made of such lists is in the systematic and economical diagnosis of pupils' needs and deficiencies. At regular intervals the pupils should be tested for knowledge of essential spellings, essential processes in arithmetic, essential handwriting elements, essential English skills, and essential reading skills, the

[1] For example, the development of the ability to outline, organize material, or to summarize what is read was well begun before the child entered school and will continue to develop through school and after.

purpose being to keep both the pupil and the teacher constantly aware of the specifics of individual development and deficiency.

Tests based on such lists or outlines can be of the informal, teacher-made type, covering the spelling list for the grade at the rate of 20 words per week, mixed fundamental problems in arithmetic covering every process learned up to the time of the test (such tests should be given weekly to maintain skills and diagnose individual needs), dictation exercises in English covering various aspects of the mechanics of writing, and diagnostic check-ups in handwriting. All this should be considered in the nature of diagnosis of specific pupil needs to guide instruction and not as a device for grading, rating, measuring, or shaming students into doing better by making them feel they are not performing up to some standard. Attention was given to this topic in Chapter 10. Here it is renewed in relation to meeting the needs of individual pupils.

Since life outside the school recognizes and rewards a great variety of aptitudes and combinations of aptitudes, the school should do the same. The traditional school has too often recognized and rewarded only docility and a facile memory. Teachers in such schools have often expressed surprise when pupils they had considered hopeless achieved considerable success in later life. The broadening of the elementary curriculum to include various forms of practical arts, fine arts, athletics, a school paper, extended educational field trips, participation in school government, the safety patrol, radio programs, and community health programs is evidence of the acceptance of this principle. The elementary school should be a proving ground in which the individual pupil discovers his peculiar strengths and weaknesses. If every child is to find himself, the schools must offer him opportunities to develop as broadly as possible but in a purposeful and meaningful way.

Administration and broad curriculum policy

In order to provide leadership in curriculum improvement, administration must be active in three areas.

First, administration must assume responsibility for seeing that available research in curriculum is used widely in the schools. If this is to be done, principals, supervisors, and teachers who work with curriculum development must come to understand the experimental nature of the educational process. In dealing in the classroom with the individual differences among children, each educational procedure is an experiment both with the class as a whole and with individual children. Teachers must regard their work in the light of objectives to be realized, of methods and procedures to be tried, and of assessment to measure effectiveness. When methods fail, there must be a re-examination of available evidence, a new hypothesis, and a new experiment. Educators must understand the essential nature of scientific method. They will understand it if, singly or in groups, they engage in individual or cooperative research on projects relating to the daily problems of teaching. Thus they will become conscious of the means by which research information is acquired, and grow accustomed to thinking of research information in terms of real situations.

If teachers and other curriculum workers are to make use of research, the research must be readily available to them. Administration must provide staff members whose function is to seek out research pertinent to the curricular problems of the moment. These staff members should have an understanding of research from having themselves participated in research projects. Thus, they should have some knowledge of statistics and experimental design and should avoid deluging teachers with an indiscriminate barrage of research findings. They should be sufficiently sophisticated to select pertinent research in various areas. Such resource people should serve not as supervisors or directors but as servants or consultants. Their positions should be purely advisory.

Second, administration must be alert to eliminate supervisory or inspectional practices that, no matter how well intended, actually serve to slow down real progress. One of these practices is to rely too much upon carefully outlined and rather specific curriculum content and upon supervisory or inspectional procedures that serve to protect the recommended or established program from criticism or change. Such supervisory programs are frequently conceived of in the kindest and most helpful of terms, and in actual practice frequently relieve teachers of worry and strain and help them to achieve what is *expected* of them. In practice, however, this tends to set up curriculum prescriptions and supervisory techniques that make progress difficult.

To overcome these failures, new concepts of leadership must be developed. Teachers must be regarded as professional workers. They are expected to exercise professional judgment, to be expert in applying professional knowledge and skill, to be alert to the various problems they face, and to be competent to make use of their professional education in a creative, scientific manner. In contrast to all this, many of our present procedures are an outgrowth of a day when teachers assumed their duties in the classroom with little more than a brief period of training during or immediately after completion of the twelfth grade. Under rigidly prescribed curriculums, teachers have little opportunity to operate as professional people. Perhaps treating teachers as professional people will hasten professionalization. Administration must take into account many of the developments in leadership that parallel the development of knowledge in group dynamics and social psychology. If teachers can be freed from the fear of being rated, transferred, dismissed, or denied promotion as the result of deviations from past practice, if they can come to regard their superiors in the educational hierarchy as friends, as helpers, as experts, as sources of information, and as bulwarks to security, morale will improve and progress will be accelerated. If administration can remove the fear that teachers have of revealing a weakness, a lack of knowledge, a lack of skill, a specific failure with a specific child, or a deviation from supervisory opinion, and in its place set up a healthy, cooperative attitude, it will have accomplished wonders in improving curriculum practice.

Administration must become active in developing a new type of public understanding. The public schools in our democracy belong in a very peculiar sense to the American people. In the final analysis, the public has a perfect right to tell the schools what shall and what shall not be done in them. By and large, the public is satisfied with American education, but this satisfaction would be increased greatly were the public really informed about the efforts that the profession, from top to bottom, is making to preserve the democratic way of life, the happiness and well-being of children, the conservation and refinement of the culture, the installation of moral and spiritual values, the teaching of fundamental knowledges and skills, and all the other objectives with which schools are concerned. Unfortunately, as schools have concerned themselves with these things, they have increasingly operated in isolation from the general public. This isolation is now being recognized as an error and steps are being taken to break it down. It cannot be done by high pressure publicity programs, by beautifully printed brochures, by hiring public relations men, by radio programs, by newspaper releases, or even by community committees of outstanding leaders who meet but to listen and approve as educators convince them of their personal competence and the purity of their ideals. Though some of these things are important, they are ineffective without something more.

The most promising administrative development in overcoming public misunderstanding is to involve more and more citizens in actual educational planning. These citizens may or may not be parents. They should sit on curriculum committees, report-card planning committees, discipline committees, subject-matter committees, mental health committees, and other committees that deal with method and content. These representatives should be chosen by various community groups. When any group or any individual in a community expresses doubt or resentment or mistrust concerning the broad directions that education is taking, their help should be enlisted if possible. By their nature, some of these committees will be statewide or citywide, but the *best work* will often be done where groups of citizens concern themselves with the problems facing their own school in their own neighborhood. The techniques for doing this type of thing are only now being developed. There are, however, some promising beginnings. It is an area where pioneering is necessary. The same psychological principles are involved here as are involved in any healthy learning situation.

Discussion Questions

1. The chief use of tests in the traditional school has been for determining grades and promotion. What are the principal arguments in support of and against this policy?
2. For what purposes should tests, measurements, and other evaluation instruments be used in a modern school?
3. In what ways can an inadequate evaluation program harm the curriculum of a school?
4. What is the nature of learning experiences in which grouping is desirable? What are the characteristics of learning experiences where grouping is not necessary?

5. How should the teaching procedures of a teacher with 20 pupils differ from those of a teacher with 40 pupils?

6. What are the advantages and disadvantages of having a teacher remain with the same pupils for several years?

7. What are the limitations of the traditional report card? How is it inconsistent with a curriculum designed to meet the needs of individual pupils?

8. Why should children be grouped with their accepted peers?

9. In what ways does a daily program give a person a sense of security?

10. Draw a diagram of what you consider to be an ideal classroom for elementary children. Indicate the location of the windows, furniture, reading center, bulletin boards, blackboards, science equipment, and everything you consider desirable and essential in a classroom.

11. What arguments can you muster in defense of the traditional curriculum that isolates the skills, the subject matter, and the feeling aspects of learning?

12. What subjects have you studied that are so remote from life that the local environment could not serve as a laboratory?

13. Make a list of learning tasks that can be completed by each member of a class varying greatly in ability, each working at his level of competency. (For example, writing a letter to a school friend who is sick.)

14. Make a list of learning tasks that can be completed only by pupils who have reached a given stage of development. (For example, reading a book of seventh-grade difficulty.)

15. In a few words, discuss each of the three areas in which administration should be active in providing leadership in curriculum development.

Selected References

Bellock, Arno, "Sequence and Grade Placement," *Journal of Educational Research,* Vol. 41, April 1948, 610-623.

Benjamin, Harold, *The Saber-Tooth Curriculum* including other lectures in the history of paleolithic education. New York: McGraw-Hill Book Company, Inc., 1939.

Bode, Boyd H., *Progressive Education at the Crossroads.* New York: Newson and Company, 1938.

Bond, G. L. and B. Handlan, *Adapting Instruction in Reading to Individual Differences,* Series on Individualization of Instruction, No. 5. Minneapolis: University of Minnesota Press, 1948.

Caswell, Hollis L. and A. Wellesley Foshay, *Education in the Elementary School.* New York: American Book Company, 1942 and 1950.

Educational Policies Commission, *Education for All American Youth.* Washington, D. C.: National Education Association, 1944.

Herrick, Vergil E. and Ralph W. Tyler, ed., *Toward Improved Curriculum Theory*, Supplementary Educational Monographs, No. 71. Chicago: University of Chicago Press, 1950.

Jersild, A. T., R. L. Thorndike, B. Goldman, and J. J. Loftus, "An Evaluation of Aspects of the Activity Program in the New York City Public Elementary Schools," *Journal of Experimental Education*, Vol. 8, December 1939, 166-207.

———, *et al.*, "A Further Comparison of Pupils in Activity and Non-Activity Schools," *Journal of Experimental Education*, Vol. 9, June 1941, 303-309.

National Education Association, *Organizing the Elementary School for Living and Learning*. Washington, D. C.: The Association for Supervision and Curriculum Development, 1947.

Otto, H. J., *Elementary School Organization and Administration*, 2nd ed. New York: Appleton-Century-Crofts, Inc., 1944.

———, *Principles of Elementary Education*. New York: Rinehart & Company, Inc., 1949.

Shores, J. Harlan, *A Critical Review of the Research on Elementary School Organization, 1890-1949*. Urbana, Illinois: College of Education, Bureau of Research and Service, University of Illinois, 1949.

PART THREE

CURRICULUM IN ACTION

*P*ART THREE portrays actual *situations in which teachers practice the principles* set forth in the first two parts of this book. A persistent reaction of teachers and prospective teachers to much of the written material designed to improve teaching has been that it is impractical. Part of this impracticality resides in the experiences that the teacher himself has had in school. Frequently he has never really experienced the kind of a classroom that the theorist discusses. There is an old saying that we tend to teach the way we were taught. This is very true. There is a strong temptation on the part of the new teacher to revert to methods and content areas that were used in the classrooms he attended.

There is another facet to the teacher's problem. Many of the people who discuss the ideal classroom have never actually run one for themselves. If they ever did any elementary teaching, it was frequently before they had specialized or before they had developed the insights that they now have. This is not said critically. A practitioner in any of the sciences must practice continually if he is to apply new knowledge in his field. This is true because of the rapid development in both theory and practice today in all fields. In education, for example, it may be demonstrated that children in a controlled situation who are subject to authoritarian domination and drilled on facts and skills will fail to develop certain desirable attitudes and social competencies. The researcher who discovers this will expect teachers to take advantage of it in the classroom situation. However, it is difficult for a teacher by himself to devise procedures to take account of all such insights.

A further source of difficulty is the variability of the situations in which the teacher may find himself. There are so many differences in communities—in groups of children and in groups of parents, in individual children and individual parents, in race, religion, and socio-economic backgrounds—that it is exceedingly difficult to establish a pattern that a teacher may follow in any situation.

Differences between schools are sometimes startling. This difference may have its source in a school board, a superintendent, a principal, a corps of supervisors, or a combination of any or all of these. The beginning teacher will find a great difference, too, between the problems he faces when he takes over a class that has been previously taught by a rigid disciplinarian, whose emphasis was on subject matter mastery, and his problems when he takes over a class that has had experience in pupil-teacher planning in terms of a realistic appraisal of growing children in their multilateral environment. Children must develop new learning skills when they are placed in a new educational environment.

Needless to say many of the things that the teacher in the modern elementary school must take into account are very subtle. Things are frequently not what they seem. An accidentally broken ink bottle may create quite a disturbance and leave a big spot on the floor but be far less significant educationally than a few unshed tears welling up in the eyes of a timid child in the cloak hall. The third-grade child who is discovered copying the spelling words from a small slip of paper in his hand may be telling the teacher something very important. He may be saying that he is developing a fear of school—a fear of failure and a lack of confidence in his ability to do what is expected of him. Or, his behavior may indicate that his intelligence, his emotional adjustment, or his available energy is not sufficient for the tasks at hand. It may even be that his tendency to copy, to search for the easiest way, may denote a lack of motivation, a feeling that the job confronting him is unimportant.

If teachers could be prepared as skilled mechanical workers it might be possible to provide them with ready answers to most of their problems. Since this is impossible it becomes necessary to prepare teachers as professional workers. They must have the background, courage, freedom, imagination, and ingenuity to approach each classroom situation with an experimental attitude. Whatever occurs in the classroom will be affected by (1) the innate complexity of the situation, (2) the basic objectives that grow out of a concern for human welfare, (3) and the learning situation, in the individual and in the group, as it develops from day to day and hour to hour.

19

MARION JOHNSON—TEACHER

$\mathcal{T}$HIS IS THE STORY of Marion Johnson. Her story should not be read as the example of the perfect teacher, nor, if she were, should her methods or the steps she took in the development of units be copied. Her story is an example of a young lady who gives promise in her beginning teaching of becoming a most excellent teacher. We see how she avoided many of the traditional pitfalls and moved confidently to experiment with methods based on new research and new insight into how desirable learnings are best brought about.

The teacher is a person, too

At the beginning of her senior year in high school, Marion Johnson had decided to become a teacher. (Now she was about to assume her duties in the Pleasant Valley School, an eight-teacher elementary school in a small community 25 miles from the city.) She had always liked children and school. She had learned easily except in mathematics. It seemed that she had always felt a bit uncertain and incompetent when faced with number problems. She knew this was probably due to some early experience, but she could not remember what it could have been. She had studied mathematics in college and felt confident she could handle the mathematics that would be required of her in the elementary schools. Her marks all through school had been good—almost all

A's in elementary school (except for arithmetic). A's and B's in high school, and a good B average in college. She regarded teaching as a highly respectable profession, and looked forward to teaching for a number of years following her graduation from college. Her parents had, in general, held teachers in respect, though they had been critical of some who had been uncouth. As a prospective teacher, Marion regarded her profession as an opportunity for a variety of experiences not available to people in other professions.

After high school, she had attended a teachers college in a small city. Her college, at one time a two-year training institution, had recently begun the four-year program which Marion took. She had participated in extracurricular activities both in high school and in college, but had never been a campus "big wheel." She had regarded her "regular" work as of prime importance, and was content with playing supporting parts in most activities.

An only child, she had grown up in a small community of 4,000 people. She was of English-Scotch ancestry, and her parents were second and third generation Americans. Her father was cashier in the Security Bank, the smaller of two banks in the community. Both her father and her mother were leaders in their community, were active in church and lodge work, and were highly respected. Neither one had ever sought public office, and were inclined to be highly critical of "politicians." In her sociology classes, she had studied the social class structure in America and could not decide whether her family should be considered a lower middle or upper middle class family. She was inclined to believe it would be the latter.

Her father had always provided well for his family. He had accumulated a little wealth as a young man, but had lost almost everything except his job at the bank during the depression. Since that time, he had been moderately successful again, and was hopeful that he could retire in his middle sixties, with enough to live on and with the hope of leaving a respectable estate to his daughter.

Marion was a neat, attractive young woman, five feet, six inches tall. In repose her face was plain, being neither beautiful nor ugly. She selected her clothes with good taste and with an eye to latest campus styles and wore them with confidence. Her off-campus clothes and party dresses were also "sharp." Her eyes were speckled

with brown and her hair was light brown. Her weight was near
the accepted norm, and she maintained it without effort. Though
she had the common illnesses, her health was good. She was not
the athletic type, but she enjoyed the exhilaration of swimming,
golfing, and skating.

She regarded herself, and her friends regarded her, as emotionally
well adjusted. She smiled easily, but with restraint. She made friends
without conscious effort, but was content with a relatively small
group of close friends. She dated boys occasionally, but had not
become emotionally "serious" or "gone steady" with any of them.
She didn't want to be "too particular" or too "reserved," but she
did not worry unduly about being so.

Marion had a mind of her own, but this was not always evident
because of the frequency with which she tended to conform. Her
parents had been strict about demanding obedience in little things,
but had taken her into partnership in planning the larger affairs
of the household, especially when such matters involved her. She
was inclined to accept the moral and social standards of her family
and her church. She enjoyed thinking things through for herself
and, as she grew up, she had upon occasion surprised her family
with the cogency and reasonableness of her thinking when it involved personal decisions. She sometimes regarded her parents as
"dated," but they amused rather than irritated her. She had a deep,
healthy affection for both, and the older she grew the more she
enjoyed her mother as a friend and adviser. As the years passed,
both parents accepted her opinions with respect, though they were
sometimes at a loss when she argued from the background of her
sociology and psychology about some of their traditional viewpoints.

Where angels fear to tread

Miss Johnson met the principal of the Pleasant Valley School at
eight o'clock on the Tuesday morning following Labor Day—the
first day of school. Miss Altonweather was a large, friendly woman
with a forceful personality. She impressed Marion as a woman with
a sense of humor, a fund of energy, a desire to do well whatever
she did, and a knack for getting things organized and keeping them
going.

"We will let the children in at nine," she said. "We will direct them to the proper rooms. Children who were here last year will know where to go, but some new ones will have to be shown where their rooms are."

There were two other new teachers and Miss Altonweather spoke to them together in her small inner office. "The other girls will know what to do," she said.

Each teacher was to keep a list of the pupils and ask all new pupils for their report cards or other records from their old school. These were to be sent to Miss Altonweather's office at the close of each day with their names. Each teacher was given a few enrollment cards. The regular textbooks were in each room. These were to be passed out and their numbers entered in the textbook record after the pupils' names. The names of the pupils should be determined. Each teacher had on her desk the promotion cards of all those who were to be in the room, except for pupils new to the district. Those who did not attend should be noted, since state law required attendance records from the first day and state aid money was allocated on the basis of attendance. However, the attendance registers should not be filled in during the first few days, until most latecomers showed up, because it was desirable that the record be as nearly alphabetical as possible. Temporary seats should be assigned, but pupils should understand that this was temporary. It was estimated that the number of pupils would average about 35 per teacher. They expected 36 in the fourth grade, many of whom would be "non-residents."

Each teacher should stand in the hall near her door as the pupils entered. The children would be excused at eleven o'clock the first day, but after that the sessions would be full length. Most of the afternoon the teacher could spend in her room, but at 2:45 there would be a general teachers' meeting.

"Do the best you can," Miss Altonweather said. "We'll iron it all out later. The children are eager and pleasant the first day. If you need me, I'll be in the office or the halls."

Marion fancied that she felt a bit like a soldier going into his first battle, but she was surprised that she was not more nervous. She thought perhaps the other new teachers were more nervous than she was. In the hall with Miss Altonweather, she met three teachers who had not previously been introduced, and had time for a quick glance over her room before the bell rang and she took her place in the hall.

The first class!

Most of the children came in with a surge, though there was a semblance of grade lines hanging over from a previous year's organization. Those who came first rushed in excitedly, and Miss Johnson could see through the door that they were anxious to claim certain seats or be near favored friends. Some smiled shyly as they passed her, a few spoke politely and with confidence, some giggled with embarrassment, but the majority ignored her for the moment, except as they eyed her with varying types and degrees of interest. Two children new to the school had to be directed to her room by others. Two others came in later in the morning, having been accompanied by their parents and taken first to the principal's office.

The halls finally emptied, Miss Altonweather serving as a rear guard in the mopping up operation, and Miss Johnson entered her room—and her profession. The room became somewhat quiet as she walked to her desk, though one or two conversations continued. She felt that most of the children were for the moment studying her carefully.

"I am Miss Johnson," she said. "I will write it on the blackboard. You will soon get to know me very well. It will be harder for me to get to know all of your names, but I will learn them as soon as I can." She remembered that names were sensitive things embedded in the national and social backgrounds of their owners. She remembered that sensitive children often resented their names and their nicknames.

"All people have names," she said, "so that we can tell one another apart. Our parents give us our names and they pick names that they like. Sometimes it is the same name they were given, or it's the name of an uncle or of someone else they like very much. If we all had the same first names, we could not tell one another apart. We wouldn't know how to deliver letters. When we hear a new name, it sometimes makes us think it's funny, but it really isn't. I like to be with people who have many different kinds of names."

A hand went up in the second row, and at her nod a little bullet-headed boy with a close crew haircut and an immense mouth said, "Lots of the kids have nicknames." (This was Russell Dickinson, she learned later.)

"That's the way it was when I was in school, too," Miss Johnson said. "People often pick out nicknames for their friends. Boys have them more often than girls, I think. We will have to talk about nicknames sometime."

But that didn't settle it. The same boy spoke again, "Some of the nicknames ain't nice. One of the boys has a name we call 'Stinky.' "

The effect on the room was immediate. Pleased anticipatory grins appeared on many faces, a few laughed aloud, while eight or ten others threw their heads into their arms on the desk tops to hide either their grins or their embarrassment. Marion was not able to determine whether "Stinky" was present or what his degree of embarrassment might be, but she guessed by the direction of a few glances that he might be in the left rear of the room. "This is it," she thought to herself. "Here are children who are moving toward social consciousness, who are not fully sensitive to the feelings of those about them, but who are interested in all the things that concern them." She felt, too, that in the remark about "Stinky," there was an implied invitation for her to visit upon the class the judgment of society concerning the use of such words in polite circles. Also there might be a problem—very real, even if minor—in the question.

"Where I went to school," she said, "we had a girl with that nickname. I'll tell you how she got it. Her very best girl friend had beautiful red hair, and all her friends called her Pinky. The girls called the other one 'Stinky' because it rhymed with Pinky. She laughed about it and didn't seem to care, but after a while the other girls stopped calling her 'Stinky' because they were afraid it might hurt her feelings. . . .

"Now I must find out your real names—perhaps the nicknames will come later. First I will call out the names of those I have here, and then we will get the names of any others."

It took one-half hour to read the names and get the new ones. One of the new pupils had his report card with him. The other did not, but said he would bring it tomorrow. The children lost interest in the mechanics of the registration process, and whispered and talked. Marion did not let this disturb her, for she knew that it would occur. She didn't wish to impose her will unnecessarily. During the name checking, Miss Altonweather came to the door with two additional new pupils, Norma Anderson and Mildred Lane. Marion met them at the door and was introduced to the mothers. They were invited in but declined at the moment, though they promised to come soon for a longer visit. Miss Altonweather stood inside the door as this conversation took place, and the children sat angelically in their seats. After Miss Altonweather and the mothers left, Miss Johnson introduced the two new pupils by name and helped them to find desks.

"Is there anyone now whose name I do not have?"

There was a pause and then two or three little hands pointed to a boy in the next to the last seat along the windows. Larger than most of the boys, he stared back at his accusers and his lips framed the whispered words, "Shut up," as the pointing spread.

"He didn't pass," two or three sibilant whispers reached all who were in the room.

"Oh! I have missed someone," Miss Johnson said and there was concern in her voice. "I am sorry." She walked back along the windows toward the boy. "What is your name?"

"Jack."

She wrote it carefully on her list. "And what is your last name?"

"Littlejohn."

"His name is Hammond," a little girl's voice corrected, "it isn't Littlejohn at all."

Jack's eyes were down and his face a blank—neither surly, nor hurt, nor red—just blank. Marion had seen the same look on a grown friend's face not too long before—at the grave of her dead soldier-husband.

"I'll put them both down," she said. "It doesn't matter which so long as we know that it is Jack." This was no time, she knew, to determine if it was Hammond or Littlejohn, Jack or John. It was no time, either, to send him back to the third grade.

Marion had seen a comedy skater on stilts one time and, as he skated among obstacles on the ice, the audience sat tense expecting him to fall. She felt at the moment that she was skating among obstacles, but it wasn't a comedy act. What a swarm of personalities!

How fast the problems presented themselves! For a few seconds, the first week stretched before her as a very long period of time.

"Now we must get at the books," she said. "We will each have an arithmetic book, a geography book, a language book, a music book, and a reading book. Perhaps later we will have a health book and a spelling book. How should we distribute the books?"

A number of hands went up, and there were many suggestions. Miss Johnson simplified them and wrote them on the board under the heading, "How to pass out the books." After a few minutes, she had the following list of suggestions: (1) Let monitors do it. (In that school, she discovered, monitors were the pupils in the front seats of each row.) (2) Form in rows and pass by table in front of room. (3) Let teacher pass them out. In simple words, Miss Johnson then raised two questions. (1) How should she go about getting a record of the numbers of the books so that ownership and responsibility could be determined? (2) Some books were newer and cleaner than others. How can we be fair about passing them out?

Again there were many suggestions. Miss Johnson saw that time was passing quickly, but she decided that the discussion was worth while. The children were interested. The problem was a real one in human relationships. She was getting to know a few of them. She saw that the problem of being efficient as a group was interesting to them, and that the fairness of the distribution had meaning for them.

It was decided finally, after a good deal of shouting and many irrelevant suggestions, that there should be five committees, one for each book. They would arrange the books into five piles of equal size. In one pile would be the books that were in the best condition, in another those just below the best, in another the average books, and so on for five groups. Then each child would get one of his books in each subject from each of the five piles. At first they had decided under Marion's guidance to divide the books into three piles, but Albert Ericson had pointed out that it would be hard to make it come out even that way—that since there were five books, there should be five piles. Marion had not seen this possibility herself, and she regarded Albert with friendly interest. Here was a young man who might be of great assistance in the arithmetic program for the year. She remembered his name easily, though this had been his first contribution. He was a quiet boy, thin but not skinny, and every so often he ran his fingers along the groove at the top of his desk as though brushing off imaginary debris from an eraser.

At 10:55, Miss Johnson started to bring the discussion to a close. After several unsuccessful attempts to silence those who were still anxious to speak, she finally waited in complete silence at the front of the room until all attention was drawn to her. She had waited expectantly and the children "read" her expectation. She quickly requested them to take the same seats tomorrow that they had today so that she could try to get to know their names, told them that at some future time they might take up the problem of selecting new seats, and said that tomorrow they would go on with the job of passing out books. She took time to remind the new students to bring the cards they had forgotten, and she found a chance to smile a friendly smile at Jack as he walked out with a sort of timid swagger. As two of her little girls walked down the hall, she was sure she heard one of them say, "She's awful nice," and though she knew it was foolish to be so pleased at a child's remark, she walked back into her room with the nicest feeling she had experienced in a long time, and then for a fleeting moment, thought of her mother.

Reconnaissance

She had from eleven o'clock until 2:45 to spend as she wished. She decided to fix up her attendance report at once and then look over the room records. First, however, she made some notes:

Check on John Littlejohn
Find out about "Stinky"
Remember the names of the new pupils
Albert Ericson—mathematics
Interest in names and nicknames
Interest in passing out books fairly

There was a folder for each child who had been promoted from the Pleasant Valley third grade. Inside the folder there was a health record card and a test record. On the folder itself there was the customary information found on cumulative record forms—spaces for yearly attendance records and subject marks, place for teachers' notes headed, "Anecdotal Record," and profile records of many of the tests given. In some of the folders there were papers. She found one "smutty note" carried on from the second grade with a teacher's note appended explaining how the affair had been handled. Also there were a few drawings labeled as an example of "the best work" —some good bird pictures by Gail Hopkins, a picture of a running boy by Andrew Larson, and some designs by Mona Carew and Stanley Smith. In Julie French's folder was a sheet of paper from the second grade on which was written:

Julie French

People in Books

People in books are not people We
dream them people to be with us

There was another folder titled, "Class Records." In this were summary sheets of how well the class did on various tests. There was an I.Q. distribution, an attendance summary, and the like. Marion knew she would spend lots of time the first few days and weeks referring to these records, but now it was time for lunch.

She went with the other teachers on what turned out to be a rather gay and happy excursion to a pleasant if somewhat smoky restaurant on the main street some four blocks away, where a limited menu of plain food was offered. She and the other two new teachers had many questions to ask about the school and the town —about where the others lived, about community standards, and the many other things young adults wish to know about any new place in which they live and work. Most of the questions dealt with rooming and boarding places, community leaders, stores and shops and recreation, and with the school—the frequency of P.T.A. meetings, the types of parents encountered, the fault finders in the community, and so forth. Marion knew that it was "surface" information, but valuable as far as it went. She learned that the teachers referred to Miss Altonweather as "Miss A." It seemed both appropriate and convenient.

On the way back to school she walked with Miss O'Leary, the third-grade teacher. Miss O'Leary had been at Pleasant Valley five years and had taught four years before that. Marion could not help asking about the Littlejohn boy.

"I didn't see him around school today or I'd have come and got him," Miss O'Leary confessed. "He's a tough little nut if there ever was one. We have all tried to help him, but he won't be helped. You never can tell what he'll do next. He lies and cheats and then he's good for a while. He won't study except by fits and starts. He comes from a broken home, you know. His real father is no good— left home when John was a baby and ran around with other women who were regular tramps. John's mother got a divorce and married Mr. Hammond when John was five. He's older than she is, and works at the bottling works. They have a child of their own now—a little girl three years old. He tries to be nice to John— course, he's strict—but Mr. Littlejohn—that's the real father—comes to see John now and then and causes trouble. John doesn't cause *me* any trouble, though, and I told Miss A. I thought he was improving some so we decided I'd keep him another year."

Marion walked on a few steps, trying to plan her next words. "I liked him, too," she said. "I talked to him a little. I rather thought I'd like to keep him, too, and see what I could do. Of course, if he's doing well in your room and you think he should stay there, I'll have plenty to do without him."

Miss O'Leary didn't answer at once, and Marion began to feel uncomfortable. She changed the subject. "That Albert Ericson certainly seemed like a bright one," she said. "I'll bet there was no question about promoting him."

"We think he's a genius," Miss O'Leary responded. "Behind his back we teachers call him 'Albert Einstein.' He is good at everything and is an excellent manager. Everything has to be just so for him. He's just the opposite of the Littlejohn kid. Albert's work is always in on time and it's neat, and he feels worse than you do if he makes a mistake. His father is a farmer who's had lots of tough luck. The mother's an invalid and the father was crippled in a tractor accident. They both come to P.T.A. They work hard and have lots of pride. Say, maybe if you want that Littlejohn kid, Miss A. would let him stay. I'll talk to her about it. She'd think it was funny if you asked."

"I like her," Marion thought as they parted in the hall. "She's big and robust and a little bit homely, but she's jolly and self-confident and somehow, I like her."

Back in the classroom, she took inventory of some of the rest of her resources. The Pleasant Valley School was an old building built in 1903, to which a new addition had been added just before the war. The old part was made up of a first floor over a half basement. The basement contained toilet rooms, a furnace room, and an activity room; the first floor contained the three upper grades and Miss Altonweather's office suite. The new addition was built at ground level and was a half flight below the level of the first floor of the old building. It contained a kindergarten and the first five grades, besides toilets, a teachers' room, and the combination gymnasium-auditorium. Miss Johnson's room was a pleasant room on the west side of the building.

In her room she found a fairly new *World Book* and an old set of *Comptons*. There were blackboards on the back and front walls and cork board all along one side. A partition separated the back of the classroom from the cloak hall. The room was larger than many classrooms she had seen, and there was space for 40 movable desk-chair combinations in neat rows and for the round library table and the rectangular work table in the rear. There was no work bench, she noted with regret. Her desk in front was close to the children. There was a 16-inch globe hanging from the ceiling and a small map case was over the blackboard in the front. The room had not been painted for four or five years, but the drab color did not show the dirt. The curtains were not bad—"Not good," she muttered to herself in fun, "not bad, but not good!" There was a pile of small dictionaries that showed little wear—and a larger abridged edition. There were bookcases set in under the windows. The heating and ventilating were of the unit type and the units were placed under the windows, too. There was a sectional bookcase in the front, but no books—obviously they were stored elsewhere. A built-in bookcase behind her desk contained the textbooks, some supplementary sets, and various other items of fourth-grade equipment—cheap rulers, scissors, paste jar, paint boxes, brushes, pans, and paper.

In her desk she found one drawer devoted to the curriculum. There were various new state courses of study that even a casual glance showed to be full of valuable materials, and, in addition, a large, old, graded course of study that Miss Altonweather would mention later and a mimeographed county course of study. There were some curriculum bulletins from the local Superintendent's office, and pamphlets on bicycle safety, first aid, the Red Cross Blood Bank Program, and so forth. She found also the teacher's manuals that were prepared by the publishers to go with adopted texts. These showed much more evidence of use than the curriculum bulletins. She had read and heard that even today textbooks frequently comprised the only real curriculum used in the schools!

The first faculty meeting

It was 2:45 before she got to the bottom of the curriculum drawer, and she hurried to the office. Miss A. greeted them all pleasantly and professionally. She devoted most of the first half hour to various routine descriptions of records and school rules. She found no fault with anyone, and took occasion to mention her pleasure with the work of all, particularly the new teachers.

Marion studied Miss Altonweather with interest. She had learned at college that the atmosphere of a school is greatly influenced by the principal. She knew that ideally the principal should be the first one to call on for assistance, the one to carry on and direct an in-service training program and be in every way the tower of strength and good will in the school. She knew, too, that not all principals approached this ideal. Marion had her own conception of the ideal classroom. The principles underlying that classroom were equally valid, she thought, for the relationships in a school between all members of the staff.

Miss A. did most of the talking and Marion noticed that the older teachers seemed content that she should. At the same time, they appeared relaxed and friendly. They laughed at the little reminiscences that bobbed up from recent years in the school. Most of the questions raised by the teachers concerned routine matters. Do you want us to take the same positions in fire drills as we did last year? Did the Superintendent get the new hectograph? Would last year's restrictions still apply to the use of construction paper and other supplies? When would Miss Altonweather wish the seventh- and eighth-grade teachers to select telephone girls? Many of the questions that might have been asked were already answered in three pages of instructions and rules that Miss Altonweather distributed.

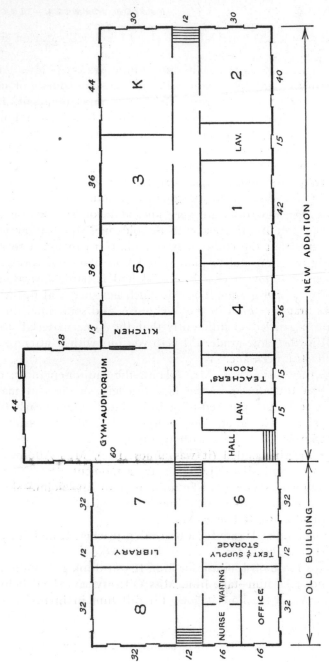

Figure 6. Diagram of Pleasant Valley School.

"What about the curriculum I should follow?" Marion asked finally.

"Each teacher's desk has a curriculum drawer," Miss Altonweather answered. "There you will find the state courses of study, and local rules and regulations from the Superintendent. From time to time I will provide you with outlines of projects and activities I would like to have you work in. I have asked all the teachers to save the old *State Course of Study*. Much of the material in it is old and you will have to bring it up-to-date, but it outlines the courses very well—much better than the new ones that are full of philosophy and theory, but that don't help much from day to day. Of course, the new ones are very fine, and you should use them all you can, but if you start with the old one, you'll know where you are and what the children have had. You can use it to make your daily program and to plan your lesson plans. Of course, you don't have to follow it exactly. You'll find it hard, anyway, especially in the upper grades. There is much new material in the new textbooks that isn't even in the old course, and sometimes the new books are organized so differently that the same material doesn't even fall in the same grade. I'll help you out with it after you get started if you need me."

Before they adjourned, Mr. Adams, the janitor-engineer, came in and was introduced to the new teachers. A pleasant man of medium stature, he appeared to be in his late forties or early fifties. "We consider Mr. Adams one of the staff," Miss A. said. "We wouldn't know what to do without him."

As the meeting ended (it was almost five), Miss Altonweather asked Marion and Miss O'Leary to stay a moment.

"Miss O'Leary says you'd like to keep John Littlejohn," she said directly and with no show of feeling in her voice.

"I would like to, if I may. Yes."

"He'll be a difficult case for a beginning teacher. If he fails, you'll have him next year, too."

"Perhaps I'm foolish to ask for him. If you think I shouldn't. . . ."

"Oh, no, take him—take him. Miss O'Leary says she'll help you with him. We'll see how it goes. I'll call him in in the morning and tell him."

"Should I tell him?" Marion asked.

"No. I will. I'll tell him he's promoted on trial."

Inwardly, Marion hoped that Miss A. would be kind when she told him.

Starting the first full day

The second day started without sufficient preparation, Marion knew. She had put up a few things that she had collected for the occasion, but there had not been time to brighten up the room as she would have wished. Interesting materials were not spread around the room in profusion. The bookcase was still bare. It was not, she knew, the stimulating learning atmosphere that the curriculum books talked about.

The main objective of the day's work, in Marion's mind, was to combine the chore of getting started with the discovery of how well her pupils could work with one another and with her and, of course, to continue getting acquainted and becoming known.

The roll was taken, but not uneventfully. A number of children came in a minute or two before the bell and moved busily about the room. One or two were vociferously trying to decide whether to take their sweaters off or leave them on. One girl took her sweater off and put it on again to be like another across the aisle. Then two boys entered, loudly and roughly pushing and shoving one another. Marion was near the door and moved near the boys. No sustained interests had yet been developed to interest the children, and unrestrained activity might lead too far. The boys paid no attention to her. One grabbed the other's foot, and down they went, wrestling furiously. Marion stepped up quickly, as a circle of small onlookers formed. She placed her hand on the shoulder of one of the boys, but she smiled as she said firmly, "It's time to get to our seats quickly so we can take roll." Amazingly enough, the boys started for their seats but there was still noise and discussion. Two of the "sweater girls" had apparently paid no attention at all to the boys. The final bell was Marion's signal to start calling the names. After three or four names, the room was quiet. It was then that Marion discovered that her legs were trembling as they had a time or two at "elocutions" when she was herself a pupil. Everyone was present, including John Littlejohn. Marion reviewed the plan they had decided upon for the distribution of the books. She had to decide whether she should determine the number of committees needed and assign the children to them, or let the pupils try to work it out. She decided to let them do the planning as far as she could contrive to do so.

"How many committees will we need?" she asked.

"One for each book." "Five," came the answers.

"Any others?" she asked, and she gave them time to think as she wrote the names of the books on the board, but there were no pertinent suggestions.

"How shall we select the members for the five committees?"

There was silence for a minute and then the suggestions that were made were not constructive. "I have an idea," Miss Johnson said. "Do you know how to count off as they do in the army?"

The children didn't know. "Well, we could start in this corner; the first one would say 'one,' the next 'two,' and so on, until you get to five. All those who are 'ones' will be on the committee for readers," and she went on to explain in more detail. The children reacted with pleasure to the suggestion and it was carried out quickly with only slight coaching. Miss Johnson tore some sheets of white paper into squares and had each child write his name and number on his square.

She then raised the question of how to rate the books. She recalled Albert's plan to divide them into five equal piles, one pile to be the best ones, one the poorest, and so forth. She assigned the groups to various parts of the room and asked the boys to carry the books to the proper stations, reminding them to ask questions if they needed help.

They seemed timid at first about moving their seats out of the neat rows in which they were arranged, but with a little coaching and directing, they moved fairly quietly to their places and were soon at work. There were seven pupils in each of four of the groups and eight pupils in the fifth group. There was some noise, of course, and a few discussions took place, but Miss Johnson was able to answer questions quickly enough and move about often enough so that the initial work progressed fairly well. She soon had to help one group decide on certain standards for rating. She helped pick a "good" book, a "poor" one, and an "excellent" one. Then she briefly called for the attention of the whole class and showed them the three books, telling them how that group had decided upon them. "Try to plan how to do it," she said. "If you don't know what to do, talk it over. Perhaps each group will need to elect a chairman.

"Who can tell us what a chairman is?" Miss Johnson asked.

Mary Friswold was called on first. As she spoke, Miss Johnson moved toward the blackboard again and prepared to write the definitions that were offered. It appeared at once that the children were not prepared to say what a chairman was, and that they had not had previous free experience in selecting their own chairmen.

"My mother is chairman of the Study Club," Mary had said glibly. "She sits in front and tells them who may talk and what to do next." Mary seemed self-confident, sure of her status in her group, proud of her mother.

"That is good," Miss Johnson said, and she wrote after number 1, "The captain of the group." Then she said, "How do we get a chairman?" The best answer came from Gail Hopkins who had been a member of the "Blue Birds." Miss Johnson wrote, "2. Elected by the group." It was clear from most of the remarks that the children did not understand about nominations and how voting took place. "We will have to study about chairmen and the rules about how to run a meeting, but we won't have time today. Perhaps today each group can talk about it and select a chairman that way. Then later we'll learn a better way to do it. The chairman will have to be the captain of each committee and call on the others to talk when they raise their hands, just as a teacher does. The chairman must not talk too much, but must let the others talk. If you can't agree, the chairman may ask me what to do next."

Miss Johnson moved quietly and pleasantly from group to group. A waving hand from a group in the far corner dropped when she glanced over and said, "I'll be there as soon as I can." In one group, Russell (the redhead) said, "I want Roger (Roger Schorn) for chairman. He's the best one;" and Helen said, "I want Janet (Janet Kremer)." "We don't want no girl for chairman," Russell replied, and then the argument was entered by two others. Miss Johnson moved to the table and listened intently for a minute or two. She knew that she could settle the matter with a word or a suggestion, but she did not want to spend her year "managing" the room. Furthermore, that was something the pupils should learn to do with constantly increasing skill if they were given the chance. "Well," she said, "You need a chairman, and you need a secretary,

too. I'll come back in a minute and see what you have decided."
As she left, she heard someone say, "Janet could be secretary," but
she heard objections to that, too.

In two groups, the chairman was picked without difficulty. In
Albert Ericson's group, he was suggested at once and the sentiment
for him was spontaneous and unanimous. In Mary Friswold's
group, Mary announced as soon as the question came up that she
would be a chairman. "I'll be our chairman," she had said. "I know
how to be a chairman. I'll show you how." Miss Johnson detected
some uneasiness on the part of one or two, but no protest was
raised as Mary took over. For one group, Miss Johnson served as
temporary chairman, received two nominations, and had an election in which Judy Norman was elected over Geraldine Reuther.
Another group selected Stanley Smith. When Miss Johnson returned
to Janet and Roger, she found that the group had decided that
both would be president and both would be secretary! Since the
children seemed satisfied, and were getting to work on the sorting
of the books, she accepted the result without protest. A compromise had been made and an agreement had been reached. It remained to be seen how the experiment would come out.

When she surveyed the room a moment later, Marion felt that
she was on the right track. She had heard experienced teachers say
that the hardest job in teaching was to get children divided into
committees and hard at work. She had been told that some teachers
teach for years and never succeed in dividing up a class for group
activities. She had heard, too, that if there was something you
wanted to do, the way to do it was to go ahead and do it. Well,
she had her committees! Now she had to take stock for a moment.
She was learning more and more about her pupils. She saw some
of the leaders, and she saw some who so far had said or done
little with their fellows. She had involved her pupils in a project
of interest to them, concerning the moral concept of fairness and
the democratic idea of equal treatment for all. She had brought
them up against the problem of parliamentary procedure and rules
of order. So far, the developing situation had held sufficient interest for all the pupils so that individual behavior had not been
troublesome.

Miss Johnson walked from group to group as they worked, trying
to limit her contribution to assisting rather than to making de-

cisions. Requests for help were frequent, but not overburdening, dealing with such questions as how a book should be classified or how to pile the books. She tried particularly to find something for each child to do. There was a good deal of noise but she saw that little of it came from discontent or disorganization, but rather from inexperience in this type of work. She suggested to some that they fit loose pages into the books at the proper places. She talked informally with a few children, getting acquainted and finding out their names. Some timid ones seemed embarrassed at this, and she did not persist in "drawing them out," being content to be friendly and wait. Some were detailed to see that legible book numbers were inside each book, and were given slips to insert in the books that needed numbers.

The daily program called for outdoor physical education and recreation at 10:30. The group did not have time to finish sorting the books before the bell rang. After recess, the children came back to their group seats and continued their work until it was finished at about 11:15.

"It is important in our room," she said, "that we treat every boy and girl fairly. We have divided the books into piles and now we must pass them out so that each one gets a book from each pile. How shall we go about passing out the books? Perhaps you could talk it over in each group for just a minute or two, and see if each group can decide on a good way to do it. See if all can agree. When any group has decided and is sure it has a good plan, the chairman of the group may stand; and when all groups are ready, if they don't take too long, we'll hear reports from them."

Marion was improvising as she went along, selecting techniques that had been suggested in college. This one had occurred to her at recess as a good starting point. It was a chance for her to study her groups, as she moved about the room again, notebook in hand. She thought the children attacked their problem with more efficiency than they had shown in the morning, but she was sure the participation was far from as wide as it should be. In some groups, one or two were bossing the others far too much. That was to be expected in inexperienced groups, she knew, and its correction would call for careful planning as the year's work developed. Those are things that can't be taught by telling the children not to be bossy or not to talk too much; they must be worked out together.

By 11:30, the last of the chairmen stood up (five minutes after they went to work at it). In the groups that finished first, some of the pupils engaged in the usual spirited conversations, punctuated by gestures and sometimes by behavior bordering on the boisterous. Marion remembered Miss Coyne, one of her favorite teachers, who had taught her in the fourth grade. Miss Coyne would have told the children to sit quietly after they reached a decision (of course, she wouldn't have had them in groups, in the first place) and would have firmly and pleasantly insisted, with a directive hand on head or pressure on arm, that her will be observed. This was sometimes necessary, Marion knew, but she believed that her children would learn more about living if they had a chance to work things out for themselves. To call them to attention, she moved to the blackboard as she said, "Now, let us see what the suggestions are," and she wrote, "Plans for passing out our books," and beneath it she wrote a "1." The suggestions were varied in detail and presented with wide differences in skill. The children had not foreseen many of the difficulties that might arise.

One had said, "Have everybody get in line and take one from each pile. Somebody could be at each pile and give them a book."

Mary said, "Have Miss Johnson pass them out so that they all come out even."

Roger was nervous and found it difficult to talk. His first few words were interrupted by a giggle, which he suppressed with an effort. "I don't know if it'll work very good or not, but you could put the books into piles and each one could get one."

When the reports were all done, Miss Johnson had written:

1. Form into a line—get a book from each group.
2. Have someone at each table.
3. Have Miss Johnson pass them out.
4. Arrange books into piles of five each.
5. Each one should take the top book in the pile.
6. No one should cheat.
7. We have to know which ones get the good books and which ones the poor books.

There was a brief discussion of the suggestions, stimulated and guided by a few questions from Marion, and quick agreement on a method. There remained 15 minutes in which they discussed their experience working in committees and what they might try to do to improve it. Additional notes were placed on the board as this discussion went along, such as, "How to talk together as friends— conversation." A number of children expressed a wish to distribute the books immediately after noon as they wanted to look at them and get their "assignments" in them.

Dirty dig or chance remark?

"How is John Littlejohn doing?" Miss O'Leary asked at noon. "Is he down to work?"

"So far, so good," Marion answered noncommittally. "He has done what the others have done. He seems quite content." She didn't want to explain what she was trying to do until she could see how it was developing. There were more important things for John Littlejohn at the moment than to get him down to work. That should come later and be an outcome, not a method. Another question bothered her a bit more. It came from Miss Janisch in the second grade.

"How do your children behave?" and then, "I thought I heard some noise from down the hall. Miss O'Leary always said they were a nice grade, too, but then she never has any trouble."

Marion had been warned to expect this reaction, but she hadn't expected it to come quite so unadorned and soon. Certainly, human behavior was predictable, even when it came to teachers!

"I hope we didn't bother you," she said and there was no edge of sarcasm in her voice, for she was sure that in her procedure so far she was on the right track; but she was not yet confident of her ability to carry it all out as she wanted it done. "We are still quite informal."

Children want to learn, but do not always know what they are learning. It is well that they see the reason for what they are doing. This gives point and intent to their work. It also allows them to answer intelligently the parental question about what was learned at school that day. These were things that Marion had remembered from many of her college courses. She wanted to bring them into focus that first afternoon.

Wednesday, after lunch, they used the first half-hour in distributing the books, and the second half-hour looking through them and discussing them with her. She noticed that the geography book and the language book got the most attention. These were new "subjects" to the fourth-graders, and most of the questions were about geography, about the manners and customs of the strange people shown in the pictures. After a while the questions began to take the direction of what they were to do with the books—what they should read and study.

"We were talking about names yesterday," Miss Johnson said. "I would like to have you look through your geography books and your readers and see how many names you can find to write down before tomorrow morning. If a person's first name and a person's last name are both given in the book, write them both down. If only the first name is used, or only the last name is used, write that down."

Pupils assess their learning

After the afternoon recess, Miss Johnson said, "Perhaps we should review what we have learned yesterday and today, and what we have found we do not know that we need to know."

There was a pause. The children were trying to recall something they had learned, but they did not do so at once. They had read no assignments, memorized no facts, drilled on no skills.

"I'll write across the top of the board two titles: 'Things we have learned,' and 'Things we need to learn.' Can someone tell me something we have learned?"

There were puzzled faces, but no answers.

"Perhaps I can help you." Miss Johnson said. "Everything we do at school, we do for some purpose because there are so many important things to learn. We learned, didn't we, that all children have equal rights so we divided our books equally? I'll write that down. Then we learned how to count off as soldiers do, in order to form committees. I'll write that, too. Now what else have we learned?" The room had come alive! The children saw now what they had been learning, and a dozen hands were asking for recognition.

It was at this fortunate point that Miss Altonweather paid her first visit to the room. Perhaps she, too, had heard some noise that morning! As she walked to the rear of the room, the children straightened virtuously in their seats, but their desire to recite was not dampened.

"We learned to appoint chairmen."
"We learned to make committee reports."
"We learned to appoint two chairmen when we got a tie."
"We found out how to get together on one plan."

Many other items were mentioned and as each point was raised, it was discussed briefly, and then Miss Johnson wrote it on the board in simple form. Then they shifted over to the other list—"Things we need to learn."

"I was secretary of our comm—comm—of ours, and I didn't know anything to do."

"That's a good point," Miss Johnson said, and she wrote, "What does a secretary do?" Each time she got a response, she contrived to pass out a word of praise, an approving nod, or a friendly smile. Only once or twice did she reject a contribution, and then she did it with great care.

"I can see that you have a good idea," she said once. "We may discuss it some other time, but it doesn't fit in here. You're doing good thinking, though. Keep it up."

The children wished to learn about parliamentary procedure and they decided to talk it over with their parents and friends that evening if the opportunity arose. Miss Altonweather stayed as the children passed out, and complimented Marion on the way the children had responded. Marion was not sure, but she thought Miss Altonweather acted the least bit surprised and puzzled, but on the whole rather pleased. Marion, too, was pleased.

She found her first full day drawing to a close and she realized that she hadn't been cross once. No child had created a violent disturbance. She began to feel that the professor had been right who suggested that when anything went awry, it was not important to affix blame or to "take steps" to insure that it never be repeated. Rather, each incident, be it a learning difficulty, a behavior difficulty, an attitudinal difficulty, or even a discipline case, should be approached calmly by the teacher and the children as an interesting problem between friendly people. The professor had said that most of the bothersome, old-fashioned problems disappear in such an atmosphere.

A quick assessment of individual differences

Wednesday after school, although Marion was dreadfully tired from her first day of teaching, she knew she would find the work less exhausting if she found out as much as she could about the class. She decided to get some first impressions concerning the range of individual differences in her classroom as shown by the test re-

RANGE IN INTELLIGENCE AND READING ABILITY OF FOURTH GRADE IN TERMS OF FIRST-GRADE INTELLIGENCE TESTS AND THIRD-GRADE READING TESTS

Range from Low to High in Detroit I.Q.'s for 32 First-Graders Now in Fourth Grade	Range from Low to High in Reading Grade Level for 32 Third-Graders Now in Fourth Grade	
	Vocabulary	Comprehension
72	1.	1.
85	1.	1.
86	1.2	1.
88	1.6	1.6
89	2.6	1.6
92	2.8	2.4
94	2.8	2.5
95	2.8	2.6
95	2.9	2.6
96	3.2	2.8
96	3.2	2.8
99	3.6	2.9
99	3.6	3.2
99	3.9	3.6
99	3.9 Median	3.6 Median
99 Median	4.0	3.6
99	4.0	3.6
99	4.2	3.8
103	4.2	3.9
103	4.4	4.0
104	4.4	4.2
105	4.6	4.4
111	4.6	4.6
113	4.9	4.6
120	5.8	4.9
124	6.5	5.2
125	6.5	5.2
125	6.5	5.8
126	7.9+	6.5
130	7.9+	7.7
141	7.9+	7.9+
141	7.9+	7.9+

sults on file. A glance at her records showed that there was a Detroit First Grade I.Q. for most of the children, and there was a second- and third-grade score in vocabulary and reading comprehension as measured by The Unit Scales of Attainment. This was little enough, but she examined it thoroughly for what it would show. She glanced first at the intelligence quotients as they were shown in September

FIRST-GRADE INTELLIGENCE QUOTIENTS AND THIRD-GRADE READING
SCORES FOR MISS JOHNSON'S FOURTH GRADE

	Detroit First Grade I.Q.	Third Grade — Unit Scales — Reading			
		Vocabulary		Comprehension	
		Reading Age	Grade	Reading Age	Grade
Affleck, Jean	99	11-8	6.5	9-9	4.6
Anderson, Norma	—	—	—	—	—
Carew, Mona	96	7-11	2.8	8-9	3.6
Carlton, Richard	—	—	—	—	—
Clarkson, Harry	94	6-0 (—)	1.0 (—)	6-0 (—)	1.0 (—)
Dickey, Carol	105	9-9	4.6	10-5	5.2
Dickinson, Russell	88	7-11	2.8	7-8	2.5
Ericson, Albert	125	13-0 (+)	7.9 (+)	13-0 (+)	7.9 (+)
Flick, Janie	125	11-8	6.5	12-10	7.7
Forsch, Larry	99	10-1	4.9	8-9	3.6
French, Julie	141	13-0 (+)	7.9 (+)	13-0 (+)	7.9 (+)
Friswold, Mary	113	13-0 (+)	7.9 (+)	11-8	6.5
Harper, Oliver	96	9-9	4.6	10-5	5.2
Hopkins, Gail	95	11-8	6.5	10-11	5.8
Knott, Esther	99	7-11	2.8	8-5	3.2
Knott, Frank	99	6-5	1.2	6-0 (—)	1.0 (—)
Kremer, Janet	124	8-9	3.6	8-11	3.8
Lane, Mildred	—	—	—	—	—
Larson, Andrew	104	13-0 (+)	7.9 (+)	9-5	4.2
Liebermann, Milton	126	10-11	5.8	10-1	4.9
Littlejohn, John	103	8-9	2.6	8-7	2.4
Murphy, Charles	89	8-1	2.9	6-0 (—)	1.0 (—)
Norman, Judy	130	9-3	4.0	9-3	4.0
Ober, Warren	—	—	—	—	—
Pogue, Sharon	120	9-0	3.9	6-9	1.6
Reuther, Geraldine	111	9-7	4.4	9-9	4.6
Sahr, Alice	85	8-5	3.2	7-11	2.8
Schorn, Roger	103	9-5	4.2	9-7	4.4
Schulz, Robert	99	8-9	3.6	7-9	2.6
Sheldon, Ray	141	8-5	3.2	7-11	2.8
Smith, Stanley	99	9-7	4.4	9-0	3.9
Stark, Edward	72	9-3	4.0	8-9	3.6
Taylor, Marjorie	86	9-0	3.9	8-9	3.6
Thompson, Helen	99	9-5	4.2	7-9	2.6
Toivenen, Selma	92	6-9	1.6	8-1	2.9
Toole, William	95	6-0 (—)	1. (—)	6-9	1.6

three years ago when the children were beginning first grade. She arranged them quickly in rank order and found that the 33 listed I.Q.'s ranged from 72 to 141. There was an 85, an 86, and there were two at 141, a 130, a 126, two at 125, a 124, and a 120. The median I.Q. was 99. These I.Q.'s, of course, were three years old. Marion wished that a more recent intelligence test record was available.

The reading scores for the third grade were not yet one year old, having been taken the previous November. The chronological age of the children that November had ranged from 8.2 to 10.5 years, but the reading vocabulary age had ranged from below 6 for two children to four others who were above 13. The reading comprehension age had ranged from below six for three children to two above 13. Reading vocabulary scores in the third grade had ranged from below first-grade level for two children to eighth grade or above for four others, while reading comprehension had ranged from below first-grade level for three children to eighth or above for two at the opposite extreme. Here indeed were the individual differences about which Dr. Cook had talked so much! Here was a third grade (now a fourth), with an eight-year spread in reading vocabulary and comprehension. Here was a group with mental ages, measured by a group test upon entering the first grade, ranging from 4.5 years to 8.4 years. Checking the chronological ages of the children, she found that they now ranged from 9.11 years to 12.5 years—a range of 2.6 years.

The test results were very inadequate when it came to deciding about the personality and ability of each individual child. There was Albert Ericson whose I.Q. in the first grade had been 125. When tested in the second grade, with a chronological age of 6 years and 10 months, his reading vocabulary age was 9 years and 10 months and his reading comprehension age was 9 years, 7 months. In the second grade, he had read as well as the average child in the fourth grade. This reading ability had held up in the third grade. There, with a chronological age of 8, he had a reading vocabulary age and a reading comprehension age of over 13. In the third grade, he was reading on the eighth-grade level or better. Mary Friswold's case was interesting, too. She had a Detroit I.Q. in the first grade of 113, but her reading age in the second grade was 10 years and 8 months in vocabulary and 9 years and 10 months in comprehension, while in the third grade her reading vocabulary was over 13 years and her reading comprehension was 11 years and 8 months. Marion guessed from these reading scores that when Mary was tested again, her intelligence quotient would show higher than 113. There was Ray Sheldon whose Detroit I.Q. in the first grade was 141, but who was reading slightly below the second-grade level in the second grade and barely on the third-grade level in the third grade. Ray had said very little in class so far, but had watched her with great, alert eyes in which there seemed to be a world of curiosity, but very little friendliness—or unfriendliness either for that matter. Then there was John Littlejohn with a Detroit I.Q. in the first grade of 103 and a vocabulary and comprehension score at the beginning of the second grade that was about middle second grade, but whose reading ability in the third grade had shown practically no improvement over his reading scores of a year below. If these test results were adequate and reliable, they indicated that John had made no progress in his reading during the year between the beginning of his second and third grade. Certainly Marion needed to know more about John Littlejohn.

Roger Schorn also had a Detroit I.Q. in the first grade of 103, and he had been only slightly better than John in vocabulary in the second grade, but had made a middle third-grade score in comprehension. The following year, in the third grade, his reading vocabulary score was 2 months into the fourth grade, and his reading comprehension score was 4 months into the fourth grade. The test scores on each child showed a little something about each one. There was the Detroit 72 I.Q. (Edward Stark) who tested low in the second grade but a bit above average in the third grade; while there was the 124 I.Q. (Janet Kremer) who was below average in reading in the second grade and only slightly above average in the third grade. There were the many I.Q.'s between 90 and 111 that were approximately normal in second- and third-grade reading.

Marion asked Miss Altonweather about the test plans for the current year. She wanted another intelligence test score on each child, and she hoped to get some other test results besides reading. Miss Altonweather said they always had the Otis Group Intelligence Test and the Stanford Arithmetic Test early in October for the fourth grade. She doubted if there would be funds for any more than that.

Marion also asked about bringing library books and supplementary books to her room, and about the purchase of a weekly newspaper. Did she have permission to take field trips? Miss A. seemed pleased at her questions. She told her to feel free to check out books for her room and told her that field trips were permissible if not "overdone." She should ask Miss Altonweather about them beforehand so as to be sure there were no conflicts and that all necessary precautions were taken. She obtained permission to take up a collection for a weekly newspaper.

She received immediate permission when she asked Miss A. if she could require each child to purchase a small ringed notebook for assignments and brief notes. Miss A. knew the kind to ask them to get—one that was stocked by the local stationer. She had some on hand and gave one to Marion to show the children. "Tell them," she said, "that if any of them can't afford to get one, to let you know privately, and you will see that one is provided. They hardly ever do, but it forestalls criticism."

Searching for interests

By Thursday, Marion was beginning to make the room look a bit more interesting. She had gone to the textbook storeroom and to the library. In the textbook storeroom she had found copies of the pre-primer, first reader, second reader, and third reader adopted as basic in Pleasant Valley. She brought one or two of each of the lower-grade language books and spellers to her room and three or four of each of the readers. She also found some supplementary readers used in the lower grades and brought copies of those. Miss Altonweather had discouraged bringing either the regular readers or the supplementary readers for the fifth and sixth grades to her room, since she thought that might destroy the interest of the children in those books when they were promoted to the next grades.

Marion found the library somewhat limited, but nevertheless there were many good things. She was able to find a lot more than she might have found in many schools. She found single copies of some fifth-, sixth-, seventh-, and eighth-grade readers and some fifth-, sixth-, seventh-, and eighth-grade geographies as well as miscellaneous textbooks for both lower and upper grades. She looked particularly for science materials and found a few, for example, the science booklets published by Row, Peterson.[1]

Miss Johnson had subscribed to a daily newspaper and she brought it to school each day. Two metropolitan newspapers were available in Pleasant Valley and Marion had chosen the one whose comics had a scientific background. Children, she knew, became interested in science in many ways, but one of the places where they picked up ideas, both true and false, was in the strips that dealt with such things as flying to other planets, highly scientific warfare, and crime detection.

Thursday morning Marion arrived at school earlier than usual. She had been searching in her mind for ways and means to find or to develop interests that could start the children on their learning activities. She knew that if she were to succeed in having the children experience a wide range of learning activities, she would have to assist them in finding materials. One of the first skills was to use reference books. This in turn depended upon such basic skills as facility with the sequence of letters in the alphabet. She had an idea the interest she had discovered and stimulated concerning names might lead into a study of the alphabet, the dictionary, and the encyclopedia.

Before the children arrived, she got out some "Zaner-Blosser" letter charts and placed them over the blackboard in the proper order. She cut some plain, heavy, white paper into pieces three inches by five inches to be used for filing cards. Glancing through the language book, she saw that there were six references to alphabetical order and five references to the use of the dictionary. Under capitalization, she found a reference to the first initials of names and a reference to making a class list. She was disappointed to find no reference to "index" or "indexing" in the index of the language book. It seemed like a strange oversight in a fourth-grade language book, and indicated something that she was to discover over and over again in her teaching—no single textbook can possibly prove adequate to the needs of an active learning class. She found that the glossary in the geography book contained the names of children from other lands, with their pronunciations and with their English equivalents in most cases, although no English equivalents were given for certain Eskimo names.

[1] See reference and treatment in Chapters 15 and 16.

She knew the arithmetic book by reputation to be a good one, but its index was of no assistance to her. The index was composed almost entirely of terms such as addition, subtrahend, and the like, rather than references to the real life situations that were used to make the basic learnings meaningful. She wished very much that the illustrative problems in the arithmetic book had been indexed according to the subjects with which they dealt. This would have made the book more usable for the kind of teaching she wished to do. She spent ten minutes thumbing through the book but could not find what she wished.

Marion was somewhat pleased with her experiences on Wednesday and had made a basic and, to her, very crucial decision. She had been faced with two alternatives. The first was to start the children with assignments in the various texts and with the various subjects separated into well-defined periods. If she had done this, she would have checked assignments, asked questions, tried to determine how much the children had memorized, drilled them on what they did not know, and then, by slow degrees, she would have tried to move into a more flexible unit-type of activity. She would have used the subject-organized, subject-centered curriculum as a crutch until she gained more power. The alternative to this was to continue an informal organization in the classroom, attempting to find intrinsic interests and real needs, and then to fit the factual learnings, the skills, and the desirable attitudes into those developing units that would spring from the needs and interests of children in a society where human welfare was of primary value. She had decided on the second course of action—at least until such time as she might be driven to use the traditional crutch.

In searching for ways to work with the children's interest in names, she saw that she could relate it to geography through the names of people in the far corners of the world. Also, she saw that she could relate it to social studies, as in understanding persons, racial backgrounds, human personality, and identity. She realized that it might develop into a study of the names connected with various racial stereotypes and result in rather careful work in human relations. She had already made her plans for relating it to the use of the alphabet, to filing and to the use of the dictionary, and to simple counting and number work. She thought that it might even develop into a study of community names, bringing the children out into their community environment.

The other interest that she thought might develop was the one dealing with parliamentary procedure and rules of order. She could see many of the same possibilities here. She knew, of course, that either one of these might fail to develop, and that she must not be disappointed if the children did not go far with either of them. She decided to stimulate these interests for a day or two to see how much "power" they would generate. If they "ran out," other incidents would arise constantly, she knew, that would give opportunity to find further interests and further needs upon which she might try to build.

There were many other things that she wished to do, but they would all have to wait their turn. She knew that she must get better acquainted with the children in order to understand their individual interests, aptitudes, and abilities. She hoped soon to talk informally about the things each one liked to do best, the things enjoyed last summer, or what each one wanted to be when grown. She was not sure that the time had arrived for this, however. Many of the children were not free yet to express themselves to her and to the class. They had not learned to speak their real thoughts. They had learned, it seemed to her, to conform, to hide their real feelings, to be suspicious of the adults about them. She knew that it would take a little while to develop the permissive atmosphere that she desired in her classroom. The children had come to expect a subject-centered, recitation-type, traditional classroom, and had developed little individual responsibility or group power. She knew that she must be patient, and wait until she could provide the conditions for it to develop. She knew, too, that its development would take much doing on her part.

Third morning

When the children came in at nine o'clock, they took their places without too much disturbance, but with enough so that Marion could not feel completely satisfied. She made a mental note that they would have to work on that. She called them to attention, however, and then said, "This morning I think we should plan our day's work." She expanded on this a bit and then went on, "Perhaps after a while, we will not have to plan each day because our plans will keep us busy for more than a day." She elaborated this point briefly, and then added, "I hope that before very long we can have the children take turns in standing up here and being chairman while we plan, and I will sit down and be a member of the group. Perhaps we can elect officers Friday afternoon if we can get our rules set up." She allowed them to ask questions and for a few minutes they talked in an informal fashion about the election, and then they reminisced a bit about votes they had taken in kindergarten, and in the first three grades.

It was easy for Miss Johnson to make the transition from this discussion to the question concerning the assignment they had given themselves the previous day to find out about rules of order, parliamentary procedure, and so forth.

She asked, "How many talked to their parents and friends last night about how to run a meeting? You remember that we decided we would find out as much as we could so that we might talk about it today."

Eleven hands were raised, with one or two others half raised in an indefinite, desultory way. Marion noted this number as a bit of group evaluation.

"Whom shall I call on first," she asked. The hands waved more insistently. "Does it make a difference whom I call on first?" The hands waved still more insistently with three or four whispered "Oh's" accompanying the waving. "Sometime we will have to decide on how to select the ones who are to talk first. Today I will start with this row by the wall and go across the room."

Five of the reports contained information valuable to the group. Mary Friswold had learned a lot from her mother about making motions, taking votes, and recognizing the speaker. Andrew Larson's father was secretary of his union and Andrew was able to tell a little bit about the way union meetings were run. Milton Lieberman's father was active in a number of Jewish organizations and had obviously helped Milton with his assignment a great deal. Milton would have talked on and on, had he been encouraged. He spoke with a shy insistence that was very appealing. Albert Ericson had gone to the county library sub-station downtown and had asked the librarian for assistance. She had shown him a copy of *Robert's Rules of Order* and he had done some work with that. It was difficult reading even for him, and he had not gotten into it very deeply. She complimented him on what he had done and offered to help him with it should he wish to continue.

When Selma Toivenen was called on, she rose carefully, brushed down her clean, starched, blue dress, and said primly, "My daddy does that, too, over at the Co-op." Then she sat down as if that settled it.

"That's good," Miss Johnson said. "They must have rules at the Co-op meeting or they wouldn't know how to run the Co-op." Selma beamed.

As usual, Miss Johnson was writing brief notes on the blackboard while the discussion went on. After all who wished to speak had spoken, some who had not done so said they would ask at home that night what their parents might know about running a meeting. Miss Johnson reminded them that some parents did not go to meetings often, and that others might not be able to take time to tell them. "It isn't necessary that everybody find out about this from their parents. We will have other things to ask parents about at other times, and everyone will get a chance sometime to tell what their parents have said."

Miss Johnson asked them if it would help them to copy from the board the rules that they had found out so far. They agreed to do so and they wrote them as carefully as possible so that they could take them home and show them to their parents and get further rules to add to the list. It was ten o'clock before Miss Johnson asked the pupils to stop copying the notes. She mentioned that time passed quickly and that sometime soon they would have to decide how much time they wanted to spend on various activities. As they had written, she had walked quietly about the room, helping some of them, and watching carefully. This had been her first opportunity to watch the children write, and she made some brief notes in a few cases.

After the writing period, Miss Johnson asked the children to get out the lists of names that they had found in their geographies and in their readers. The three by five slips of paper were passed out and the children were asked to write as many names as they could, one name on each slip of paper. She showed them how to write the last name first, a comma, and then the first name, and how to use a straight line where one of the names was missing. The children worked at this task until 10:30. Those who finished sooner were given the privilege of working at anything else they wished. Some read their textbooks; a few moved to the reading table and examined the materials beginning to accumulate there.

In writing the names and capitalizing them, Miss Johnson made reference to the page in the language book where capitalization of the first letter in names (and in some other contingencies) was discussed. After the recreation period, Miss Johnson told the children to save the name slips for later use. She asked those who could do so to arrange their cards in alphabetical order. There were some questions and some confusion when this suggestion was made, so she asked how many knew how to arrange the cards alphabetically. A number of hands were raised but she was not sure from their hesitant manner how many had confidence in their ability. She asked how to find words in the dictionary. If they knew that, she said, they would know how to arrange names alphabetically. She passed out the dictionaries and they discussed and studied them to determine how the words were arranged. There was quite a bit of interest in this activity. Some of the children knew how the words were arranged, at least in part, and they led the discussion. The other children thumbed through the pages and many of them were able to make some progress.

She asked questions about what everyone must know in order to use the dictionary, and they agreed that everyone should know the alphabet. Some already knew the alphabet, they said, and one or two volunteered to recite it, and did so very quickly. Miss Johnson suggested that some of them might wish to learn the alphabet backwards and forwards. She said that in a day or two they might have a game similar to a spell-down that they would call a dictionary game. This suggestion was received enthusiastically by many of the children. She said that some of them might wish to study to prepare for this game. By working with the children, she found something for each one to do. Those who didn't know the alphabet studied that; those who didn't know how to arrange words within the letter groupings were asked to study it out by seeing how it was done in the dictionary. Those who felt competent, arranged the list of names they had in alphabetical order.

In their discussion, they decided that it would be desirable for each child to have a card index of all the children in the room.

This decision was not arrived at spontaneously; Miss Johnson had to hint at it. She told them that if they were to work in groups and decide many of the other questions that had been raised already about classroom management, it would be convenient if each child had a card index of all the children in the room. The class decided that each child would prepare 37 cards upon which he had written his name in neat, legible form. One of these would be given to each child and one to Miss Johnson. This would be of great assistance to the new students, of whom there were four. Those who had time, started their cards immediately. Some of the others continued to work on the alphabet and on the arrangement of the names from the books in alphabetical order.

The Littlejohn kid

As they were discussing the desirability of a card for each child in the room, Miss Johnson noticed that John Littlejohn was growing decidedly restless. She noticed this first when he reached across the aisle and struck at Ray Sheldon. When he did this, she looked at him seriously and calmly for a moment and he straightened up in his seat and stared at the desk in front of him. As the discussion went on, she heard another noise, and glancing back she saw that Robert Schultz, who sat behind John, was drawn down in his seat. She knew that John had grabbed him by the foot and pulled him forward. When the noise became noticeable, John released his hold and straightened up, whereupon Robert straightened himself in his chair and struck John between the shoulders with his fist. As this was occurring, Miss Johnson moved quietly in their direction. Standing beside John's seat, she glanced down at him and said, "Can I help you, John?" John answered something that sounded like a low, snarled, "Naw." "Have you started to make your cards yet?" she asked. Then suddenly it happened. John was looking at her, the same cold, deadpan expression in his face that she had seen the first day, but his voice was saying over and over again heatedly, "I ain't gonna, I ain't gonna! I won't! You can't make me! I won't!" His voice was nervous and tight very much like a suppressed scream.

Marion remembered the things she had been told so often in her class in mental hygiene, and she wondered if she had the self-control and the courage to try it now when it was necessary. She felt somewhat as she had felt when as a little girl she was taking swimming lessons. "Place yourself in the water face up, put your head way back and your arms by your sides and take a deep breath and you can't sink," the instructor had said. He had demonstrated it, too, but it didn't seem reasonable to Marion. She was sure she would sink, but she knew she had to try it anyway. She remembered how much courage it took the first time. After that it was fun. And now she had to do something that seemed equally unreasonable to her. She thought for a fleeting moment what Miss Coyne might have done. Miss Coyne would have settled the problem quickly and surely, and she would have done it in a way that would have won the approval of all the "good" little boys and girls in the room. She would have shown John Littlejohn once and for all who was the boss in that room. But Miss Johnson had to make her experiment. She looked at John and she tried to keep all trace of irritation or of personal insecurity out of her voice as she said to him calmly and firmly, "You are mad at me now. You are very mad at me. Sometimes children get very mad at their parents and at their teachers." And then she turned and walked away from him to the front corner of the room, and continued the discussion with the rest of the class.

At noon, when she had time to think over the incident, she saw where she had made her first big mistake. Two days before, she had sensed that John Littlejohn was not sure whether he was John Littlejohn or Jack Hammond. She had felt that there was social disapproval in the group over his use of the name, Littlejohn. Also, she had discovered that he was a sensitive child and not well adjusted, and yet she had led him into a situation, without thinking about it, where he had become so insecure that he had to fight back to maintain his status with himself. She was interested in John. She had asked to have him in her room, and had made up her mind, with a wry inward grin at herself, that John's problem would not go unsolved for lack of effort on her part. She knew some of the theory about how to do it, and hoped she would be adept enough to put it into practice.

It had been decided before noon dismissal that those children who had time would try to find at home some examples of ways in which alphabetical arrangements were used outside of school. The telephone book was mentioned at once and one or two children thought they had extra telephone books at home that they could bring to school either that afternoon or tomorrow.

First week's ending

Thursday afternoon and Friday continued along the lines of Thursday morning. Quite a few of the children found out at noon some interesting applications of the alphabet in everyday life. Two of the children brought old telephone books to school, one brought a little black address book with alphabetical divisions in it, and another brought an alphabetical shopping-list booklet distributed free by one of the stores. But the most interesting of all was the information that Roger Shorn brought in about the arrangement of the avenues north of Main Street. His father had told him that Main Street was really "A" street; that First Avenue was really "B" street; and from then on the names were all in alphabetical order. There was Cranberry Avenue, Duluth Avenue, Emerson Avenue, Foster Avenue, and so forth. Roger didn't know how far it went, but he thought it went almost through the alphabet. The children were very interested in this bit of information; probably few of them had heard of it before, and certainly none of them had thought about it seriously. Miss Johnson could find no map of Pleasant Valley Township at school, but she thought they could make a map if they could get one to copy from, and two boys, Roger and Oliver, were appointed by their classmates to find a map, borrow it, and bring it to school on Monday morning. It was suggested that they might go to the bank or to the newspaper office or to Mr. Radke's real estate and insurance office. There was some discussion about what size map they should get. The question also arose over how the streets were named that ran in the other direction and also about the streets south of Main Street. It was decided to try to get a map of the whole village.

The children worked on their name cards and on getting sets of names for all the children in the room, though these were not completed by all the children. Two children in the room wrote with so much difficulty that they were far from finished with the proper number of cards. Miss Johnson discovered that two children did not know how to count to 37, so she knew she would have to start their arithmetic there. Others completed the cards easily and she had them read in their geography books and write on their cards some brief biographical notes about the children who lived in the various lands, showing one or two of them how to make such brief notes. During much of this time, she walked about the room helping and observing and directing attention to things they seemed in need of knowing.

Miss Johnson had prepared a seating chart of the room with a small square for each child and on this she was able to make many little notes about the children as she located their various strengths and weaknesses. For group work, she had them divide into the same groups that they had used for the distribution of books. In these groups, they discussed some of the things they had learned about parliamentary procedure. Upon another occasion, in these groups, they worked together preparing a filing system for the whole room. Each child was to have a file folder suitable for holding papers up to eight and one-half inches by eleven inches in size. These folders were to be arranged in boxes at the back of each row. Miss Johnson used her copies of last year's report cards to pick out the children who received "A" in number work the previous year. They were, in general, those who needed extra duties. So she

Miss Johnson's Daily Log

Tuesday: Got names
             Planned on how to distribute books—5 books, 5 committees,
             5 piles of books
Wednesday: 9:00- 9:10 Took roll—routine
             9:10- 9:30 Counted off and divided into committees
             9:30-10:00 Discussed chairmen and rules of order, and selected
                        committee chairmen
            10:00-10:30 Started sorting books
            10:30-10:45 Recreation break
            10:45-11:15 Finished sorting the books
            11:15-11:45 Studied in committee as a whole group how to
                        pass out books
            11:45-12:00 General discussion and evaluation of how they had
                        worked as groups and how to improve
             1:00- 1:30 Distributed books
             1:30- 2:00 Discussed books. Noted interesting pictures and
                        stories

JEAN	MILTON	SHARON	ALICE	GERALDINE	WARREN
I.Q. 99-?!	Father active in Jewish Commu. Arith. Commu.	High I.Q. Low achiever?		Defeated in group chairmanship. Arith. Commu. Reading P.O. Read a poem	New this year.
JULIE Very quiet. Looks well. Identify from 2nd grade. Read a poem	**MARY** Mother-very flirty girl. Slumps the self appt. droll reader? I.Q. too low? Arith. Commu.	**RUSSELL** Good arith. Mentional nicknames.	**ALBERT** Arith. + + ! Perfectionist? Prob. of group. Arith. Commu. Farm boy	**STANLEY** Artistic. Chm. of group. Read poem	**JANIE** Mother upper upon arith. Commu. Brother home.
ESTHER Twin. She mothers her brother. Arr. student	**JUDY** Chm. of group. Elected 1st room chairman.	**GAIL** Blue Bird member. L.Q. accurate? Artistic. Arith. Commu. Brother in thy bonts	**JANET** Co-chm. of group. High I.Q. Art. achiever	**SELMA** Dad active in corps. Beautiful writer! Cleans happy; well dressed? Poor reader	**ANDREW** Dad - union secretary. Artistic
CAROL Artistic	**MONA**	**FRANK** Twins - depends on arith. Below avr.	**OLIVER** Looks out as 1st room chairman. Arith. Commu. Read in granite hun. I.Q. Leonardo?	**ROGER** Laughs when talks. Co-chm. of group. Good achiever. Avr. ability	**MILDRED** New in P.V. this year. Older than most
JOHN West Poor achiever	**RAY** Mormont. Unaccept. High L.Q.- low achiever. Good in arith. Uncivilized rebel.	**HARRY** Doesn't know alphabet.	**EDWARD** Good reader for low L.Q. Can't count 72 I.Q.	**WILLIAM** Stutters some. Does not volunteers. Farm boy	**CHARLES** Had the nickname. Doesn't know alphabet. Farm boy
ROBERT Pays little attention	**HELEN** Mother ill.	**MARJORIE** Good in arith. Didn't get 3rd grade 8 A's	**NORMA** New in P.V. this year - oldest girl in room. 11-5	**RICHARD** New in P.V. this year. Farm boy	**LARRY** Broken home. Stepmother loves lovers? Strong extroverted

Figure 7. Seating chart and notes—first week.

2:00- 2:30 Assigned making name cards for names in geographies and readers. Read to note names which will be placed on 3 x 5 name slips tomorrow

2:30- 2:45 Recreation break

2:45- 3:45 Review of what we have learned so far

Thursday: 9:00- 9:15 Discussion of teacher-pupil planning

9:15- 9:45 What we learned at home about rules of order. Carried over assignment till tomorrow for those who forgot. Made list of points.

9:45-10:00 Writing—copied list of rules to take home for further hints

10:00-10:30 Made name cards; mentioned alphabet game

10:30-10:45 Recreation

10:45-11:15 Alphabet and alphabetizing

11:15-12:00 Dictionary study. General activity—pupil name cards made so each child may have room file

1:00- 1:30 Telephone books and other alphabetical applications learned at home and reported. Alphabetical street arrangement. Interest in a map.

1:30- 2:00 Reading about names—started making notes on cards about characters in books

2:00- 2:30 Group work—started making folders for each child. Decided on folder boxes and where to get them. Arithmetic committee set up.

2:30- 2:45 Recreation

2:45- 3:00 Distribution of art materials

3:00- 3:45 Free reading period

Friday: 9:00- 9:20 Taking roll. Why we take roll
1. Check on health
2. Everyone safe
3. State aid and taxes
4. Credit for school work. Records of education
5. Good citizenship

9:20-10:00 Letters home about attendance and state aid

10:00-10:30 Committees studied letters

10:30-10:45 Recreation

10:45-11:15 Some wrote letters
Some worked on pupil name cards
Some worked on reading name cards
Some studied the alphabet and/or arranged cards in order
Some studied how to count

11:15-12:00 Sorted cards and studied names and arranged cards
Criticized poor writers
Adopted rule "Always write your best."

1:00- 2:00 Review of week's work. Listed 30 items

2:00- 2:30 Elected chairman and settled on temporary "rules
of order"
2:30- 2:45 Recreation
2:45- 3:45 Planned next week's work

formed them into a committee to decide what size the boxes should
be to hold these card files. They thought they could get some cartons the right size at Martinelli's grocery store. She suggested that
they write a letter to Mr. Martinelli asking him if he would cooperate with the class, but the committee thought that would be
silly—the committee could select members (Milton and Andrew) to
call on him after school much easier than that. She had to agree
that they were right and that's the way it was done. When they over-
rode her suggestion in this respect, she had a feeling that she was
making progress. Certainly the atmosphere she was creating was
not overly restrictive. Certainly the children were thinking realistically about their objectives and the best way to attain them. The
class discussed with the committee the kind of boxes wanted, and
it was decided that if Mr. Martinelli had plenty of boxes, they
should get more than one size and try them out. They also discussed
certain rules of etiquette that should be observed as they approached
Mr. Martinelli for cooperation, such as how to ask him for the
boxes, explain their need, and thank him for them.

On both occasions, so far, when children were called on by their
fellows to do errands for the class, the "better pupils" had been
selected. Marion wished they had selected John, Ray, Robert, Edward or various others. She knew that this would only come as they
gained power in planning and in assigning to each of their fellows
duties that would allow everyone to help and that would tend to
recognize individual talents and interests. At this point, she did not
wish to make such assignments herself. She wished, rather, to see
which of their classmates the children would select in order that
she could assess the group structure, and the maturity of judgment
that the group would show. She felt that these skills were not highly
developed. In order to get that type of measure, she resolved to
make a sociogram as soon as a good opportunity presented itself.

Marion's progress with John Littlejohn remained an unknown
quantity through Thursday afternoon, but Friday morning he gave
her a shy fleeting grin as he entered the room and she grinned back

at him in friendliness as other children came by. He behaved well all day but he did not prepare his name cards, nor did Marion tell him to. The work was arranged so that there was plenty else for him to do.

Friday

The Friday morning opening period had been taken up partly with further contributions from children who had learned something about parliamentary law from their parents and partly with a report from Milton and Andrew. The latter brought in 14 cartons. There was a discussion of classroom management with specific reference to the reasons for taking roll and keeping attendance records. The children contributed some reasons and Marion contributed some until the list was as follows:

Reasons Why We Take Roll
1. Check on health of children
2. Check on safety of children
3. Check on good citizenship—reliability
4. Keep records for credit and promotion
5. How many books to buy
6. How many teachers to hire
7. How much taxes we need
8. State aid money depends on attendance

These reasons were written in their notebooks. Their discussion brought out the need for care on the part of the pupils who would soon take roll. Marion was pleased at the interest the children showed. She found that many of the children thought it was expected that they attend school every day, no matter how good their excuse. They thought their parents did not know about state aid and would not keep them out of school to shop or go to the dentist if they knew that.

"What could we do so they would understand that?" she asked.
"We could tell them."
"What would be the best way to tell them?"
"Put it in the newspaper."
"Have Miss Altonweather tell them."
"Write them letters."

"How many think we should write letters about it?"

Over half the hands in the class were raised, but Selma said she didn't think she could because she had to finish her name cards and her folder file and read about the children in the books.

"How many won't have time to write letters today?"

Many hands were raised, some of them very doubtfully and timidly. Selma had not been timid. She seemed to believe implicitly in the kindness and friendliness of her environment and in the simple happy rightness of being "Selma." Marion felt that she was wonderfully well adjusted. "I must visit her home soon," she thought. "She will be of help in making the slow academic achievers feel respectable."

As they planned the day's work, they decided that those who wished could write letters, but that first they should all study how to write letters in their language books. They decided that they would study in committees and that each of the five committees would select the best letters written by its members and make up a committee letter that all members of the committee could send. That way those who were too busy would not need to write letters, but they would still have a letter to send and they would learn by discussing and helping in the committee.

After the recreation period, the children worked for 45 minutes at various jobs. Those who had not finished their pupil name cards worked at that. Miss Johnson found a chance to tell John Littlejohn he need not make his 37 name cards. She found that four others had not completed that job: Harry, Edward, Mildred, and Charles. She helped them finish. She was surprised that Frank had his, but saw without saying anything about it that on some of his cards (the neat ones) his name was in another hand that she guessed to be his sister's. Some of the children's name cards were very poorly written, but she made no point of that at the moment. She had previously written 37 cards for John Littlejohn.

The children passed the cards around until each child had 36 different cards. Miss Johnson got the thirty-seventh set. The children read the cards over and learned to read the names. Some were not legible!

"I can't read some of mine."

"Is this a 'F' or a 'T'?"

"I can't tell the first names and last names."

There were many objections. Here was a good lesson in group responsibility!

"What should we do?" Miss Johnson asked.

The children who felt sure of the legibility of their own cards were very critical and were ready to visit heavy penalties on those who had not done so well. Typical remarks were:

"Make them do them over."

"Make them stay after school and write them."

"Make them write a hundred cards."

"Don't give them a set of our cards."

Marion did not summarize these remarks on the board. She knew that their effect would be to show that the group wanted a high standard of work when they were working together and providing one another with material. She knew, too, that many of their suggestions were childish interpretations of what a teacher should require and were the result of their experience in school so far.

"Perhaps I did not tell you it should be done very neatly, and perhaps some of you have not done much writing during vacation. Perhaps we can correct or rewrite the cards we have and then we can ask that next time we all write our very best. Some children can write real well, and some can't. It's just like swimming, or roller skating, or making candy, or sewing, or playing ball, or anything else."

So a writing rule was adopted, "Always write the best you can," and it was a majority decision. Perhaps in time it would become a unanimous one. That would have to be another of Marion's objectives, but she couldn't achieve it by requiring it. She would have to watch for her chances to develop it in the same way that she had started.

Friday afternoon, Marion reviewed with the children the things they had been doing during the week. She wrote on the board the title, "Things We Are Studying and Doing," and underneath she wrote: "(1) Committee work; (2) Names we find in our geography and reading books; (3) Our names; (4) Making our folders; (5) Learning to count; (6) Using alphabet lists; (7) Learning the alphabet; (8) Who the people are in our books; (9) Get and prepare file boxes and folders for each row; (10) Study the rules of order; (11) How to work in groups; (12) How to talk together as friends—conversation; (13) How words are arranged in the dictionary; (14) Getting ready to play a dictionary game; (15) Making a class-list file; (16) Getting to know and work with each other; (17) Finding alphabetical arrangements outside of school; (18) How to approach adults for help; (19) How to thank people who help us; (20) How to take notes; (21) How to be good citizens; (22) How to write plainly; (23) Art; (24) How to write letters; (25) How to be a 'pupil-teacher;' (26) Reasons for taking roll; (27) What we can find in our textbooks; (28) What maps are—what they show; (29) Use of the alphabet in the community; (30) Names and people in various countries."

The children listed the 30 items.

Following the review period, and growing out of it, the children reviewed their material on parliamentary procedure. It was time to elect the first slate of classroom officers—a chairman and a secretary.

"Let us review what we know about our rules of order," Miss Johnson said. "Our notes so far are as follows:

"A chairman
1. Is captain of the group
2. Is elected by the group
3. Does not talk too much
4. Decides who may speak first
5. Sees that everyone is treated fairly
6. Calls the meeting to order

"A secretary
1. Writes down what is decided by the group
2. Reads the report of what the group does
3. Puts down the names of those who 'make motions'
4. Puts down the names of those who are 'nominated'
5. Puts down the number of votes and who is elected
6. Writes down the names of those on committees

"A treasurer
1. Keeps the money
2. Keeps a record of the money
3. We have no money yet
4. We need no treasurer yet

"Committees
Sometimes the chairman appoints committees

Sometimes the group elects committees
Sometimes the first one named is the committee chairman
    (this saves time)
Sometimes the committee chairman is elected by the committee
    members
Sometimes the committee needs a secretary
The committee selects its own secretary

"Order of business
1. Chairman opens meeting
2. Secretary reads minutes
3. The group may correct the minutes
4. The group accepts the minutes
5. The chairman asks if there is any old business
6. He asks for committee reports
7. He asks for any new business
8. He tells them what they should decide that day
9. He asks them to decide on time of the next meeting
10. When everything is finished, he asks for a motion to adjourn

"General rules
1. Each person votes only once
2. You may vote by saying 'Aye' or 'Nay'
3. You may vote by a 'show of hands'
4. You may vote by ballot
5. On personal matters, it is best to vote by ballot

"Making motions
To ask to speak, you stand and say, 'Mr. (or Madam) Chairman.'
    The chairman says your name if you are to speak. You then
    make your motion.
You say, 'I move that . . . .'
Someone who agrees must second the motion
Then you discuss the motion
Then others may speak for it or against it
Then the chairman takes a vote on it

"To get the floor
You must speak on the subject that is being talked about, or the
    Chairman should stop you
You may ask a question
You may ask to have a vote

"To make nominations
You say, 'Mr. Chairman, I nominate . . . .'
More than one may be nominated
When all who wish to do so have spoken, someone should say,
    'I move that the nominations be closed.'
This must be seconded and passed
The names should be written on the board and one ballot passed
    out to each one
Only one position should be voted on at a time

"Special rules
Officers will be elected in the fourth grade each week
No one can serve twice in one month."

Albert was not satisfied with the rules. "They are not right," he said. "We must have a constitution and by-laws to go by. Then there are all kinds of motions and some are more important than others and come first. Then there is something where you lay motions on the table and vote on it and that puts it off."

"I believe Albert is right," Miss Johnson said. "We will have to work on our rules and try to make a constitution if we want one. There are other rules, too, that we must learn as we go along. Those are things we must consider. What do you think we should do, Albert?"

"I think we should do it the right way—the way it says in the books—in the books for grownups."

"That is what I want, too."

"Then we have to have a constitution and by-laws."

Marion saw then what was bothering Albert. He wanted things just right and was not content to see them evolve, if that seemed a careless and slipshod way to do it.

"The United States has a Constitution, too," she said. "We will study it when we can. But when our country first started we did not have a Constitution until 1787, 11 years after the Declaration of Independence. Of course, that was a very big job, but it took 11 years to get a constitution. You have to start having meetings and then work out the constitution."

Albert looked straight into Marion's eyes for two or three seconds, then he smiled slightly, and sat down. He was satisfied.

Miss Johnson then said, "When people first start a club, someone stands and says, 'I nominate Mr. Smith (or someone) as temporary chairman,' and that person is elected without much trouble because the temporary chairman serves just long enough to select a permanent chairman. Today, if you do not object, I will serve as temporary chairman."

There were no objections.

"Are there any nominations for chairman?"

"I nominate Judy Norman," Mary Friswold said.

Miss Johnson wrote Judy's name on the board as she asked for further nominations.

"I nominate Oliver Harper," said Albert Ericson.

Before anything more could be said, Milton loudly moved the nominations be stopped. The motion was hastily seconded and passed.

As Miss Johnson passed the ballots, she explained that the secretary would do that next time, or else a committee appointed by the chairman. The result was close, but Judy was elected by what appeared to be an almost solid boy *versus* girl vote. Counting the votes provided a demonstration lesson in arithmetic—marking off fives.

The contest for secretary was between Milton and Gail and Gail won, also by a small margin. The boys grumbled a bit at the result, but Miss Johnson was not bothered by it.

"Fourth-grade children," she said, "almost always start out with most of the boys voting for boys and almost all the girls voting for girls, but after a while they vote for those they think will make good officers, or for those they think need practice so they can learn to be good officers too." She said this without sarcasm, without a superiority of manner, and without humor. It was advanced as a statement of fact.

It was time for recess. "After recess," Miss Johnson said, "we will plan the work we want to do next week. Judy is your chairman and will preside. I will write what I want to do next week on the board and you can decide what you want to do. Then we will fit it together."

On the blackboard, Miss Johnson wrote:

Next week I want to

1. Find out how much arithmetic you remember from last year

2. Give each one a chance to read for me from one of the books

3. Get to know more about each one of you through conversation.[2] What do you like to do? What do you want to be when you are grown up? What are your hobbies? What do you like to read? Who are your best friends? What did you do last summer that was most fun?

Next week the pupils want to
1.
2.

Miss Johnson's list proved so interesting that it was some time before the children got around to discussing their own plans. When the class came in from recess, Miss Johnson had taken a seat at the rear of the room and waited. Judy looked around questioningly.

"Go ahead," two or three whispered to her.

She stood and went to the front of the room.

"Come to order," she said. "What shall we plan to do next week?"

"We can have an arithmetic test."

"We would have to study first."

"We could all take turns reading."

"One could read and then another."

"I want to be a truck driver and go to the coast."

"I want to be a camp counselor."

"I want to be an aviator—jets—zoooooom!"

"They don't sound like that. Zee-ee-ee-p! That's what they sound like."

"Naw, they go Fee-ee-eerze. They whistle after they are gone past."

"Yeah—you gotta look ahead of where you hear them. I can always see them, but my dad, he never sees them because they're gone first. Every time it's like that!"

The room was seething with snorts and whistles and Judy was a bit nonplussed at her responsibility and the vigorous freedom of expression. She had started by nodding to the pupils who raised their hands instead of having them request recognition. Soon, many didn't wait for her nod. There was much interest and free expression, however, and Miss Johnson did not intefere.

After a time, Albert raised his hand and turned in his seat to face

[2] The first three chapters in the fourth-grade language books were on conversation.

Miss Johnson. She smiled at him and pointed to Judy. He turned and, after a moment, stood up.

There was no immediate silence, but when he slowly and loudly said, "Madam Chairman," there was a focus in his direction and the room became calm. "You should make each one say 'Madam Chairman,' and they should not talk until you say their name."

Judy looked at Miss Johnson. Marion looked pleased and interested, but she resisted the impulse to nod and thus solve the problem for the class.

"Well," Judy said, as she looked with some irritation across the great fourth-grade barrier of the sexes. Words failed her for the moment.

Mary saved the day. "Madam Chairman."

"Mary."

"I think the teacher has to tell us what books to read and the arithmetic problems to do, and correct them and show us how because we wouldn't know." (Miss Johnson made a note of this remark.)

That set the children off again, but this time they did generally address the chair and await recognition.

"The teacher has to give permission."

"Miss O'Leary made us sit in the back of the room when we didn't get our work done."

"Yeah! She made us stay after school, too, when we didn't, or when we sassed her."

"She never let friends sit near each other 'cause they whispered."

"When the kids were bad, she made them do extra work."

"Oh! She didn't either."

During the discussion, Marion had moved up to Gail's desk and had talked quietly to her, coaching her a bit, and then she moved to the back again as Gail got the floor.

"I move," she said, "that we talk about what we will do on Monday at nine o'clock and at ten o'clock—and like that—and after recess and after dinner, so I can write it down."

"I second the motion," Mary said.

"What do I do now?" Judy asked Miss Johnson.

"If I were you, I'd ask those who think that Gail's plan is a good one to raise their hands. Gail is secretary and can count the hands. Then those who are opposed to the plan should raise their hands

and be counted." With a bit more coaching the voting was carried
through successfully.

There were no unfavorable votes though four or five didn't vote,
among them Ray, Robert, Charles, and Norma.

"We have to take the roll first, and see who's here and who's
late," Russell said.

"We have to do that every day," Janie said.

"I move we do that every day."

"I second the motion," Albert said.

"Those who want it, raise your hands," Judy said. It was unanimous.

Miss Johnson coached Gail again so quietly that the others did
not hear. "I'll help you afterwards because it is all so new. Do the
best you can. . . ." Gail smiled in appreciation.

"I move that we have arithmetic next." It was Milton's motion
seconded by Oliver and passed unanimously.

"Madam Chairman." Thus Miss Johnson rose and addressed
the chair.

Judy did not recognize her at first, but looked at her in silence,
expecting her to speak on without official recognition. Then she
suddenly remembered. "Miss Johnson," she said with dignity.

"I move that we spend the time from afternoon recess until closing each day as long as is necessary taking turns having each one
tell the class what he or she did last summer that was fun, or what
he or she wants to do next summer. Perhaps we can talk over—
discuss—each one's report in class and make notes on their name
cards about their interests—what they say they like to do." This was
seconded and passed.

Gail said, "What shall we do after recess in the morning and before recess in the afternoon?"

Miss Johnson said, "Madam Chairman, I suggest that we get
some ideas by looking at our list of things we are studying and
doing." Marion paid close attention to the discussion that followed,
for in it she found leads to interests that could be built upon to
give direction to the development of the possible units that were
taking shape in her mind. They decided that they should plan for
an alphabet game, work on their Pleasant Valley maps, study how
to work in groups, and study how to carry on the conversations
about what they liked to do. It was recalled that the committee's

letters to parents about attendance were not completed yet. They thought they should study more about writing letters. Some suggested further reading about the people whose names they found in the books. There would not be time to do all these things, so they decided that various pupils and committees could do different jobs. The day was over before all the plans were made. Miss Johnson and Gail agreed to try to finish the program and present it Monday after roll. A motion was made and passed to adjourn. Gail seemed restless about staying after school, so Miss Johnson said it would only take a minute and some of the other girls could stay and wait for her if they wished. While they waited, Miss Johnson discussed the plan with them, meanwhile writing rapidly on the board.

Monday's Program

9:00- 9:30   Take roll

           Led by Judy $\left\{\begin{array}{l}\text{Discuss outside assignments}\\ \text{Discuss program for rest of day}\end{array}\right.$

9:30-10:00   Arithmetic
10:00-10:30   Reading
10:30-10:45   Recess
10:45-11:30   Study about conversations
11:30-12:00   (1) Plan for alphabet game $\left.\right\}$ individual
               (2) Select proper size boxes for folders   and com-
               (3) Finish other jobs that may come up   mittee work
 1:00- 1:30   Study maps—geography books [3] and reading table
 1:30- 2:30   Discuss maps and start work on Pleasant Valley map
 2:30- 2:45   Recess
 2:45- 3:30   Pupil reports—vacation interests, led by Judy
 3:30- 3:45   Plan for Tuesday, led by Judy

Gail approved it as fast as Miss Johnson wrote it and was soon able to run off gaily with her friends.

Pulling the week "together"

At the week's end, Marion's note pad contained many remarks, a number of which had been checked to show that they had been

---

[3] There were an introduction to maps, an aerial photograph, and a map of a small town in the first part of the geography book.

partly cared for, and many of which remained unchecked. "Check on John Littlejohn. Check on 'Stinky.' Remember the names of new pupils. Albert Ericson—mathematics. Capitalize on interest in names and nicknames. Interest in passing out books fairly. Make seating chart. Need for individual folders. Get to know Mr. Adams—janitor. More about each child. Need for skill in committee work. Interest in rules of order. Children must learn to arrive at group opinions—consensus. Need for additional testing. Prepare for alphabet game. Arithmetic committee—third-grade A's. Find materials at various levels of interest in reading ability. Prepare children for larger part in classroom management: (a) skill and dispatch in getting seated and started; (b) pupil-teacher planning; (c) pupils to serve as chairmen; (d) increase interest in carrying out group assignments for home work; (e) means of deciding who shall recite first; (f) pupil participation in checking attendance and tardiness; (g) pupil care of room housekeeping."

Marion had a good start on her committee work. She had five committees that had been set up on a random basis by counting off. Then she had set up her special arithmetic committee composed of all those children who had an "A" in third grade in arithmetic. She would have preferred to select the committee on the basis of more objective evidence. In any case, her arithmetic committee was composed of Janie Flick, Milton Liebermann, Oliver Harper, Gail Hopkins, Albert Ericson, Geraldine Reuther, and Mary Friswold. She intended to add other children to the committee who showed high ability or interest in numbers. (The second week she added Ray Sheldon and Russell Dickinson and the third week she added Marjorie Taylor. After the October standardized tests, she also added Julie French and Janet Kremer.)

Early Committees

(1)	(2)	(3)
Larry	Janie	Andrew
William	Geraldine (secretary)	Stanley (chairman)
Oliver (secretary)	Edward	Alice
Gail	Frank	Norma
Mary (chairman)	Judy (chairman)	Harry
Jean	Julie	Mona
Robert		Esther

(4)	(5)	(Arithmetic Committee)
Mildred	Charles	Milton
Albert (chairman:	Roger (chairman)	Oliver
Sharon	Janet (chairman)	Gail
Marjorie	Russell	Albert
Ray	Milton	Geraldine
Carol	Helen	Mary
	John	

The rooming house a valuable but biased resource

Miss Johnson, Miss Huderle, who taught the eighth grade, and Miss Sandusky, who taught the kindergarten, roomed at the Gilbert home. Mrs. Gilbert, a middle-aged widow, was a good sport and teachers said it was fun to stay at her place. She allowed them kitchen privileges and they all planned to eat cooperatively after the first week.

Friday night after dinner, Marion had a get-acquainted chat with her new landlady. She learned that Mr. Gilbert had worked in the bank in Pleasant Valley until his death five years before. He had left her the home and sufficient money on which to live, but she welcomed the opportunity to supplement her income from her home. She was thrilled to find that Marion's father was a bank cashier also.

"I hear you've got that Littlejohn kid in your room this year," Mrs. Gilbert asked. "He's a little devil, they say."

"He's been good so far," Marion said defensively.

"Yes, he's good, all right and then he isn't good at all," Mrs. Gilbert answered professionally. "These poor kids from broken homes have a tough time. His mother should have known better than to marry his father. She came from a nice home. She had every opportunity. Her mother has told me many times how she warned her about that good-for-nothing Littlejohn. But she wouldn't listen. She fell in love head-over-heels. After he got her and got married to her, then she wasn't good enough for him. What that man didn't do."

While they were talking, Miss Huderle joined them. She said, "Mrs. Hammond seems awfully nice but somehow beaten up. I think she just feels ashamed of herself. She married Mr. Hammond

almost as soon after the divorce as she could, and he's really a nobody, although he's a nice enough man, I guess. But he's really
just a laborer over at the bottling works. He doesn't really amount
to anything. I don't know where he came from, but he's worked
around town for a long time. He's a good deal older than she is,
and he's a good enough provider, but he really hasn't anything."

Marion began to see that John Littlejohn's problem was a matter
of community concern. As the year went along, Marion found this
out more and more. Her problem in dealing with him was a far
greater one than merely adjusting him to a classroom situation.
She had to teach him to live with confidence and security in a
world where his chances of being hurt were very great. How much
more fortunate he would have been had his mother not been expected to be "somebody" among the young people in the community.

Two other children in Marion's room were from broken homes,
but apparently they were not the subject of community discussion.
Janie Flick's mother had been divorced two years ago and was
now living with her mother. During her marriage, she had lived in
the city where Mr. Flick was a prominent junior executive in a
large manufacturing establishment. Mrs. Flick received adequate
alimony and expense money for Janie. Gossip had it that the reasons back of the divorce were very similar to those in the case of
Mr. Littlejohn. Mrs. Flick was a quiet, competent, good-looking
woman who was devoting her life to her daughter and to a few
of the women's activities in Pleasant Valley. Janie was a very bright
little girl, well dressed, and well trained, and seemed secure, confident, and well adjusted. As nearly as Marion was ever able to find
out, there was no community disapproval of Mrs. Flick.

Larry Forsch's parents had also been divorced. Larry lived with
his father and his stepmother. Marion found it more difficult to
find out much about that divorce. The Forsches were not people
who were well known among those with whom Marion associated
It was said that his mother would not take care of the children,
that she drank and caroused, but Mr. Forsch's reputation was not
much better. The present Mrs. Forsch had been a waitress before
her marriage and then had worked in a war plant. She was the
mother of two young children who had not yet started school.
Larry seemed to be a normal boy—his I.Q. was measured at 99 in

the first grade. He was strong and extroverted, and, as far as Marion could see, well adjusted emotionally.

Marion saw that it was difficult to find simple answers to the causes of the children's difficulties. One of her sociology professors had pointed out the danger in relating delinquency and emotional disturbance to the presence of broken homes. The controlling factors involved, he had said, might not be in the broken home at all, but in a lot of things that may or may not go with it.

Planning the second week

Over the week end, Marion had time to plan her second week's work. The work so far had given her many leads. Her problem now was to get things going in such a way as to keep the majority in the room busy at useful learning experiences while she found time to diagnose individual differences and find learning experiences for those who were not able to work with the rest of the children, either because they were too far behind or too far ahead.

In the typical old-fashioned fourth-grade reading lesson, for example, the children open their books and, one after another, read to the teacher. Some children go so fast that the teacher criticizes them for their speed. Others read at a reasonable speed and with a few mistakes, but many will have difficulty with the typical basic fourth-grade reader, and some will read seldom and very haltingly. While one child is reading, in such classes, the other children are learning little or nothing. Those who can read well are wasting time watching the words someone else reads. Those who are unable to read lose interest and, if they are able, watch only close enough to keep the place while they hope they will not be called on. The fact is that they are seldom called on, for their reading is poor and irritating both to the class and to the teacher. Marion did not believe in this kind of wasteful teaching, and she had no intention of doing it. She hoped to plan so they would read for a purpose and would strive to understand because they needed what they were reading either for pleasure or information or both. She wanted them, *all* of them, to learn to enjoy reading rather than to detest it.

She intended to carry out the same plan in other subjects. She did not wish all children to work the same arithmetic problems because she knew if she did, she would be wasting the time of most of them. All this added up to the need for developing self-sustaining activities where children's interests, motives, and needs would carry them along, while she assisted first one and then the other. Three days, she knew, were not sufficient to get her class well organized along this line, particularly since it had been taught in a rather traditional, albeit kindly and friendly way the year before.

She was able, however, to see various possibilities. The children had shown a spontaneous interest in names that had led to a real interest and concern about the alphabet. This in turn had involved them in the study of the dictionary and the telephone book, and now gave promise of leading them out into the community, into a study of the map of the community and from there into various aspects of community life. The interest in their own names and in each other's names was closely related to their social interests. They were beginning to make notes on their cards about people whose names they found in their readers and their geographies. Some of them were learning a few things about how to make brief, pointed notes. They were learning to file alphabetically. They had experience in preparing cards in a more legible form for other members of the group to use, so that each one's card record of the whole class was in a sense a group product since each child had prepared his own card. The file boxes they were preparing for each row also were to be arranged alphabetically and each child's name would be on his individual folder. The maintenance of these folders, Marion hoped, would last through the year. She had great hopes for developing their interest in what went into these folders. From them she could develop self-evaluation. Through their interest in names, she knew that she could keep them busy with silent and work-type reading, with writing, and with various other projects that would carry them along without constant prodding and domination on her part.

The children had also shown much interest in the mechanics of running a meeting according to some rule or discipline. They had already collected much information about how to hold meetings, and Marion felt sure they would develop great skill in conducting meetings, in having a secretary who would keep minutes, and in making some sort of group decisions both on a voting and on a consensus basis. At first, however, she was concerned with setting up conditions under which children would assume more and more responsibility in classroom management. The main reason for this was to give practice in the processes of democracy, including the simple responsibilities that teachers so frequently burden themselves with, never realizing that while such routine is time-consuming drudgery to them, it is highly interesting and educational to children. Her secondary reason was to free herself from the routine and the policing duties that occupy most of the attention of some teachers, so that she could perform more of the highly professional duties that she was trained to do. She realized soon that there would be some members of the class who would find it extremely hard to learn these new procedures or to keep at any one activity for any sustained length of time. There could be no "perfectly" organized class, but there could be genuine adult tasks, however small, for everyone.

She hoped to bring the classroom into close contact with the community. A start was being made here in going to the store for boxes, going to the bank and other places for maps, and in seeking information at home about the use of the alphabet in the outside world and about the rules of order for running meetings. These were preliminary activities, however, and merely icebreakers as far as Marion's ultimate plans were concerned.

In preparing her work for Monday, Marion secured some large sheets of white wrapping paper upon which the children could draw maps in groups. She secured six rules each 18 inches long and some dividers from the supply department in the principal's office. There was a science kit in the storeroom and from this she secured a bar magnet and provided herself with a needle and a cord and some glasses for water. One of the science pamphlets told about how to make a classroom compass and she intended to introduce this experiment at the same time the children located north on their maps, to test their interest and backgrounds in science. They would also examine some of the maps in the map case at that time to see where north was. Some of the brighter ones could try to study about north on the globe, too. She thought they could have some fun with puzzles such as, "Where on the earth could two men both walking straight north bump into one another face to face?" "Where on the earth can you suddenly change from going north and start going south without turning around?"

She dropped into a filling station and secured free of charge several copies of the map of the state and of the surrounding states, and going by the lumber yard, she had an inspiration and walked in and asked the manager for some floor plans that might no longer be usable. The lumber yard manager was very interested and asked Marion many questions about why she wanted this material. She was able to enlist his interest and a promise to come to school some time and explain how new buildings are built. In the course of their conversation, he mentioned that they had some blueprints suitable for use in constructing lawn furniture, kitchen cabinets, and various other items around the home. He provided her with copies of much of this material. He also had some plans for building outside grills of brick, mortar, and stone, and he had some samples of painted bits of wood to demonstrate different colored paints, and had various samples of woods of all kinds. Marion didn't feel able to carry all the things that he offered her, and she asked him to save them for her, but he promised instead to deliver them at school himself on Monday morning.

Marion knew that the University maintained an air field about six miles from Pleasant Valley, so she telephoned there to see if they had any aerial photographs or prints of aerial photographs that might show the topography of the surrounding country from the air. The people at the University said that they could let her have some that had been used for training purposes, and she made arrangements to have them left for her at Peterson's Restaurant on Main Street. She had a last inspiration along the line of maps and charts. She examined some of the educational magazines in the teachers' library and discovered plans for school buildings and classroom furniture layouts, drawn to scale so that they could be used as examples of classroom maps or school maps.

More study of individual pupils

It was Marion's intention to find time to work with some of the children at both extremes of ability in an effort to discover individual interests or abilities of the children that might contribute to the total classroom situation and serve as motivational spring boards from which learning for all might take place. At one extreme she was interested in children like Albert, Julie, Judy, Milton, and Janie.

An examination of the third-grade reading scores showed that Janie, Jean, Milton, Oliver, Carol, Andrew, Gail, Albert, and Mary were reading from one and one-half to four and one-half grades above their grade level. It was obvious that if these children were really reading so much above their own grade level, it would be a waste of time under ordinary circumstances to ask them to do much formal reading with the other children since it could do little but bore them and waste their time.

At the other extreme there were the Knott twins, Esther and Frank, both with first-grade I.Q.'s of 99, but Esther was achieving at about average, while Frank was decidedly below average. There was Charles Murphy with a first grade I.Q. of 89, whose reading in the third grade was below the first-grade level in comprehension. There was William Toole with an I.Q. of 95 in the first grade and Harry Clarkson with an I.Q. of 94 in the first grade, both of whom were reading in the third grade at or below the first-grade level. Sharon Pogue with an I.Q. of 120 in the first grade was reading below third-grade level. There were those who seldom or never participated, such as Ray and Robert, and there was Edward with an I.Q. of 72.

She wanted a chance during the second week to hear these children read, to listen to them talk, to see them try some simple arithmetic in order to place their abilities. Even more important, because it was more difficult, she wanted to discover their interests and motives. She wanted to find out things they were able to do that would benefit them and provide practice in learning things they should learn. She knew that some of those of low ability in her classroom would probably be very ordinary workers in the adult world, and she knew that some of those with high ability in her classroom might be the future professional and business leaders of their community. She knew that she could not reasonably expect all of them to do, learn, and appreciate the same things. She knew, too, that double promotions or accelerated programs for the brighter children and failure and retention for the slower children would not reduce the range of abilities in the various classrooms. She knew that the older these children got, the more difficult they would be. Hence, time, even double-time in a grade, would not serve to bring them up to some imaginary standards. She knew that the only alternative left to her was to find out what their abilities were, what their interests were, what their needs were, and what the best judgment was concerning what they should be able to learn and to go on from there. She knew, finally, that she could not tell for sure which were the dullards and which the potential leaders. She had read of too many cases where serious errors had been made in such cases, even when based on careful testing.

Miss Johnson considers her objectives

Thus Miss Johnson began the development of her fourth-grade units. Her objectives she drew from the curriculum that had been given her to use, from her own conviction that education should be based on the broad basic objective of human welfare, and from her insight into the purposes of education as she had worked them out at college. The local curriculum outline stated the general objectives under four categories—physical, social, intellectual, and ethical—under one or more of which there were specific references to individual health, and health and safety for all; skills and techniques in the worthy use of leisure; freedoms and responsibilities; worthy group membership; wholesome human relations; mastery of the common and necessary knowledge and skill for effective living; critical, discriminating thinking and problem-solving; curiosity and interest and their satisfaction; the development of ideals; and the appreciation of beauty, truth, justice, freedom, and a respect for the opinions of all.

These were valid objectives though she would have stated them differently and expanded them somewhat. She wanted to be more explicit in her statement of attitudes, somewhat as follows: cooperation, appreciation of each other, high standards of workmanship set by each one for himself and by the group for the group, thoroughness the same way, application, curiosity, tolerance, resourcefulness, open-mindedness, and scientific attitude.

In mentioning skill objectives, she also wanted something more definite: skill in using sources of information—books, pictures, maps, magazines, newspapers, radio, excursions, and the like. The variety of communication and aesthetic skills needed more extensive enumeration—dramatization, oral and written reports, letter writing, pageantry, costuming, use of clay, paint, wood, tools, paper—as media of expression, in addition to handwriting, arithmetic, and an ever-to-be-increased skill in all kinds of reading.

Objectives intertwined with the psychology of learning

She believed that finding and developing goals is essential to real learning, that fragmentized learning is ineffective, and that processes and skills must be used in the effort to attain goals if they are to be effectively learned; that learning must involve invention and discovery by the learner, rather than being limited to memorizing things that others have already learned or discovered; and that what is learned must be organized and interrelated, generalized about, and tested for its worth. She planned her units to take advantage of these well-established principles of learning, instead of depending upon mechanical, verbal, memoriter mastery of assignments.

Administrative prescriptions affect the curriculum

In the Pleasant Valley outline, the fourth grade was the first year in which the children moved beyond the study of their more immediate home, church, and school neighborhood into the broader world of the city, county, state, and (in general terms) the whole world.

The time schedule (suggested) for the fourth grade gave a daily 120 minutes to the social studies *and science,* 100 minutes to the language arts, 40 minutes to health, safety, and physical education, 40 minutes to mathematics, and 45 minutes to crafts, art and music, and other aesthetic experience. Marion knew, of course, that it was psychologically impossible to break up a day in this fashion, but she felt that she could carry out its spirit and felt free to try, since the outline made clear that it was a suggestion only.

Three possible learning units appeared to be growing

She thought that the units themselves might ultimately shape themselves into three studies:

(1) A study of group management
(2) A study of the community
(3) A study of world background

Social competence in
working as a group

Miss Johnson wanted her classroom to have an atmosphere of freedom under mutually agreed upon rules and to have the pupils participate in setting goals, in planning to reach them, and in evaluating the effectiveness of efforts to carry out plans and reach goals. She wanted all children to feel at ease, to succeed according to their abilities, and to be free of the fear of failure to achieve as well as others. She wanted to develop group loyalty and pride, and the social skills and attitudes essential to democratic living.

Children's interests easily lead
to the community and its resources

For the social studies subject matter in the first units that she hoped to develop, she planned to draw on the civic, social, scientific, economic, and industrial resources of the community. She planned to lead out into the community first through a search for help in "running meetings," selecting officers, working in committees, and the like. This was an interest that had seemed real to the children as the first week's work had progressed. She hoped to bring parents into her room to tell the children how to be a chairman, a secretary, a committee member, and so forth. Before the parents came, the children would work hard to decide what to ask, how to ask it, how to take notes, and other things. Then there might be a visit to a school board meeting, a city council meeting, a labor union meeting, a bank directors' meeting, a parent-teachers' meeting, a co-op meeting, or any other meetings that they might discover. Many letters would be written inviting, thanking, and asking for information; and many oral interviews would be made.

The interest in names might also lead out into the community. The pupils might find a Scandinavian parent, for example, who would visit them some day and tell them what the "son" and "datter" meant at the end of their names. Or it might be a Scot (if one could be found, and the search would be fun) who could tell what "Mac" meant. These people from other lands could at the same time tell the children many other interesting things about the old country, the trip to America, and so forth. This type of activity could easily lead to the construction of a map of the world with ribbons springing from Pleasant Valley (and its fourth grade) to nations far away, and to invitations from immigrants and world tourists in the community to come and tell about distant places.

Names also could lead into a study of the history of the locality and the state—who the first settlers were, their names and nationalities, and the waves of immigration. Much of this information could be obtained from the Mayor's Council on Human Relations in the nearby city, from the county and state historical societies, and other similar bodies. The local newspaper office would be plumbed for historical data.

The children's interest in fairness in the classroom in the distribution of books could lead, too, to a study of fairness in the community. Fair laws, fair traffic courtesy, fair treatment for all groups, and fair law enforcement.

The children's immediate interest in the alphabetical street arrangement and in the preparation of a map of the town would easily lead to the location on it of the various community industries and businesses. The pattern of community development would emerge from this. A model community made to scale might be constructed if it caught the interest of the children. Then the industries and businesses could be studied. The bottling works offered a fine chance to talk about state health rules, pure food laws, sterilizing, preservatives, and mechanical shortcuts. Here would be science, health, and social science combined! There were other businesses to study, too. The lumber yard, the power plant, creamery, monument works, telephone office, butcher shop, barber shop, bakery, garage, cooperative market and warehouse, and wholesale oil company.

A study of the names of streets, and the names on the fronts of some of the old buildings in town might lead by another avenue to a study of the people who built the town and county—the history of the pioneers.

Health and safety would easily become a part of such work. The factor of traffic safety could be introduced while a study of the map and the location of businesses was being undertaken. An actual traffic count by students might work in here and what an opportunity to motivate arithmetic if that should catch their interest! The doctors and dentists would certainly be interviewed, and the services of the local hospital studied. The children could formulate a set of rules concerning what fourth-graders should do in case of accidents of various kinds. (1) Call for adult help—police, doctor, parents, teacher, depending upon when and where the accident occurred. (2) Simple first aid. (3) Electric wires to be feared and other hazards to be avoided. This certainly would get cooperation from the Civil Defense Authorities as valuable whenever the threat of war was on the horizon.

Science information would come in on all points. Health could provide many openings here—the clinical thermometer, the stethoscope, and vaccination and other immunizations. The Junior Red Cross would be a valuable resource here. Then the students could turn their attentions to industry in the community. In addition to the bottling works, there was the granite industry. There an introduction could be made to geology. Fossils, crystallization, stone cutting, and the health hazard of silicosis could be studied. Insofar as safety was concerned, the identification and dangers of dynamite caps could be learned.

The creamery should provide a multitude of interesting science experiences. Milk, butterfat content, cream, pasteurization, souring, bacteria, and cheese cultures might be a few. The centrifugal butterfat tester would likely be of interest to children. In all this, there were countless mathematical possibilities. Marion sighed as she dreamed up the outlines of her resource units. "How much I'll learn myself," she thought. She knew little or nothing except "words" about granite and quarries, and pasteurization, and cheese, and yogurt, and her knowledge of bottling was limited to opening bottles and reading about the dangers to humans of certain types of food preservatives.

The study of the creamery would lead out to the farms around Pleasant Valley, to the dairy herds, the forage crops, the silos, the tractors, the farm homes, all the farm animals, and to conservation, to man's dependence on his environment and his need to take care of it—to interdependence of man and environment and to interdependence of all people such as the farmers in the country and the workers in the city.

In all this, Marion knew that her children would develop and learn literally thousands of valuable attitudes, abilities, problem-solving techniques, and facts and skills. She knew that planning was necessary in order that mastery of the facts and skills be made a conscious motive and goal. She felt that perhaps half of each day could be spent profitably in concentrated work devoted to skill subjects, the need for which should spring from group activities. She knew, too, that *some important skills* and the chance to use and learn them *might not grow out of the units as they developed and that these should be taught and maintained without reference to the unit.*

The individual differences in the class
set the curriculum patterns

She needed, as soon as possible, to learn more about the individual interests and hobbies of her pupils and their ability levels in various areas. She had some knowledge of these factors already. She knew the third-grade reading scores and who had received A in mathematics in the third grade. She knew about Albert's high mathematical ability, the verbal ability and extroversion of Mary, Andrew, Janie, Gail, Jean, and Milton and to a lesser extent Oliver, and Judy, and Geraldine. These were the talkers, the ones who raised their hands. Julie, too, also had high verbal ability and a high first-grade I.Q., but she was very quiet.

She knew something about the occupations of a few of the parents and about their homes, socio-economic status, and the like, but for the vast majority she had little to go on but first impressions. She had to get acquainted.

She had to learn soon about who could draw, paint, sing, play musical instruments, run, jump, throw, dance, sew and weave, make things with tools, make rhymes and odd sounds, who had lived in or traveled to distant places, knew foreign languages, rode horseback, delivered papers, or had coin, or stamp, or butterfly collections—and all the other things that the cumulative record should show, but didn't.

These were things she had to know before she could really assist the children in planning units in terms of their needs and abilities. She had her plans made to start learning. Each child now had a file holder in which he would put things of interest to himself. These were the files that were to be kept in the boxes at the ends of the rows. They would be open to inspection by other children and by Miss Johnson at any time their use was necessary.

She had some notes of her own, too, in a set of confidential file folders that she was building up. These were in addition to the permanent individual folders that would pass on from grade to grade. Marion wanted a file where she could put notes about each child as she made important observations. For example, Helen Thompson's mother was mentally ill, had delusions of persecution, and it was sometimes feared she might harm other members of her family. Under such conditions it would take unusual human understanding to help Helen meet the problems facing her as an immature and inexperienced child. There was a note too on Roger Schorn, who volunteered sometimes, but who giggled nervously as he talked and seemed under tension when he became the center of attention in his learning group. As these notes accumulated in the file, a fund of information of the type she needed would gradually be built up.

Official curriculum outlines as a resource

In addition to the local curriculum outline already mentioned, the State Guides for instruction proved to be most valuable. The general guide had a chapter on "Using Community Resources in Learning" [4] that was very helpful. A 14-page outline had one column devoted to sources of community information and a parallel column devoted to suggestions for coordinating school and community activities. As a book salesman might say it, "The suggestion that the names of the winners at the local fair would provide a list of resource people was worth the price of the book!" These pages became an important part of the resources on the community that she was building up.

In a chapter on "Helpful Information for the Elementary Teacher" she found suggestions for evaluating pupil progress under

[4] *A Guide for Better Instruction in Minnesota Schools.* St. Paul: State of Minnesota, Department of Education, 1946, pp. 147-167, 179-197, Chapter IX.

each of the following headings: careful observation, records by former teachers, informal teacher tests, standards set up on a pupil-teacher cooperative basis, group and individual progress charts, standardized tests, and promotion policies (the futility of expecting good results from non-promotion). Marion was a bit shocked by the warning she found against placing workbooks in the hands of all pupils for group work. She had assumed that all teachers were familiar with this danger. She liked the last chapter on "Significant Curriculum Trends." It made her feel professional, experimental, alert.

In the State Guide for Social Studies in the Elementary Schools, Miss Johnson found a chapter on "The Student Council in the Elementary Grades." She studied this carefully, as she wished her room to assume more and more of its own management. She thought that many of the suggestions for activities for a student council were not significant enough really to challenge pupils, but she found an excellent set of "Questions and Answers Relative to Rules of Order for Children's Meetings." [5] It was just what she needed, and it was written simply enough for some of the better readers in the grade to read for themselves. The suggestions on map use were also very valuable.[6] The State Guide in Arithmetic [7] strongly emphasized the need for caring for individual differences and the futility of trying to assign the same work to all pupils on the assumption that grade standards could be preserved.[8] Particular stress was given to the importance of mental age in assaying ability with numbers.[9] She found throughout the bulletin many good suggestions on the objectives, methods, materials, and the use of arithmetic in reaching goals real to the pupils.

In the State Curriculum Bulletin on Guidance,[10] the chapter on "Guidance in the Elementary School" proved to be another curriculum resource. She found support for her plan for cumulative folders

[5] *A Guide for Instruction in the Social Studies.* St. Paul: State of Minnesota, Department of Education, 1949, pp. 41-44.

[6] *Ibid.*, pp. 22-35, 80-93.

[7] *A Guide for Instruction in Arithmetic.* St. Paul: State of Minnesota, Department of Education, 1948.

[8] *Ibid.*, pp. 7, 8, 9.

[9] *Ibid.*, pp. 21-23.

[10] *Guidance Services for Minnesota Schools.* St. Paul: State of Minnesota, Department of Education, 1951, pp. 29-32.

for the teacher's use, though she had gone even further in having another set for the pupils' use. She intended to use a sociogram very soon, as an outgrowth of the name cards the pupils had prepared. There was a brief description of that technique in the bulletin,[11] though she preferred the treatment in the 85-page pamphlet, Sociometry in Group Relations,[12] which she had in her files.

The State Guide for Instruction in Art [13] was another valuable resource. She regretted that it was not a wider treatment—a guide to aesthetic experiences in general, for the arts are not to be separated from one another any more than from the other areas of living. There were suggestions for the use of art in a community survey [14] and in democratic experience. Many of the suggestions for art materials were novel to Marion, and inexpensive.[15] A page [16] on what "child art is" and what "child art is not" was thought-provoking and reassuring to a teacher with Marion's convictions.

Curriculum resources upon which Miss Johnson planned to draw

As background for herself in approaching the study of the community, she reviewed again material she had collected for her own use, such as How to Know, How to Use, Your Community [17] and Field Trips—Suggestions for Plans and Procedures.[18] She also used as resource units the Unit of Work on Community Life [19] and the Unit of Work on Home, School and Neighborhood Life [20] from the

---

11 Ibid., pp. 31-32.

12 Jennings, Sociometry in Group Relations.

13 A Guide for Instruction in Art. St. Paul: State of Minnesota, Department of Education, 1948.

14 Ibid., pp. 46-49.

15 Ibid., pp. 55-79.

16 Ibid., p. 14.

17 Committee on Community Study of the Department of Elementary School Principals, How to Know, How to Use, Your Community. Washington, D. C.: National Education Association, 1941-42.

18 Katherine V. Bishop, Field Trips—Suggestions for Plans and Procedures. Garvey, California: Garvey School District, 1951.

19 Ruth Newby, et al., Unit of Work on Community Life. Pasadena, California: Pasadena City Schools, Elementary Curriculum Department, 1948.

20 Ruth Newby, et al., Unit of Work on Home, School and Neighborhood Life.

Pasadena Schools. Though these were prepared for the primary grades, there were countless suggestions in them suitable for all levels of ability.

Also from Pasadena was a *Unit of Work on the Food Market* [21] prepared by second-grade teachers. This contained many ideas that she could adapt to the study of any business or activity in the community. These lower-grade units would prove of special value in dealing with the slow readers and the children who were immature for their grade, as she sought to adjust activities to their individual differences—("Take them where they are and go on from there.") [22] Valuable suggestions on a plane suitable for slower children were also to be found in her copy of *Social Studies, Primary Grades* [23] from Omaha.

Very suggestive as to community study was *Improving the Quality of Living—A Study of Community Schools in the South*,[24] prepared at Peabody College. It was full of illustrations of how pupils and parents could come to grips with day-to-day problems covering food, shelter, and survival.

Marion had in her file *The Curriculum Plan for the Utopian Public Schools* [25] prepared by a class of which a friend of hers was a member at the University of Oregon. This bulletin discussed the physical, mental, social, and emotional traits of children and the various subject-matter experiences in terms of factors operative in four periods of development—post-infancy, pre-adolescent, adolescent, and post-adolescent. She also had *The Teaching of Current Events*,[26] *How Are We Doing?* [27] and *Sources for Free and Inexpens-*

Pasadena, California: Pasadena City Schools, Elementary Curriculum Department, 1948.

21 Ruth Newby, *et al.*, *Unit of Work on the Food Market*. Pasadena, California: Pasadena City Schools, Elementary Curriculum Department, 1948.

22 Ruth Newby, *et al.*, *Unit of Work on the Farm*. Pasadena, California: Pasadena City Schools, Elementary Curriculum Department, 1949.

23 Omaha Public Schools, *Social Studies, Primary Grades*, Curriculum Bulletin No. 1. Omaha, Nebraska: Board of Education, 1949.

24 W. K. McCharen, *Improving the Quality of Living*. Nashville, Tennessee: George Peabody College for Teachers, 1947.

25 Hugh B. Wood, ed., *The Curriculum Plan for the Utopian Public Schools*. Eugene, Oregon: University Cooperative Store, 1949.

26 Hugh B. Wood, ed., *The Teaching of Current Events*. Eugene, Oregon: University of Oregon, 1950.

27 Hugh B. Wood, ed., *How Are We Doing?* Eugene, Oregon: University Cooperative Store, 1950.

ive Teaching Materials.[28] From the University of Minnesota, she had a *Bibliography of Lists and Sources of Free and Inexpensive Learning Materials.*[29]

She also had a fine field trip bulletin from the St. Paul, Minnesota, Public Schools.[30] This gave her many ideas of how she might enlist the constructive cooperation of local institutions.

A bulletin of the schools of Springfield, Massachusetts, on *Contributions of the Elementary Schools to the City-wide Program of Education for Democratic Citizenship* [31] told briefly how schools there, including the middle grades, had utilized the community for the purpose named in the title. Also highly suggestive was *A Study of Community Needs* [32] from Newark, New Jersey. In it, she found listed many sources of information about the community, some of which she might have missed, such as the welfare offices, state and local youth agencies, State Board of Guardians, insurance companies, milk inspection officials, and many others. It also suggested techniques for community study.

The Indianapolis Social Studies Program, Grades 1-6, had nine pages for grades three and four on "Expanding Community Life" [33] with suggested activities, teaching procedures, topics (very valuable to Marion), and available materials. There was also much useful material in *Course of Study, Fourth Grade, Social Studies Supplement* [34] from Dallas, which showed how the teacher might include, within a unit on transportation, the various fourth-grade areas of learning.

The development of competence in the physical, biological, and social sciences requires an open mind. The bulletins prepared in

[28] Hugh B. Wood, ed., *Sources for Free and Inexpensive Teaching Materials.* Eugene, Oregon: University of Oregon, 1949.

[29] Arthur Adkins, *Bibliography of Lists and Sources of Free and Inexpensive Learning Materials.* Minneapolis: University of Minnesota, Curriculum Workshop for the Experimental Schools, 1949.

[30] Warren Panushka, *This Is Your Town, A Field Trip Handbook.* St. Paul: Curriculum Bulletin No. 43, St. Paul Public Schools, 1951.

[31] *Contributions of the Elementary Schools to the City-wide Program of Education for Democratic Citizenship.* Springfield, Massachusetts: Springfield Public Schools.

[32] *A Study of Community Needs.* Newark, New Jersey: The Curriculum Improvement Program, 1941.

[33] *Indianapolis Social Studies Program, Grades 1-6.* Indianapolis, 1948.

[34] *Course of Study, Fourth Grade, Social Studies Supplement.* Dallas, Texas: Dallas Independent School District, 1947, p. 9.

The Open Mindedness Study [35] in the Philadelphia Public Schools were one of Marion's resources here. They contain illustrations of how teachers used classroom statements or incidents to motivate valuable lessons, as when children fought over a reference book, when a boy said that all politicians are grafters, or when another said that Chinese children were funny because they write "backwards."

To Marion, without an extensive science background, her most valuable science curriculum resource was the *Course of Study in Science* from Chicago.[36] Six units were suggested for the third grade on (1) plants and animals supply necessities, (2) water, its forms and uses, (3) animals need protection, (4) air, (5) birds, and (6) machines. The important things to Marion in this bulletin were the many pages of information *for the teacher only*—literally hundreds of romantic and exciting bits of information that could be used to interest children and lead them to adopt scientific attitudes and habits of thought. "Contrary to common belief, a porcupine does not throw its quills," "The bee dies after stinging its enemy," "The shell of the snail is formed from a secretion from the soft part of its body," "Frogs remain dormant . . . and their body machinery seems to stop completely," "Some of the finer grades of [hog] intestines are used to seal the tops of perfume bottles," "Gelatin, obtained from the calf's head, is prepared as a stiffener for ice cream and fancy foods." There was an interesting comparison of birds, bats, airplanes, and kites (hollow bones, for example) and material about thermometers, air, and air currents. Many references and teaching activities were mentioned.

The Chicago fourth-grade *Course of Study in Science* [37] was similarly organized and equally valuable. Subjects for units were "Insects and Spiders," "Changes in Plants," "The Sun, Moon, Stars and Planets," "The Earth in Motion," "How 28 Different Animals Are Fitted for Their Environment," "Plant Study," and "Magnets."

---

[35] This series, prepared by the Philadelphia Public Schools, Curriculum Office, contains the following titles: *Open Mindedness Can Be Taught* (1949); *Toward the Open Mind* (1950); *Creating Good Climate* (1950); *Making Decisions* (1950); *Thinking Critically* (1950); and *Building Desirable Values* (1950).

[36] *Course of Study in Science*. Chicago: Bureau of Curriculum, Board of Education, Chicago Public Schools, 1944.

[37] *Course of Study in Science for Grade Four*. Chicago: Bureau of Curriculum, Board of Education, Chicago Public Schools, 1944.

Hundreds of unusual bits of knowledge for the teacher regarding all of these areas were invaluable and the suggestions for activities were very good too.

Of assistance for science ideas was the March-May 1951 issue of the *Baltimore Bulletin of Education* [38] which was devoted to science at all levels. An article on "Science in the Elementary Program" suggested how individual differences in interest and ability may actually be an asset in the science program. "Children do not select interests from a vacuum." [39] "Children studying the Panama Canal may feel the need for learning the life cycle of the mosquito. . . ." The article on "Science at Work" among other things gave meaningful suggestions on such items as how to capitalize on pupils' lead questions. It is not necessary that the teacher know the answers. They all can search together. When a light bulb is replaced in the classroom, why does the bulb no longer burn? There was the story of an interesting study of pigeons by an opportunity class. [40]

Another pamphlet from Philadelphia, *Science—An Approach in the Elementary School*,[41] contained this jewel, ". . . we aren't teaching science at all unless we show people how to look for answers to questions they really care about." This pamphlet suggests how to find the questions children do care about, and approach these questions scientifically.

Two resources indicative of the immediate concern that science has for all children were *Garden Enemies* published by the University of Kentucky Bureau of School Service under a Sloan Foundation grant, and *Tales from the Salvage Can* by the University of Vermont, also under a Sloan grant.

Many ideas on how to locate science materials in rural areas and small towns, how to discover children's interests, how to use the resources "across the way and down the road," and how science enriches rural living, Marion found in *Science Teaching in Rural and Small Town Schools*,[42] prepared in the United States Office of

[38] *Baltimore Bulletin of Education*, Vol. XXVIII, No. 4, March-May 1951.
[39] *Ibid.*, 4-7.
[40] *Ibid.*, 7-12.
[41] *Science—An Approach in the Elementary School*. Philadelphia: Philadelphia Public Schools, Curriculum Office, 1945.
[42] *Science Teaching in Rural and Small Town Schools*, Bulletin No. 5. Washington. D. C.: Office of Education, Federal Security Agency, 1949.

454 MARION JOHNSON—TEACHER

Education. A fourth-grade unit of real value was one on spring planting, with an actual day-to-day diary of what the class did, including letter writing for materials and the planning for a classroom visit by the county agent.

Training Young Hands in Modern Living [43] dealt with plans for home economics and industrial arts experiences in the upper grades in Chicago. It contained many ideas that Marion could adapt to the work benches and tables in her room for boys and girls— balanced meals, care of kitchen equipment, use of plastics, basketry, soap carving, ceramics, and so forth.

Mathematics as Learned and Used in the Seattle Public Schools, while written in 1943, contained excellent aids and suggestions. Marion was interested in all the material for grades one through six, since she was sure she had that great a range of ability in her classroom. The pictures were suggestive of many arithmetic activities that she could work into the units she hoped to develop—"Pecks and Bushels," "Measures of Distance," and "Body Temperature." She found the suggestions on the content of a high-school course in general mathematics to be practical and real for middle-grade children, as were some of the suggestions for high-school laboratory and shop mathematics and for "materials of instruction."

Stimulating instructional materials of many kinds
are necessary to sustain and develop interest
and guide activity

In the library room Marion found some fine material for her reading table. Later, she hoped the children would explore the library for pertinent materials. For alphabet and dictionary practice, she selected a very simple book, five by eight inches in size, called *Railroad A B C,*[44] and, much larger, the *A B C and Counting Book.*[45] These were on a pre-primer reading level. She selected *My First Dictionary,*[46] a delightful picture dictionary with a second-

[43] *Training Young Hands for Modern Living,* Curriculum Brochure No. 1. Chicago: Bureau of Curriculum, Board of Education, Chicago Public Schools, 1949.
[44] *Railroad A B C.* New York: Franklin Watts, Inc., 1948.
[45] Phyllis Frazer, *A B C and Counting Book.* New York: Wonder Books, 1946.
[46] Laura Oftedahl, and Nina Jacobs, *My First Dictionary—The Beginners Pic-*

or easy third-grade vocabulary. Another find was the colorful *The Golden Encyclopedia*,[47] 12 by 18 inches in size, with 125 pages of pictures. Here there were many brief articles about things her children would wish to know, such as maps, music, aircraft, farming, food, games, history, Indians, insects, fish, magnets, mammals, and man. The article on names fell in with the class interest. Glancing at it, Marion learned for the first time the meaning or reason for the two surnames seen in the Spanish. She also found references to alphabetical order and dictionary usage in other elementary textbooks besides those used as basic in her grade. She selected a number of these at various grade levels.[48]

Her best find on names in the library was *People Are Important* [49] by Eva Knox Evans. She found that this was a very interesting and highly factual book written in easy fourth-grade language about things fourth-graders love to know. One chapter dealt with names, and the whole book was full of important information on how to establish good human relations.

In her search for materials on parliamentary law, Marion found two books on a junior high-school level, both old. She thought they might interest some of the good readers.[50] She also found some textbooks that had simple illustrations of club meetings.[51]

Marion also located a dictionary of names. She borrowed the *Webster's New International Dictionary, Unabridged*, in which first names could be found with their meanings. She had the telephone

---

ture Word Book, Laboratory Schools, University of Chicago. New York: Grosset & Dunlap, 1948.

[47] Dorothy A. Bennett, *The Golden Encyclopedia*. New York: Simon & Schuster, Inc., 1946.

[48] Mabel E. Simpson and Mary A. Adams, *Growth in English*, Book One, Part Two. New York: Newson and Company, 1934, pp. 184-5, 212.

[49] Eva Knox Evans, *People Are Important*. New York: Capital Publishing Co., Inc., 1951.

[50] Alta B. Hall and Alice Fleenor Sturgis, *Textbook on Parliamentary Law*. New York: The Macmillan Company, 1923; Emma M. Wines and Marjory W. Card, *Come to Order*. Garden City, New York: Doubleday, Doran and Company, Inc., 1930.

[51] Harry G. Paul, Isabel Kincheloc, and J. W. Ramsay, *Junior Units in English*, New York: Lyons and Carnahan, 1940, pp. 36-49; Mildred A. Dawson and Jonnie Washburne Miller, *Language for Daily Use—Grade 4*, New York: World Book Company, 1948, p. 154; Mildred A. Dawson and Jonnie Washburne Miller, *Language for Daily Use—Grade 5*, Yonkers, New York: World Book Company, 1948, pp. 192-200.

books that had been previously brought. In the library she had found a copy of *Robert's Rules of Order* and she had found as well some other books that contained information about how young people should conduct meetings.

Since Marion wanted to stimulate interest in science, she was glad to find *The Big Book of Real Trucks*,[52] 12 by 18 inches, that told in simple words and colored illustrations about gooseneck trailers, tank trucks, diesel freighters, airport fire trucks, automobile carriers, concrete mixers, and many other vehicles that the children would like to read about. To make it better, the book ended with diagrams and simple explanations of what makes a gasoline truck engine operate. *The Story of Sound* [53] told what sound was— discussed church bells, bands, violins, tuning forks, pipes, door bells, comb music, the whirr of wings, running water, thunder, and told how and why Indians listened with an ear to the ground, how sailors make soundings, and many other interesting things about sound. She found the "Encyclopaedia Britannica Picture Stories" in two series of twelve books each—the *True Nature Series*,[54] and the *World's Children Stories*.   These were fine, colorful, authentic nature and geographic booklets. *Tools for Andy* [56] and *Tim and the Tool Chest* [57] were books with easy lower-grade vocabularies designed to catch and hold the interest of youngsters who like to make things.

[52] George J. Jaffo, *The Big Book of Real Trucks*. New York: Grosset & Dunlap, 1950.

[53] James Geralton, *The Story of Sound*. New York: Harcourt, Brace & Company, Inc., 1948.

[54] Britannica Encyclopaedia, *True Nature Series*, "Animals of the Woods," "Gray Squirrel," "Snapping Turtle," "Water Birds," "Black Bear Twins," "Three Little Kittens," "Pride, the Saddle Horse," "Shep, the Farm Dog," "Goats and Kids," "Adventures of Bunny Rabbit," "Animals of the Farm," "Elephants." New York: Encyclopaedia Britannica Press, 1946.

[55] Britannica Encyclopaedia, *World's Children Stories*, "Mateo and the Mexican Fair," "Anaghalook, Eskimo Girl," "Dark Eyes and Her Navajo Blanket," "Shin Ming, Chinese Boy Scout," "French Canadian Children," "A Day With Dutch Children," "Hans of the Swiss Alps," "Pedro Picks Coffee in Brazil," "Yukiko and a Japanese Carnival," "Children on England's Canals," "Kana, Prince of Darkest Africa," "Pauli and His Hawaiian Feast." New York: Encyclopaedia Britannica Press, 1947.

[56] James S. Tippett, *Tools for Andy*. New York: Abingdon-Cokesbury Press, 1951.

[57] Jerrold Beim, *Tim and the Tool Chest*. New York: William Morrow & Company, 1951.

The Noisy Book [58] told of a little dog who heard and tried to identify many noises. Through the interest it might arouse, Marion hoped to involve the children in the "sound" world around them, and from there stimulate real interest in both science and music (a partnership that extends through all kinds of music education). Other books that she found helpful in this respect were *The Merry Fiddlers,*[59] a story primarily of crickets, though other animals play minor roles; *Song of the Swallows,*[60] a story of Capistrano; *Ruby Throat,*[61] the story of a hummingbird; *Stories that Sing;* [62] and the delightful *Cow Concert,*[63] the story of the little Swiss girl who in her dream taught her cows to ring their cow bells (as the Swiss bell ringers do), to play the Blue Danube and other Strauss waltzes as she stood in the barn and directed them.

To interest the girls in science, and in other things too, she found *A Child's First Cook Book* [64] for girls from age seven to twelve, and *The Junior Party Book* [65] with suggestions for parties on all occasions. For both boys and girls, to help build an interest in graphic art, she found numerous books by Amy Hogeboom from which she selected six.[66] She selected for general reading *Indians and Cowboys,*[67] *Daniel in the Cub Scout Den,*[68] and *You and the Constitution of the United States.*[69]

[58] Margaret Wise Brown, *The Noisy Book.* New York: Harper and Brothers, 1939.

[59] Alice E. Goudey, *The Merry Fiddlers,* Aladdin Books. New York: American Book Company, 1951.

[60] Leo Politi, *Song of the Swallows.* New York: Charles Scribner's Sons, 1949.

[61] Robert M. McCluny, *Ruby Throat,* Morrow Junior Books. New York: William Morrow & Company, 1950.

[62] Ethel Crowinshield, *Stories That Sing.* Boston: Boston Music Company, 1945.

[63] Earle Goodenow, *Cow Concert.* New York: Alfred A. Knopf, Inc., 1951.

[64] Alma S. Lack, *A Child's First Cook Book.* New York: Henry Holt & Company, Inc., 1950.

[65] Bernice Wells Carlson, *The Junior Party Book.* New York: Abingdon-Cokesbury Press, 1948.

[66] The six chosen by Marion were *Forest Animals and How to Draw Them* (1950); *Wild Animals and How to Draw Them* (1947); *Dogs and How to Draw Them* (1944); *Birds and How to Draw Them* (1945); *Boats and How to Draw Them* (1950); and *Horses and How to Draw Them* (1948). All are published by The Vanguard Press in New York.

[67] Sanford Tousey, *Indians and Cowboys.* New York: Rand McNally & Company, 1948.

[68] Julilly H. Kohler, *Daniel in the Cub Scout Den.* New York: Aladdin Books, 1951.

[69] Paul Witty and Julilly Kohler, *You and the Constitution of the United States.* Chicago: Children's Press, Inc., 1948.

Films and filmstrips are used too

From her catalogues and notes she had taken in her course in visual education, Marion compiled a list of films and filmstrips that were available for small rental fees from the University and from the State Education Office. This list she planned to show to Miss Altonweather and then to schedule as far in advance as developing plans might justify.[70]

Monday's room

Monday morning, Marion had the books on the reading table and on the bookcase shelves. She had 53 library books and brochures in addition to over 90 graded textbooks in various subjects and on various levels. She put road maps of three states on the bulletin board, as well as some blueprints of house plans, some of the aerial photographs from the airport, and some classroom plans from an old professional journal. A roll of white wrapping paper was placed conspicuously on her desk, along with large rulers and some dividers. Other blueprints of buildings and lawn furniture and extra copies of the road maps were placed on the work tables along with the daily newspaper.

Judy and the monitors took roll as Miss Johnson worked at her desk. Three or four children had come in early and gone to work. The program for the day was on the board and Gail presented it. Roger was appointed to see that each child's parents received a letter on attendance and state school aids.

At the opening of the arithmetic period at 9:30, Miss Johnson told the children she wanted to find out how much they remembered from the third grade. "Some remember better than others," she said. "There is no need to study things you already know." She wrote the following page numbers on the board: 2, 3, 16, 17, 44, 88, 128, 145, 182. They were pages that contained inventory tests ranging from the very simplest to rather complex problems in addition, subtraction, multiplication, and division.

"Try to work the hardest ones you can," she said. "See how far you can go all by yourself. I won't mark you on it, so don't worry if you can't go very far. When you have gone as far as you can,

[70] See Selected Films—Fourth Grade Units. pp. 487-488.

put your name on a sheet of paper and put down the answers of
the problems on that page. Some of the first pages review what you
had in the third grade. I want you to do the problems on pages
2 and 3 and then turn over to pages 16 and 17, and keep on working as far as you can go. I will walk around the room and help you
and see how far you can go. Do not worry if you can't do the hard
problems. Many of us forget a lot during the summer. I just want
to find out how much you have forgotten and how much you can
work."

Albert started in at top speed. He wrote the numbers carefully
and neatly but very rapidly and without apparent effort. Marion
noticed very quickly that Julie and Milton were competing with
one another—Julie in her shy, bashful way glancing over Milton's
left shoulder occasionally and Milton frankly turning around every
now and then to see how far Julie had gone. They were both pro-
ficient in their work. Before the period was over, Marion had quite
a few new impressions of the children, though she knew those relating to arithmetic skill would not be too reliable until she had
some standardized test results. She was surprised to see Marjorie Taylor working quickly and competently. Although her first-grade I.Q.
was 86, and her third-grade reading scores were only slightly above
average, she was apparently working with more speed and accuracy
than most of the other children. Miss Johnson had taken little note
of Marjorie up to this point. She had not volunteered or attracted
attention to herself in any way. She was not on the arithmetic committee since she had not received "A" in arithmetic in the third
grade. It struck Marion that Marjorie did not look scholarly. She
sat in the back near poor achievers; she seemed less neat and girlish
than the other girls and was not quick to respond to ordinary motivation. "I must study her," Marion thought. "What is there about
her that suggests poor academic ability aside from the low first-
grade I.Q.?"

Marion noticed that some of the children were making no
progress at all. Edward Stark stared at the pages and fingered his
pencil in a desultory fashion. Selma worked methodically and happily, using the fingers of her hands to count surreptitiously now
and then. Ray Sheldon, slumped in his seat, made good progress.
Larry Forsch, Charles Murphy, Sharon Polk, and Mona Carewe
seemed to be working fairly slowly. Robert Schultz fussed with the

papers in his desk and didn't get around to doing much work. As Marion walked about the room, she made no critical remarks about anyone's arithmetic ability. She asked a few questions and made a few suggestions. She showed the children in one or two instances how to write the problems and space them so that they did not become run together and confused. She smiled and was helpful and unruffled by any show of inability. She allowed pleasure and encouragement to show in her voice when even the simplest addition fundamental was done correctly.

After a half hour, she suggested that they place their papers in a safe place until tomorrow, or later in the day if they had time from other work. "I would like you to save them even if you didn't get very far."

During the rest of the week, she divided the children into four working groups to work on basic arithmetic skills. This was much simpler for those who were poor in arithmetic than for the more advanced. The latter were capable of doing arithmetic on an upper-grade level. Her problem with them would be to help them find constructive, interesting opportunities to learn mathematics in relation to the developing units. The slow groups seemed relieved when they discovered they were not to be rushed or pushed to overtake the more gifted groups. They became more interested in arithmetic as they found how they could apply it with profit in their work.

Marion used the reading period in much the same way. Each child found a page in a book that he would volunteer to read to her, except that "you will not know all the words, because we haven't studied the words in the reading books this year. You can ask the meaning of words you don't know when you read, or wait and look them up in the dictionary." After they found a page they wanted to read, they were free to do other work or read at random.

She found that Julie, Stanley, and Geraldine chose poems to read. Albert read an editorial from the daily newspaper about the need for flood control along the middle reaches of the Mississippi River; Jane and Mary read perfectly from sixth-grade textbooks. Some of the children had selected fourth-grade material they could not read at all well, but a sense of pride and insecurity prevented them from selecting lower-grade material. Others showed no such hesitancy, among them Selma who had selected a second-grade reader and read from it competently. Miss Johnson complimented Selma on having found something she could do well.

Many were able to read material they had mastered in their search for data about the children in the various books. It took two days before each one had a chance to read for her. She then had a basis for tentative reading groups, and the children planned with her on reading assignments. Where possible, these were made in terms of the needs of other activities. This was to be both a recreation and a work-type reading period, Marion decided, but the two would not be mixed. Things the children read for profit or for entertainment would not be spoiled by injecting into them the mechanics of reading. Lessons devoted to the mechanics of reading would make no attempt to find facts or ideas for other projects such as pleasure and beauty in literary expression or vicarious adventure and experience in fiction or biography.

After recess, the children had a language lesson in preparation for their afternoon oral reports. The first chapters of the language book were of great assistance as the children began to make a list of "good rules when we talk with one another." The development of this list took more than the one week. Some of the children with more time than the others worked in groups preparing surprisingly good conversations to demonstrate the rules they had developed.

The most important part of the day to Miss Johnson was the actual reports and the conversations about them that came after recess in the afternoon. She sat in the rear of the room where she could take notes more easily. Judy called on Janet, Jean, and Geraldine first, and then followed with Oliver, Russell, and Gail. Janet's interests were not bookish. She talked of her month at the lake, and was interested in the beach and in fishing (she said, though the conversation showed little real experience), swimming, and playing on the dock. The high point of her summer had been the discovery of riding stables where she had taken eight one-hour lessons ($25.00) and had learned to ride well enough to "pass" on three gaits. Albert knew quite a bit about horses, and so did Richard, Charles, and William, all of whom lived on farms near town. Richard rode horseback also and had the most to offer.

Marion's notes in this matter were of assistance later in the year when discussion of the rapid changes in ways of living and the contrast between the horse-drawn age and the motor age came up.

These children had by then become the room authorities on horses and other farm animals, and what the class didn't know they were expected to find out. Various other notes were also important. Marion was surprised to see how diverse their interests and experiences were. Ray was interested in his uncle's "tool shed." His uncle was a well driller and had a tool shed full of vises and a lathe and a forge with an electric bellows. Larry lived nearby and Ray's uncle "let Larry come in too, but not other kids 'cause they swiped things and fooled around and might get hurt or ruin the tools."

Ray's uncle as well as his tool shed proved to be a *most* valuable find—the tool shed as a place to have things made, and Ray's uncle as a man who knew a lot about local geology and the changing water level of the region. He was an observant man. The many wells he had driven had given him a wide fund of information of this sort, information he was ready to share with others.

Through the week, Miss Johnson got much better acquainted with the children and they got better acquainted with each other. She made suggestions concerning notes about one another that they could write on their name cards. After the children had a chance to discuss their interests and experiences with the class, Miss Johnson suggested that they consider how she should reassign the seats for the enrollment and recitation periods.

"You will remember," she said, "that the seats you have are those that you selected the first day. Now it is time for me to try to work out a better seating arrangement. As far as it is possible to do so, I would like to have you sit near the people you wish to be near. Of course, I won't be able to work it out exactly that way, but I'll do my best." Slips of paper were passed out. "Will each of you write three names on each slip, numbering your choices one, two, and three. . . ?"

There was the usual childish shuffling and inefficiency in promptly writing the names, but there wasn't the shouting and questioning that had sometimes broken out during the first few days of school. Marion found that her choice of which pupils' questions to answer was important in helping the class to pull together. She continued to use patience and tolerance in overlooking occasional noisy distractions.

A sociogram is prepared

Miss Johnson used the customary techniques in arranging the names and drawing the diagram. She discovered that the pattern was rather typical of fourth grades in many schools. The small number of choices between sexes was typical of classrooms where children do not work much in groups. The number of choices ranged among the boys from Oliver with six and Russell, Roger, and Stanley with five to Charles and William who were chosen by none and Edward and John who were chosen only once. Among the girls, Judy received seven choices and Janet and Marjorie each received five, while Carol and Mildred were chosen by none. Janet and Judy were mutual choices, as were Mary—Janie, Marjorie—Norma, and Marjorie—Helen. Mutual choices among the boys were Albert—Oliver, Harry—Edward, and John—Ray.

Miss Johnson recalled her surprise at Marjorie's arithmetical

SUMMARY OF FIRST SOCIOGRAM

	Choices			Choices	
Boy's Name	Received	Made	Girl's Name	Received	Made
Oliver	6	3	Judy	7	3
Roger	5	3	Janet	5	3
Russell	5	2	Marjorie	5	3
Stanley	5	3	Gail	4	3
Larry	4	3	Mona	3	3
Albert	4	3	Norma	3	3
Milton	3	3	Janie	3	3
Ray	3	3	Geraldine	3	3
Andrew	3	3	Jean	3	3
Richard	3	3	Helen	3	3
Warren	2	3	Sharon	3	3
Harry	2	3	Julie	3	1
Robert	2	3	Selma	3	3
Frank	2	3	Esther	3	3
Edward	1	3	Mary	2	3
John	1	3	Alice	2	3
William	0	3	Mildred	0	3
Charles	0	3	Carol	0	3

Choices between sexes—6
Mutual choices—girl and girl—4
Mutual choices—twins, boy and girl—1
Mutual choices—boy and girl—3

ability. Now she saw that Marjorie had received five choices. She noticed that none of the five girls who chose Marjorie also chose Judy, but that Marjorie herself chose Judy. This could be contrasted with Janet. Janet and Judy were mutual choices and Mildred and Mary chose both Janet and Judy. This pattern suggested numerous interesting possibilities, among them that some sort of social division existed within the group, and that Marjorie might feel that Judy's group had greater status.

Among the boys, none of the five who chose Stanley chose Oliver, but again Stanley chose Oliver. None of the five who chose Russell chose Oliver, but Oliver chose Russell. These also suggested groupings of which Miss Johnson had not been conscious.

Frank's position on the sociogram was interesting. Miss Johnson had previously noticed his dependence on his twin sister Esther, but found on the sociogram that he and his sister made each other mutual choices and that he had also been made a choice by Carol who was a close friend of his sister. No boy had chosen Frank, but Frank had chosen Sharon, who had in turn chosen his sister Esther. This might indicate nothing more than that Frank's dependence on his sister had extended itself to his sister's friends, and that an increase in his ability to stand alone would change his dependency all around. It might indicate a healthy heterosexuality due to an opportunity through his sister to enter the girl groups. His position was so clearly set forth, however, particularly in contrast to the general room pattern, that the possibility of an incipient feminine pattern of behavior should not be entirely discounted. Miss Johnson was not alarmed at it, but decided to study it closely as opportunity presented.

There were six choices between boys and girls. Frank figured in four of these—his choice of his sister and Sharon, and his sister's and Carol's choice of him. The other two choices were from Roger to Mona and from Albert to Julie. Albert and Julie were similar in being wide readers. The reason for Roger's choice of Mona did not correspond to any impression of either that Miss Johnson had, nor, of course, was it necessary that it ever should. Mona was sweet, pretty, and artistic—perhaps that was enough.

Of particular interest were the groups within groups that showed in the sociogram. Not all of these were apparent at first glance, but Marion noticed the Marjorie to Helen to Gail to Marjorie triangle,

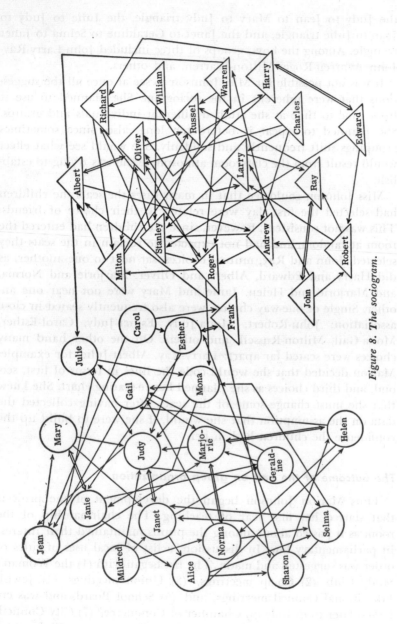

Figure 8. The sociogram.

the Judy to Jean to Mary to Judy triangle, the Julie to Judy to Jean to Julie triangle, and the Janet to Geraldine to Selma to Janet triangle. Among the boys, groups of three included John-Larry-Ray-John, Warren-Roger-Milton-Warren, and others.

It was not possible for Miss Johnson to see at once all the suggestions that were inherent in the sociogram. She planned to use it from time to time as she studied different individuals and groups. She planned to repeat it before too long, also, since sometimes groupings shift frequently and suddenly. She would see what effect would result from the classroom atmosphere she was trying to establish.

Miss Johnson could see that in many cases the seats the children had selected the first day were related to their choice of friends. This was not consistent, however, since the children had entered the room at random, and had not expected to remain in the seats they selected. John and Ray, mutual choices, sat next to one another, as did Harry and Edward, Albert and Oliver, Marjorie and Norma, and Marjorie and Helen. Janie and Mary were not near one another. Single or one-way choices were also frequently seated in close association: John-Robert, Mona-Judy, Esther-Judy, Carol-Esther, Mona-Gail, Milton-Russell, and others. On the other hand many choices were seated far apart: Larry-Ray, Albert-Julie, for example. Marion decided that she would code the lines in terms of first, second, and third choices as she planned her re-seating chart. She knew that she must change some of the seats, after having collected the data on the assumption that she would, if she were to build up the confidence the children had in her.

The outcome of the unit on group organization

Thus Marion Johnson began the development of the projects that started her first year of teaching. The chairmanship of the room as it passed about among the pupils maintained their interest in parliamentary law. In discussion, a list of local uses of rules of order was suggested and made. The list began with (1) the Woman's Study Club, (2) Co-op meetings, (3) Union meetings, (4) Jewish Educational Council meetings, and (5) School Board, and was enlarged later to include (6) Chamber of Commerce, (7) City Council, (8) Parent-Teacher Association, and (9) Toastmasters Clubs.

Mrs. Friswold came to school and talked with the children about parliamentary law and a report was made of her discussion and the questions it raised. Albert asked questions that could not be answered. It was decided to ask the Chamber of Commerce for a speaker, and Mr. Anderson, its secretary and parliamentarian (a lawyer), came one morning at nine o'clock. The children prepared for him, and he for them. He called Miss Johnson at home to find out "what it was all about." She was confident of her group and told him to be prepared for hard questions and to feel free to answer them fully. Mr. Anderson was so enthusiastic after his visit that he arranged for the whole class to visit a regular Chamber of Commerce meeting. Later the class visited a City Council meeting. Meanwhile, the children did a great deal of reading.

The Mayor, who was a member of the Chamber of Commerce, also became interested and wrote a letter suggesting that the class choose a team to come and put on a program for the newly organized Pleasant Valley Improvement Association. This gave Miss Johnson an excellent chance to provide work for the better students, while the rest learned from them. The final scene was a demonstration of parliamentary law in action put on by 16 of the pupils, followed by a panel where the audience asked the "experts" difficult questions, such as: which motions have precedence, which motions are debatable, what is meant by a point of order, and many others. The panel of experts was made up of Albert, Gail, Milton, Judy, and Mary. The demonstration was built around an imaginary "Community Improvement Council" and featured debating and voting about the expenditure of money on a conservation program for the area. In preparing the script, the whole class studied a great deal of science, including agriculture, water supply for humans and for crops, soil erosion, water power, utilization of waste land, and similar subjects.

The project was so unusual in that school and community that it created some problems for Miss Johnson. At the request of the local Chamber of Commerce, a daily paper in the city sent out a feature writer and a photographer. The local weekly also wrote up the project. Miss Altonweather was quite pleased, too, but there was some frostiness on the part of two of the teachers. Marion refused to let this bother her, however. She did not talk about her work with the other teachers in any way that she thought would set her apart from them, nor did she criticize what they did in any way. She acted as surprised as they were at the attention the project received, and in fact she was. She knew in her own mind that the unit was far from perfect; she could see many inadequacies as it developed. She judged it not by the attention it received but by the contribution it made to all her pupils.

The final activity in the unit was the presentation of the model of parliamentary procedure and the panel of experts at the crowded P.T.A. meeting. In the course of the unit, the pupils had read widely, written letters, made reports, made up the skit, practiced answering questions before a microphone, used a tape recorder to study their diction, learned about government, about community activities, about everyday science, and about how to work together to attain mutual purposes. At the final meeting, when the "experts" were asked where they had seen the best examples of running a meeting according to rule, Albert, who was moderator, referred the question to Mary Friswold who said, "I think the grownups who did it best were at the union meeting of the truckdrivers."

By any other name

The interest in names was not carried through in a formal way for as long a time as was the unit on parliamentary law. Marion used it to stimulate reading and to lead into other areas. From it the students learned (1) the nationality backgrounds of each pupil's name, (2) the mechanics of using names in marriage, in legal papers, and the like, (3) the use of nicknames, (4) the meanings of names, (5) how names evolved historically, (6) how names could be legally changed, and (7) how names did not necessarily indicate nationality.

The pupils examined the names of early pioneers in Pleasant Valley at the County Historical Society for leads about which peoples had first settled the region. They found out about the people whose names appeared on some of the older buildings in town. They tried to get people to come to school to tell them about the origin of names in various foreign countries, but found that they already knew more about it from their reading than any of the people they could find. They did find two families (in the room) who had kept rather complete "family trees" (Friswold and Hopkins). The pupils who discovered what their names meant wrote papers on their findings and took them home. The names of various parks and streets led also into the history of the community.

Miss Johnson felt that the main outcome of the study of names was in the emphasis it gave to people, their importance as individuals, their contributions to their fellows, and their right to be treated with respect. Unusual names in the community were brought in and discussed, not as being funny but as having use and meaning.

These results were tied up in reports that were given by late November, and the children went on into two other areas that had been opened up through their interest in names. These were units on old world background and on the local community.

The study of the community

The map of Pleasant Valley when completed in outline was four by six feet in size. On it were streets, parks, schools, public buildings, and other places of general interest. A smaller map on a larger scale showed the business section with every business building located on it. Another map showed the trade, industrial, and farming area surrounding the town. Here the homes of all the pupils were located. A traffic map was made showing the intersections having the most automobile and pedestrian traffic. Actual counts were made by committees at various times of the day. The cooperation of the Chief of Police and a Deputy Sheriff was secured in this work. New maps and traffic counts were made that were more complete and accurate than those previously at hand. Some changes in "police routes" for pupils as they came to school were made as a result of the survey. The pupils were astonished to find that there were chain drugstores on two of the three busiest intersections in the community, with a locally owned drugstore on the third one. They found out from the community librarian that large businesses paid premium prices for such locations and agreed with her that her library should have space on one of those busy corners, since "people should be able to get books about things when they need them."

In making the maps, the pupils learned how to read maps in general, how to construct and read maps to a scale, and, as a consequence, discovered mathematics to be a valuable tool. They made sample counts during carefully spaced and measured periods and then estimated total traffic. As the year advanced, the arithmetic books were used less and less as a source of problems, and more and more as a reference and as a place to find drill materials through which to memorize materials that were too time-consuming to look up all the time.

In the survey of the community, visitors came to school in great numbers. They came from the monument factories, the quarries, the bank, the truck transfer company, the creamery, and the farmers marketing cooperative. Three farmers came. One of the best presentations was made by the lumber yard manager. The airport sent a dispatcher. Whenever possible, representatives were chosen from the families of pupils. Mr. Hammond came, as did Ray's uncle, the well digger. After Mr. Hammond's discussion of the bottling business, another bottler sent word to school that his business had been missed. The notice came verbally from Larry, whose father drove a truck for a "bottled gas" company. The petroleum company supplying the gas had a great deal of informative material to send to school, and Larry's father brought it when he came. He also left a film that his company used with its salesmen-drivers. Larry and two of his friends carried that project still further, reading about petroleum and its sources in the *National Geographic* and the *Junior Scholastic.*

By the latter part of the school year, the children's interest in the community had extended to the agricultural area surrounding Pleasant Valley. The children were seeking to understand the value of soil, the relationship of soil to their welfare, the different kinds of soil, the fertility of the soil, the danger of soil erosion, the ways to prevent or control erosion, and the factors that make for good fertility. In discussing the conservation of soil, the children made a list of places where help might be secured in conserving soil. Under improvement of soil, the children discussed the composition of soil, the kinds of crops that improve soil, and the use of fertilizers. The children read about the effect of weather on soil, particularly heavy rainfall. For example, the composition of the soil affects its reaction to rain, hence some soils get dry and hard after being wet. The cash value of crops came in for study. The use of income crops that may be rotated to build up the soil were read about and discussed.

The children built up a terrarium in which they placed soil and earthworms. They found that the earthworm was a soil helper and they read about why this was true. The county agent visited the school and gave them many pamphlets to use in their search for answers. They also received help from 4-H club leaders. The children read poems about farm life, and they composed some poems about growing things. They learned to test the acidity of soils. On a field trip they observed signs of erosion and noted soil conservation practices on a farm and studied top soil and sub-soil along roadside banks. On their field trip they collected vegetation to plant in the terrarium. The weather was studied in relation to soil conservation. The children drew pictures showing good farm practices, and they used clay to model farm animals. On the field trip they measured the depth of the gullies and estimated the square yards of top soil and sub-soil that were lost in such gullies. They used mathematics also to study the number of acres in various farms, the crop production per acre, the price of crops per bushel, the consumption of grain by farm animals, and the resultant comparative desirability of different kinds of farming.

It was possible to introduce many music experiences in the development of the unit. Some of the children were interested in the Pleasant Valley Brass Band, an organization that had been active in Pleasant Valley for 50 years. The oldest member of this band, and at one time its director, came to school to tell the children its history. He told them how important music was in the life of a community, described many of the celebrations at which the band had played, and gave the children the names of many of the pieces that the people loved the most.

Music contributes to finer living, but if a child is to become sensitive to beauty in music, music must contribute to his happiness. Marion devoted many periods to listening to music with her pupils, though they seldom exceeded 15 and never 20 minutes in length. Marion tried to find records or tapes appropriate to the interests the children were pursuing at the time. She also introduced many creative music activities. For example, after the children had visited the farms, a group of boys experimented with imitating the sounds of animals. They went to the auditorium and used the piano. Julie and Mona went with them and helped them make a poem from the sounds they devised. They used the sounds and the poems as the basis for a rhythmic dance in which various children played the parts of the farm animals. They called the dance the "Big Kids' Kindergarten," and they burlesqued it just a bit to show their superiority to the thing they were doing. Marion was quite pleased at the humor displayed in this part of the project.

In studying the health of the community, committees of children visited the doctors' and dentists' offices, the local veterinarian's office, and one of the pharmacists at Peterson's Drugstore. One of the doctors gave them a copy of an article from the *American Medical Association Journal* that told about the ratio of doctors to population. The children used this material as the basis for a number of arithmetic lessons. The dentists gave them some materials about composition of teeth, fluoridization of water to prevent tooth decay, and the necessity for certain elements in the diet if growing children were to have good teeth. The pharmacist told them about the vitamins and minerals in drugs and a lot about chemistry that served to develop the children's interests in science.

Entirely unrelated to health, the children were reading one day about how Indians communicated great distances with smoke signals. One of the boys thought the Indians might have done much better if they could have used chemical smoke instead of the smoke from fires. They asked their friend the pharmacist about it, and he volunteered to help them produce chemical smoke. This led the children to an interest in dots and dashes by which they could send words with their smoke signals. They went to the local telegraph office and got a copy of the Morse code and planned a short message. They decided on, "What hath God wrought?" The children brought two pieces of canvas to hold and release the smoke and then sent messages from one end of the school grounds to the other, using dots and dashes made of smoke. The pharmacist assisted them in the chemical part of the experiment. The children learned how to produce the smoke and planned to try it on a larger scale the coming summer at camp.

The veterinarian gave them much information about the proper feeding of farm animals. He told them that you could tell how fat or how lean the meat of an animal was before you butchered it by weighing it when submerged in water up to its neck, and he told them how this was done. This was an item of great interest to them. It led to discussions involving diet and the weight of substances submerged in water. It presented an opportunity for the extensive use of mathematics.

The pharmacist told the children about the poison signs on bottles and he warned them of the danger of saving old medicines. He told them how you could put pins through the corks on bottles of poison so that you would not pick them up by accident in the dark. He told them how frequently young children got possession of sleeping pills and other medicines that could cause sickness or death. These instructions led the children to read a great deal about safety. They made surveys of medicine chests in their own homes. They collected a list of common poisons and the common medicines that are dangerous if taken in large doses. This project aroused a good deal of parent interest and many parents complimented Miss Johnson and Miss Altonweather on the interest the children were showing in things around the home related to their own welfare.

One of the physicians talked to the children about immunization. As a result, the children made a survey among their number of vaccinations and diphtheria immunizations. They studied chest x-rays and other public health measures. After they had studied for some time, a number of questions came up upon which they needed more help so they invited the county nurse to visit them as soon as possible. When she came, they showed intelligent interest in many of her instruments. She used a tongue depressor and had the children look into each other's throats. They saw how the throat opened up at the whispered "Ah" and examined the clinical thermometers. They felt each other's pulses. At Miss Johnson's suggestion, the nurse took the pulse rate of three children and then had them run outside around the building and back, and then took their pulse again. The nurse explained that there were temperature variations, too, in terms of the time of day, the amount of activity, and various other factors besides illness. The children showed curiosity about the hypodermic needles used in immunization, but the nurse did not have one with her. She promised to come again and show them one.

The final report on the community study was organized in four headings, with various sub-topics upon which one or more papers were written.

A. What does it take to have a community
  1. People
  2. Government
  3. Business
  4. Money
  5. Food
  6. Shelter and clothing
  7. Roads and highways
  8. Homes
  9. Land
B. What goes on in our community
  1. Trade and business
  2. Agriculture
  3. Health service
  4. Schools
  5. Churches
  6. Shows, parks, and recreation
C. What makes a good community
  1. A clean and healthy place
  2. A safe place
  3. Good buildings
  4. Beautiful parks, streets, and homes
  5. Good laws
  6. Good churches
  7. Good schools
  8. Good people
D. How can we improve our community
  1. Be good citizens
    a. Obey laws
    b. Do not destroy property
  2. Pay taxes
  3. Get a public swimming pool
  4. Get a public skating rink
  5. Treat all citizens alike—be democratic
  6. Help those who need help—be kind
  7. Use knowledge of science to improve living conditions
  8. Practice conservation
  9. Better schools—night schools
  10. Contribute to Community Chest
  11. Vote
  12. Attend school board meetings and city council meetings

Under trade and business, for example, there were many reports on the various types of industries. The essays under Parts A and D were far less extensive than was the material in Parts B and C. The organization was not entirely consistent and there was overlapping, but Miss Johnson knew that it was exceptionally good work for a fourth grade, and she refused to refine and organize it according to her own ideas. The essay on better schools and night schools ended with this statement, "There are lots of things to learn that people don't know. They have night schools for this. There should be one in Pleasant Valley."

Fourth-grade intelligence tests

Late in September, Miss Altonweather brought in Otis Intelligence Tests that Marion administered and corrected. She compared the results of these tests with her impressions of the children and with the Detroit Intelligence Tests that had been given in the first grade. She knew that the Otis tests tended to group the children around the center of the curve and to reduce the number of scores at the very low and the very high levels. However, in most cases the children's I.Q.'s did not change greatly. This was true for William, Harry, Janie, Milton, Larry, Charles, Carol, John, Mona, Andrew, Geraldine, Roger, Russell, Robert, Stanley, Selma, Helen, Esther, and Frank. There were some significant drops in measured intelligence: Sharon 120 to 94, Ray 141 to 102, Judy 130 to 116, Janet 124 to 109, and Julie 141 to 128. There were some significant increases as well: Jean 99 to 118, Oliver 96 to 117, Gail from 95 to 119, Albert 125 to 139, Marjorie 86 to 109 and Mary 113 to 132.

November arithmetic tests

Early in November, Miss Altonweather brought in fourth-grade Stanford Arithmetic tests in computation and reasoning. The results showed that the fourth grade ranged from some children whose scores were below the third-grade level to one whose score was three months into the sixth grade. The median score in arithmetic computation was the first month of the fourth grade, and the median score of arithmetic reasoning was the second month of the fourth grade.

Marion saw that Marjorie was second highest in arithmetic reasoning, although she was very high, too, in arithmetic computation. Her new I.Q. of 109 was more in keeping with such high arithmetic achievement than her first-grade I.Q. of 86, but Marion was not yet satisfied with the measures she had on Marjorie. Ray's marks in the arithmetic tests placed him in the upper five or six in the room, but his fourth-grade I.Q. of 102 was much different from his first-grade I.Q. of 141. This was another case where Marion thought further testing should be done. Albert Ericson's test pattern was consistently high. Julie was much higher in arithmetic reasoning than she was in arithmetic computation. It seemed clear that her

FOURTH-GRADE TEST RESULTS IN INTELLIGENCE AND ARITHMETIC

| | | Stanford Arithmetic | | | |
| | | Computation | | Reasoning | |
Pupil	Fourth Grade Otis I.Q.	Age	Grade	Age	Grade
Affleck, Jean	118	9-2	4.2	8-9	3.8
Anderson, Norma	84	8-9	3.8	9-6	4.5
Carew, Mona	95	8-6	3.5	8-9	3.8
Carlton, Richard	103	7-9	2.8	7-10	2.9
Clarkson, Harry	94	9-3	4.3	9.2	4.2
Dickey, Carol	101	9-7	4.6	9-6	4.5
Dickinson, Russell	92	10-3	5.2	9-5	4.4
Ericson, Albert	139	11-0	5.9	11-4	6.3
Flick, Janie	121	8-9	3.8	10-2	5.1
Forsch, Larry	94	8-5	3.4	8-4	3.4
French, Julie	128	9-0	4.0	10-3	5.2
Friswold, Mary	132	9-0	4.0	9-8	4.7
Harper, Oliver	117	9-2	4.2	9-11	4.9
Hopkins, Gail	119	9-6	4.5	9-11	4.9
Knott, Esther	101	9-1	4.1	9-5	4.4
Knott, Frank	102	8-9	3.8	8-9	3.8
Kremer, Janet	109	10-3	5.2	9-6	4.5
Lane, Mildred	90	8-6	3.5	8-4	3.4
Larson, Andrew	103	9-0	4.0	8-9	3.8
Liebermann, Milton	120	9-2	4.2	10-3	5.2
Littlejohn, John	105	8-1	3.0	8-3	3.2
Murphy, Charles	90	8-5	3.4	8-7	3.6
Norman, Judy	116	9-0	4.0	9-6	4.5
Ober, Warren	103	8-9	3.8	8-9	3.8
Pogue, Sharon	94	8-8	3.7	8-7	3.6
Reuther, Geraldine	108	9-1	4.1	10-2	5.1
Sahr, Alice	103	9-0	4.0	8-7	3.6
Schorn, Roger	107	8-8	3.7	9-6	4.5
Schultz, Robert	94	9-8	4.7	9-0	4.0
Sheldon, Ray	102	9-7	4.6	10-2	5.1
Smith, Stanley	108	8-9	3.8	9-5	4.4
Stark, Edward	90	8-5	3.4	8-1	3.0
Taylor, Marjorie	109	9-8	4.7	10-8	5.6
Thompson, Helen	105	8-9	3.8	8-7	3.6
Toivenen, Selma	94	9-8	4.7	8-7	3.6
Toole, William	91	9-0	4.0	8-8	3.7

interests were not primarily mathematical. With such high intelligence and with such high ability in arithmetic reasoning, Marion resolved to be on the lookout for chances to motivate and interest Julie in mathematics. To do so she knew that she would have to show Julie how mathematics could contribute to her literary, artistic, and poetic tendencies.

RANGE IN RESULTS IN MISS JOHNSON'S AUTUMN FOURTH-GRADE TESTING

Range in Grade Level from Low to High in Arithmetic Computation of 24 Fourth Graders	Range in Grade Level from Low to High in Arithmetic Reasoning of 34 Fourth Graders	Range in Otis I.Q. for 36 Fourth-Graders Tested in Fourth Grade
2.8	2.9	84
3.0	3.0	90
3.4	3.2	90
3.4	3.4	90
3.4	3.4	91
3.5	3.6	92
3.5	3.6	94
3.7	3.6	94
3.7	3.6	94
3.8	3.6	94
3.8	3.7	94
3.8	3.8	95
3.8	3.8	101
3.8	3.8	101
3.8	3.8	102
4.0	3.8	102
4.0	4.0	103
4.0	4.2	103
—— Median	—— Median	—— Median
4.0	4.4	103
4.0	4.4	103
4.0	4.4	105
4.1	4.5	105
4.1	4.5	107
4.2	4.5	108
4.2	4.5	108
4.2	4.5	109
4.3	4.7	109
4.5	4.9	116
4.6	4.9	117
4.6	5.1	118
4.7	5.1	119
4.7	5.1	120
4.7	5.2	121
5.2	5.2	128
5.2	5.6	132
5.9	6.3	139

There were many interesting individual differences to be seen even with the small number of test results available in Miss Johnson's room. William Toole was about average in fourth-grade arithmetic, but he had been far below average in third-grade reading. William stuttered slightly. Harry rated even better in fourth-grade arithmetic than did William and even lower in third-grade reading than did William. Harry's reading was not as good as one would expect from his 94 I.Q. Janie was better in reading than she was in arithmetic and this was true also of Jean, Andrew, Gail, Mary, and Julie. On the other hand, many of the children scored relatively higher in mathematics in the fourth grade than they had in reading in the third. This was true of Ray, Charles, John, Geraldine, Alice, Russell, Selma, Esther, and Frank.

John Littlejohn becomes a person

The break in John's problems came when his stepfather, Mr. Hammond, was invited to visit the classroom to tell about the bottling industry. Marion found him a serious-minded man and, contrary to Mrs. Gilbert's opinion, destined soon to become local manager for his company. Marion had visited the Hammond home before the invitation. John's mother had greeted her in a friendly but somewhat subdued manner. She did indeed seem a bit crushed and beaten. Marion saw that social disapproval of her two marriages, or something else, had driven her to retreat into her home and into herself. Perhaps her first marriage had been the result of an inability to cope with her problems—probably an unresolved conflict with her mother.

These were purely matters of speculation, Marion knew, but they offered clues to the problem facing John. Obviously his mother felt some sort of social inferiority and disapproval and probably guilt. Mr. Hammond did not seem to be a party to this feeling at all. A serious man without great imagination, he saw his wife as a fine woman with an education and background he admired. He went about his work honestly and conscientiously. He regarded his stepson as difficult to discipline and he accepted as natural the fact that John seemed to resent him. He did not see John's difficulties at school or elsewhere as having any connection with his mother's first marriage or with her marriage to him. He was apparently unaware of any community disapproval, which, in fact, was not directed at him. He was fond of John and assumed that he would grow up to be either good like his mother or bad like his father. He had not considered the part played by Mr. Littlejohn in John's life as being anything that he should attempt to limit or control.

Marion had discussed John with Mrs. Hammond as a boy that she was fond of, as a boy who had problems just as all other children had problems, as a boy whose experiences should be planned to be of help to him. Marion did not discuss John's deeper emotional needs and his probable feeling of insecurity, because she was not sure of her diagnosis or of his mother's ability to understand her theories or their tentative nature. She did, however, discover that John had not been legally adopted by Mr. Hammond and that Littlejohn was in reality his legal name, that generally in such cases children go by the step-father's name, but that Mr. Littlejohn insisted that John use his name. (Mrs. Gilbert heard of her visit and tried to get the "low down" on it, but Marion was pleasantly and disarmingly uncommunicative.)

The children were interested in studying various industries in the community one by one. They made an extensive list and then decided on those they wished to hear more about or visit. They thought it would be wise to start with those parents who worked in the various industries, since they would be better able to fit into the plan. Mr. Hammond was third on the list, following Mr. Harper, who had told about the granite and monument business, and Mr. Reuther, who was a post office employee.

The children had delegated John to ask his stepfather to visit the class. They had previously developed an outline to be given ahead of time to all visitors from community businesses, so that they would know what the children wished to have covered. In this case, because it was crucial, Miss Johnson called Mr. Hammond by telephone after John had given him the message. She did not discuss John, but tried to insure that his contribution would be of great interest in order that John would gain status from it.

His presentation did, in truth, gain this objective. He had many pamphlets, charts, and colored pictures, an analysis of the nutritional qualities of many beverages, and he told about sanitation and cleanliness in the bottling plant. Miss Johnson had referred to him casually as John's stepfather. The children accepted him as an adult who was important in providing them with one of the luxuries of their living. As they planned later for the visit to the bottling works, John took a leading part because of his greater knowledge. Miss Johnson treated both John and his father with great respect. She asked questions about things she did not know.

The visit to the plant was even more interesting. The bottle-capping machines, the sterilizers, the loading platforms, the trucks, the syrups, the carbonating machines, and the safety devices, all got their share of attention. Miss Johnson discussed the importance of the project with Miss Altonweather, who drove over for the last part of the visit and for the refreshments that followed the tour. Miss A. sometimes did not understand just why Marion did things the way she did, and at times interfered at the wrong time, but Marion knew these were mistakes of the mind and not of the heart, and she refused to be disturbed by them. In this case, she was interested in status for John and for his stepfather and she had been able to make that point with Miss A. without being offensively superior. Miss A. played her part well. She thanked Mr. Hammond on behalf of the school and acted obviously pleased at his knowledge and hospitality.

John played an increasingly active part in class affairs during this time, and so did Ray, Larry, and Robert.[71] After it was all over, he seemed aware that his stepfather was accepted as important by the children, and that the stepfather relationship was something that could be referred to publicly and openly. Marion saw that John was more at ease and more self-confident, but she did not allow herself to forget that this was not due alone to the role she played or to her acceptance of John, but also, and more important, to increased standing with his peer group. She knew that his long-standing problems could not be solved entirely by a few months in an improved school environment and she was right. He continued upon occasion to withdraw from his group and to strike back, particularly in his life outside the classroom and the school, but there was distinct improvement even there.

When she met Mr. Hopkins, Gail's father, who was a scout-

71 See sociogram.

master, she found an occasion to tell him about the fine cooperation Mr. Hammond had given to her room and of his interest in
youth. Before Christmas, John told the class that his stepfather
had a troop. Through this activity, Miss Johnson saw that Mr.
Hammond would gain further prestige among John's peers and
among adults in the community. When she met Mrs. Hammond
shortly afterward, she made a point of telling her how fine everyone
at school thought it was that her husband was helping the scouts.

In other activities, Miss Johnson also found a chance to help
John. A good illustration was in the study of names and nicknames. The pupils listed many names with their customary idio-
matic variations. They studied the way the same name appeared in
different languages. They studied the necessity for using the real
name in official papers, so that clear identification could be established. They found out how the wife takes the husband's name,
and how the children take the father's name. Casually and without
emphasis, but in the background of its legal and social necessity,
the case of children living with stepfathers was discussed. They
found that both John and Nathan mean "gift," Charles means
"strong," Richard means "powerful," and so forth.[72] They found
out how names like Greenfield, Whitehill, Washington, and Littlejohn got started. In all this, involving the nationality and meaning
of names, the children grew to regard names as primarily a means
of identification.

This story could be continued. Mr. Hammond became more important in John's eyes, and his community status improved in Mrs.
Hammond's eyes as did John's assessment of his own place in the
scheme of things. He became a real part of his peer group, accepted
by it. He found in the classroom many opportunities to do constructive things. He found a teacher who was not concerned with
dominating him, but who somehow seemed interested in helping
him. He found that what he said did not bring forth a correction or
a re-phrasing in better style (or fulsome praise, for that matter).
He and others found it easy to say what they thought. For the first
time in his life John found an adult (Marion) to whom he could
talk frankly without getting buried in shock, good advice, or acclaim.

[72] Evans, *People Are Important,* pp. 23-34.

Discussion Questions

1. Is Albert Ericson a potential problem? What might Marion be doing to guard against the development of an unhealthy perfectionism in Albert? Complete the story of how she may have dealt with him.

2. Evaluate the inadequate testing program in the Pleasant Valley School and suggest some improvements.

3. Discuss the rather impromptu way that John's provisional promotion was made. Did Marion's attitude have anything to do with it? Is this the way such decisions should be made?

4. What lesson for modern education can you draw from the incident where Gail Hopkins drew on her experience in the "Blue Birds" to tell how chairmen are selected? How much did the children know about rules of order when the question first came up?

5. When the children in our group were arguing over whether Roger or Janet should be chairman, why did Marion point up the question, make a suggestion, and then move away? Should she have been offended that her suggestion was not accepted? Pleased?

6. Mary Friswold was extroverted and dominating but not overly popular with her peers. What type of assistance did she need? Give your answers in terms of a developing curricular situation.

7. Notice evidences as the story goes along of the expectation and desire of the children to drop into the conventional classroom behavior, where the teacher makes decisions and the children carry out assignments. Discuss the significance of this tendency.

8. What would you think when you discovered that John Littlejohn's reading had not improved during the year he was in Miss O'Leary's room? Should Marion have mentioned this to Miss O'Leary? What had been Miss O'Leary's apparent objective in dealing with him?

9. Miss Altonweather's policy in regard to the required purchase of notebooks by those who can't afford them seems fairly enlightened. Discuss some of its strengths and shortcomings.

10. Do you believe Marion should have used the prepared letter charts or written the alphabet on the board herself?

11. Why did Miss Johnson tell the children that all parents did not go to meetings and that some parents might not be of help in their study of rules of order?

12. How do you suppose Marion worked with Selma in order to gain her help in giving status to slow achievers?

13. Discuss Marion's early attempts to adjust the work to individual differences. Use the letters written home on the first Friday as one example.

14. When Miss Johnson told the class that fourth-graders frequently voted

boys versus girls, how might this have been done in an awkward or unfortunate way?

15. Was it just a passing, kindly whim that made Marion suggest that some of the girls stay and wait for Gail that first Friday evening, as she worked with Gail on the next week's plan?

16. What were some of the differences between the broken home situations of John and of Larry?

17. Discuss Marjorie's failure to gain Marion's attention at first in the light of her later achievement and her position on the sociogram. Do teachers see in pupils what pupils see in one another?

18. Marion's interest in the "real whole child" led her to notice many things that other teachers miss. As the children selected things to read to her, why did she notice (and make notes on) the children who selected poetry? Find other illustrations of things Marion noticed that you might have disregarded.

19. Can you imagine some of the changes that the socialized atmosphere will bring about in Marion's next sociogram?

20. Write a case study of Frank, as you imagine he progressed during the year.

21. The trick, in the first days of an experience with a class, is to avoid setting a pattern or atmosphere that will later inhibit what you wish to accomplish. Discuss Marion's efforts to avoid early "authoritarianism." Discuss where she "directed" and where she elected to let the children develop power.

22. Do you believe Marion will have sufficient time for remedial work as her program develops?

Selected References

Adkind, Arthur, *"Bibliography of Lists and Sources of Free and Inexpensive Learning Materials.* Minneapolis: University of Minnesota, Curriculum Workshop for the Experimental Schools, 1949, mimeographed.

A Guide for Better Instruction in Minnesota Schools, Curriculum Bulletin No. 1. St. Paul: State of Minnesota, Department of Education, 1946.

A Guide for Instruction in Arithmetic. St. Paul: State of Minnesota, Department of Education, 1948.

A Guide for Instruction in Art. St. Paul: State of Minnesota, Department of Education, 1948.

A Guide for Instruction in the Social Studies. St. Paul: State of Minnesota, Department of Education, 1949.

A Study of Community Needs. Newark, New Jersey, The Curriculum Improvement Program, 1941.

Britannica Encyclopaedia, *True Nature Series,* "Animals of the Woods,"

"Gray Squirrel," "Snapping Turtle," "Water Birds," "Black Bear Twins," "Three Little Kittens," "Pride, the Saddle Horse," "Shep, the Farm Dog," "Goats and Kids," "Adventures of Bunny Rabbit," "Animals of the Farm," "Elephants." New York: Encyclopaedia Britannica Press, 1946.

————, *World's Children Stories*, "Mateo and the Mexican Fair," "Anaghalook, Eskimo Girl," "Dark Eyes and Her Navajo Blanket," "Shin Ming, Chinese Boy Scout," "French Canadian Children," "A Day With Dutch Children," "Hans of the Swiss Alps," "Pedro Picks Coffee in Brazil," "Yukiko and a Japanese Carnival," "Children on England's Canals," "Kanz, Prince of Darkest Africa," "Pauli and His Hawaiian Feast." New York: Encyclopaedia Britannica Press.

Baltimore Bulletin of Education, Vol. XXVIII, No. 4, March-May 1951.

Beim, Jerrold, *Tim and the Tool Chest.* New York: William Morrow & Company, 1951.

Bennett, Dorothy A., *The Golden Encyclopedia.* New York: Simon & Schuster, Inc., 1946.

Bishop, Katherine V., *General Supervision.* Garvey, California: Garvey School District, 1951, mimeographed.

Brown, Margaret Wise, *The Noisy Book.* New York: Harper and Brothers, 1939.

Building Desirable Values. Philadelphia: Curriculum Office, Philadelphia Public Schools, 1950.

Carlson, Bernice Wells, *The Junior Party Book.* New York: Abingdon-Cokesbury Press, 1948.

Committee on Community Study of the Department of Elementary School Principals, *How to Know, How to Use, Your Community.* Washington, D. C.: National Education Association, 1941-42.

Contributions of the Elementary Schools to the City-wide Program of Education for Democratic Citizenship. Springfield, Massachusetts: Springfield Public Schools.

Cooperative Planning in Education. Bureau of Publications, Teachers College, Columbia University, 1947.

Course of Study, Fourth Grade, Social Studies Supplement. Dallas, Texas: Dallas Independent School District, 1947.

Course of Study in Science. Chicago: Bureau of Curriculum, Board of Education, Chicago Public Schools, 1944.

Course of Study in Science for Grade Four. Chicago: Bureau of Curriculum, Board of Education, Chicago Public Schools, 1944.

Creating Good Climate. Philadelphia: Curriculum Office, Philadelphia Public Schools, 1950.

Crowninshield, Ethel, *Stories That Sing.* Boston: Boston Music Company, 1945.

Dawson, Mildred A. and Jonnie Washburne Miller, *Language for Daily Use—Grade 4*. Yonkers, New York: World Book Company, 1948.

————, *Language for Daily Use—Grade 5*. Yonkers, New York: World Book Company, 1948.

Elliott, Eugene B., *Planning and Working Together*, Bulletin No. 337. Lansing, Michigan: State Department of Public Instruction, 1945.

Evans, Eva Knox, *People Are Important*. New York: Capital Publishing Company, Inc., 1951.

Frazer, Phyllis, *A B C and Counting Book*. New York: Wonder Books, 1946.

Geralton, James, *The Story of Sound*. New York: Harcourt, Brace & Company, Inc., 1948.

Goodenow, Earle, *Cow Concert*. New York: Alfred A. Knopf, Inc., 1951.

Goudey, Alice E., *The Merry Fiddlers*, Aladdin Books. New York: American Book Company, 1951.

Guidance Services for Minnesota Schools. St. Paul: State of Minnesota, Department of Education, 1951.

Hall, Alta B. and Alice Fleenor Sturgis, *Textbook on Parliamentary Law*. New York: The Macmillan Company, 1923.

Hogeboom, Amy, *Birds and How to Draw Them*. New York: The Vanguard Press, 1945.

————, *Boats and How to Draw Them*. New York: The Vanguard Press, 1950.

————, *Dogs and How to Draw Them*. New York: The Vanguard Press, 1944.

————, *Forest Animals and How to Draw Them*. New York: The Vanguard Press, 1950.

————, *Horses and How to Draw Them*. New York: The Vanguard Press, 1948.

————, *Wild Animals and How to Draw Them*. New York: The Vanguard Press, 1947.

Indianapolis Social Studies Program. Grades 1-6. Indianapolis, 1948.

Jaffo, George J., *The Big Book of Real Trucks*. New York: Grosset & Dunlap, 1950.

Jennings, Helen Hall, *Sociometry in Group Relations*. Washington, D.C.: American Council on Education, 1948.

Lack, Alma S., *A Child's First Cook Book*. New York: Henry Holt & Company, Inc., 1950.

Making Decisions. Philadelphia: Curriculum Office, Philadelphia Public Schools, 1950.

McCharen, W. K., *Improving the Quality of Living*. Nashville, Tennessee: George Peabody College for Teachers, 1947.

McCluny, Robert W., *Ruby Throat,* Morrow Junior Books. New York: William Morrow & Company, 1950.

Newby, Ruth *et al., Unit of Work on Community Life.* Pasadena, California: Pasadena City Schools, Elementary Curriculum Department, 1948, mimeographed.

——, *Unit of Work on Home, School and Neighborhood Life.* Pasadena, California: Pasadena City Schools, Elementary Curriculum Department, 1948, mimeographed.

——, *Unit of Work on the Food Market.* Pasadena, California: Pasadena City Schools, Elementary Curriculum Department, 1948, mimeographed.

——, *Unit of Work on the Farm.* Pasadena, California: Pasadena City Schools, Elementary Curriculum Department, 1949, mimeographed.

New York Public Schools, *Curriculum Development in the Elementary Schools,* Curriculum Bulletin No. 1. New York: Board of Education, 1946.

——, *Exploring a First Grade Curriculum,* Publication No. 30. New York: Board of Education, 1947.

Oftedahl, Laura and Nina Jacobs, *My First Dictionary—the Beginners Picture Word Book,* Laboratory Schools, University of Chicago. New York: Grosset & Dunlap, 1948.

Omaha Public Schools, *A Library Program for Elementary Schools,* Curriculum Bulletin No. 3. Omaha, Nebraska: Board of Education, 1948.

——, *Social Studies, Primary Grades,* Curriculum Bulletin No. 1. Omaha, Nebraska: Board of Education, 1949.

Open Mindedness Can Be Taught. Philadelphia: Philadelphia Public Schools, Curriculum Office, 1949.

Panushka, Warren, *This is Your Town, A Field Trip Handbook.* Curriculum Bulletin No. 43. St. Paul: St. Paul Public Schools, 1951.

Paul, Harry G., Isabel Kincheloc, and J. W. Ramsey, *Junior Units in English.* New York: Lyons and Carnahan, 1940.

Petersburg Builds a Health Program, Bulletin No. 9. Washington, D.C.: Office of Education, Federal Security Agency, 1949.

Politi, Leo, *Song of the Swallows.* New York: Charles S. Scribner's Sons, 1949.

Railroad A B C. New York: Franklin Watts, Inc., 1948.

Science—An Approach in the Elementary School. Philadelphia: Philadelphia Public Schools, 1945.

Science Teaching in Rural and Small Town Schools, Bulletin No. 5. Washington, D.C.: Office of Education, Federal Security Agency, 1949.

Simpson, Mabel E. and Mary A. Adams, *Growth in English,* Book One, Part Two. New York: Newson and Company, 1934.

The Place of Subjects in the Curriculum, Bulletin No. 12. Washington, D.C.: Office of Education, Federal Security Agency, 1949.

Thinking Critically. Philadelphia: Curriculum Office, Philadelphia Public Schools, 1950.

Tippett, James S., *Tools for Andy*. New York: Abingdon-Cokesbury Press, 1951.

Tousey, Sanford, *Indians and Cowboys*. New York: Rand McNally & Company, 1948.

Toward the Open Mind. Philadelphia: Curriculum Office, Philadelphia Public Schools, 1950.

Training Young Hands for Modern Living, Curriculum Brochure No. 1. Chicago, Illinois, Bureau of Curriculum, Board of Education, Chicago Public Schools, 1949.

University Elementary Demonstration Faculty, *Illustrative Teaching Units for the Elementary Grades*. Minneapolis: University of Minnesota Press, 1941.

Wines, Emma M. and Marjory W. Card, *Come to Order*. Garden City, New York: Doubleday, Doran and Company, Inc., 1930.

Wood, Hugh B., ed., *The Curriculum Plan for the Utopian Public Schools*. Eugene, Oregon: University Cooperative Store, 1949, mimeographed.

———, *Sources for Free and Inexpensive Teaching Materials*. Eugene, Oregon: University of Oregon, 1949, mimeographed.

———, *The Teaching of Current Events*. Eugene, Oregon: University of Oregon, 1950, mimeographed.

Selected Films
Fourth-Grade Units

Airport. Collaborator, Paul R. Hanna. Wilmette, Illinois, Encyclopaedia Britannica.

Are You a Good Citizen? Collaborator, Jerome G. Kerwin. Chicago, Coronet Instructional Films.

Building a Highway. Collaborator, Maurice B. Lagaard. Wilmette, Illinois, Encyclopaedia Britannica.

Caravans of Trade. Collaborators, Twentieth Century Fox. New York, Films, Inc.

Cotton. Collaborator, Harriet L. Herring. Wilmette, Illinois, Encyclopaedia Britannica.

Developing Responsibility. Collaborator, I. O. Foster. Chicago, Coronet Instructional Films.

Fireman. Collaborators, Ernest Horn, Arthur I. Gates, and Celeste C. Peardon. Wilmette, Illinois, Encyclopaedia Britannica.

Food Store. Collaborator, Marjorie D. Sharpe. Wilmette, Illinois, Encyclopaedia Britannica.

Foods and Nutrition. Collaborators, A. J. Carlson and H. G. Swan. Wilmette, Illinois, Encyclopaedia Britannica.

Fred Meets a Bank. Collaborators, Dr. I. Owen Foster and Dr. Frederick G. Neel. Chicago, Coronet Instructional Films.

Living in a Metropolis. Collaborator, Louis de Rochemont Associates. New York, United World Films.

Maps and Their Uses. Chicago, Coronet Instructional Films.

Maps Are Fun. Chicago, Coronet Instructional Films.

Policeman. Wilmette, Illinois, Encyclopaedia Britannica.

Safety Begins at Home. New York, Young America Films.

Vitamin-Wise. Chicago, National Film Board of Canada.

Water Supply. Hollywood, Academy Films.

What Is Money. Collaborator, Paul L. Salsgiver. Chicago, Coronet Instructional Films.

Wool. Collaborators, Robert H. Burns and Alexander Johnson. Wilmette, Illinois: Encyclopaedia Britannica Films.

Wonders in Your Own Backyard. Los Angeles, Churchill Wexler Film Producers.

Selected Filmstrips
Fourth-Grade Units

Bacteria, Good and Bad. Young America Films, Inc., 18 E. 41st St., New York 18, N.Y.

Body Defense Against Disease. Encyclopaedia Britannica Films, Inc., 1150 Wilmette Ave., Wilmette, Illinois.

Building a House (Country Life Series). Modern Teaching Aids, Eye Gate House, Inc., 330 W. 42nd St., New York 18, N.Y.

Eat Well, Live Well. Popular Science Publishing Co., Audio Visual Division, 353 4th Avenue, New York 10, N.Y.

Firemen at Work (Community Helpers Series). Eye Gate House, Inc., 330 W. 42nd St., New York 18, N.Y.

Foods and Nutrition. Encyclopaedia Britannica Films, Inc., 1150 Wilmette Ave., Wilmette, Illinois.

Foods for Health. Young America Films, Inc., 18 E. 41st St., New York 18, N.Y.

Larry Helps the Police. Eye Gate House, Inc., 330 W. 42nd St., New York 18, N.Y.

Living in a Machine Age. Young America Films, Inc., 18 E. 41st St., New York 18, N.Y.

My Father Is a Bus Driver. Instructional Films, Inc., 330 West 42nd St., New York 18, N.Y.

My Father Is a Garbage Man. Instructional Films, Inc., 330 West 42nd St., New York 18, N.Y.

My Father Is a Postman. Instructional Films, Inc., 330 West 42nd St., New York 18, N.Y.

Our Homes and Communities. Popular Science Publishing Co., Audio Visual Division, 353 4th Avenue, New York 10, N.Y.

Plays and Recreation. Popular Science Publishing Co., Audio Visual Division, 353 4th Avenue, New York 10, N.Y.

Strong Teeth. Young America Films, Inc., 18 E. 41st St., New York 18, N.Y.

Transportation. Popular Science Publishing Co., Audio Visual Division, 353 4th Avenue, New York 10, N.Y.

Using Our Forests Wisely. Popular Science Publishing Co., Audio Visual Division, 353 4th Avenue, New York 10, N.Y.

Wool (Clothing and Shelter Series). Encyclopaedia Britannica Films, Inc., 1150 Wilmette Ave., Wilmette, Illinois.

20

A MAN IN THE GRADES

$\mathcal{H}$ERBERT ZAN had taught for five years before he came to Amber City to teach sixth grade in the Columbus School. Amber City had two hundred and fifty thousand people and an extensive suburban population. Its school system, with over 2,200 teachers and other employees, seemed to him to be a big institution. He had previously taught two years in a nine-teacher district and three years in a twenty-two teacher district. After having grown up in a small town, he had attended a metropolitan university for four years and two subsequent summers, and had spent four years in military service. Almost 30 years old, he had acquired a wife and two babies since the war.

Getting settled in the city was in itself a bit unsettling. He was not able to find the desirable living quarters that he and Mary wished, and the rent seemed extremely high. They hoped that soon they could find a home to buy, but that would have to wait.

The Amber City schools had developed an orientation plan for new teachers. There were bulletins telling of the school calendar, salary schedule, current and cumulative sick leave, retirement, various rules and regulations, school board organization, reporting and record keeping, school organization, functions of executive and administrative officers, probation and tenure, community resources, various special school services, other community agencies that co-operate with the schools, audio-visual aids available, and various general and specialized curriculum bulletins. Some of the bulletins were helpful and complete, while others were sketchy, out-of-date, or ambiguous and obscure. There was a planned program by which new teachers could get acquainted, and it assisted Herbert and Mary in getting started in the schools of the community.

Miss Tate was the principal in the sixteen-teacher Columbus School to which Herbert was assigned. She eyed Herbert speculatively when he first appeared and told him that the last two men assigned to her school had not been successful. She softened somewhat when she heard of his wife and two children, but wondered audibly how they would make ends meet on a teacher's salary.

"I expect each teacher to handle his own discipline," she said upon one early occasion. "Extreme cases only should be sent to the office. This is a difficult community. The people here think they can get special privileges for their children by 'getting in' with the teachers. Some of them read a lot and think they know more about running schools than the teachers do. They had trouble here for years until I came. I let them know that I run the school. They were always running downtown to the office, but I've shown them that doesn't pay."

"Do you have a good P.T.A.?"

"Yes, the P.T.A. is pretty good. They raise money for our library and have purchased playground equipment. I go to all the meetings and I expect each teacher to attend twice each year—once at open house night and one other time, generally when you have a program. Mr. Sarholm last year went every time. He tried to get in with them all the time, but they were on to him. He's teaching over in Michigan this year. He'll probably do better in a small town where the discipline is easier."

Herb was a bit disappointed in Miss Tate, to say the least.

"I've seen ninety-day-wonder lieutenants like her," he told Mary that first evening, "but she takes the cake for a woman of her age—a principal in a large city."

"She may not turn out to be so bad," Mary said, "and anyway you won't have to stay in that school forever."

As time went on, Herbert's initial irritation changed a bit to amusement. Miss Tate, he found, was not all bad. She was concerned that her leadership be accepted, and her technique was to weave a web of minor orders and regulations about those who worked for her and to insist on their observance. She was temporarily reassured of her status when teachers deferred to her or asked her advice. She was fearful when those "under" her were complimented on original work, and she guarded against that eventuality by modifying each one's work with her own ideas so that she could claim a part in any activity in her school. She tried to stand between her staff members and the community.

Herbert found that she knew the children and the parents in her district well. She had friends and enemies in the community and she seemed to take as much pleasure in pleasing the former as she did umbrage in circumventing the latter. She was willing to express opinions on almost any subject, educational or otherwise, and except for a few relatively liberal ideas about the need for better salaries for teachers, and freedom from political domination of the schools, her convictions tended to be conservative politically and traditional educationally. She used much of the new educational terminology, but she seemed to miss the connotation of the words. She confessed this, unconsciously, when she said, as she often did, "If you want to be progressive, just think up a new word for one of the same old ideas."

"There are lots of new things, Miss Tate, and we must have new words to describe them," Herbert had said once in a rash moment. "I saw Hiroshima, and what happened there wasn't a new word for the same old warfare. We need new words to describe new educational procedures also."

Miss Tate did not argue with this, but she looked at him with new interest. "What I mean," she said, "is when you use a new word and the procedure is not new. There is little that is really new."

"I have two babies at home that are really new," Herb answered, though he knew it would appear *non sequitur* to her. "No one just like either of them ever occurred before, and that's true of every little boy and girl in school."

Miss Tate agreed with that. She was honestly interested in the children in her school and, in her way, did the best she could to see that they grew up to be model young men and women.

"At times I almost admire her," Herb told Mary later, "only she is so sure she knows all the answers. If she could just be up against something tough with hundreds of others in the same boat and find out that her minor standards of deportment and method are really unimportant, she might be O.K. She needs to be disturbed."

"Or else she is disturbed," Mary answered practically, "and doesn't dare to face it."

"Only I'd hoped to go to work with someone who would be able to help me work out some of my ideas. These sixth-grade kids in my room may be carrying guns in six or eight more years. Chasing them down the hall because they bang their lockers isn't going to help one bit to get them ready for that, or help to prevent it from happening either. A big city like this should be leading the way. It was better in the small towns."

Mary was not disturbed at all this. She had fallen in love with a fellow who wanted to do his part to make the world a saner, better place to live, and who was impatient to get at it—a fellow who had stumbled onto teaching and found there the promise of a deeply rewarding career. She knew he'd found his chance to be a hero more than once, though he didn't want it talked about. "It's the time and the place that make a hero, not the man," he'd said heatedly once. "It's in every man to be a hero." Mary knew better, of course. There were few who would be like Herb. She knew that Herb could have been a small town principal this year, but had wished to teach longer—and to be in a city near the University.

She liked it better when he told her how his classes were going. Then he was enthusiastic, even if sometimes impatient. He described the various children to her: the shy little girls who admired him so much; the braver ones who smiled at him coyly; the reserved ones who were remote and distant; the boys who pushed and shoved and showed great scorn for girls, except once in a while; the boys who were timid and withdrawn; the boys who slouched and stamped and yelled and acted silly in their search for status; the children who seemed to be seeking to learn or to experiment, frequently without regard to what had been outlined for them in the curriculum.

There were 32 children in Herbert's room—20 boys and 12 girls. The ratio of the sexes was about reversed in Miss Brown's sixth grade across the hall. Apparently Miss Tate had felt that Herbert might be better able to discipline the older boys than Miss Brown, and had assigned most of them to him. After a day or two, he learned that he had all the "live wires."

An intelligence test given when his group had been in the fourth grade showed a range in I.Q. from 79 to 131. Other low I.Q.'s were 85, 86, two 89's and two 90's. High I.Q's besides the 131, were 124, 121, 116, 115, 108, 107, and three 105's. The median I.Q. was between 102 and 103. At the end of the fourth grade the median achievement test scores in the group had been at standard. Fifth-grade reading scores available for 25 of the 32 children ranged from low second-grade to above the eighth-grade level. In October of the fifth year, six of the 25 children had been reading at or above the seventh-grade level while three others had been at least one year advanced. In language too, the group was approximately average, though the range was from the third- to the eleventh-grade level. In spelling, the range was from third to tenth grade level.

A sociogram of the room showed an interpersonal structure with moderate interaction. With three choices, there were four children who were not chosen. There were three or four small closed groups in the room between whose members and the rest of the grade there was not much interaction. The most favored positions fell to four students rather than to one or two. In general, the social pattern was typical of classrooms where there had been an authoritarian atmosphere and where there had been little interaction between pupils in the room.

Getting started

Mr. Zan began his sixth-grade work in a forthright and business-like manner. Textbooks were passed out, seats assigned, the roll taken, study assignments made, and recitations held. He felt that the students expected this sort of regime. Having assessed the school as being relatively traditional, he adapted his beginning work to it. A relatively conventional daily program was outlined and followed. From the very first, however, he set aside one hour a day for conversation and discussion. In these periods, he let the pupils express themselves freely about their likes and dislikes, their hobbies and activities, their problems and their hopes for the future. He was interested particularly in finding out what the attitudes of the children were toward the school and the subjects they studied in the school. He was interested in their attitudes toward the teacher as a position rather than as a person. He studied their attitudes toward one another. He was interested in obtaining frank statements from them concerning their ideas about discipline, playground conduct, classroom conduct, and out-of-school conduct.

He got some ideas about the family standards of the children by discussing with them their activities during the summer. Of the 32 children in the room, seven had spent from one week to a month in summer camps away from their parents, while eight others had had the privilege of getting away from the city with their parents to lakes or farms in the suburban or rural areas. Seventeen had stayed the whole summer at home in the city, weekend trips not counted. Sixteen pupils, one-half the class, had earned money from other than their parents one way or another. Mowing neighbors' lawns and baby-sitting were the two most popular money-making activities. Mr. Zan made notes of as many of these observations as he could.

From these discussions, an interest was developed in recreational facilities in the neighborhood, and a unit began to develop along that line. At the start, the students talked about the part of the city in which they lived and listed the recreational areas. There was a large city park at the extreme western end of the district and another one at the extreme eastern end. In one or both of these parks there were public golf courses, baseball or softball diamonds, tennis courts, swimming pools, greenhouses, extensive flower and botanical gardens, a zoo, and equipment for water sports such as boating, water polo, and surf-riding.

Both of these parks were too far away from the homes of most of the boys and girls to be of ready use. To get to them, an automobile or bus was necessary unless permission was received from home for a rather long bicycle ride. In the more immediate neighborhood, there was a city playground upon which the children could play baseball, football and softball or, in the winter, skate. The playground had a small clubhouse in which were toilets and washbowls and a small space used in the winter as a warming house. In addition, there was an office for the playground director and a storage room for playground equipment. There was no place for indoor play on rainy days or cold winter days. The school playground also was available, but this comprised only half of the city block upon which the school was built. The other half was taken up with the building and with the landscaped lawn upon which play was not permitted. The school playground was unsupervised during the summer months. All this was information that the children already had and that came out in the discussions.

The children became interested in making a survey of these facilities near at hand. As a first step, they needed a map showing the playground and recreational facilities upon which children resident in the area could be located by placing dots. A committee was assigned the job of making a map of the school attendance district upon which the dots could be placed.

"We need people to do it who can draw well and who know how maps are made," Mr. Zan said. "What do we need to know in order to make a map?" He thought the discussion of such a question would give the children some background in selecting a good committee. The answers came rapidly, from seven or eight of the students.

"You have to know where north and south and east and west are."

"You have to know the streets."

"You have to show the stop streets and the bus lines."

"You have to know how to get the distances all the same."

As the suggestions were made, Mr. Zan wrote them on the board and made brief comments. It was a fine opportunity to build vocabulary. For example, "Show North, South, East and West— *cardinal* points of the compass;" "Show stop streets (*arterial*);" "Show distances—draw them to *scale*." The last item led to a brief discussion of *ratio* and *projection*. Few if any of the children understood the words at first, but some followed the discussion as Herbert used some simple illustrations. He told them a brief, true story of how important maps were to soldiers in the field. A committee of three boys, John, William, and Lars, was selected at the end of the discussion. Herbert thought it best to use a small committee the first time to see how well it would work. He wanted to make committee membership desirable and pleasant as well as educationally profitable. "I will see if Miss Tate has a small map we can use to make our large map from. Meanwhile, I think the committee members should examine some maps and see what you can find about map making in your texts and references. I'll find some time for you to start on the map tomorrow."

Miss Tate had a map of the attendance district that she was glad to loan to Mr. Zan and the committee. She also had a roll of wrapping paper in the storeroom suitable for map making. "I got it through the Art Department," she said, "for making murals and things like that, but we haven't used much of it. It goes a long way."

The next day when the time for geography came, Herbert said, "The map committee can work at the big table while the rest of us have geography." There were some study questions on the board relating to the text to occupy the class while he got the committee started. "Feel free to talk quietly and to consult the reference books. We will try not to let you bother us."

Activity outcomes begin to show

At the end of two days, the map was ready. There had been some false starts, but the final map was neat and clear, with streets, school, and playground carefully named. The committee presented the map to the class by describing what it showed. One of the boys was able to answer questions about the scale of the map.

"Miss Tate's map didn't have any scale on it," he said. "So we took a city map and found the scale on that—three inches for 5,000 feet. On Miss Tate's map, things were ten times bigger, so the scale was three inches for 500 feet. We made our map three inches for 250 feet, so that on our map one mile—that's 5,280 feet— is a little more than 21 inches long."

"How big is a block?"

"Some blocks are different than others. Some are long and narrow. The long ones have eight blocks in a mile so that's two and five-eighths inches long on our map or about 220 feet." The three boys demonstrated some of their arithmetic on the blackboard. "You gotta know about fractions to do this part," one said.

"Now we have to put the spots on the map, where we live."

"All the kids or just our room?" came the question.

The committee members looked at Mr. Zan, expecting him to decide.

During the early days of the term, Herbert had made the decisions and established the discipline with a swift and a sure hand. Now, it was necessary to "pass the ball" to the children as fast as they could be prepared to carry it.

"I don't know which is best," he said. "Perhaps you should discuss it with the class."

It was decided to put in spots just for the children in the room, since they were well spread over the district. Without help from their teacher, they passed out slips of paper and each one wrote his name and address. The next day the map was finished and placed on the bulletin board.

"Any good map shows something important. What does our map show?"

The discussion brought out the need for a summary and with two girls, Alice and Wendla, added to the committee, a summary was made. Mr. Zan showed them how to tabulate the material, and they placed their summary on the board.

NUMBER OF CHILDREN AND DISTANCE FROM PLAYGROUNDS

Item	Distance from School Playground	Distance from McDounough Playground
Less than ¼ mile	8	3
¼ to ½ mile	10	5
½ to ¾ mile	12	4
¾ to 1 mile	2	7
1 to 1¼ miles	0	6
1¼ to 1½ miles	0	7

The discussion of playground needs then turned to the facilities for play at the two playgrounds. There was a need for space for touch football and regular football for the younger fellows. In winter, the skating problem was the same. Older boys and young men at hockey pushed the younger ones aside. In the discussion period on Friday of the first week, a list was made (and saved) of needed facilities for existing playgrounds. Herbert wanted the children to save the list so that they could add to it as their conception of recreation widened. The list included space for the common outdoor games and it also included a swimming pool and a gymnasium for basketball and volleyball. The girls wanted a special rink for figure skating. One or two mentioned outdoor tennis, but indoor table tennis received a larger vote. Herbert thought that a warming house for skaters would be essential if there was to be skating. The warming house might include space for storage of shovels and other tools. It might be possible also to enlarge it sufficiently for informal club meetings.

They move into pupil-teacher planning

The last thing on Friday, Mr. Zan held a planning period for the next week. "Should we do any more with our recreation survey and if so, what?" he asked.

"Why can't we have a better playground? Where my cousin lives, they have a swell playground and a big community house. They even have a stage and they have shows and everything."

"Why can't we use the schoolhouse on nights in the winter? My dad says that's what they do in some cities."

"Our gym ain't no good anyway!"

"Yeah! We could use the mats for tumbling."

"Who wants to tumble! Basketball! I'm going to be a forward in high school like my brother."

"I'll be a guard."

"You won't be a guard. You won't be nothing. Somebody'd come down the floor rat-tat-tat-tat-tat-tat-boom and you'd be knocked out —boom! Georgie Price, he'd do it. Down you'd go."

"Yeah! Georgie Price—ping, ping, ping—basket, basket, basket!"

"Georgie Price, sure! What's he got to do with it. He's professional. You guys couldn't play with him either. You couldn't reach his knee hardly."

The boys engaged in an orgy of fantastic imagination and recrimination, not waiting for one another to finish before interrupting, and not caring to listen as they belittled one another and expressed their own exuberant intentions. Mr. Zan spotted three or four boys who seemed particularly aggressive in the discussion, and noted that though they had participated capably in the physical education classes, they had not been overly aggressive there. John was the boy who had suggested being a guard. He had not appeared either exceptionally good or inept in physical education, but he was a good, if quiet, scholar. He had been chosen on the map committee. Apparently, and this Herbert would later have to confirm or reject, the children accepted his academic leadership but evened the score in other activities. He had not been rejected on the sociogram.

Herbert did not worry about the lack of order in this discussion or its seeming lack of bearing on the planning of the next week's work. It gave him a chance to observe his group in a new light and to assess individuals in other than purely academic endeavor. Were they, in their minds, playing basketball successfully with the great professionals while their fellows were being trampled and found incompetent? Were they projecting themselves forward into the exciting activities of young manhood with all the energy of their young bodies? Or were they running wild, since their teacher had relaxed his firm grip for a moment, trying to make noise, waste time, show off, try out the teacher, and buck the school discipline?

Herbert was conscious of the passage of time and was desirous that some group planning take place. He waited to see if the children would return to the map project, but decided they wouldn't without some assistance from him. He rapped sharply on his desk.

"Ruby, what do you think?"

Ruby looked at him blankly. She had been listening to the basketball chatter with only half an ear, but had forgotten the original question. Herbert thought she was probably at the stage where this boyish talk seemed very silly.

"I mean," he continued, "what should we do with our recreation survey?"

"There is a lot more than just the playground and the gym. I go to the parks even if they are far away. I took sketching last summer in a class at the Institute and we went to Indian Head Park for our classes."

The discussion came down to earth then. Some of the girls said there should be things for girls in the survey, too, and some of the boys said that boys were interested in other things besides games. They decided to seek answers to the following questions.

1. What recreation facilities do we have outside our school area?

2. Do we have as much in the Columbus School area as in other parts of the city?

3. What do our parks have for us, in addition to our playgrounds?

The map committee volunteered to make another map, this one to show the whole East Side of the city with its two big parks as well as various playgrounds and schools outside the Columbus School district. The committee agreed to make the map as meaningful as possible so that by looking at it, any person in the community could visualize the needs of the whole area. The committee was anxious to make the map helpful in planning the best use of space in the East Side.

Transfer boy

Friday after school, Mr. Zan was in the office with Miss Tate when she was called to the telephone. He paid little attention to the conversation until he heard her say, "I think it would be unfair to Mr. Zan. He is new here this year and has a difficult grade. I'm willing to take my share of them, and I think I have, but I don't see why some other schools can't take their share, too." There was some more conversation and then the following, "Well, let me think it over. If I have to take him, I suppose I have to. Mr. Zan is in the office now, I'll talk to him."

Mr. Zan learned that the neighboring district to the west was often termed a delinquency area. Children in that area frequently got into trouble. A boy from there had been sent to a "home school" the previous March and had finished his fifth grade there. He was now being returned to the regular schools. He had attended his old school for two days the first week and then had "ratted." A vigilant principal had reported him, a visiting teacher had interviewed his parents, and the boy had finally agreed that he would be willing to try another school. The boy had said he would rather go back to the home school than to attend school in his own district.

"I don't object to handling our own problems, but I don't see why we have to take problems from other schools. I don't ask other schools to take my problems. I heard about this boy last spring. He kicked his teacher in the shins and swore at her viciously. They put him in another room in the same school, but the next week he broke into a parked delivery truck and stole some stuff and tried to sell it. That's when they sent him to the home school. Parents in our district won't like a boy like that being with their children."

"I wonder why he kicked his teacher?" Mr. Zan asked.

Miss Tate knew the story and told Mr. Zan. It had been a case of an order that the boy refused to obey and that the teacher was enforcing. Mr. Zan was curious concerning the boy's earlier history and concerning the practices being followed generally in schools where there was a high delinquency rate. Miss Tate answered him as well as she could.

"There was a kid like that in the school I went to," Mr. Zan said. "He quit school in the seventh grade. He swore at all the teachers. He and I enlisted the same day. He is buried out in the Pacific now and his mother's got a nice letter from the War Department. He cursed a lot, but he stuck with his buddies and got killed doing it."

Miss Tate looked at Mr. Zan with renewed interest. His intensity and his seriousness in such discussions were always intriguing to her. "Perhaps I should find out more about this boy. Perhaps you'd like to take him?" she asked.

"Sure," he answered, "why not? He's probably a good enough kid. After all, what are schools for if not to help the kids that need help?"

And so it was arranged. The record of the boy was to be sent to Mr. Zan before the boy appeared. The visiting teacher was to meet with him ahead of time and discuss the case. The boy was to be admitted without being made to feel that he was considered a bad boy. He was to understand that Miss Tate and Mr. Zan knew why he had not been successful in the other school and that a mutual arrangement had been made for him to try out in the Columbus School to see if everyone concerned could get along better.

From junk box to bulletin board

Mr. Zan had been building up his room resources during the first week in an effort to stimulate wide interests and discussions. In a box at the rear of the room beside the reading table he had put a flashlight of his that no longer lit up when the button was pressed. In the box also were a mouse trap that worked, some dry cells, some wire, a magnet, some rollers made by sawing up a broom handle into eight inch lengths, some nails, a spring scale, an old brownie camera, a string of Christmas tree lights, a medicine dropper, some marbles, some steel ball bearings, a metal measuring cup, a four-inch clamp, some electric sockets and plugs, some glass rods and some wool, some silk and a piece of fur, a cigarette lighter that didn't work, a small mirror, a "burning glass," and a faucet. Through the first week he had not said anything about his collection, though he had added to it while the children were in the room. He had brought the faucet and the medicine dropper from home on Friday and had "discovered" them in a package on his desk during the geography period and had brought them back and put them in the box at that time. Five or six of the children had looked into the box and handled some of the items while at the reading table, but had shown no great interest as yet.

He had discovered some science kits in the storeroom where the curriculum bulletin said they would be. These provided some basic materials that would be of use but that he did not wish to place out for the children.

The bulletin board also was being used. Articles in the newspaper by Howard Blakeslee, Associated Press Science Editor, were put up whenever he found them. One headline had said, "Amazing Heat Major Space Ship Problem." Scientists from the United States Air Force School and from some of the great universities were quoted concerning the heat from the naked sun's rays that would strike space ships when they passed beyond the atmosphere, and about the dangers of being hit by small meteors that would pass right through a space ship, since they travel as fast as 100,000 miles an hour. Articles such as this one were read by a number of the children. Another Blakeslee article told how new superstitions arise to take the place of the old ones. Some of the superstitions listed were that waving a red flag excites bulls, that all criminals are feebleminded, that Indians see better than white men, that lines in the hand foretell a person's future, and that you can make a person turn around by staring at his back. The science columns in *Newsweek* and *Time* magazines provided some good background. A newspaper article discussed accident-prone children. Several articles, later in the fall, explained how to handle guns safely and this was followed by news articles of hunting accidents.

Pictures were used, too. An illustrated story dealing with erosion was placed along the blackboard to the side. Herbert put up pictures of new types of airplanes as fast as he found them. A diagram map of the oil wells of Iran held a lot of science and geography. As time went on, more and more interest was shown in the exhibits. Mr. Zan asked Miss Tate for a subscription to a daily newspaper. She said she would try to figure out where to get the money for it, but her questions and remarks led him to believe that she was not sure it was a good idea.

As the year went along, the children began to bring bulletin-board items. Mr. Zan's effort was not to have them search for spectacular or even indiscriminately interesting items. He encouraged them to bring articles that were indicative of their own personal interests. Ruby, Joan, and Lars brought in much material about painting, drawing, and sketching, while Tommy, Jimmy, Marvin, Mary, and Lucille concentrated on music of various kinds. Jimmy was also interested in science as was John, Lawrence, William, and Ella. These activities developed as the year went along and did not spring up all at once.

A small but significant study bobs up

One of the first bulletin-board items that aroused sustained attention was a feature story about two people who make a business of extracting snake venom for sale to experimental laboratories. The headline had said, "Snake Venom May Be Polio Remedy." The children were interested in polio (they learned to spell *poliomyelitis* though it was not in the article). The article told how the owner of the "serpentorium" developed immunity to snake bites through injecting venom into his body. It also told how he financed his work in part by charging admission to see his snakes. The story said, "No announcements have been made, but reports of astonishing results have been drifting out of the laboratory" of the university that purchased the venom.

Some of the children were interested in snakes and lizards, and had handled and observed garter snakes. Many had watched Marlin Perkins' television show, "Zoo Parade," and had learned much about snakes from that source. The article was made to order for discussion. Did the data prove that the man's self-injections made him immune? Did it really indicate that venom might soon be a cure for polio? Did it give a good example of scientific method? Did it play up the idea of "easy" discovery and forget the hard systematic laboratory work? William offered to ask some of these questions of his father who was a physician. Later, after William reported his conversation with his father, Dr. Lervine accepted the invitation to talk to the class on the scientific method in medicine. Dr. Lervine had not been favorably impressed by the article, nor had Mr. Zan. They both wished to see it dealt with critically.

"William told me to study up on it before I came," Dr. Lervine told Mr. Zan later. "He said the kids were reading about it and knew a lot about it. He was right, too."

The playground and recreation study expands

During the first part of the week, the map committee was able to finish its map of the East Side. It had been made from a city map and had been blown up in size to twice the scale of the original. In their discussion of the parks, the children and Mr. Zan asked many questions that no one could answer: How many acres were in the park? How did the city get parks? How many people visited the parks? Who ran the concessions in the park? How much money did it cost to run the parks? Who hired the park policemen (the children knew they wore different uniforms and had different cars from those of the regular policemen)? How much vandalism was there in the parks and what was the cost of vandalism to the city? How did one get to schedule games in the parks?

It was decided that a letter should be written to the Park Department asking that an appointment be made for a small committee to come down and get any printed material that might tell about the parks. Letters had been written on similar occasions in the earlier grades, and some of the children showed good understanding of what should go into them. As Herbert reviewed letter writing with them, he was pleased at how much many of them knew, though, as it always is with each subject, there were some who made no contributions and showed no interest. He tried to remember those who did not contribute. All people should know how to write letters. It would be necessary later to get them into activities in which they were interested and in which it would be profitable to use the mail for communication. Three children were selected to go to the City Hall for the interview, and they were delegated to write their own letter. The letter was prepared and mailed on Tuesday. The following Monday an answer came, setting the appointment date for Thursday at 9:30 A. M. That would be the third week of school.

Herbert regretted a bit that he had not gone down for the material himself without an appointment, since he feared the long wait would tend to slow up the development of the activity. There could have been other opportunities for the interview and the letter writing, but what was done was done. He put the problem up to the children after the letter was mailed.

"Is there anything we can do to learn more about our problem while we wait for an answer?"

"We could study about the clubs we belong to, and what they do to furnish recreation," John said.

"We could study about other things we do, too. I sing in the choir at our church, and we practice Thursday nights and Saturdays," said Eunice.

"We could find out about the camps we go to in the summer," Albert suggested.

"There are free camps for poor kids," said John. "My father belongs to the Kiwanis Club. They have a camp for kids who can't afford to pay. He helps them get it started every summer. I've been out there and, boy, they've got a lot of stuff—boats and a dock and everything."

The room was divided into five committees for this study. There was a scout committee for boys, another for girls. There was a church activity committee, a committee on activities sponsored by men's service clubs, and one on junior lodge organizations. Members of each one were to find out all they could about the activities sponsored for boys and girls from 11 to 13 years of age. They were to inquire at home, bring manuals, use the telephone, write letters, or invite speakers or visitors. A new committee was added before long. The Community Chest drive was announced and a committee was set up to see what that organization did for recreation.

The service club committee was the first to invite in a speaker. They decided to have Mr. Deppelman, John's father, tell them about the Kiwanis Camp and any other camps he knew about. He came on Friday at 2:45.

Before he came, the question arose about how the children would entertain him. It was decided that one of the children should introduce him. Ruby was chosen as chairman because she lived right across the street from Mr. Deppelman and knew him well. It would be better for her to do it than John, because he would ask John all about it, and it would seem more real if someone else did it. The children thought Ruby should tell Mr. Deppelman what they were studying and why. Then she would tell the children who he was.

"Generally," Mr. Zan said, "a chairman greets a speaker and talks privately with him for a minute, telling him what the group expects and asking him how he wishes to be introduced."

The children assess the curriculum

There was quite a bit of uncertainty when the children began to outline what Ruby should say to Mr. Deppelman. They didn't seem able, at first, to express clearly their reasons for studying recreation.

"It's part of our study," Wendla said.

"We're supposed to know about it," said William.

"It's something to do when we're not studying our assignments," said Orville, who wasn't interested in book assignments.

"It's more fun to do than old book assignments," said Frank, who was Orville's chum.

"Our recreation study is about us. It's about things that give growing children exercise and recreation, so we don't have to play in the streets, and get into trouble," said Lester, who had said he wanted to be a lawyer.

Starting thus, and guided by questions from Mr. Zan, they developed a statement of reasons for studying recreation. They also reviewed some of the interesting and valuable things they had already learned. Mr. Zan had noticed many times in his work, and had studied many times in educational psychology, that people learn most efficiently when they know what they are learning and why. As he taught, he frequently asked, "Why do you suppose we are studying this?" or "Why did the author of the book put in a chapter like this for people of your age and grade?" Each time he started with a new group, he found the children prone to answer that they needed to know about China or India, for instance, in order to be educated, in order to know about all the world, in order to pass the tests, or to get into high school or college. Seldom at first were they able to see how such learning might directly affect their living or the living of people in a world devoted to the advancement of human welfare in either its broad or its specific instances. He knew, of course, that children could become interested and learn much valuable information without a mature assessment of all its implications, but he knew that the best motivation involved some conception of the real function or use of the information being learned.

Mr. Zan tried to assist his pupils in understanding the importance of learning to read, write, spell, and use arithmetic, of learning good individual work habits, of learning to attack problems in an orderly and systematic fashion, of learning good attitudes and appreciations, and of learning the skills necessary to work together democratically. In order to further this objective, he held frequent informal reviews, sometimes briefly at the end of a period or sometimes at the end of a project or part of a project, in which the pupils tried to put into words the things they had learned. When they knew and could state what they were learning, their enthusiasm was keener and their progress was accelerated. In such reviews he felt rewarded by answers such as the following:

"We learned that it costs more money to provide parks and playgrounds in the city than in the small towns."

"Yes, but we need them more in the city."

"Because in the city, there are not so many things to do to keep busy as on a farm, for instance."

"We learned the meaning of lots of new words such as 'delinquency area' and 'recidivism'. We studied the spelling of the words we didn't know so we could write up our findings."

"We found out how to use fractions in order to draw our maps to scale and we had to learn about ratio."

"We learned how to interview and introduce a guest speaker."

First visiting expert

After the noon recess on the day Mr. Deppelman was to come at 2:30, Mr. Zan called him on the phone. They had talked before and were acquainted.

"I am going to leave the room as you arrive," Mr. Zan told him. "I want the class to get you started without my help. They still tend to depend upon my guidance in too many small ways. I wish you would act as you would with any group of adults. Let them carry on as best they can."

Herbert knew the children had planned carefully, but he wanted them to build self-confidence.

When Mr. Deppelman appeared at the door, he turned to Ruby and said, "Mr. Deppelman is here, Ruby. You know him, of course. Will you take charge, see that our project is explained to him, and introduce him. I'll be gone for a few minutes, but will be back before he finishes."

When Herbert returned 15 minutes later, Ruby was seated at

ease in the front of a classroom of orderly children, all of whom were listening courteously. There was a spirited question and answer period, the children were on their best behavior, and Ruby's job was performed excellently and easily. Mr. Deppelman expressed his enthusiasm for the skills the children were developing. "They didn't do things like this when I was in school. It's bound to develop good citizens. Could you come sometime and tell about this type of work to one of our noon luncheons?"

"Perhaps it would be much better to have a group come from the class to tell the conclusions of their study of recreation in Amber City."

That was what happened, too. The invitation came and was accepted for a suitable future date.

Visits to the park

At the interview with the Park Department officials on Thursday of the third week, a great deal of material was collected. In addition to a history of the parks, telling their size and how they were secured and developed, there were bulletins of activities carried on in the parks, schedules of games and concerts during the past summer, statistics on attendance in the parks, and budgets that included the cost of vandalism. They got a copy of the City Charter, setting forth the organization and function of the Department and authorizing a definite tax levy with a millage limitation. There was a description of the plants in the greenhouse and another on the animals in the zoo. There was a separate bulletin on the golf courses in each of the parks. In addition to such information, they were given copies of recreation and sports magazines for their reading table. Before the committee left, it made a date for the whole class to meet with Mr. Neale, the Superintendent of Parks, at Indian Head Park on the following Tuesday, weather permitting (and it did).

The meeting and the tour through the park were the source of much learning. There were the mechanical details of getting permission from the parents, for this was the first field trip by the whole class. Transportation was solved by a call to the bus company, since no school buses were available that day. The bus company ran two buses instead of one on its 9:15 East-Side circuit. There would be ample room on the midday buses for the trip back.

In the park, the children had decided they would not spend time at the zoo. Many of the animals were in their inside cages, and autumn attendance was too low to justify keeping all the exhibits open. Furthermore, all the children had seen the animals more than once.

"We need to study more about the animals in the materials they gave us, and in our library before it would pay us to see them again," Lawrence had said, and the group had approved in its planning meeting.

"We are going there to study, not to have a good time," Ella had added.

Mr. Zan hoped they'd have a good time anyway. Somehow, he disliked the dichotomy and hoped in time he could start to remove it from their thinking.

The children made rules before they went. "Stay together. Spend no money for eating or riding at the concessions. Look out for one another. See that no one is left out of anything. Make individual lists of things to see and try to find out the answers. Bring small notebooks. Dress according to the weather. Report at once to Mr. Zan if anybody gets ill or too tired." Some of the rules were the result of parental suggestions. Each of the five committees wanted to find out how the parks and playgrounds served the groups in which they were privately interested.

In the park, the children became interested in Indian Head Lake. "Why can't we have a swimming beach in the lake?"

"The lake is artificial. There is not sufficient water in it for bathing. It is not pure fresh water."

Many questions were asked about fresh water and notes were made to find out more about the aeration of water, its self-purification, and the like. Later this was extended by a group of the girls into a study of swimming pools, bacteria, chlorination, and related topics.

Then a group of the boys asked how artificial lakes were made. Superintendent Neale told them how the water was pumped in through underground pipes and how the levels were determined by automatic valves.

"There are automatic valves in the flush tanks of toilets," one of the boys said.

"That's true," Mr. Neale answered. "But those are float valves. These work on the same general principle, but are pressure valves. The weight of the water opens and closes them." The children were so interested that he later showed them a diagram and also some replacement parts for the valves when they went through the maintenance engineer's shop.

"Could anyone make an artificial lake on his land?" the children wanted to know.

"You could if you had enough water and if you had the right kind of soil and rock under your lake. Our lake started to leak a few years ago. We began to lose water. It was during the drought and water was hard to get, so we had to find the leak or else let the lake shrink or even dry up."

Questions were asked about the drought, and about how the leak was found and plugged. Mr. Neale told them about the instruments and observations that were used to locate the seepage, how the engineers drilled holes surrounding the lake both to determine ground water levels and to provide samples of the ground water— samples that would show traces of chemicals placed in the lake water. He told them how the engineers then drained the lake in the suspected parts and lined the lake bed with a type of clay that was relatively impervious to seepage. "The bottom of an artificial lake is called a waterpan," he said. In answer to other questions he told them that the leak was first discovered by reading the water meters on the inlet pipes. Later, in mathematics and science, the children studied about water meters.

All this information interested some of the boys to the extent that they later interviewed the engineers and park employees who had done the work, got samples of the clay in question and experimented with it in school, studied ground water and made both a model and a diagram of the underlying rock and soil structure of the region, and found out that lakes bedded on pure rock may seep more than those whose beds have a coating of sand or clay, since faults in the rock (even igneous rock) funnel off the moisture, while moisture-bearing rocks absorb water. They found out some of the differences between various kinds of rocks.

One good thing leads to another

All this led to two further studies. One, relatively brief, dealt with oil-bearing rocks and shales. The other, and longer one, dealt with the chain of lakes that provided Amber City with its water supply. Much initial material for the latter study was obtained from the City Water Department, but the study went far beyond that. It dealt, too, with the drought, with the watershed beyond the lakes, and with state forests far up in the watershed. It involved the use of a number of films on water supply including one on sewage disposal.

By this time, the members of one group in the class were becoming expert young hydraulic engineers. They were soon off on the track of sewage disposal. Here again, while one committee studied the mechanics, the chemistry of the subject, other committees studied river beautification, the smothering and killing of fish and other wildlife by untreated sewage including industrial wastes, and the control of disease through proper disposal. By spring, a valuable field trip was made to the sewage disposal plant and the river. A whole day was taken for another trip through the lakes and pumping stations in the water supply basin and to the filtration plants.

Units are not to entertain

These things were taken up as opportunity permitted. Mr. Zan had found early in his experience that activities could range from being very educational to being only superficially entertaining. He had found that to maintain classroom interest with a succession of superficially entertaining projects was a greater strain on a teacher than was the policing and driving that is typical of very "traditional" classrooms. Many teachers give up the idea of activity units after rushing through a succession of exciting adventures where the children throw off restraint, look for one readymade thrill after another wherever they are, become spectators, and like a crowd at a boxing match, boo the fighters the instant they stop slugging.

The development of educationally productive units takes planning—careful planning. Much of this planning must be leisurely and pleasant. It involves dreaming of an imaginative and constructive kind. "Here is an interest," Mr. Zan would say to himself upon occasions such as the one where the boys asked questions about the seepage from the artificial lake. Their interest was the more obvious because of their animation as they examined the lake shore and piled question upon question about water levels, fish, and so forth. "What can I do or say to capitalize on it?" He made notes of such interests and of questions that might lead into the development of interests, so that he could think about them later.

Films were a possibility to develop interests in the initial period, but there was always the question of whether to use the films to arouse interest early in the study or to defer the use of them to provide information and inspiration later. The early use of the film before the children are alert to the questions involved in an activity will not provide the learning outcomes that will result if its use is deferred until the children know enough really to see and understand the content. Some films are best used to stimulate interest while others are best used to sustain interest or to assist in "tying things up." The decision regarding the use of films depended upon a number of other considerations.

When Mr. Zan felt that a particular area of learning was so important that all children should gain familiarity with it,[1] and if the interest did not develop without it, he might use films or any other motivational device such as field trips in order to get the thing started. He frequently used films with which he was not familiar in this broadly exploratory way. After having used them once, he was better able to place them so that they made more subtle or more substantial and specific contributions if used again. He found that as he became familiar with films and film strips, he could time them much more effectively. As he developed power in using committees in his classes, he found that films and film strips and tapes, and other recordings, too, could be used by small groups engaged in intensive committee study. There were materials of this nature that could be used with both high- and low-ability learners, but more frequently the divisions in the use of such materials were not on an ability basis but rather on the basis of special interests or special assignments by the whole group to sub-group committees. He even found it possible, when committees were at work, for one committee to

1 See Chapter 12 for a discussion of the criteria by which the significance of curriculum content may be determined.

use the movie projector (sitting close to a small screen) while the other children worked at other things.

Unit planning is not prescribing

Mr. Zan knew of films to use in the work on sewage disposal and water supply, but he knew little himself about water seepage and artificial lakes and impervious clays. He began to imagine what the children might do with such a project. Perhaps they could take a tub, he thought, and place a screen on some supports above it. Then they could place clay and other materials such as fine sand and coarse gravel in the form of artifical lakes on top of the screen. They could fill the little lake models with water and watch the seepage. The children never did this, however. When the pupil-teacher planning stage came, his suggestions in that respect were not adopted, but others were adopted that were better because they were in terms of the imagination and experience of the children, and strangely enough (though this no longer surprised Mr. Zan) they were better plans than the ones he had thought up alone.

Had he said to them, without preliminary pupil-teacher planning, "Let's get a tub and some screen and some clay and sand and make some lakes. . . ." that is what the obedient children would have done. A few would have been interested because it would have involved activity and concrete materials. The brighter children would have guessed how it would turn out long before the experiment had run its course. If they had been right in their guesses, their main learning would have been that Mr. Zan knew a lot about how water seeped through the soil. Bored, they might have made mud pies on the side, or molded marbles out of the clay, or they might have smeared and thrown the clay and water in an effort to inject some interest or life into the project. If they were wrong in their guesses, they might learn to have less faith in their teacher. Actually, however, the possibilities for learning would be increased if the guesses were wrong. This is the weakness of many projects such as those on the feeding of white rats. Instead of trying out the rats on diets that are unknown to the children (or even to the teacher) in their effects, foods are used that guarantee anticipated outcomes. Mr. Zan had used rat-feeding experiments with what he considered great success. He found them good with younger children who were inclined to be gratified with the achievement of the anticipated result and valuable for children who needed reassuring activity. Also, such experiments were good with groups just moving into pupil-teacher planning of units and in the organization of the many contributory activities of units, such as the use of oral and written skills and arithmetic in its application to the measurement of diet, weight and time, health, and so forth. As he and the pupils gained experience, however, he found his classes planning newer and less cut-and-dried projects. He found it less necessary, too, that he himself be expert in all the areas of learning involved in the projects.

Perhaps the hesitancy of teachers to develop units in areas where they are not expert has resulted in some of the "feminizing" of the elementary schools that was once obvious. Perhaps it was a subtle part of the reason why active upper-grade boys sometimes rebelled at the orientation of their school work. Mr. Zan thought of this early in his career as a teacher when faced with interesting his pupils in units. The girls, he found, sometimes had interests that surprised him, and stores of knowledge in areas where he was a rank tyro. Until he learned to work with them in their areas of interest and excellence, he found it hard to draw them out as he did the boys. "Why couldn't that be true in reverse with women teachers?" he asked.

Unit activity is not superficial

Mr. Zan did not wish the boys to get too involved in their study of water seepage until the results of the study of the parks and play-grounds were realized, but neither did he wish their interest to flag until he discovered whether or not it was substantial enough to build upon. The day after their field trip, they discussed it in class. The various committees reported on what they had learned and what they wished to learn more about.

The service club and the lodge committees had found that during the past summer 24 picnics had been held in the park by fraternal groups and that all of these had been attended by husbands, wives, and children. They learned that most such groups did not take full advantage of the facilities the parks provided. There were playground supervisors who would organize games, and trained guides who could be scheduled free for descriptive trips through the zoo and the greenhouse. There was a "bird man" who would take scheduled groups into a wooded section to observe bird-life, and "three power" sport binoculars could be rented for this trip. There was a "botany" trail also. They had found out that each spring the Park Department sponsored a series of radio programs on the parks and was hoping to expand into a companion television program.

"They might need some kids—some children to help in that," Ruby said. "That would be fun."

"Yeow! A mob scene. That's for me. Boom! Boom! Marching! Bugles! Raw-tah tah tah—tah tah!" That was a joke and its humor was accepted quietly and pleasantly by the group since it was also accepted by Mr. Zan.

"Let's ask Mr. Neale."

"That's not till spring."

"Oh! Who wants to be on television?"

"I think it would be fun." It was Ruby holding to her original idea.

"I think it would be fun, too."

"On Zoo Parade, Marlin Perkins handles snakes. He hands them to other people and they get scared."

"I don't mean that. There would have to be a program about people in the park."

"Let's ask him."

After a few more remarks, "Let's ask him," got attention.

"Write him a letter."

"He might forget before spring."

"Let's write in the spring, then."

"How will we remember?" asked Mr. Zan. He had the germ of another idea!

"Ruby can remember."

"Yes, Ruby could remember," Mr. Zan said. "But by that time we will probably have a lot to remember. You people are planning an awful lot."

"We could make a list."

And so they set up a calendar of future events and possible events that, as it grew, became a constant source of ideas for possible new activities. The letter was never written as that interest did not maintain itself. It was not forgotten, however. It just couldn't compete with other choices when the time came. Sixth-grade children can and frequently do maintain interest for long periods of time, but more frequently they do not. The calendar that was started, however, was maintained and many other items placed on it were carried out.

In their review of the field trip, the discussion finally came to the artificial lake.

"There are fish in the lake, but he said it was too dirty for people to swim."

"Mud bottom, too, and people throw broken glass and cans in it. They have to clean it out all the time. That costs money that they could spend for equipment."

"They aren't game fish—they're bullheads."

"Ah! They have pan fish in it. They're game fish."

"Yeah! But they just bring them in tank trucks and dump them in for the kids to fish. They die pretty soon and they all winterkill. That's what Mr. Neale told us. He said they have a man to pick up the dead fish when they come to the top or drift up on shore."

"They smother in winter under the ice."

"Why don't they smother in big lakes?"

Nobody knew. Neither did Mr. Zan for sure.

"I don't know either," he said. "Who'll volunteer to look it up for us?"

Somebody would (and did).

"My dad said he never knew that lakes leaked."

"My dad told me about a man that lives over in Lichen Hills that made a swimming pool in his back yard. He had a man come with a steam shovel and dig a big hole and they put roofing paper all over the bottom and used tar to stick it together just like a roof. They filled it with water and it didn't leak."

"I read about that in one of my science magazines. You have to use chlorine if very many people use it."

"Couldn't they use clay?"

"It's a special kind of clay."

"Where does the water go when it leaks out of the lake?"

"That's what we have in our notes. It becomes ground water and it forms lakes and springs in low places, and it is pumped up in pumps where people have pumps instead of faucets."

"Let's get some impervious clay and see how it works."
"Let's ask the men who fixed the lake how they did it."
"Let's get some books about it."

After some more discussion, it was decided to write some letters to find out where to get some clay, and to inquire at the reference division of the city library for suggestions about reading about the topic. A group of nine children wished to do special work on that project.

"It will be some time before we can really get going on it," Mr. Zan said. "We'll have to order the clay and get the reference books and read them. Meanwhile, we'll finish our project on the parks and playgrounds."

Some outcomes of the parks and playgrounds unit

The written reports on recreation contained a great mass of interesting information. The children had found a relationship between their part of the city and municipal recreation facilities that was of long standing. The area surrounding the Columbus School had been built up and populated in the years just prior to World War II. It was essentially a new part of town. It had been developed during a period when times were hard and money scarce. The lots on which the homes were built were small. The real estate promoters had not felt it advisable to set aside any large sections of the subdivision for recreational purposes since they did not feel that they could add that much money to the cost of the lots they were selling. The City Council had not foreseen the future development of that section of the city and had not set aside land for recreation. These were typical of things the students found out as they studied the situation.

In the register of deeds office in the County Court House, a well-informed and instructed committee found that at the time home building in the district was just getting started, there had been much land upon which taxes had not been paid. The City Parks Department could have obtained this land for playgrounds at no cost. The Department had not been alert to the possibility. This discovery led to some very serious discussions about the responsibility of city officials remaining alert to the needs of their growing communities.

The study of recreation in Amber City spread to the state and another unit was developed in that area, led by a special committee of ten. The State Department of Parks and Conservation had much material available here, as did some of the publishers' state supplements to their elementary social science series. Books and pamphlets dealing with the state were good beginning sources. Films on forest fires, rivers, soil erosion, wild life propagation, and similar topics were used. Many of the children had visited the state parks. A collection of pictures and post cards from home was made and displayed.

This study served to keep the project interest alive until the time came for the visit to the Kiwanis luncheon. A panel of five was selected. Each prepared a two-minute presentation, and then the panel answered questions. Mr. Zan merely stood and took a bow. The children did the rest. The men were amazed at the answers. Some questions were passed up and down the panel with the final answer being, "We don't know." The men remarked that they noticed the children making notes of each unanswered question.

Cross section of a unit

Six weeks later the children returned to their experiment with the clay, better able to appraise the problem as a result of the research they had conducted since it was first discussed.

"We have to use something porous and then treat it with clay," said one of the boys who had read the pamphlets and advertisements obtained from the engineers.

"Cloth is porous unless it's chemically treated," said Louise, whose father was a dry cleaner and who had stated her ambition to be a stylist and designer of clothes. "Well, I guess it's porous even then, only it resists water."

"Well, we could use some cloth and cover it with clay."

And so they started planning. The boys made some frames, eight inches square, out of a one-by-four inch board. They covered one of these loosely with a light cotton cloth tacked around the edges, one with cheesecloth, and one with canvas. They experimented by putting the covered frames in pans and pouring water over them. Then they experimented with thin layers of clay on each one. After a day, they decided they needed a control for the factor of evaporation, so they covered another board with cloth sealed with an asphalt roofing compound. They finally got around to using beakers to measure their water carefully. They decided they had to make allowance for the amount of water absorbed and held by the fabric. One of the boys who had camping experience remembered that if one rubbed the inside of the top of a tent while it was raining, the tent might leak. They experimented along that line, too, and at Mr. Zan's suggestion, read about surface tension and the action of molecules in either attracting or repelling moisture. They experimented with piercing the canvas with nail holes and seeing how effective the clay was in such cases.

Louise and two other girls were interested in "Cravenetting" fabrics. They obtained some sample treated fabrics from Mr. Kohen, Louise's father, and tested them. He gave them a small bottle of the concentrated solution used in making fabrics water resistant. "It has," he said, "a paraffin base." In dry cleaning, this solution was dissolved in the dry cleaning fluid and dried into the fabrics in a centrifuge. The girls wanted to use the solution according to directions, but it was decided not to use inflammable materials.

They brought some paraffin from home that their mothers used to seal jelly and tried rubbing it cold on the fabric. They melted some and tried to brush it on the fabric, but that wouldn't work and they discussed why. They discussed, too, the safety precautions they should take before they melted and used the paraffin. They experimented with some fabrics soaked in a light oil. This brought up the question of instantaneous combustion. The oiled rags were kept in jars, and some of the girls read to find out why this procedure should be followed. They developed some fire safety rules regarding paint rags and oily dust mops around the house and communicated these rules and the reason for them to their parents. They observed the difference between the same fabric, treated and untreated. They saw that the water resistant factors were only effective to a certain point. They washed out some of the cloth with soap and water and saw that its resistant quality was removed. Mr. Zan demonstrated the action of soap in various ways such as its effect in reducing surface tension in water. They obtained some "liquid rubber" and really waterproofed one piece of cloth. As a result of their reading, the children became interested in fire resistant fabrics and obtained some waterglass (potassium and sodium silicate) and treated and tested fabrics with it.

Both the boys and the girls learned that imperviousness to water was largely a matter of degree as it applied either to waterpans or fabrics.

One day the spelling and vocabulary list on the blackboard included the following words: porous, centrifuge, paraffin, Cravenetting, impervious, waterpan, aeration, tension, molecules, asphalt, beaker, repellent, resistant, solution, evaporation, absorption, and chemical.

Each day the pupils used their arithmetic books to find such things as how to read the marks on the side of a beaker or how to set up their data in tables. There were many thought questions involving addition, subtraction, multiplication, and division. These problems involved understanding how the comparisons between different frames could be made, how great the differences were, and so forth.

The class schedule grows more flexible

The study of artificial lakes was only a small part of the whole unit on water supply, ground water, water conservation, erosion, and the geology of the region. As the class worked with units, the scope of the units developed and grew. Mr. Zan found it possible to spend more time on them profitably. He had started the year with a rather formal time schedule, saving one hour a day for conversation and get-acquainted activity. For some time an hour a day proved sufficient to select, plan, and carry through on the small activity involved in surveying and making a map of the immediate recreation area. One small committee with at first three and later five members had worked on the map. The rest of the class was involved only in the planning and in the conversation that still served the primary purpose of getting acquainted so that teacher and pupils could deal with one another as real persons possessed of strengths and weaknesses, interests and aversions, talents and shortcomings. By slow degrees, Mr. Zan let the students make decisions regarding the projects, such as which children to include in the spot map. Pupil-teacher planning was used in an elementary way in discussions about what the maps showed and how they should be summarized. The whole group discussed the criteria for a good playground and community house. Greater freedom and informality of discussion gave Mr. Zan an opportunity to know the children as real people, not as little pretenders. By the end of the first week, he had learned a little about each child and a lot about ten or twelve of them. The bulletin board and the science "junk" box offered additional opportunities to find out about the children's interests and capabilities.

When the study expanded beyond the local school area, the map committee undertook a wider assignment. When Mr. Deppelman came to school to talk about the summer camps supported by various service clubs, an important school-community contact was made and the pupils began to develop self-confidence in seeking community assistance. In the snake venom episode, there was a chance to bring in another visitor, an M.D., and to help lay the basis for future pupil-teacher-parent planning.

Community recreation was studied by five committees (soon changed to six) with every child being on one committee or another. The map committee was now disbanded, though it could be reactivated at any time. The maps were still on display. As this work went forward, Herbert tried to have the children realize why they studied certain things and what they really learned. As this developed, an improvement in classroom morale became obvious. The pupils made rules for themselves as a group before they went to the park. These were revised for each trip in terms of the contingencies of the time, place, and past experience.

In each unit, there were the seeds of interest in further units. The unit on city recreation was followed by a similar unit, statewide. Then came the inception of the committee on lakes, ground water, and geology, followed and in part paralleled by units on oil wells and oil deposits, and on the water supply of Amber City. As these committees ended their units in various ways, the children, organized in other committees, studied sewage disposal and the related problems of river beautification, river pollution, industrial sewage, and disease control through sewage disposal.

By this time, the unit activities occupied the full afternoons. The mornings were spent on the formal subjects such as arithmetic, reading, geography, spelling, and hygiene. Much of what transpired in the morning was an outgrowth of the afternoon's work, but much of the morning work could not be related to the units in progress and Herbert made no farfetched effort to do so when it would have been artificial and unnatural to try.

Attention to individual differences

Mr. Zan made little attempt to do ability grouping in the activity units. He did that more frequently in the more formal part of the program when, for example, children poor in mathematics studied the things they were able to learn, while the better mathematicians went far beyond the typical sixth-grade textbook. In the activity units, there was plenty of constructive work for children at all levels working side by side on the same general project. In order to realize on this opportunity, it was necessary, Herbert had found, to give the children the freedom and then the necessary assistance in learning to plan the details of their work for themselves. No single human could possibly get around to directing the activities of all the children where individual differences are taken into account, and it would not be desirable if he could. Children must learn to be self-reliant, cooperative, and secure in their groups without outside domination and direction.

Frank, Orville, and Grant were probably the slowest boys, academically, in the class. Under the direction of some of the others, they made the frames for the experiment with clay and the waterproofing of fabrics.

"We'll have to cut them so they are eight inches square on the outside or they won't fit into the pans," William had told the three boys, "so each piece should be seven and one-eighth inches long."

Jimmy who was standing by the bench said, "Here, I'll show you. That's the one-eighth mark on the square. Mark it across there right after the seven." A stubby finger marked the spot.

The three workmen took their instructions with no show of resentment. They were interested and contributing members of their group. When the first four pieces were cut, they held them together and measured them before they nailed them. The first nailing split one of the boards and Mr. Zan was consulted. He had to find some brads. Then the boys were more successful. Frank measured, Orville sawed, and Grant nailed. They measured each frame when it was finished and, to make sure, they fitted each in turn into the pans.

Jimmy and William had joined another group that was discussing the planning of the experiment. A committee of girls cut the cloth, allowing extra goods to fold under along the tacking edge. A consultation was held over how deep into the box the fabric should hang.

"It has to hold enough water," Lawrence said. "There has to be some pressure and it has to be enough to measure."

Decisions were reached, trials made, and specifications set up. Again a group of workmen took over, tacking on the fabric. This time there were both boys and girls. The boys did not fold the fabric under on the first one they tacked, but upon criticism from the girls and demonstration that the fabric would tend to pull apart under pressure, they took the fabric off, folded it, and tacked it again.

Later some of the slower children assumed the duty, at proper intervals, of examining the pans, measuring and recording the seepage in graduates, adding carefully measured amounts of water, and duly recording all that they did on charts. The children on the planning committee instructed them in these duties, showing them how to read the measures and where to record it. "Never measure or write it down alone," was one rule. "Have two do it, and each one check so as to be sure it's right."

There were other specific jobs to do that were assigned to or assumed by those able to do them. As examples, the clay was to be mixed and kept moist, trials were necessary until a suitable consistency for the clay was determined, a small wooden paddle was carved to use in applying the clay, cold paraffin was to be rubbed by hand on the surface of fabrics, fabrics were to be washed in soap and water and dried, paraffin solutions were to be used in Cravenetting, and waterglass was to be used in fireproofing.

In getting these and countless other things done, Mr. Zan did not strive for an outwardly orderly and quiet room. Instead, he encouraged the children to plan and work together. As he got to know the children better, he found this easier to do. When he saw some of the superior students doing work that mainly required manual dexterity, he might say, "Perhaps you can find someone to do this, while you go to the library. . . ." If he found some children unable to agree on the necessary consistency of the clay, he might say, "Why don't you ask some of the others to help you decide—some who have done more reading and who know how they plan to use it?" Sometimes his guidance was more direct, but when he was direct in his suggestions, he was conscious of it and of its limitations in building initiative and enterprise. "There are some better ones over there. Look at them and see if you can get yours more like them." "Be careful. Never leave a saw so that it may fall or be knocked against another child. Think, each time you use it or put it down, so that you don't injure anyone."

Discussion Questions

1. Marion Johnson began with her class in a socialized manner and worked in the direction of a schedule of planned activities. Herbert Zan began with a formal subject schedule and worked in the direction of experience units and activities. Discuss the differences in the two approaches.

2. Which approach would you prefer to use? If you elect Mr. Zan's approach, is it because you fear to try the other? What do you fear, the criticism of fellow teachers, of principal, or of community?

3. Are you afraid of lack of discipline? Does that mean you fear that you may not be able to dominate the situation? If so, is it based on your lack of faith in your professional training, in the skill to do the job in the new way? Is it based on lack of faith in your own personality, sensitivity to other personalities, empathy? Or is it based on your belief, or in an unwillingness to discard your belief, in the educational effectiveness of autocratic procedures?

4. You saw Miss Johnson work with John Littlejohn? How do you think Mr. Zan should begin with his "home-school" boy? What of his first days in the room? How make him feel at home? How find a place in the "group" for him? How "evaluate" him, to find out where to begin? Take an imaginary boy, or a real boy from your own experience, and trace an imaginary story of what might happen. Can Mr. Zan expect everything to go "smoothly" with this boy?

5. Assume that Mr. Zan's father was an immigrant from central Europe who came to America as a young married man, became a cobbler, and earned a modest living repairing boots and shoes in a small town. Contrast Herbert's background with Marion's. What insights might he have to develop? Would his attitudes toward those struggling with less success than his father and himself necessarily be more wholesome than hers?

6. Contrast Miss Altonweather and Miss Tate. Are they typical, do you think, or is the ordinary principal superior to these stereotypes? What could Miss Tate have said or done to assist Mr. Zan in his first days, so that he would not have felt so discouraged? What seems to have been her primary failure in Mr. Zan's eyes? Was he too visionary and idealistic?

7. What items can you think of that might be added to Mr. Zan's science junk box? Discuss the use of such resources. What items might the pupils bring? What was his purpose in building the collection without discussing it? Was this good or bad technique?

8. Evaluate Herbert's use of the parent as a visitor upon the occasion when he left the pupils alone to greet the visitor.

9. Describe some places where you think Mr. Zan carried over or should have carried over the project work into some real honest-to-goodness drill on facts and skills.

10. Discuss the things in Mr. Zan's beginning work that show a definite plan on his part that the children move in the direction of certain important learnings. Then point out instances, within that plan, where a happy circumstance or chance remark led to interesting and new activities contributory to that over-all plan.

Selected References

Audio-Visual Education, Publication No. 16, 1948-49. Pasadena, California: Pasadena City Schools, 1949.

Color, School Publication No. 432. Los Angeles: Los Angeles City Schools, 1947.

Curriculum Guide, English and Social Studies, Grades Seven, Eight, Nine. Minneapolis: Board of Education, Minneapolis Public Schools, 1951.

Elkhart Into the Air Age. Elkhart, Indiana: Elkhart Public Schools, 1946.

Everett, Samuel, *School and Community Meet.* New York: Hinds, Hayden and Eldredge, Inc., 1948.

Fenner, Phyllis R., *The Library in the Elementary School.* New York: Hinds, Hayden and Eldredge, Inc., 1945.

Guide to Social Education, A. Glencoe, Illinois: Board of Education, 1944.

Healthful Living in School and Community. Montgomery, Alabama: Division of Instruction, State Department of Education, 1946.

Home and Family Living. Pasadena, California: Pasadena City Schools, 1949.

Living and Learning in the Elementary Grades. Gainesville, Florida: College of Education, University of Florida.

Science in Our Schools. Newark, New Jersey: Board of Education, Newark Public Schools, 1951.

Olsen, Edward G., *Social Travel, A Technique in Intercultural Education.* New York: Hinds, Hayden and Eldredge, Inc., 1947.

Physical Education and Health Instruction. Dallas, Texas: Dallas Public Schools, 1947.

Your Ticket to Popularity—Good Manners. New York: The Girl Scouts of the U.S.A. and The Boy Scouts of America, 1950.

21

MAXINE SCHMIDT—SUPERVISOR

$\mathcal{T}$HREE YEARS AGO when I accepted the position as supervisor in Hampton Rapids, I had taught only seven years, two years in a rural school and five years in the middle grades in a small community. I had then returned to school for three years and had finished work for my Bachelor's and Master's degrees.

The position at Hampton Rapids interested me very much and I was very pleased that I was the successful candidate. Hampton Rapids is a town of 5,000 people and the school district contains, in addition, three other small communities, 8, 9, and 15 miles from Hampton Rapids. The position I was to fill was a new one; I was to supervise 26 elementary teachers in Hampton Rapids and six in each of the three outlying communities. When Superintendent Walker first interviewed me, I was very thrilled and would have accepted the position immediately if it had been offered to me. As it was, I had time to think it over before the offer came, and in the meantime I had time to dream. If it should come through, I thought, it was the opportunity of a lifetime. I hoped it would present a chance to do the kind of permissive supervision that I had studied about. My major advisor assured me that my chances for the position were good and that I should view the position from the standpoint of what I wished the job to be, as well as from the standpoint of what Superintendent Walker might want. The placement bureau officials said it was entirely proper to discuss in detail the conditions under which I would accept the position.

When Superintendent Walker invited me to Hampton Rapids to look over the situation, my ideas were well formulated. Hampton Rapids was an attractive community with two elementary schools, one quite old and one fairly new. Each of these schools had a principal, while the three schools in the small neighboring communities had teaching principals. I saw the small but attractive office that might be mine some day and was told that the supervisor would have an office secretary. There was a conference room adjacent to my office that I could use with the rest of the staff.

I discussed with Superintendent Walker the working conditions that I desired. First, I did not wish to participate in the selection of teachers. I would rather concentrate my efforts on the improvement of instruction. Second, in the interest of better rapport, I wished to have nothing to do with the rating of teachers for purposes of determining whether they should be retained at Hampton Rapids or promoted to administrative or other positions. Third, I wished to talk over with Mr. Walker the possibility of having a definite budgetary allocation for the purchase of professional materials that might be useful in an in-service training program and for the conducting of workshops and study groups involving the employment occasionally of outside experts on problems that the teachers might wish to study. Fourth, I wanted to discuss the possibility of having a budgetary fund which could be used for the employment of substitute teachers while regular teachers visited other teachers in the school system or perhaps farther away. I wished also that at some time we might have a budget for carrying on workshops. Fifth, I wanted permission to work with community groups, parents, businessmen, laboring men, and citizens of every description who might become interested in planning with teachers and students for the improvement of classroom instruction. Finally, I wanted to have a meeting with the principals in the various schools to see whether or not we might agree on an acceptable method of working together in the improvement of instruction.

Superintendent Walker was interested in my suggestions and he asked many questions about them. I agreed with him that, in any specific matter, his judgment would be final and I assured him that I would welcome all the help he could give me. I told him, however, that I would dislike having him evaluate my work at the end of one year, since I felt that it would take longer than that before the things that I wished to do would bear tangible fruit. Mr. Walker has told me since that it was my presentation of the conditions under which I wished to work that really settled in his mind the conviction that he wished to employ me. The meeting with the principals was easily arranged and they readily agreed with me on a program under which we would work together. After I met briefly with the Board of Education and discussed my hopes, the Superintendent recommended my appointment and I left with a signed contract.

As I drove back to the University, I couldn't resist patting myself on the back. I could see my name, "Maxine Schmidt," on that office door! I couldn't resist thinking back to those two years at teachers college, to those two years in the rural schools, and to those five years of teaching in town—each summer working to get a little extra money, waiting on tables in Glacier National Park, doing office work, and working in war plants. I couldn't help remembering that sometimes it had seemed a bit hopeless and dreary.

After a bit, I began thinking about the responsibility that was to be mine. After all, I had never taught the way I wanted to have teachers teach who would work with me in Hampton Rapids. My teaching had been very much the same as that of the teachers who had taught me when I was in school. Two years in teachers college had not given me a very broad or deep understanding of what education was all about. I don't think I was a poor teacher, but I certainly had been far from an ideal teacher. I am afraid that I had been a rather authoritarian teacher in a pleasant sort of way. I had made the decisions in my classroom, handed out the assignments, and decided upon the projects and the problems to study. I had been the dominating teacher. In seven years, I had developed some pretty good techniques for managing my classroom. I found out how to maintain discipline and how to be pleasant without losing control of my class. I had worked in the summers and saved my money so that I might complete my degree all at one time.

Now I was faced with a real problem. As I studied at the University, I saw that the way I had been teaching was not as good as I thought it was when I was doing it. I decided that there were better ways to teach. Unfortunately, I had never actually used the methods that I wanted to see used. As a teacher, I had not used the methods in which I now believed. When I began to think of what

I was setting out to do in Hampton Rapids, I became just a little unsure of myself. I wondered if perhaps I should not have gone back to teach for a year or two myself before I allowed myself to be set up as a supervisor. By the time I arrived home that evening I was not sure whether I was to be congratulated or commiserated.

A second grade to remember

When I arrived on the job in the fall, I decided to spend the first month in getting acquainted with as many teachers as possible. I told them at an opening teachers' meeting that I would try to get around to all of them as soon as possible. I explained a bit about my philosophy of working with them, but I knew that little I would say would have much effect. I knew that I would have to wait until they got acquainted with me before they would understand what I meant.

There was one thing that I had in mind to do first. I wanted to see if there were teachers in the district who knew how to do, and were doing, the things that I had only learned about theoretically. I can still remember the thrill I had when I went into Miss Wolitarsky's second grade on Wednesday of the second week. I arrived shortly after ten o'clock and I stayed all day. I had a feeling when I had been in the room a short time that she knew what she was about. The first thing I can remember now occurred when the pupils found that the gymnasium would not be available to them for their recreation period. It was raining outside and play facilities in that old building were at a minimum. The children talked over the problem and decided upon a game—a simple game for second-graders. A child ran about the room, tagged someone who was sitting down, and then ran about through the aisles until he was either caught or succeeded in getting back to the seat that the other child had left. Several children who were caught took seats in the front of the room. After a while, one little boy was caught, but he insisted that he had not been and returned to his seat. The child who had tagged him looked protestingly at Miss Wolitarsky but she did not seem concerned. Two or three children seated near the little boy also protested, both in the direction of Miss Wolitarsky and to the little boy himself, but he sat stubbornly in his seat. After a moment or two, the child who had tagged him went on playing the game with the others and the little boy sat on. As I watched, I could see that the children were leaving him out of the game. He looked around and the only eyes he met were disapproving ones. After a little while he got up, moved quietly and almost surreptitiously up to the front of the room and took a place with the other children who had been tagged. Arriving there, he talked to the others, but it was some few minutes before they accepted him into the group again.

As I sat there watching, I saw what Miss Wolitarsky had done and I thought back to what I would have done when I was teaching. I knew I would have stepped in pleasantly and made a ruling one way or other. I would have said, "Oh! I think you were caught. You'd better sit up in front with the other children," and I would have smiled and patted him on the head and he would have gone up in front perfectly contented, and the game would have gone on. I might have ruled the other way and said, "Well, it was pretty close. I'm not sure whether you were caught or not. What do you say, class, if we let him take his seat and not be caught?" And I would have smiled again and the class would have smiled with me and all would have been forgotten. But Miss Wolitarsky was smarter than that. She was wise enough to build a group control. In a week's time she had built well enough so that she could withhold herself while the group enforced its own standard. I spoke to Miss Wolitarsky about the incident at noon. I complimented her on what I had seen, and I told her that I was afraid if I had been in her place I would have thoughtlessly made the decision myself. I asked her what she had done with the class to prepare them to handle the matter the way they did. She seemed a bit embarrassed at the question. "Children know how to do a lot of things," she said, "if we just give them a chance. It didn't take too much planning. We have talked each day a little bit about how to play together and how to work together and how to set up rules. While the children made suggestions, I put a list on the board."

There on the board, sure enough, was the list. It was headed, "Be Happy at Work and Play." Beneath it were the rules as Miss Wolitarsky had interpreted them while the children made their suggestions. (1) Don't be noisy. (2) Mind the teacher. (3) Pass quietly. (4) Don't talk when you shouldn't. (5) Don't yell. (6) Be polite. (7)

Work hard. (8) Be neat. (9) Don't fight. (10) Don't tell lies. (11) Don't play with naughty children. (12) Don't play with children who don't play nice. (13) Don't laugh at naughty children. (14) Don't be a tattletale. (15) Make ours the best room. (16) Play nice. (17) Do what the rules say. (18) Don't sass each other. (19) Don't hit each other. (20) Don't say bad words. (21) Be good.

That was the list. You could see that as far as possible Miss Wolitarsky had used the words the children had used. You could see that she must have simplified some of it so that the words could be as easy as possible. You could see, too, where Miss Wolitarsky had made remarks and had guided the discussion. The first rules seemed to follow the sort of thing that children had heard teachers and parents say over and over again. Almost all the rules were prohibitions rather than statements of positive behavior. You could guess that some place along in the list Miss Wolitarsky had suggested that they think about things that they might do when some children did not live up to the rules. Then you could see a little bit later that she might have asked them what they would do as a group to bring about a room where there would be happy children at work and at play. Though I thought I could see these things in the list, I could also see where one rule had suggested others to the children. I could see where rules had been suggested that did not fit into the things the rest were thinking about at the time. Miss Wolitarsky explained that the list was incomplete, that they used the list as the basis for discussions and that they intended to add to it from time to time.

I asked her what she would do as the list became longer. I asked how long they would leave the list on the board and what they would do with it afterwards. "I'm not sure," she answered. "Perhaps the children will decide that some of them can copy the rules into a little book of rules, or perhaps each child will wish to have a book of rules. It might be that we could use it in a second-grade newspaper. I will be concerned that we do something with it to help the children understand the meaning of the rules. The main thing is to get them to set up rules as a group. So far, each of these rules has only been suggested by one child. Perhaps the time will come when we can set up some rules by group action. It's hard to tell now just what will come of it."

Meet some other teachers

All of the teachers were not as discerning as Miss Wolitarsky. There was Miss Smith, a sincere, hardworking teacher whose room was orderly at all times and whose discipline was of the best. In her fourth grade the first day I visited, she was having a spelling lesson. She dictated 15 words and then had the children sit quietly at their seats while she passed up and down the aisles and marked each child's paper. Most of them had but one or two words wrong, or else they were all correct. When she found one or two words misspelled, she chided a bit. She succeeded in dictating the 15 words and getting around the room in 25 minutes. She completely wasted 25 minutes of time for the ten children who had the words all right. Except for getting the marks, which she later wrote into her book, she had not succeeded in achieving anything that could not have been achieved by having the children check their own words and study those they did not know. The words had been taken from a spelling book and had no relationship to any need to learn those words that the children had at that moment.

There was Miss Gabriel who arranged her class according to the marks on arithmetic tests each six weeks. The child with the highest mark got the seat on the inner row next to the door, and the child with the poorest mark got the seat in the last row next to the windows. In between, all the children were arranged according to their arithmetic scores. Each six weeks there was a new arrangement. During the year, Miss Gabriel continued this practice. It was interesting to note that Mike Martin always sat in the last seat in the last row. He was the room dumbbell. It was interesting to note, too, that most of the discipline problems in Miss Gabriel's room were in the row along the window. Most of the children admired Miss Gabriel because she had, indeed, a great fund of knowledge and told the children many things that stimulated them and interested them, but her room was seldom calm and placid. She was the boss in her room. The children knew that she got angry and they talked about how mad she got. She sent children to the office for discipline quite frequently; she had them stand in the hall; sometimes she shook them and on rare occasions paddled them across the seat with a ruler; most of her discipline cases arose when children became frantic or discouraged because they could not achieve up to the standards she set for them.

During reading lessons, she stood with her book open while the children took turns reading. When one finished reading, he was generally given the privilege of calling on another to read next. The children seldom called on the poor readers since it bothered them to hear the poor ones struggle and stammer over the words. She divided her day's work into reading, writing, spelling, arithmetic, history, art, geography, health, and music. She opened her day with a brief opening period in which she made announcements and checked on attendance and discipline. She was ambitious, sturdy, intelligent and "all in" when the day was over. She was known as a hard marker; the children respected her; the parents respected her; and she was considered an asset to the school.

It seemed a great tragedy to me that she should waste so much talent. The test results in her room showed the same wide range of abilities that there was in other rooms.

If her discipline was measured not by the quietness and inactivity of the room, but by the number of violations of the standards of behavior that she set for the room, it was not a well-behaved room. A particular bit of misbehavior that seemed most frequent in her room consisted in throwing things—wads of paper, paper airplanes, and even an occasional spitball.

Miss Holden's room was always pleasant to observe. She developed fine units that were planned with care. She decided on her objectives and located a wide range of materials. She assigned work in the units in terms of the abilities of the children as nearly as she could determine them. They did work of a research nature; they drilled on facts and skills that they needed to know; they prepared booklets on what they were doing; and they always ended the unit with a culminating activity in which the brighter children always played the main parts and wore the costumes. The whole thing was carried off with a flair.

It was not until I had an opportunity to visit her two or three times that I became somewhat less enthusiastic about her work. This occurred as I discovered that the children did not participate in planning the units; she planned everything for them. She assigned every job to them, set up and selected the committees, and furnished the committees with instructions. She told them on their

Mexican unit just how to set up the little stalls at the Mexican Fair. She told them what to look for at home to decorate the stalls; she told them how to nail and hammer and paste. She told them what to prepare to put in their booklets. She wrote the dramatic sketches for them in their committees while they listened. When I asked the children where they got this idea or that idea, they said with great pride in their teacher that they got the idea from her. She seemed very pleased at their willingness to give her credit for what she had done. I classified her work in my mind as far superior to much that one would see in the traditional school where the subject matter was less real to the children, but I regretted very much that she did not see the opportunity she was missing to train the children in working together, in self-reliance, in planning, in problem-solving, and in writing and reading for a purpose.

She always followed each unit and its culminating activity with a long period of formalized drill and fact-learning from the textbooks. As she put it, they had had their unit—now it was time for the children to "catch up."

Miss Holden's Mexican unit, I found out later, was known throughout the schools and the community. Those who had not seen it for years described it to me in surprisingly accurate detail for it changed little from year to year. She knew which families in town had "Mexicana" that could be borrowed. Her own supply of gourds served over and over again. The children drew many of the same designs year after year. The children enjoyed the exhibits and the pageantry and learned a great deal, but most of them knew the resources of the pageant from previous years in the school, and their enthusiasm was somewhat tempered.

A teacher who started with pupil interests

Miss Wickersham was one of the teachers about whom I could grow honestly enthusiastic. She had a sixth grade in rural Woodlot. Most of her boys seemed large for this grade and their fifth-grade teacher the year before had been replaced because she could not handle them. Miss Wickersham had begun the work by finding out who the children were, where they lived, and what they were interested in. Five of the boys were interested in hunting. They were studying guns, their bore and gauge, the differences between buckshot and bird shot, the differences in "spread," and the range of different charges. They were studying the game laws of the state, and were branching out from that into the study of conservation. They had written letters to the Isaac Walton League, the State Department of Conservation, and the Wild Life Service. They were beginning to read about wild life in different places of the world: big game hunting in Alaska and Africa, elephant hunts in India, hunting moose in Canada, and all sorts of game in the Rockies. There was much emphasis on safety.

A group of boys and girls were studying poultry farming, discussing banding, trap nests, housing, breeding, marketing, and the like. From this they were becoming interested in city markets, in transportation, in diet, in climate and weather, and in farm construction.

Another group started out with a study of the local rural electrification project. They were able to get two speakers to visit class from the R.E.A. They studied electricity, wiring, candle power, various household uses of electricity, and water power. They became interested in conservation, too, from the study of power and rivers. They saw the movie, "The River," and became interested in the T.V.A. They ran across pamphlets from the private power companies and from R.E.A. and some of them were able to read them and understand them with help from the home and the community. They, too, wrote to many sources for information about their various interests.

There was a state forest near Woodlot and some of the children were interested in that. In all the projects, Miss Wickersham found opportunity to have them learn and apply mathematics, citizenship, geography, science, history—and to do it in terms of current community interests. There were many occasions when farmers, foresters, hunters, the proprietor of the local sporting goods store, a salesman for an appliance company, and an old-timer known as a hunter and a trapper visited and addressed the pupils. "Every gun is loaded, but it is always the unloaded gun that accidentally kills people. Never point a gun at another even in fun, or even if it's a play gun made out of wood. Train yourself to circle people with your gun until it's second nature." All these safety facts about firearms the children were absorbing.

When I complimented Miss Wickersham on her knowledge of

rural affairs, she said, "Why I never knew a pullet from a hen until I started this year's work. I had never shot a gun in my life and didn't know the difference between a rifle and a shotgun. I do not find it necessary to know more than the children about a new project. Some of my children always know more about some things than I do. I went out with the boys and Mr. Pogue last Saturday and I shot a twenty-two for the first time. The big boys were so proud to show me how to shoot and how to hit the target every time. I regard myself as the adult in the classroom, the one to help them find out more about what they already know and want to know, to direct their interests and to help them with the mathematics, history, social science, and communication skills they need and that I know."

Barriers to supervision

In many cases, as I visited the schools, it was difficult at first to get a real insight into my problem for I was constantly faced with an artificial situation. If I visited a school, it was only a minute or two until all teachers in the building had been "warned" of my presence. Many of the teachers quietly "shifted gears" into some activity that they felt would be pleasant to me. Others continued what they were doing with a tense and unconsciously antagonistic attitude as if to insist that I could find fault if I wished. I knew that many teachers "resent" unexpected visits by supervisors. They feel that they are entitled to a warning. In many cases the pupils had been warned, too, by the time I arrived in the class. I found it relatively easy to spot rooms where pupils were supposed to make a "good impression" on the visitor. The over-acting of the conscientious and "good" little citizens was a cue, as was the barrage of quick, appraising glances thrown at me. Most damaging, it seemed to me, however, was the knowing and sphinx-like regard that many of them had for their teacher in this situation. Children know how many times their parents and they, themselves, feel it necessary to put on a good front. Unless teacher has their approval and unless they have developed common objectives and sympathies, the teacher loses caste when he demands their cooperation in "saving face." When the teacher says, "We want them to know at the Superintendent's office that our room is the best one," the children know perfectly well what the teacher means. Sometimes the teacher felt that the preliminary warnings were not sufficient and so he subtly repeated them when I was introduced by telling the pupils pointedly who I was and where I was from. Seldom was I introduced at first as a friend or a helper.

I hoped that the time would come (and it did) when I could enter a room without any fanfare at all. Children need feel no strangeness when adults enter a room. They will get acquainted in their own way if that becomes necessary. As schools expand into the community, the number of visitors increases so greatly that constant formality becomes obstructive. It is probably true that visitors are disturbing when most of the visits presage trouble for someone— a principal on the prowl, an attendance officer, or a probation investigator.

Despite our agreement the previous spring, I found that the principals were also on edge when I made my first visits. I found that I got some insights into the principal's philosophy by noticing the teachers to whose rooms he guided me first, or those of whom the principal felt "proud." In general, they were the teachers whose rooms were fairly quiet, neat, orderly, and attractive. It seemed to me they were, in general, the teachers who were most competent and who had the greatest potentialities, but frequently they were teachers whose insights into the nature of the learning process, as related to the basic objectives of education, were not clear and whose procedures were not consistent with the social and psychological nature of the learners and with the wide range of individual and trait differences in a classroom.

Discomfiture with supervision is the result of the kind of supervision on the part of all administrators that has been common in the past 50 years. It was my faith that it would disappear as teachers gained confidence in their own abilities and were given the chance to work freely and cooperatively in meeting their problems. It would persist as long as they felt they were being rated, weighed, analyzed, and improved. It would be increased by "kindly and pointed" suggestions given in a "My-Dear,-I-love-you-and-have-so-much-experience-and-want-to-help-you" attitude. It would also be increased by "Do-it-this-way" instructions. It would tend to disappear as mutual goals were discovered toward which we could work together, both of us in the role of seekers and both of us as contributors.

Despite the strain and the play-acting, it was possible for me to meet the teachers in a friendly way and to discuss their problems with them. I made mental notes as we talked and wrote them down as soon as I had the opportunity.

"Large classes" was the number one item of irritation. Closely related, but further down the list, were "too much to do," and "too many interruptions and extra duties." The second item was "how to cover the work." Many of the teachers felt that they were expected to cover an impossible amount of material. Not enough supplies and equipment and educational facilities of all kinds was third on the list. "Too much clerical work and testing and record keeping" was another frequent objection. "Discipline" and "getting parental cooperation" were mentioned. Low salaries were mentioned frequently, particularly in relation to large classes.

It was from leads such as these that I hoped to build staff projects or building projects. These, I knew, would not spring up quickly and could not be framed and implemented by me. It was very probable that the teachers had not been entirely free in stating their problems and that some difficulties might exist about which I had not been informed. It was probable that group attacks on common professional problems were already in process, either in structured form or informally. If so, they should not be interfered with nor should they necessarily fall either within or outside my orbit of activity. The things that developed would depend upon many factors and the way I would fit into it all would depend upon where I was capable and needed.

Mrs. Greatheart

Mrs. Greatheart was principal of the Woodlot School. A married woman, she had lived in the community for many years. She was healthy, wholesome, intelligent, energetic, and sympathetic, with a deep interest in the various teachers and children in the school. She took a personal, friendly interest in the teachers and they loved her for the freedom she gave them to work creatively and for the help she gave them when they requested it. If she had a hobby, it was the study of the personalities of various children. As I walked about the school with her, she gave me thumbnail sketches of many of them.

When we entered the fifth-grade room, Mrs. Greatheart stood with me in the front corner. "You see that girl, second one in the second row. She's the one I was telling you about in the office—the one who stole the money at Larson's store last week."

The little girl had glanced at us as we entered. Her face had been clear and happy. She did not hear what Mrs. Greatheart said, but I knew as I glanced at her and caught her eye and saw her lower her eyes to her desk that she knew what Mrs. Greatheart was saying to me, and that she knew that I knew about her theft.

I remembered the time in the hospital when my surgeon came to the door with a staff physician. He passed the time of day pleasantly with me and with my two roommates, but as he turned to leave I heard him say to his companion, "That's the case I was telling you about." Had he been talking about me or was it one of my roommates? Was there something wrong that he had held back? Why should he be discussing me with the staff physician if everything was as good as I had been led to believe? I can still remember how I worried about that remark. I wondered, too, how much worrying the little girl would do—the little girl who had taken some money—the little girl who probably needed more than anything else to feel that she was not set apart from other children, that she was not the object of unfavorable attention.

Later, as we walked down the hall, Mrs. Greatheart met a little boy on his way to the third grade from the lavatory. "This is Albert Smith," she told me. "He is a new boy in Woodlot. He is learning to get along with the strange children now. At first he had a lot of trouble. Have you had a fight today, Albert?"

He hadn't.

"The children fight with new boys when they come here. After a while they'll get to know you and they'll stop. Run along now."

Mrs. Greatheart knew and had great sympathy for all the children. She knew a great deal about what went on in her classrooms, on the playground, and on the way to and from school. In the fourth-grade room, she fixed her attention on a boy in the first row. "Do you see that one," she said to me in a confidential whisper. "He's the one who carried the main part at our P.T.A. last week. He's a good one, he is. He can sing and recite, and he's a regular mimic. We certainly are proud of him." The boy knew that we were discussing him. He probably knew that he was being discussed favorably, but he, too, grew uneasy and restless.

In the third-grade room later in the day, after Mrs. Greatheart had left me, I discussed classroom procedures with the teacher. We discussed the new boy in the Woodlot School. I discovered that the advent of the new boy had not been taken as an opportunity to teach citizenship, human relations, or hospitality.

I knew that this was no time to suggest such procedure. Supervision is apt to defeat its own end if it becomes directive. I felt that it was no time either to suggest to Mrs. Greatheart that her remarks about children were disturbing to them and to the friendly school atmosphere she really worked so hard to achieve. These were things for me to remember and to try to bring out in such a way that teachers, principals, and others might come to see for themselves, the factors involved.

A second-grade unit takes shape

A month passed before I found another chance to visit Miss Wolitarsky. Her class had progressed a great deal. When I entered the room, just before nine o'clock, I found that some of the children were already busy at their work. Some rolls of Scotch Tape were on a table at the front of the room and children were bringing in boxes and cans for their store. A number of children had brought Wheaties boxes, oatmeal boxes, Cream of Wheat boxes, and the like. Others had coffee cans, Jello boxes, ice cream cartons, and other items in great variety. The children closed the boxes and sealed the cans with Scotch Tape. Two children were placing the contributions on shelves made from eight orange crates. As more children arrived, there was much inspection of each other's contributions. As they arrived, Miss Wolitarsky checked their attendance in her book and did other work at her desk. I sat in the rear of the room, except as I walked about observing things on the bulletin boards. The rest of the children came in when the bell rang. Almost all of them, even those who brought nothing, went past the table and shelves to inspect the new additions. A few showed Miss Wolitarsky what they had. She was interested, but not effusive. Her attitude was friendly, but adult. I noticed that a child in each row seemed to be checking row attendance. One by one they went up to Miss Wolitarsky and reported—all but one.

"Have you a report, Adelle?" Miss Wolitarsky asked.

Adelle arose quickly from her knees by the shelves and checked her row. She looked around the room for those not in their seats and found that all were present. She went up to the desk and made her report. Miss Wolitarsky's attitude was that of one adult listening to another.

Miss Wolitarsky then took out some modeling clay, some paper pulp, paste, and other materials and placed them on the work table. "This is for the candy committee," she said.

Five or six children came forward, two of whom went to their store for a box of candy wrappers. There was a difference of opinion and a clash of wills over which one should bring the box to the committee. In the tugging, the box was pulled apart and the wrappers fell to the floor. I saw that Miss Wolitarsky was conscious of this activity but remote from it. The two children exchanged a word or two of recrimination and a light blow was struck before the box was placed on the floor and they began picking up the wrappers. The other children had arranged their desks face to face and were placing the materials on them preparatory to their work. One or two of them watched the progress of their wrappers with only slight impatience. They seemed to know that the wrappers would arrive in good time, and that differences of opinion were things that happened naturally.

"Here is some paper for the sale signs," Miss Wolitarsky said. She had a small roll of white wrapping paper. Another group began to detach itself and arrange the seats. One or two helped Miss Wolitarsky get crayons, pencils, and rules.

At this point the other committees began to form without any cues from the teacher. When all were in groups, I could see that a great deal of flexibility existed. Some children left their groups to wander about and see what others were doing. In many cases, busy little eyes assessed every detail, and an occasional question was asked or suggestion given. Not all the remarks were either quietly given or graciously received, but it was plain that there was much goal-directed activity, much persistence, and much purposeful learning. Sometimes one committee member noticed the absence of another and set forth to bring him back.

One group worked on price tags—its members had scissors, thumb tacks, and tack hammers, as well as white tag board from which they cut out price tags to place on the edges of the shelves. One group was trying to make a grocery push cart, using a paper carton and four roller skates at the corners. There was much experimental trial-and-error activity and some serious discussion. This group was making use of the vise, tools, and work table at the rear of the room to cut blocks of wood to place in the roller skates and strips to make handles. They also used a ruler to measure lengths on a number of occasions.

One group was taking an inventory, or rather adding to it, counting the new accessions and correcting and amending yesterday's list. One group had taken form and left the room, to return in ten minutes with the building engineer. The committee was pointing out to him some chalk marks on the floor and some wall dimensions. Miss Wolitarsky did not assist in this discussion. When the engineer made some suggestions, the children listened, but were not entirely satisfied.

"No," one little girl said, "we must have a wall here because we must have a window to have light." The engineer's argument that no wall at all on that side would give even more light was not at all satisfactory.

"If a store hasn't got a wall, how could you lock it up?"

That was the carpenter crew and they would need to do some of the large dimension work in the janitor's workroom.

As the work began, I saw that the candy committee was modeling candy bars to fit into the candy wrappers the children had saved. These were sometimes wrapped and sealed with tape. The construction of a fairly good "life-saver" roll by one of the girls was hailed with approval. When it was wrapped, one boy said, "Boy, that would fool me!" The sale-sign committee was making a bargain announcement. A large mailed sale ad from a supermarket and a full page newspaper advertisement were serving as sources for ideas. This committee consulted Miss Wolitarsky frequently about unknown words, but she offered little more than what was asked of her. They cut off pieces of wrapping paper experimentally and measured and worked. They checked spelling and lettering against their models and occasionally checked their prices with those the price tag committee was placing on the shelves. Not all the spelling was correct.

So far in the day, Miss Wolitarsky had not addressed the whole group once. She had initiated the work by starting two committees. Her most important overt contribution was in answering questions. I was deeply pleased and complimented that she had paid so little attention to me. She was secure so she did not have to justify. I hope that she did not explain because she felt I understood! She watched the groups rather closely and listened a good deal, but I noticed that she found time to examine some outlines and make some notes at her desk as the children worked.

At ten o'clock, she selected 12 children from the committees to take places in a reading circle. I was not sure what group it was until I saw that the book they selected from their desks was a primer. In it there was a story about a visit to a toy store, a story about a clothing store, and one about a pet store. The children read the stories quite well and with considerable interest since they discussed it all in terms of their own grocery store. This group was followed by two other groups who had also selected stories dealing with retailing, such as child experiences at a road-side vegetable stand, an ice cream and candy store, and a fruit peddler with his truck. Their stories were from second- and third-grade books.

Two of the groups ended by reading from some of the cartons in the store. A few of the children could read almost all the words on them, while almost all could point to and pronounce the key words on the packages, such as "coffee," "Jello" and "corn flakes."

Before noon, Miss Wolitarsky rang a small bell on her desk, at which signal the children put away their group work and put their desks into rows. Three children approached Miss Wolitarsky immediately after she rang the bell, waiting only long enough to ask others to take care of their work. Miss Wolitarsky talked with them and answered their questions. It turned out that they were the room officers.

Miss Wolitarsky seizes an opportunity
to promote mental hygiene and motivate her class

As I look back on my visits to Miss Wolitarsky's room, it seems that each time, in addition to its general excellence, I came away with a special example of her keen insight. This day was no exception. As the committees broke up, one little boy said to Miss Wolitarsky, "Teddy is taking some of our candy bars. He is going to sell them and fool the kids."

Miss Wolitarsky smiled and said, "That would be a good way to start a story, wouldn't it? Perhaps we can plan a story where a boy would do that. Teddy can help us with the story. If you want, you can make up a story."

The suggestion was well received and a number of hands were raised. "We won't have time to plan it now, but we can talk about it tomorrow. It will be fun to see how the story comes out."

The room became almost quiet then, but the little boy who was chairman was not patient.

"Tommy and Lacey and Mary—be quiet and sit down."

The children looked at him with no dismay or apparent resentment and came to order as quickly and, it seemed to me, more thoughtfully than if an adult had addressed them.

"We are going on our visit to the Bargain Market after dinner. Janet's committee is going to tell us what to do."

Janet took the floor.

"We are going to walk over from here," she said. "We are not going to touch things in the store. We are not going to bump into things." She looked at her notes. "If we do, we are going to pick them up. We are not going to shove. We will make a line outside the store and John will go in and tell Mr. Max that we are ready. John!"

John came forward and began, "I'm going to say, 'Mr. Max, we appreciate (he stumbled over the word and smiled and bobbed his head as he finally got it out) coming to your store. We want to learn about stores because we have to shop and buy things for our parents and we are having a store in our second grade at school.' "

In turn, various children told what they were going to see. Their assignments followed quite closely their committee work. Two boys and one girl (Esther) were going to count the push carts. (It developed later that they became interested in the kind that had a seat for infants, and they devised a classroom model in which they seated a doll.) Other assignments were to see how the cash registers worked, visit the stock rooms behind the store, see the refrigeration units, find out how many people come to the store each day, the best time to shop, how often the store had sales, where the items for sale came from, how much money the store took in, how to make change, and how to find things that were not displayed. Tom was to ask about the cash register, since he had a toy cash register at home that he was going to bring when the store was ready for it. All the children were to watch for items they would like to have in their store and for the prices that were charged for them. Janet was to ask for any printed materials they could have, such as advertisements, window signs, sale ads, and the like. Erland was to ask for any cardboard display stands that were of no more use and that could be put into their store. (They obtained five display boxes that stood on the floor and were counter high. One had contained a soap display, another had held pocket library books, another whiskbrooms and brushes, and so forth. In some cases these were remodeled, painted, and printed.)

A safety committee was to study the parking lot at the store, and where the cars entered and left it. Mr. Max was particularly helpful with that committee.

I found out later that Mr. Max had arranged the visit with great care. He had been a guest at school before my visit when the children were beginning the project and had invited them to come on an acceptable day. He had arranged for a newspaper reporter and had himself employed a photographer so that he could report the project in his company's house organ. He had located some simple printed materials and had obtained some children's books about stores from the publisher who provided him with his juvenile literature. He gave these to the children for the classroom library. He had coached his staff in the store so that each child could have his questions answered by the person who did the job in the store. He also had treats for the children to eat.

Miss Wolitarsky directs pupil energies into constructive channels

As time went by, it was interesting to watch Miss Wolitarsky's units develop. Because of the youth of the children, there was much more independent work within the groups than one finds in older grades. They did not plan far in advance of where they were at any particular time, but they had definite goals they wished to achieve.

Their interest in one another was not long sustained. They wanted to follow through on their ideas at once, and were consequently impulsive and thoughtless. They were inclined to ignore the rights of others and to lack self-restraint. Sometimes their shyness and their disturbance at an unexpected change in routine showed itself in aggressiveness or stubbornness. Miss Wolitarsky's planning took these factors into account. She let the children know what was to be expected of them. Their routine emerged naturally from these expectations. This had been seen when the committees formed around the materials she placed out for them.

It always intrigues me to watch Miss Wolitarsky and teachers like her. They are thoughtful and careful, but seldom seem to be subject to the strains and tensions that afflict a Miss Smith, a Miss Gabriel, or even a Miss Holden. Miss Wolitarsky reminded me of my own experience as a waitress at Glacier Park. Each day of my first month in the dining room there had left me tired and irritated. Then I had learned to organize my side stands and stations, and to plan the work in cooperation with the hostess so that I worked with rather than against my customers. I had learned to lift the heavy trays with my hand back over my wrist so that my legs and my whole body did the lifting and not my back alone. I had learned to move with and not against my environment.

Miss Wolitarsky did the same thing in her room. Children are reasonable creatures who want to learn. She did not try to force them to do her way what they would do equally or more effectively their own way. She helped them to do it their own way, which was in accord with the basic drives and natural interests that dominated them at the various stages of their development. She did not deal with them as an adult who felt it necessary to dominate them, but as a trained student of child nature and learning who took advantage of all the forces at work within them. Her children, she knew, were active, energetic, intelligent, striving to learn and communicate, observant, primarily self-centered and family centered, but in process of becoming increasingly competent in ever larger social groups. To impose a traditional subject-matter curriculum on them would require discipline, constant attention, endless policing, and constant drill with one group after another, while the others were occupied with more or less identical preparatory assignments. Instead, she started with the basic nature of the growing, developing, and learning child, and sought to develop competence in the skills and factual learnings, while at the same time stressing attitudes, social skills, and competency in meeting and solving new problems. Her attempt was to provide a wide range of educative experiences through a variety of books and periodicals, simple science equipment, tools and work bench, simple musical instruments, and all the other enrichments that can be made available in a second grade. She gave her students opportunities to make individual and group decisions, to communicate and to listen, to struggle to lead, not dominate, to accede, and to follow through on group decisions. She encouraged them to work independently and creatively, rather than in passive imitation, with sounds and colors and shapes, and to become sensitive to the beauty of words, music, form, and color and to enjoy the grace and rhythm of movement.

In all this she was tapping the happy, cooperative side of the children. She was working with the forces that make little boys and girls grow up into fine men and women, that lead to sympathetic, generous, and understanding personalities. Her role was one that brings a daily pleasantness and that has a healthy, friendly, wholesome emotional tone.

A first cooperative staff study emerges

The opportunity for the first staff study project came in late October at the State Education Association Convention. We held a Hampton Rapids breakfast the last morning and the conversation got onto the problem of substituting informal notes and parent-teacher conferences for report cards. A speaker had discussed the problem and four or five of our teachers had attended a follow-up panel.

"Teachers who had tried it said it helped solve many of their problems," said one.

"It brings the home and school closer together," said another.

"I sure hate filling in those report cards every six weeks. They mean so little."

"Sometimes I think they do more harm than good."

"I'd like to write notes and hold conferences if I could find time to do it. As it is, I'm so busy teaching that I don't know how I'd ever get it done. It's not that I don't believe in it. It's just that I can't see how it could be worked out."

"I was talking to a teacher from Oak Heights. She said they do it during school time."

"The notes or the conferences?"

"Both. That's what she said."

"Do they send the children home?"

"She said they didn't need to. The children work while she works or meets the parents."

"Well, I'd like to see them do it. I'll bet they couldn't do it in my room. I'd like to know how they do it. Perhaps they let the children play."

"Teachers could join up and take double groups."

Finally someone said, "Miss Schmidt, what do you think?" I could have hugged her, as I wanted to say something, but had resolved to wait until asked. When I became known and accepted, perhaps I would not need to be so careful.

"I don't know much about the details of how they work such plans. I know they seem to work well when they are done carefully. I'll be glad to collect some materials for us to study."

In no time at all it was all decided. I had an assignment and it was about a problem that had sprung from the teachers themselves. It involved much more than the writing of notes and the holding of parent-teacher conferences. It involved planning for desirable ends and for interpreting changes in pupil behavior (learning) in meaningful terms. It involved gaining greater cooperation between school and home, and offered a chance to move in the direction of the community school. It might affect the educational and social tone of some of our classrooms, as teachers might learn to free themselves from the need for constant guiding and dominating and move in the direction of becoming professional architects of human behavior, of manipulating the latent but potentially dynamic psychosocial forces in each class so that they become self-directing.

I was able to find many professional references to new reporting procedures, some of which were available in the professional library in Hampton Rapids, and others that I ordered immediately.[1] I spent part of the day at the University libraries and seminar study

1 See bibliography, pp. 569-571.

rooms. I ran across two of my former professors who recommended colleagues who might be of assistance as consultants if the teachers decided they wanted them.

At dinner I met Superintendent Walker and told him what had occurred. I have never told him since how he failed me then. I was so enthusiastic and thrilled that I had found the chance I had been seeking. I had told him a number of times how I hoped to work things out, and he had been so encouraging. Now that the chance had come, he seemed not to see it for the opportunity that it was. I have learned since that each of us has problems in which we become immersed. Sometimes when other's problems have been as important as mine, I have not been able to see the implications of theirs or they of mine. I still feel that top administrators in school systems must come to regard the curriculum problems of the schools, and the methods by which teachers best work to improve their practice as deserving of more attention and more encouragement than they generally receive. In the final analysis, what goes on in the school situation under the direction of teachers is the be-all and the end-all of all administrative effort, from the legal machinery for taxing and managing to the final penny for cleaning and polishing. In my experience, Superintendent Walker has never failed to support the improvement of educational practice with money and facilities. He is far superior to most superintendents I know, but a new bus, a new device for better classroom lighting, or a district athletic championship brings a gleam to his eye that I have never seen over a successful workshop or a curriculum unit that is a symphony in human development.

Some early general impressions

I would not wish to give the impression that I considered the professional level in Hampton Rapids to be low. In many ways it was superior to that in most communities. The staff morale was good, the teachers were interested in their work, the salaries compared favorably with the best in similar sized communities in the state, and the equipment and supplies available were relatively good. As I visited the schools, I was pleased with what I saw. It was my responsibility, however, to improve instruction. My first interest was to assess what I found as well as I could. I made notes of what

I saw and by slow degrees tried to organize my impressions into broad categories. Some of the headings into which they fell were: (1) need for curriculum planning involving the community; (2) more attention to mental health of pupils; (3) greater use of basic interests and drives of pupils; (4) imposed control used when democratic control would be more effective; (5) too great relative emphasis placed on rote memorization, on factual verbal learnings and automatic skills, rather than on democratic attitudes, social skills, and learning through doing; (6) too rigid daily schedules with consequent fragmentation of the learning emphases; (7) regard for discipline as imposed control and deportment rather than as growth in self-control and in group control; (8) evaluation largely in terms of factual learnings; (9) hesitancy to use new techniques and methods.

Vandalism at Forest Lake

One day in December, when I approached the Forest Lake School, I knew that something was amiss. Though it was only 8:15, a number of children stood excitedly at the door, where a teacher was on guard.

"We've been broken into!" she exclaimed to me as I entered. "Poor Mr. Black, he's collapsed. I'm afraid he's dead."

I rushed in and found a sad state of affairs. Mr. Black, the janitor-engineer, was lying unconscious at the foot of the stairs leading to the second floor. His eyes were closed and his face pale, but I saw that he was breathing regularly. Some of the teachers had already loosened his clothing and covered him with warm blankets. An ambulance had been ordered.

All around was confusion and destruction! The building had been entered during the night and ransacked. The drawers of the teachers' desks had been pulled out and emptied, bottles of ink had been thrown about and smashed, tables overturned, books scattered and torn, and a phonograph broken, a radio smashed, a tape recorder destroyed and four rolls of recorded tape unrolled, the office desk forced open and a small sum of money taken, some kindergarten and primary chairs broken, pupils' desks upturned and emptied, bookcases thrown forward on the floor, a world globe crushed, some maps torn from the cases. . . .

Clearly, a number of people had spent a busy hour doing damage. It was surmised that when Mr. Black entered the building he became excited, rushed about, and suffered a heart attack.

The police arrived soon after I did. Superintendent Walker came at about the same time. An ambulance took Mr. Black to the hospital. A hurried conference resulted in sending the children home for the day. The local radio station broadcast the news. Rumors spread throughout the community that were far from the truth, but the reality itself was bad enough.

The police asked that nothing be disturbed until they had time to look for clues. They wanted the teachers to remain at school to help identify any objects that might serve as clues. Word from the hospital indicated that Mr. Black was alive and would probably recover (which he did, but only after a long convalescence and then not to return to his job). He could not be questioned for some time, but had nothing to offer when he was queried. It was determined that a large bruise on his head was the result of his fall and not of a blow.

While the investigation was in process, the teachers gathered in the lunch room and talked about the terrible thing that had happened. For some time the discussion concerned Mr. Black's illness and the extent of the damage. It then turned to possible culprits.

"I'd just like to know who did it," Miss Swanson (sixth grade) said, and there was righteous anger in her voice.

"I know one or two who might be in it," Miss Antoine (fifth grade) volunteered.

"I can't think it was any of our children," said Miss Jackson (principal). "It looks like the work of older, stronger children."

"I hope," said Miss Jones (second grade), "that we don't find out who did it, particularly if Mr. Black should die."

"You don't! Well I do. They should be taught a lesson!"—Miss Swanson.

"Oh, I suppose you're right. It's just that I am afraid we don't really know how to teach that lesson, and instead we may make a bad situation worse. Just imagine how a group of bad little boys could break into the school. They got started and didn't know where to stop. One threw ink. Another had to top him by upturning a bookcase. They didn't know how to stop. None of them thought that a man might die as a result of their escapade. Imagine how the thought of that evil result might ruin a boy's life."

"Wouldn't it be best to know so we could help the boys to live it down?" asked Miss Jackson.

"Yes, if we really know how to help."

(That problem was later solved as far as we were concerned. The culprits were four older boys from a neighboring town, three of whom had dropped out of school.)

"I think we should use the incident as the basis for our curriculum work for a while." This was Mrs. Ernst, a very fine third-grade teacher. "Our children will be shocked and bewildered by what has happened. They will want to know all about it. They will hear their parents and friends talking about it. People in the community will wonder if there is something wrong with our schools, when youngsters do things like this. The children's interest and excitement concerning school will be at the highest point ever. The incident represents great opportunity to motivate some real learning."

"How would you go about using it?" I asked.

"Well. It is hard to say how it will develop," Mrs. Ernst said. "I believe I would like to have them come to school and find the room just the way it is now. I would like to have them pick up and straighten up and make a list of all the damage. I am sure the talk at home will have aroused their interest in the cost of the destruction. Some of them can use a lot of arithmetic in estimating that. They will need some help in lifting up some of the bookcases, and they won't be able to remove the ink from the floor and cork boards, but they can list what needs to be done. They can use the event in speaking, writing, and in citizenship."

"I wonder what Mr. Walker would think of our ideas," I said, and I went in search of him. When we returned, the fifth-grade teacher, Miss Antoine, was talking.

"The children could write a story of what happened. It would give them an opportunity to practice English. We could dramatize a report of it for radio presentation."

"We could study community recreation to see what the community provides for children," Miss Swanson suggested.

"My children would be interested in the duties of the janitor and the care of the building," Mrs. Ernst said.

Mr. Walker was impressed with all the many suggestions made

except the one about having the children find the building in disarray.

"I don't think it would work," he said. "I doubt in any case that we can have school tomorrow. I will have cleaners in to scrub and bleach the ink spots. We will have to assess the damage and report it to the Board of Education. The telephone has been pulled from the wall. The broken glass from the bookcases, doors, and aquariums is dangerous. The parents will want it all cleaned up. The police will not want us to touch anything for at least a few hours yet."

"I really believe," I said, "that Mrs. Ernst has an unusual and a challenging idea. I can see an opportunity in it to enlist community participation in school planning. It may be, however, that our pupils, our parents, and our Board of Education are not ready to handle it that way."

"I'm sure that most of what has been suggested would work out well," Superintendent Walker said. "But I am afraid that parents would not understand the reasons for not having the building cleaned up. I believe that you can still use the incident to motivate the pupils and I will cooperate in every other way I can. I believe we can use it, too, to stimulate parent and citizen interest in our school, its problems and procedures."

After he left, there was a spirited discussion. Two of the teachers seemed doubtful, but not unwilling. The others were more interested. Miss Burns expressed the majority opinion when she said, "I believe that we can use it as curriculum motivation."

That night of vandalism resulted in some good projects in the Forest Lake School. Superintendent Walker was pleased and commended the teachers, as did many of the parents. The most dramatic was a radio skit, "Vandalism Doesn't Pay," with sound effects and announcer, recorded on tape and used at the local radio station. Most of the projects were of short duration, however, and I was disappointed in our lack of ability to motivate and develop them further. I visited on the day that school reopened and for two or three days afterward. Throughout the school, there was an air of hushed suppression among the children, though the culprits had been identified and there was no suspicion on any of our pupils. The teachers worked hard to get school back on an even keel; they discussed the damage with the children; the children wrote letters to Mr. Black and some of them took him flowers; the cost of the damage was computed; mock trials were held; upper-grade children studied the juvenile court laws; lower-grade children discussed the duties of policemen, ambulance drivers, and janitors; a school citizenship pledge was composed in one room.

I never determined that the teachers were disappointed in these outcomes. They probably were not. It seemed to me, however, that except for the radio script, there was a lack of enthusiasm on the part of the pupils in sharp contrast to that in Miss Wolitarsky's store or in Miss Wickersham's projects on hunting, wild life, and rural electrification. I have thought about it frequently and discussed it with others, but I am not sure why this should have been.

1. Did the evil elements in the incident discourage the pupils and dampen their interest?

2. Was the unconscious shock of the teachers the discouraging factor?

3. Did I press too hard to seize a chance to demonstrate a point?

4. Are pupils repelled by incidents that bring forth adult "moralizing" and "lesson drawing"?

5. Would the outcomes have seemed more real if Mrs. Ernst's suggestion had been adopted?

6. Was there a lack of real pupil motivation because the project was not in keeping with basic needs and drives?

7. Was the problem too adult in nature?

The second grade goes into business

Colorful signs on stakes announced to passers-by the great news!

GRAND OPENING

SECOND GRADE

SUPER MARKET

November 10, 2 P. M.

Carefully written invitations inviting the parents as special guests to the grand opening had been prepared and delivered. "There will be prizes and free treats. R.S.V.P."

The schoolroom had atmosphere as the visitors arrived. One of two doors led from the hall to the cloak hall and from thence into the room. This area represented the rear entrance and back room of the store as well as "backstage" for the demonstration. The "front part" of the store stretched three-fourths of the way across the front of the classroom. The remainder was a small area shut off by a curtain for "out of the store" dramatizations.

The "store" was furnished with homemade shelves made from boxes and crates, display racks (redecorated) obtained from Mr. Max, and with piles of "bargains" built in pyramids on the floor. Boxes and cartons had been cut in various shapes for bins. Over and around everything there were bargain announcements. There were price tags in profusion. Every item had a price written on it. When the audience was seated, the small curtain was pulled.

Seated at a little breakfast table were three children, playing the part of father, mother and son:

Father: Here is some money. Go to the store and get some groceries.
Mother: Thank you. How much money is it?
Father: It is 14 dollars. You should get some change.
Son: Can I go, too, and get some candy?
Mother: We'll see.
Son: I want some picture books, too.
Mother: You have brushed your teeth and eaten your cereal. You can have them.
Father: I must go to work now.
Mother: I will go to the store as soon as it opens.

Curtain

The children read some of their lines from manuscripts on the table. Some parts they remembered. ("They read on television," one boy had said. "You can see them.") The parents laughed a good deal as the father counted out the 14 dollars. The children smiled, too, but their smiles showed that they did not see the same humor in the situation that their parents did. The 14 dollars had been arrived at only after much study. Children had talked over the amount at home. They had counted and added at school. The sum as it was finally arrived at was a unanimous opinion. So much consideration had gone into it that in their opinion it had to be the right sum.

The children talked quite slowly and clearly. They had tried out parts of their speeches on a tape machine and had listened and discussed their work with great interest and critical spirit. Miss Wolitarsky had tried to make a second tape of the children discussing their tape. We wanted it for later use in in-service study. In many parts, there were too many voices and too many undistinguishable remarks. One part, however, went like this:

"Miss Wolitarsky says we should say 'May I,' not 'Can I.' "

"I say, 'Can I.' "

"So do I."

"Well," this from the member of the committee that authored that part of the drama, "this is a daddy and a mother, not a school."

The teachers considered this remark to be significant, particularly since it went unchallenged by the other children. What was there in our schools or in our culture that, even at such early ages, there should be a behavioral dichotomy between school world and home world—where never the twain meet?

The curtain opened again. A little girl held a paper clock face while a little boy placed the hands at nine o'clock.

"The store opens at nine o'clock."

He turned the hands to twelve o'clock.

"The clerks go to lunch at twelve o'clock."

With appropriate changes, he continued: "Some other clerks go at 12:30—the store closes at six o'clock."

He worked hard at his job. The little girl watched as best she could as she held the clock. He didn't make a mistake, but it was obvious that he had studied hard to do it.

As he turned the clock back to nine, Esther came in and struck a cymbal softly and rhythmically nine times, counting silently but visibly with her lips as she did.

Curtain

Esther had not been able to count to beyond five when she entered second grade. Her ability with numbers was low, but was improving as she saw some uses and meaning in them. She had worked with four other children on the time-telling scene. They were proud of it and the other children were too.

The next activity took place in the store. The clerks and a cashier came in. The "mother" came in with her son. She selected a grocery cart (a small doll buggy that had been given a double deck by placing a piece of cardboard on the springs). She had a list to which she referred frequently. The little boy began to look at some Little Wonder Books. Another mother came in with two little girls and a baby (a doll). She selected the homemade cart that ran on roller skates. She strapped the doll into the "baby seat." You could best distinguish the "mothers" from the "children" by the ladies' hats they had brought from home, though there were other bits of adult dress—costume jewelry, sashes, and the like, as well as adult mannerisms—particularly a peculiar swing of the hips. The little girls went to the candy counter.

Each shopper bought many health foods—milk, oatmeal and other cereals, cheese, eggs, meat, fresh fruits and vegetables, some real and some made from paper, clay, and so forth. As the shelves were emptied, clerks brought in more supplies. Each shopper used a list, had a pencil, and checked prices. The "mothers" were very strict with the children, despite their good behavior. One mother found it necessary to lead her child by the ear when he persisted in not staying near her. This brought gales of laughter from the audience. The store scene was played not for its dramatic effect with a "center stage," but for its realism. The actors each played their roles and spoke their lines with no thought of scene stealing or mugging. At times they dropped out of character temporarily to watch their fellows. There were one or two minor accidents, but they were not at all disturbing because the children played their parts as freely and imperturbably as small children play house. When early in the act a cart tipped over, the audience giggled and laughed, but the children went on methodically. It did not seem to have occurred to them that a cart should not tip over in any store. They had not planned that it should tip and were definitely "out of character" until it was righted and refilled. Then they went on. By slow degrees, the parents laughed less and watched more closely. It seemed that most of them sensed to some extent the imagination and constructiveness that was being developed, as well as the hard basic knowledges and skills that had been learned.

The adding machine-cash register was the wonder of all. A calculator had been borrowed from the office. This machine adds without a tape. A group of seven who were good at arithmetic had worked long on that project. The final result was the placement of Tom's toy cash register beside the calculator to hold the money.

At one time they had planned to place Lilly and Bobby out of sight beneath the table to take the lists and add them while Luella, the cashier, pretended to work with the cash register. They would then pass the answers up to her. This had presented too many difficulties when it was tried. Neither Lilly nor Bobby had been able to do the job quickly and reliably enough to satisfy themselves or their committee, though Miss Wolitarsky later professed her humorous regret that the plan was abandoned. "How hard they practiced quick addition," she said. "The members of the committee are now able to add on the fifth-grade level, using decimals to separate dollars from cents. How scornful they were when they found problems in the third-grade book giving pre-inflation prices for lettuce and bread! When I tried to explain that prices had gone up since the book was written, Lilly had said, 'We ought to get some new books.' Tom had said, 'Ma says that's all prices do—go up.' "

The shift to the calculator had been made at Jean's suggestion. Her mother worked in an office and used an adding machine. Jean had visited there and played with the typewriter and seen the adding machine. The committee had borrowed the machine from the office for the day, but had done most of their practicing in the office. They had learned to use the dollars and cents columns with some insight. They had felt impelled to add some "big" numbers by themselves and then on the machine to check its accuracy. When the machine had been demonstrated to the whole class one day, Betty, an average student, had said, "When I get big I'll have one of those and I won't have to add." This had served as the basis for a discussion and the boys had pointed out some practical difficulties. "You have to learn anyway. You can't carry around a big adding machine wherever you go."

Before long, the shopping scene was completed. The shopping carts were filled, the columns totaled, and the change made with money the children had made. Miss Wolitarsky's first participation occurred here. Up to this point she had sat in the audience, but in one instance Luella got stuck making change. Without the slightest sign of embarrassment or self-consciousness, she turned to her teacher and asked, "How do you do it when it ends in 99?" Miss Wolitarsky came forward and showed her, without attempting at that time to build any insights. She then sat down again in front.

The last customer left the store, and the clerks and cashier went backstage.

There was some applause, but it was cut short by the opening of the curtain.

"We learned many things in our store," Carl said. "We will tell you what we learned." One by one, children who had not yet participated, told something they had learned.

"We learned to make signs. We learned to paint them ourselves and to print the words and the prices and all that."

"We learned to run an adding machine and you can multiply with it, too, but we don't know how yet. That comes in high school, Miss Wolitarsky says."

"We learned to tell time and know when the store opens. If you go in the morning, Mr. Max says it's better because a lot of people come when it's when there's a big crowd."

"We learned to print. We learned to spell. We learned to read what's on the packages. We learned to read many new words."

"We read stories about stores. We read all about stores. We read the ads in the newspaper."

"We visited Mr. Max's store. We learned how to shop. We learned to be polite."

"We studied all about good foods to eat and not all ice cream and candy and cake. You should eat things that make you grow big and strong. You should eat hot cereal, fresh vegetables, and drink milk."

"We learned to make things. At first we didn't know how to make a cart but Mr. Johnson helped us. We made the counters out of boxes and Mr. Johnson helped us with the wall."

"We learned how to add. We learned about sales and prices. We learned how to read prices. You have to save money by low prices."

"We learned about money and how to count money and many of the children learned how to make change."

"We learned how to paint and to draw signs and we decorated our store ourselves. Miss Wolitarsky says we thought of a lot of good ideas."

In the final part of the program, two children held and described the scrap book they had prepared about their store and about stores in general. They read two poems the children had written about visiting stores. When the program was over, the children picked things up and left for home. Most of the parents stayed for tea and cookies with Miss Wolitarsky.

The program itself had been carefully planned. Every effort was made to get parents to attend, particularly the parents of those children that Miss Wolitarsky thought needed the thrill of having their parents see them perform. Each grocer in town had been invited in previously to see the store and most of them had come. Together they had suggested that each one contribute attendance prizes to all parents who would attend. They decided to do this without identifying their firms with the gifts. As a result the children had been able to tell their parents that merchandise worth $37.83 would be given away as door prizes. There was cocoa, coffee, Spry, Crisco, Swiftning, canned pineapple, peaches, berries, pears, various kinds of soaps, and canned fish and meat. The children had found the prices of each contribution and the best arithmeticians had added them up to arrive at the total value.

We meet some parents

I overheard Mrs. Aitkin talking to Miss Wolitarsky at tea. She had been a teacher, too. "When do you find time to teach the children their reading, arithmetic, spelling, and writing? Maybeth certainly has learned to read, and reads more than ever and does wonders in arithmetic, but she never talks about her lessons."

"We study these things all the time," Miss Wolitarsky said. "I have never had a grade that wanted to work harder. We have a regular arithmetic group with about 15 in it. Then we have three other groups with from five to seven each. One group is developing arithmetic readiness, one is reviewing simple number concepts, and one is working on more advanced work. The children have found out that they must try to know a lot about numbers and they study it as much as a whole hour some days. Much of it has been in relation to our project, but much of it has been drill. As soon as they see the need for knowing and are mature enough to understand it, they love to drill on it until they master it. Maybeth is in the large group. Her arithmetic is above average, but she is not ready for more advanced work yet. She needs experience with numbers as she goes along. Like most children her age, she needs to regard the things she lives with—her dolls, her books, her spending money— as things that are described by numbers. She needs to find out how larger and larger numbers are used as quantities get larger. She is an intelligent little girl and she will advance in arithmetic very well. Relative to her arithmetic, she is more competent in reading and spelling. She knows the meaning of many words and is thus better able than most to learn to recognize the words in printed sentences. Because she learns easily, she has a feeling of competence and security and happiness in her school work and this helps her to take her part in activities with other children. She gets along well with them. She helps them generously and accepts help gracefully. She loves to compete with the other children and is learning to do her best and to be a good sport whether she wins or loses."

"We certainly appreciate what you are doing for her. Schools have changed a lot, even since I was a teacher." She ended by asking Miss Wolitarsky to come soon for a visit at her home.

Later Miss Wolitarsky said to me, "She is an unusual mother. Ex-teachers are often the hardest ones to talk to, particularly if their children are as bright as Maybeth is."

I noticed another woman who hadn't talked to many of the others. Twice, as she drifted toward the door, Miss Wolitarsky had detained her by asking her to look at something Esther had done. Finally when only three or four were left, Miss Wolitarsky introduced me to her.

"Keep her here if you can," she had said to me.

She joined us a moment later.

"We'll walk out with you." In her casualness, there was no hint of a special message—no feeling of pressing or urgency. As we put on our wraps, we discussed the store.

Then came the question, "How is Esther doing?" Dreadful question! I found out later that Esther had been passed on probation. Esther did not read well at all. On a sociogram no child had chosen her as best friend or the one to sit near. Sometimes she cried without great provocation. The morning of the day the first report cards were to be ready she had vomited and had to go home early. An individual Binet had shown an I.Q. of 85.

"I think she is making very good progress," Miss Wolitarsky said. "She was slow getting started last year, but she is beginning to get the hang of things now. She was a great help in planning our store.

She brought many packages and she can tell the difference between the different boxes of cereal and can point out the names of the contents of the boxes. We cut out the names from the boxes and used them as cards. Even that way she knows many of them. She is beginning to enjoy finding printed words that name things she knows. She is learning to count, too. Best of all, she enjoys being with other children more and more. She can be shoved and shove back without worrying about it as much as she did."

"We try to make her study and learn, but she doesn't bring her books home. We'd make her study at home if she had some books."

"I'd let you know if I thought that was necessary, but Esther does not need homework yet. She is a child who starts her school work slowly. We don't know how fast she may go later, but I feel sure she will do much better than she has so far. I know you and her father are busy, but if you would read stories to her sometimes in the evening, there are some books in our library that I could recommend. It would be nice if we could get Esther to regard books as things that bring pleasure. Somehow, she has not learned to love books. That can be done only if she finds out that they are sources of fun or information. She likes to know. The more fun that she can have reading stories or having them read to her, the better it would be."

"We would read stories to her," the mother said, "but my sister's girl reads to her and she doesn't like that. We tell her she should learn to read like her little cousin does."

"It would be better if adults read to her," Miss Wolitarsky said diplomatically. "She hears many children read at school. If you read to her at home, she may sometimes tell the stories to the other children at school. I want you to tell her tonight that I told you she was doing better all the time. That is true. She is working hard and needs to know that she is getting credit for it."

We walked out of the building and were quiet for a while. Miss Wolitarsky was waiting for a remark and when it came I remembered it from my own experience and knew that Miss Wolitarsky had been waiting for it *and wanted it.* When I had heard it as a teacher, I had sighed and thought, "That's what they always say," I hadn't known how to use it.

"She really is bright enough, you know. She learns the things she wants to learn. Her father was just saying the other day that perhaps we should just *make* her study. She knows lots of things that would surprise you when she wants to."

In this remark there was an implied and very natural criticism of the school that Miss Wolitarsky chose to ignore. She was secure and confident.

"I'll bet that's true," she answered encouragingly. "I have noticed the same thing." Again she waited for the mother to answer.

"The other day, when her father slammed the car door to close it, she told him that if he opened the car window first, he wouldn't have to slam so hard. He had never heard of it, but he knew it was true. She wouldn't tell where she learned that.

"She knows how to watch her brother, too,—he's four. I never worry when she's watching him. She doesn't let him put things in his mouth—he wants to put everything in his mouth—and she's careful closing the car door so she doesn't catch his hand. He minds her, too, and it's funny because she doesn't get mad at him even when he's mean."

"What's her brother's name?" Miss Wolitarsky asked. That was something for the teacher to remember, I knew.

"It's Robert,—and Esther is so careful of needles and pins. She never leaves them where he can get them. When she sews, she won't let him help. She's gotten so she sews at the dining room table—:puts a box on one of the chairs to sit on. He can't reach up so easy."

"Does she sew much?"

"She'd do it all the time if I'd let her. When she was little, Grandma Dusek—that's my mother—gave her some cards with yarn to sew through with. The cards had holes. She did it just like the pictures showed her to do. She has been sewing ever since. I never did sew much—my sister was the sewer in our family—but her Grandma shows her how to make stitches and sometimes helps her cut the doll clothes. Her father says it shows what she can do when she wants to."

We came to the parting of the ways. Esther's mother said again that she was glad she came and glad she met me. Though it seemed on the tip of her tongue, she didn't extend an invitation to either of us to visit her home.

"She works part of the time," Miss Wolitarsky explained, "when Grandma Dusek is strong enough to care for the baby. Her husband is caretaker for Tom Adkins who is the largest local stockholder in the mill. I've heard the Adkins like her very much. She takes marvelous care of their nice things. I wonder if she has so little company at her home because she thinks it shabby by comparison. I did want to meet her. Now I can talk to Esther about her brother, Robert, and get her to talk about child care. I can also try to interest her in sewing and fabrics and dress design at school, and see if I can find books and problems about these things to indicate word meanings. She dislikes books. She seemed to fear to try to do arithmetic or read when she came. In her small arithmetic committee, she has learned to count and she can tell time on the hours, and the half pasts, but beyond that—no soap yet. She is learning to try, however. She is no longer without hope of learning. She is now a part of her small group, and takes part with the others. In September, she took no part at all in group play or work. I haven't been able to find an art interest so far. She doesn't like printing or drawing. Sewing may do it. She may learn to draw patterns or read simple patterns.

"Do you know any place to find simple patterns for doll clothes with simple words and large print?" Miss Wolitarsky asked me.

I didn't and I felt inadequate. I almost went defensive and said I wouldn't have time to locate things like that. Instead I said nothing and resolved to try and, if successful, let my actions speak louder than my words.

"I wish I did," I answered. "That would be good motivation for a child like her."

"I'll have to remember about that car door, too. It may be that she has an interest in science. Some children can think very clearly about things like that. I wonder if she knows or senses something about air pressure. I had never heard about car doors closing easier with open windows."

Evaluation was a constant process, I had learned. It was testing; but more than that, it was constant intuitive observation, piling up impression and observation, detail after detail, until there was a great store of information about each child.

The way Miss Wolitarsky taught, she had opportunity to study and collect information to use in the evaluative process, and she had enough theory to make use of the things that were at hand every day to be observed.

Miss Wolitarsky, too, was bringing the parents into her planning. In some cases, this was relatively easy, but she sought opportunities when and where they were needed. She brought community leaders into her classroom as easily as she brought parents. In the case of the store, it was mainly the grocers who were involved, although the attention of many others had been attracted to it.

Retrospect

After three years at Hampton Rapids, I can look back with some pride and, of course, some disappointment. I have not been able to bring about all the changes I had hoped for. Some things I have not changed at all; some have changed. but not enough; while in some areas the improvement has been most gratifying. I have learned that changes come slowly and that the best insurance for improvement really is to enlist the creative thinking of more heads than my own on each problem. That in itself, I learned, sometimes takes a lot of doing.

The teachers' study of reporting practices carried through the first year. Each P.T.A. appointed a committee to work with the teachers and we had our first workshop when interest on the part of parents justified Mr. Walker in taking two Friday afternoons in April for parent-teacher study groups. A new report card was prepared and, for a year's experiment, the number of written reports during the year was reduced, with provision for time off for two parent conferences during the year.

In April and May of the next year, conferences and evaluative discussions were held with parents. Most of the parents favored the new procedure, but a respectable minority still believed the old marking methods were better. It was finally decided that for the second year each parent who wished should have two report cards of the old type during the year, one in November and one in May. They were insistent on having the conferences in addition, however, which indicated a growing conviction that the parent conferences were the most important practice of all. Both parents and the teachers made up their minds on the basis of study as well as observation of the children.

This last spring, the decision was made to ask the Superintendent to have the new report cards formally approved and to continue granting time for parent conferences. The demand for the continuance of the old marking system, even twice a year, was dropped.

The main factor involved in this decision was the success we had in getting parents to study the evidence and to approach the problem with open minds. They reached the same conclusion the teachers did when they studied it along with the teachers.

I am not half so proud of the new reporting procedure as I am of two things that it helped bring about. First, it demonstrated to parents that the schools are their schools and that we as teachers are anxious to provide the kind of schools our community wants, with the kind of methods and content that they believe in. Second, it demonstrated to all of us that methods can be developed right in each school community for mutual study, with give and take, experimentation, willing postponement of final decisions, and eventual agreement.

Of course, the teachers learned many other things besides new theories and practices in reporting. They gained new insights into motivation, evaluation, mental health, the psychology of learning, the broad objectives of education, and a host of other things. Further, they learned, and their principals and I learned, a lot about working together freely and equally on our common problems.

Discussion Questions

1. Why did Maxine not want to "rate" the teachers? Was it merely because she didn't have faith in present rating techniques?
2. Why didn't she wish to assist in hiring teachers?
3. Discuss the fallacy, if fallacy it is, in Miss Holden's idea that children had to "catch up" after the conclusion of a unit.
4. Discuss the implications of Miss Wickersham's statement that some of her children know more about things than she does. Would it be true that some children in almost every grade will be "brighter" than the teacher? What does this mean in terms of "good" teaching?
5. Should teachers insist, as a right, that they be warned when a supervisor is coming? Under what conditions might this be a fair demand? Under what conditions might it be superfluous and silly?
6. Why, when Maxine Schmidt was so anxious to speak at the breakfast where the teachers were discussing reporting to parents, did she say so little when her chance came? She merely offered to help find materials for study.
7. Why did she not speak until she was asked?

8. How do you think a supervisor might get teachers and principals like Mrs. Greatheart to see that discussing the children in whispers in their presence was bad? Could the approach be made by a study of the personalities of the various pupils as it was carried on by Marion Johnson? Would more than that be necessary? What about group demonstrations with adult study groups, where roles would be played and someone might discuss other adults in the same obvious but secretive way?

9. Discuss answers to the seven questions Maxine Schmidt asked in regard to the projects that followed from the vandalism at the Forest Lake School.

10. Evaluate Miss Wolitarsky's visit with Maybeth's mother, Mrs. Aitkin, as a teacher-parent conference.

11. Do the same with her conference with Esther's mother.

12. It has been said that when a small child really misbehaves or vomits in school, what he is really doing is telling the teacher he needs help. Was this true of Esther? Is it generally true, do you think? Would your own introspective memory necessarily be reliable as a source of information here?

13. What do you think of Miss Wolitarsky's plan in having the children cut out names from cereal boxes with which to make flash cards, thus combining reading manipulation, measurement, drill, and the like?

14. What do you think of Miss Wolitarsky's remark when Esther's mother mentioned how well Esther's cousin could read?

Selected References

A Forward Step, The Improvement of Teaching through the Stimulation of Teacher Growth, Curriculum Bulletin No. 7. Augusta, Maine: State Department of Education, 1948.

A Reading Readiness Program, Curriculum Bulletin, Volume I, No. 3. Milwaukee: Milwaukee Public Schools, 1945.

Division of Instructional Service, *Library Practice, A Manual for Students,* Publication No. 22. Pasadena, California: Pasadena City Schools, 1950.

Educational Policies Commission, *Education of the Gifted.* Washington, D.C.: National Education Association, 1950.

Health and Physical Education in the Elementary Schools, Curriculum Bulletin No. H.P. 102. Montebello, California: Montebello Unified School District, 1950.

Living and Learning Experiences in the Elementary Schools of South Carolina. Columbia, South Carolina: State Department of Education, 1948.

Miel, Alice, ed., *Teacher's Role in Pupil-Teacher Planning.* Bureau of Publications, Teachers College, Columbia University, 1947.

New York Public Schools, *School Civic Clubs.* Curriculum Bulletin 1950-51 Series, No. 1. New York: Board of Education, 1951.

We Go to School in the Primary Department. Arlington, Virginia: County Public Schools.

Miss Schmidt's Bibliography on Reporting Procedures

Anderson, Robert H. and Edward R. Steadman, "Pupils' Reactions to a Reporting System," *Elementary School Journal,* Vol. 51, No. 3, November 1950, 136-142.

Anderson, Vernon E., *et al.,* "Evaluating and Reporting Pupil Progress," *Principles and Practices of Secondary Education.* New York: The Ronald Press Company, 1951, pp. 264-288.

Ayer, Fred C., "Teachers' Marks," pp. 96-111; "Reporting Practices—Philosophy and Itemization," pp. 112-130; "Reporting Practices—Methods and Practical Considerations," pp. 131-154, *Practical Child Accounting.* Austin, Texas: Steck Company, 1949.

Beaumont, Henry and Freeman Glenn Macomber, "The Reporting and Interpreting of Pupil Growth to Parents Is an Essential of Evaluation," *Psychological Factors in Education.* New York: McGraw-Hill Book Company, Inc., 1949, pp. 255-257.

Bolmeier, E. C., "Principles Pertaining to Marking and Reporting Pupil Progress," *School Review.* Vol. 59, No. 1, January 1951, 15-24.

Chamberlain, Leo M. and Leslie W. Kindred, "Reports to Parents," *The Teacher and School Organization,* 2d ed. New York: Prentice-Hall, Inc., 1949, pp. 452-459.

DePencier, Ida B., "Trends in Reporting Pupil Progress in the Elementary Grades, 1938-1949," *Elementary School Journal,* Vol. 51, No. 9, May 1951, 519-523.

D'Evelyn, Katherine E., *Individual Parent-Teacher Conferences,* Practical Suggestions for Teaching, No. 9. New York: Bureau of Publications, Teachers College, Columbia University, 1945.

Elsbree, Willard S., *Pupil Progress in the Elementary School,* Practical Suggestions for Teaching, No. 5. New York: Bureau of Publications, Teachers College, Columbia University, 1943.

Fostering Mental Health in Our Schools, 1950 Yearbook of the Association for Supervision and Curriculum Development. Washington, D.C.: National Education Association, 1950.

Frank, Mary and Lawrence K. Frank, *How to Help Your Child in School.* New York: The Viking Press, 1950, pp. 312-317.

Hightower, H. W. and V. L. Mitchell, "Reports to Parents of Children in Primary Grades." *Nation's Schools.* Vol. 46, No. 3, September 1950, 59-60.

LeBaron, Walter A., "What Shall We Tell the Parents?" *Elementary School Journal,* Vol. 51, No. 6, February 1951, 322-326.

Long Beach Public Schools, *Teachers' Guide for Reporting Pupil Growth.* 1948, pp. 7-9.

Mary Gabrieline, Sister, "Oral or Written Reports?" *Catholic School Journal,* Vol. 50, No. 9, November 1950, 278-279.

Morrissy, Elizabeth and J. Ben. Robinson, "Reporting Pupil Progress in Elementary Schools," *Baltimore Bulletin of Education,* Vol. 26, No. 4, June 1949, pp. 1-10.

Muellen, T. K., "An Experiment in Reporting Pupil Progress," *Elementary School Journal,* Vol. 52, No. 1, September 1951, 42-44.

Odell, C. W., "Marks and Marking Systems," *Encyclopedia of Educational Research, Rev. ed.* New York: The Macmillan Company, 1950, 711-717.

Patton, Lucie Dean, "Parent-Teacher Conferences," *California Teachers Association Journal,* Vol. 47, No. 7, October 1951, 15.

"The Problem of Reporting to Parents," *Journal of Education,* Vol. 133, No. 2, February 1950, 43-44.

"Pupil-Progress Plan in Berkeley," *Elementary School Journal,* Vol. 50, No. 6, February 1950, 315.

Richey, Robert W., "Reporting Pupil Progress to Parents," *Indiana University School of Education Bulletin,* Vol. 25, No. 1, January 1949, 29-34.

Ross, C. C., *Measurement in Today's Schools.* New York: Prentice-Hall, Inc., 1947, pp. 397-422, 476-479, 521-527.

Starbeck, Catherine, "Parent-Interview Day in Chicago Public Schools," *Elementary School Journal,* Vol. 51, No. 3, November 1950, 143-145.

Strang, Ruth M., "What a Report Card Really Means," *Better Homes and Gardens,* Vol. 28, No. 2, October 1949, 202-205.

Wrinkle, William L., *Improving Marking and Reporting Practices in Elementary and Secondary Schools.* New York: Rinehart & Company, Inc., 1947.